The Latvian Gambit Lives!

Tony Kosten

B.T. Batsford Ltd, *London*

First published in 2001

ISBN 0 7134 8629 5

British Library Cataloguing-in-Publication Data.
A catalogue record for this book is
available from the British Library.

Printed in Great Britain by
Creative Print and Design (Wales), Ebbw Vale
for the publishers,
B.T. Batsford Ltd,
9 Blenheim Court,
Brewery Road,
London N7 9NT

A member of the Chrysalis Group plc

A BATSFORD CHESS BOOK

Contents

Acknowledgements

For this new work I am indebted, once again, to John Elburg, editor of the *Latvian Newsletter*, and Georgio Ruggeri Laderchi who sent me a copy of their CD *Latvian Gambit into the next Millennium,* plus numerous updates, and other material, and who were happy to discuss variations with me.

I would also like to thank these last two, plus Hagen Tiemann, and Mauro Voliano for consenting to play a training Latvian Gambit tournament with me, so that I could run through some of my analysis, and, finally to Stefan Bücker for sending me copies of his excellent publication, and unpublished analysis.

Bibliography

Books

The Latvian Gambit, by Tony Kosten

Developments in The Latvian Gambit, by K.Grivainis & J.Elburg

The Latvian Gambit, by K.Grivainis

Latvian Gambit made easy, by K.Grivainis & J.Elburg

Le Gambit Letton, by F.Destrebecq

Encyclopaedia of Chess Openings 'C'

Sahovski Informators #55 and #56

Frank Marshall's Best Games of Chess, Frank J. Marshall

NCO, J.Nunn, G.Burgess, J.Emms & J.Gallagher

Magazines

Kaissiber, ed. Stefan Bücker

Latvian Correspondence Chess & Latvian Gambit

Electronic

Latvian Gambit into the next Millennium, by John Elburg & Georgio Ruggeri Laderchi

The Latvian Newsletter, edited by J.Elburg

I was also assisted by ChessBase 7.0 and Fritz 6

Introduction

The Latvian Gambit can be thought of as a sort of King's Gambit played by Black:

1 e4 e5 2 ♘f3 f5

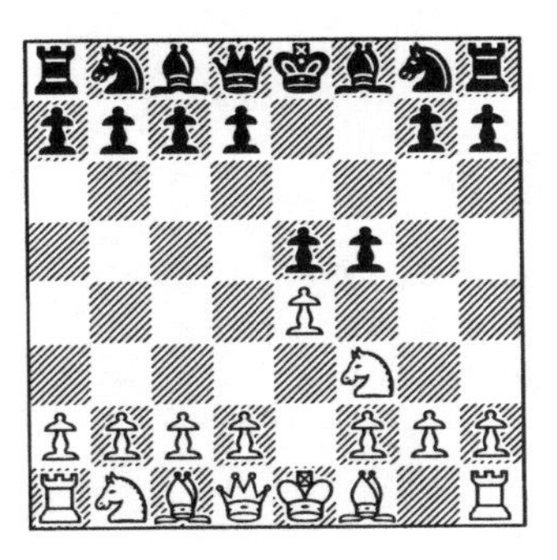

The move 2...f5 was originally quoted by Damiano in 1512 (and not in the Gottingen Manuscript, which only mentions 1 e4 e5 2 ♘f3 d6 3 ♗c4 f5 4 d3 f4), and for centuries the opening was known as the Greco Counter Gambit after the Italian Gioachino Greco (1600-1634). Then, from around 1900, the Latvian Karlis Betinš started to play and analyse the opening, winning many exciting games. He was joined by other Latvian masters, and from 1934 to 1936 the Seniors Club of Riga, under Betinš, employed the opening to gain a famous victory in the correspondence match against Stockholm. Recognizing the contribution of the Latvian chess players to the renewal of interest in the opening, it was renamed the Latvian Gambit at the 1937 FIDE Congress.

When I agreed to revise my book *The Latvian Gambit* for Batsford, I told them that I did not want to spend more than a week or two over it. Fortunately for the reader, and unfortunately for my free time, that was four months ago! This revision has become a labour of love for me. I have been through all 9000 or so Latvian Gambits ever published, with the help of the *ChessBase* 'Tree' function to catch any transpositions, and have deeply analysed all the critical lines.

Although I have kept the same basic structure (after all, it seemed logical to me in 1994, and it still does) the contents have been thoroughly reworked, and updated. There is no subjective bias, this is no 'Winning with ...' book—when a line is good for White I say so.

Interestingly, when I wrote the original tome, I based it around games of the strongest over-the-board players (in particular Jonny Hector), because the standard of many correspondence games was not that high. However, seven years on, it is the games by the correspondence players that are the real mainstay of the book. Not only are these players now armed with databases containing all the relevant games and can use published literature to recite the most theoretical lines, but they also have access to powerful analytical engines. This means that many correspondence games are now tactically flawless, and that the theory has been pushed to new limits.

The Latvian Gambit is now a mature opening, and it is possible to say which lines are definitely good, which bad. I hope the reader gets much enjoyment out of reading this work, and scores many points!

Tony Kosten,
Chamalières, March 2001

Symbols used in this book

+	check
+/-	winning advantage for White
±	large advantage for White
⩲	slight advantage for White
-/+	winning advantage for Black
∓	large advantage for Black
⩱	slight advantage for Black
=	level position
!	good move
!!	outstanding move
!?	interesting move
?!	dubious move
?	bad move
??	blunder
1-0	the game ends in a win for White
0-1	the game ends in a win for Black
½-½	the game ends in a draw
corr.	correspondence game
ch	championship
m	match

1 Main line: 3 ♘xe5 ♕f6 Introduction and 7 f3

1 e4 e5 2 ♘f3 f5 3 ♘xe5

This is White's most natural continuation and also traditionally considered to be his strongest, capturing the important e5 pawn and simultaneously threatening ♕h5+.

3...♕f6

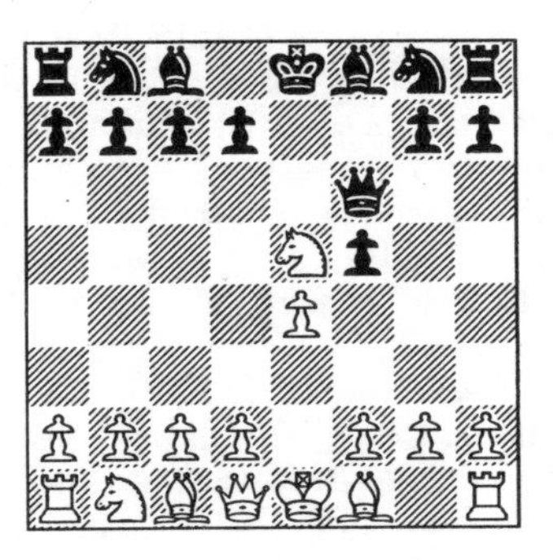

At first sight a strange reply, immediately throwing the black queen into the fray before developing any of the other pieces. The mundane tactical point is that Black parries the ♕h5+ menace whilst attacking the white knight on e5, thus guaranteeing the recapture of the pawn on e4. Less obviously, although Black suffers temporarily from a lack of mobilization, in the long term he hopes to be able to profit from the aggressive placement of his queen on the kingside which, when combined with the rook on the open f-file, opens possibilities of an eventual attack on the white king. Other third moves for Black, more in keeping with real gambit play, are considered separately, in Chapter 6.

4 d4

Apart from this, most obvious of moves, White can also play the 4 ♘c4 of Chapter 5, but should certainly avoid:

a) 4 f4?! d6 5 ♘c4 fxe4 (6 ♘c3 can be met by either 6...♕g6, or by 6...♕xf4 7 d3 ♕g4! with a very pleasant endgame in store) 6 d4 ♕g6 7 ♘c3 ♘f6 8 ♘e3 c6 9 ♗e2 d5 10 0-0, Izuel-Cordoba, corr. 1975/76, when the simple 10...♗d6 grants Black an edge.

b) 4 ♘f3?! fxe4 5 ♕e2 d5 (5...♕e7! 6 ♘d4 ♘f6 which is quite equal after 7 d3 [7 ♘c3 d5 8 d3?! c5 9 ♘b3 ♗g4! and White is losing, Vaernik-Dreibergs, corr., USA 1968] 7...exd3 8 ♕xe7+ ♗xe7 9 ♗xd3 0-0 and Black has an extra central pawn) 6 d3 ♗f5 7 dxe4 dxe4 8 ♘fd2?! (8 ♘bd2) 8...♕e6 9 ♘c4 ♘c6 10 ♗e3 0-0-0 11 ♘bd2 ♘f6 12 h3 ♗b4 13 g4!? ♘xg4?, Alden-Sawyer, USA 1990, and now both players overlooked 14 hxg4! ♗xg4 15 ♕xg4! ♕xg4 16 ♗h3 when Black has only two pawns for the piece.

4...d6

Chasing the knight away, 4...♘c6?! 5 ♘xc6 dxc6 6 e5 ♕f7 transposes to Chapter 6, whilst 4...fxe4? 5 ♗c4, 4...d5? 5 exd5 ♗d6 6 ♗b5+, and 4...♕h4? 5 exf5 are all terrible.

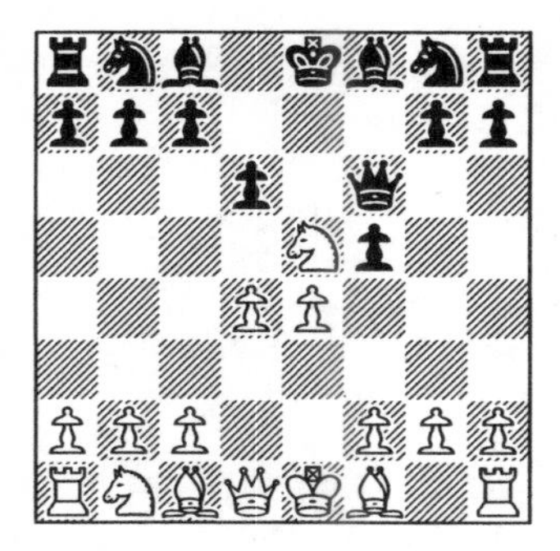

5 ♘c4

Otherwise:

a) There is no reason to give Black free tempi by 5 ♘f3 (Fine's recommendation, although first played by Staunton in 1841), 5...fxe4 6 ♘g5 (6 ♕e2?! ♕e7! 7 ♘g5 [7 ♘fd2 is no better, 7...♘f6 8 c4 ♗f5 9 ♘c3 Landgren-Zalitis, Sweden 1978, when 9...♘c6! would have been difficult to meet, e.g. 10 ♘b3 ♘b4-d3+] 7...♘f6 8 ♘c3 d5 9 ♗f4 h6, when White is forced to play the ugly move 10 ♘h3, Polland-Pupols, USA 1968, and 6 ♗g5?? loses a piece, 6...♕g6 [6...♕f5 amounts to the same] 7 ♕e2 ♗e7 8 ♗xe7 exf3 0-1, Deronne-Gedult, Paris 1975) when 6...d5 with the threat of ...h6 is best, e.g. 7 c4 h6 (probably Black should withhold the move ...h6 until it is most effective: 7...c6! 8 ♘c3 ♗b4 9 ♕b3 [9 cxd5 cxd5 10 a3 ♗xc3+ 11 bxc3 ♘e7 12 c4 0-0 with an edge, as ...h6 is coming, Martinez-Krustkains, Atars 1979] 9...♗xc3+ 10 bxc3 h6 11 ♘h3 ♘e7 12 ♗e3 0-0, and the h3-knight is offside, Destrebecq-Sénéchaud, corr. 1997) 8 ♘h3 ♗xh3 9 ♕h5+! (9 gxh3 Steiner-Apsenieks, Kemeri 1937, 9...♗b4+!? [or 9...dxc4 10 ♗xc4 ♘c6—Destrebecq] 10 ♘c3 ♘e7 11 cxd5 0-0 equal) 9...g6 10 ♕xh3 ♘c6 11 ♗e3 ♘b4 12 ♘c3! ♘e7 (if 12...♘c2+ 13 ♔d2 ♘xa1 14 ♘xd5 ♕f7 then 15 ♕g4! intending 16 ♕xe4+, followed by 17 ♗d3 and 18 ♖xa1—Destrebecq) 13 ♖c1 c6 14 a3 with some advantage, Destrebecq-Zerbib, corr. 1997.

b) Similarly, 5 ♘d3 fxe4 6 ♘f4 has little to recommend it, 6...c6 (6...♕f7 looks like a good response, planning ...d5 and ...♗d6) 7 c4! ♕f7 8 ♘c3 ♘f6 9 ♗e2 ♗e7 10 0-0 0-0 11 d5 is slightly better for White, Franco-Hector.

5...fxe4

Black sometimes tries 5...♘c6? here, but White has at least two good replies: 6 d5 ♘e5 7 ♘c3 ♘e7 8 ♘xe5 ♕xe5 9 f4 ♕f6 10 ♗d3 g6 11 ♘b5 ♔d8 12 ♗e3 c5 13 ♗d2 ♗d7? 14 ♗c3 1-0 Schilling-Scott, corr. 1988, and 6 e5 dxe5 7 dxe5 with advantage: not then 7...♘xe5?? Vitols-Vildavs, Latvia, when 8 ♕e2 ♗d6 9 f4 appears to win a whole piece.

6 ♘c3

Immediately attacking the e4 pawn. The drawback of the text compared with the moves 6 ♗e2 and 6 ♘e3, which are covered in Chapters 3 and 4, respectively, is that c4 is no longer possible. Instead, Bronstein mentions the possible pawn sacrifice 6 ♕h5+!? g6 7 ♕e2 (7 ♕d5 is met by 7...♕f5 8 ♘e3 ♘f6! 9 ♕xf5 gxf5 10 c3 d5 with extra space, Cabanas-Aziz, Madrid 1999) 7...♕xd4?! (too risky for practical play, 7...d5 is best, 8 ♘e5 ♘d7! 9 f4 c6 and Black has nothing to fear, Collins-Hage, corr. 1999) 8 ♘c3 (but 8 ♗d2!, threatening ♗c3, looks unpleasant) with a useful lead in development: a likely continuation is: 8...d5 9 ♘b5 ♕g7 10 ♗d2, unclear.

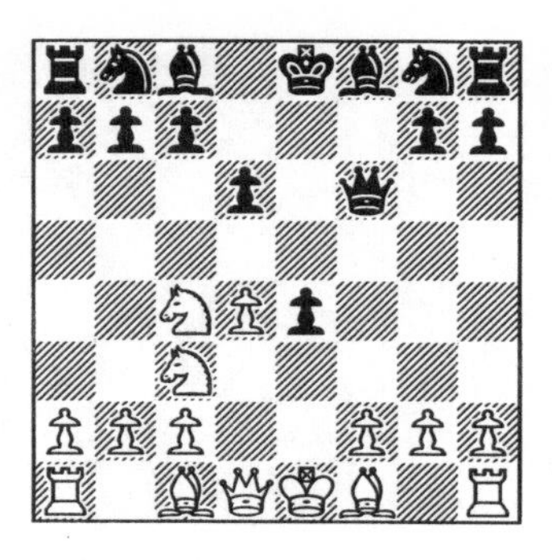

6...♕g6

A key move for Black—he will decide on the placement of his minor pieces according to his opponent's play. In the meantime White will have to find time to defend his g2 pawn. Other, less well documented, possibilities:

a) 6...♗f5?! with,

a1) 7 ♘e3 ♗g6 (conceding the important light-squared bishop is dangerous for Black: 7...c6?! 8 ♘xf5 ♕xf5 9 ♗e2 ♘f6 10 0-0 ♗e7 11 f3 exf3 12 ♖xf3 ♕d7 13 d5 0-0 14 ♗g5 ♕c7 15 ♗d3 ♘bd7 16 ♖h3 ♖ae8 17 ♗f5 ♗d8 18 ♕d3 h5, Grivainis-Diepstraaten, corr. 1977/80, and now 19 ♗e6+ is a killer, and 7...♘e7!? is probably best met with 8 d5, rather than by 8 ♘cd5 ♘xd5 9 ♘xd5 ♕d8 10 c4 ♘d7 with no particular problems for Black, Haluska-Stepanski, USA 1987) 8 ♘ed5!? ♕f7 9 ♗c4 c6 10 ♘b6 d5 11 ♘xa8 dxc4 12 d5 (12 ♕g4! ♕d7 13 ♕g3 might just allow the knight to escape) 12...♗c5 13 ♗e3 ♗xe3 14 fxe3 ♘f6 15 ♕d4 0-0, Grivainis-Pupols, corr. 1971/72, and now 16 d6 gets the knight out.

a2) White can try for a refutation with 7 g4!? ♗g6, and now 8 ♗g2 (8 h4!?) 8...c6? (8...♘c6 is Black's best chance: 9 d5 [9 ♗e3?! d5 10 ♘e5 0-0-0 is fine for Black, Zjajo-Steinhart, Untergrombach 1999] 9...♘e5 10 ♘xe5 ♕xe5 11 ♕e2 0-0-0 12 ♗e3 a6 13 0-0-0 with a small advantage, Hernandez-Bedevia, corr. 1990) 9 ♗xe4 ♗xe4 10 ♘xe4 ♕e6 11 ♕e2 d5 12 ♘f6+!! (12 ♘cd6+ is also emphatic, 12...♗xd6 13 ♘xd6+ ♔d7 14 ♕xe6+ ♔xe6 15 ♘xb7, Gåård-Svendsen, corr. 1994/98) 12...♔f7 13 ♘e5+! ♔xf6 14 ♗g5+! ♔xg5 15 ♕f3 ♗b4+ 16 ♔f1! (this wins the black queen, not 16 c3? g6! 17 cxb4 ♘d7 18 ♕e3+ ♔f6 19 ♘xd7+ ♕xd7 20 ♕e5+ ♔f7 21 ♕xh8 ♖e8+ 22 ♔d2 ♘f6 winning! Jackson-Svendsen, corr. 1991) 16...g6 17 ♘f7+ ♕xf7 18 h4+ ♔h6 19 ♕xf7 with mate to follow, Kozlov-Svendsen, corr. 1994/98.

b) 6...♕f7?! and

b1) Note that 7 ♗e2! is very strong here, forcing a transposition into Chapter 4, variation (d).

b2) Also, it is not clear whether the e4 pawn is really immune from capture in this position after all, 7 ♘xe4!? ♕e7?? 8 ♗d3! ♘f6 (there are no better alternatives for Black on move 8 either, i.e. 8...d5 9 ♕h5+ ♕f7 10 ♕xf7+ ♔xf7 11 ♘e5+, or 8...♗f5 9 ♕e2 d5 10 ♘cd6+ cxd6 11 ♘xd6+ ♔d7 12 ♘xf5, both crushing for White.) 9 0-0 ♗e6 10 ♖e1 ♔d7 11 ♘g5 1-0, Gaard-Lemay, corr. 1989.

The question remains: what would White have played against the somewhat superior 7...♕e6 ? Perhaps he intended something like 8 ♗d3 (my suggestion 8 f3 d5 9 ♘e5 dxe4 10 ♗c4 ♕d6 11 0-0 gives White an attack for the piece) 8...d5 9 ♘e5 dxe4 10 ♗c4 ♕b6 (10...♕f5

11 ♘f7) 11 ♕h5+ g6 12 ♗f7+ ♔e7 13 ♗g5+ ♘f6 14 ♗xg6 ♕xd4 (14...♗g7 15 ♗xh7! ♖f8 16 ♕g6 ♗h8 17 ♕xe4 ♗e6 18 0-0-0 1-0, Dorer-Stader, corr. 1982) 15 ♗e8! ♗e6 16 ♘g4 ♗g7 17 c3 ♕c4?! [17...♕d5!] 18 ♘xf6 ♗xf6 19 ♗xf6+ ♔xf6 20 ♕h4+ ♔g7 21 ♕g5+ ♔f8 22 ♗b5! ♕d5 23 ♕f6+ ♔g8 24 ♖d1 winning, Novak-Bonte, corr. 1995.

b3) 7 ♘e3 ♘f6 (7...c6?! loses a pawn, 8 ♘xe4 d5 9 ♘g5 ♕f6 10 ♘g4 ♗b4+ 11 c3 ♕e7+ 12 ♘e5 ♗d6 13 ♕h5+ g6 14 ♕e2 ♘f6 15 ♘gf7 0-0 16 ♘xd6 ♕xd6 17 ♗h6 with advantage, Rittenhouse-Krantz, corr. 1993) 8 ♗c4 ♗e6 9 d5 (9 ♗xe6 ♕xe6 10 d5 ♕e7 11 0-0 with some advantage, Grivainis-Morgado, corr. 1977/79) 9...♗c8 (9...♗d7?! obstructs the b8-knight 10 f3 exf3 11 ♕xf3 g6 12 0-0 ♗g7 13 ♗d2 0-0 14 ♖ae1 and Black has problems developing his queenside, Jelling-Bruun, Denmark 1980) 10 0-0 ♗e7 11 f3 exf3 12 ♖xf3 (if 12 ♕xf3 ♘bd7 intends ...♘e5) 12...0-0 (now 12...♘bd7!? also with the idea ...♘e5 (Melchor) can be met by 13 ♘b5 ♗d8 14 ♘f5, but 12...a6 may be better, 13 ♘f5 ♗xf5 14 ♖xf5 ♘bd7 is reasonable, Diepstraten) 13 ♘b5 ♘a6 14 a3 with the knight aiming for d4, thence e6, Ruisdonk-Peet, corr. 1977.

c) 6...c6? 7 ♘xe4! ♕e6 8 ♕e2 d5, von Bilguer-von der Lasa, Berlin 1839, when 9 ♘ed6+ ♔d8 10 ♘xb7+ ♔c7 11 ♕xe6 ♗xe6 12 ♘ca5 would have been convincing.

d) 6...♘c6? 7 d5 ♘e5 8 ♘xe4 ♕g6 9 ♘g5 with advantage, Downey-Oren, corr. 1994/98.

e) 6...♘e7!? 7 d5 ♕g6 8 ♕d4 ♗f5 9 ♘e3 ♘d7 10 ♗d2 ♘f6 ∓ Mileika-Benins, Latvia 1977, is more interesting.

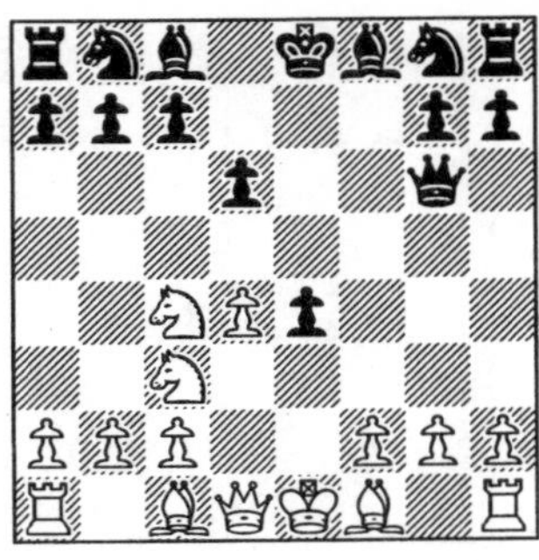

And so we come to the first major crossroads, how should White proceed? If Black can successfully complete his development, he will be fine. His position is solid and robust. On the negative side, he is temporarily behind in development and his e4 pawn is exposed. It is perhaps not surprising, therefore, that White is most successful with 7 f3, attacking the e4 pawn head on and immediately opening up the position. More positional methods fail to trouble Black, partly because White has already slightly compromised his position by blocking his c2 pawn.

7 f3!

Chronologically one of the first moves employed against the Latvian Gambit. The alternatives are considered in Chapter 2.

7...exf3

Normal, although recently 7...♘f6?! has been attracting more attention, but the doubtful assessment remains (7...♗e7?! 8 fxe4 [but 8 ♘xe4 is possible, for if 8...d5 9 ♘e5] 8...♘f6 transposes). 8 fxe4 (8 ♘e3 is sometimes preferred, and transposes into a sub-variation of B), Chapter 2: 8...♗e7 9 ♗c4 etc.) 8...♗e7 (Black is in no position to recapture the e-pawn, 8...♘xe4? loses after the obvious 9 ♗d3 when 9...d5! is the only move to avoid losing a piece [9...♗f5?! 10 ♕e2, viz 10...♗e7 11 ♘xe4 d5 12 ♘e5 ♕b6 13 ♘c5 with advantage Schaller-Zernack, corr. 1992, and 10...d5 11 ♘xd5 ♗d6 12 ♘xd6+ cxd6 13 ♘f4 1-0, Marin-Harju, corr. 1971] 10 ♘xd5 [10 0-0! is a good, and simple alternative] 10...♕xg2 but I would not fancy Black's chances after 11 ♕h5+ ♔d8 12 ♖f1 ♘f6 13 ♘xf6 gxf6 14 ♘e5!. Neither are 8...♗g4?! 9 ♗e2 a6 10 0-0 ♘bd7 11 e5 ♗h3 12 ♗f3, Rehfeld-Rebber, corr. 1992, and 8...♘c6 9 ♗e3? [9 ♘e3! leaves White a pawn to the good] 9...♘xe4!? 10 ♗d3 ♗f5 11 ♕f3 d5? [11...♘xc3 12 ♗xf5 ♕f7 is playable] 12 ♘xd5 0-0-0 13 ♘f4 ♕e8 14 g4 ♘xd4 15 ♗xd4 ♖xd4 16 0-0-0 ♗d7 17 ♖he1 ♗c6 18 c3 with advantage Svendsen-Jackson, corr. 1990, any improvement) 9 e5! is the theoretical 'refutation' (although a simple continuation like 9 ♕d3 is possible, 9...0-0 10 ♘e3 [10 ♗e3 can't be bad either, of course, Black has no great lead in development to speak of] 10...♘c6 11 ♗d2 Rajlich-Lapshun, New York 1999 [the further pawn grab, 11 ♕c4+?! ♔h8 12 d5 ♘e5 13 ♕xc7 ♖f7 is far too risky], when the evident 11...♘g4! 12 ♘xg4 [12 ♘cd5?! ♗h4+ 13 g3 ♘f2] 12...♗xg4 traps the white king in the centre; Black will continue ...♖ae8, and obtain good play).

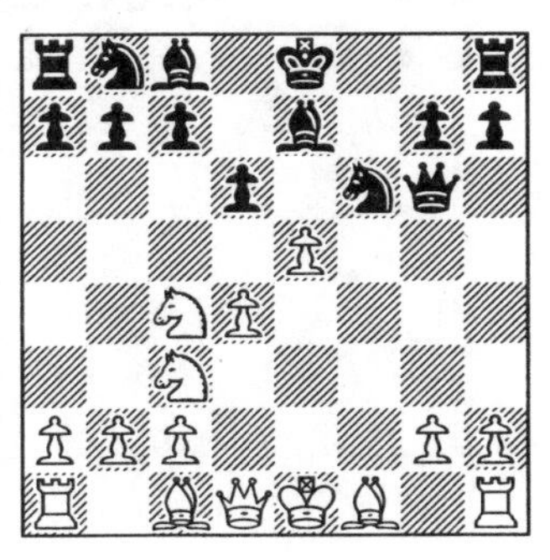

Now Black has three alternatives:

a) 9...♘h5 10 ♗d3!? (10 ♗e3 0-0 11 g3! ♘c6?! [11...♗g4 12 ♗e2 ♗xe2 13 ♕xe2 is a better chance, but still excellent for White] 12 ♗e2, Hempel-Grava, corr. 1971/72, is probably even stronger, showing up the awkward placing of the h5-knight, and on 12...♘xg3 13 ♖g1 should win) 10...♕xg2 11 ♕xh5+ g6 12 ♗xg6+ ♕xg6 13 ♕xg6+ hxg6 14 0-0 ♗e6 (14...♗f5 15 exd6 ♗xd6 16 ♘xd6+ cxd6 17 ♘d5 ♔d7 18 ♘e3 ♗e4?! 19 d5 ♖e8 20 ♘g4 1-0, Grivainis-Callinan, corr. 1971/72, or 14...dxe5 15 ♘d5 ♗h3?! 16 ♖e1 ♗h4 17 ♖e3! ♗e6 18 ♘xc7+ ♔d7 19 ♘xe6 winning quickly, Grivainis-Zemitis, corr. 1970) 15 d5 ♗h3 16 ♖e1 with advantage Grivainis-Gabrans, corr. 1969/70.

b) 9...♘g4!? First played by Ionescu, but popularised by Krantz, this move is the reason for the renewed interest in this pawn sac line. Black plans tactics involving ...0-0, and ...♗h4+.

10 ♗d3, as usual, is the sharpest (10 exd6!? is greedy, but might just be possible, 10...♗h4+!? [10...cxd6 11 ♗d3 ♕h5 12 ♕f3 is clearly good for White, as in Ghinda-Ionescu, Odorheiu Secuiesc 1993, the inaugural game in this line] 11 g3 0-0 12 dxc7?! hardly necessary, [12 gxh4! is strong, as after 12...♘f2 White saves material with the tactic 13 ♘e5! and the queen has no satisfactory square, e.g. 13...♕xd6 14 ♘b5 ♕f6 15 ♗g5] 12...♘xh2!! 13 cxb8=♕ ♗xg3+ 14 ♕xg3? [14 ♔d2 ♖xb8 15 ♘e2 is a better defence] 14...♕xg3+ 15 ♔d2 ♘f3+ and White should have given his queen to avoid mate, Svendsen-Krantz, corr. 1994/98), 10...♕h5 with a choice:

b1) 11 ♗f4!, the kingside needs defending, 11...0-0 (11...♘c6? 12 exd6 ♗h4+ 13 g3 0-0 14 ♕d2! ♘xd4 15 0-0-0! led to a quick loss for Black in Fressinet-Sénéchaud, Créon 1996) 12 ♕f3!. Heap has been very successful with this move, White defends the bishop, and prepares to castle (once again 12 ♘d5?! tempts fate, 12...♗h4+ 13 g3 c6!? [13...♖xf4 14 ♘xf4 ♗xg3+ 15 hxg3 ♕xh1+ 16 ♔d2 is unclear] 14 ♘c7 ♖xf4 15 gxh4? dxe5 16 ♘xe5? ♕xh4+ 17 ♔d2 ♘xe5 18 dxe5 ♕g5 19 ♘xa8 ♖e4+! 0-1, Gåård-Krantz, corr. 1994/98, 20 ♔c3 ♕xe5+ 21 ♔b3 ♖b4+!! 22 ♔xb4 ♕xb2+ leads to mate) 12...♘c6 (12...dxe5 13 ♘xe5 ♗d6 14 0-0 ♔h8 15 h3 ♘f6 16 ♕xh5 ♘xh5 17 ♘g6+! 1-0, Heap-Sireta, corr. 1994/98, as 17...hxg6 18 ♗xd6 ♖xf1+ 19 ♖xf1 cxd6 20 ♖f8+ ♔h7 21 ♘e4! is soon mate) 13 ♕d5+! ♔h8 14 exd6 (the point, White offers the exchange of queens, and kills the black attack) 14...♗h4+ (14...♕e8 15 0-0! cxd6 16 ♘xd6 is crushing for White, Heap-Kozlov, corr. 1994/97, and 14...♕xd5 15 ♘xd5 ♗xd6 16 ♘xd6 cxd6 17 ♗xd6 ♖d8 18 0-0 is also hopeless for Black, Heap-Sénéchaud, corr. 1994/96) 15 g3 ♕e8+ 16 ♔d2 ♗e6 17 ♕e4 ♘f6 18 ♕g2 ♘h5 19 ♗e3 and Black's initiative has ground to a halt, Heap-Krantz, corr. 1994/96.

b2) 11 ♘d5 courts danger, 11...♗h4+ 12 g3 0-0 (12...♗xg3+? 13 ♔d2) 13 ♗e4 (13 ♘xc7?! allows Black good play: 13...♗xg3+ 14 ♔d2 ♗f4+ 15 ♔c3 dxe5 16 ♗xf4 exd4+ [17 ♔b3!? ♘a6! {17...♖xf4 18 ♖e1!} 18 a4 ♘xc7 19 ♗xc7 b5 is unclear] 17 ♔d2 17...♖xf4 18 ♔c1 [18 ♘xa8 ♕h6!] 18...b5 19 ♘xa8 ♕h6 20 ♕d2 ♘f2 21 ♘c7? [21 ♖e1] 21...♘xh1 and Black should win, Villar-Radovic, 3rd Latvian Gambit WCh 1999; 13 gxh4 ♕xh4+ 14 ♔d2 ♘f2 15 ♕e1 ♕xd4 is also wild) 13...♘c6!? (development!) 14 ♘xc7 (14 ♘f4) 14...dxe5 15 ♘xa8 exd4 16 ♕e2 ♖f2 17 ♕d3 ♘b4 Black starts throwing the kitchen sink at White! 18 ♕b3 d3! 19 ♘e3+! (19 ♘d6+ ♔h8 20 ♗xd3 ♗xg3 21 ♘e4 ♖xh2+ 22 ♘xg3 ♕e5+ is good for Black) 19...♔h8 20 cxd3 ♖xh2 21 0-0! ♗e7 22 ♘xg4 ♗xg4 23 d4 ♖e2 24 ♗g2 (it seems that White is consolidating, but Black throws some fresh wood on the fire) 24...♘c6 25 ♕d5 ♖xg2+! 26 ♕xg2 ♘xd4 27 ♕xb7 ♘e2+ 28 ♔f2 ♗d6 29 ♔e1 ♗xg3+ 30 ♔d2 ♕g5+ 31 ♔d3 ♕d8+ 32 ♔c2 ♘d4+ 33 ♔c3 ♗e5 34 ♗g5 ♘f3+ 35 ♔b3 ♗e6+ 36 ♔a4 ♗d7+ 37 ♔b4 ♗d6+ 38 ♔b3 ♗e6+ 39 ♔a4 and now, rather than 39...♘xg5!? playing for the win, but going on to lose, Downey-Krantz, corr. 1994/98, Black should probably take the perpetual check by 39...♗d7+.

c) 9...♘e4 10 ♕f3 ♗h4+ 11 g3 ♘xg3 12 hxg3 ♗xg3+ 13 ♔d2 ♖f8 14 ♕d5, Grivainis-Strautins, corr. 1971/72, is also insufficient.

8 ♕xf3

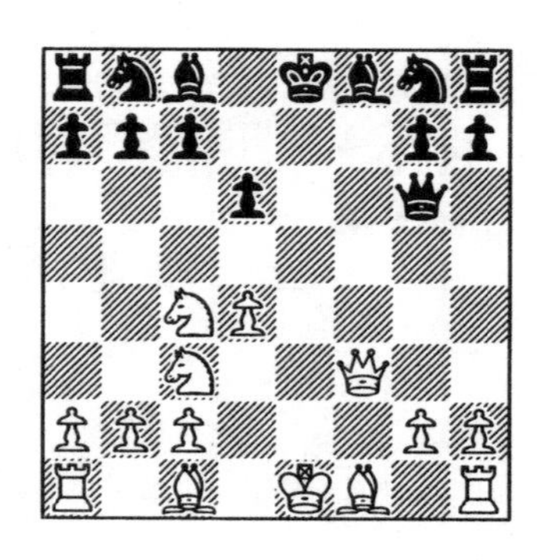

The key opening position, White enjoys a lead in development and will use the open e and f files for his rooks. Black will often need to try to exchange queens on g4 to blunt the white attack, but the ensuing endgame (assuming White cannot advantageously avoid it) favours White who can often play ♘e3-f5, gaining the bishop pair.

Now we have:

A 8...♘f6,
B 8...♗e7!?
C 8...♘c6?!

Others:

a) After 8...♕g4?! 9 ♕f2, keeping queens on the board, probably Black should try 9...♘f6 (as, unfortunately, 9...♘c6 fails to force a transposition to the main line, White can answer either 10 ♘b5 or 10 ♘d5, and 9...♕f5?! wastes more time with the queen, 10 ♗f4 ♘f6 11 0-0-0 ♗e7 12 ♘e3 ♕a5 13 ♗c4 and Black was in trouble, Morgado-Pupols, corr. 1970/72) 10 ♗e2, the problem, 10...♕e6 11 ♘e3 (menacing ♗c4) 11...d5?! (11...c6 was necessary) 12 ♘cxd5! ♘xd5 13 ♗g4 ♗b4+ 14 c3 ♘xc3 15 0-0! ♖f8?! (this loses a piece, 15...♕c6 16 ♕f7+ ♔d8 17 bxc3 is not particularly appetising, though) 16 ♗xe6 ♖xf2 17 ♗xc8 and the threats to both c3, and b7, are decisive, Downey-Cattermole, corr. 1999.

b) 8...c6? is a luxury Black can ill afford: 9 ♗d3 ♕f6 10 ♕e3+ (10 ♗f4!? d5 [10...♕xd4? 11 0-0-0 must win quickly] 11 0-0-0! with advantage, Clarke-Kozlov, corr. 1987) 10...♕e6, Endzelis-Strelis, corr. 1970/72, when 11 ♘e4! d5 12 ♘cd6+ would have been most unpleasant.

A 8...♘f6

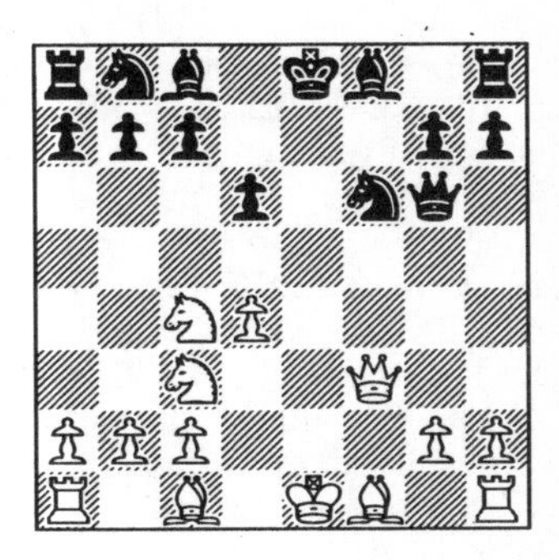

This quiet move aims to complete kingside development, and is recommended by the German theoretician Bücker.

9 ♗d3

Otherwise, 9 ♘e3!? is an interesting idea, as Black often seeks the exchange of queens on g4 in this variation, White decides to make this square unavailable, even if it means sacrificing a pawn. 9...♘c6 (9...c6?! is passive, 10 ♗d3 ♕f7 [the endgame after 10...♕h5 11 ♕xh5+ ♘xh5 12 0-0 ♗e7 is also unpleasant for Black after the standard 13 ♘f5, Clarke-Elburg, corr. 1994/95] 11 0-0 ♗e7 12 ♖e1! [even stronger than 12 ♘f5] 12...0-0 13 ♗c4 ♗e6 [forced, 13...d5? 14 ♘cxd5! cxd5 15 ♘xd5 wins] 14 d5! Clarke-Svendsen, corr. 1987, and now only 14...cxd5 15 ♘exd5 ♔h8 avoided immediate loss) 10 ♗d3!? (a pawn sac, 10 ♘b5!? also causes a certain amount of inconvenience, and may be superior, 10...♔d8 11 ♗d3 ♕e8 12 c3 a6 13 ♘a3 although 13...♗g4 14 ♕g3 d5 15 0-0 ♗d6 16 ♕h4 ♕h5 kept White's advantage to a minimum, Pihlajasalo-Hamalainen, Helsinki 1996) 10...♕f7 (10...♕h5? loses to 11 ♕xh5+ ♘xh5 12 ♘ed5, Tzermiadianos-Fragiadakis, Hania

1995) 11 0-0 ♘xd4 12 ♕d1 ♗e6 13 ♗e4! ♘c6 (Bücker's 13...c5 is also possible) 14 ♘ed5 and now, rather than 14...♔d7?! 15 ♗g5 with some pressure, Svendsen-Melchor, corr. 1990, Bücker points out that 14...0-0-0! is simple, 15 ♘xf6 (15 ♗g5 ♗e7 16 ♘xf6 gxf6 17 ♗xc6 bxc6 18 ♕d4 c5 is also fine for Black) 15...gxf6 16 ♗xc6 bxc6 17 ♕d4 I had previously intimated that this was good for White, but now Bücker suggests the line 17...c5 18 ♕a4 ♔b7 when White can force a draw by 19 ♕b5+ ♔a8 20 ♕c6+ but no more.

9...♕g4

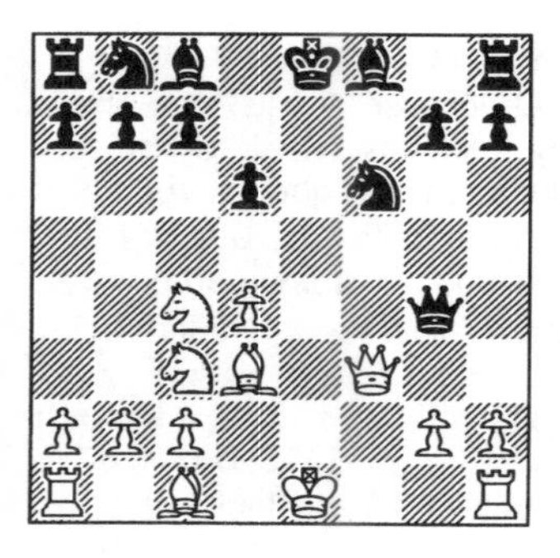

10 ♕e3+

The endgame following 10 ♕xg4 offers White a small plus, as Black no longer has the resource ...♘c6-b4, as in the main line C: 10...♗xg4 11 0-0 ♘c6 12 ♗g5 ♗e7 13 ♖f4! (13 ♖ae1 0-0-0, Hempel-Strautins, corr. 1970, and now 14 ♘e3-♘f5 is best) 13...♗h5!? (13...♗d7 14 ♗xf6 ♗xf6 15 ♘d5, Downey-Elburg, corr. 1994/96, when Bücker suggests 15...♗g5 16 ♖e1+ ♔d8 17 ♖f7 g6 but I don't like the look of the rook on the seventh rank, myself) 14 ♗xf6 (critical, 14 ♖e1 0-0-0 15 ♖f5 ♗g6 16 d5 ♘e5 17 ♘xe5 dxe5 18 ♖fxe5 ♗c5+ 19 ♗e3 ♗xe3+ 20 ♖5xe3 ♘xd5 is equal, and 14 d5!? ♘e5 15 ♘xe5 dxe5 16 ♖h4 ♗f7 17 ♖e1 ♗d6 18 ♗xf6 gxf6 19 ♖h6 ♗e7 20 ♖xh7 ♖xh7 21 ♗xh7 ♖d8 22 ♖d1 c6 grants Black sufficient play thanks to his bishop pair) 14...♗xf6 15 ♘d5 ♗xd4+ 16 ♖xd4 ♘xd4 17 ♘xc7+ ♔d7 18 ♘xa8 ♖xa8 19 ♖e1 (if 19 ♗xh7 then Black obtains a useful initiative by 19...d5! 20 ♘e3 ♘e2+ 21 ♔h1 d4 22 ♘c4 ♖f8 23 ♗d3 ♖f2 24 ♖e1 ♘f4) 19...♗f7 20 c3 ♘c6 21 a4 h6 22 ♗f5+ ½-½ Elburg-Kosten, email 2001.

However, 10 ♕f2 appears to make more sense here than in the main line, as White does not lose his d-pawn: 10...♗e7 11 0-0 0-0 the disadvantage is the white queen's placing on the f-file, opposite the black rook, 12 h3 ♕h5 13 ♗f4 ♘c6 14 ♖ae1 ♗d7 White has more space, but Black is solid, Bergsma-Wijnands, Rotterdam 1939.

10...♗e7 11 0-0 ♕h5!?

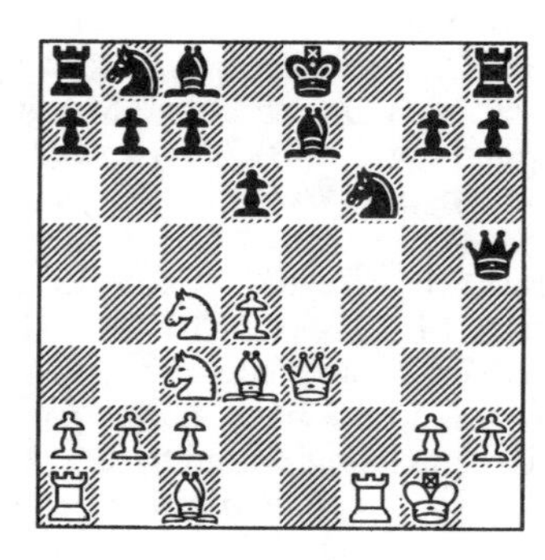

Bücker adorns this move with two exclamation marks, the point being that d5 is further controlled, and White's d5-push stopped.

Instead, 11...♘c6 forces a transposition to the main line, and offers Black the dual advantage of avoiding the line with 9 d5, and 9 ♘b5.

Bücker's analysis continues:

12 ♗d2

12 ♘b5 can be met by 12...♘a6 now, e.g. 13 ♗d2 when 13..0-0 is possible, as 14 ♕xe7!? ♖e8 traps the queen 15 ♕xc7 ♘xc7 16 ♘xc7 although White may be better here, anyway.

12 ♖e1 is easily met by 12...♘c6 now, as 13 d5?! (13 ♗e2 ♗g4) 13...♘xd5 14 ♘xd5 ♕xd5 15 ♗e4 ♕f7 is fine for Black.

12...♘c6 13 ♘b5

13 ♖ae1 0-0 14 d5!? ♘xd5 15 ♖xf8+ ♗xf8 16 ♗xh7+ [16 ♘xd5 ♕xd5 17 ♕e8? ♗h3] 16...♔xh7 17 ♕d3+ ♗f5 18 ♕xd5 ♗g6 seems OK for Black, who can rely on his bishop pair.

13...♔d8

The black king's position is awkward but, as Bücker notes, 'the white pieces aren't ideally placed', either.

14 ♘a5

If 14 h3 ♕xb5!? (instead, Bücker indicates 14...a6 15 ♘c3 ♘b4) 15 ♘e5 ♕xb2 16 ♘f7+ (16 ♖fb1 ♕xb1+ 17 ♖xb1 dxe5 18 dxe5 ♘d7 should favour Black) 16...♔d7 17 ♘xh8 (17 ♗c3 ♕a3) 17...♕xd4 appears very promising for Black.

And a 'sensible' move like 14 ♘c3?! is met by 14...♘g4 e.g. 15 ♕f4 ♘xd4!? (or 15...♖f8 16 ♕g3 ♗f6) 16 h3 ♕c5 17 ♔h1 ♖f8.

14...♘xa5 15 ♗xa5 b6 16 ♗d2 ♖e8 17 ♕g3 ♕g4 18 ♕xg4 ♗xg4 19 ♗f4

Else Black plays ...c6.

19...a6 20 ♘c3 c6 21 ♖ae1 ♔c7

...when White's advantage is tiny. This line is certainly worth testing.

B 8...♗e7!?

This move has the advantage that Black can offer the exchange of queens from f6, as well as from g4.

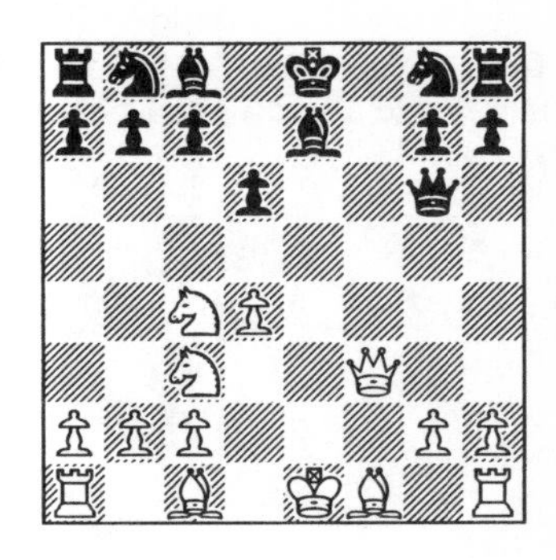

9 ♗d3

9 ♘d5 ♗h4+ 10 g3 ♗d8 11 ♗d3 ♕g4 12 ♕e3+ ♕e6 is not too frightening, Downey-Malmström, corr. 1994/96.

9...♕g4

All the same, Black should prefer this square here, when White can play an endgame with an edge, but no more, as after 9...♕f6?! 10 ♗f4! is a problem 10...♕h4+ (10...♕xd4? loses after 11 ♘b5 ♕c5 12 ♗e3) 11 ♗g3 ♕g4 (11...♕xd4? again loses to 12 ♘b5 i.e. 12...♕c5 13 ♗f2 ♕b4+ 14 c3, soon winning, Elburg-Yus, corr. 2000) 12 0-0 (12 ♕f2 looks more aggressive) 12...♘f6 13 ♖ae1 and Black suffers considerably, Grivainis-Castelli, corr. 1970/72.

10 ♕xg4

10 0-0!? ♕xf3 11 ♖xf3 ♘f6 12 ♘e3 0-0 13 ♘ed5, White has some pressure, but the black position is solid, Kosten-Voliani, email 2001.

10...♗xg4 11 ♘e3 ♗e6

11...♗d7 is similar, 12 0-0 c6 13 ♘f5 ♗xf5 14 ♗xf5 with the bishops, and some advantage, Downey-Grivainis/Hayward, corr. 1997.

12 0-0

12 ♗e4!? c6 13 ♘f5 ♗xf5 14 ♗xf5—White has the bishop pair, Heap-Melchor, corr. 1994/96.

12...♘f6 13 ♗f5 ♗d7 14 ♘ed5

14 ♗xd7+ ♘bxd7 15 ♘f5 ♔f7 offers White a small plus.

14...♗d8

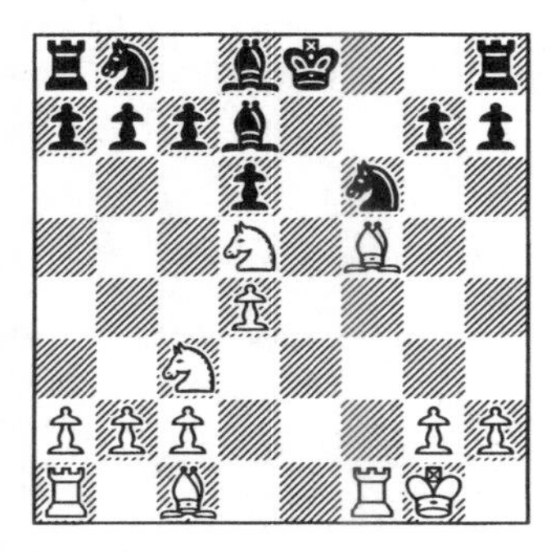

15 ♗g5?! ♘xd5! 16 ♘xd5 ♗xg5 17 ♘xc7+ ♔d8 18 ♘xa8 ♘c6

But the knight never escaped from a8, and Black won, Grivainis/Hayward-Strautins, corr. 1999.

C 8...♘c6?!

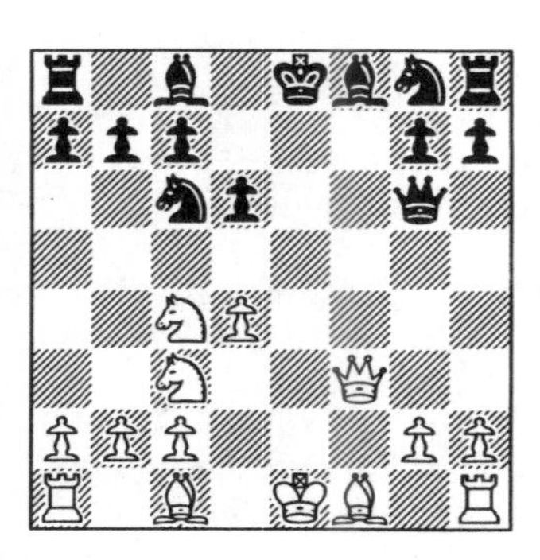

By far the most popular, Black hopes to gain time counterattacking the d-pawn, but the disadvantage is that White's pawn push to d5 will gain a tempo at some time.

White has four dangerous replies:

C1 9 ♘d5,
C2 9 ♘b5!
C3 9 d5
C4 9 ♗d3

Otherwise, 9 ♗e3 is harmless, 9...♘f6 (but not 9...♘b4? when, rather than 10 ♘a3?! c6 11 d5, Webster-Crimp, Australia 1994, after which 11...♘f6 is fine, 10 ♘b5! is strong, i.e. 10...♘xc2+ 11 ♔d2 ♘xa1 12 ♘xc7+ ♔d8 13 ♗d3 ♕f6 14 ♘xa8 which should win) 10 ♗d3 ♕g4 11 0-0 Sprod-Krustkains, corr. 1979, and now 11...♘b4 is best.

9 ♗e2? ♘xd4 10 ♕e3+ ♘e6 11 ♗d2 ♘f6 12 0-0-0 ♗e7 13 h3 0-0 ∓ Stockholm-Riga, corr. 1934/36.

C1 9 ♘d5

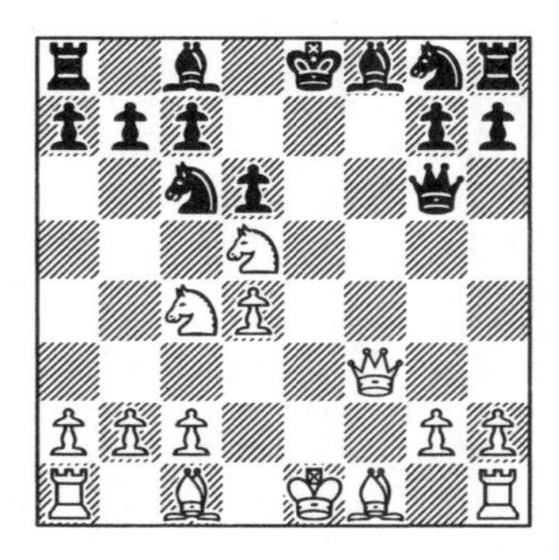

9...♗g4!

There is no other sensible way to defend c7.

10 ♗d3!?

10 ♕e3+ also has its points, 10...♔d7 (or 10...♔d8 11 ♗d3 ♕e6 12 0-0 ♘ge7 ±) 11 ♗d3 ♕f7 (but not 11...♗f5 12 ♘f4 ♕f6 13 ♗xf5+ ♕xf5 14 0-0 with a dangerous initiative, or 11...♕e6?! 12 ♘f4!) 12 ♕g5 and now, instead of 12...♕e6+? when either knight to e3 wins a piece, i.e. 13 ♘de3 (13 ♘ce3 ♘h6 14 0-0 also wins) 13...d5 14 ♘e5+ ♘xe5 15 dxe5 ♘h6 16 ♘xg4 and the knight cannot be recaptured without allowing a fork with ♗f5+, Schrader-Mlotkowski, St.Louis 1904, my old suggestion 12...♗e6 13 ♖f1 ♕e8 still looks unclear.

10 Qf2?! allows the king to escape, though, 10...0-0-0 11 Bd3 Qh5 12 Nf4 Qe8+ 13 Be3 d5 14 Nd2 and now, rather than 14...Nxd4?! 15 0-0 Nc6 16 Bxa7 d4?! 17 Bb5 g5 Endzelis-Tomson, corr. 1974, when 18 Rae1 is strong, 14...Nb4 or a sensible developing move like 14...Nf6 is fine.

10...Bxf3

The simplest, 10...Qe6+?! is best answered by 11 Nce3! Bxf3 12 Nxc7+ Kd7 13 Nxe6 Kxe6 14 gxf3 Nxd4 (analysis of Malmström) when 15 Kf2 is better for White, due to his bishops (15 0-0 was also reasonable, Stevens-Poland, corr. 1993, but why not keep the king close to the centre?).

10...Qh5!? is ambitious, but rather than 11 Qe4+ Kd7 12 0-0 Re8 13 Qf4 Be6 14 Nde3 (14 Nce3!? Bxd5 15 g4 is possible) 14...g5 15 Qf2 Nxd4 which won a pawn, although the position remains messy, Charlick-Mann, corr. 1881, 11 Qe3+ Kd7 12 Nf4 Qf7 13 Qg3 is promising.

11 Bxg6+ hxg6 12 Nxc7+?

A typical computer mistake, 12 gxf3 Nxd4!? (12...Kd7 is safer) 13 Nxc7+ Kd7 14 Nxa8 Nxc2+ should be tried.

12...Kd7 13 Nxa8 Bxg2 14 Rg1 Be4 15 c3 Be7!

The bishop goes to h4 to keep the e7-square free, 15...Nf6 16 b4! b5 17 Ne3 Be7 18 a4! is quite unclear, Kharitonov-Vujadinović, corr. 1998.

16 b4 Bh4+ 17 Kd1 Nf6 18 b5 Ne7 19 Ba3 Nf5!

There is no rush!

20 Kd2 Rxa8

Black has a winning material advantage, Fritz 3 - Tasc R30 Ver.2, Bauermeister 1995.

C2 9 Nb5!

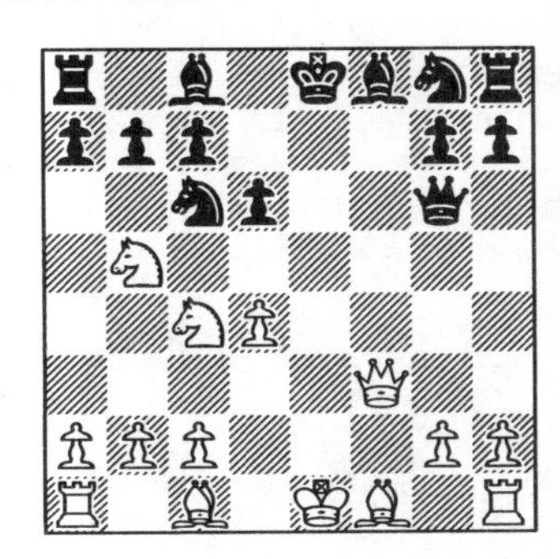

This rare line looks very similar to the previous variation, is even more dangerous, and comes close to being a refutation of 8...Nc6.

9...Bg4

9...Qe6+ 10 Be2 Qd7 is the only sensible alternative, but it doesn't look especially tempting.

10 Qc3!

The latest idea, White prepares threats to c7. Others:

a) 10 Qe3+?! is less effective, 10...Kd7 11 Bd3 Qf7! to stop White from castling short, 12 Rf1 (12 Qg5 Be6 13 Rf1 Nf6) 12...Nf6 13 Qf4 Qh5! (even stronger than 13...Re8+ 14 Be3 Be6 as, although Black obtained the advantage after 15 Ne5+!? dxe5 16 dxe5 Nd5?! [16...a6!] 17 Qxf7+ Bxf7 18 Rxf7+ Kc8 19 Bf4? g6 20 Bg3 Nxe5 and went on to win in Macht-Betinš, corr. 1933/34, 19 Nxa7+ Nxa7 20 Bxa7 Rxe5+ 21 Kd2 looks playable, and good, as 21...b6 can be met by 22 Ba6+) 14 Ne3 Nb4! 15 Bf5+ Bxf5 16 Qxf5+ Qxf5 17 Rxf5 Re8 18 Kd1 c6 19 Nc3 d5 and after some forcing play Black has a plus, Grivainis/Hayward-Downey, corr. 1997.

b) 10 Bd3?! Bxf3 (10...Qe6+?! 11 Ne3! Bxf3 12 Nxc7+ transposes to 9 Nd5) 11 Bxg6+ hxg6 12 gxf3

(12 ♘xc7+? also transposes to the above) 12...♔d7 13 d5 (13 c3?! ♖e8+ 14 ♘e3 d5 menaces ...a6, and favours Black) 13...♘b4 14 ♘e3 ♘f6 is very pleasant for Black, whose kingside pawns are no weaker than White's.

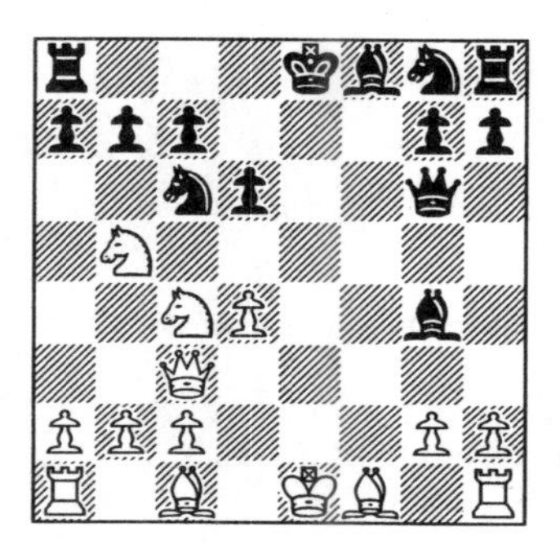

10...♖c8

This is not completely satisfactory, but what else?

a) 10...0-0-0?! loses: 11 d5 a6 (obviously the c6-knight cannot move without allowing mate) 12 dxc6 (12 ♘xc7 is also convincing: 12...♔xc7 13 dxc6 ♖e8+ 14 ♗e3 [14 ♘e3!?] 14...d5 15 ♕a5+; this looks horrific for Black although in Malmström-Hage, corr. 1999, Black discovered considerable resources: 15...♔b8 16 c7+ ♔c8 17 ♘b6+ ♔xc7 18 ♘xd5+ ♔b8 19 ♕c7+ ♔a8 20 h3? [20 ♗b5! axb5 21 0-0 wins] 20...♕g5! 21 ♕b6 ♖xe3+ 22 ♕xe3 ♕xd5 23 hxg4 [23 ♕e8+ ♔a7 24 ♕xf8 ♕e5+ forces a perpetual] 23...♘f6 24 ♗e2 ♗c5 25 ♕d3 ♕e6 26 ♕f5 ♕d6 27 ♖h3 ♖e8 with a powerful attack on the dark squares surrounding the uncastled white king) 12...axb5 13 ♘e3 ♕h5? (13...d5 14 ♗d3 ♕e8 is better) 14 a4! bxc6 15 ♕xc6 ♘e7 16 ♕a6+ ♔d7 17 ♗xb5+ c6 18 ♕b7+ and Black is quite lost, Malmström-Van Gameren, corr. 1999.

b) and 10...♕f7?! 11 d5 leaves the knight without a square, e.g. 11...♘d8 12 ♘e3.

c) 10...♔d8?! 11 d5 a6 12 ♘xc7 ♔xc7 13 dxc6 is also very strong.

11 d5 ♘ce7 12 ♘e3 ♘f6

As Ruggeri Laderchi pointed out to me after our game, 12...a6?! is worse, 13 ♘a7! (13 ♘xc7+ ♔d7 14 ♗d3 ♕h5 15 ♕d4 ♔xc7 16 ♘xg4 ♕xd5 and at least Black is not material down) 13...♖a8 14 ♕xc7! ♖xa7 15 ♗d3 ♕h5 16 ♕b8+ ♘c8 17 ♗e2! and White regains his piece, with interest.

13 ♗d3 ♕h5 14 ♘xc7+! ♔d8 15 ♘xg4 ♖xc7 16 ♘xf6 ♕h4+ 17 g3 ♖xc3

Following 17...♕xf6 18 ♕xf6 gxf6 19 c4 the endgame is hopeless for Black, Gentinetta-Rosso, corr. 1998.

18 gxh4 ♖xd3 19 cxd3 gxf6 20 ♖g1 ♘xd5 21 ♗d2

Black has no compensation for the exchange, Kosten - Ruggeri Laderchi, email 2001.

C3 9 d5

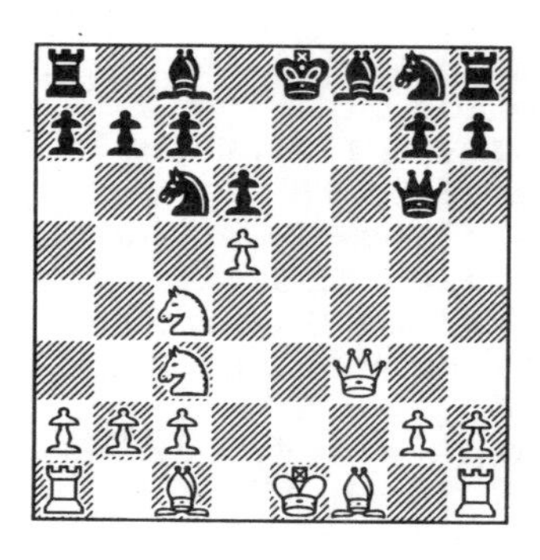

9...♘b4

9...♘e5?! 10 ♘xe5 dxe5 11 ♗d3 ♕f6 12 ♕g3 ♗d6 13 ♘e4 ♕f7 14 ♖f1 ♘f6 15 ♗h6!, undermining the black knight, with a crushing

position, Noomen-Simmelink, email 1999.

10 ♘e3

10 ♘b5? is not as ridiculous as it appears, 10...♘xc2+ 11 ♔f2 ♘xa1? meets the rejoinder 12 ♗d3! ♕f6 13 ♘xc7+ ♔d8? 14 ♗g5! ♕xg5 15 ♕xf8+ ♔xc7 16 ♕xd6 mate! But Black has the interposition 11...♗g4! and should win.

10...♘f6

Black has tried finding another move here to avoid problems, but each move has its drawbacks, i.e. 10...♗e7 11 ♗b5+ ♔d8 12 0-0 ♘f6 13 ♕e2! (making a3 a serious menace, the b4-knight is very exposed) 13...c6?! 14 dxc6 bxc6 15 a3! ♘xc2 16 ♗xc6 ♘xa1 17 ♕b5 1-0, Downey-Sireta, corr. 1994/95.

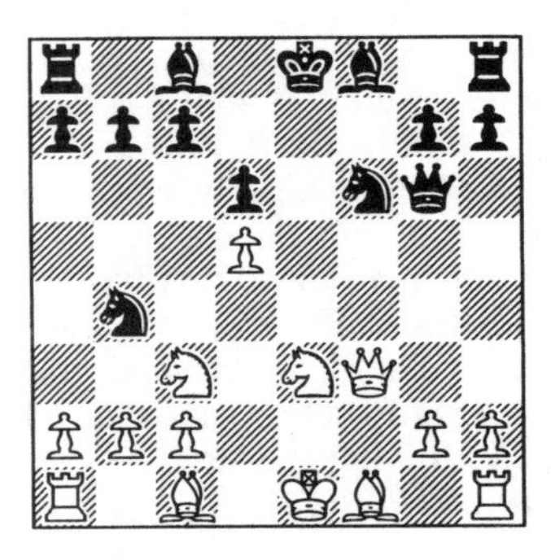

11 a3

a) 11 ♗b5+!? is unusual, but good: 11...♗d7 12 ♗xd7+ ♘xd7 (12...♔xd7?! has been played, but apart from 13 ♕h3+ ♔d8 14 0-0 with some advantage, Svendsen-Spiegel, corr. 1991, 13 ♕e2, threatening ♕b5+, 13...♘a6 14 ♕b5+ ♔c8 15 0-0 is simple, and strong) 13 ♗d2?! (13 0-0! is better, 13...0-0-0 14 ♕f2 and 15 a3 with a significant plus) when, in the game Dutreeuw-Hector, Geneva 1990, the Black position became very uncomfortable following 13...♗e7? 14 ♕e4! ♕xe4 15 ♘xe4 ♘a6 16 0-0 ♘f6 17 ♘g5 ♔d7 18 ♖ae1 c6 19 ♘f5 ♗f8 20 dxc6+ bxc6 21 ♘e6 ♘d5 22 c4 with advantage. I think that Black should take the bull by the horns: 13...♘xc2+! 14 ♘xc2 ♕xc2 15 ♖c1 ♕xb2 16 ♖b1 ♕c2 17 ♕e2+ ♗e7 18 0-0 (not 18 ♖xb7? when 18...0-0! wins) with compensation for the two pawns.

b) 11 ♕e2!? is untried, and yet threatens both ♕b5+ and a discovered attack with the knight; 11...♗d7 seems best, 12 a3 ♘a6 13 ♕f3 with some advantage.

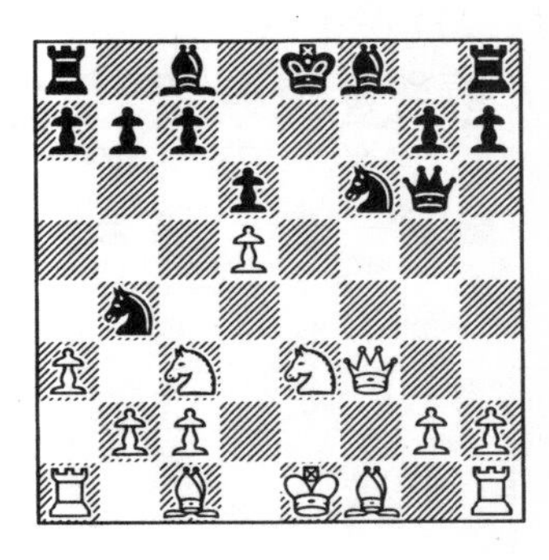

11...♘a6

Forced, 11...♘xc2+? is now known to lose: 12 ♘xc2 ♕xc2 13 ♗d3 ♕b3 14 ♘e4! (not 14 0-0?! which gives Black time to recover, 14...♗g4 15 ♕e3+ ♔d8 16 ♕g5 h6 17 ♕h4 ♗e7, Gaard-Malmström, corr. 1991, White's compensation is not quite sufficient) 14...♔e7 (this loses, but so does everything else, 14...♕a4 15 ♘xf6+ gxf6 16 ♕xf6 ♕a5+ [if 16...♖g8 17 0-0 wins on the spot, i.e. 17...♕d7 18 ♗g5 1-0, Clarke-Logunov, corr. 1994/95] 17 ♗d2 ♕xd5 18 0-0! ♕xd3 19 ♕f7+ ♔d8 20 ♗g5+ ♗e7 21 ♕xe7 mate, Heap-Jackson, corr. 1994/95, 14...♗e7?? is quickest of all, 15 ♘xf6+ 1-0, Lane-Valverde Lopez, corr. 1995, as 15...♗xf6 16 ♗g6+

wins the exposed black queen, and 14...♘xe4?? 15 ♕xe4+ is also hopeless 15...♔f7 16 0-0+ ♔g8 17 ♕f3) 15 ♗g5 ♕xb2 (15...♕xd5 16 ♗xf6+ gxf6 17 ♕xf6+ ♔d7 [17...♔e8 18 0-0-0 ♕e5 19 ♘xd6+ ♗xd6 20 ♖he1 1-0, Trani-Rebaudo, corr. 1999] 18 ♕xh8 ♕xd3 19 ♘c5+ dxc5 20 ♖d1 winning the queen, Downey-Rosso, corr. 1999) 16 0-0 ♕d4+ (16...h6 17 ♘xf6 hxg5 18 ♖ae1+ 1-0 Svendsen-Browning corr. 1991) 17 ♔h1 ♕xd5 18 ♗xf6+ 1-0, Ruggeri Laderchi-Elburg, corr. training game 1998.

12 ♗d3

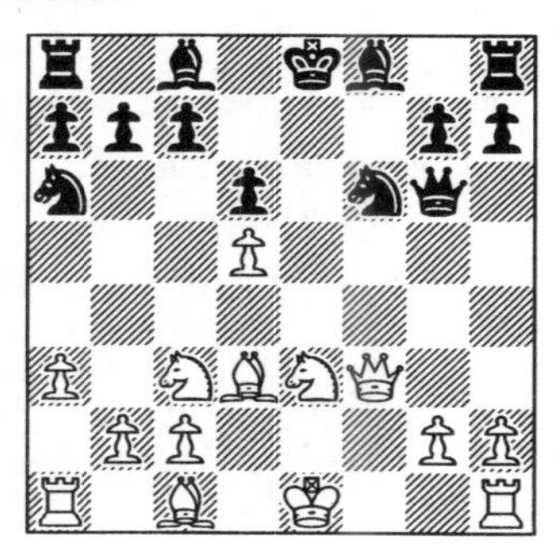

12...♕h5

White maintains the advantage in the endgame after this, the most popular choice at the present time. But 12...♕f7?! is worse, 13 b4! (to keep the black knight offside, although 13 0-0 will probably amount to the same, as 13...♘c5 is countered by 14 ♗b5+ ♗d7 15 b4! a6 16 bxc5 axb5 17 c6 bxc6 18 dxc6 ♗e6 19 ♘xb5 ♔d8 20 ♘d4 which is very unpleasant for Black, Kruijer-Schoesser, corr. 1998) 13...♗e7 (13...♗d7 14 0-0 0-0-0 15 ♗xa6 bxa6 16 ♕e2 ♕e8 17 ♕xa6+ ♔b8 18 ♘c4 with advantage, Gaard-Nyman, corr. 1991) 14 0-0 0-0 15 ♘f5 (currently favoured, although 15 ♗b2 would be my preference, 15...♗d7 16 ♖ae1 [16 ♘e4!?] 16...♕h5 17 ♕g3 with a very aggressive set-up, Svendsen-Heap, corr. 1991) 15...♗d8!? (to conserve both bishops, 15...♗xf5 16 ♗xf5 ♔h8 17 ♗g5 ♖ae8 18 ♖ae1 ♗d8 19 ♖xe8 ♖xe8 20 ♕h3 g6 21 ♗e6 with considerable advantage, Clarke-Gaard, corr. 1990) 16 ♗h6!? (aiming for a direct refutation, 16 ♗g5 is also good, with the point that 16...h6? loses to 17 ♗xh6 1-0, Clarke-Borrmann, corr. 1992, and 16 ♗b2 likewise) 16...♕h5 17 ♗xg7! ♕xf3 18 ♖xf3 ♗xf5 19 ♗xf8 ♗xd3 20 cxd3 ♔xf8 21 ♘e4 ♔g7 22 ♖af1 ♘xd5?! (22...♘xe4 23 dxe4 ♗g5 is a better chance) 23 ♖f7+ ♔g6 24 ♖f8 ♖b8? (24...♔h6 had to be tried) 25 ♖g8+ ♔h6 26 ♖f3 and the threat of mate forces the gain of material, Svendsen-Stummer, corr. 1994/95.

13 ♕xh5+ ♘xh5 14 0-0

14 b4, immediately confining the a6-knight to the edge, 14...♗e7 (14...g6!? is an alternative, 15 0-0 ♗g7 16 ♗d2 ♘f6 17 ♘b5 0-0 offers Black a playable position, Sénéchaud-Budovskis, corr. 1994/95) 15 0-0 transposes.

14...♗e7

Trying to bring the knight back into the game by 14...♘c5?! is most simply answered by 15 ♘b5, forcing the retreat 15...♘a6 when Black's position has only worsened, Heap-Elburg, corr. 1994/97, as 15...♔d8 loses a pawn to 16 ♗xh7. The simple 14...♘f6?! is also possible, 15 b4 ♗e7 16 ♗b2 0-0 17 ♖ae1 ♘d7 (17...♗d7?! 18 ♘f5 ♗d8?! 19 ♘xg7! winning, Ruggeri Laderchi-Trani, corr. 1999, as 19...♔xg7 20 ♘e4 threatens the almost unstoppable 21 ♘xf6 ♗xf6 22 ♖e7+) 18 ♖xf8+ ♗xf8 19 ♘e4 h6 20 c4 and White enjoys a very consequent space advantage, Simmelink-Bartsch, corr. 1999.

15 b4

Once again the key to White's play, the a6-knight is shut out.

15...♗f6

15...♘f6?! transposes into the previous note.

16 ♗d2

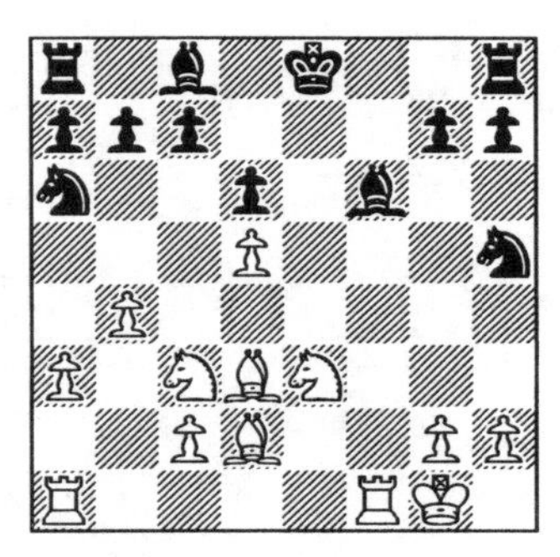

16...♗d4

The bishop seeks greener pastures, and anyway, 16...0-0? 17 g4 forces Black to exchange this one active piece, 17...♗xc3 (17...♖e8 18 gxh5 ♖xe3 [unfortunately, 18...♗xc3 19 ♗xc3 ♖xe3 20 ♖ae1 ♖xe1 21 ♖xe1, intending 22 ♖e7, is also hopeless for Black] 19 ♗xe3 ♗xc3 20 ♖ab1 gives Black precisely zero compensation for the exchange, Ruggeri Laderchi-Malmström, corr. 1997) 18 ♖xf8+ (18 ♗xc3? ♘f4 is less convincing, Svendsen-Sénéchaud, corr. 1990) 18...♔xf8 19 ♗xc3 ♘f6 20 ♖f1 ♔e7 21 g5 winning material.

17 ♔h1

17 ♖ae1 ♘f6 18 ♘b5 (18 ♖f4 ♗b6 19 ♗b5+?! ♗d7 20 ♗xd7+ ♔xd7 21 g4 ♖hf8 22 ♔g2 offers White a slight edge, Svendsen-Niemand, corr. 1994/96, and 18 ♔h1 transposes) 18...♗b6 19 a4 0-0 20 a5 ♗xe3+ 21 ♖xe3 ♗d7 22 c4 ♘g4! heading for e5, Black is only slightly worse, Stockholm Vasa Chess Club - Riga Seniors Chess Club, corr. 1934/36.

17...♘f6 18 ♖ae1 0-0 19 ♘f5 ♗xf5 20 ♗xf5 ♔h8 21 ♗e6

White has a slight advantage, Sakellarakis-Gåård, email 1998.

C4 9 ♗d3

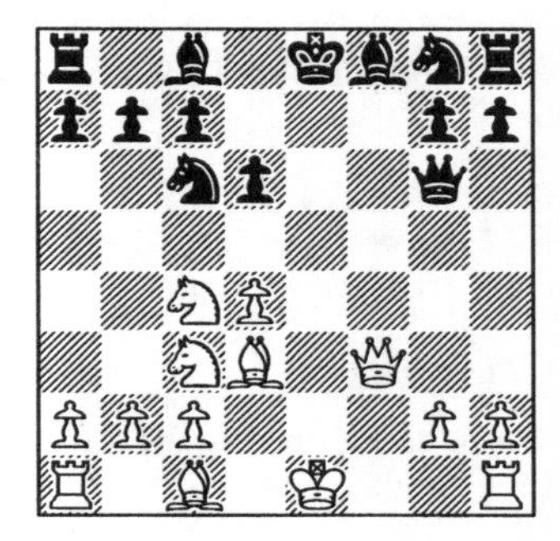

The most logical, not being afraid to give up the d-pawn, if need be.

9...♕g4

Black attempts to cover his development problems by entering the endgame.

9...♕e6+!? is possibly not as bad as I originally thought, 10 ♗e3 (10 ♔f2?! leads nowhere, 10...♘xd4 11 ♘d5 ♘xf3 12 ♘xc7+ ♔f7 13 ♘xe6 ♗xe6 14 ♔xf3 ♖c8 15 ♘e3 level, Riga-Trani, corr. 1997) 10...♘xd4 11 ♕f4 ♘c6 12 0-0 ♘f6 (12...♘ge7!? is interesting: 13 ♖ae1 ♕g4 14 ♕f7+ ♔d8 15 ♖f4 ♗e6! 16 ♘xd6! cxd6 17 ♕xf8+ ♖xf8 18 ♖xf8+ ♔d7 19 ♖xa8 ♘c8!? which is messy, Elburg-Sveinsson, corr. 2000) 13 ♖ae1 ♗e7 (13...♘d5?? is a blunder, 14 ♘xd5 ♕xd5 15 ♗e4! ♔d8 [pointless, but 15...♕h5 allows 16 ♗xc6+ bxc6 17 ♕xf8+! and mate in 6] 16 ♗xd5 1-0, Dzervenis-Zagata, corr. 1993) 14 ♗d4 ♕f7 (14...♕g8? 15 ♘xd6+! cxd6 16 ♕xd6 ♕f7 17 ♗xf6 gxf6 18 ♘d5 proved decisive in Meyers-Crowl, Australia 1930) 15 ♗xf6 gxf6 16 ♕xf6 ♕xf6 17 ♖xf6 ♘e5! 18 ♘xe5 ♗xf6 19 ♘g6+ ♔d8 20 ♘xh8 ♗xh8 21 ♗xh7 and Black's powerful dark-squared bishop is not enough compensation for the two passed pawns, Melchor-Crimp, corr. 1995.

Now White has a choice between the endgame, and two more complicated lines:

C41 10 ♕xg4
C42 10 ♕f2
C43 10 ♕e3+

C41 10 ♕xg4

White can gain a small edge after the exchange of queens:

10...♗xg4

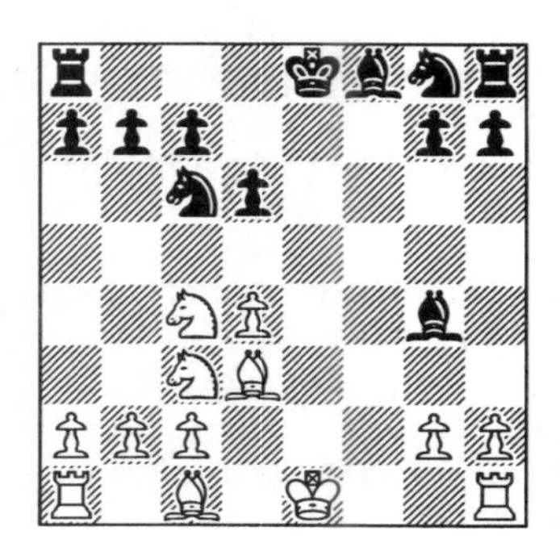

11 ♘e3

Best, other moves led to a small advantage for Black in both Alberts-Strautins, corr. 1969, after 11 ♗e3?! ♘b4! 12 ♗e4 ♘f6 13 a3 ♘xe4 14 axb4 ♘xc3 15 bxc3, and in Schmidt-Hempel, Germany 1969, which went 11 0-0?! ♘b4! (White's lead in development means little in this ending, whereas possession of the two bishops is important) 12 ♗e4 (White could have tried to muddy the waters a little with 12 ♘b5!?) 12...♘f6 13 ♗xb7? ♖b8 14 ♗f3 ♗xf3 15 ♖xf3 ♘xc2 16 ♖b1 ♘xd4 ∓.

11...♗d7 12 ♘ed5 0-0-0 13 ♘b5 ♘f6 14 ♘bxc7 ♖e8+!? 15 ♔f2

15 ♘xe8? ♘xd5 traps the e8-knight.

15...♘xd5 16 ♘xd5 ♘xd4 17 ♗e3 ♘c6 18 ♖he1

...with an edge, because of the isolated d6-pawn, Scarani-Rosso, corr. 1998.

C42 10 ♕f2

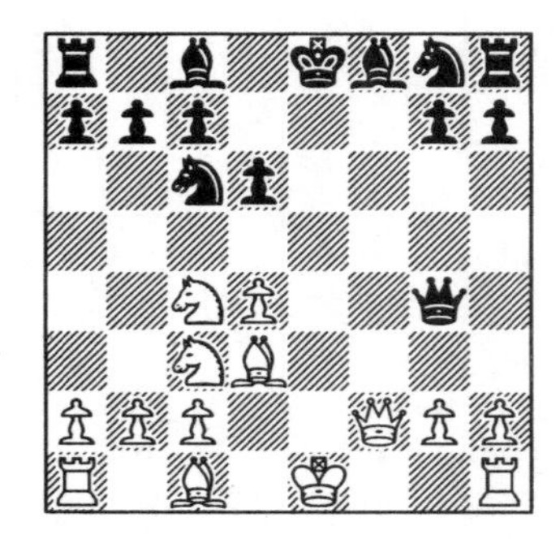

10...♕xd4

Taking the d4 pawn whilst at the same time continuing to offer the exchange of queens. Apart from its basic numerical value, the gain of this pawn is also strategically desirable for Black as he no longer has to worry about White pushing d5, and he can now use the e5 square. Nevertheless, if the note to White's next move proves convincing Black may have to resort to 10...♘f6 which is tried occasionally: 11 0-0 (11 h3?! ♕e6+ 12 ♗e3 d5?! [12...♘b4!] 13 ♘b5 ♗b4+ 14 c3 ♕e7 15 ♘d2? [15 ♘e5! is clearly better] 15...a6 16 ♘xc7+ ♕xc7 17 cxb4 ♘xb4 18 ♗b1 [18 ♕e2 ♘xd3+ 19 ♕xd3 ♕g3+ is also terrible] 18...♕c1+ 19 ♔e2 ♕xb2 20 a3 0-0 ∓ Yudovich-Elzov, Moscow 1941) 11...♗e7

(11...♘b4 is more combative) 12 ♘b5 (12 h3?! ♕h5 13 ♗e3 0-0 14 ♕g3 is level, Gåård-Müller, corr. 1988) 12...0-0 13 ♘e3 (13 ♘xc7?! ♘d5) 13...♕d7 14 ♘f5 ♘b4 (14...♗d8 15 ♕g3 ♘b4 might be more accurate) 15 ♕g3 ♘h5? (15...♗d8 16 ♗c4+ ♔h8 17 ♕b3 ♘c6 is fine for Black) and now, as well as the 16 ♘xe7+ ♕xe7 17 ♖xf8+ ♕xf8 18 ♕h4, with advantage, of Grivainis-Eglitis, corr. 1977/79, White also had 16 ♕e1! ♖xf5?! 17 ♗xf5 ♕xb5 18 ♗xc8 winning. Incidentally, at the end of this game White makes the most awful blunder, that I can only explain in one of two ways: a) it was a slip of the pen or b) he had the wrong position set up on his board!

Otherwise 10...♗e7?! allows 11 ♘d5, Medina-Delara, Caracas 1954.

11 ♗e3

The most common, by far, but not the best.

11 ♕e2+! creates more problems, 11...♘e5 (11...♗e7? 12 ♘b5) 12 ♘b5! (if 12 ♘xe5 then going for the endgame by 12...♕xe5 is simplest, e.g. 13 ♘d5 ♕xe2+ 14 ♗xe2 ♔d8 15 0-0 ♘f6 [15...♗e7!? 16 ♘xe7 ♘xe7 17 ♖f7 ♗e6 18 ♖xg7 ♘f5 is also feasible] 16 ♗g5 h6!, as 12...dxe5? is too risky, 13 ♕h5+ ♔e7 14 ♗g5+ [14 ♕g5+! ♘f6 15 ♗e3 ♕d6 16 0-0-0 is really nasty] 14...♘f6 15 0-0-0!? [15 ♖f1] 15...♗g4 16 ♘d5+ ♔d6 17 ♘xf6?! [whilst amusing, this is hardly correct! 17 ♕f7! ♘xd5 18 ♗f5 must be better for White] 17...♗xh5 18 ♘xh5 ♔c6 19 ♖he1 ♕a4!, good for Black, Frolik-Grünfeld, Torremolinos 1986) 12...♕h4+ 13 g3 ♕e7 14 ♘xe5 dxe5 15 ♗g5 ♘f6 (15...♕xg5!? 16 ♘xc7+ ♔f7 17 ♘xa8 ♘f6 might be a better practical try) 16 0-0-0 (threatening 17 ♗xf6 gxf6 18 ♕h5+) 16...♗g4 (going into a difficult endgame, but there is nothing better) 17 ♗xf6 ♗xe2 18 ♗xe7 ♗xd1 19 ♗xf8 ♗xc2 20 ♗xc2 ♔xf8 21 ♖e1 c6 22 ♘d6 b6 23 ♖xe5, White is clearly better, Zaniratti-Tatlow, corr. 1999.

11...♕f6

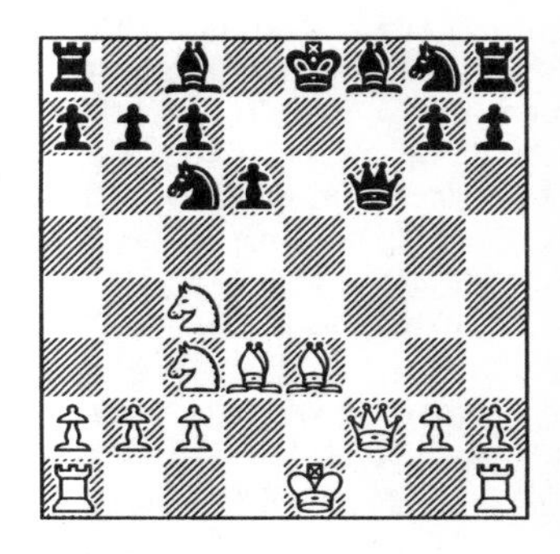

12 ♕g3

The other possibilities:

a) 12 ♕e2 also avoids the ending but 12...♗e6 gives Black good play:

a1) 13 ♘e4?! ♕h4+! (better than 13...♕e7 14 ♗g5 ♕d7 [14...♘f6? 15 0-0 ♗xc4 16 ♗xc4? ♕xe4 17 ♕xe4+ ♘xe4 18 ♖ae1 with enough play for a draw, Grivainis-Hempel, corr. 1970/73, but White missed 16 ♖xf6! ♗xd3 17 cxd3 which wins material] 15 0-0 ♗e7 16 ♗xe7 ♕xe7?! [16...♘gxe7!? 17 ♕h5+ ♔d8 keeps the game alive] 17 ♖ae1 ♗xc4 18 ♕h5+! g6 19 ♘f6+ ♔d8? [19...♘xf6 20 ♖xe7+ ♘xe7 offers some drawing chances] 20 ♖xe7 gxh5? 21 ♖e8 mate, Grivainis-Gunderam, corr. 1970) 14 ♗f2 (White wants to keep the queens on, alternatively: 14 ♘g3 ♕g4 15 ♕xg4 [15 ♕f2? ♗xc4] 15...♗xg4 16 0-0 ♘f6 [16...d5! is even better] 17 h3 ♗d7 18 ♗g5 ♗e7, White doesn't have enough for a pawn, Grivainis-Budovskis, corr. 1977/79, or 14 g3

♕g4 15 ♕f2? [15 ♘g5 ♕xe2+ 16 ♔xe2 ♗g4+ 17 ♔f2 ♘f6 does not really give White much compensation for the pawn, Zabaznov-Tatlow, email 1998] 15...♗xc4! also Grivainis-Budovskis, when White tried a good bluff 16 h3!?, as he saw that 16 ♗xc4? ♕xe4 17 ♕f7+ ♔d8 18 ♕xf8+ ♔d7 loses after both 19 ♕xa8 ♕xe3+! and 19 ♕f7+ ♘ge7 20 ♔d2 ♖af8. In the game Black could have won by 16...♕e6, but instead he played 16...♕g6? and White saved himself by 17 ♗xc4 ♕xe4 18 ♕f7+ ♔d8 19 ♕xf8+ ♔d7 20 ♕xg7+ ♘ge7 21 ♕g4+!, revealing the importance of the h3 move.) 14...♕g4 15 ♕e3!? d5 (15...0-0-0!? 16 h3! ♕xg2 17 ♘exd6+ ♗xd6 18 ♕xe6+ ♔b8 19 ♖g1 is unclear) 16 h3 d4 17 ♕d2!? (17 hxg4 dxe3 18 ♘xe3 is about equal) 17...♕xg2 18 ♘g3? (18 0-0-0 is stronger) Knudsen-Hayward, corr. 1986, 18...♘f6 with two extra pawns.

a2) 13 ♖f1 ♕e7 14 0-0-0 (14 ♘e4? ♗xc4 ∓ Swafield-Dreibergs, corr. 1968) 14...0-0-0 (14...d5? meets the rejoinder 15 ♘xd5! ♗xd5 16 ♗c5) 15 ♖de1 d5 16 ♗c5! ♕g5+ (16...♕xc5?! 17 ♕xe6+ ♔b8 18 ♘xd5!) 17 ♗e3 =, Zschorn-Tiemann, corr. 1989/90.

a3) 13 0-0-0 0-0-0 14 ♘e4?! (14 ♖hf1 ♕e7 transposes into the previous note) 14...♕e7 15 ♘g5 d5! (15...♘f6 is not bad, either, 16 ♘xe6 ♕xe6 17 ♖hf1 [17 ♖he1?! and now, instead of the catastrophic 17...♔b8?? 18 ♗xa7+ 1-0, Hailey-Kennedy, email 1993, 17...d5 18 ♕f3 ♘e4 is perfectly reasonable] 17...♔b8?? [the same blunder, better is 17...♕f7] 18 ♗xa7+ 1-0, Niemand-Tiemann, corr. 1983 15...♗d7?! 16 ♖hf1?! [16 ♘xh7] 16...♘f6 17 h3 h6 18 ♘f3 d5 Black is back on top, Niemand-Tiemann, corr. 1983) 16 ♘d2 d4 17 ♗f4 ♗xa2 with a clear Black advantage.

a4) 13 ♘b5?! ♕f7 14 ♗f2 ♔d7! (♕xe6+ was the threat) 15 0-0-0 ♖e8 16 ♖hf1 ♘f6, threatening ...♗g4, and consolidating, Behrmann-Parzefall, corr. 1996.

b) 12 ♘d5?! ♕xf2+ 13 ♗xf2 ♔d8 14 ♗h4+ ♘ge7 (14...♗e7 15 0-0) 15 0-0 ♗e6 16 ♘f4 ♗f7 17 ♘h3 ♗xc4 18 ♗xc4 ♘e5?! (18...h6! is more accurate, when Black remains a sound pawn up) 19 ♘g5! c6 20 ♘f7+ ♘xf7 21 ♖xf7 ♖c8 22 ♖e1 (22 ♗e6 looks interesting; if then 22...♖c7? 23 ♖d1 d5 24 ♗g3) 22...♖c7 Grivainis-Kozlov, corr. 1978/9, when 23 ♗e6 keeps White on top.

c) 12 0-0!? ♕xf2+ 13 ♖xf2 ♘f6 (13...♗e6!? 14 ♖e2 ♔d7 15 ♘b5 ♗xc4 16 ♗xc4 ♘e5 Diepstraten) 14 ♗g5 ♗e7 15 ♗xf6 ♗xf6 16 ♘d5 Snayer-Goedhart, corr. 1981, when 16...0-0 17 c3 (17 ♘xc7?! ♗d4) 17...♖f7 is level.

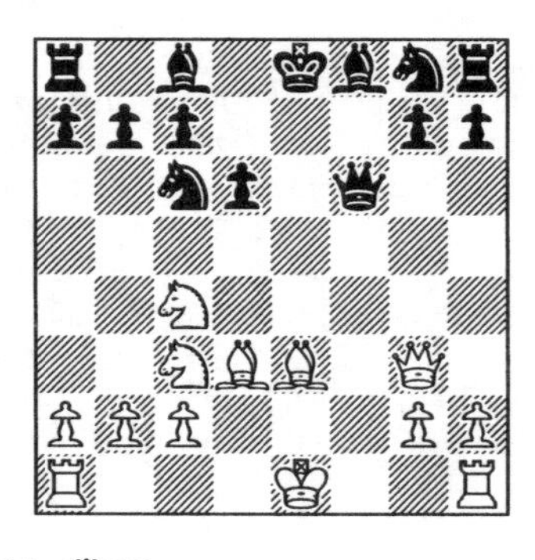

12...♕f7!

The most common, and clearly best, although 12...♗e6? has also been seen, but without success: 13 ♘e4 ♕e7 14 ♗g5 ♕d7 (14...♘f6 15 0-0 ♘xe4 16 ♗xe4 ♕d7 17 ♖ae1 [17 ♕h4 is also strong, 17...♗e7 {17...♗xc4? 18 ♗xc6! winning} 18 ♗g6+! ♔d8 19 ♕xh7! ♕e8

{19...♖e8 20 ♗xe8 ♕xe8 21 ♕xg7 with advantage} 20 ♗xe7+ 1-0, Winkelmann-Schlenker, corr. 1989, as 20...♘xe7 21 ♗xe8 ♖xh7 22 ♖f8 c6 23 ♖e1 ♗xc4 24 ♗xc6+ ♔c7 25 ♖xe7+ ♔xc6 26 ♖xa8 is crushing] 17...♗e7 [17...♘e7 18 ♗xb7 ♖b8 19 ♘a5 is no improvement, Gåård-Hayward, corr. 1990] 18 ♗xc6 bxc6 19 ♗xe7 ♕xe7 20 ♖xe6 ♕xe6 21 ♖e1 wins, Pape-Jackson, corr. 1994/95) 15 0-0 d5 (this loses, but the others are even worse: 15...♘ge7? 16 ♘exd6+! cxd6 17 ♘xd6+ ♔d8 18 ♖ad1 is overwhelming, 15...♗xc4? 16 ♗xc4 ♘e5 17 ♖ae1 wins, Tiemann-Fiorito, corr. 1980, but misses the elegant 17 ♘c5! ♕c6 18 ♕xe5+! dxe5 19 ♗f7 mate, 15...♗e7? 16 ♗xe7 ♕xe7 17 ♖ae1 and the threat of ♘g5 is decisive, and finally, 15...h6? Becker-Gonschior, corr. 1979, allows a couple of immediate wins, for example: 16 ♘c5 dxc5 17 ♗g6+) 16 ♖xf8+! ♔xf8 17 ♖f1+ ♗f7 18 ♘c5 ♕e8 19 ♕xc7 ♘f6 20 ♗xf6 decimating the black position, Tiemann-Grivainis, corr. 1985.

13 ♘e4

The knight covers the g5-square to deter Black from playing ...♗e6, 13 0-0-0 ♗e6 gives White a problem with his c4-knight, 14 ♘e4! (14 ♘d2?! is too acquiescent, 14...0-0-0 [14...♘f6!] 15 ♖hf1 ♘f6 16 ♘ce4 ♘xe4 17 ♘xe4 ♕h5 White doesn't have quite enough for the pawn, Terblanche-Doyle, corr. 1994) 14...0-0-0?! (14...♗xc4 should be tried, 15 ♘g5 ♕d5 16 ♗e2 [16 ♗g6+? is too generous, 16...hxg6 17 ♖xd5 ♗xd5] 16...♕e5 17 ♗xc4 ♕xg3 18 hxg3 ♘e5, about level) 15 ♖hf1 ♘f6?? (blundering a piece, 15...♕d7 is OK) 16 ♘g5 ♕d7 17 ♘xe6 winning immediately, Pape-Evans, corr. 1994/95, as 17...♕xe6? drops the queen to 18 ♗f5.

13...♗e7

13...♘b4!? is a good plan, the white light-squared bishop is an important piece, so Black liquidates it, 14 ♘g5 (14 ♖f1!?) 14...♘xd3+ 15 cxd3 ♕g6 16 0-0 h6 17 ♘e4 (17 ♖ae1 ♗e7 also forces the exchange of queens) 17...♕xg3 18 ♘xg3 Reinke-Stummer, corr. 1994/95, and Black is better.

14 ♗g5

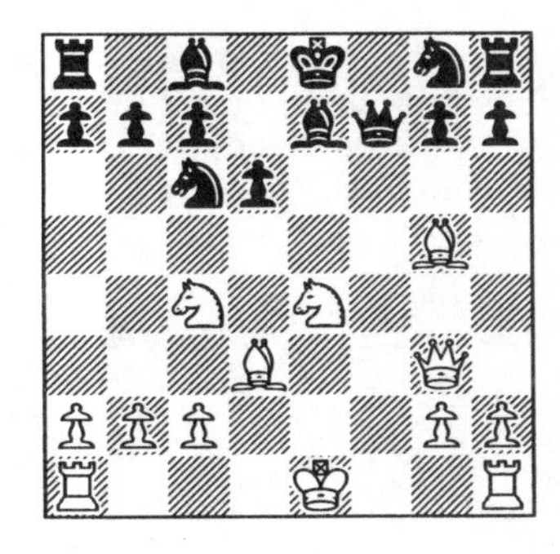

14...d5

The sharpest, although 14...♘f6 turned out well in Svendsen-Elburg, corr. 1990: 15 0-0 ♗d7 (15...♘xe4? 16 ♗xe4 ♕xc4 17 ♗xc6+ bxc6 18 ♖ae1 ♗e6 19 ♗xe7 is unclear) 16 ♗xf6 gxf6 and now, 17 ♖xf6 ♕d5 18 ♖af1 0-0-0 should be equal.

15 ♖f1

And certainly not 15 ♕xc7?? ♗b4+ 0-1, Leisebein-Gaard, corr. 1992, or 15 0-0-0? dxe4 0-1 Jensen-Melchor, corr. 1989/90.

15...♘f6!

This seems to win 'by force', so there is little need to bother with the old line 15...♕e6 16 0-0-0 (rather than 16 ♘e3?! dxe4 17 ♗c4 ♕d6 18 ♗f7+ ♔f8 19 ♗b3+ ♘f6 defending, Krantz-Downey, corr. 1990) 16...dxe4 17 ♗xe7 ♕xe7 18 ♗xe4

♗e6 19 ♗xc6+ bxc6 20 ♖de1! 0-0-0 21 ♘e5 which is tricky for Black, Weber-Doyle, corr. 1993.

16 ♗xf6 gxf6 17 ♖xf6 ♕g8 18 ♕xc7 dxe4 19 ♖xc6 exd3 20 ♘d6+ ♗xd6 21 ♖xd6 ♕g5!

White can't be allowed to castle.

22 ♖xd3 ♖f8 23 ♖ad1 ♗g4 24 ♕g3 ♔f7! 25 ♖e3 ♖ae8 26 ♖dd3 ♖xe3+ 27 ♖xe3 ♖d8 0-1 Melchor-Downey, corr. 1994/96.

C43 10 ♕e3+

I am not so sure that this move is White's best any more, it rather depends on the outcome of 15...♕xc8, in the main line.

10...♗e7

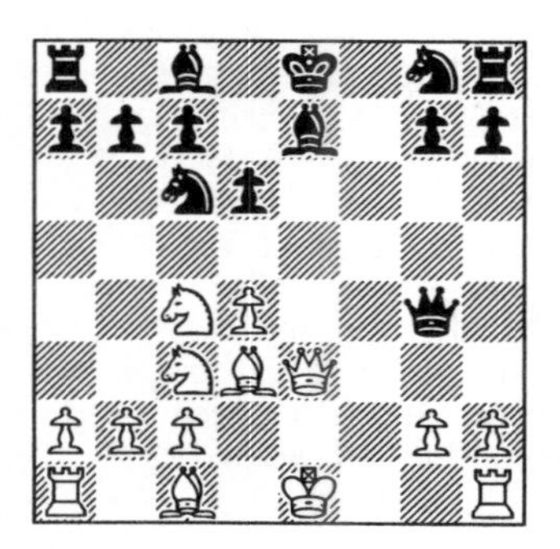

11 0-0

As it appears that Black cannot take the d4 pawn, this would certainly seem to be the best choice here, but White does have other options:

a) 11 d5 ♘b4 (11...♕xg2!? 12 ♗e4 ♗h4+ 13 ♔d1 ♗g4+ 14 ♗f3+ ♘ge7) 12 0-0 ♘xd3?! (it is probable that 12...♘f6 is the best, transposing to the main game) 13 ♕xd3 ♗d7 (to castle queenside, but it is quite risky; the unplayed 13...♘f6 is almost certainly better) 14 ♘a5! is tricky: (14 ♗d2 0-0-0?! 15 ♖f4 ♕h5? [15...♕g6!] 16 ♕d4 b6 Heap-Sawyer, corr. 1988, and now 17 ♕xg7 ♕g6 18 ♕xg6 hxg6 with advantage to White) 14...0-0-0?! (14...♗f6?! is met by 15 ♘b5 with advantage, Sclart-Menta, corr. 1972/74, but Black can try 14...♘f6 answering 15 ♘b5?! with 15...0-0! 16 ♘xc7 ♖ac8, and 15 ♘xb7? with 15...♕b4 16 ♕a6 ♕b6+ when a white knight is trapped; unfortunately, 15 ♖f4 ♕h5 16 ♘xb7 wins a pawn without fuss) 15 ♗e3 ♔b8? 16 ♖f4 ♕h5 17 ♖b4 1-0, Morgado-Priede, corr. 1970/73.

b) 11 ♘b5? ♕xg2! 12 ♖g1 ♕xh2 13 ♘xc7+ (White might as well take this, neither 13 c3 ♔d8 14 ♖xg7 h5 15 ♕f2 ♕xf2+ 16 ♔xf2 a6, Ilyin Genevsky - Betinš, corr. 1921/23, nor 13 ♗d2 ♕h4+ 14 ♖g3 ♔d8 15 ♕f3 ♘h6, Neff-Dreibergs, corr. 1964, hold out much hope for White) 13...♔d8 14 ♘xa8 ♗h4+ 15 ♔d1 ♘f6 16 ♖xg7 ♖e8 (but 16...♗g4+! 17 ♖xg4 ♘xg4 is crushing) 17 ♕g1 ♖e1+ 18 ♕xe1 ♗xe1 19 ♔xe1 ♕h4+ with a powerful attack, Stebahne-Brusila, 1986.

c) 11 ♗e4? ♘f6 12 ♗xc6+ bxc6 13 0-0 ♗a6 14 ♖f4 (14 ♖e1 0-0 15 b3 ♖ae8 was also much to Black's liking in Purins-Tomson, corr.) 14...♕d7 15 b3 0-0 16 ♗d2 ♘d5 17 ♖xf8+ ♖xf8 18 ♕e4 ♘b6 19 ♘xb6 axb6 20 d5? ♗f6 21 ♕a4 (21 dxc6 ♕f7, threatening some nasty bishop moves) 21...♕f5 0-1. This looks a little premature, but 22 ♕xa6 ♗d4+ (or 22...♕xc2) 23 ♔h1 b5 24 h3 ♕xc2 should certainly win for Black, Bernsdorfer-Hazenfuss, corr. 1937/38.

d) 11 ♘d5? blunders a pawn, 11...♕xg2 12 ♕e4 ♕xe4+ 13 ♗xe4 ♗h4+ 14 ♔d2 ♔d8, Nobbe-Hage, corr. 1982.

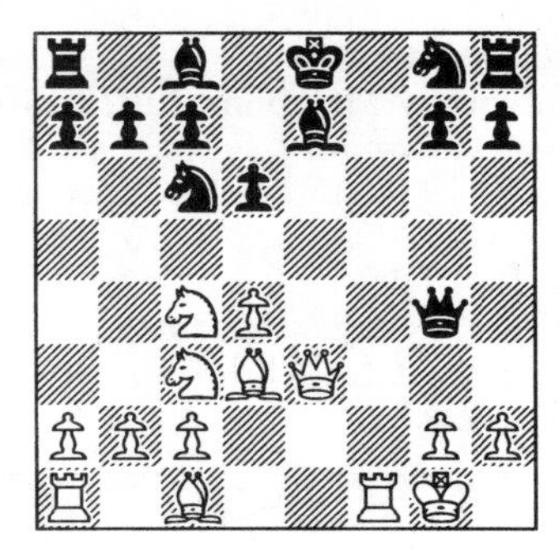

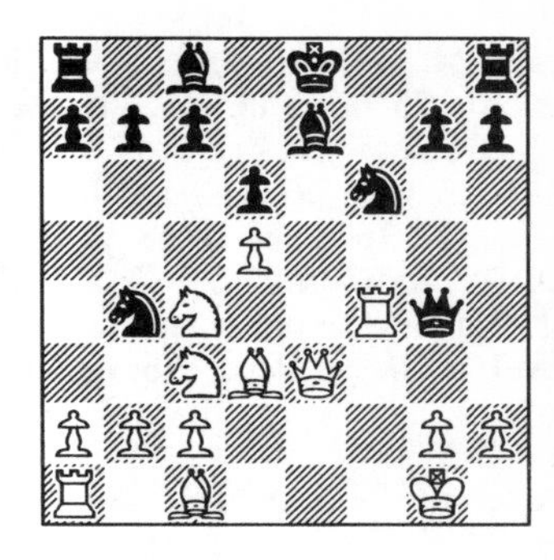

11...♘f6

11...♘b4?! is a new try, but will soon be discarded, no doubt, 12 ♗d2 ♘xd3 13 ♘d5! (13 ♕xd3 ♗d7 14 ♖ae1 0-0-0 15 ♘d5 ♗f6 16 ♖e4 ♕g6 17 ♘a5! c6 18 ♕b3 is not bad either, Villar-Profeta, corr. 1999) 13...♔d8 14 ♕xd3 ♘f6 15 ♘xe7 ♔xe7 16 ♖ae1+ ♔d8 17 ♘e5! dxe5 18 dxe5+ ♗d7 19 exf6 gxf6 20 ♖xf6, winning quickly, Downey-Destrebecq, corr. 1997.

The ending that follows 11...♕xd4?! 12 ♘b5! ♕xe3+ 13 ♘xe3 is not favourable to Black, by any means, 13...♔d8 14 ♘d5 ♘f6 15 ♘bxc7 ♘xd5! 16 ♘xd5 Grivainis/Hayward-Budovskis, corr. 1997.

12 d5

12 ♘b5 ♔d8 13 c3 ♖f8 14 h3 ♕h5 is fine for Black, Doplmayr-Bonte, corr. 1995

12 ♖f4!? ♕e6 13 ♘b5 (13 ♕f2 can be met by 13...♘b4) 13...♘d5 (13...♕xe3+ 14 ♗xe3!? ♘d5 15 ♗e4! ♘xf4 16 ♘xc7+ ♔d8 17 ♘xa8 ♘e2+ 18 ♔f2 ♘exd4 19 ♗xd4 ♘xd4 20 ♖d1 ♖f8+ 21 ♔e3 ♘f5+ led to equality in Pape-Reinke, corr. 1994/95) 14 ♕xe6 ♗xe6 15 ♖e4 ♗f7 is very comfortable for Black, Decker-Beutel, corr. 1997.

12...♘b4 13 ♖f4

12...♕d7

At the present moment in time, the text seems adequate, however the alternative 13...♘bxd5!? has now received some attention, 14 ♖xg4! (14 ♘xd5 ♘xd5 15 ♖xg4 ♘xe3 16 ♘xe3 ♗xg4 17 ♘xg4 0-0, and an endgame is reached where White has bishop and knight for rook and pawn. Black should strive to exchange a pair of rooks and the dark squared bishops, bring his king to the centre, and mobilize his queenside pawns. I would evaluate this as ±, but not without practical prospects for Black, 18 ♗d2 d5 19 ♖f1?! ♗c5+ 20 ♗e3 ♗xe3+ 21 ♘xe3 ♖xf1+ 22 ♔xf1 c6 and Black eventually managed to draw, Holt-Major, corr. 1995) 14...♘xe3 15 ♖xg7 (+/- *NCO*), but 15...♘xc4! (15...♘eg4?! 16 ♗g5 ♔d8? 17 h3 [17 ♖xe7! ♔xe7 18 ♘d5+ ♔f7 19 ♖f1 is even simpler] 17...h6 18 ♗h4 with a decisive advantage, Downey-Melchor, corr. 1994/96) 16 ♗xc4 ♘h5, curiously nearly trapping the rook! 17 ♗h6! (if 17 ♖f7 c6 and ...d5) 17...♘xg7 18 ♗xg7 ♖f8 19 ♗xf8 ♗xf8 (after the forcing play, Black is behind in development, but enjoys a useful pair of bishops) 20 ♘d5 (otherwise, 20 ♖f1 c6! 21 ♗d3 ♗g7 22 ♗xh7 ♗e6, or 20 ♘b5 ♔d8 21 ♖f1 ♗e7 22 ♖f7 d5 23 ♗d3

♗c5+ 24 ♔f1 c6 and Black has chances, 25 ♘c3 h6 26 ♖h7 ♗e3 etc.) 20...♔d8 21 ♖f1 ♗g7 22 ♖f7 ♗d4+ 23 ♔f1 c6 24 ♘c7 ♖b8 25 ♗e6 ♗xb2 26 ♗xc8 ♖xc8 27 ♘e6+ ♔e8 28 ♖xb7 ♗e5 29 ♖xa7 ♖b8 and Black eventually managed to grovel a draw, Pepe-Elburg, corr. 1999.

14 ♗f5

After 14 ♘b6 axb6 15 ♖xb4 0-0 (15...♘g4! looks interesting) 16 ♗d2, Castelli-Hempel, corr. 1970/71, Black is a little worse, but no more.

Otherwise, the tactical continuation 14 ♘xd6+?! ♕xd6 15 ♘b5 is not quite correct, 15...♕c5 16 d6 ♘xd3 17 ♘xc7+ ♔d8 18 ♘xa8 ♗xd6 19 cxd3 ♘d5 20 ♕xc5 ♗xc5+ 21 ♔h1 ♗e6! 22 ♖c4 ♗d6 23 ♖a4 ♗b8!?, definitively trapping the white knight, 24 b3 ♗d7 25 ♗g5+ ♔c8 26 ♖e4 ♖f8 27 ♗e7 ♖f7 28 ♖c1+ ♗c6 and, inexorably, Black rounded up the knight, and won, Pape-Krantz, corr. 1994/95.

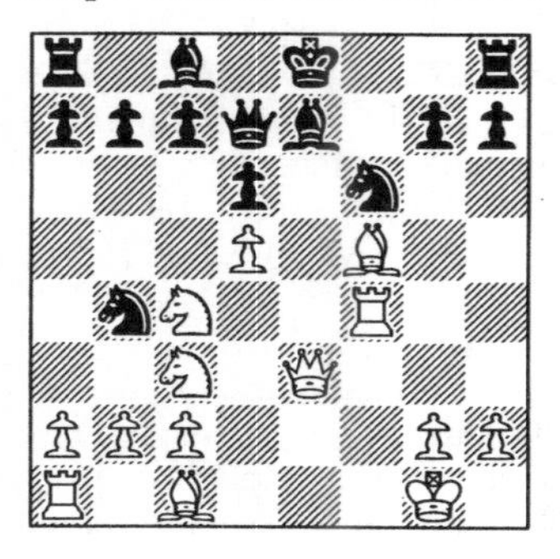

14...♕d8

The queen sacrifice 14...♕xf5? is no longer considered Black's best chance, 15 ♖xf5 ♗xf5 16 ♕f4! (16 ♘b5?! is a slip, 16...0-0! 17 ♘xc7 [and not 17 ♕xe7? ♖ae8 18 ♕xc7 ♖e1+ 19 ♔f2 ♘xc2 20 ♘bxd6 ♗g6 handing Black a powerful attack.] and instead of 17...♘bxd5? Rublevsky-Malyutin, Russia 1992, Black missed 17...♘xc2! 18 ♕xe7 ♖ae8! 19 ♘xe8 ♖xe8 with equality) 16...♗g6 17 ♘e3 ♘a6 18 ♘f5 ♗xf5 19 ♕xf5 0-0 20 ♗e3 maintains a large advantage, Trim-Vaughan, CSA Ch 1993.

15 ♗xc8

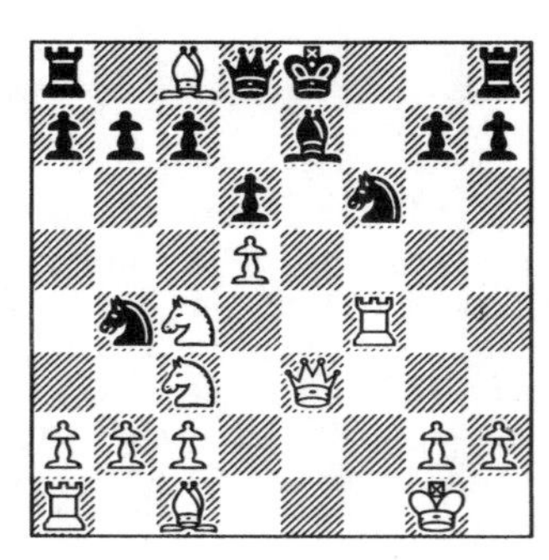

15...♕xc8!

The best, otherwise, we have the following possibilities:

a) 15...♘xc2? 16 ♕d3 ♘xa1 17 ♗xb7 0-0 (17...♖b8 18 ♗c6+ ♘d7 19 ♕b1 with advantage) 18 ♗xa8 ♕xa8 19 ♘e3 c6 20 dxc6 ♕xc6 21 ♕b1, winning the stranded knight, Gurnhill-Monciunskas, Brighouse 1966.

b) 15...♖xc8 16 ♕xa7! (16 ♕e6!? ♘xc2 17 ♖xf6! gxf6 18 ♘e4 ♖f8 19 ♘cxd6+ cxd6 20 ♘xd6+ ♕xd6 21 ♕xc8+ ♔f7 22 ♕xc2 ♕c5+ only leads to a draw, Downey-Reinke, corr. 1994/96) 16...♘bxd5 17 ♘xd5 ♘xd5 18 ♖f5! ♘b4 (18...♘b6 19 ♘xb6 with advantage) 19 ♗d2 ♕d7 20 ♖af1 is better for White, Foulds-Ottenbreit, corr. 1997.

c) 15...♘bxd5?? 16 ♘xd5 ♘xd5 fails to the shot 17 ♗xb7! 1-0, both Melchor-Krantz, corr. 1994/95, and Downey-Vitols, corr. 1994/95 as 17...♘xe3 18 ♗c6+ recovers the queen with interest.

16 ♘xd6+ cxd6 17 ♖xb4

This position was considered (even by myself) to give White the advantage, however...

17...0-0!

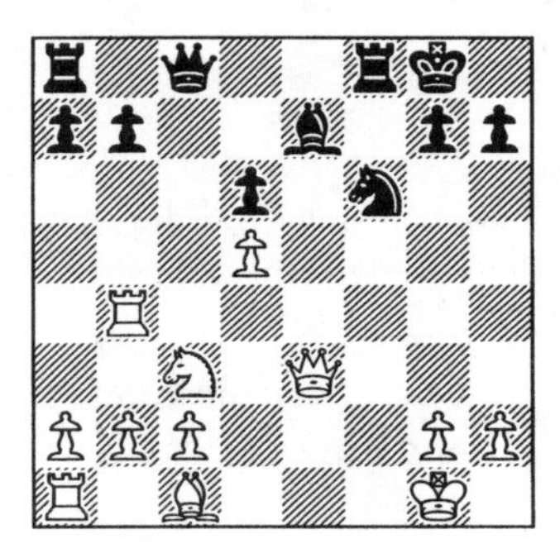

Black moves over to the attack!

18 ♗d2

Alternatives:

a) 18 ♕e6+ ♕xe6 19 dxe6 d5! 20 ♖xb7 (20 ♖b5 a6 21 ♘xd5 might pose more problems) 20...♗c5+ 21 ♔h1 (21 ♔f1!?) now, instead of 21...♘e4!? 22 g3 ♖f1+ 23 ♔g2 ♖g1+ 24 ♔h3 ♘f2+ 25 ♔h4 ♖h1 26 g4 ♗d6 27 ♗f4! ♗xf4 28 ♖xh1 ♘xh1 29 ♘xd5 which is wild, Hunwick-Tatlow, corr. 1994, 21...♘g4 is simpler, 22 ♖f7 ♘f2+ 23 ♔g1 ♘e4+ 24 ♔f1 ♘xc3 25 bxc3 ♖xf7+ 26 exf7+ ♔xf7 with equality.

b) 18 h3?! ♗d8! the bishop finds a perfect diagonal! 19 ♕e6+ ♕xe6 20 dxe6 ♗b6+ 21 ♔h2 ♖ae8 22 ♗g5 ♖xe6 23 ♗xf6 ♖fxf6 24 ♘d5 ♖f2 25 ♘xb6 ♖ee2 Black has no problems, Turley-Tatlow, corr. 1996.

c) 18 ♕xe7? ♕c5+ forks rook and king.

18...♗d8! 19 ♕e6+ ♕xe6 20 dxe6 ♗b6+ 21 ♔h1

21 ♖xb6!? axb6 22 ♖e1 might be a better try.

21...♖ae8 22 ♖e1

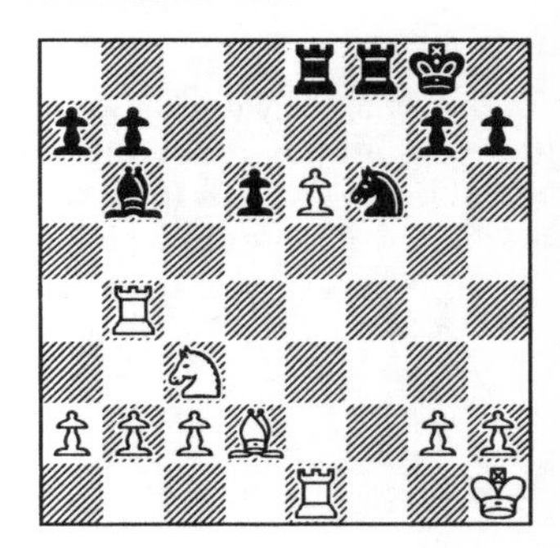

22...♖xe6! 23 ♖xe6 ♘d5

Simultaneously hitting the b4-rook, and threatening a back rank mate.

24 ♖e8 ♘xb4 25 ♖xf8+ ♔xf8 26 ♘b5 ♘xc2 27 ♘xd6 ♗d4 28 b3 b6 29 ♘b5 a6 30 ♘c7 ♔e7 31 ♘xa6 ♔d6 32 ♘b4 ♗e3 ½-½

Arias-Miguel, corr. 1995, the active black king holds the balance.

To sum up, the main line with 8...♘c6 seems fine for Black if White plays 10 ♕e3+, and also after 10 ♕f2 ♕xd4 11 ♗e3, but in this last line 10 ♕e2+ is rather more worrying. Furthermore, both 9 ♘b5! and also 9 d5 are also disturbing for Black.

Perhaps Black should prefer 8...♘f6, currently bolstered by Bücker's ideas, or even 8...♗e7.

2 Main line: other seventh moves

In this chapter we look at White's other possibilities following **1 e4 e5 2 ♘f3 f5 3 ♘xe5 ♕f6 4 d4 d6 5 ♘c4 fxe4 6 ♘c3 ♕g6**, which are:

A 7 ♗f4
B 7 ♘e3
C 7 ♗e3
D 7 ♘d5
E 7 ♕e2
F 7 d5
G 7 g3
H 7 h4

A 7 ♗f4

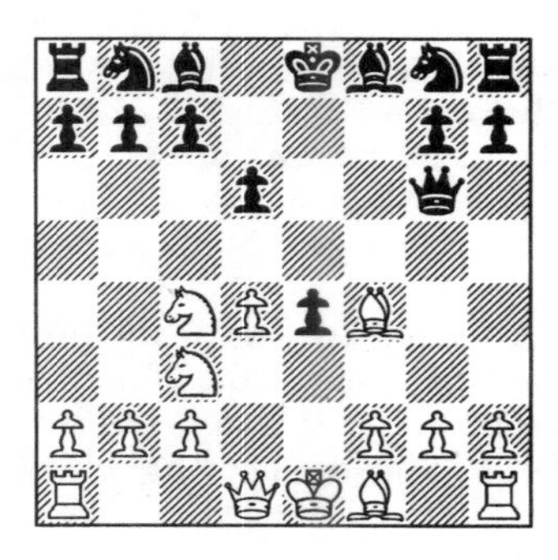

As White's king's knight almost invariably finds itself hopping back from c4 to e3, it is evidently very logical for White to develop his bishop to f4 beforehand, thereby avoiding the possibility of its incarceration on c1. This move can also be a precursor to a quick queenside castling. The most obvious drawback, however, is the likely exposure of the bishop on f4. If Black can play ...♘h5 when the bishop is bereft of retreat, he will be doing well.

7...♘f6

Now the alternatives are:

A1 8 ♘e3
A2 8 ♕d2

Lesser moves:

a) 8 h3 ♗e7 9 d5 0-0 10 ♕d2 ♗d7!? (10...♘bd7 11 0-0-0 [11 ♘b5?! ♗d8 12 0-0-0 a6] 11...a6 will effect a transposition to the main game) 11 ♘e3 ♘a6 12 0-0-0 ♘c5 13 ♔b1 b5? (this is a little impatient, 13...a6 is more sensible) 14 ♗xb5 ♖ab8 15 ♗xd7?! ♘fxd7 16 ♗g3 ♗f6 17 b3 (17 ♔a1? ♖xb2 18 ♔xb2 ♘a4+) 17...♖b4 18 ♖de1 ♖fb8 with a strong attack, Borochow-Zemitis, USA 1961. White's fifteenth move was very obliging, and allowed the black pieces to take up very aggressive positions without loss of time. Black would have had a harder time justifying his sacrifice after 15 ♗c4.

b) 8 ♘b5?! is pointless now, 8...♘a6 9 d5 ♗e7 10 g3?!, very ugly, Ribes-Melchor, Barcelona 1997, as now 10...♗g4 11 ♕d4 ♗f3 with a sizeable advantage, or 11 ♗e2? ♗xe2 and no matter how White recaptures, the d-pawn will be lost, i.e. 12 ♔xe2 ♕h5+. Typical of OTB play!

8 ♘e3 ♗e7

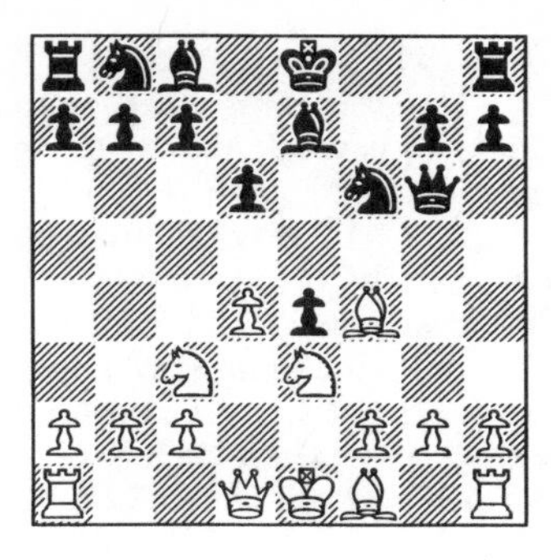

9 ♗c4?!

Very popular, but not very good. Other moves are:

a) 9 ♗e2! 0-0 10 ♗g3 (10 ♕d2 would be inaccurate, see (b) 10...c6 (10...a6!? 11 a4 ♘c6!? [profiting from the hole on b4 created by 11 a4] 12 a5 ♗d7 13 ♘cd5 ♗d8?! 14 ♘f4 ♕h6 15 ♗c4+ ♔h8 16 ♗e6 with an edge, Small-Hector, Royan 1988) 11 d5 a6 12 0-0 c5, setting up a Benoni-style position 13 a4 (13 ♘c4 is more awkward) 13...♖d8 (13...♘bd7?! 14 ♘c4 ♖d8 15 ♗xd6!? ♗xd6 16 ♘xd6 ♘b6 17 ♘xc8, Lorand-Destrebecq, Belfort 1983, 17...♖axc8 regaining the pawn, with near equality) 14 a5 ♘bd7 15 ♘c4 ♘f8 16 ♖e1 ♗f5 17 ♕d2 h6 18 ♖ab1 ♖ac8 19 b4 cxb4 20 ♖xb4 (White's play is logical, but the black position is solid, and not without counter chances) 20...♖c7 21 ♖eb1 ♗c8 22 ♕d4 ♘8h7 23 ♘e3 (surrounding the e-pawn, but in return Black will get the a5-pawn) 23...♖c5 24 ♖a1 ♕f7 25 ♘xe4 ♘xe4 26 ♕xe4 ♗g5 27 c4 ♗f6 28 ♖a3 ♕c7 29 ♖b1 ♘f8 30 ♗g4 ♗xg4 31 ♕xg4 ♖xa5, unclear, Nevanlinna-Hector, Jyvaskyla 1993.

b) 9 ♕d2 c6 10 ♗e2 (10 d5?! transposes to 9 ♘e3 in the main line) 10...0-0 11 0-0 (11 d5 ♘h5 12 ♗xh5 ♕xh5 13 dxc6? ♖xf4 14 ♕d5+ ♕xd5 15 ♘cxd5 ♖f7 16 ♘c7 bxc6 17 ♘xa8 ♘a6 traps, and wins, the errant knight, Cherner-Clarke, corr. 1998) and rather than 11...d5 12 f3 exf3 (this is more sensible than 12...♗e6?! as occurred in Rehfeld-Schmidt, corr. 1992, when, instead of the dreadful 13 ♘g4?? ♘xg4 14 fxg4 ♗xg4 15 ♗xg4 ♕xg4 ∓ White should certainly have played 13 fxe4 dxe4 with some advantage; and 12...b5?!, intending the typical tactic 13 fxe4 b4, is met, unexpectedly, by 14 ♘cxd5 cxd5 15 e5 ♘e4 16 ♘xd5 with advantage) 13 ♗xf3 ± Flohr-Vecsey, Prague 1930, 11...♘h5! is again possible.

9...c6 10 d5

This is the logical follow up, but 10 ♗e2 might be better, despite losing a tempo on note a), just above. The game Alonso-Desoto, Spain 1942, went instead: 10 0-0? d5?! (of course, instead of all this, 10...♘h5 11 ♗g3 ♘xg3 12 hxg3 d5 13 ♗e2 0-0 would have been wonderful for Black) 11 ♗e2, reaching a similar position, and continued 11...0-0 12 f3 ♘h5? when 13 ♗xb8 ♖xb8 14 fxe4 would have been strong, but Black should prefer 12...exf3.

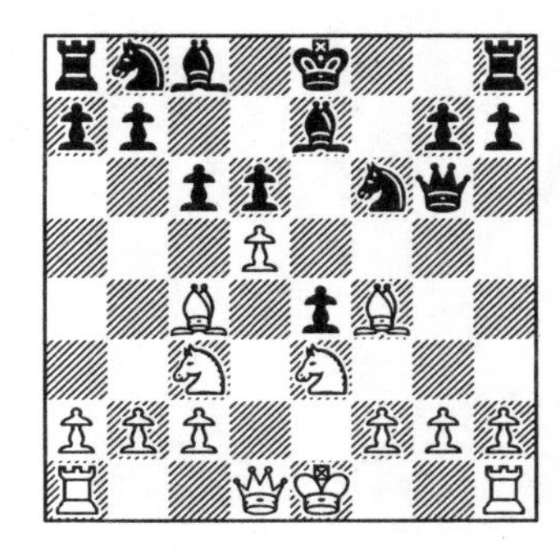

10...♘h5!

Black exchanges the f4 bishop, when his own dark-squared bishop has the potential to become very powerful.

10...b5?! is worse: 11 ♗e2 (11 ♗b3!? b4?! [11...♘h5] 12 ♘e2 c5 13 ♗g3 ♘g4 14 ♘c4 Olafsson-Diepstraten, simul, Hilversum 1976, when 14...0-0 limits White's edge) 11...b4 12 ♘a4 0-0 13 a3 ♘g4! (a big improvement on the game Sir G.Thomas-Tartakower, England 1926, which continued: 13...bxa3?! 14 ♖xa3 ♗d7?! 15 ♘b6 axb6 16 ♖xa8 ♘xd5 17 ♘xd5 cxd5 18 ♗g3 with advantage) 14 ♗g3? (14 ♗xg4 ♗xg4 15 ♕xg4 ♕xg4 16 ♘xg4 ♖xf4 17 ♘e3 should keep some advantage) 14...♘xe3 15 fxe3 ♕g5 16 axb4 ♗b7 when White has problems finding a safe haven for his king, Dagenais-Polland, corr. 1984.

11 ♗g3 ♘xg3 12 hxg3

I don't believe that 12 fxg3!? can be good. Perhaps 12...♗g5 is the sharpest reply, with the two possibilities: 13 ♕d4 c5 14 ♗b5+ ♔d8! 15 ♕d2 ♕h6 16 ♘cd1 ♖f8, and 13 ♕e2 b5!? 14 ♗b3 b4 15 ♘cd1 c5 16 0-0 ♖f8.

12...♘d7

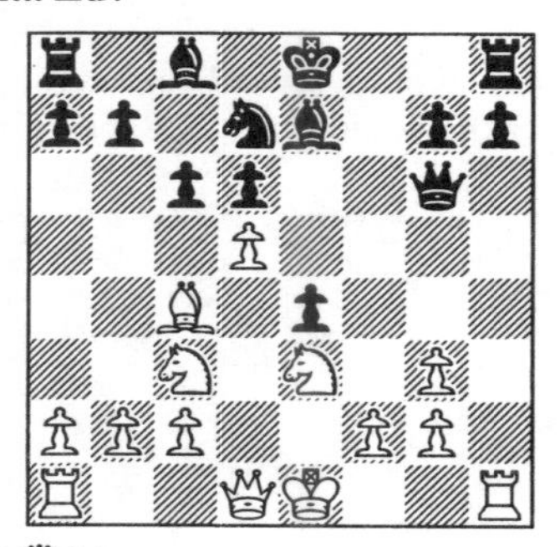

13 ♕d4

Otherwise:

a) 13 ♕d2, in Littrell-Dreibergs, corr. 1964, Black was successful with 13...♗f6! (13...♘e5?! 14 ♕d4 wins a pawn by 14...♘xc4 15 ♕xc4 ♗g5 16 ♕xe4+ ♕xe4 17 ♘xe4 ♗xe3 18 fxe3, rather than 14 0-0-0?!, Bullockus-Schild, corr. 1979, when 14...♘xc4 15 ♘xc4 ♗g5 16 ♘e3 0-0 is clearly good for Black, f2 is weak and Black has the two bishops) 14 0-0-0 ♗e5!? (14...♗xc3 15 ♕xc3 c5 may be simpler) 15 ♖h4 (15 dxc6 bxc6 16 ♖h4 ♘f6 transposes) 15...♘f6 16 dxc6 (16 ♗b3! intending ♘c4) 16...bxc6 17 ♕e2?! (17 ♘xe4? ♘xe4 18 ♗d3 ♗xb2+ 0-1, Bullockus-Scott, corr. 1971) 17...♗xc3 18 bxc3 d5.

b) 13 ♗e2, with a threat! 13...0-0 (simple and good, 13...♘f6? 14 ♗h5 ♘xh5 15 ♕xh5 ♕xh5 16 ♖xh5 g6 17 ♖h2?! 0-0 18 ♘xe4, when White has won a pawn, although Black's bishops offer some compensation, La Mar - Portillo, corr. 1971) 14 dxc6!? bxc6 15 ♘ed5 ♗g5 16 ♘c7 ♖b8 17 ♗c4+ d5 18 ♘3xd5 ♔h8! (18...cxd5 19 ♕xd5+ ♖f7 is interesting, but not 19...♔h8?! 20 ♘e6) 19 ♘f4 ♗xf4 20 gxf4 ♘b6 21 ♗f1 ♗g4 and the active black pieces are well on top, Sowden-Saunders, corr. 1996.

c) 13 ♘e2?! ♘e5 (it seems to me that 13...♗g5! is a better choice here; ...♗xe3 is the threat, and 14 ♘f4 appears to lose a pawn to 14...♗xf4 15 gxf4 ♕f6) 14 ♘f4 ♕f6 15 ♗b3 ♗d7? 16 dxc6 bxc6, Toro-Saaveira, corr. 1967/68, when 17 ♕e2 is unclear, and 17 ♘ed5!? cxd5 18 ♘xd5 ♕g5 19 ♘c7+ ♔d8 20 ♘xa8 e3! likewise.

13...♘f6

13...♘c5! 14 0-0-0 ♗f6 15 ♕d2 ♗e5 is worth serious consideration, Black seems to be better.

14 0-0-0

The 14 ♘e2 c5 15 ♗b5+ ♔f7 16 ♕d2 a6 17 ♘f4 ♕g5 18 ♗e2 b5 19 0-0-0 ♕e5 of Veiss-Dreibergs, corr. 1952, is similar.

14...c5!?

14...♗d7 avoids the displacement of the king, 15 ♘e2 c5 16 ♕d2,

Wang-Dreibergs, corr. 1965, when 16...♘h5 would stop the e2-knight coming to f4.

15 ♗b5+ ♔f7 16 ♕d2 a6 17 ♗e2 b5 18 ♖h4 ♖f8

18...b4 19 ♘a4 ♖b8 of Alexander-Hasenfuss, Folkestone 1933, weakens the c4-square.

19 ♖dh1 ♔g8

Black has a promising Benoni-style position, McKenna-Saunders, corr. 1990.

A2 8 ♕d2

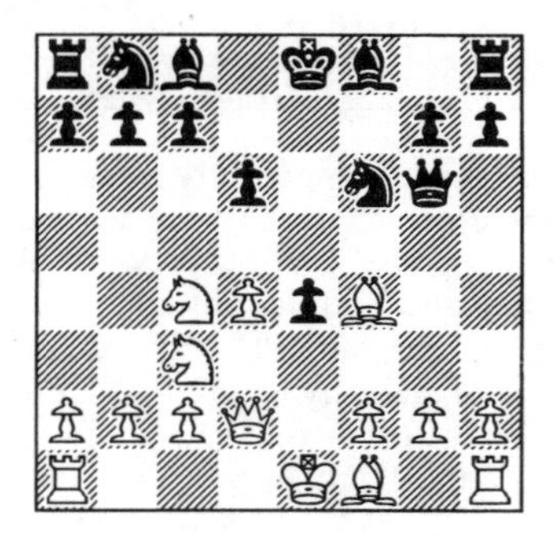

White intends to castle long, but Black is well placed to meet this.

8...♗e7 9 0-0-0

9 ♘e3 c6 10 d5?! (10 ♗e2! transposes to the note 9 ♕d2 of 8 ♘e3) 10...♘h5! 11 ♗g3 0-0 12 ♗c4 (12 ♗e2) 12...c5 13 0-0 a6 14 a4 ♘d7 15 ♖ae1 ♘xg3 16 fxg3 (unfortunately for White, 16 hxg3? is impossible: 16...♘e5 17 ♗a2 ♗g5 18 ♕d1 ♗xe3 19 ♖xe3 ♘g4 20 ♖xe4 ♕h5 winning the exchange) 16...♖xf1+ 17 ♖xf1 ♘e5 18 ♘e2 ♗d7 19 ♘f4 ♕h6 20 a5 ♖f8 21 ♖e1? ♗g5 0-1, Schabanel-Kosten, French League 1994, since 22 ♗a2?! say, is answered by 22...♖xf4 23 gxf4 ♗xf4 24 h3 ♕g5 25 ♔h1 ♗xh3 26 gxh3 ♕g3.

9...0-0 10 h3

Black was actually threatening a tactical operation involving ...♘g4, followed by ...♖xf4 and ...♗g5, and this move is played to control g4, and prepare a retreat square for the bishop. Other possibilities:

a) 10 ♔b1 takes the king off the exposed diagonal, 10...a6 11 ♗e2 b5 (11...♕xg2!? is possible as is 11...♘bd7 like the main game) 12 ♘e3 c6 13 ♗g3 (13 g4!? Badii-Lopez de Castro, Paris 1994, is more aggressive, but 13...♕f7 looks like a good reply, or 13...d5 followed by bringing a piece to c4) 13...d5 14 h4 ♗e6 15 h5 ♕f7 16 f4 ♗d6 17 ♗h2 ♕c7 with chances for both sides, Sigurjonsson-Gundersen, Graz 1972.

b) 10 h4? controls g5, but it is unwise to weaken g4, i.e. 10...♗g4 11 f3?! exf3 12 ♗d3 ♗f5 13 ♗xf5 ♕xf5 14 ♖hf1? (14 ♖he1 was only ∓) 14...b5! (winning!) 15 ♖de1 ♖f7 0-1, Lynberg-Hector, Malmö 1990.

c) 10 ♗e2? instructively ignores the threat: 10...♘g4 11 ♗e3, Vutov-Dimov, Teteven 1991, when I can see nothing wrong with the evident 11...♘xf2 12 ♗xf2 ♖xf2.

10...a6!

In Ciocaltea-Destrebecq, Val Thorens 1980, Black tried 10...♘bd7 11 ♔b1 ♘b6?!, but this left the queenside pawn formation somewhat inflexible after 12 ♘xb6 axb6 13 d5!.

11 d5 ♘bd7 12 ♔b1

A necessary preparation for g4, which, if played immediately, loses at least a pawn to 12 g4? ♘xg4! 13 hxg4 ♖xf4 14 ♕xf4? ♗g5.

12...b5

Not the prelude to a queenside onslaught, as one might expect, but part of a strong plan to artificially isolate White's d5 pawn, and re-arrange Black's minor pieces. The knights are aiming for b6 and c5, respectively, and the dark squared bishop for f6.

13 ♘a5 ♘b6 14 a3

There is nothing to be gained by 14 ♘c6 as 14...♕f7 followed by...♗b7 puts great pressure on the d-pawn.

14...♘fd7 15 g3

Of course, with the knight on a5 instead of e3, 15 ♗e2? would leave the g-pawn en prise.

15...♘c5 16 ♗g2?

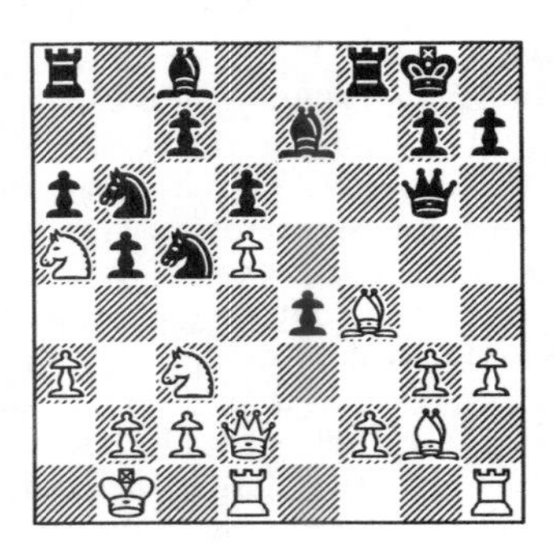

Allowing a small combination, but 16 ♗e3 ♗f6 is also better for Black.

16...♖xf4! 17 ♕xf4

Or 17 gxf4 ♕xg2 18 ♖dg1 ♕f3 19 ♕d4 ♗f8 ∓ as now 20 ♖xg7+?? fails to 20...♗xg7 21 ♖g1 ♗g4 22 ♖xg4 ♕xg4!.

17...♗g5 18 ♗xe4 ♘xe4 19 ♕xe4 ♗f5 20 ♕d4

White cannot defend the c-pawn with 20 ♕e2 because of 20...♖e8.

20...♗xc2+ 21 ♔a2 ♗f6 22 ♕d2 ♗xd1 23 ♖xd1

The net result of the combination is a vulnerable d-pawn for White, and a strong bishop for Black. Considerable advantages in the hands of Sokolov.

23...♖e8 24 g4 ♕f7 25 ♔a1 ♗e5 26 ♕d3 ♕xf2 27 ♖f1 ♕g2 28 ♕f5 ♗f6 29 ♖f2 ♕xh3 30 ♘c6 ♕h6 31 ♔a2 ♕g5 32 ♕xg5 ♗xg5 33 ♘b4 ♗f6 34 ♘xa6 ♗xc3 35 bxc3 ♘xd5 0-1, Apicella-I.Sokolov, European Teams ch, Debrecen 1992.

B 7 ♘e3

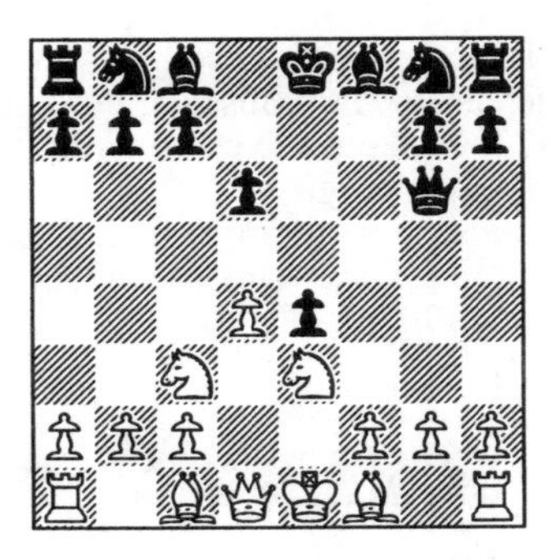

Although apparently impeding the movement of White's queen's bishop, the knight is well placed here, and should the f-file become open the knight can often hop advantageously to f5.

7...♘f6

Natural, and best.

If 7...c6!? 8 f3 is a good choice, (8 d5 ♘f6 9 ♗e2 transposes to the main line) 8...d5 9 fxe4 dxe4 10 ♗c4 and, although Black has some space, the fact that he cannot castle kingside, because of the open a2-g8 diagonal, is going to be a problem, Pedersen-Taksrud, corr. 1979. And 7...♘c6?! 8 ♘ed5 (8 ♗e2 ♘f6 9 ♘cd5, French-Zemitis, corr. 1968, is less effective) 8...♔d8 9 ♘b5 ♗g4 10 ♕d2 is awkward.

8 ♗e2!

Not the sharpest move, but the most sensible, and strongest. The others are:

a) 8 ♗c4 c6 9 d5 (White does not want Black to play ...d5, 9 0-0?! d5 10 ♗b3 ♗d6 11 f3 [it is difficult to arrange to play c4, as 11 ♘e2?! meets 11...♘g4! 12 ♘g3 h5 13 ♖e1 ♘xh2?! 14 ♘xd5! Galje-De Vries, corr. 1991, when the natural 14...cxd5 15 ♗xd5 ♔d8 16 ♘xe4 leaves the situation somewhat confused, but 13...h4 14 ♘gf1 h3 15 g3 0-0 is exceedingly dangerous for White] 11...exf3 12 ♕xf3 0-0 13 h3 ♗e6, the white queen is awkwardly placed on the f-file, Black is better, Lonsdale-Svendsen, corr. 1987) 9...♗e7 (the immediate 9...♘bd7! is even better, 10 0-0 ♘e5 11 ♗e2 ♗e7 12 ♘c4? ♘xc4 13 ♗xc4 ♗h3 14 g3 ♗xf1 15 ♗xf1 0-0 0-1, Mazuchowsky-Dreibergs, Michigan 1963) 10 a4!? (played by the great Bobby Fischer although he was only a lad at the time, and it was a long time before he was to become World Champion! 10 0-0 ♘bd7 11 f3 exf3 12 ♕xf3?! ♘e5 = Gabrans-Tomson, corr. 1974) 10...♘bd7 11 a5 ♘e5 12 ♗e2 0-0 13 0-0 ♗d7 14 ♔h1 ♔h8 15 ♘c4 ♘fg4 with plenty of activity, Fischer-Pupols, US Junior ch, Lincoln 1955.

b) 8 ♘cd5 (8 ♘ed5 ♘xd5 transposes, of course) 8...♘xd5 9 ♘xd5 ♕f7 10 ♗c4 c6

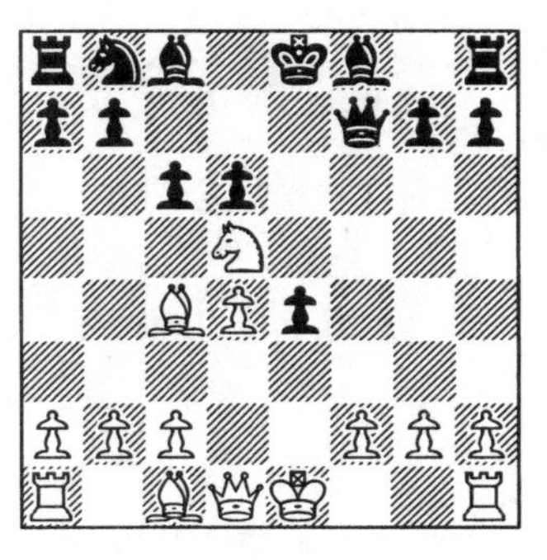

b1) White can take the exchange here, but he is well advised not to: 11 ♘b6?! d5 12 ♘xa8 (White can gain a pawn, at the cost of a tempo, by 12 ♗xd5!? cxd5 13 ♘xa8 ♗d6 14 0-0 0-0 15 ♗e3 ♘c6 16 c4 [16 f3 appears more to the point, but after 16...♕h5 17 h3 Black wins by 17...♗xh3! 18 gxh3 ♕xh3 19 ♖f2 exf3, without even having to capture the a8-knight!] 16...dxc4 17 d5 ♘e5 18 ♕a4 ♘f3+! forcing mate, Spaans-Diepstraten, Hilversum 1988. 12 ♘xc8?? is just a blunder, though, 12...dxc4 13 ♕g4 ♘d7 14 ♕xe4+ ♔d8 trapping the knight, 15 ♘xa7 ♗b4+ 16 ♔d1 ♖xa7 and White can resign, Ravel-Sireta, Auvergne 1993) 12...dxc4. Clearly White will be unable to extract his knight from a8 and when Black eventually takes it he will have two pieces for a rook. What can White do in the meantime? The evidence is: not very much; there is only one file for the white rooks, furthermore, Black has the use of the d5 square. Some examples:

b11) 13 d5 ♗d6! 14 ♗e3 (14 dxc6 0-0 15 0-0 ♖d8 16 ♕e2 ♘xc6 also favours Black) 14...c5 (14...cxd5!?) 15 ♕e2 0-0 16 ♕xc4 ♘a6, Hohnes-Dreibergs, corr. 1954, when 17 ♕xe4 ♗f5 18 ♕c4 ♖xa8 favours Black.

b12) 13 f3!?, Sloan-Elburg, corr. training game 1999, is most simply answered by 13...e3!? keeping the f-file closed, e.g. 14 ♗xe3 ♗d6 15 0-0 b5 16 a4 b4.

b13) 13 ♕e2 ♗d6! 14 ♕xe4+ (14 f3 e3 15 ♕xe3+ ♕e7!? [15...♗e6 resembles the main line] 16 0-0 ♕xe3+ 17 ♗xe3 ♘a6 18 c3 ♗f5 19 ♗f2 ♔d7 and ...♖xa8 ∓ Baxter-Dreibergs, corr. 1951) 14...♗e6 (14...♕e6 is also reasonable, 15 ♕xe6+ ♗xe6 16 ♗e3 ♗d5 17 b3 c3 18 0-0 ♘d7 19 ♖fe1 0-0 with the usual two piece for rook advantage, Walter-Purser, corr. 1977) 15 0-0 (15 ♗e3 0-0 16 0-0-0 ♗d5 ∓ Gabrans-Purins, corr. 1974/76) 15...0-0 Farooqui-Smit, Teesside 1973. Black will move his knight and capture its white counterpart; the 15...♔d7?! of Harris-Kampars, corr. 1969, looks too contrived.

b2) 11 ♘e3 d5 12 ♗b3 ♗e6 (12...♗d6 is also good, not fearing c4: 13 0-0 0-0 14 f4 [14 f3 ♕h5 15 f4 Grivainis/Hayward-Malmström, corr. 1997, and I would be happy to play the endgame here, 15...♕xd1 16 ♘xd1 ♗e6 etc.] 14...♘d7 15 c4 ♘f6 = Doelling-Dreibergs, corr. 1952) 13 0-0 ♘d7 14 f3 (or 14 f4) 14...exf3 15 ♖xf3 (15 ♕xf3 ♕xf3 16 ♖xf3 0-0-0 = Fletcher-Dreibergs, corr. 1966) 15...♘f6 16 ♕e2 0-0-0 = Venesaar-Kampars, corr. 1967/68.

c) 8 f3 ♗e7!? (not completely necessary, 8...exf3 9 ♕xf3 ♘c6 leads to a set up examined in the previous chapter, after 8...♘f6 9 ♘e3)

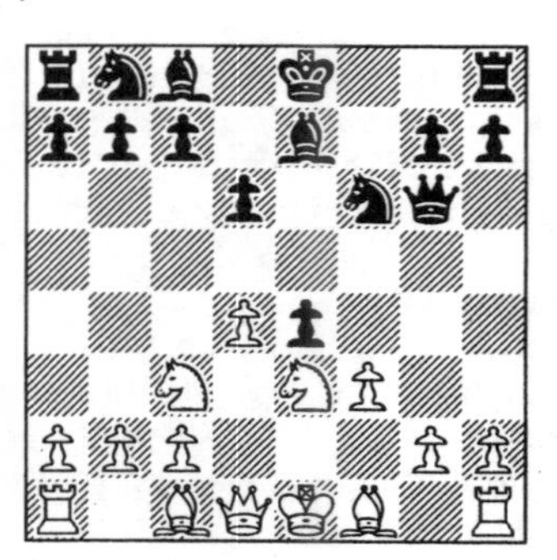

c1) 9 ♗c4 c6?! (I feel that Black should take on f3 now: 9...exf3 10 ♕xf3 c6!?) 10 fxe4 (10 d5?! ♘bd7 11 ♕e2 exf3 12 ♕xf3 ♘e5 Jackson-Hayward, corr. 1991) 10...♘xe4 11 0-0!? (not 11 ♗d3?? ♗h4+ winning on the spot, but 11 ♘xe4! ♕xe4 12 0-0 d5 13 ♗d3 also gives a clear edge, the knight will come to f5 in due course) 11...♘f6 12 d5 ♘bd7? 13 dxc6 bxc6 14 ♘f5 is awful for Black, Cirić-Strobel, Imperia 1966.

c2) 9 ♘ed5 ♘xd5 10 ♘xd5 ♔d8!? (10...♗d8! is superior, as the attempt to win the e4 pawn backfires: 11 ♕e2 0-0 12 ♘f4 [12 fxe4 ♖e8 13 ♘c3 ♗f5] 12...exf3! 13 ♘xg6 fxe2 14 ♘xf8 exf1=♕+ 15 ♖xf1 ♗e7 and the knight is lost!) 11 ♘xe7 ♔xe7 12 fxe4 (12 ♕e2, Logunov-Elburg, corr. 1994/96, is risky, for Black can try 12...♖e8! 13 fxe4 ♔d8 and the white king is also not ideally placed) 12...♕xe4+ 13 ♕e2 and White has an edge, Bakker-Diepstraten, corr. 1975.

c3) 9 ♗e2 0-0 10 ♘xe4? (10 0-0 exf3 11 ♗xf3 c6 transposes to a later line) 10...♘xe4 11 fxe4 ♕xe4 12 ♗f3?! ♗h4+ 13 g3? ♖xf3 14 gxh4 ♖xe3+ is a catastrophe, Weening-Backhuijs, corr. 1982.

c4) 9 fxe4 ♘xe4 10 ♗d3?? 0-1, Walther-Traut, corr. 1986, but in Heisterhagen-Huehn, Hessen 1992, White actually played on seventeen moves! 10...♗h4+ 11 ♔e2 ♗g4+ 12 ♘xg4 ♕xg4+ 13 ♔f1 0-0+ 14 ♔g1 ♗f2+ etc.

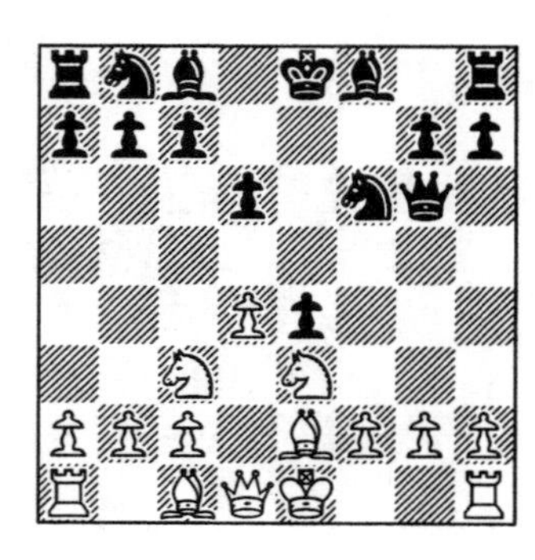

8...c6

There was a threat of ♘cd5 to contend with, so 8...♗e7?! is worse, 9 ♘cd5! (9 0-0 0-0 10 f3 exf3 11 ♗xf3 c6 12 d5 transposes to the main line, once again) 9...♗d8 (9...♘xd5?? 10 ♗h5) presents White with a choice of two good lines:

a) 10 ♘f4 finds the black queen embarrassed for squares. 10...♛g5!? 11 g3 (11 g4!? succeeded admirably in Kvist-Bondick, corr. 1977, 11...c6 [11...♛xf4? 12 ♘g2 wins the queen for two pieces, but 11...0-0 is clearly best, when White may regret his kingside weaknesses] 12 ♘f5! ♝xf5 13 h4 and Black resigned as his queen is once again lost. However, he should have continued, as after 13...♛xg4 14 ♗xg4 ♝xg4 15 ♕d2 0-0 Black has a certain amount of compensation!) 11...♛a5+ 12 ♗d2 ♛b6 13 ♗c3 c6 14 d5 ♛c7 15 ♕d2 0-0 16 h4 with advantage to White, Rocha-Cruz, Lisbon 1997.

b) 10 ♘xf6+ ♛xf6 (10...♝xf6?? 11 ♗h5) 11 0-0 ♘c6 12 c3 0-0 13 f3 ♛g6? (13...exf3 14 ♗xf3 ♛e7 is not very nice, but better than that played) 14 fxe4 ♜xf1+ 15 ♕xf1 ♛xe4? 16 ♗c4+ ♝e6 17 ♗xe6+ ♛xe6 18 d5 1-0, Müller-Gorla, Switzerland 1979, by transposition.

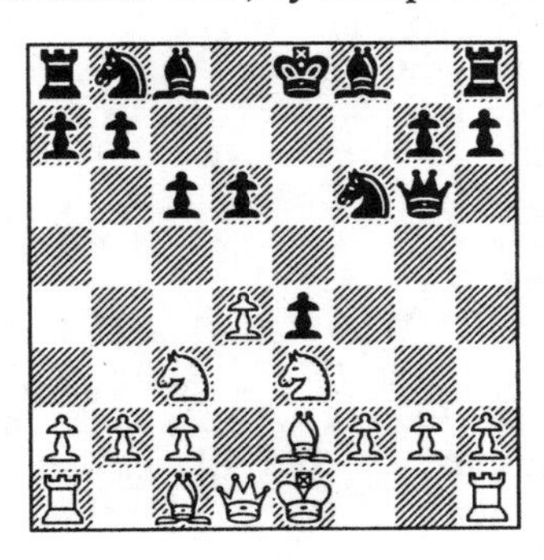

9 0-0

a) Play can transpose into the main line on 9 d5 ♝e7 10 0-0, but Finnish Grandmaster Westerinen tried 9...♞bd7!? against Prié at Fourmies, 1988, and although the game did not turn out too well, this was not because of the move itself: 10 b3 ♞e5 11 ♗a3 c5 (11...♞f7) 12 ♘b5 ♛f7 13 ♗b2 a6 14 ♗xe5 dxe5 15 ♘c3 b5 16 0-0 ♝b7? (16...♝d6 is fine) 17 ♗g4! ♜d8 18 ♗e6 ♛h5 19 ♘xe4 and White was already winning.

b) Otherwise, the immediate 9 f3 is possible 9...exf3 10 ♗xf3 d5!? (the most ambitious, Black wants to develop his dark-squared bishop straight to d6; 10...♝e7 is safer, 11 ♗e2!? 0-0 12 0-0 d5 13 ♗d3 ♛e8?! [13...♛f7 looks more active] 14 ♘f5 ♝xf5 15 ♗xf5 ♝d6 16 ♕f3, Rittenhouse-Svendsen, corr. 1992, when Black missed the simple 16...g6! 17 ♗d3 ♞e4 18 ♕e2 ♜xf1+ 19 ♕xf1 ♞xc3 20 bxc3 ♞d7 fairly level) 11 0-0 (Although I cannot find any games featuring 11 ♕e2!? it seems interesting, 11...♚d8 [11...♝e7? 12 ♘cxd5 cxd5 13 ♘xd5] 12 0-0 ♝d6 brings about a similar position to that after 11 0-0, but with the black king in the centre. 11 ♘cxd5!? is optimistic, 11...cxd5 12 ♘xd5 ♚d8!? [12...♞xd5?? 13 ♗h5, Zschorn-Melchor, corr. 1987, 12...♝d6 13 0-0 transposes into a later note] 13 ♘xf6 gxf6 White's compensation should not be sufficient) 11...♝d6 12 ♘exd5!? (this is quite popular, although 12 ♗e2 is probably stronger, 12...0-0 13 ♗d3, fairly level, Albisetti-Faraoni, Zurich Open-B 1990) 12...cxd5 13 ♕e2+ (13 ♘xd5?! 0-0 14 ♗f4 ♞xd5 15 ♗xd5+ ♚h8 16 ♗xd6 ♛xd6 17 ♕h5 ♞d7 18 ♖xf8+ ♛xf8 19 ♖f1 ♞f6, Black is consolidating, Zschorn-Strelis, corr. 1987; 13 ♘b5 ♚d7! 14 ♘xd6 ♚xd6 15 ♗f4+ ♚d7 16 c4 ♚d8 17 cxd5 ♝g4 18 ♕b3 ♝xf3 19 ♖xf3 ♛f7 unclear, Szabo-Eberth, Miskolc 1998) 13...♚d8 14 ♘xd5 ♞xd5 15 ♗xd5 ♞c6 16 c3?! ♜e8 (16...♝xh2+?! looks tempting, but 17 ♔xh2 ♛d6+

18 ♔h1 ♕xd5 19 c4 is actually very messy) 17 ♕b5 a6 18 ♕b6+ ♗c7 19 ♕c5 ♗d6 ½-½ Niermann-Leisebein, East Germany 1983.

9...♗e7

Again, Black can consider playing 9...d5 and putting his king's bishop on d6: 10 f3 (10 ♘cxd5? is worse here than after 9 f3, or 10 f3, as White has no open f-file to use; on 10...cxd5 11 ♘xd5 ♗d6 12 ♗f4 ♗xf4 [12...♘xd5 13 ♗h5 ♗xf4 14 ♗xg6+ hxg6 15 h3 is unclear] 13 ♘xf4 ♕g5 14 g3 0-0 the white compensation is quite insufficient, Zschorn-Kozlov, corr. 1987) 10...exf3 11 ♗d3! (this idea was not possible previously; the automatic 11 ♗xf3 is considered in the note to 9 f3) 11...♕h5 12 ♕xf3 ♕xf3 13 ♖xf3 ♗d6 14 ♗d2 0-0 15 ♖af1 ±, Marić-Smit, Strasbourg 1973.

10 f3

10 d5 0-0 11 f3 exf3 12 ♗xf3 transposes.

10...exf3

Black's position after 10...d5!? 11 fxe4 dxe4 12 ♗c4 ♖f8, Svendsen-Downey, corr. 1990, is compromised, but as the main line is also favourable to White, this is no worse. 13 ♘e2 ♘h5 (else 14 ♘f4 with advantage) 14 d5?! (I don't like this, why open the g1-a7 diagonal? 14 ♖xf8+ ♗xf8 15 ♗d2) 14...♖xf1+ 15 ♕xf1 ♗c5 16 ♗d2 ♕g5!? 17 ♕f2 b5 18 ♗b3 is close to equality.

And 10...0-0 11 fxe4 ♘xe4 12 ♖xf8+ ♗xf8 13 ♘xe4 (13 ♗c4+!? ♔h8 14 ♕f3 ♘f6 15 ♗d2) 13...♕xe4 14 ♗d3 ♕h4, Christoph-Cherubim, 1959, is also a little better for White after 15 c3.

11 ♗xf3

White has two other good alternatives:

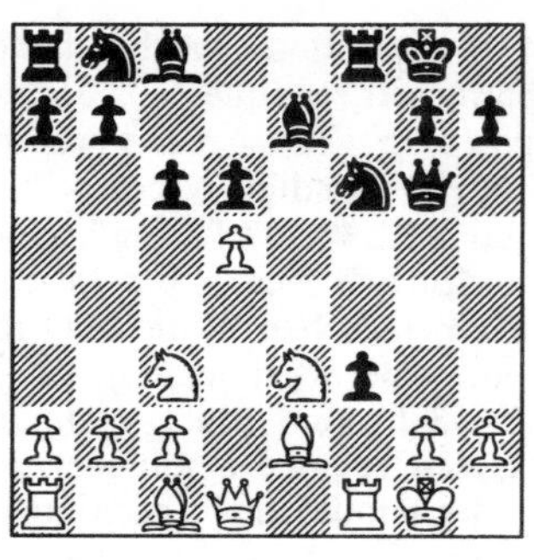

a) 11 ♗d3 ♕h5 12 ♕xf3 (exchanging the queens makes Black's defence more difficult, 12 ♖xf3 transposes to 11 ♖xf3, below) 12...♕xf3 13 ♖xf3 d5 (13...0-0 14 ♘f5 ♗xf5 15 ♖xf5 [15 ♗xf5! is better as the bishop is more active on the h3-c8 diagonal] 15...♘bd7 16 ♗g5 ♖ae8 Black enjoys near equality, Boudre-Destrebecq, Belfort 1983) 14 ♘f5 (14 ♗d2 is also good, 14...0-0 15 ♖e1 ♗d6 16 ♘f5 ♗xf5 17 ♗xf5 with a plus, Nilsson-Niemand, corr. 1991) 14...♗xf5 15 ♗xf5 0-0 16 ♗g5 ♘a6 17 ♖e1 ♗d6?! (17...♖ae8 18 ♖fe3 ♗d6 limits White's advantage) 18 ♖e6 ♖ad8?! 19 ♖h3 winning a pawn, Bengtsson-Ekstroem, Sweden ch 1977.

b) 11 ♖xf3 0-0 12 ♗d3 ♕h5 13 ♘f5 (13 ♗d2 d5 14 ♕e2 ♖e8 15 ♖af1 ♘a6 16 h3 ♗d6 is quite reasonable for Black, Ladisic-Destrebecq, corr. 1984) 13...♗xf5 14 ♗xf5 ♔h8!? 15 d5? (opening the position prematurely, 15 ♕e1 maintains a plus) 15...cxd5! 16 ♘xd5 ♘xd5 17 ♕xd5 ♘c6 18 ♗e4 ♕xd5 19 ♗xd5 ♘d4 and White is in trouble, Svendsen-Koser, corr. 1992.

11...0-0 12 d5

White can also consider 12 ♗e2-d3, as per the Rittenhouse-

Svendsen game in the note to White's ninth move.

12...c5 13 ♕e2

It is a matter of taste how best to tackle this Benoni-style position. Other moves:

a) 13 ♖e1 is also good, 13...♘bd7? (in light of the problems Black had in this game, 13...♘a6 would seem to be an improvement, keeping an eye on the c7 square, e.g. 14 ♘c4 ♖e8 15 ♗f4 ♘b4!?) 14 ♘c4 ♖e8 15 ♘b5 ♗d8 16 ♘bxd6 ♖xe1+ 17 ♕xe1 ♘f8? 18 ♕e2 b6? 19 ♘e5 1-0, Gaard-Jackson, corr. 1993.

b) 13 ♗e2 ♘a6 14 ♗d3 ♕e8 15 ♘f5 ♗xf5 16 ♗xf5 ♘c7 17 ♕d3 ♕h5 18 ♗d2 ♘g4 and Black has enough play, Merenyi-Spielmann, Budapest 1928.

13...b6!?

13...♘bd7?, Piris-Loureda, Spain 1995, whilst tempting (Black hopes to establish this knight on e5, when all his troubles will be behind him), is again a mistake, 14 ♘c4 ♕f7 15 ♗f4, there is no way to defend d6, i.e. 15...♘e8 16 ♗h5 g6 17 ♗h6.

14 a4

14 ♘c4 ♗a6 15 ♕xe7 ♗xc4 16 ♕e6+ is also possible.

14...♖d8

Black embarks on a lot of unnecessary prophylaxis, 14...♗a6 15 ♘b5 ♘bd7 16 ♘c4 ♖ae8 is more active, although White has a certain advantage.

15 b3 ♘a6 16 ♘b5 ♕e8?! 17 ♗b2 ♕d7 18 ♖ae1 ♖e8 19 ♘c4 ♗b7?!

19...♗f8.

20 ♕e6+! ♕xe6 21 ♖xe6 ♘xd5 22 ♘cxd6 ♘ac7 23 ♘xb7 ♘xe6 24 ♗xd5 1-0

Bauer-Sénéchaud, Metz 1997, a model White victory.

C 7 ♗e3

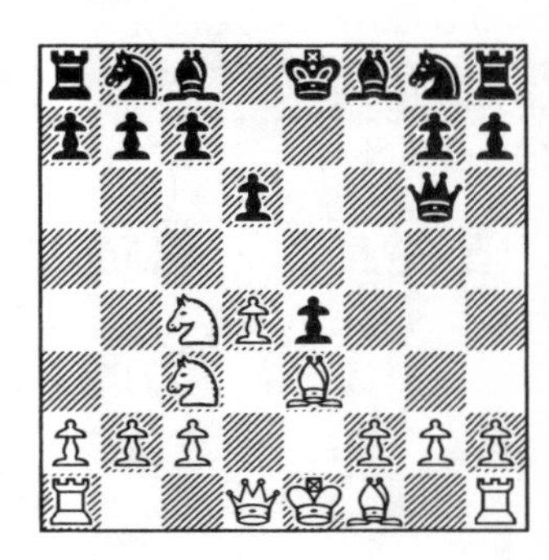

Quite a popular move in OTB games.

7...♘f6 8 h3

In order to prevent the possibility of the ...♘g4 sortie, but in Kraus-Dreibergs, corr. 1954, White continued 8 ♕d2 ♗e7 9 0-0-0 anyway, 9...0-0 (as after 9...♘g4 White can reply 10 ♘d5! ♗d8 [10...♘xe3? 11 ♕xe3 ♗g5 meets 12 f4 as the e4-pawn is pinned] 11 f3 exf3 12 gxf3 ♘xe3 13 ♕xe3+ gives White a certain initiative) 10 f3 (10 h3 transposes to the main line) 10...exf3 11 gxf3 with some play down the g-file. 8 d5 is common, and transposes into F.

8...♗e7 9 ♕d2

In order to castle; 9 g4!? is sharper, but weakening, 9...0-0 10 ♗e2 c6 (intending the standard ...b5) 11 g5 ♘d5! 12 ♘xd5 cxd5, forking a piece, and a pawn, 13 ♗h5 ♕f5 14 ♗g4 ♕f7 15 ♘d2? (15 ♗xc8 ♖xc8 16 ♘d2 is OK) 15...♗xg5!, winning an important pawn, Lillo-Cueto, Santiago de Chile 1997.

9...0-0

So far both players attempt to complete their mobilization in the most straightforward manner, but in Oren-Krantz, corr. 1990, Black went in for a bit of restraint: 9...h5?! 10 0-0-0 ♗d7 11 ♗e2 a5 12 a4?! ♘c6 13 ♘b5?! ♘d5! 14 ♔b1 0-0 with complicated play.

10 0-0-0 c6

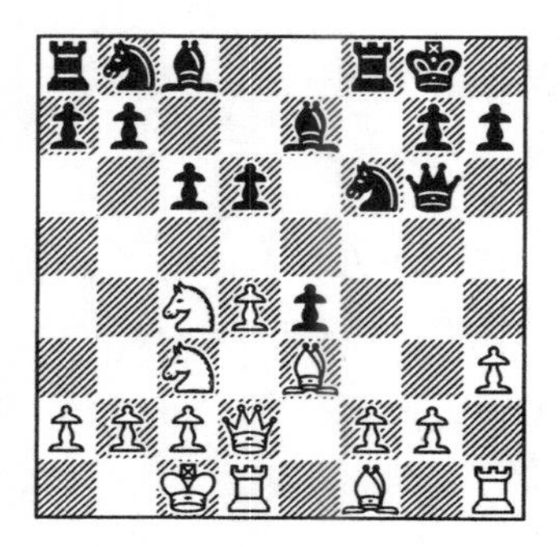

Unanimously preferred here, ...b5 becomes an unpleasant threat.

11 g4?!

White continues his kingside plan, but this is dubious.

11 ♗f4? stops ...b5, but allows something even nastier: 11...♘d5! when 12 ♗e3 is virtually forced, leaving Black on top, Meyer-Haenisch, Hessen 1990; not 12 ♘xd5? cxd5 13 ♘a5 ♖xf4 when the white king and queen prove to be on an embarrassing diagonal.

11 d5 is probably the best move, as then 11...b5 12 ♘a5 b4 13 ♘e2 frees the c4-square for the knight, 13...♘xd5? losing a piece to 14 ♘xc6 ♗e6 15 ♕xd5!.

11...b5

In the game Oren-Melchor, corr. 1990, Black played the awful move 11...a5? and was severely punished following 12 ♘b6 ♖a7 13 d5! c5 14 ♗xc5! (although 14 ♘xc8 ♖xc8 15 g5 ♘fd7 16 ♗g2 can't be bad either) 14...dxc5 15 d6 ♗xd6 16 ♕xd6 ♘fd7 17 ♗c4+. Curiously this strange idea (...a5) has something of a history, because in the game Roach-Gabrans, corr. 1968/69, they reached the same position except that the white queen was on e2 and the white g-pawn on g3: after 11...a5? 12 ♘b6 ♖a7 13 ♗g2? d5, this time it was Black who quickly came out on top.

12 ♘a5

With the bishop on e3, this knight has nowhere else to go.

12...♗d8!

The point!

13 ♘e2 ♘d5 14 ♘g3 ♘xe3 15 fxe3 ♖f3 16 ♘h5 ♗g5 17 ♘f4

Oren-Svendsen, corr. 1990, when in place of 17...♗xf4? 18 exf4 ♕f7 19 d5 e3 20 ♕d3 ♕xf4 21 ♗e2 ♖f2 22 dxc6 ♗e6 23 ♕xd6, with advantage, 17...♕f7! would have been difficult to meet.

D 7 ♘d5

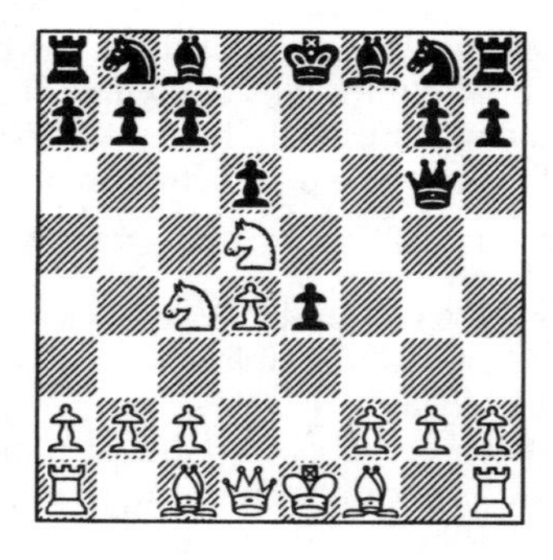

This whole idea looks suspiciously like a waste of time to me. These knight sorties in the Latvian tend to be playable if associated with a specific tactical idea, but here Black's simple reply defends c7 and attacks the knight, gaining time.

7...♕f7 8 ♘de3

This suffers from the disadvantage of occupying the c4-knight's logical retreat square, but other moves also have drawbacks:

a) 8 ♘c3?! is actually the most common in practice! 8...♗e7! (Of course, 8...♕g6 is possible, offering a repetition, but why not exploit White's loss of tempi? Meanwhile, 8...♘f6?! is less accurate, for after 9 ♗g5 White will capture on f6, e.g. 9...♗e6 Carlsson-Stalne, Vaxjo 1992, 10 ♗xf6 gxf6 [10...♕xf6 11 ♘xe4] 11 d5 ♗f5 12 ♕e2) 9 ♗e2 (White is unlikely to get enough compensation for the piece on 9 ♘xe4!? ♕e6 10 ♗d3 d5) 9...♘f6 10 0-0 0-0 11 ♗e3 ♘c6, equal, Voigt-Mlotkowski, Philadelphia 1921.

b) The 8 ♘f4 of Heilmann-Moll, Berlin 1907, is slightly better, 8...♘f6 9 ♗e2 (White can also consider playing for control of e6 by an immediate 9 d5 ♗e7 10 ♘e3 0-0 11 ♘e6 [White has no time to increase his hold on e6 by 11 ♗c4 as 11...♘fd7 gives him severe problems on the f-file, 12 ♘g4 ♗g5 13 ♘e6 ♗xc1 14 ♖xc1 ♘e5! winning] 11...♗xe6 12 dxe6 ♕g6 13 f4 exf3 Van Nouhuys-De Raadt Offerhaus, Zuidhorn 1883, 14 ♕xf3 ♘e4 15 ♕g4 ♕xg4 16 ♘xg4 d5 favours Black) 9...♗e7 10 0-0 0-0 11 ♘e3 c6 12 d5 g5!? 13 ♗c4? (13 ♗h5) 13...b5 14 ♘e6 bxc4 which should have been winning.

c) 8 ♘ce3?! allows Black to expand in the centre with gain of time, 8...c6 9 ♘c3 d5 (good, now that White cannot play c4, or ♘c4-e5) 10 ♗e2 ♘f6 11 0-0 ♗d6 12 f3 exf3 13 ♗xf3 0-0 14 ♕d3! ♘a6 15 a3 with preference for Black, if anyone, Baudry-Destrebecq, Belfort 1983, by transposition from 4 ♘c4 (misplayed by White), and with a move more for each side.

8...♘f6

Neither 8...d5? 9 ♘e5 ♕e6 10 c4 c6, Humphreys-Simons, England 1992, 11 cxd5! cxd5 12 ♗b5+ with advantage, nor 8...c6?! 9 d5 c5, Castelli-Morgado, corr. 1970, 10 a4! with a good Benoni-style position, are as good, but 8...♘d7!? has more to it, 9 ♗e2 d5 10 ♘d2 ♗d6 with a good position.

9 ♗e2

9 g4!? has to be taken seriously, as it was played by a FIDE KO World Champion, albeit a rather young one, 9...h6?! (9...♗e7 10 g5 ♘d5 appears simpler) 10 c3 ♗e7 11 h4 ♗e6 12 ♖g1?! ♘h7 13 ♖h1 c6 14 ♕c2 0-0 15 ♖h2 ♘d7 16 ♗d2? ♗xh4 and Black went on to win, Anand-Destrebecq, simul, Lyon 1988.

9...♗e7

This is more straightforward than 9...c6 10 0-0 b5? 11 ♘d2 with advantage, Goncalves-Grivainis, Munich 1958.

10 0-0 0-0 11 f3

11 d5 a5!? 12 b3!? b5 13 ♘a3 b4 14 ♘b5 ♗d8 15 c4 ♘bd7 16 a3! favours White, Nieber-Diepstraten, Hilversum 1977.

11...exf3 12 ♗xf3 c6 13 d5 c5 14 a4

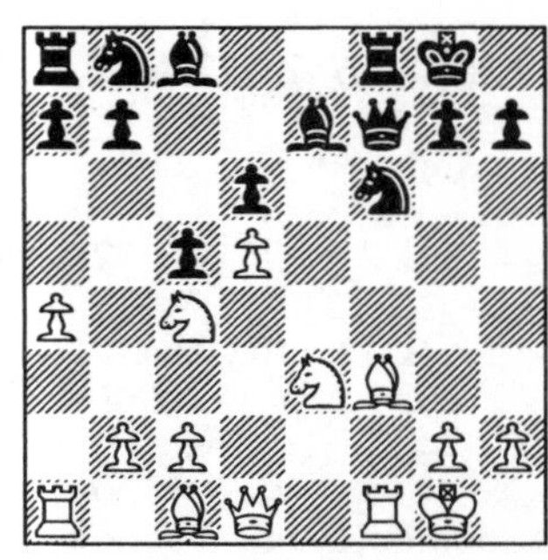

...with a slight edge in this Benoni-style position.

E 7 ♕e2

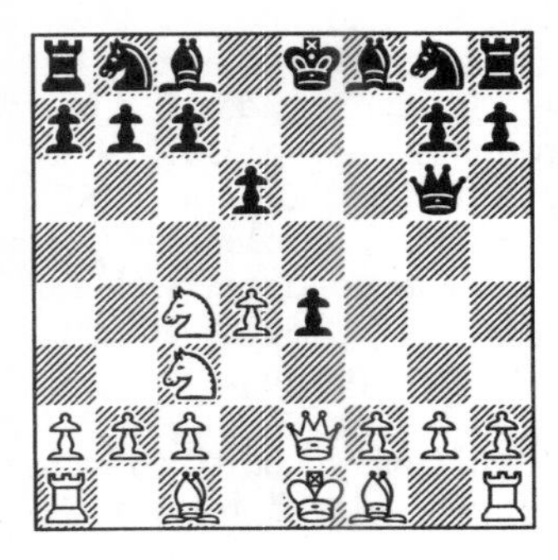

7...♘f6 8 f3

The point behind White's strange 7th move is this attempt to win the e4 pawn, but the weakness of White's d4 pawn gives Black his counterplay.

White can also try to pick up the e-pawn by 8 d5 ♗e7 9 ♘d2!? but he risks falling behind in development, (9 ♗e3 0-0 10 h3 a6 11 g4?! b5 12 ♘d2?! [12 g5] 12...b4 13 ♘a4 ♗d7 14 b3 ♗b5 15 ♘c4 ♘xd5 is crushing, Schulz-Menningmann, Duisburg 1991, or 9 h3 0-0 10 ♗f4 ♘bd7 11 0-0-0 ♘b6 Leibsen-Alberts, corr. 1978/80, although I would prefer 11...♘c5) 9...0-0 10 ♘dxe4 (10 g3?! weakens the light squares, 10...c6! 11 dxc6 ♘xc6 12 ♘dxe4 ♗g4 13 ♘xf6+ ♗xf6 14 ♕c4+ ♔h8 15 ♗g2 ♖ae8+ 16 ♗e3 ♘e5 17 ♕a4?! ♘d3+! winning, Burke-Stobbe, Upton, USA 1989, as 18 cxd3 ♗xc3+ 19 bxc3 ♕xd3 20 ♕xg4 ♖xe3+ 21 fxe3 ♕xc3+ 22 ♔e2 ♕c2+ 23 ♔e1 ♕xg2 is very good for Black) 10...♘xe4 11 ♘xe4 (11 ♕xe4?! ♗f5 12 ♕b4 ♘d7 13 ♕xb7 ♖ae8 14 ♕xa7? [single-minded! 14 ♗e3 ♗g5 15 ♕xa7 ♘c5 is also unpleasant, but does offer chances of defending] 14...♗h4+ 0-1, Pavilons-Grabans, corr. 1968, as after 15 ♘e2, say, 15...♗g4 16 ♗e3 ♕xc2 there is no real defence against the black knight hopping in to d3) 11...c6 12 ♕c4? (12 ♕d3 retains the possibility of defending the d5-pawn with c4) 12...♕f5! 13 ♕d4 cxd5 14 ♘g3 ♕f7 15 ♗e3 ♘c6 16 ♕d2 d4! 17 ♗xd4 ♘xd4 18 ♕xd4 ♗f6 19 ♕b4 (trying to improve on 19 ♕d2? ♗xb2 20 ♖b1 ♕xa2 ∓ Trull-Dreibergs, corr. 1953) 19...a5 20 ♕a3 ♗g5! 21 f3 ♖e8+ 22 ♗e2 ♗f4 23 ♘e4 d5 24 ♘c3 ♕h5, the white king is uncomfortably stuck in the centre, Knorr-Dravnieks, corr. 1992.

8...♘c6!

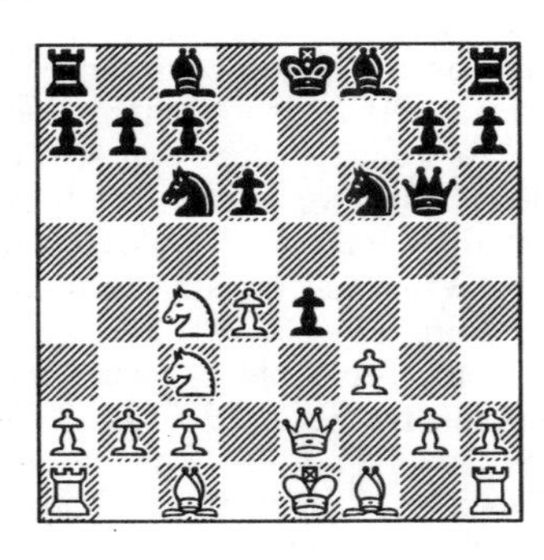

9 ♗e3

White has no better than to play this and take the pressure off e4, as the other moves offer little:

a) 9 ♘xe4?! ♘xe4 10 fxe4 (10 ♕xe4+ ♕xe4+ 11 fxe4 ♘xd4 12 ♗d3 ♗e6 13 ♘e3 ♗e7 14 c3 ♘c6 is nice for Black, Jurgenson-Tiemann, corr. 1987, 10 c3 looks tempting, after all the e4-knight is still pinned, but following 10...d5 11 ♘d2 ♗e7! 12 fxe4 0-0, ...♗h4+ is a threat, 13 g3 ♗g4 and Black has a strong initiative) 10...♘xd4 11 ♕d3 ♘c6 12 ♗d2 ♗e7 13 0-0-0 0-0 is, once again, comfortable for Black, Fabian-Pupols, Philadelphia 1974.

b) 9 d5!? is very wild, but I don't really believe it...

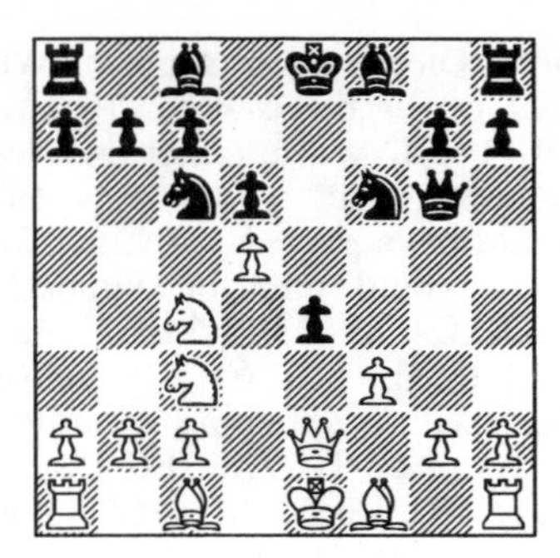

9...♘d4 10 ♕d1 (10 ♕d2 exf3 11 ♕xd4 merely transposes) 10...exf3 11 ♕xd4 fxg2 12 ♗xg2 ♕xg2 13 ♖g1 ♕xh2!? (it is probably best not to take the c-pawn, although this is also played: 13...♕xc2 14 ♘b5! [14 ♗f4 ♗f5 15 ♖g3? 0-0-0?! 16 ♕xa7 ♘g4 17 ♖d1?! ♖e8+ 18 ♔f1, Destrebecq-Gaard, corr. 1993, when 18...♖e4!, Downey, wins] 14...♔d8 15 ♗g5 ♗e7 16 ♖c1 ♕xh2 17 ♘xc7! ♔xc7 18 ♘xd6+ Roscher-Polland, corr. 1992, and 18...♔d7! is best, 19 ♕a4+ b5 20 ♕xb5+ ♔xd6 21 ♕c6+! ♔e5 22 ♗xf6+ gxf6 23 ♕c3+ forces a draw) 14 ♗f4 (14 ♘b5? meets the rejoinder 14...♘xd5!) 14...♕h5 (14...♕h4+ 15 ♔d2 h6 16 ♖h1 ♕g4 17 ♖ag1 ♕f5 is not too clear, Destrebecq-Downey, corr. 1993, White will play his king to safety on c1, and then attack) 15 ♔d2! (again the right idea, 15 ♘b5?! ♔d8 16 ♗g5 ♗e7 fails to solve White's king problem, 0-1, Reinke-Clarke, corr. 1994/95) 15...♗d7 16 ♖ae1+ ♔d8 17 ♔c1 b6 18 ♗g5 ♔c8 19 a4 ♔b7 and, having also brought his king to relative safety, Black could start exchanging some pieces, Oren-Krantz, corr. 1994/97.

c) 9 ♘b5?! seems to confuse two plans, Borochow-Mlotkowski, Los Angeles 1919, continuing 9...♔d8 10 ♗e3 a6 11 ♘c3 exf3 12 gxf3 b5 13 ♘d2 ♕xc2 14 ♖b1 ♗f5 with a clear black advantage.

9...♗e7 10 0-0-0 0-0

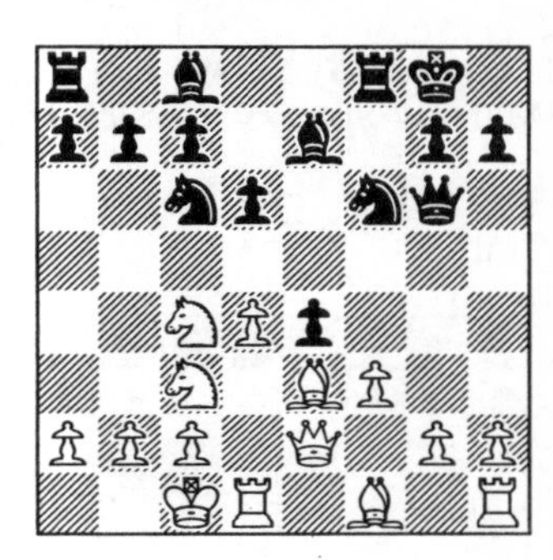

11 d5

Gaining space and displacing the c6 knight. 11 ♕d2?! is worse: 11...exf3 12 gxf3 ♔h8?! 13 ♖g1 ♕f7 14 ♔b1 a6 15 ♕g2 b5 16 ♘d2 ♗f5= Zschorn-Hayward, corr. 1991.

11...♘b4 12 a3 a5!?

A sharp piece sacrifice, opening up the a-file, but 12...♘a6 is quite adequate: 13 ♖g1 ♗d7 14 ♘d2 ♗f5 15 ♕b5 ♘c5 16 b4?! c6, unclear, Hempel-Castelli, corr. 1970/71.

13 axb4 axb4 14 ♘b1 ♖a1 15 ♘cd2 exf3 16 gxf3 ♘xd5 17 ♘e4

Black also has compensation after 17 ♘b3 ♘xe3 18 ♘xa1 ♗g5.

17...♘xe3 18 ♕xe3 ♗e6 19 ♖g1 ♕f7?!

19...♕f5 would have been better.

20 ♘ed2?

Missing 20 ♘g5 ♗xg5 21 ♕xg5 with an edge: 21...♗a2 (or 21...♖fa8?! 22 ♗d3 ♖1a5 23 ♕h4 g6 24 ♖g5, Hempel-Gunderam, corr. 1970, but 21...♕f4+ is better) 22 ♔d2 ♕f4+ (note that 22...♖xb1?? 23 ♖xb1 ♗xb1 loses to 24 ♗c4) 23 ♕xf4 ♖xf4, Hempel-Grivainis, corr. 1970/72.

20...♗f6 21 ♗d3 ♖a2 22 ♖de1 ♗xb2+ 23 ♔d1 ♗d5 24 ♖g5 ♗e5 25 ♖eg1 ♖a1 26 ♖xe5 dxe5 27

♕xe5 ♖a5 28 ♔c1 b6 29 ♕d4 ♕e7 30 ♕g4 ♔h8 31 h4 ♖e8 32 ♘e4 b3 33 cxb3 ♗xe4 34 ♗xe4 ♕c5+ 35 ♗c2 ♕e3+ 36 ♔b2 ♕d4+ 37 ♔c1 ♖a2 38 ♗e4 ♕b2+ 39 ♔d1 ♖d8+ 0-1 Muratov-Spassky, USSR 1959.

F 7 d5

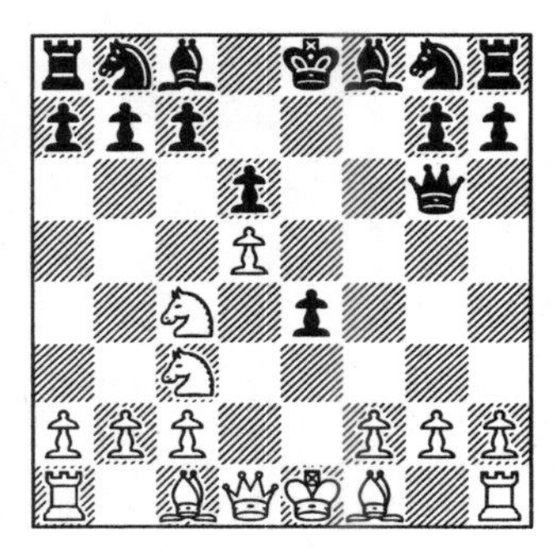

Another attempt to isolate and surround the black e-pawn, but again Black finds himself with a lead in development which more than compensates.

7...♘f6 8 ♗e3

White would transpose into Burke-Stobbe, E above, with 8 ♕e2?!.

8...♗e7

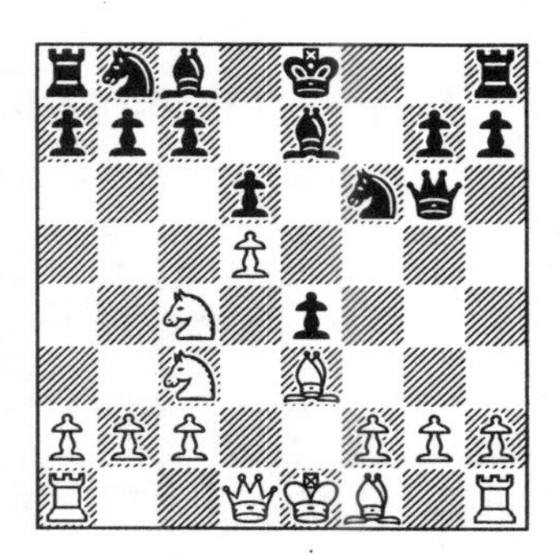

9 ♕d4

9 ♘b5 cannot be good, 9...♘a6 10 ♕d2 (In the correspondence game, Diepstraaten-Hundley, White went in for the esoteric 10 ♘a5?! 0-0 11 ♕d2 when, rather than wasting time with 11...♔h8?!, Black should have played 11...♘g4! ∓. 12 0-0-0 would then be impossible: 12...♖xf2! 13 ♗xf2 ♗g5 ∓. Pawn-grabbing by 10 ♘xa7?! presents Black with a whopping initiative after 10...♗d7 11 ♘a3 0-0 12 ♘7b5 ♘g4) 10...0-0 11 h3 ♔h8 12 a4?! ('positional', but sometimes tactics are more important!) 12...♘xd5!? (Good, but so is 12...b6 which intends rounding up the d5-pawn by ...♗b7) 13 ♕xd5 c6 14 ♕d2 cxb5 15 axb5 ♘c7 16 g3 ♗e6 17 ♘a3 ♘d5 and Black is in charge, Semenova-Varga, Zalakaros 1993.

9...0-0 10 ♘d2

10 0-0-0 is treated similarly 10...c5! 11 dxc6 ♘xc6 12 ♘d5? ♘xd5 13 ♕xd5+ ♗e6 14 ♕d2? (14 ♕b5 d5 15 ♕xb7 is the only hope) 14...d5 15 ♘a3 (15 ♘a5 ♗b4) 15...d4! 0-1, Pirk-Kulaots, corr. 1991, White loses a piece: 16 ♗xd4 ♘xd4 as 17 ♕xd4? ♗g5+ 18 ♔b1 ♖ad8 wins the queen.

10...c5! 11 dxc6

If 11 ♕c4 then 11...a6 12 ♘cxe4 b5 13 ♕d3 ♗f5.

11...♘xc6 12 ♕c4+ ♔h8 13 0-0-0

13 ♘dxe4? d5 wins a piece.

13...♗g4 14 f3 d5!

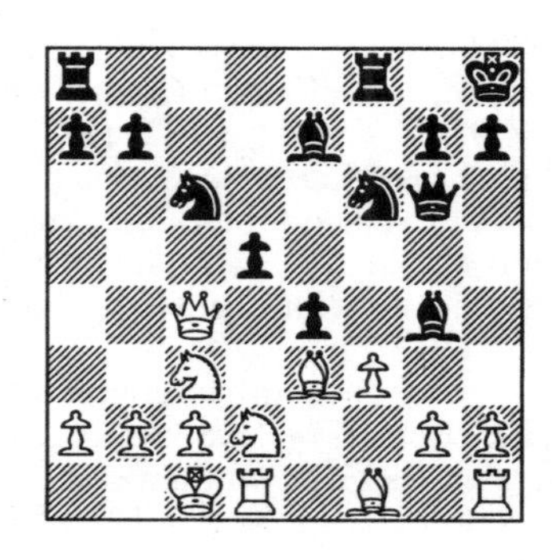

Opening up White's position.

15 ♘xd5 ♘xd5 16 ♕xd5 exf3 17 gxf3 ♖ac8?

A bad slip, 17...♕xc2+ 18 ♔xc2 ♘b4+ was possible, when Black has the tiniest of edges in the endgame, but, instead, 17...♘b4! 18 ♕b3 ♖ac8 19 c3 ♗e6 was a real crusher.

18 ♗d3

White is back in the game, Spielmann-Nimzowitsch, Semmering 1926.

G 7 g3

Another rare idea, but it does look quite sensible, attacking the e4 pawn with the g2 bishop. The negative side of the move is the weakening of the kingside light-squares.

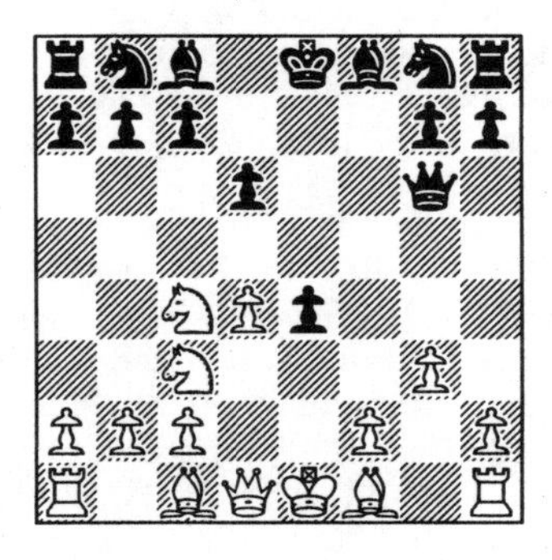

7...♘f6 8 ♗g2 ♗g4!

This is the right time for this move. 8...d5? 9 ♘e3?! (9 ♘e5 ♕f5 10 h4 will win the black queen by ♗h3!) 9...c6 10 ♗d2 ♗e7 11 ♕e2 ♘a6 12 0-0-0 ♘c7 = Lejarza-Purins, corr. 1968/69.

8...♗e7 9 0-0 0-0 (now, 9...♗g4 is more simply answered by 10 ♕e1 ♗f3, Murray-Owens, Electro game 1995, after which 11 ♗xf3 exf3 12 ♕e6 renders Black's further development difficult) 10 ♖e1 ♕f5 (10...♗g4 11 ♕d2) 11 ♘e3 ♕e6 12 d5 ♕f7 13 ♕e2 and Black has problems defending his e4-pawn, Dupont-Lescot, corr. 1994.

9 ♕d2

9 f3 exf3 10 ♗xf3 ♗xf3 11 ♕xf3 ♘c6 12 d5 ♘e5 13 ♘xe5 dxe5 is good for Black, whose bishop will find a more active post than the habitual e7.

9...♘c6 10 0-0 0-0-0 11 ♘e3

11 d5!? ♘e7 12 ♕d4 c5.

11...d5 12 ♘e2?

12 ♘xg4 ♕xg4 is equal.

12...♗xe2 13 ♕xe2 ♘xd4

Winning a crucial pawn, Latch-Kampars, corr. 1966.

H 7 h3

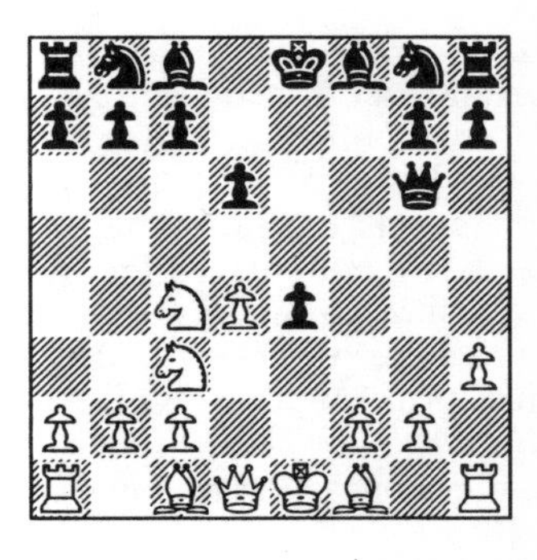

A similar idea to G was seen in the game Rauzer - Ilyin Genevski, Leningrad 1936.

7...♘f6 8 g4!?

8 ♗e3 transposes to line C, and 8 ♗f4 to line A.

8...♗e7 9 ♗g2

The g-pawn can also continue on its route, 9 g5!? ♘fd7 10 ♗e3 (10 ♗g2 ♗xg5 11 ♗xe4 ♕h6 12 ♗xg5 ♕xg5 13 ♕f3 can be met by 13...♖f8 14 ♕e2 ♔d8 unclear) 10...c6 11 d5 0-0 12 ♕d2 ♘b6! as the e3-bishop is required on the c1-h6 diagonal to defend the g-pawn, 13 0-0-0 with sharp play, Gåård-Zschorn, corr. 1989.

9...0-0 10 ♗e3 c6 11 d5
And now, pinning the d5-pawn by
11...♕f7
gives Black good chances.

I 7 h4!?

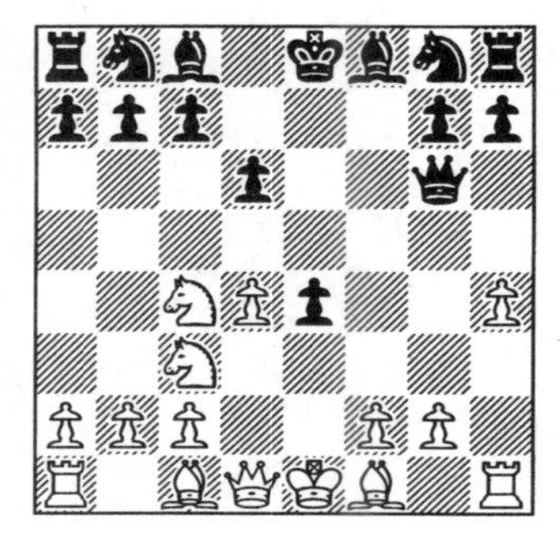

I thought that this was an idea of Grandmaster Yaacov Murey, one of the most original players in the world. He mentioned it to me over dinner one evening after a club match (we both played for Auxerre, in the French League), however I have since discovered that none other than the then World Champion Alekhine played it twice in a simultaneous display in Lisbon, 1940!

7...♘f6

Others:

a) 7...♗g4?! Several of Murey's games against a computer opponent went like this, 8 h5! ♕e6 (8...♕f5 9 ♗e2 ♗xe2 10 ♕xe2 ♘f6 11 ♘d2 wins a pawn, although 11...♘c6 12 ♘dxe4 ♘xe4 13 ♘xe4 0-0-0 14 ♘g3 ♕d5 generates plenty of play) 9 d5 ♗xd1 10 dxe6 ♗xc2 might be playable, then 11 ♘b5 ♘a6 12 ♘e3 ♗d3 13 ♗xd3 exd3 14 ♘d5 with the initiative.

b) 7...h6?! 8 h5 ♕h7 9 f3 exf3 10 ♕xf3 ♕f5 11 ♕e3+ with a big plus.

c) 7...h5?! 8 ♗g5 again with the advantage, the g5 square is weak (as Murey pointed out, this is reminiscent of the main variation of the Lowenthal Sicilian).

8 h5!

As played by Alekhine, 8 ♗g5 is how Murey intended to play, putting pressure on e4, 8...♗e7 9 ♕d2 0-0 10 0-0-0 with interesting play.

8...♕f7 9 ♗g5

9 ♗f4?! ♗e6.

9...♗e6?!

No better than 9...♗e7?! 10 ♘e3! 0-0 11 ♗xf6 ♗xf6 12 ♘xe4 with an extra pawn, however, 9...d5!? might be the best, avoiding problems with the e4-pawn, 10 ♘e5 ♕e6 11 h6 c6 and Black seems to be OK, e.g. 12 hxg7 ♗xg7 13 ♗e2 ♘bd7 14 ♗h5+ ♘xh5 15 ♕xh5+ ♔f8.

10 d5!?

10 ♘e3 d5 11 h6 ♘bd7 12 hxg7 ♗xg7 13 ♕d2 0-0-0 is fine for Black, Mainka-Pape, Bad Mergentheim Rapidplay 1994, but 10 ♗xf6! is rather more worrying, 10...♗xc4 11 ♗h4! ♗xf1 12 ♕g4!, threatening mate in one and winning the e-pawn with check.

10...♗xd5 11 ♘e3!? ♗e6 12 ♕d2 a6? 13 ♗xf6 gxf6 14 ♘xe4 ♘c6 15 ♕c3 ♗e7 16 ♘g5 fxg5? 17 ♕xh8+ ♗f8 18 ♗d3 0-0-0 19 ♕xh7 winning in a few moves, Alekhine-Braumann, simul, Lisbon 1940.

3 Nimzowitsch's variation 6 ♘e3

1 e4 e5 2 ♘f3 f5 3 ♘xe5 ♕f6 4 d4 d6 5 ♘c4 fxe4 6 ♘e3

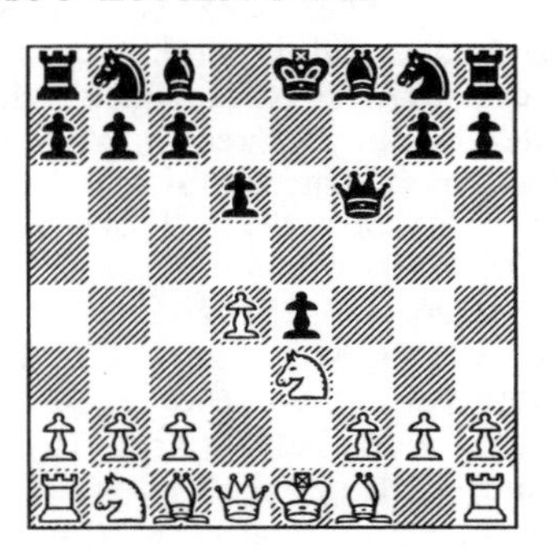

It is perhaps not surprising that Nimzowitsch held this move to be White's strongest, as the blockading knight formed an intrinsic part of his system. Nowadays, however, the line is not much in vogue, preference being given to sharper systems. Black has two continuations:

A 6...c6
B 6...♘c6

Other moves like 6...♕g6 are sometimes played, but often transpose into 7 ♘e3, in the previous chapter, i.e. 7 ♘c3 (7 ♗c4 or to other lines in this chapter, 7...♘f6 8 0-0 c6 for instance) 7...♘f6.

A 6...c6 7 ♗c4

Nimzowitsch's original idea, provoking ...d5, gives White a target for his c4-blow, however, Black has several ways to achieve equality. White sometimes plays 7 c4 instead, gaining space on the queenside, and, objectively speaking, I believe this is stronger: 7...♕g6 8 ♗e2 ♘f6 9 ♘c3 ♗e7 10 0-0 (10 b3 is also a logical choice, 10...0-0 11 ♗b2, Moskovic-Gabrans, Latvia, when 11...♗e6!? [11...♘a6] 12 d5 ♗f7 13 0-0 ♘bd7 14 f3 ♖ae8 15 fxe4 ♘xe4 16 ♗d3 ♗g5 17 ♘f5 favours White, Moskovic-Gabrans, Riga 1985. 10 h3?! is not the most pertinent: 10...0-0 11 ♕c2 ♘a6 12 a3 c5 13 d5 ♘c7 14 ♗g4 ♗xg4 15 ♘xg4?, a misjudgement, [15 hxg4 is superior] 15...♘xg4 16 hxg4 ♖ae8 17 ♕e2 ♗f6 18 ♖h3 ♗d4! 19 ♗e3 ♕f6 20 ♗xd4? cxd4 21 ♘d1 b5!? 22 b3 bxc4 23 ♕xc4 e3 24 fxe3 dxe3 25 ♖a2 ♕f2+! 26 ♘xf2 exf2+ 0-1, Tefedor-Hector, Manresa 1990) 10...0-0 11 f3 exf3 12 ♖xf3! (and now I prefer this move to have the possibility of bringing the bishop directly to d3, to molest the black queen; the alternative is 12 ♗xf3 ♘a6 13 ♗e2 [13 d5 c5 {13...♗d7!? intending ...♖ae8, is more flexible} 14 a3 ♘d7?! {too ambitious, 14...♘c7} 15 ♗e4 ♖xf1+ 16 ♕xf1 with advantage, Pineau-Sénéchaud, Avoine 1995] 13...♗d7 14 a3 ♖ae8 15 ♗d3 ♕h5 16 ♕xh5 ♘xh5 17 ♘f5?!, Leenes-Yska, Groningen 1984, when 17...♗xf5 18 ♖xf5 ♗f6 shows the d4-pawn to be underdefended) 12...♘a6 13 ♗d3 ♕h5 14 ♕e2 Harris-Destrebecq, France

1977, and now 14...♖e8 15 ♘f5 ♗f8 limits White's advantage.

7 d5 ♕g6 8 ♘c3 ♘f6 transposes into Chapter 2.

7...d5

Black is also able to defer this move: 7...♕g6 8 0-0 ♘f6, for instance, waiting for White to unveil his plan. 9 f3 (9 ♗b3?! d5 10 c4 ♗d6! [going for a direct KO! 10...dxc4 11 ♗xc4 ♗d6 12 ♘c3 transposes into a line from Chapter 2] 11 cxd5 ♘g4 12 ♘xg4 ♗xg4 13 ♕d2 h6 14 ♘c3 ♗f3 15 g3 and White's king was a problem throughout the game, which Black won nicely, Fossan-Eilertsen, Randaberg 1989) 9...d5 10 ♗b3 exf3 11 ♕xf3 ♗d6 12 c4 ♖f8! 13 ♗c2?! (better to remove the queen from the f-file; 13 ♕e2! ♕e4! 14 ♘c3 is sharp, but promises some advantage, 14...♕xd4 15 cxd5 ♗g4 16 ♕e1) 13...♘e4 14 ♗xe4?! dxe4 15 ♕e2 ♖xf1+ 16 ♕xf1 ♘a6 17 a3 ♕h5 18 h3 ♗d7 19 ♘c3 ♕g6 with threats, Diepstraten-De Boer, corr. 1982.

8 ♗b3

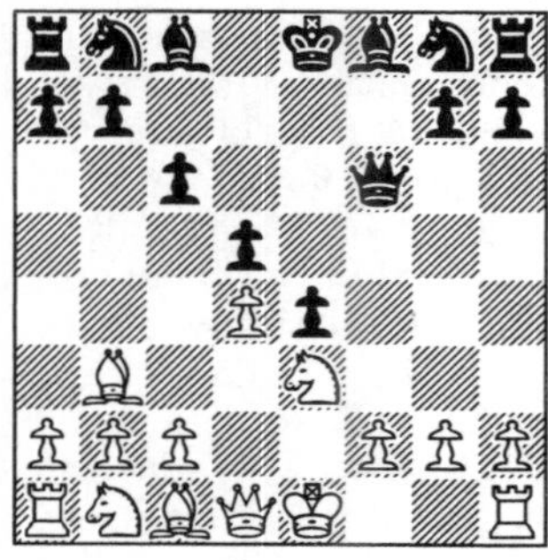

8...♗e6

Attempting to reduce the impact of White's next. Other moves are:

a) 8...♕g6!? 9 c4 dxc4 10 ♗xc4 (Black's idea, forcing White to capture with the bishop as 10 ♘xc4? ♕xg2) 10...♗d6 11 ♘c3 ♘f6 12 a4?! (the immediate 12 f3? allows 12...♗xh2 but 12 0-0 is simple and good, with f3 to come) 12...a5 13 ♗d2 ♘a6 14 ♕b3 ♘b4 15 0-0-0?! ♗d7 16 ♖he1 ♔e7!, intending ...b5 with dangerous counterplay, Santo Roman - Destrebecq, Uzes 1988.

b) 8...♗d6?! 9 c4 dxc4 10 ♘xc4 ♗b4+ (too many moves with this piece is a sign that something has gone wrong) 11 ♘c3 ♗e6 12 0-0 ♗xc3 13 bxc3 ♗d5 14 ♗a3 with advantage, Eglitis-Strelis, corr 1979.

c) 8...b5? 9 ♘xd5! (Black's elaborate attempt to forestall White's c4 was more successful in Eglitis-Kozlov, corr. 1978: 9 a4 b4?! 10 0-0?! [10 ♘xd5! is still good] 10...♗e6 11 a5 ♗d6 12 f3 ±) 9...cxd5 10 ♕h5+ g6 (10...♔d7? is catastrophic, 11 ♕xd5+ ♔c7 12 ♗g5! ♕d6 [12...♕g6?? 13 ♗d8 mate] 13 ♕xa8 ♗b7 14 ♕xa7 ♘c6 15 ♕c5 ± Destrebecq-Kozlov, corr. 1982) 11 ♕xd5 ♘c6 12 ♗g5 ♕e6 13 ♕xb5!? (13 ♕xe6+ ♗xe6 14 d5 should be simple enough) 13...♕d7? (13...a6! 14 ♕a4 ♕d7 15 d5 ♘e5 16 ♕xe4 ♕f5 offers some chances) 14 ♗d5?! (giving Black another chance, 14 ♗a4 ♗b7 15 d5 is decisive) 14...♗b7? (14...♘xd4! 15 ♕xd7+ ♔xd7 16 ♗xa8 ♘xc2+ 17 ♔d2 ♘xa1 18 ♘c3 is good for White, but Black is still playing) 15 ♗xc6 ♕xc6 16 ♕e5+ winning, Preikschat-Jaeckel, Porz 1984.

d) This variation, in general, suffers from too few practical trials. It occurs to me that 8...♘h6!? might be playable, with the possible continuations: 9 c4 dxc4 (10 ♘xc4 ♘f5 11 ♘e5 ♗e6 or 11...♘d7!?) 10 ♗xc4 10...♘f5 11 d5? ♗b4+ 12 ♔f1 (12 ♘d2 ♘xe3 13 fxe3 ♕g5 is little improvement) 12...♗c5 13 ♕c2?! ♗xe3 14 ♕xe4+ ♔d8 15 ♗xe3 ♖e8 16 ♕f3 ♘xe3+ 17 fxe3

♕xb2 18 dxc6 ♕xa1 19 ♕d5+ ♘d7 0-1, Hellberg-Ringoir, Belgium-Norway 1993.

Or 9 0-0 ♕h4!? 10 c4 ♗d6 11 g3 ♕h3 12 f3 (12 f4 ♘g4) 12...dxc4.

9 c4

9...♕f7

Bolstering d5, but it might be better to concede it, 9...dxc4!? 10 ♗xc4 ♗xc4 11 ♘xc4 ♘d7 12 0-0 0-0-0?! (sharp, but 12...♕e6! 13 ♕e2 ♘gf6 is very comfortable for Black) 13 ♘c3 ♕e6 14 ♕b3 (threatening a nasty discovered attack on the queen, and gaining a tempo) 14...♖e8 15 ♗f4 ♘gf6 16 ♖ac1 and White has a strong attack on the c-line, Destrebecq-Grivainis/ Hayward, corr. 1997

9...♗b4+?! is very popular, but why exchange White's passive bishop? 10 ♘c3 (10 ♗d2 ♗xd2+ 11 ♕xd2 ♕f7 12 cxd5 cxd5 13 f3 exf3 14 0-0 ♘c6 15 ♖xf3 ♘f6 16 ♘c3, White has a slight, but persistent, positional advantage, Huewels-GGAT, Compuserve, corr. 1993) 10...♘e7 11 0-0 ♗xc3 12 bxc3 0-0 13 f3 ♕g6 14 ♗a3 which must have made Black doubt the wisdom of conceding his dark-squared bishop! Megier-Crimp, Australia 1995.

10 ♕e2

10 cxd5 may be superior, 10...cxd5 11 0-0 ♘f6 12 ♘c3 ♗b4 13 f3 ♗xc3 14 bxc3 exf3 15 ♗a3!? (confining the black king to the centre, at the cost of a pawn) 15...♘c6? (15...fxg2 is critical, 16 ♖e1 ♔d8 17 ♕f3 ♖e8 18 ♖e2 when White has compensation for the pawn, but possibly not enough) 16 ♕xf3 ♘e7? (16...0-0-0) 17 ♖ae1 ♖d8?! 18 ♘f5 winning, De Firmian - Church, Hollywood 1985.

10...♘f6 11 0-0 ♗b4?!

Black might be more successful with 11...♘bd7!?, answering 12 ♘c3 with 12...♘b6 trying to fix the central pawns, and 12 f3?! with 12...♕h5 13 ♘c3 ♗d6, but 11...♗d6! 12 ♘c3 0-0 is surely the simplest, with a level game.

12 ♗d2 ♗xd2 13 ♘xd2 0-0 14 f4!? dxc4 15 ♘dxc4 ♕e7 16 f5 ♗d5?!

Conceding a useful bishop, 16...♗f7 is fine.

17 ♘xd5 cxd5 18 ♘e3 ♕d7?

18...♕f7.

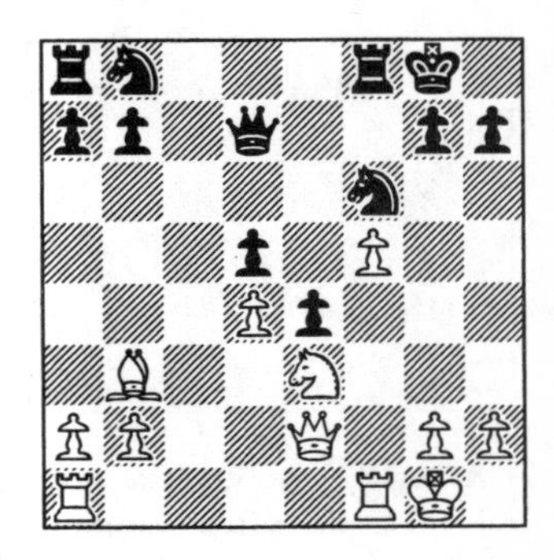

19 ♘xd5! ♘xd5 20 ♕xe4 ♖d8 21 f6 gxf6

Forced, in view of 21...♘c6 22 f7+ ♔f8 23 ♕xh7 +/-

22 ♖f5 ♔h8 23 ♖xd5 ♖e8 24 ♖xd7 ♖xe4 25 ♖d8+ ♔g7 26 ♖g8+ ♔h6 27 ♖f1 1-0

Nimzowitsch-Betinš, Latvia 1919.

B 6...♘c6

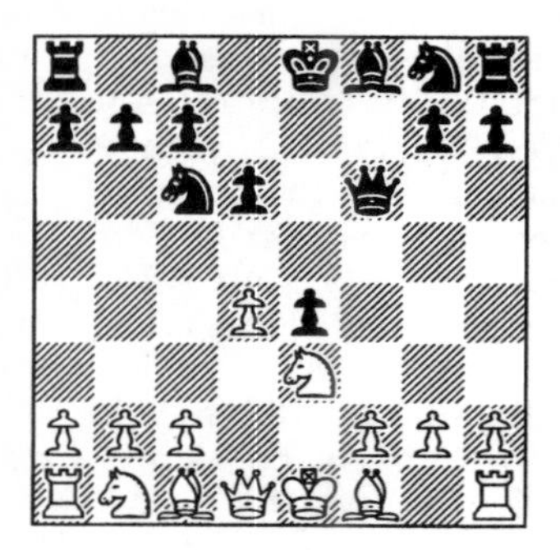

The modern preference, hitting d4. It was actually first proposed by Betinš after his defeat at the hands of Nimzowitsch.

7 d5

Conceding the e5 square is not a serious problem, but there are sound alternatives:

a) 7 ♘d5 ♛f7 with:

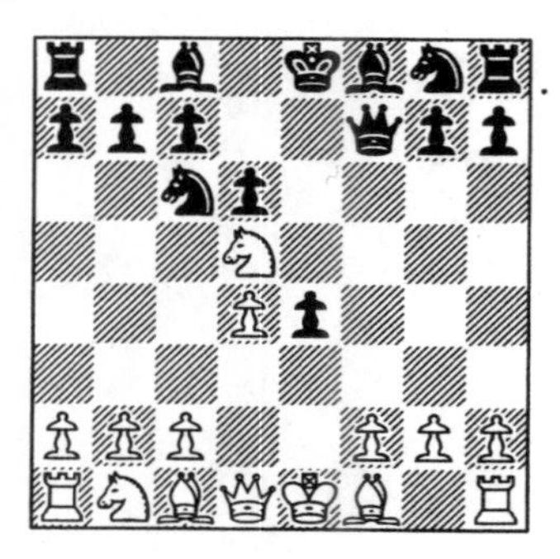

a1) 8 ♗c4?!, hoping to win the a8-rook but, as often happens in these type of positions, this tends to rebound. 8...♘a5 9 ♘b6 (9 ♘f6+? ♛xf6 10 ♛h5+ ♛g6 11 ♛xa5 ♛xg2 12 ♖f1, Golob-Thoma, corr. 1982, when 12...c6 is best, as 13 ♗xg8 ♖xg8 14 ♛h5+ g6 15 ♛xh7 ♖g7 wins for Black, i.e. 16 ♛h4 ♗h3 17 ♘d2 ♖f7 menacing ...e3, and winning) 9...♘xc4 10 ♘xa8 b6 (the 10...d5!? 11 f3 exf3 12 0-0 of Crimp-Destrebecq, corr. 1999, may be playable, but leaves Black further from recovering the a8-knight) 11 b3 (11 ♘c3 ♗b7 12 ♘xc7+ ♛xc7 13 0-0 ♘f6 14 d5 ♗e7 15 ♛e2 0-0. Black's two pieces are far stronger than the rook, Golob-Van Houten, corr. 1982, and 11 c3 a6 12 b3 ♘a5 13 d5 ♗b7 14 ♛g4 ♚d8! must also favour Black) 11...♘a5 12 ♗d2 ♘c6!? (12...♗b7 13 ♗xa5 bxa5 14 ♛g4 ♘h6 is simpler, Black is clearly better) 13 d5 ♘e5 14 ♛e2 ♗b7?! (returning a piece for the attack, 14...♘f6 15 ♛b5+ ♚d8 is messy but good for Black) 15 ♛xe4 ♗xa8 16 f4 ♘f6 17 ♛e2 ♛xd5 18 fxe5 dxe5 (18...♛xe5 leads to a promising ending) 19 ♘c3 ♛d4 20 0-0-0 ♘e4 21 ♛g4?? (losing on the spot; 21 ♘b1 defends, and leaves White in the driving seat) 21...♗a3+ 22 ♚b1 ♘xc3+ 23 ♗xc3 ♛xg4 0-1, Smit-Diepstraten, Hilversum 1991.

a2) 8 ♘bc3 ♗e6 9 ♘xc7+?!

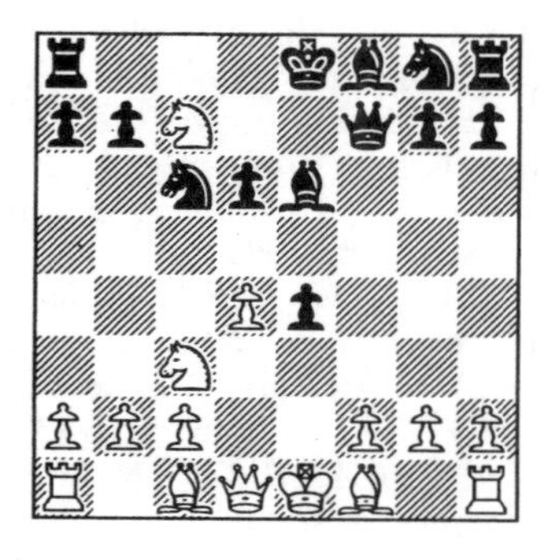

(this theoretical continuation almost loses by force, so perhaps White should prefer 9 ♘f4) 9...♛xc7 10 d5, now the theoretical choice is 10...♘f6 (10...♗f5!?, unusual, but quite reasonable, 11 dxc6 [11 ♘b5 ♛d7] 11...bxc6 12 f3 ♘f6!? 13 fxe4 [13 g4!?] 13...♘xe4 14 ♛f3! ♘xc3 15 bxc3 [15 ♛xf5 ♛e7+] 15...g6 16 ♗d3 ♗g7 17

♗xf5 when, instead of 17...0-0?! sacrificing a piece for doubtful attacking chances, Torrecillas-Hector, Barcelona 1988, 17...gxf5 was perfectly adequate, 18 0-0 0-0) 11 dxe6 d5! (-/+ *ECO*), and now:

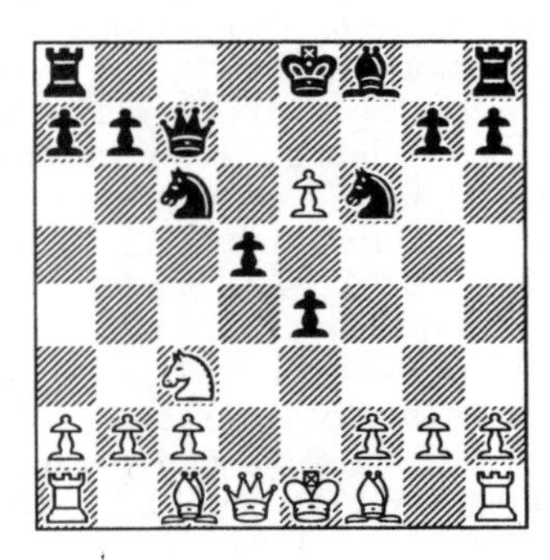

a21) 12 ♘xd5 ♕a5+ 13 ♘c3 ♗b4 14 ♗d2?! (but 14 ♗e2 ♗xc3+ 15 bxc3 ♖d8 [15...♕xc3+ 16 ♗d2 ♕e5 should be OK for White] 16 ♗d2 ♕d5 17 ♖b1 and White can hold with precise play) 14...0-0-0 15 ♕c1? (Betinš originally analysed 15 ♗e2 ♖xd2? 16 ♕xd2 ♖d8 17 ♕e3 ♘d5 18 ♕h3 ♘f4, overlooking 19 ♕g4! ♗xc3+ 20 ♔f1 and the threat of e7+ allows White to win the exchange. Instead, 15...♗xc3 16 bxc3 ♖d6 is quite satisfactory) 15...♖xd2! 16 ♕xd2 ♖d8 17 ♕e3, ♘d5? (according to the Betinš recipe, but 17...♘g4! 18 ♕h3 e3 cuts the queen's defence of c3, and wins) 18 ♕h3 ♘f4 19 ♕e3 ♘d3+! 20 ♗xd3 ♗xc3+ 21 bxc3? (21 ♔f1 ♗xb2 22 ♖e1 [22 ♖b1?! exd3 23 e7? dxc2!! 24 exd8=♕+ ♕xd8 wins] 22...exd3 23 cxd3 is unclear) 21...♕xc3+, winning, Reyburn-Downey, corr. 1980.

a22) 12 ♗g5 0-0-0 13 ♗b5 d4 14 ♗xc6 (14 ♗xf6 gxf6 15 ♕g4 ♘e5 16 ♕f5 ♔b8 17 ♘xe4 ♕a5+ 18 ♔d1 ♕xb5 19 ♕xf6 ♗e7!! 20 ♕xe7 d3 21 ♔c1 dxc2 22 ♘d6 ♘d3+ 0-1, Pretto-Ortiz, corr. 1994, as 23 ♔xc2 ♕c5+ 24 ♔xd3 ♖xd6+ 25 ♔e2 ♕c4+ leads to a swift end) 14...♕xc6 15 ♗xf6 gxf6 16 e7 ♗xe7 17 ♕g4+ ♔b8 18 ♘xe4 ♗b4+ 19 ♔d1 ♖he8 with an attack, Stockholm-Riga, 1934/36.

a3) 8 c4 logical, and best, White simply gains space:

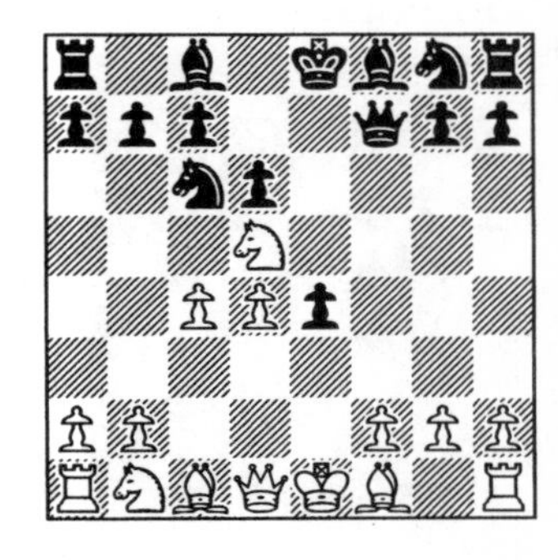

8...♗f5 (or 8...♘f6 9 ♘xf6+ [9 ♘bc3 ♗f5 transposes] 9...♕xf6 10 ♗e3 ♗f5 11 ♗e2 0-0-0 12 0-0 Wright-Boisvert, corr. 1973, with an edge to White) 9 ♘bc3 0-0-0!? (9...♘f6 10 ♗e3 ♘xd5 [10...0-0-0 transposes] 11 cxd5 ♘e7 12 ♕b3 [12 ♕a4+] 12...0-0-0 13 ♖c1 Destrebecq-Downey, corr. 1997, 13...a6!? is playable.) 10 ♗e3 (alternatively, 10 b4!? has aggressive intentions, 10...♘f6 11 ♘e3 ♗g6 12 ♖b1 [12 b5 ♘e7 13 ♕a4 is more direct] 12...d5!? 13 c5 ♔b8 14 ♗e2, Hanisch-Schneider, corr. 1987, White's queenside build-up is making life very uncomfortable for Black. 10 ♗e2 ♘f6 11 0-0 ♘xd5 12 cxd5!? ♘e7 13 ♕a4 ♔b8, Schwartz-Dreibergs, corr. 1961, 14 f3 exf3 15 ♖xf3 with a plus, or 10 ♘b5 ♖d7) 10...♘f6 11 ♕a4 a6 (rather than 11...♔b8?! 12 ♘b5! [12 ♘xf6 ♕xf6 13 d5 ♘d4 14 0-0-0 c5 15 dxc6 ♘xc6 16 ♘d5 is also very difficult for Black, Destrebecq-

Svendsen, corr. 1997] 12...♘e8 13 ♘dxc7! ♘xc7 14 d5 ♘xb5 15 cxb5 ♘e5 16 ♕xa7+ ♔c8 17 ♖c1+ ♔d7 18 ♖c7+! ♔xc7 19 b6+ ♔d7 20 ♗b5+ ♔e7 21 ♗g5+ analysis by Melchor.) 12 b4 ♘b8?! 13 b5 ♘xd5 14 cxd5 ♕e8 15 ♖b1 ♗d7 16 bxa6!? ♗xa4 17 a7, regaining his queen, with advantage, Destrebecq-Clarke corr. 1997.

b) 7 ♗b5

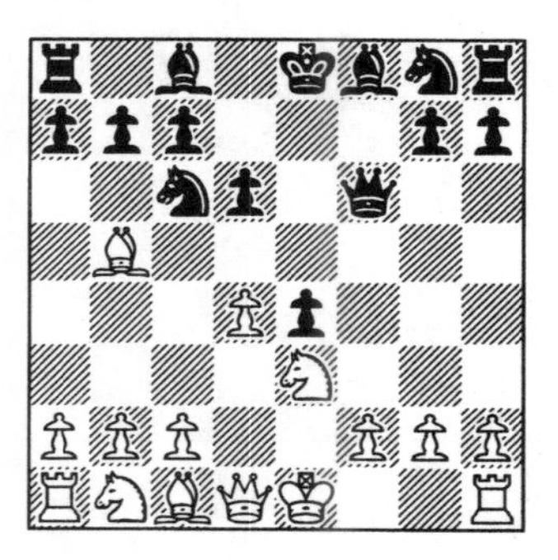

7...a6 (I am not too keen on 7...♗d7?, White can play 8 ♘d5! [rather than 8 ♗xc6? ♗xc6 9 c4 ♕g6 10 0-0 ♗e7 11 ♘c3 ♘f6, Waserman-Dreibergs, USA 1957, and Black is doing fine] when 8...♕d8 [passive, but probably forced as 8...♕g6?! 9 ♘xc7+ ♔d8 10 ♘xa8 ♕xg2 11 ♖f1 ♘f6 looks completely insufficient] 9 ♕e2 ♘f6 10 ♘xf6+ ♕xf6 11 d5 ♘d4 12 ♕xe4+ grabbing a pawn) 8 ♗xc6+ bxc6 9 d5 (9 c4 ♕g6 10 ♘c3 [10 d5 can now be met by 10...cxd5 as 11 ♕xd5 ♖b8 and the e4-pawn is defended] 10...♘f6 11 0-0 ♗e7 12 ♕c2 0-0 [12...♔f7!?] 13 f3 exf3 14 ♕xg6 hxg6 15 ♖xf3 ♗e6 and Black's bishop pair provides compensation for the structural weaknesses, Krempl-Sireta, corr. 1995. 9 0-0 ♕g6 10 f4!? ♘f6 11 f5 ♕f7 12 c4 ♗e7 = Donoso-Carmona, Chile 1974) 9...c5 (9...cxd5? 10 ♕xd5 wins the e4-pawn, but 9...♗b7 is a possibility, avoiding the fixing of the black queenside pawns) 10 c4 (10 ♘c3 ♕g6 11 0-0 ♗e7=) 10...♕g6 11 ♕a4+ (11 0-0 ♗e7 12 ♘c3 ♘f6 13 ♘e2 0-0 14 ♕c2 ♘g4!? with interesting play, Malmström-Budovskis, corr. 1994/95) 11...♗d7 12 ♕a5 ♘f6!? 13 ♘c3 (White's queen is misplaced after 13 ♕xc7 ♗e7 14 0-0 0-0 but this is clearly critical) 13...♗e7 14 ♘b5? 0-0 15 ♘c3, handing Black two useful tempi, Johansson-Gåård, Sweden 1994, as 15 ♘xc7?? ♗d8 16 ♕b6 ♖c8 loses a piece.

c) 7 c3 is solid, and reasonably common in OTB games, 7...♕g6 8 ♗e2 ♘f6 9 0-0 ♗e7 10 ♘d2! 0-0 11 f3 exf3 12 ♘xf3 ♔h8 13 ♘h4 ♕e8 14 ♘ef5 with a plus, Pantaleoni-Destrebecq, Bagni di Luca 1979.

7...♘e5

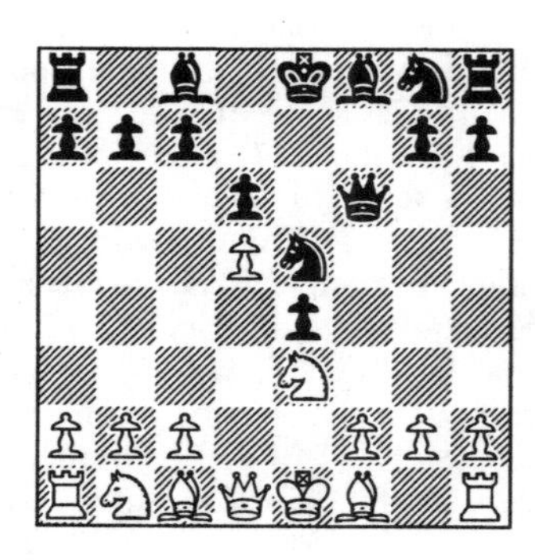

8 ♗e2

Stopping the black queen from reaching its ideal square on g6.

a) Alternatively, 8 ♗b5+!? is inaccurate, 8...c6! (8...♗d7?! 9 ♗xd7+ ♘xd7 10 ♘c3, when Black should reply 10...♘c5 ± keeping control of d4, rather than 10...♕g6?! 11 ♕d4 when Black has the choice between losing his e-pawn, or allowing ♘b5: 11...♗e7 12 ♕xe4 with advantage, Frommel-Dravnieks, 1988) 9 dxc6 bxc6 10 ♗e2 (10 ♕d5!? is more enterprising, 10...♗d7 11 ♕xe4 ♖b8 [not 11...d5?! 12 ♘xd5! ♕d6 13 ♘dc3 ♘f6 14 ♕e2 cxb5 15 ♗f4 regaining the piece, with interest] 12 ♗e2 d5 13 ♕a4 ♗c5 with plenty of activity) 10...d5 11 ♘xd5!? (11 0-0 ♗d6 is pleasant for Black, with his strong centre) 11...cxd5 12 ♗b5+ ♗d7 13 ♗xd7+ ♘xd7 14 ♕xd5 ♖c8 and White can get three pawns for his piece, Pintado-Busom, corr. 1995.

b) White has an interesting alternative in 8 ♘c3 ♕g6 9 ♕d4 (9 ♗e2 ♘f6 10 0-0 ♗e7 11 ♘b5 ♗d8 12 ♘d4 0-0 13 f3 c5?! 14 dxc6 bxc6 15 fxe4?! [15 f4!] 15...♗b6 with active play, Grey-Zemitis, USA 1974) 9...♘f6 10 ♘b5 ♔d8! (for tactical reasons this is best, 10...♕f7?! 11 ♘xa7 ♗d7 12 ♘b5 ♖c8 13 ♗e2 ♗e7, Black has some compensation for the pawn, but not enough, Serpi-Negrini, corr. 1994) 11 ♘xa7 ♗d7 12 c4 (12 ♘b5? reveals the point of no longer having the black king on e8: 12...♗xb5! 13 ♗xb5 ♕xg2! [this combination was first given by Betinš] 14 ♘xg2 ♘f3+ 15 ♔d1 ♘xd4 16 ♗c4 b5 17 ♗f1 ♘xd5 with advantage, Lawrence-Andersen, corr. 1998) 12...♗e7 13 h3 (13 ♗d2?, cutting off the queen's escape route, 13...♘fg4 [a good move, with the right idea, but 13...♘e8! is a killer, 14 ♘d1 {14 ♘b5 ♗f6 wins the white queen} 14...♗h3!! winning] 14 ♘xg4 ♘xg4 15 ♗e3 ♗f6 16 ♕d2 ♘xe3 17 ♕xe3, Koemskoj-Manaspoetra, corr. 1990, when 17...♗xb2 18 ♖b1 ♕f6 is emphatic) 13...♖f8 14 ♘b5 ♗xb5 15 cxb5 ♘fd7! (intending ...♘c5-d3) 16 ♗e2?! ♘c5 17 0-0 ♘b3 (and did I mention ♘c5-b3, as well?) 18 axb3 ♖xa1 with a sound extra exchange, Pape-Niemand, corr. 1994/96.

8...♕f7 9 c4

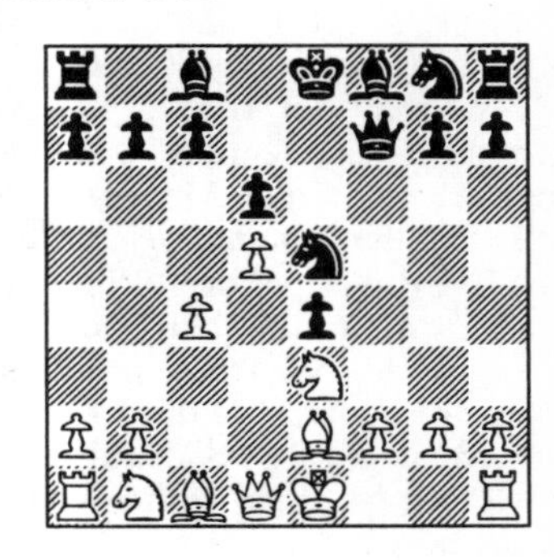

The positional line, White can also go after the e4-pawn again, much as in the previous note: 9 ♘c3 ♘f6 10 ♕d4 (10 h3 ♗e7 11 g4?! is inappropriate, 11...0-0 12 g5?! ♘fg4! ouch! 13 ♘xe4?! [13 ♘xg4 ♗xg4 14 f4 is forced, if somewhat gruesome for White] 13...♘xf2 14 ♘xf2 ♕xf2+ 15 ♔d2 ♗xg5 0-1, Evans-Niemand, corr. 1994/95) 10...c5! (10...♕g6 is playable, although it does leave Black a tempo down on the line 8 ♘c3 ♕g6 9 ♕d4, as he has played ...♕f6-f7-g6, instead of ...♕f6-g6, 11 ♘b5 ♔d8 [11...c5? 12 dxc6 ♘xc6 13 ♕d1 forces the ugly move 13...♔d7 as 13...♕f7? 14 ♘c4 blows Black apart, Littleboy-Svendsen, corr. 1985] 12 ♕c3!? [12 ♘xa7 ♗d7 13 c4 certainly should be less risky now] 12...♕f7 13 ♕b3 c6?! [13...♗d7] 14 ♘xa7 ♘xd5 15 ♘xd5 ♕xd5 16 ♕b6+ is promising for White, Kozlov-Tiemann, corr. 1989) 11 dxc6 (11 ♕a4+ ♗d7 12 ♗b5 a6 13 ♗xd7+ ♕xd7 14 ♕xd7+ ♔xd7 15 a4 ♖e8?! [15...g6 16 a5 ♗h6 looks right, this Benoni-type endgame is fine for Black, with the caveat that his e4-pawn can be a problem] 16 a5 g6 17 ♖a4! ♘f7 18 b4! White has an edge, Kozlov-Destrebecq, corr. 1992; 11 ♗b5+ ♗d7 12 ♕a4 a6 amounts to the same) 11...♘xc6 12 ♗b5 (12 ♕a4?! d5 13 ♘b5 ♗c5 14 0-0 0-0 15 c3 ♗d7 is great for Black, who will soon turn his attention to White's kingside, Sprenkle-Magee, USA 1998. But the 'unintuitive' 12 ♕d1! ♗e6 13 f4! is superior—White must try to restrain the black d-pawn) 12...♗d7 13 ♕a4?! (once again White loses control of d5, 13 ♕d1 is best) 13...d5 14 0-0, Sadeghi-Gåård, corr. 1990, 14...♗d6 with a wonderful position.

9 ♘d2 ♘f6 10 c4 transposes, as does 9 0-0 ♘f6 10 c4 ♗e7 11 ♘d2.

9...♘f6 10 ♘d2!

In order to play f3, White must be ready to recapture on f3 with a knight.

10...♗e7

In the game Graber-Leisebein, 1986, Black essayed the radical 10...h5!? 11 0-0 g5 12 f3 exf3 13 ♘xf3 ♘xf3+ 14 ♖xf3 g4 15 ♖f1 ♗d7 16 b4 ♕e7 and ...0-0-0 with double-edged play.

11 0-0 0-0

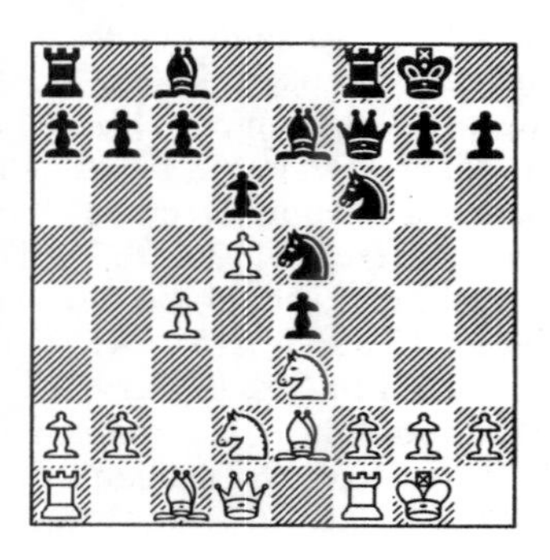

12 f4!?

This seems more accurate than 12 f3, when Black can also continue 12...♕g6!? 13 fxe4 ♘fg4! (However, 13...♘xe4?? is disastrous: 14 ♖xf8+ ♔xf8 15 ♗h5, deflecting the queen from its defence of the hapless e4-knight, Van Vuuren-Van Bree, corr. 1982) 14 ♖xf8+ ♔xf8 15 ♘xg4 ♘xg4 16 ♗f3?! (White should try to obtain some control over e5 by 16 ♘f3 ♗f6 17 ♕c2 ♘e5 when Black has minimal compensation for the pawn) 16...♗f6 17 ♘f1 ♔g8 18 ♖b1 ♘e5 19 ♘e3 ♗d7 20 ♗d2 ♖f8 with a firm grip on the dark squares, as in Destrebecq-Elburg, corr. training game 1993.

12...exf3 13 ♘xf3

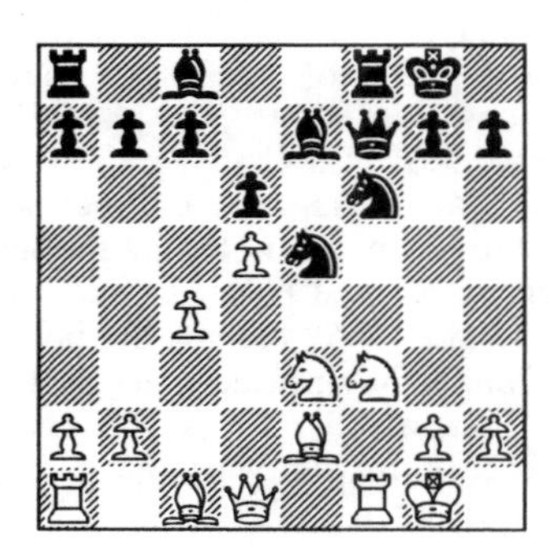

13...♕g6?!

Both 13...♘xf3+ 14 ♗xf3 ♗d7 and 13...♕h5 14 ♘d4 (14 ♘xe5 ♕xe5) 14...♕g6 15 ♘ef5 ♗d8 require investigation, although in both cases White retains a small advantage.

14 ♘h4! ♕e8 15 ♘hf5

Tasc R30-Mephisto Berlin, corr. training game 1994, when **15...♗d8** is best.

4 Bronstein's variation 6 ♗e2

1 e4 e5 2 ♘f3 f5 3 ♘xe5 ♕f6 4 d4 d6 5 ♘c4 fxe4 6 ♗e2

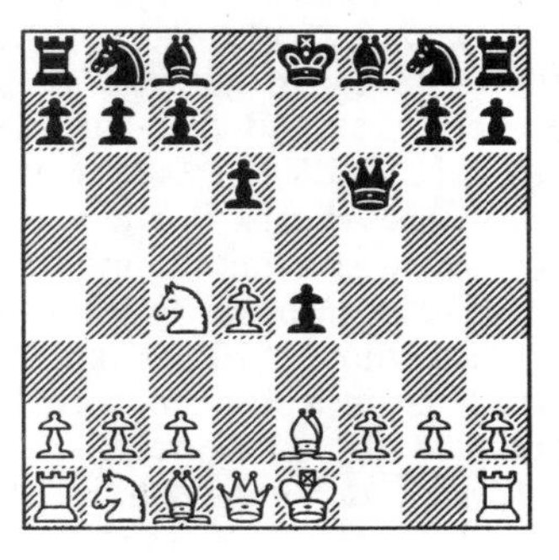

In his excellent book *200 Open Games*, David Bronstein goes into a deep discussion of how he came to discover the strong move 6 ♗e2 (which is odd, as it had already been analysed by Betinš). In essence, his idea is to stop Black's queen from settling on the important square g6, from where she simultaneously surveys g2, protects the e4-pawn, and also allows the king's knight to develop naturally on f6. The other advantage of 6 ♗e2 is its flexibility: White can attack the black e-pawn with ♘c3, and, if necessary, with f3 and yet is ready, should Black play...d5, to play ♘e3 and c4.

Black has tried many replies:

A 6...♘c6
B 6...♕d8
C 6...d5?!
D 6...♕f7?!
E 6...h5?

... without ever finding one that is completely satisfactory.

A 6...♘c6

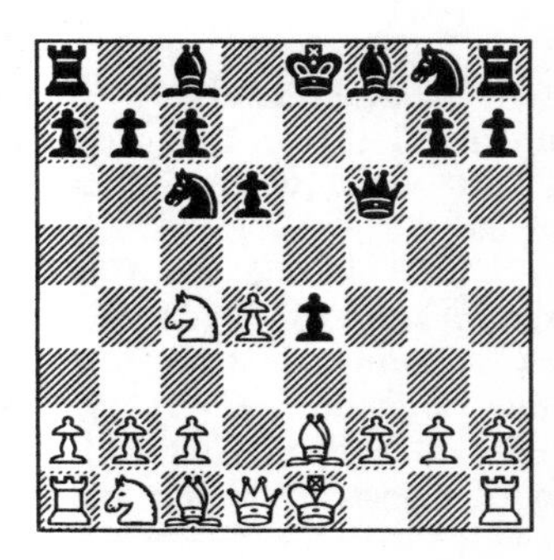

Immediately counter-attacking the white d-pawn.

7 d5

This 'isolates' the black e-pawn, whose subsequent defence causes the second player no end of problems, and is really the only move worth considering, 7 c3 being rather too passive, and allowing Black an easy game, 7...♕f7 (7...d5?! gives White a target, 8 ♘e3 ♗e6 9 0-0 0-0-0 [9...♗d6?! 10 f3 exf3 11 ♗xf3 leaves Black in trouble, 11...♕h6 12 g3 0-0-0 13 ♘f5 ♕f6 14 ♘xd6+ ♖xd6 15 ♗xd5 and White has an extra pawn, and the better position, Goldgewicht-Sénéchaud, Parthenay 1992] 10 f3 ♕h4 11 fxe4 dxe4 12 ♗g4 ♗xg4 13 ♕xg4+ ♕xg4 14 ♘xg4. White has an edge in this endgame because of the weakness of the e4-pawn, Bademian-Burgos, Mar del Plata

1993) 8 0-0 ♘f6 9 f3 exf3 10 ♖xf3 ♗e7 11 ♗g5 (11 ♘e3 d5 12 ♘f5 gains the bishop pair) 11...♗g4 12 ♖f4 ♗xe2 13 ♕xe2 0-0-0 which is close to equality, Johner-Grob, corr. 1940.

7...♘e5

Much the best square for the knight, although 7...♘d4?! has been seen: 8 ♘c3! ♗f5 9 ♘e3 (9 ♗h5+ g6 10 ♗e3 is tempting, but less good, 10...♗g7! [10...♘xc2+? 11 ♕xc2 gxh5 12 ♕a4+ is awkward] 11 ♗e2 [the obvious 11 ♗xd4 ♕xd4 12 ♕xd4 ♗xd4 13 ♘b5 encounters 13...♗g7! 14 ♘xc7+ ♔d7 15 ♘xa8 gxh5 when the knight is trapped] 11...♘e7?? [11...♘xe2 12 ♕xe2 ♕f7 is fine for Black] 12 ♗xd4 ♕xd4 13 ♕xd4 ♗xd4 14 ♘b5 winning material, Levene-Lynn, Dunedin 1983) 9...♘xe2 (9...♕e5 10 ♘xf5 ♘xf5 11 ♗b5+ may be objectively better, but is still difficult for Black, Watson-Pascute, corr. 1998) 10 ♕xe2 0-0-0 11 0-0 (11 ♘xe4! ♗xe4 12 ♕g4+) 11...♗g6 12 ♘xe4! ♕e5 (as 12...♗xe4 is again met by 13 ♕g4+) 13 ♘c3 ♘f6 14 ♕c4 ♔b8 when, instead of 15 ♘b5 ♖c8 16 f4?! ♕e4 with some chances for Black, White would have retained a clear advantage, in the game Oren-Rittenhouse, corr. 1993, by the simple 15 ♗d2 ♖d7 (else ♘b5 and ♗c3) 16 ♖ae1.

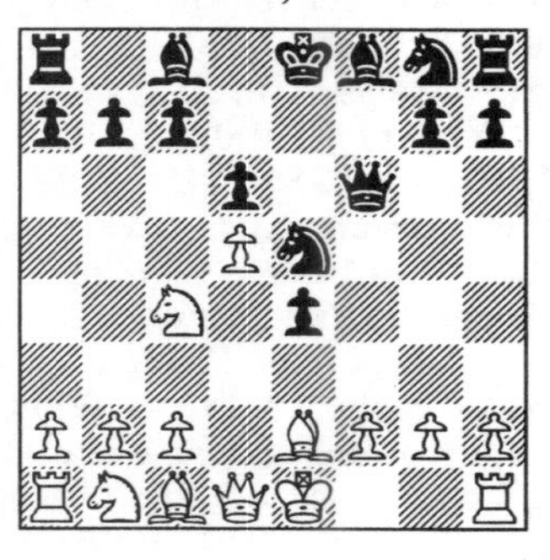

8 0-0

Alternatively:

a) 8 ♘xe5 ♕xe5 9 0-0 (Obviously, 9 ♗b5+?! is met by 9...c6 10 dxc6?? ♕xb5, but, nevertheless, White can continue here with 9 ♘c3 ♘f6!? [I believe that Black would be better off avoiding the annoying check on b5, perhaps 9...♗d7!?, or 9...c6] 10 ♗b5+ ♔d8 [10...♔f7!?, hoping to 'castle' by hand] 11 ♗e3 a6 12 ♗e2 ♗e7 13 0-0 ♗f5 14 ♗d4 ♕f4 15 f3 e3 16 g3 ♕g5 17 ♗d3 Ziecher-Urban, Bundesliga 1989, when 17...♘xd5 18 ♘xd5 ♗xd3 19 ♕xd3 ♕xd5 keeps White's advantage down to a minimum) 9...♘f6 (9...♗f5?! transposes to the note to the next move) 10 c4 g6!? (the game Nilsson-Korhonen, corr. 1988, continued most bizarrely: 10...h5? 11 f3 g5?! In for a penny! 12 ♘c3 h4? 13 f4! ♕e7 14 fxg5 1-0) 11 ♘c3 ♗g7 12 f3 0-0 13 f4!? ♕e7 14 ♗e3 h5!? (14...c5 immediately may be the most accurate) 15 h3 a6 16 ♖c1 ♗f5 17 a4 c5 with a fairly level position, Elburg-Sénéchaud, corr. 1994/95.

b) There is a further option in 8 ♘c3, putting immediate pressure on e4: 8...♘xc4 9 ♗xc4 ♕g6! (this is more interesting than 9...♗f5?! 10 ♗b5+ when the black king must move, as 10...♗d7? loses to 11 ♗xd7+ ♔xd7 12 ♕g4+) 10 ♗b5+ (if 10 0-0? ♗h3 picking up the exchange, although White has a fair deal of compensation: 11 g3 ♗xf1 12 ♕xf1 0-0-0!? [there is nothing drastically wrong with 12...♘f6 13 ♗b5+ ♔d8 for Black] 13 ♗e3 ♔b8? [this loses by force, although I do not really blame Black for missing White's next; 13...a6 14 ♗xa6 bxa6 15 ♕xa6+ ♔d7 16 ♕a4+ ♔e7 17 ♘xe4 is dangerous, but Black does own an extra rook!]

14 ♗a6! A bolt from the blue! 14...♕e8 15 ♗b5 ♕e7 16 ♗c6 a6 17 ♕c4 1-0, as 17...♔c8 18 ♕b4 and mate in five more moves, Huldin-Rantalainen, corr. 1983) 10...♔f7! (10...♗d7?! 11 ♗xd7+ ♔xd7 12 0-0 ♘f6 transposes to a later note) 11 ♔f1?! ♘f6 12 h3 ♗e7 13 ♘e2 ♖f8 14 ♕d4 ♔g8 and the respective positions of the two kings speaks volumes, Browning-Sadeghi, corr. 1991.

c) The popular 8 ♘e3 transposes to Chapter 3.

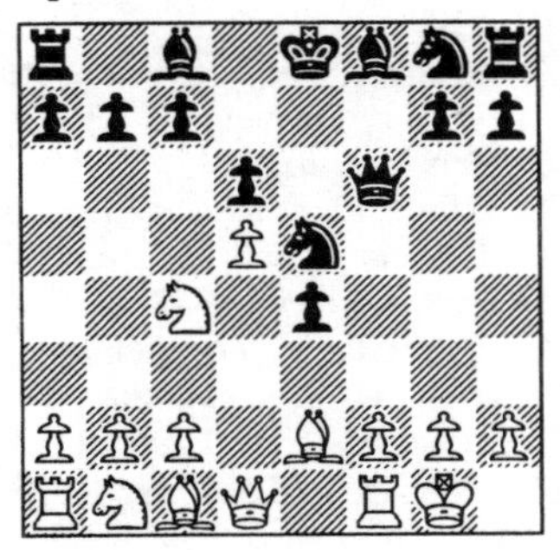

8...♘xc4

Black can thereby bring his queen to the desired square g6, and develop his g8-knight to f6. The alternatives:

a) 8...♗f5?! seems the most obvious but 9 ♘xe5 (9 ♘c3 is also quite good, as 9...0-0-0 10 ♗e3 leaves the black king poorly defended, 10...♔b8 11 ♕d2 ♘xc4 12 ♗xc4 ♕g6?! [12...♘e7] 13 ♕d4 b6 14 a4 and White will crash through on the a-file, Canal Oliveras-Clarke, corr. 1999) 9...♕xe5 (9...dxe5!? needs to be examined, although 10 ♗b5+ c6 [10...♔d8!?] 11 dxc6 bxc6 12 ♗g5! ♕e6 13 ♗a4 certainly favours White) 10 ♗b5+! (again, 10 ♘c3 is a good alternative: 10...♘f6 [10...0-0-0 is a risky try] 11 f3! exf3?! 12 ♖xf3. White threatens ♖e3, the black queen has nowhere to go, 12...♘g4 13 ♗f4 ♕f6 14 ♘b5 ♔d7 15 ♘xc7 Elburg-Gåård, corr. 1994/95, and Black is losing, for 15...♔xc7 16 ♖c3+ ♔d8 17 ♗xg4 regains the piece) 10...c6? (this loses by force, 10...♔f7 is not much of an improvement as 11 f3 ♘f6 12 ♘c3 plans to expose the black king on the f-file; 10...♔d8! is always awkward, but is best, 11 ♘c3 ♘f6 12 ♖e1 [for once, 12 f3?! is not very effective, 12...exf3 13 ♖xf3? ♗g4] 12...a6?! [driving the bishop to a good square, I prefer 12...♗g6] 13 ♗d3 ♕d4 14 ♗e3! ♕b4 15 a3 ♕xb2 16 ♗d4 exd3 17 ♖a2 winning the queen for insufficient compensation, Tatlow-Goedhart, corr. 1995) 11 f4! Deflecting the queen from its defence of c6, or opening the e-file, 11...exf3 12 ♖e1 f2+ 13 ♔xf2 ♗e4 14 ♘c3! (this is simpler than 14 dxc6 ♕c5+ 15 ♔g3 ♕xb5 16 ♖xe4+ ♗e7 17 cxb7 ♕xb7 18 ♘c3 ♘f6 19 ♖d4 0-0 which leaves White's king somewhat exposed) 14...♕f5+ (14...♘f6 15 dxc6 ♕c5+ 16 ♗e3 [16 ♔g3!? ♕e5+ 17 ♗f4 ♘h5+ 18 ♔f2 ♕xf4+ 19 ♔g1 also seems very strong] 16...♕f5+ 17 ♔g1 when Black was lost, e.g. 17...bxc6, Rittenhouse-Heap, corr. 1992, 18 ♘xe4! ♕xb5 19 ♘xd6+ ♗xd6 20 ♕xd6) 15 ♔g1 0-0-0 16 ♖xe4 cxb5 17 ♕d3 ♘e7 18 ♗e3 a6 (18...♔b8 19 ♘xb5 a6 20 ♗a7+ ♔a8 21 ♗b6 1-0, Downey-Clarke, corr. 1997) 19 ♗b6 ♖d7?! 20 ♖xe7! 1-0, Svendsen-Clarke, corr. 1999, 20...♕xd3 21 ♖e8+ and mates.

b) 8...♗d7?! 9 ♘c3 ♕f5 (9...♘xc4 10 ♘xe4! ♕e5 11 ♗xc4 wins a pawn for nothing) 10 ♘e3 ♕f4 11 ♕d4 ♘f6 12 ♘g4 ♕f5 13 ♘xf6+ removing the e-pawn's defender, Rittenhouse-Grivainis, corr. 1992.

c) 8...h5!? 9 ♘c3 ♗f5 10 ♘xe5 dxe5 (10...♕xe5 11 ♗b5+ ♔d8 12 ♖e1 ♘f6 13 f3 h4 14 ♗g5 ♗e7? 15 f4 1-0, Kozlov-Leibson, corr. 1979, was positively disastrous) 11 ♗e3 (11 ♗b5+ ♔d8 12 ♖e1 ♕g6 is not too bad for Black) 11...♗d6 (11...♕g6!?) 12 ♗xh5+!? risky, 12...g6 13 ♗g4 (13 ♗e2? ♕h4 14 h3 ♗xh3 wins) 13...♕h4 14 h3 ♘f6 15 f3, Rittenhouse-Melchor, corr. 1992, and now 15...exf3 16 ♗xf5 gxf5 17 ♕xf3 ♖h5 is not too clear.

9 ♗xc4

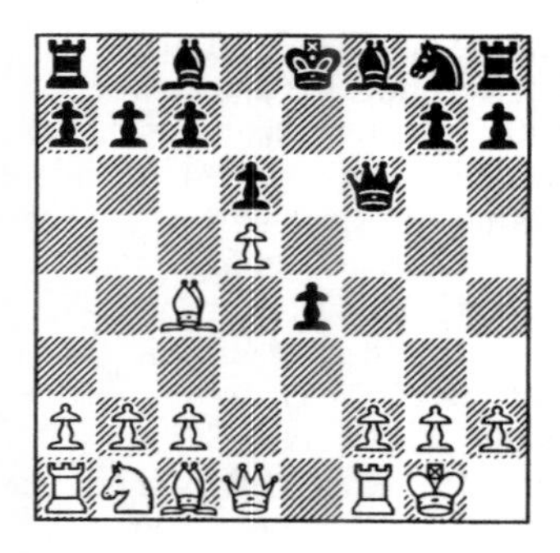

9...♕g6

The move 9...♕g6 was chosen by Black in the beautiful game, Bronstein-Mikenas, Rostov 1941:

9...♗e7 should be similar, or may even transpose, if White plays ♗b5+, 10 ♘c3 (10 ♗b5+ ♔d8 11 ♘c3) 10...♕g6 11 ♕e2 (again 11 ♗b5+ is reasonable and 11 f3, although apparently unplayed, deserves serious consideration, e.g. 11...exf3 12 ♕xf3 ♘f6 13 ♗d3 ♕g4 14 ♕e3, very reminiscent of Chapter 1) 11...♘f6 12 ♗b5+ (ganging up on the e4-pawn by 12 ♖e1?! Kozlov-Müller, corr. 1979, is less precise, as 12...♗h3 13 f3 0-0! 14 ♘xe4?! [14 fxe4? ♘g4] 14...♘xe4 15 fxe4? [15 ♗d3 ♗h4 16 ♗xe4 ♕xg2+ is only slightly better for Black] 15...♗h4 wins for Black) 12...♔f7 13 f3 a6! (13...exf3 is slightly less accurate, 14 ♕xf3 ♗g4 [14...♕xc2?? loses to 15 ♗d3] 15 ♕f4 ♖hf8 16 ♗d3 ♕h5 17 ♗e3 ♔g8 18 ♕c4 ♗d8 19 ♖ae1, White has more space, Svendsen-Melchor, corr. 1997) 14 ♗a4 b5?! (too weakening, 14...exf3 15 ♕xf3 ♖f8 is almost level) 15 ♗b3 exf3 16 ♕xf3 ♖e8 17 ♘e2! (e6 and c6 beckon) 17...♔g8 18 ♘f4 ♕f7 19 ♗d2 ♘g4 20 ♖ae1 ♗f6 21 ♘e6 ♘e5? 22 ♖xe5! dxe5 23 ♘xc7 winning quickly, Silavs-Cuba, Latvia 1963.

10 ♗b5+

Tempting, and almost unanimously played, yet 10 f3 is also extremely logical, 10...exf3 (10...♘f6?! 11 fxe4 ♗e7 [the pawn can't be recaptured, 11...♘xe4? 12 ♗d3 wins a piece] 12 ♗d3 ♕g4 13 ♗b5+ and Black's compensation for the pawn is non-existent, Genius 5-Comet test game 1996) 11 ♕xf3 ♘f6 12 ♘c3 ♗d7 13 ♗d3 ♕g4 14 ♕xg4 ♘xg4 15 ♘b5 ♔d8 16 ♗g5+ ♗e7 17 ♗xe7+ ♔xe7 18 ♖ae1+ ♘e5, Alvarez Villar - Gåård, corr. 2000, and as 19 ♘xc7 ♖ac8 20 ♘e6 ♗xe6 21 dxe6 g6 regains the pawn, Black is OK.

10...♔d8!

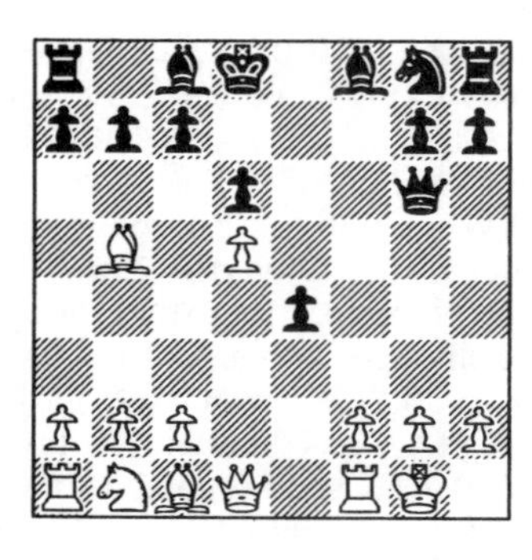

Black prefers to keep his light-squared bishop for use on the king-side (for instance, ...♗h3, or ...♗g4, can sometimes prove useful resources). However, as Black has less space to manoeuvre, swapping a pair of pieces also has to be considered:

10...Bd7 11 Bxd7+ Kxd7 12 Nc3 (12 c4?! Be7! 13 Nc3, Simcoe-Campbell, corr. 1978, and now 13...Bf6! intending ...Bxc3, or ...Be5, and then ...Nf6) 12...Nf6 13 Re1 (13 Ne2 -f4-e6 can also be considered) 13...Re8? (13...c5) 14 Qd4 Qh5 15 Qxa7 Nxd5 16 Qxb7 Nxc3 17 bxc3 g6 18 Be3 Bg7 19 Bd4 and White has a significant advantage, Borisek-Picco, Nova Gorica 2000.

11 Bf4

Bronstein's move, defending against the threatened ...Bh3 (as Bg3 would follow), but the bishop can prove a target here for a knight hop to h5.

11 f3! is objectively stronger, 11...exf3 12 Qxf3 Be7 (12...Nf6 13 Bd3 Qg4 14 Nc3 Qxf3 15 Rxf3 Be7 16 Bf4 and White has the more pleasant position, Harper-Tatlow, corr. 1999) 13 Nc3 Nf6 14 h3! (14 Bd3 Qg4 should transpose to the previous game) 14...Bd7 15 Bd3 Qh5 16 Qxh5 Nxh5 17 Be3 Nf6 18 Rae1 c6 19 Re2 (maybe 19 g4 h6, first, is more precise) 19...Re8 20 Rfe1 Bf8 21 Bg5 Rxe2 22 Nxe2 h6 23 Bxf6+ gxf6 24 Nf4, White has a nagging edge, Ruggeri Laderchi-Kosten, email 2001.

11...Nf6

11...h5?! is overly aggressive, 12 f3 Bf5 13 Nc3 exf3 14 Qxf3 Bxc2? (exceedingly risky) 15 Bg5+! Nf6 (15...Qxg5?? allows mate in one) 16 Rae1! c6 (and now 16...Qxg5? is met by 17 Qxf6+! and 18 Re8 mate) 17 Bxf6+ Qxf6 18 Qe2 Qd4+ 19 Kh1 Bg6 20 Rxf8+ Kc7 (20...Rxf8 21 Qe7+) 21 Bxc6 (21 Rxa8 and other moves also won, if somewhat mundanely) 21...bxc6 22 Nb5+ cxb5 23 Qxb5 Re8 24 Re7+ 1-0, as 24...Rxe7 25 Qc6 mate.

However, 11...Be7!? 12 f3 exf3 13 Qxf3 Bf6 14 Nc3 Ne7 is an interesting attempt to improve the black piece coordination, 15 Bd3 Qg4 16 Qe3 Qh5 and Black is doing well, Elburg-Malmström corr. 1994.

12 Nc3

12 c4?! is worse, 12...Be7 (12...Nh5 13 Bg3 Nxg3 14 hxg3 Be7 to f6, seems simple, and good) 13 Nc3 Bf5 (and again, 13...Nh5 gives the bishop a hard time) 14 Qe2 with chances for both sides, Terlecki-Tscharuschin, corr. 1990.

12...a6 13 Ba4 b5!?

13...Nh5 14 Qd2 Be7 15 Be3 Rf8 is a logical line, intending to play ...Bf6.

14 Bb3

Svendsen-Gåård, corr. 1990, when, once again,

14...Nh5

is worth consideration.

B 6...Qd8

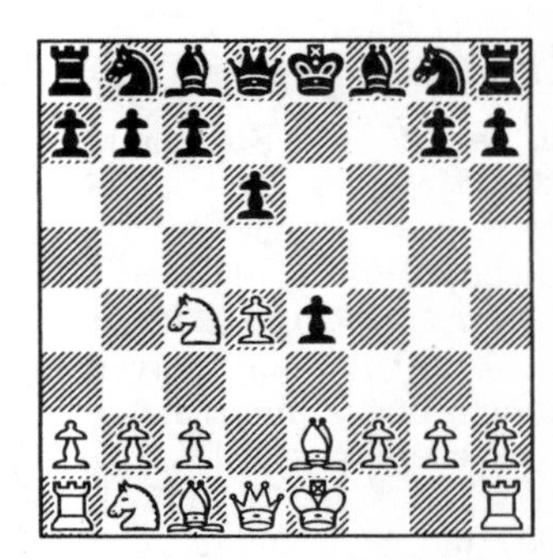

This seems very retrograde, but is in fact one of Black's two strongest possibilities.

7 0-0

Other tries:

a) 7 d5 Gaining space and isolating the e4-pawn, but this is probably not a necessary precaution as Black will not be playing ...d5 himself for a while. There are two main alternatives:

a1) 7...♘f6

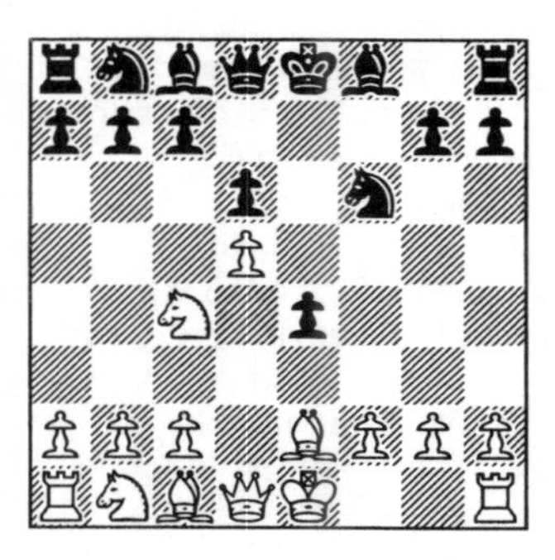

8 ♘c3! (In the 15-minute game Jackson-Mephisto, London 1992, after 8 ♕d4 ♗e7 9 ♘c3 ♗f5 [9...c5 is tempting] 10 ♘e3 ♗g6 11 0-0 0-0 12 ♘g4 ♘bd7 13 ♗e3 ♘c5 14 b4 ♘xg4 15 ♗xg4 ♗f6 16 ♕c4, the computer showed its greedy nature with 16...b5? [16...♘d7 is level] 17 ♘xb5 ♗xa1 18 ♖xa1 a6 19 ♘xd6 cxd6 20 bxc5 when White had more than enough compensation for the exchange and went on to win. 8 ♘e3 g6!? 9 h4 [9 c4 ♗g7 10 ♘c3 0-0 = Fiorito-Borrmann, corr. 1983/85] 9...h6 10 ♘c3 ♗g7 11 ♗c4 ♘bd7 12 h5 ♘e5 13 hxg6, Littleboy-Borrmann, corr. 1983, 13...♘xc4 14 ♘xc4 ♗f5 with good play. 8 0-0 is rarely played in this position, but is important for transpositional purposes, 8...♗e7 9 ♘c3 [9 ♘e3 0-0 10 f3 exf3 11 ♗xf3 ♘bd7 and, by bringing the knight to e5, Black solves his main development problem, Elburg-Downey, corr. 1994/96] 9...0-0 10 f3 exf3 11 ♖xf3 [11 ♗xf3] 11...♘a6 12 ♗e3, Warnock-Hayward, corr. 1986, when 12...c6 and ...♘c7 will oblige White to exchange his d5-pawn) 8...♗e7 and White does dispose of a wide choice at this juncture:

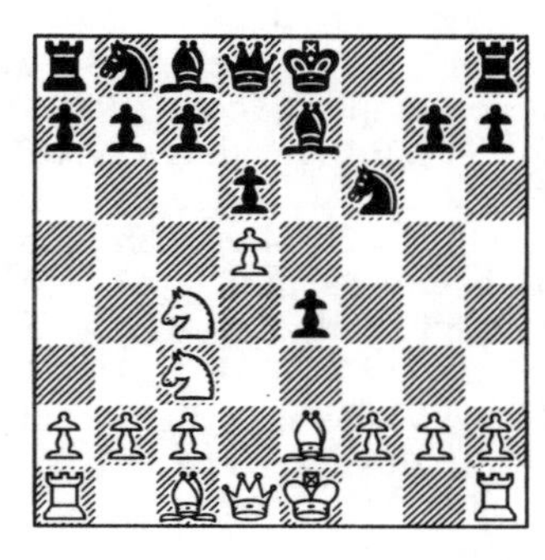

a11) 9 ♗e3 0-0 10 ♘d2!? c5!? (immediately giving up the pawn in return for an active position, if 10...♗f5 then 11 g4! ♗g6 12 g5 ♘fd7 produces a fairly typical position for this variation, 13 ♘dxe4 ♘c5 14 ♘xc5 dxc5 15 ♕d2 ♘d7 16 0-0-0 a6, Coqhill-Elburg, corr. training game 1999, 17 h4-h5 clearly favours White) 11 ♘dxe4 ♕b6 12 ♖b1 (perhaps 12 ♗c1 is more accurate, as it does leave White a solid pawn up, 12...♘xe4 13 ♘xe4 ♘a6 [13...♗h4?! 14 0-0 ♗f5 15 ♘d2 ♘d7 16 ♘c4 ♕c7 17 ♗f4 forces the dark-squared bishop to return, Ruggeri Laderchi-Cramton, corr. 1999] 14 0-0 ♗f5 15 ♘g3 ♗g6 16 ♗h5 and Black has no compensation, Ruggeri Laderchi-Elburg, corr. training game 1998) 12...♘xe4 13 ♘xe4 ♗f5 (13...♕a5+! 14 ♘c3 ♗f6 15 ♗d2 ♗f5 may be a better continuation) 14 ♘d2 ♘a6 15 a3 ♘c7 16 b4! the sharpest possibility, 16...♘xd5 17 ♗c4 ♗e6 18 ♘f3 ♘c3! (this is better than 18...♘f4 19 ♗xe6+ ♘xe6 20 ♕d5 ♖f6 21 ♗g5 ♖xf3 22 gxf3 ♗xg5 23 ♕xe6+ ♔h8 24 0-0 with advantage) 19 ♗xe6+ ♔h8 20 ♕d3! (20 ♕c1 ♕b5 [20...d5!?] 21 ♘g1 d5 22 ♖b3 d4 looked awkward to me, and certainly not the sort of position to play against Jonny) 20...♘xb1 21 0-0 ♘xa3 22 ♕xa3 ♕xb4 23 ♕d3 b5 24 c3 ♕a5 25 ♘g5 ♗xg5 26 ♗xg5 ♕b6 27 ♗a2 c4 28 ♕g3 d5 29 ♖d1 ♕e6 30 ♗e3 a5 31 ♗b1 b4 32 ♖d4 (the black queenside is beginning to look menacing, so White stakes everything on the attack) 32...bxc3 33 ♖h4 h6 34 h3 ♖ab8 35 ♗g6 ♖b6 36 ♗c2? (as my opponent pointed out to me after the game: 36 ♖xh6+! gxh6 37 ♗d4+ ♖f6 38 ♕c7 ♕g8 [38...♔g8? and mate in 5: 39 ♕h7+ ♔f8 40 ♗c5+ ♖d6 41 ♕h8+ etc.] 39 ♕xb6 ♕xg6 40 ♗xf6+ ♔g8 41 ♕d8+ ♔f7 42 ♕e7+ ♔g8 43 ♗xc3 wins) 36...♖f6 37 ♖g4 ♕d6 38 f4 ♖b7 39 ♗d4 ♖bf7 40 ♕xc3 ♔g8 41 ♗xf6 ♖xf6 42 ♕xa5 ♕b6+ 43 ♕xb6 ♖xb6 44 ♖g6 ♖b2 45 ♗f5 c3 46 ♖c6 d4 47 ♗g6 ♔f8 48 ♖e6 and White easily rounded up the pawns, Kosten-Hector, Torcy 1988.

a12) 9 g4 is very dangerous, White tries to displace the e4-pawn's defender. 9...h6 (Black should probably stop the advance of the g-pawn thus, and then develop his minor pieces, waiting to see where White will castle. 9...0-0!? 10 g5 ♘e8?!, this avoids losing the e-pawn but the knight is horribly placed, [10...♘fd7!? is more natural, but Black's compensation after 11 ♘xe4 ♘c5 12 ♘xc5 dxc5, Ruggeri Laderchi-Villar, corr. 1999, 13 h4 is not that obvious] 11 h4 ♗f5 12 ♘e3 ♕d7 [12...♗g6?! 13 ♖g1 ♕d7 14 ♗g4 ♕d8 15 h5 is horrible for Black, Tatlow-Niemand, corr. 1995] 13 ♘xf5 ♕xf5 14 ♗e3 c5 15 ♗g4 ♕e5 16 ♗e6+ with a crushing position, Liardet-Nyffeler, corr. 1992) 10 ♘d2 (White picks up the e-pawn. 10 g5?! hxg5 11 ♗xg5 ♗f5 12 ♘e3 ♗g6?! 13 h4?! [13 ♖g1 is more awkward] 13...♘g8?! [13...♘fd7] 14 ♗xe7 ♕xe7 15 ♕d4 ♖xh4 16 ♖xh4 ♕xh4 17 ♕xg7 ♕h7 18 ♕xh7 ♗xh7 19 ♘b5 with an edge, Gåård-Kozlov, corr. 1994/97) 10...e3 11 fxe3 0-0 12 0-0 ♘bd7 13 h3 ♘e5 14 ♘c4, Tatlow-Svendsen, corr. 1996, when 14...♘xc4 15 ♗xc4 ♘d7 would replace the e5-knight. The looseness of White's pawns provides some compensation for the e-pawn.

a13) 9 ♗g5 is not effective here, 9...♗f5 (9...♘xd5!? 10 ♕xd5 ♗xg5 11 ♘xe4 might be playable, although it does leave Black somewhat behind in development) 10 ♘e3 (10 ♕d2 ♘bd7 11 ♘e3 ♗g6 12 h4 h6 13 ♗f4 a6, fairly equal, Deacon-Cavendish, corr. 1991) 10...♗g6 11 ♕d4 ♘bd7 12 f3 exf3 13 ♗xf3, Evans-Heap, corr. 1994/95, 13...♘e5 with equality.

a14) 9 ♘d2!? heads directly for the e-pawn, 9...♗f5 10 g4 ♗g6 11 g5 e3! 12 fxe3 ♘fd7 13 h4 ♘e5 with some positional compensation for the pawn, Davies-Crimp, Australia 1995.

a2) 7...♗e7 8 0-0 ♗f5!? (8...♘f6 transposes to 7...♘f6) 9 ♘e3 (the correspondence game Strautins-Borrmann, 1990, came to a rapid conclusion following 9 ♗g4!? ♗xg4 10 ♕xg4 ♘f6! 11 ♕xg7 ♖g8 12 ♕h6 ♕d7 13 ♖e1 ♖g6 14 ♕d2 [14 ♕h4 c6 15 dxc6 ♘xc6 is very risky for White] 14...♖xg2+ ½-½, as 15 ♔xg2 ♕g4+ leads to perpetual check) 9...♗g6 10 ♗h5! ♘f6!? (Latvian Gambit players like using an open h-file!) 11 ♗xg6+ hxg6 12 ♘c3 (12 f3?! exf3 13 ♕xf3 ♘bd7 14 ♘c3 ♘e5 15 ♕e2 ♕d7. Black is very well placed, with the e5-square for his knight, 16 ♗d2 0-0-0 17

♕b5 c6! 18 ♕a5 ♔b8 19 ♖ae1 ♖h5 20 ♖f4 ♖dh8 21 h3? [21 ♘f1] 21...♖xh3! 22 gxh3 ♕xh3 23 ♔f2 ♘h5 0-1, Niemand-Krantz, corr. 1995) 12...♕d7 13 ♕d4 c5 14 ♕c4 ♖h4 15 f4 (15 g3?! ♕h3! 16 gxh4 ♘g4 17 ♘xg4 ♕xg4+ forces a perpetual check, but 15 f3 a6 16 ♘xe4 ♘xe4 17 fxe4 ♗f6 18 ♕d3 appears strong) 15...♘a6 16 ♘xe4 0-0-0 17 g3?! (17 ♘g5) 17...♖h5 18 ♘g5 ♘g4 when White had problems turning his extra pawn to account, Kozlov-Krantz, corr. 1993).

b) 7 ♘c3 d5! (the logical riposte now that White cannot avail himself of the flanking blow c4. 7...♘f6? is much worse: 8 ♗g5 ♗f5 9 ♗h5+! g6 10 ♘e3! gxh5 [or 10...♗e6 11 ♘xe4 with a good pawn more] 11 ♘xf5 ♗e7? 12 ♘xe7 ♕xe7 13 ♘d5 1-0, Rittenhouse-Elburg, corr. 1990) 8 ♘e5 ♘f6 and:

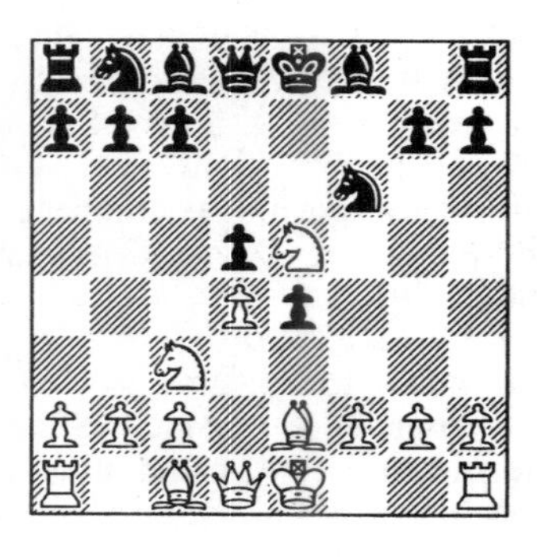

b1) 9 ♗g5 ♗e7 10 ♗h5+!? (White invests a tempo in order to weaken Black's kingside dark squares, 10 0-0 0-0 11 f3 exf3 12 ♗xf3 c6 is far from frightening for Black, 13 ♕d3 [13 ♘e2 ♘bd7 14 c4?! Elburg-Keller, corr. 1994. Black can now gain the upper hand by 14...♘xe5! 15 dxe5 ♘g4] 13...b6?! allowing a tactic, [13...♘bd7 is OK] 14 ♘xc6!? ♘xc6 15 ♗xf6 ♖xf6 16 ♗xd5+ ♔h8 17 ♖xf6 ♗xf6 18 ♗xc6 ♕xd4+, regaining one pawn, with some drawing chances because of the bishop pair, Shortland-Crimp, corr. 1996) 10...g6 11 ♗e2 ♗f5 12 0-0 ♘bd7 13 f3 exf3 14 ♗xf3 ♘xe5?! (initiating a sharp tactical sequence, much in keeping with Hector's 'no-holds-barred' style, but 14...c6 was somewhat simpler) 15 dxe5 ♘e4 16 ♗xe7 ♕xe7 17 ♕xd5 ♘xc3 18 ♕xb7 ♕c5+ 19 ♔h1 ♖d8 20 bxc3 0-0 21 c4 ♗e6 22 ♗d5 ♖xf1+ 23 ♖xf1 ♗xd5 24 cxd5 ♕c4! and Black had just enough initiative to make a draw, Ivanović-Hector, Metz 1988.

b2) 9 0-0 ♗e7 (Black could probably try 9...c6, or 9...♗f5 to avoid the problems associated with ♗h5+ in this line) 10 ♗h5+! g6 11 ♗e2 c6 12 ♗h6 ♘bd7 (12...♗f5 13 f3 ♘bd7? [of course, 13...exf3 was better] 14 fxe4 dxe4?? [and 14...♗xe4 15 ♘xe4 dxe4 was also superior to the move played, although 16 ♗c4 or 16 ♘xd7 gives the advantage] 15 ♖xf5 1-0, as 15...gxf5 16 ♗h5+ leads to mate, Rittenhouse-Hayward, corr. 1990) 13 f3 exf3 14 ♘xf3 ♘g4 15 ♕d2 ♘xh6 16 ♕xh6 ♗f8 17 ♕f4 ♕f6 18 ♕d2 ♗e7. Black is reasonably placed, Downey-Heap, corr. 1994/96.

7...♘f6

Averkin's suggestion 7...♗e7 might be more accurate as 8 ♗g5 is thereby avoided, e.g. 8 f3 (8 ♘c3 d5 9 ♘e5 ♘f6 transposes to 7 ♘c3) 8...exf3 9 ♗xf3 ♘f6 transposing to 7...♘f6.

Otherwise, 7...d5?! is best met by 8 ♘e3, c4, ♘c3, etc. rather than 8 ♘e5 ♘f6 9 ♗g5 ♗e7 10 c4 c6 11 ♘c3 ♗e6 12 ♕b3 ♕b6 13 ♕xb6 axb6, Liepins-Gubats, Latvia 1963, although even here White has a small edge.

8 f3

8 ♗g5 (the most common, but avoided by 7...♗e7) 8...♗e7 9 ♘e3 (9 f3 exf3 10 ♗xf3 0-0 11 ♘c3—Keres, transposes to a later variation) 9...0-0 (9...c6 10 c4 is a more common move order, but can Black forego ...c6?) 10 c4 (White is targeting the e4-pawn, 10 ♘d2 d5 11 c3 c6 12 ♕b3 ♔h8 [12...a5!?] 13 f3 exf3 14 ♘xf3 Correa-Kozlov, corr. 1976/79, when Black could have played 14...♘bd7 15 ♖ae1 ♘e4 16 ♗xe7 ♕xe7 17 ♗d3 ♘df6) 10...c6 (far from forced) 11 ♘c3 ♘bd7 12 ♕c2 ♖e8 13 ♖ad1 (13 f3?!, Aalzum-Reurich, corr. 1982, allows the surprising tactic 13...♘d5!? 14 ♗xe7 ♘xe3 with near equality) 13...d5? (the only chance is 13...♕a5 when 14 ♗xf6 ♘xf6 15 ♘xe4 ♘xe4 16 ♕xe4 ♕xa2 appears fine for Black) 14 cxd5 cxd5 15 ♘b5, winning material, Zier-Tiemann, corr. 1979.

8 d5 transposes to 7 d5.

8...exf3 9 ♗xf3 ♗e7 10 ♘c3

10 ♗h5+!? is a typical idea, weakening the black kingside dark squares. 10...g6 (10...♘xh5!? 11 ♕xh5+ g6 12 ♕d5 ♖f8 might be playable) 11 ♗g5!? (the most fun, although 11 ♗f3 0-0 12 ♗h6 ♖f7 13 ♘c3 c6 14 d5 c5 15 ♗f4 favours White, Harabor-Downey, corr. 1995) 11...♘xh5 (critical, 11...0-0 12 ♗f3 c6 13 ♘c3 ♘a6 14 ♕d2 with a typical white space advantage, Strautins-Kozlov, corr. 1990 and 11...gxh5!? 12 ♗xf6 ♗xf6 13 ♕xh5+ ♔e7 14 ♘c3 certainly looks like it could be winning for White!) 12 ♗xe7 (12 ♖e1!? ♘c6 13 ♘a5 ♘e5 14 ♗xe7 ♕xe7 15 dxe5 dxe5 is also unclear) 12...♕xe7 13 ♖e1 ♗e6 14 d5 0-0 15 dxe6 ♘c6 16 ♘c3 ♘f4 and the e6-pawn may be just a weakness, Strautins-Krantz, corr. 1990.

10...0-0 11 ♗g5

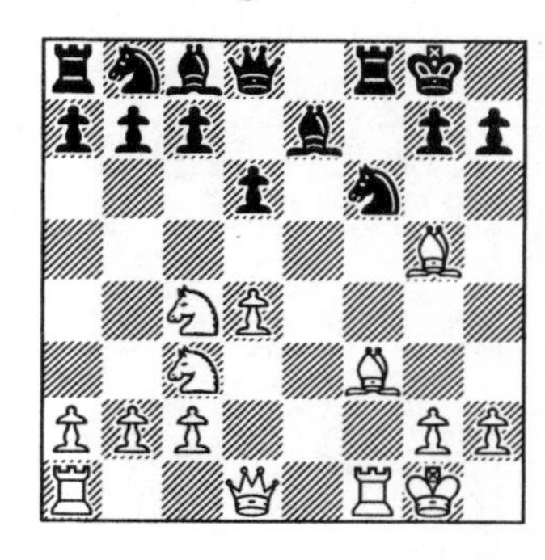

This position was considered by Keres to be advantageous for White.

11...♘bd7

11...c6 is more common, but after 12 d5 White is better, e.g. 12...♔h8 (12...c5 leads to an unfavourable Benoni-type position) 13 ♕e2? (missing Black's threat, 13 ♗f4 maintains a plus, and 13 ♕d2 likewise, Harper-Van de Velden, corr. 1999) 13...♘xd5! 14 ♗xd5 ♗xg5 15 ♖xf8+ ♕xf8 16 ♖f1 ♗f6 and Black has a solid extra pawn, Berg-Loon, corr. 1982. 11...h6!? 12 ♗f4 d5 is possible.

12 ♘d5

12 ♕e2 is stronger, 12...♖f7 13 ♖ad1 ♕f8 14 ♘b5 ♗d8 and Black is under pressure, Berg-Den Hertog, corr. 1982.

12...♘xd5 13 ♗xd5+ ♔h8 14 ♗xe7 ♕xe7 15 ♖xf8+ ♕xf8 16 ♕f3 ♕xf3 17 ♗xf3 ♘f6 18 ♖e1 ♔g8 19 ♘e3

19 ♖e7 ♔f8 20 ♖xc7 ♘e8 traps the rook, although White will obtain sufficient compensation.

19...♔f8 20 ♘d5 ♗d7 21 c3 c6 22 ♘xf6 gxf6 23 ♔f2 a5 24 ♔g3 b5 25 a3 b4! 26 axb4 axb4 27 cxb4 ♖b8

...which is equal, although Black managed to grind out the win on move 58 in the game Fransson-Hector, Gausdal 1990.

C 6...d5?!

This move is a mistake, providing White with a target.

7 ♘e3

This puts immediate pressure on d5 and is much stronger than 7 ♘e5?!, which, although appearing to be more aggressive, achieves little: 7...♗d6 8 f4 ♕h4+!? (8...♘e7 is simpler) 9 g3 ♕h3 10 ♗f1 ♕e6 11 h4?! ♘e7 Black is at least equal, Comer-Johnsrud, corr. 1999.

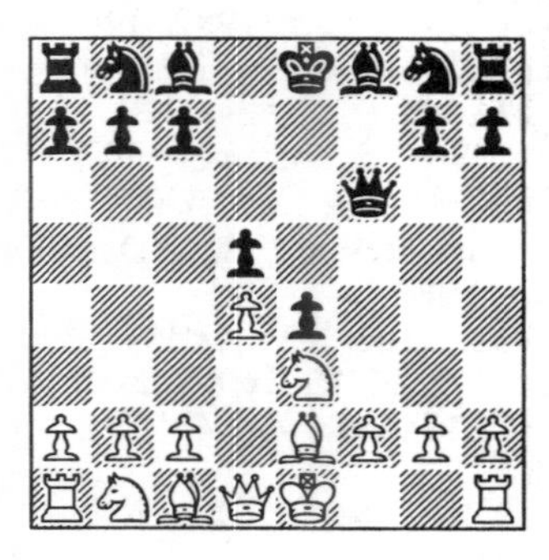

7...♘e7

None of Black's alternative moves are satisfactory, but I prefer this to the attempt to hold on to the centre by:

a) 7...c6 8 c4 (8 0-0 does not have quite the same 'bite', although after 8...♗d6 9 f3 ♕h4 10 g3 ♕e7 11 c4!? [11 fxe4] 11...♘f6 12 ♘c3 ♗e6?! 13 cxd5 cxd5 14 fxe4 [14 ♕b3 wins a pawn] 14...dxe4 15 ♘f5 White still had the better play in Gaard-Strelis, corr. 1992) 8...♗b4+ (Black hereby gains time, but he will be obliged to concede his dark-squared bishop, and this brings its own problems. Anyway, 8...♗e6?! 9 ♘c3 ♕f7 fails to defend the centre, 10 cxd5 cxd5 11 ♗g4!, the d-pawn's defender is exchanged, 11...♗xg4 12 ♕xg4 ♘c6 13 ♘exd5 ♖d8 14 ♕xe4+. Black has zero compensation, Ruggeri Laderchi-Scherman, corr. 1999) 9 ♘c3 ♘e7 10 0-0 0-0 (Black might just as well get his king into safety, the alternatives are no better: 10...♕d6? 11 ♕b3 ♗xc3 12 bxc3 dxc4 13 ♗xc4 with advantage Strautins-Budovskis, corr. 1970, is even worse, 10...♘f5? loses on the spot, 11 ♘cxd5! cxd5 12 ♘xd5 forking queen and bishop, Strautins-Krustkains, corr. 1990, and 12...♕d6? is no defence, 13 ♗f4, 10...♗xc3 11 bxc3 ♗e6?! [11...0-0 12 ♕b3 transposes into the next note] 12 f3 ♕g6 13 fxe4, Strautins-Grava, corr. 1970/1, is already too dismal for words, if now 13...♕xe4? then 14 ♗f3 ♕h4 15 g3 ♕h3 16 ♗g2 wins) 11 ♕b3! (11 cxd5 ♗xc3 12 bxc3 cxd5 [12...♘xd5 13 ♕b3 ♕f7, Strautins-Nyman, corr. 1990, seems worse after 14 f3] 13 ♗a3 is less precise, as Black now has the c6 square available, 13...♘bc6 14 f3 with an edge, Schuttrich-Mathe, corr. 1973) 11...♗xc3 12 bxc3 ♕f7?! 13 ♗a3 ♖d8 14 ♗xe7 ♕xe7 15 cxd5 with a big advantage, Silavs-Vildavs, Latvia 1963, is fairly typical of the problems facing Black here: behind in development, he is incapable of countering White's pressure.

b) 7...♗e6 8 c4 ♗b4+ 9 ♘c3 ♘e7 10 0-0 ♗xc3 11 bxc3 ♘bc6 12 f3 and Black is already losing, Curdo-Hayward, New Hampshire 1976.

c) 7...♕d8!? is a better idea, 8 0-0 ♘f6 9 c4 dxc4 (the best, for, as usual, holding on to the centre just wastes time, and gives White a ready-made target) 10 ♗xc4 ♘c6 11 ♗b5 a6!? (11...♗d7 12 ♘c3 ♗d6 is playable) 12 ♗xc6+ bxc6 13 ♘c3 with a plus, Elburg-Budovskis, corr. 1994/95.

8 c4

This is strong, but 8 0-0 is also reasonable; 8...♘bc6, counterattacking d4, 9 c3 ♗d7!? 10 ♕b3?! (10 f3 is more testing, as the black queen is exposed on the f-file, e.g. 10...exf3 11 ♗xf3 ♕d6 12 ♗xd5! ♘xd5 13 ♕h5+ g6 14 ♕xd5, winning a good pawn) 10...0-0-0!? 11 ♘xd5 ♘xd5 12 ♕xd5 ♗f5 13 ♕b3 ♗d6 14 ♗e3 ♕h4 15 g3 ♕h3 16 ♘d2 h5 with some counterplay, Nilsson-Svendsen, corr. 1991.

8...dxc4

Rather than defend the d-pawn, which as we have seen in a previous note is too passive. Black can also try the counterattack 8...♘bc6 9 ♘c3 ♕xd4 (9...dxc4!? 10 d5 ♘d4 is worth a try), now there is much to be said for the simple 10 cxd5 (better than the 10 ♗d2?! of From-Harju, corr. 1975/77, when 10...dxc4 11 ♘b5 ♕d8 is unclear) 10...♕xd1+ 11 ♗xd1 ♘b4 12 0-0, winning the e4-pawn, 12...♗f5 13 ♗a4+ ♗d7 14 ♗xd7+ ♔xd7 Malmström-Krustkains, corr., 15 ♖d1 etc.

9 ♘c3 ♗f5 10 ♗xc4

10 g4?! ♗g6 11 h4 is too loosening, 11...h6 12 ♗xc4 ♘bc6 13 ♘b5 0-0-0, winning quickly, Niermann-Elburg, corr. 1999.

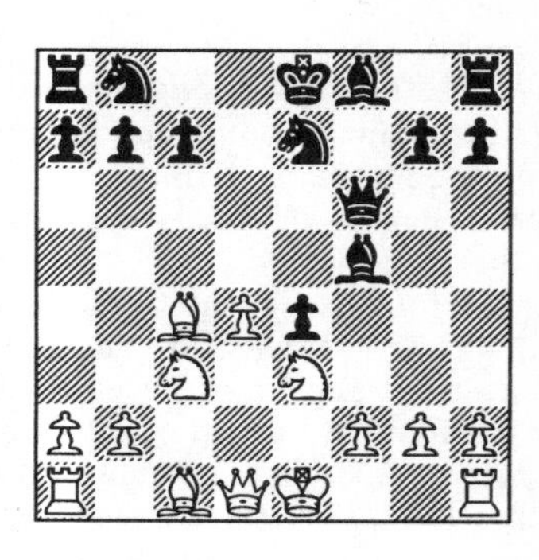

10...♘bc6 11 d5!

The alternative 11 ♘xf5 ♘xf5!? 12 d5 0-0-0 is quite double-edged.

11...♘e5 12 ♕a4+ ♗d7

12...♔d8!?.

13 ♕b3 ♕b6 14 0-0

14 ♘xe4.

14...♘c8 15 ♘xe4 ♘xc4 16 ♘xc4 ♕xb3 17 axb3 ♗b4 18 ♗d2 ♗xd2 19 ♘cxd2 0-0

...when White's tatty pawn structure allowed Black certain drawing possibilities, Rittenhouse-Downey, corr. 1992.

D 6...♕f7?!

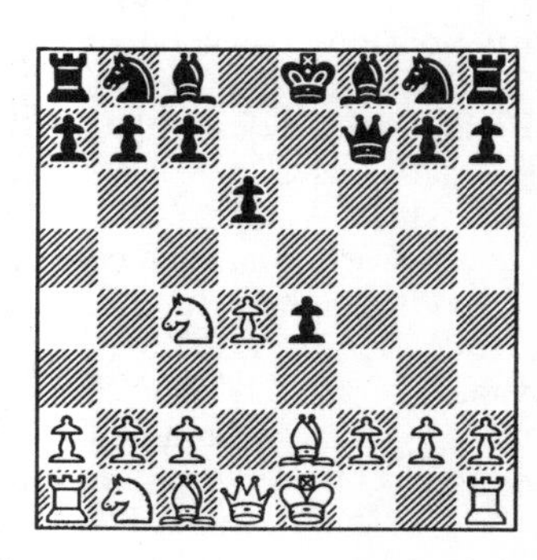

In an ideal world, this is where Black should like to put his queen.

Unfortunately, White appears to be able to build up a large advantage almost by force.

7 ♘c3!

As this move is strong, there is no need to concern ourselves too much with the alternatives, most of which allow Black a relatively easy game. In brief:

a) 7 0-0 also promises some advantage, 7...♘f6 8 ♗g5 (8 ♘c3 c6 [8...♗e7 9 ♗g5 transposes] 9 ♗f4 ♕e6 and now, instead of 10 ♘e3 d5 11 ♗e5?! ♘bd7 = Trutmann-Purins, corr. 1971/72, 10 d5! was good) 8...♗e7 9 ♘c3 ♗f5?! (9...♘bd7 is considered in the main line) 10 ♘e3 ♗g6 11 ♗c4 ♕f8 12 f3 exf3 13 ♕xf3 c6 14 ♖ae1 with a considerable advantage, the black king is stuck in the middle, Van Willigen-Keijzer, corr. 1982.

b) 7 d5 ♘f6 8 ♘c3 ♗e7 9 ♘b5 ♘a6 10 ♘e3 0-0 11 0-0 ♗d7 = Strelis-Maly, corr. 1970.

c) 7 ♘e3 ♘f6 8 0-0 ♘c6!? 9 f3 exf3 10 ♗xf3 ♗d7, unclear, Simila-Zalitis, Sweden 1978.

d) 7 c3?! ♗e6!? 8 b3 ♘d7 9 0-0 ♘gf6 10 ♘bd2 0-0-0 11 ♘e3 d5 12 a4 h5 13 f3 ♕g6 14 f4 ♘g4 with the makings of a strong attack, Karlsson-Zalitis, Sweden 1978.

7...♘f6

Black must defend the e-pawn, and 7...d5? loses to 8 ♘e5 ♕e6? 9 ♗g4, whilst 7...♗f5?! 8 ♘e3 is most awkward, for instance 8...♗g6 9 0-0 (9 ♗c4 ♕d7 10 ♗d5 wins a pawn) 9...♘d7? (9...♘f6 10 f3 with advantage.) 10 ♗c4 ♕e7 11 ♘ed5 ♕d8 12 ♘b5 winning, Downey-Logunov, corr. 1994/95, as the defence 12...♖c8 meets 13 ♘f4 ♗f5 14 ♗e6 which is awful for Black.

8 ♗g5 ♘bd7

There is little choice, 8...♗f5?! 9 ♘e3 ♗g6 10 ♗c4 ♕d7 11 ♗xf6 gxf6 12 ♗d5 wins a pawn, 12...c6 13 ♗xe4 d5 14 ♗xg6+ hxg6 15 ♕f3 ♕f7 16 0-0-0, Schultz Pedersen -Kozlov, corr. 1976 and Black has no real compensation.

9 ♘b5

9 0-0 is also dangerous, 9...♗e7 10 ♘b5 (forcing the black king to move, although 10 f3 also looks good) 10...♔d8 11 f3 exf3 12 ♖xf3 h6 13 ♗h4 a6 14 ♘c3 g5 15 ♗g3 ♕g7 16 a4, Downey-Sénéchaud, corr. 1994/95, and now 16...♘h5 17 ♗f2 ♘f4 is playable.

9...♔d8 10 ♕d2 ♗e7 11 0-0-0 b6!?

Not a good move to play against any member of the Littlewood family: it allows White to wrap up the game in typical, incisive fashion. To be fair to Black, his position was already quite unpleasant. 11...a6 12 ♘c3 ♖e8 keeps things intact for a while, though.

12 ♘e5!?

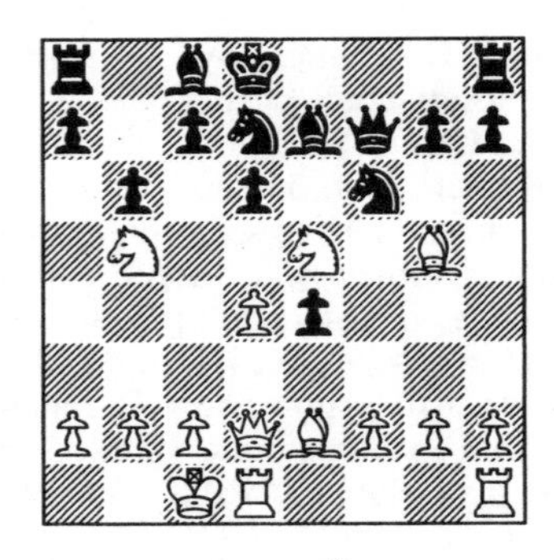

12...dxe5 13 dxe5 ♘g8?

13...♕xa2 14 ♘c3 ♕a1+ 15 ♘b1 ♕a4 is not so clear.

14 ♗g4 ♗xg5 15 ♕xg5+ ♕e7 16 ♕f4 h5 17 ♗xd7 ♗xd7 18 ♕xe4 ♖b8 19 ♕c6 ♔e8 20 ♘xc7+ ♔d8 21 e6 ♘f6 22 exd7

1-0, P.Littlewood-Kindermann, London 1978.

E 6...h5?

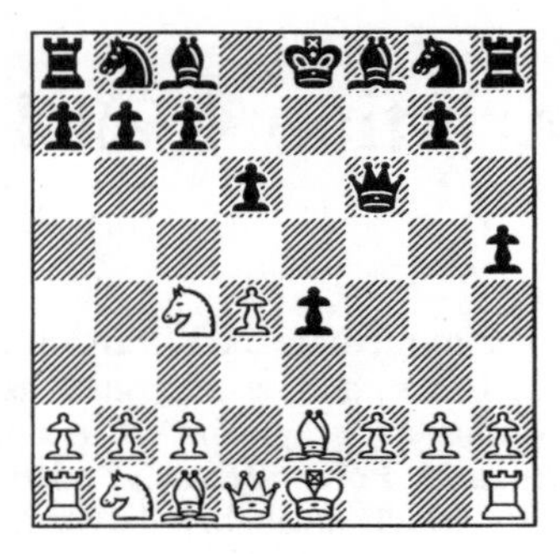

Black plays a game of bluff, since if White doesn't take this pawn for fear of opening the h-file, Black will be able to develop his queen on g6 after all, the h5 square now being additionally defended by the rook. That said, if White does take the pawn (and he should) the open h-file does sometimes come in useful.

7 ♗xh5+

If instead 7 ♘c3 then Black should reply 7...♕g6 (rather than 7...♗f5?! 8 f3 exf3 9 ♗xf3 c6 10 0-0 d5? [10...♕g6 was more circumspect, although still not very good] 11 ♗xd5! cxd5 12 ♘xd5 ♕c6 13 ♕e2+ ♗e6 14 ♕xe6+ ♕xe6 15 ♘c7+, winning, From-Keffler, corr.) when the game Destrebecq-Jurgenson, corr. 1992, went on 8 ♘e3 ♘f6 9 0-0 ♘c6 10 f3 exf3 11 ♗xf3 ♗d7 12 ♘cd5 ♘xd5 13 ♗xd5 0-0-0 14 ♗f7 ♕e4 which looks OK for Black.

7...g6 8 ♗g4

Possibly 8 ♗e2 is more accurate.

8...♗f5 9 ♘c3 c6 10 ♗f4

10 d5 ♘d7 11 ♗e2 ♘c5 12 ♗e3 ♕e7 13 ♕d4 is also very good for White, Van der Hauw-Diepstraten, corr. 1975.

10...♖h4!?

The h-file!

11 ♗xf5 ♖xf4?! 12 ♗xe4?!

Both 12 ♗c8! and 12 ♘xe4 look better, and with great advantage.

12...d5 13 ♗xg6+?

13 ♗xd5!.

13...♕xg6 14 ♘e5? ♕xg2 ∓

Kloss-Diemer, corr. 1959.

F Apart from the five moves mentioned, Black might also be able to essay **6...♘e7!?**

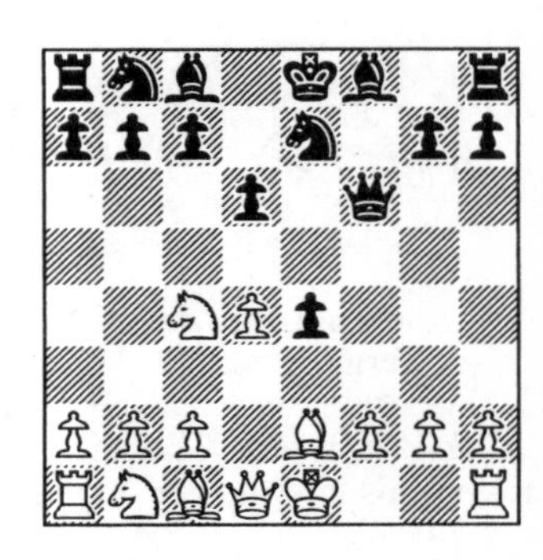

7 d5

The idea is to answer 7 0-0 with 7...♘f5, hitting d4, and 7 ♘c3 with 7...d5 as 8 ♘e3 c6 is fine since White can no longer play c4.

7...♗f5 8 ♘c3 ♘a6 9 ♗e3 c5??

Losing a piece, 9...♕f7 is considerably better.

10 g4! ♗g6? 11 g5

1-0, Crimp-Clarke, corr. 1998, the queen is lost.

5 Leonhardt's variation 4 ♘c4

1 e4 e5 2 ♘f3 f5 3 ♘xe5 ♕f6 4 ♘c4

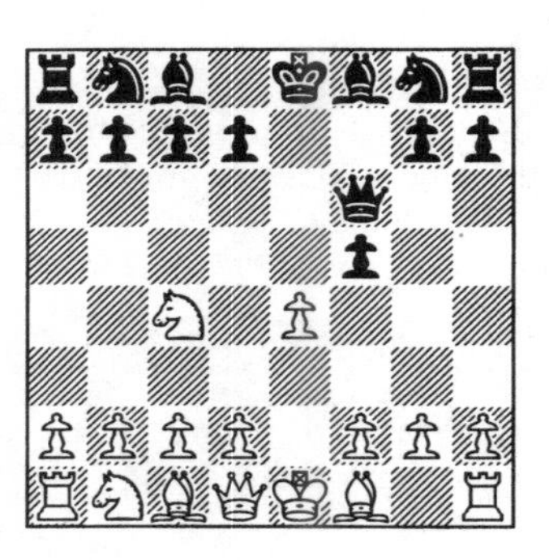

This variation was recommended by the German master Leonhardt (1877-1934) but was also mentioned by Cozio in 1760. The difference between this and the previous chapters is that White will have the possibility of attacking Black's e4 pawn with d3 at some point. Instead of playing strategically, White aims for rapid piece play.

This is now White's most popular line.

4...fxe4

Neither 4...b5? 5 ♘e3 fxe4 6 ♘c3 with advantage, nor 4...♕e6?! 5 ♘e3 f4 (5...fxe4 6 ♗c4 ♕g6 7 d3 exd3 8 ♗xd3 leaves White a useful lead in development, Van de Pol-De Boer, Dutch Junior ch 1990) 6 ♘d5 ♕xe4+ 7 ♕e2 with advantage, Pupols-Zemitis, corr. 1970, represent improvements in any way.

5 ♘c3

The immediate 5 d3 is also played sometimes, and is not quite as innocuous as it appears. 5...exd3 (In the game Foltys-Petrov, Podebrady 1936, Black, probably the strongest Latvian chessplayer before the advent of Tal and numbering Alekhine amongst his many victims, played 5...d5!? 6 ♘e3 [but 6 ♕h5+ ♕f7 7 ♕xf7+ ♔xf7 8 ♘e3 Halstead-Smith, Lansing ch 1985, gives White a small plus] 6...♗e6 7 dxe4 dxe4 8 ♘c3 ♗b4 9 ♗d2 ♘e7 10 ♘xe4 ♗xd2+ 11 ♘xd2 0-0 12 ♘e4 ♕xb2 =) 6 ♗xd3 d5 7 ♕h5+ (after 7 ♘e3 Black should be OK as compared to the main line he has not wasted a move with his queen, for instance 7...♗e6! 8 0-0 ♘c6 [or 8...♗d6] 9 c4 dxc4 10 ♗xc4 ♗d6 and ...0-0-0) 7...♕f7 8 ♕xf7+ ♔xf7 9 ♘e5+ ♔f6 10 ♘f3 ♗d6 11 ♗g5+ ♔f7 12 ♘c3 c6 13 0-0 ♘f6 14 ♖fe1 ♗g4 and Black is fine, Hunon-Destrebecq, Brest 1978.

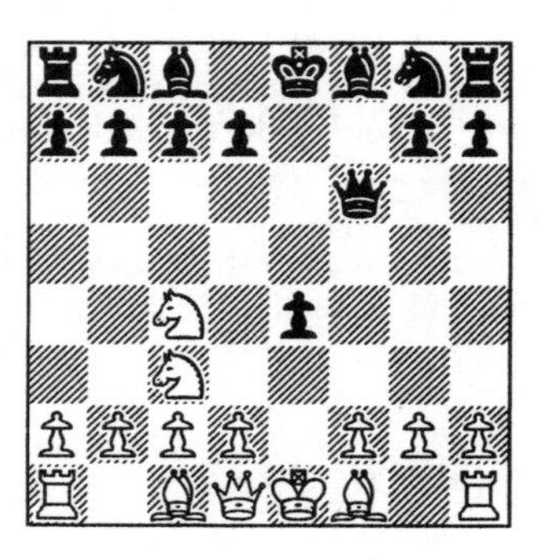

At this juncture there is a wide range of options but only the following three come anywhere near being satisfactory.

A 5...♕g6
B 5...♕e6
C 5...♕f7!

Nevertheless, other moves are played:

a) 5...c6?! this is surprisingly popular, 6 ♘xe4 (this time Black is well placed to meet 6 d3?! d5 7 ♘e3 ♗b4 8 d4? [8 ♗d2] 8...♘e7 9 a3?! 0-0 10 ♕d2 ♗d6 and White is in trouble, Dagendhart-Krull, corr. 1971, but 6 ♕g4!? is interesting, 6...♘h6 7 ♕xe4+ ♗e7 8 ♕e5, Castelltort-Julbe, Barcelona 1996, although Black obtains some play for the pawn, 8...d5 9 ♕xf6 ♗xf6 10 ♘d6+ ♔d7 11 ♘xc8 ♖xc8) 6...♕e6 7 ♕h5+ (7 ♕e2!? appears tempting, but 7...d5! 8 ♘cd6+ ♔d8 9 ♘g5 ♕xe2+ 10 ♗xe2 ♗xd6 11 ♘f7+ ♔e7 12 ♘xh8 and can the knight escape? 12...♘f6 [12...♗e6! is more accurate] 13 g4! this pawn will save the knight, 13...♘a6 14 ♗xa6 bxa6 15 g5 ♘g4 16 g6 ♗f5 17 ♘f7 ♗xh2 18 f3 ♗g3+ 19 ♔f1 ♗xg6 20 fxg4 ♔xf7 21 d3 and White is better, Malmström-Goedhart, corr. 1995) 7...g6 (7...♔d8? 8 ♕e5 d5 9 ♘g5!, Black is in a bad way, Matwienko-Borner, corr. 1974) 8 ♕e5 (8 ♕e2!? is still possible, as the g6-move has its advantages, and its disadvantages: 8...d5 9 ♘ed6+ [now 9 ♘cd6+?! is worse, 9...♔d8 10 ♘g5 ♕xe2+ 11 ♗xe2 ♗xd6 12 ♘f7+ ♔e7 13 ♘xh8 ♗e5 and the knight is captured] 9...♔d8 10 ♘xb7+ ♔c7 11 ♕xe6 ♗xe6 12 ♘ca5 ♗c8 13 d4!, Crimp-Svendsen, corr. 1997. White is winning as 13...♗xb7 14 ♗f4+ ♔b6 15 ♘xb7 ♔xb7? 16 ♗e5 wins the rook) 8...♕xe5 9 ♘xe5 d5 (9...d6 10 ♘c4! ♔d7 [10...d5 11 ♘ed6+ ♔d7 12 ♘f7 dxc4 13 ♗xc4] 11 ♗e2 ♔c7 12 d4 and Black still cannot play ...d5, Migala-Melchor, corr. 1998) 10 ♘g5 ♘h6 11 d4 ♗f5 12 ♗d3 ♗xd3 13 ♘xd3 and one can't really say that Black has much in the way of compensation for his pawn, Whiteside-Silverman, corr. 1980.

b) 5...♘e7? clogs up the kingside, 6 ♘e3!? (this is better than 6 d3?!, Bendig-Leisebein, corr. 1987, when Black can play the obvious 6...exd3 7 ♗xd3 d5 with a fine position. However, 6 ♕h5+ g6, Frommel-Leisebein, corr. 1987, 7 ♘xe4 ♕e6 8 ♕e5 leads to a favourable ending for White) 6...♕e5 7 d4 exd3 8 ♗xd3 d5 9 0-0 ♗e6 (9...c6 is no better: 10 ♖e1 ♕c7 [10...♕d6 11 ♘exd5! cxd5 12 ♘b5 ♕c6 13 ♗f4 is also crushing] 11 ♘exd5! cxd5 12 ♘xd5 with a winning advantage Vitomskis-Krustkalns, Latvia 1973) 10 ♖e1! (10 f4 ♕d6 11 f5 ♗f7 12 ♘g4 is less convincing, Pachman-Florian, Prague 1943) 10...♕d6, Müller-Grott, corr. 1986, and others, and now 11 ♗f5 wins immediately, i.e. 11...d4 (11...c6 12 ♘e4 ♕e5 13 ♘c4!) 12 ♘b5 ♕b6 13 ♘xd4.

c) 5...d6?! 6 d3!? (this is reasonable, as is 6 ♘e3 ♕g6 7 d3 exd3 8 ♗xd3 ♕f7 9 0-0 [9 ♗c4 ♗e6, the point of playing an early ...d6, 10 ♗xe6 ♕xe6 11 0-0 ♘c6 12 ♘ed5 0-0-0 13 ♖e1 ♕f7 14 b4 ♘f6 and White has a space advantage, Kozlov-Grobe, corr. 1991] 9...♘c6 10 f4!? ♘h6 11 ♕f3 ♗e7 12 ♘cd5 with a plus, Reitstein-Grivainis, corr. 1957, but the evident 6 ♕h5+! g6 7 ♕a5 wins the e-pawn for nothing) 6...exd3 7 ♗xd3 ♕f7 (perhaps

7...♗e6!? is playable, e.g. 8 ♕h5+ ♕f7, Mozota-Parzefall, corr. 1996, Black is not too badly placed) 8 0-0 ♘c6 9 ♖e1+ ♔d8 (9...♗e6 10 ♕g4 ♘d8 11 ♗f5 with advantage, Morgado-Korsmaa, corr. 1975) 10 ♗g5+?! ♗e7 11 ♗xe7+ ♘gxe7 12 ♘e4 d5?!, Gaard-Kozlov, corr. 1992, when 13 ♘e3 favours White.

d) 5...♘a6?! 6 d3 (more accurate than 6 ♘xe4 ♕e6 7 ♕h5+ g6 8 ♕e5 ♕xe5 9 ♘xe5 ♘b4 10 ♔d1 ♗g7 with a very slight compensation for the pawn, Destrebecq-Kozlov, corr. 1981) 6...♗b4 7 ♗d2 ♕e6!? (but 7...exd3 8 ♗xd3 ♘e7 9 0-0 leaves White well ahead in development) 8 ♘e3 (8 dxe4!? ♘f6 9 ♕e2 wins a pawn) 8...♘f6 9 dxe4 ♘xe4 (9...♗xc3?! 10 ♗xc3 ♘xe4? 11 ♗xg7 ♕f7, Dravnieks-Svendsen, corr. 1992, and now 12 ♕d4 wins on the spot, Black only has one check!) 10 ♗c4 ♗xc3 11 ♗xe6 ♗xd2+ 12 ♔f1 dxe6 13 ♕h5+ ♔f8 14 ♕f3+ with a winning advantage, Budovskis-Müller, corr. 1979/81.

e) 5...♘c6?! 6 ♘d5 (6 ♕g4 is also strong, 6...d5!? 7 ♕h5+ g6 8 ♕xd5 ♗e6 9 ♕b5 0-0-0 10 ♘a5 with a quick white win on the cards, Malmström-Triantafillopoulos, corr. 1997) 6...♕d8 7 ♕g4 ♘f6 8 ♘xf6+ ♕xf6 9 ♕xe4+ ♗e7 10 ♘e3 and Black's compensation for the pawn is very slight, O'Bee-Howes, corr. 1995.

f) 5...♕f5?! 6 ♘e3 ♕e5 7 d4 exd3 8 ♗xd3 ♘f6? (8...♗b4 9 ♗d2, Morgado-Atars, corr. 1977, and now 9...♘f6 10 0-0 0-0 leaves Black worse, but not terminally so) 9 0-0 ♘c6 10 ♖e1 and Black is already lost, 10...♔d8 11 ♘ed5 ♕d4 12 ♗e3 ♕h4 13 g3 ♕h3 14 ♘f4 ♕h6 15 ♘e6+, winning the black queen, Krustkains-Lonsdale, corr. 1986.

A 5...♕g6

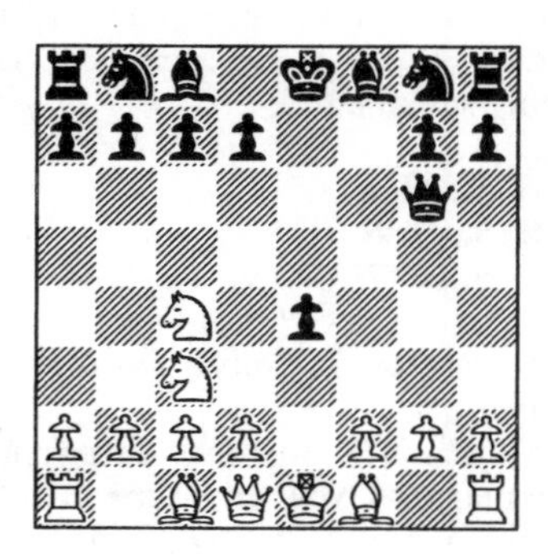

6 d3

Thematic. If Black captures on d3, then ♗xd3 will gain time on the black queen.

a) Leonhardt's original intention was to continue with 6 f3 but, as Betinš pointed out, 6...♗e7! is then good: 7 fxe4? ♗h4+ 8 g3 ♗xg3+ 9 hxg3 ♕xg3+ 10 ♔e2 d5 11 ♘e3 d4 ∓.

b) White can also play 6 ♘d5!? and this is quite dangerous, 6...♘a6 (according to Bücker, 6...♔d8 is a better bet, 7 d3 [7 d4 d6 8 ♘f4 ♕f7] 7...exd3 8 ♕xd3 ♕xd3 9 ♗xd3 ♘c6 10 ♗f4 d6 11 0-0-0 ♘f6 and White has a development advantage, but the black position is solid) 7 d4! (7 ♘ce3 ♗d6 8 ♗e2 ♘f6 = Atars-Tomson, corr. 1974/5) 7...exd3? (7...c6?! 8 ♘e5 ♕e6 9 ♘f4 ♕f6 10 ♗xa6 bxa6 11 f3 with a clear advantage; a better chance is offered by either 7...d6 8 ♘ce3 c6 9 ♗xa6 cxd5 10 ♗b5+, the doubled black d-pawn is a weakness, Pickles-Slaven, corr. 1996, or by 7...♕f7 8 ♘ce3 c6 9 ♗xa6 cxd5 10 ♗b5 with similar problems) 8 ♗xd3! ♕xg2?! 9 ♕h5+ (9 ♕e2+! also wins by force, 9...♗e7 10 ♗e4 ♕h3 11 ♗g5 ♕e6 12 ♘f4 ♕f7 13 ♘e5 ♕f8 14 ♘e6! dxe6 15 ♕b5+ c6 16 ♗xc6+ ♔d8 17 0-0-0+ ♔c7 18 ♖d7+!

♗xd7 19 ♕xb7+ ♔d6 20 ♘c4+ ♔c5 21 ♕b5+ ♔d4 22 ♗e3 mate, Bücker) 9...♔d8 10 ♗g5+ ♗e7 11 ♘xe7 ♘xe7 (11...♕xh1+ 12 ♔d2 ♕xa1 13 ♘xg8 mate) 12 0-0-0 h6 13 ♗xe7+ ♔xe7 14 ♘e5 and the black king is not long for this world, Fantoni-Richard, email 1999.

c) 6 ♘e3?! allows Black a simple route to equality, 6...♘f6 7 d3 ♗b4 8 ♗d2 Spiel-Antusch, Bayern 1988, and now 8...♗xc3 9 ♗xc3 0-0.

6...♗b4

Black will lose his queen if he tries 6...exd3?! 7 ♗xd3 ♕xg2?? 8 ♕h5+ ♔d8 9 ♗g5+ ♘f6 10 ♗e4, and 6...♘f6?! 7 dxe4! (7 ♘xe4 ♘xe4 8 dxe4 ♕xe4+ 9 ♘e3 ♕e5!? 10 ♗c4 b5!? Bücker) 7...♘xe4?! (Black's compensation for the pawn is insufficient after the superior 7...♗b4 8 f3 ♗xc3+ 9 bxc3 d6, Rozzoni-Zaniratti, corr. 2000) 8 ♕e2!? (8 ♗d3! ♗b4 9 0-0 ♗xc3 10 bxc3 is very effective and without risk [for White, that is!]. After 10...d5 11 ♘e3 ♕f7 12 ♘xd5 ♕xd5 13 ♗xe4 etc.) 8...♗b4 9 f3 d5 10 ♘d2 ♗xc3 11 bxc3 0-0 12 fxe4 White has some problems developing his bits, but it is difficult to believe that Black has enough compensation for a piece.

7 ♗d2!

White can transpose into B with 7 dxe4?! ♕xe4+ 8 ♘e3 ♗xc3+ 9 bxc3 ♘e7 10 ♗d3 (or 10 ♗c4 as per *NCO*, but this offers White nothing).

7...♗xc3

Universally played, as the alternatives are worse: 7...exd3?! 8 ♗xd3! ♕xg2 9 ♕h5+ (White can also continue 9 ♕e2+ ♔f8 10 ♗e4 ♕h3 11 ♘d5 ♗xd2+ 12 ♕xd2 with advantage, Wei-GGAT, corr. 1993) 9...♔d8 (9...♔f8) 10 0-0-0 (not 10 ♗e4?! ♘f6 11 ♕h4 ♕g4 nor 10 ♗g5+ ♘f6) 10...♘f6 11 ♕h4 ♕g4 12 ♕xg4 ♘xg4 13 ♖hg1 (or 13 ♗g5+ ♗e7 14 ♗xe7+ ♔xe7 15 ♖hg1 d6 16 f3 ♘f6 17 ♖xg7+ and Black is in difficulty, Strautins-Jackson, corr. 1991) 13...♘xf2 14 ♖de1 (14 ♗g5+ ♗e7 15 ♗xe7+ ♔xe7 16 ♖de1+ ♔d8 17 ♘e5 offers good chances, too) 14...♖e8? 15 ♗g5+ ♗e7 16 ♖xe7 ♘xd3+ 1-0, Elburg-Michalek, corr. 1988.

7...♘f6?! loses a pawn: 8 ♘xe4 ♗xd2+ (8...♘xe4 9 ♗xb4) 9 ♘exd2, Schuh-Hohnemann, corr. 1990.

8 ♗xc3 ♘f6

The game Smyslov-Kamyshov, Moscow 1944, continued 8...d5?! 9 ♘e5 (9 ♘e3 ♘e7 [9...♗e6?! 10 dxe4 dxe4 11 ♕d4 is strong] 10 dxe4 dxe4 11 ♕d4 is a good alternative) 9...♕f5 10 dxe4 ♕xe4+ 11 ♗e2 ♘f6 12 0-0 c6?! (12...♕f5 is better, but 13 ♗d3 ♕f4 14 g3! ♕h6 15 ♗b4 keeps the king in the centre, with a clear plus) 13 ♗h5+ ♔f8 14 ♖e1 ♕h4 15 ♗g6!? ♘a6?! (15...♘bd7) 16 ♕e2 ♗h3?! 17 ♘f3 1-0.

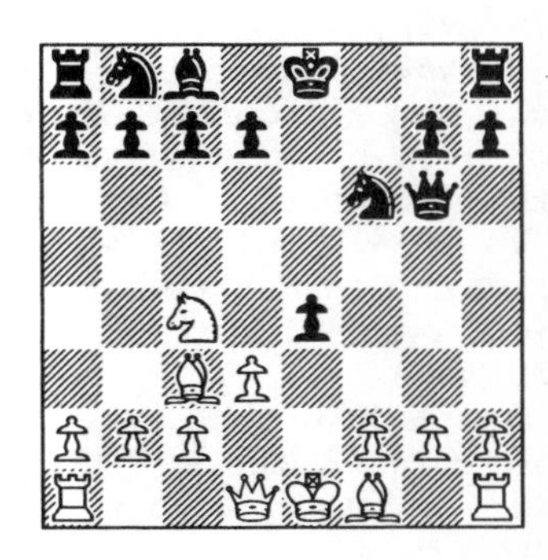

9 ♗xf6!

9 dxe4?! is much less convincing, 9...♘xe4 10 ♗d3 0-0 11 0-0 ♘xc3 12 bxc3 ♕f6 (12...♕g5! 13 ♘e3 c6 14 f4 ♕c5 15 ♕f3 d5 16 ♔h1 ♘d7 17 ♖ae1 ♘f6 is very comfortable

for Black, Grobe-Robins, corr. 1972) 13 ♕h5 g6 14 ♕a5 ♘a6 (14...c6? 15 ♕a3! ♘a6 16 ♘d6 cuts the black position in half, Dubois-Strautins, corr. 1973) 15 ♘e3 c6 16 ♗xa6 bxa6 17 ♖ae1 and White has a small pull, Morgado-Eckenfels, corr. 1968.

9...gxf6

This disfigures the pawn structure, but otherwise Black sheds a pawn, 9...♕xf6?! 10 dxe4 0-0 11 f3 (the simplest, 11 ♕d2?! b5! 12 ♕d5+ ♔h8 13 ♕xa8 ♕xf2+ 14 ♔d1 ♘c6 15 ♘d2 ♗a6 16 ♕xf8+ ♕xf8, Jackson-Svendsen, corr. 1994/96, might favour White on 17 a4, but it is messy, while 11 ♕d5+ ♔h8 12 0-0-0 ♘c6 [12...♕xf2? loses: 13 ♗d3 ♕f4+ 14 ♔b1 ♕f7 15 ♕xf7 ♖xf7 16 ♖hf1 loss of material is inevitable, the black queenside pieces are too far away, Grobe-Kozelek, corr. 1976] 13 f3 transposes) 11...♘c6 12 ♕d5+ ♔h8 13 0-0-0 d6 14 ♕d2 ♗e6 15 a3 a5 16 ♘e3 and White has an extra pawn, and more space, Budovskis-Hempel, corr. 1970.

10 ♘e3!

10 dxe4?! ♕xe4+ 11 ♘e3 (11 ♗e2?! ♕xg2 12 ♗f3 ♕g5 13 ♕e2+ ♔d8 14 ♘e3 ♕a5+ 15 c3 d6 ∓ Siklosi-Westerinen, Copenhagen 1988) 11...♕b4+ 12 c3 ♕xb2 13 ♖c1 ♕a3 is far from clear, Gebuhr-Vitols, corr. 1972/74.

10...♔d8

Black is in trouble, 10...c6?! 11 dxe4 ♕xe4 12 ♕d6 ♕e5 13 0-0-0 with advantage Filipovs-Zarins, corr. 1991, or 10...d6 11 ♗e2 0-0 12 ♗h5 ♕g7 13 dxe4 with a pawn more, Budovskis-Grivainis, corr. 1977/79.

11 dxe4 ♕xe4 12 ♕d2 ♘c6 13 0-0-0 d6 14 ♘d5 ♖f8 15 f3 ♕e5 16 ♗c4

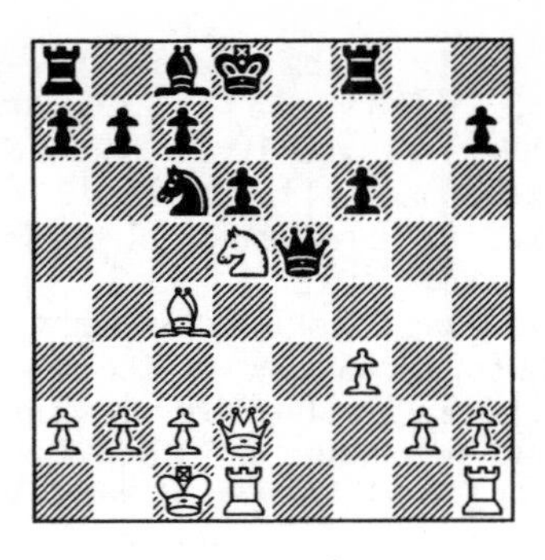

16...♕g5 17 f4

Black's position is extremely uncomfortable, Gaard-Jensen, corr. 1990.

B 5...♕e6

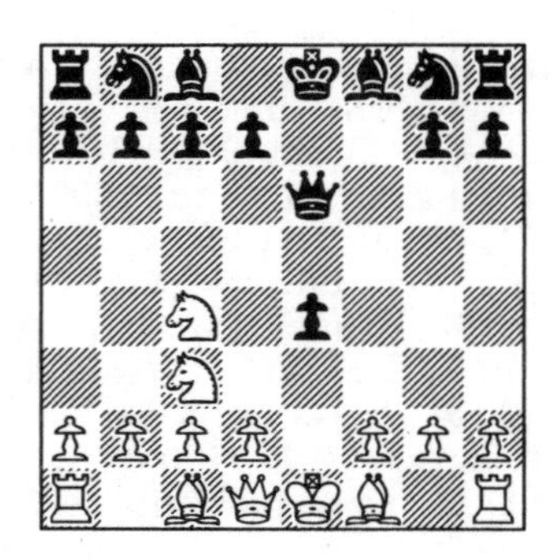

6 ♘e3!

Stronger than

a) 6 d3 ♗b4 (6...exd3+!? 7 ♘e3 dxc2 is risky, but playable; 8 ♕xc2 c6, else White plays ♗c4, and Black will be unable to castle, [8...♘f6?! 9 ♗c4 ♕e5 10 0-0 ♗d6 11 g3 ♘c6 12 ♘f5 with dangerous threats, Parant-Baudoin, corr. 1988] 9 ♗d3 ♘e7 [9...♘f6 10 0-0 ♗e7? 11 ♘f5 0-0 12 ♗h6 gxh6 13 ♖ae1 and Black is crushed, Müller-Gagsch, 9...d5?? 10 ♗f5 ♕e7 11 ♗xc8 d4 12 ♕e4! ♘d7 13 ♗xd7+ ♔xd7 14 ♕xd4+ 1-0, Prat-Bravo, corr. 1986] 10 0-0 ♘a6!? [10...d5 11 ♕d1!? d4?! {11...♘d7 is safer} 12 ♗c4 ♕f6 13

♘e4 ♕e5 14 ♕d3 ♘g6 15 f4! ♘xf4 16 ♖xf4, Sidenko-Collier, email 1998, Black is in trouble, as 16...♕xf4 17 ♘d5 ♕f7 loses the queen after 18 ♘df6+] 11 ♗xa6 bxa6 12 ♗d2 d5 13 ♖fe1 ♕d6, Morgado-Atars, corr.1967, and now Lein likes the positional 14 ♘a4, but Black has chances here) 7 dxe4 ♗xc3+ (7...♘f6!? 8 ♘e3 [8 f3 d5 9 ♘e3 c6 transposes to a later line] 8...♘xe4 9 ♗c4 ♘xc3 10 bxc3 ♗xc3+ 11 ♗d2 ♕e5 12 ♖b1 ♕d4 and Black was hanging on, Elburg-Kozlov, corr. 1992) 8 bxc3 ♕xe4+ 9 ♘e3 ♘e7 with a choice:

a1) 10 ♗d3 (chases the queen to a safer square, but it avoids Black's principal defensive idea: ...♗e6) 10...♕h4 11 ♗c4 ♘bc6 (11...c6!? is possible as, although it weakens the dark squares, the king will be able to castle. 12 ♗a3 d5 13 ♗d3 0-0 14 0-0 with chances for both sides, Morgado-Strelis, corr. 1974/77) 12 0-0 (12 a3?! is less logical, 12...♘e5 13 ♗a2 ♖f8 14 0-0 d6 and Black has a solid position, Kozlov-Svendsen, corr. 1990) 12...d6 (or 12...♘e5!? 13 ♖e1 d6 14 ♕d4 ♕xd4 15 cxd4 ♘xc4 16 ♘d5 ♔d8 17 ♗g5 h6 18 ♗xe7+ ♔d7 19 ♗h4 g5 20 ♗g3 Bücker) 13 g3 ♕f6 14 ♖e1 ♖f8 15 f4 ♔d8 16 ♖b1 ♖b8, 'unclear with complicated play'—Bücker, 17 ♗d3 g5!?.

a2) 10 ♗c4 d6 11 0-0 (+/- *NCO*) 11...♗e6 (exchanging one of the bishop pair is the positionally right decision) 12 ♕h5+ (12 ♗d3 ♕c6!? [12...♕h4] 13 ♖b1 ♘d7 14 ♕h5+ [14 ♗b5 ♕c5 15 ♗xd7+ ♔xd7 16 ♖xb7 ♗xa2! is fine, as 17 ♕g4+? ♗e6 18 ♕xg7 sets White up for tactics on g2, 18...♕c6 19 ♖b2 ♖ag8 with a useful attack] 14...♗f7 15 ♕g5, Nigg-Agarkoff, corr. 1939, 15...♗xa2 with fair chances; 12 ♗b3 might be White's best, as he will iron out his pawn structure when Black captures on b3) 12...♔d7 13 ♗xe6+ (13 ♕b5+ ♔c8 14 ♗xe6+ ♕xe6 15 ♖b1 b6 16 a4 ♘bc6 equal, Strelis-Tomson, corr. 1974. Black's queenside is solid as a rock) 13...♕xe6 14 c4 ♘bc6 15 ♖b1 (15 ♗b2 g6 16 ♕h4 ♖hf8 17 ♕xh7 ♖f7 18 ♕h4 ♘f5) 15...b6 and Black doesn't have any problems, Castelli-Gabrans, corr. 1970.

b) 6 ♕h5+ leads nowhere: 6...g6 7 ♕d5 ♕xd5 8 ♘xd5 ♘a6 9 ♘ce3 c6 10 ♗xa6 cxd5 11 ♗b5 ♘f6. Sawicki-Lewandowski, 1997.

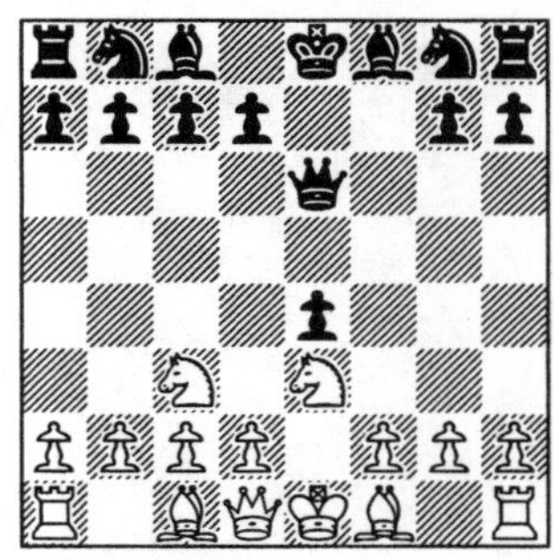

6...♘f6!?

Black can take measures against the threat of ♗c4 by playing 6...c6 and this may be stronger: 7 d3 ♗b4 (7...d5?! 8 dxe4 dxe4 9 ♗c4 ♕e5 10 ♗xg8! ♖xg8 11 ♘c4 with advantage, Grobe-Strelis, corr. 1974/5, 7...♘f6 8 ♘xe4 ♘xe4 9 dxe4 ♕xe4 10 ♗d3 ♕e5 11 0-0 d5 12 ♖e1 ♔f7 13 c4 ♗b4 14 ♗d2 ♗xd2 15 ♕xd2 ♕g5 16 f4 is crushing for White, Elburg-Nilsson, corr. 1988) 8 dxe4 (8 ♗d2 exd3 [8...d5?! 9 dxe4 d4 10 ♘f5; 8...♘f6] 9 ♗xd3 ♘f6 10 0-0 0-0 11 ♗c4!? d5 12 ♘cxd5 cxd5 13 ♘xd5 ♘xd5 14 ♗xb4 ♖d8? [14...♖f5 is the only chance] 15 ♖e1, White wins, Marin-San Pedro Fraga, corr. 1975) 8...♘f6 (8...♕xe4 9 ♗d3 ♕h4 10 ♘f5 ♕f6 11 0-0 d5

12 ♖e1+ ♔f7 13 ♕g4 is very good for White, Krustkains-Kozlov, corr. 1979) 9 f3 (9 ♗d2 might offer more, 9...♘xe4 10 ♘xe4 ♕xe4 11 ♗d3 ♗xd2+ 12 ♕xd2 ♕f4?!, Gnirk-Jove. corr. 1998, and White can infiltrate on d6 by 13 ♘c4! ♕xd2+ 14 ♔xd2) 9...d5 10 exd5 cxd5 11 ♕d4 ♘c6 12 ♗b5 0-0 (12...♗a5! 13 0-0 0-0 is interesting as the bishop will come to the sensitive g1-a7 diagonal) 13 ♗xc6 ♗xc3+ 14 bxc3 (14 ♕xc3 is more logical) 14...bxc6 15 0-0 is better for White, Diepstraten-Oren, corr. 1992.

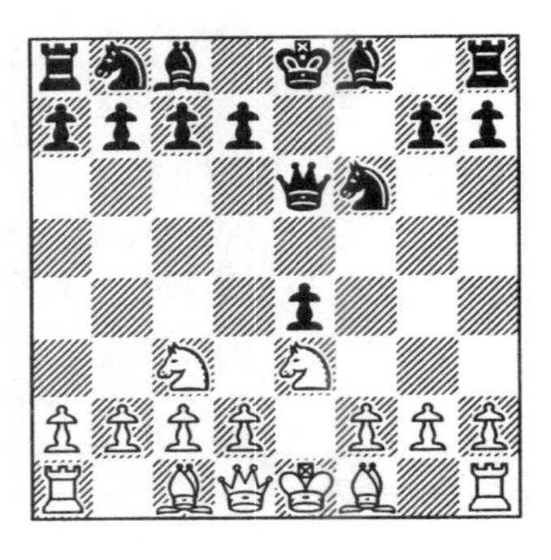

7 ♗c4

7 d3?! is worse, 7...♗b4 8 ♗d2 d5? (this is tricky, but incorrect, 8...♘c6! is stronger, 9 dxe4 ♘xe4 10 ♗c4 ♗xc3! 11 ♗xe6? [11 0-0 is superior] 11...♗xd2+ 12 ♔f1 dxe6 13 ♕g4 ♗xe3 14 ♕xe4 ♗c5 with three pieces and a solid position for the queen. Black is winning, Risto-Kilpela, corr. 1993) 9 dxe4? (but White had a lot of opportunities to improve, for instance 9 ♘exd5! ♘xd5 [9...exd3+ 10 ♘e3 dxc2 11 ♕xc2 is also good for White] 10 ♕h5+ Destrebecq, and 9 ♘cxd5! ♗xd2+ 10 ♔xd2 ♘xd5 11 ♕h5+ is also convincing) 9...d4 10 ♘f5! (in the games Eiken-Svedenborg, Norway 1969, and Doroftei-Vaisman, Soutcheava 1971, White was crushed after 10 ♘cd5 dxe3! 11 ♘xc7+ ♔f7 12 ♘xe6? [12 fxe3 ♕xe4 13 c3 ♗d6 is less clear] 12...♗xd2+ 13 ♔e2 ♗xe6 14 h3 ♘c6 ∓) 10...♕b6 (this time, 10... dxc3? is a mistake, 11 ♘xg7+ ♔f7 12 ♘xe6 cxd2+ 13 ♔e2 ♗xe6 14 c3) 11 ♘a4 ♕c6 12 ♘xg7+ ♔f7, Melchor-Svendsen, corr. 1994/95, when 13 ♗xb4 ♕xa4 14 ♕xd4 is critical.

7...♕e5

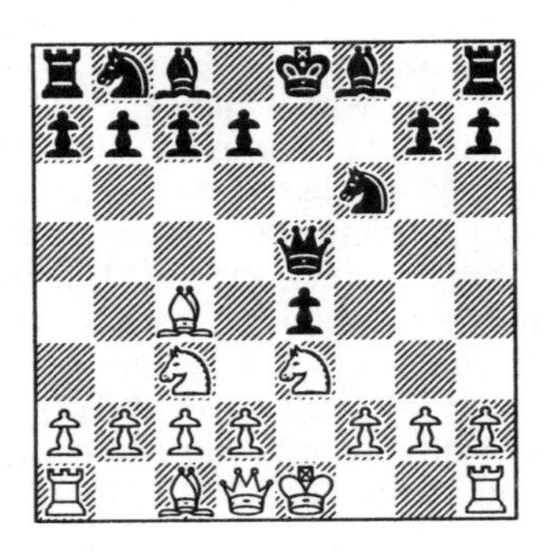

8 d3

The most dangerous. Others:

a) 8 ♘g4!? ♘xg4 9 ♕xg4 ♗b4! 10 ♘xe4? (a typical 'computer mistake', White wins a pawn, but loses his head! 10 ♕xe4?? ♗xc3 is even worse, but 10 ♔d1!? is a possibility, and 10 ♘d5 is best, 10...♘c6 [Bücker prefers 10...♘a6!? 11 ♕e2 c6 12 f4 ♕d6 13 ♘xb4 ♘xb4 14 d3 ♕e7 15 dxe4 d5 with play for the pawn] 11 0-0 ♗d6 12 ♕h4 ♗e7 13 ♘xe7 ♘xe7 14 ♖e1 d5 15 ♗b3 and Black's centre is difficult to maintain, Kozlov-Destrebecq, corr. 1981) 10...♘c6 (menacing ...d5) 11 ♕f3 ♘d4 12 ♕d3 (12 ♕f7+? ♔d8 13 ♗d3 ♘e6! threatening to win the queen, 14 ♕f3 d5 15 ♕g3 ♘f4 16 ♕g5+ ♕xg5 17 ♘xg5 ♖e8+ 18 ♔d1 h6 19 ♘f7+ ♔e7 20 ♘e5 ♔f6 21 ♘f3 ♗g4 22 h3 ♗xf3+ 23 gxf3

♘xd3 24 cxd3 and White's position is a mess) 12...d5 13 c3 dxc4 and Black is better, Owens-Kravitz, email 1998.

b) 8 0-0 ♗b4 (8...♗d6!? 9 g3 b5!? 10 ♘xb5 ♗b7 11 ♘xd6+ ♕xd6 12 d3 ♘c6 13 ♘f5 ♕f8 14 dxe4 ♘e5 doesn't look completely correct, Atars-Saavedra, corr. 1969) 9 d4 exd3 10 ♕xd3 ♗xc3 11 bxc3 d6 12 ♗b2 ♘c6 13 ♖fe1 ♔d8, with a typical position where Black's superior pawn formation provides ample compensation for his misplaced king, Krustkains-Strelis, corr. 1990.

c) 8 d4 exd3 transposes.

8...exd3 9 0-0 ♔d8

Black doesn't need his two most important pieces on the same open file.

10 ♗xd3

10 ♕xd3 c6 11 f4 ♕h5 12 ♗d2 ♗c5 13 ♘a4 ♘g4 14 h3 ♗xe3+ 15 ♗xe3 ♘xe3 16 ♕xe3 Borrmann-Kozlov, corr. 1991, when 16...b5 might be best, e.g. 17 ♗e2 (17 ♘b6?! ♖e8 18 ♕a3 axb6!? 19 ♕xa8 ♔c7 20 ♗d3 ♘a6, trapping the queen) 17...♖e8 18 ♗xh5 ♖xe3 with equality.

10...d6 11 ♖e1

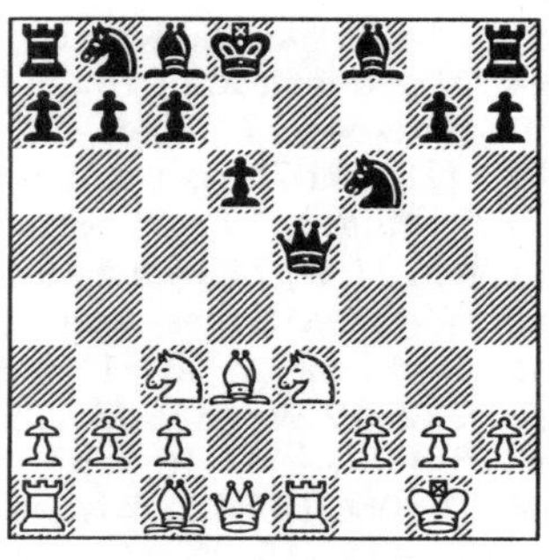

11...♕h5 12 ♕xh5 ♘xh5 13 ♘ed5 ♗d7 14 ♗g5+

...with advantage Budovskis-Atars, corr. 1974/75.

C 5...♕f7!

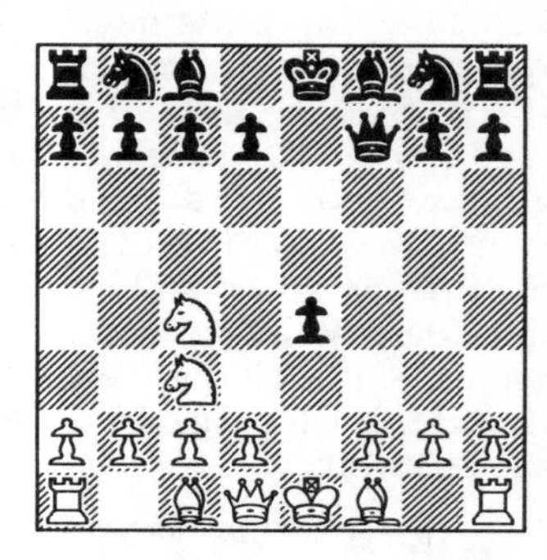

This idea of Gunderam's is by far the most popular move at this stage. Black is ready to solve his development problems by gambiting his e-pawn.

6 ♘e3

a) For once 6 d3 is well met by 6...d5 7 ♘e5 ♕f6! (but not 7...♕e6 8 ♕h5+! g6 9 ♘xg6 ♕xg6 10 ♕e5+ ♔f7 11 ♘xd5 which is very messy; however 7...♕f5 is also fine, 8 f4, with the threat of g4, 8...exf3 9 ♘xf3 ♘f6 10 ♗e2 ♗c5 equal, Bering-Nilsson, Copenhagen 1993) 8 d4 (if 8 ♘g4 ♕e6 9 ♗e2 Endzelis-Kozlov, corr. 1981, then, instead of 9...exd3?!, Black could have essayed 9...d4!? with the two lines 10 ♘xe4 h5 or 10 ♘b5 ♕b6 11 dxe4?! ♗xg4, winning a piece in both instances) 8...c6 9 ♗e2 ♗d6 10 ♘g4 ♗xg4 (more straightforward than 10...♕h4) 11 ♗xg4 ♘e7 12 0-0 0-0 13 ♗e3 ♘f5, regaining a bishop, with comfortable equality, Clayton-Peters, corr. 1995.

b) There is a major alternative, though, in 6 d4 ♘f6 (the others: 6...♗b4 7 ♘e5 ♕f5 [7...♕e6?! 8 ♕h5+! g6 9 ♘xg6 ♘f6 10 ♕h4 ♖g8 11 ♘f4 {simpler than 11 ♘e5 ♘c6 12 ♗c4 d5 13 ♗b5 ♖xg2 14 ♗g5 with advantage, Weber-Fox, corr. 1989} 11...♕f5 {11...♕f7 12

♗e2 with advantage} 12 ♗e2 d5 13 0-0 c6 14 f3 Black has nothing for his pawn, Zink-Lopez, corr. 1993] 8 ♗c4 ♘e7 9 ♗f7+ ♔d8 10 g4 ♕f6 11 g5 ♕f5 is unclear, Haas-Schlenker, corr. 1988; 6...d5!? 7 ♘e5 ♕e6 8 ♘xd5!? ♕xd5 9 ♗c4 ♕d6 10 ♕h5+ g6 11 ♗f7+ ♔e7 12 ♗xg6, Maier-Rafnung, corr. 1984, when 12...♘f6! 13 ♗g5 ♕xd4 14 ♗e8 ♗e6 15 ♘g4 ♗g7 16 c3 ♕d5 is unclear) with:

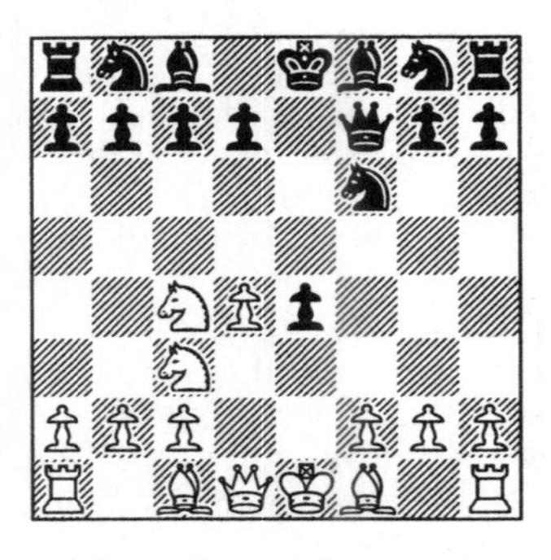

b1) 7 ♘e5 ♕e6 8 ♗g5 (8 ♗c4 d5 9 ♘xd5? ♘xd5 10 ♕h5+ g6 11 ♘xg6 ♕xg6 12 ♕e5+ ♘e7 13 ♕xh8 ♕xg2 ∓ Gabrans-Zemitis, corr. 1970/73) 8...♗b4 9 ♗c4 (9 ♗e2 0-0 10 0-0 d5 is b3 below, but in this move order, 10...♗xc3 11 bxc3 d6 12 ♘c4 b6 is simpler, with a balanced position in both cases, or 12...♘d5!?) 9...d5 (better than 9...♕f5?! 10 ♗xf6 gxf6 11 ♘g4 ♕g6 12 ♘e3 f5 13 ♘ed5 with advantage, Dubinsky-Tchebotariev, USSR 1968) 10 ♗xf6 (going in for the complications, although 10 ♗b3 is not so bad, 10...0-0 [10...c6 11 0-0 ♘bd7 12 ♗xf6 ♘xf6 13 f3 exf3 14 ♕xf3 0-0 is safer, Trigance-Tatlow, corr. 1995] 11 0-0 ♗xc3 12 bxc3 ♘c6 13 f3 exf3 14 ♕xf3 ♘xe5 [14...♘e7? 15 ♖ae1 ♕d6 16 c4 ♗e6 17 cxd5 ♘fxd5 18 ♕e4 with advantage, Grobe-Magee, corr. 1989] 15 dxe5 ♕xe5 16 ♗xf6 ♖xf6 17 ♕xd5+ ♕xd5 18 ♗xd5+ ♔f8 which is quite equal, Malmström-Budovskis, corr. 1997) 10...♗xc3+ (this move can be played at various moments, without changing anything) 11 bxc3 gxf6 12 ♕h5+ ♔e7 13 ♘g6+ (13 ♗xd5? ♕xd5 14 ♘g6+ ♔d6 15 ♕xd5+ ♔xd5 16 ♘xh8 ♗e6 17 ♖b1 ♔c6 [17...♘d7!? 18 ♖xb7 ♔c6 ½-½, Yagolnitzer-Elburg, corr. training game 1999, but Black can continue without risk as his minor pieces have good light squares to settle on] 18 c4! ♗xc4 19 ♖b4 b5 20 ♖xc4+ bxc4 and Black is better, Grobe-Elburg, corr. 1994/95) 13...hxg6 14 ♕xh8 dxc4 15 d5!? (better than 15 0-0?! ♘d7! [or 15...b6 16 d5 ♕f5 {16...♕d7? 17 ♕g7+ ♔d8 18 ♕xf6+ ♕e7 19 ♕xg6 with advantage, Grobe-Svendsen, corr. 1990} 17 f3 e3?! {17...♘d7!? 18 fxe4 ♕g5} 18 g4! ♕d7 19 ♕g7+ ♔d8 20 ♕xf6+ ♕e7 21 ♕xg6 and again White is well on top, Yagolnitzer-Elburg, corr. training game 1999] 16 f3 [16 d5?! ♕f7 {there is nothing obviously wrong with 16...♕xd5!?} 17 ♖ae1 f5 18 f3 ♕f6 19 ♕h7+ ♔d6 20 fxe4 ♘e5 and Black is slightly better, Grobe-Krantz, corr. 1994/95] and instead of 16...b6!? 17 d5?! [17 fxe4] 17...♕xd5 18 fxe4 ♕f7? [18...♗b7! is strong, 19 ♕xa8?? ♕c5+] 19 e5! ♘xe5 20 ♖ae1 ♕e6 21 ♕g7+ with a powerful attack, Grobe-Melchor, corr. 1991, there is 16...e3! 17 ♖ae1 ♘b6 18 ♕g7+ ♔d6 19 ♕xg6 ♘d5 ∓. However 15 0-0-0 ♘d7 16 ♕h7+ ♔d6 17 ♕xg6 ♘b6 18 h4 f5 ∓ is interesting) 15...♕f5 (15...♕e5!? is worth consideration: 16 ♕g7+ [16 ♕xc8 ♕xc3+ 17 ♔e2 ♕xc2+ 18 ♔f1 ♕d3+ 19 ♔g1 ♕xd5 ∓] 16...♔d6 17 ♕f8+ ♔d7 18 0-0 ♘a6 19 ♖ad1

♕e7 and Black has the better chances, Grobe-Clarke, corr. 1994/96) 16 0-0 ♘d7 17 f3 ♕xd5?! (Black can try to keep files closed with 17...e3!? 18 ♖ae1 ♕e5 19 ♕h6 ♔d6 [19...g5 20 f4 gxf4 21 ♖xf4 is also unclear] 20 ♖xe3 ♕xd5 21 ♖fe1, Grobe-Jackson, corr. 1994/95, and now 21...g5 22 f4 b6 is unclear, or go in for the complicated 17...exf3!? 18 ♖ae1+ ♔d6 19 ♖xf3 ♕xd5 unclear) 18 fxe4 ♕f7 19 e5! f5 20 e6 ♔xe6 21 ♖ad1 ♕f8 22 ♖fe1+ again with a strong attack, Grobe-Clarke, corr. 1991.

b2) If instead 7 ♗e2 d5 8 ♘e5 (8 ♘e3?! c6 9 f3 exf3 10 ♗xf3 ♗d6 11 0-0 0-0 12 ♗d2 ♗e6 13 ♕e2 ♘bd7 14 ♖ae1 ♖ae8 =, Zschorn-Clarke, corr. 1991) 8...♕e6 9 ♗g5 then, as well as 9...♗b4 transposing, there is the simple 9...c6! 10 0-0 ♗d6 =.

b3) 7 ♗g5 is actually the most common move, but normally transposes, 7...♗b4 8 ♗e2 (8 ♘e5 ♕e6 transposes to the above, but 8...♕e7 is also a possibility, 9 ♗c4 d6 10 ♗f7+!? ♔f8 11 ♗h5 ♗xc3+ 12 bxc3 dxe5 13 dxe5 ♕xe5 14 ♕d8+ ♘e8 15 ♕xc8 ♕xc3+ 16 ♗d2 ♕xa1+ 17 ♔e2 ♘c6 18 ♕xa8 ♘d4+ 19 ♔e3 ♘xc2+ 20 ♔e2 ♘d4+ ½-½, Grobe-Melchor, corr. 1994/95; perhaps Black can risk 20...♕e5) 8...d5 9 ♘e5 (9 ♘e3 0-0 10 0-0 c6 11 f3 exf3 12 ♗xf3 ♗xc3 13 bxc3 ♕g6 equal) 9...♕e6 (or 9...♕e7) 10 0-0 0-0!? (chancing his arm a little, but if 10...♗xc3 11 bxc3 0-0 then 12 c4 is possible, although the reply 12...♘c6 seems reasonable) 11 ♗xf6!? (this is completely obscure, but if 11 f3 then not 11...exf3? 12 ♗xf3 c6 when, instead of 13 ♘e2? ♘bd7 14 ♗xf6 = Gyuricza-Carlsson, corr. 1978, there is 13 ♗xf6! ♖xf6 14 ♗g4 ♖xf1+?! 15 ♕xf1 ♕e8 16 ♗xc8 ♕xc8 17 ♕f7+ ♔h8 18 ♖f1 +/-, but 11...♗xc3 12 bxc3 ♘bd7! 13 ♘xd7 [or 13 fxe4?! ♘xe4 14 ♖xf8+ ♘xf8 =] 13...♗xd7 14 ♗xf6 ♖xf6 15 fxe4 ♖xf1+) 11...gxf6 12 ♘xd5 fxe5 13 ♘xb4 (13 ♘xc7 ♕g6 14 ♘xa8 ♗h3 15 g3 is also far from certain) 13...a5 14 b3, blow for blow!, 14...♔h8 15 ♗c4 ♕g6 (15...♕d7?! 16 ♘d5 b5 17 f3 ±) 16 ♘d5 ♗g4 17 ♗e2 (I cannot find anything wrong with 17 ♕d2!? ♗f3 18 g3 but it is very risky) 17...♗h3 18 g3 ♘c6 19 dxe5 ♗xf1 20 ♗xf1 ♘xe5 21 ♕d4 ♕g7 22 ♔g2 ♖ad8 23 ♕xe4 ♘g4 0-1, Lindgren-Hector, Rilton Cup 1990.

c) 6 ♘e5!? is tricky, but 6...♕f5! 7 d4 (7 ♘g4 c6 8 ♘e3 ♕f7 9 ♘xe4 transposes to the main line) 7...exd3 8 ♘xd3 ♘f6 9 ♗f4 d6 10 ♗e2 ♗e7 11 0-0 0-0 is nearly level, Forte-Ruggeri Laderchi, corr. training game 1999.

d) and naturally not 6 ♘xe4?? d5 7 ♘e5 ♕f5, winning a knight.

6...c6!

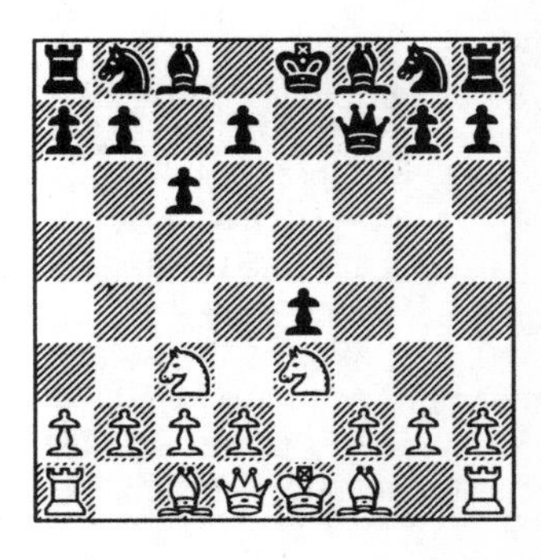

Calmly leaving the e4 pawn to its fate. What exactly does Black obtain in return? Objectively, very little, just a slight lead in development and a lot of fun. In other words, all the things that he is denied in the other lines!

The alternative 6...♘f6 is worse: 7 ♗c4 ♕g6 8 d3 (White cannot afford to hang around, 8 0-0?! c6 9 d3?! [9 d4 d5 transposes into Chapter 3] 9...d5 10 ♘exd5 cxd5 11 ♘xd5 ♘xd5 12 ♗xd5 exd3 and White does not have enough for the piece, Gabrans-Kotek, corr. 1972) 8...♗b4 9 0-0 (9 ♗d2 is also effective, 9...exd3 10 ♗xd3 ♕f7 11 ♗c4 ♕g6 12 0-0 and Black is behind in development, and cannot castle, Sireta-Bonte, corr. 1995) 9...c6 (9...♗xc3 10 bxc3 d6 [10...b5?! smacks of desperation, 11 ♗xb5 c6 12 ♗a4 0-0 13 ♗a3 is overwhelming for White, Marciano-Debard, Val Thorens 1990; 10...c6 11 dxe4 transposes to the next note] 11 ♖e1 ♔d8 12 dxe4 ♘xe4 13 ♗d3 ♘d7 14 f3! ♘xc3 15 ♗xg6 ♘xd1 16 ♘d5! ♘f6 17 ♗g5 winning material, Sharkow-Malmström, corr. 1988) 10 ♘xe4 (10 dxe4 is also strong, 10...♗xc3 11 bxc3 ♘xe4 12 ♕e1 with advantage, Budovskis-Gunderam, corr. 1970) 10...d5 11 ♘xf6+ gxf6 (11...♕xf6? 12 ♗xd5!) 12 ♗xd5!? (this is not necessary, 12 ♗b3 leaves White a solid pawn up, Kozlov-Littleboy, corr. 1977/80) 12...cxd5 13 ♘xd5 ♗d6 (or 13...♘c6!? 14 ♘xb4! [14 ♘c7+!? ♔f7 15 c3 {15 ♘xa8 ♗g4 16 f3 ♗h3 gives Black good play} 15...♗h3 16 ♕f3 ♕xg2+! 17 ♕xg2 ♖ag8!! 18 ♕g3 ♗d6, winning the exchange for two pawns] 14...♗h3 [14...♘xb4 15 ♕e1+] 15 ♖e1+ [15 g3 may be superior] 15...♔d7 16 ♕f3 ♗xg2 17 ♕xg2 ♘xb4 is good for White, but Black does have some drawing chances) 14 ♖e1+ ♔f7 15 ♗f4! (to gain entry to the e7-square) 15...♖g8? (this is not too useful, 15...♕f5!? 16 ♗xd6 ♕xd5 17 ♖e7+ ♔g6 seems playable) 16 ♕f3 ♗xf4 (16...♗g4? loses brilliantly: 17 ♗xd6! ♗xf3 18 ♖e7+ ♔f8 19 ♖xh7+ ♔e8 20 ♘c7+ ♔d8 21 ♘e6+ 1-0, Hergert-Schott, Mainz 1990, it is mate next move) 17 ♖e7+ ♔f8 18 ♘xf4 ♕f5 19 ♖ae1 and White has a winning attack, Walther-Gebuhr, corr. 1971.

Now White comes to another crossroads, does he take the pawn, or go for quick development?

C1 7 ♘xe4
C2 7 d3!

C1 7 ♘xe4

This move is analysed by Nunn in his *Practical Chess*, and he even goes so far as to prefer this line to 7 d3! in *NCO*. However, this must be one of the most 'impractical' lines he could possibly have recommended as White goes pawn hunting, and find himself subjected to a violent attack!

7...d5

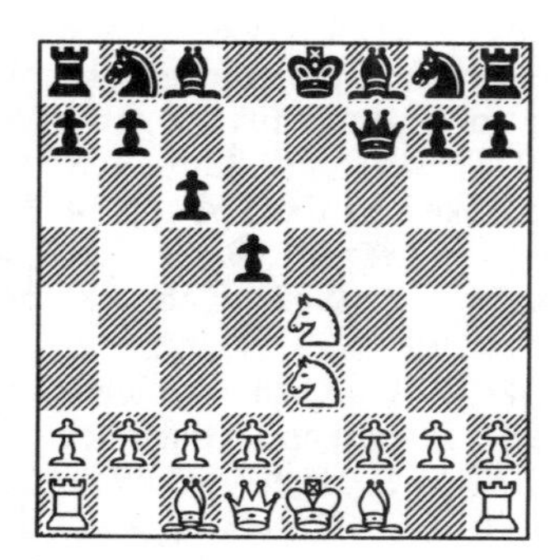

8 ♘g5

This knight's destination is f3 as he cannot return whence he came, 8 ♘c3?? d4, and the other possibility is less natural: 8 ♘g3 h5! (a common device) 9 h4 (to stop the further advance of the h-pawn, 9 ♗e2 h4 10 ♘gf1 ♗e6 11 d4 ♘d7 12 ♘g4?! [12 c3 ♗d6 13 ♕b3 0-0-0 is also fine for Black] 12...0-0-0 13

♘fe3 ♗d6 14 ♕d3 ♘e7 15 ♗d2 ♘g6 16 ♗f3?! h3 17 0-0-0 ♘h4 18 ♕e2 ♗xg4 0-1, Parraga-Zemitis, corr.) 9 d4 h4 10 ♘e2 ♗d6 11 ♘c3 ♗e6 12 ♗e2 ♘h6!? 13 ♘g4 ♘f5 14 h3 ♘d7 15 ♗e3 ♘xe3 16 ♘xe3 0-0-0 17 ♕d2 ♖hf8 18 ♗f3 ♘b6 19 0-0-0 ♗f4 20 ♕d3 ♘c4 with sufficient compensation, Cursoux-Kosten, Aurec Rapidplay 2001) 9...♗d6 10 d4 ♘e7 11 ♗d3 g6!? (Black might forego this and aim to castle long, instead, i.e. 11...♗e6 12 c3 [12 ♕e2 menaces ♘f5, so 12...g6 transposing] 12...♘d7 13 ♕b3 0-0-0 ∓) 12 ♕e2 0-0 13 ♘ef1 ♘a6!? ± Kozlov-Budovskis, corr. 1978/79.

8...♕f6 9 ♘f3

9 h4!? is occasionally played, but can make it difficult for White to castle short, 9...♗d6 (9...h6!? 10 ♕h5+ g6 11 ♕e2 ♘e7 12 ♘f3 ♗g7 13 d4 0-0 14 h5, Schott-Kempf, corr. 1994, and now 14...g5 is very playable for Black) 10 d4 ♘e7 11 ♗d3 h6 12 ♘f3 ♗e6 13 ♗d2 0-0 14 ♕e2 ♘g6 15 ♗xg6 ♕xg6 and the light-squared bishop provides some compensation for the pawn, Walther-Strautins, corr. 1974.

9...♗d6

Probably best, and certainly the most popular. Others:

a) If Black wants to castle queenside, and, despite Nunn's opinion, I still think that this is not a bad idea, he should make his plans now: 9...♗e6 10 d4 ♘d7 11 ♗d3 (Simplest. 11 g3 0-0-0 [11...♗d6 transposes to a later line] 12 ♗g2 g5! 13 0-0 h5 14 h4 [14 ♘xd5!? ♗xd5 15 ♗xg5 is possible] 14...gxh4 15 ♘xh4 ♗e7 Black has kingside attacking chances, Kinnes-Kozlov, corr. 1977 11 c4 ♗b4+ 12 ♗d2 ♗xd2+ 13 ♕xd2 ♘e7, Tiemann-Jackson, corr. 1989, 14 ♕b4!? with a plus.) 11...0-0-0 (11...♗d6 will transpose here if Black continues with ...0-0-0, and to the main line if he castles short) 12 0-0—Nunn's recommendation, not fearing 12...g5!? (12...♗d6 13 c4 ♘e7 14 cxd5 cxd5 15 ♗d2 ♘c6 is possible, Malmström-Strautins, corr. 1997, Black will first play his king to b8, and then start his kingside march) 13 c4 as 13...g4?! (13...dxc4 14 ♘xc4 [14 ♗xc4, Zaniratti-Van de Velden, corr. 1999, 14...g4 15 ♘d2 ♗xc4 16 ♘dxc4 h5] 14...g4!? is superior) 14 cxd5! cxd5 15 ♘xg4 (15 ♘e5 is also OK, 15...♘xe5 16 dxe5 ♕xe5 17 ♘xg4 ♕g7 18 ♕e1! 1-0, Kure-Orr, corr. 1997, as 18...♗xg4 19 ♗f4 menacing ♖c1+, leads to a decisive attack) 15...♗xg4 16 ♗g5 is strong 16...♗xf3 17 ♗xf6 ♗xd1 18 ♗xh8 and White will capture on h7 and create three passed pawns.

b) However, 9...d4? is definitely misguided, Black concedes the e4-square, 10 ♘c4 b5 11 ♕e2+! ♔d8 (11...♘e7 12 ♘ce5 ♘d7 13 c3 dxc3 14 dxc3 does not help, White has an extra pawn, and the better position, Nimzo-Comet test game 1997) 12 ♘ce5 (12 d3?! is less accurate, 12...♗b4+ 13 ♔d1 h6 14 ♘ce5, although White is still clearly better, Peters-Bie, corr. 1982) 12...♗d6 13 d3 (+/- *NCO*) 13...h6 14 ♕e4!? (14 ♗d2 ♔c7 15 ♕e4 is safer, Zecha-Traut, corr. 1987, as

White can castle long when the black rook comes to e8) 14...♘e7 15 ♕xd4 ♘f5 16 ♕e4 ♖e8, Grobe-Szilagyi, corr. 1983, when 17 d4! ♘xd4 18 ♕xd4 ♘d7 19 ♗f4 ♘xe5 20 0-0-0 ♔c7 21 ♕xd6+! ♕xd6 22 ♖xd6 ♔xd6 23 ♘xe5 is crushing.

10 d4 ♘e7

10...♗e6 will transpose.

11 c4

The most important move, although there are two reasonable alternatives:

a) 11 g3 ♗e6 (if 11...0-0 12 ♗g2 ♘f5 [12...♗e6 transposes] 13 h3! ♘xe3 14 ♗xe3 followed by c3, ♕b3, 0-0-0 with advantage, whilst the attempt to stop the king from castling, 11...b6?! 12 ♗g2 ♗a6, should not be met by 13 c4?! dxc4 14 0-0 0-0 [14...♘d7!?] 15 ♘g4 ♕f5 16 ♘ge5, Tiemann-Krantz, corr. 1991, when White is only slightly better, but by 13 ♘e5 0-0 [if 13...♗xe5 14 ♘g4 with advantage] 14 f4, and now Black erred with 14...♘g6? when 15 ♘xd5! cxd5 16 ♗xd5+ wins material, Malmström-Elburg, corr. 1994/95) 12 ♗g2 ♘d7 13 0-0 0-0 (unfortunately, the natural 13...0-0-0 allows 14 ♘g5! h5?! [if 14...♕xg5?! 15 ♘c4 ♕f6 16 ♘xd6+ ♔b8 17 ♗f4 ♔a8 leaves the d6 knight trapped, but there is no way of getting at it, i.e. 18 ♖e1 ♘g6 {or 18...h6 19 ♕e2 with advantage} 19 ♗g5 with advantage; 14...♗g8?! 15 ♘g4 ♕g6 16 f4 h6 17 ♘h3 ♗e6 18 ♘e5 and White has a dominating position; so perhaps Black's best bet is 14...♗f5 15 ♘xf5 ♘xf5 16 c3 h6 17 ♘f3 g5, but White is better] 15 ♖e1 ♗g8 16 ♘f3? [16 h4 is good] 16...g5 ± Borrmann-Krustkalns, corr. 1991; 13...g5? is a blunder, 14 ♘xg5! winning quickly, Morgado-Grivainis, corr. 1977, but 13...h6!? is the best alternative, 14 b3 0-0-0 15 c4 g5 16 ♗b2 h5, with fair attacking chances, Budovskis-Svendsen, corr. 1998) 14 b3 (14 ♗d2 is more passive, 14...♖ae8 [14...♘f5 is also reasonable, 15 ♘g4 ♕g6 16 ♘fe5 ♘xe5 17 dxe5? {17 ♘xe5 is forced} 17...♗c5 {17...♘xg3! is possibly even stronger} 18 ♗f4?! ♘h4! winning material, Borrmann-Tiemann, corr. 1988] 15 ♗c3 ♘f5 16 ♘g4 ♕g6 17 ♘fe5 ♗xe5 18 ♘xe5 ♘xe5 19 dxe5 ♘h4! with good chances on the light squares, Korchnoi-Destrebecq, simul, Lyon 1979) 14...♘g6!? (14...♖ae8! 15 ♗b2 ♘f5 is also possible, and should be similar to the 14 ♗d2 lines) 15 ♗b2 h5?! (15...♖ae8 first, is more accurate) 16 h4 ♖ae8 17 ♘g5! (17 c4!? is more common, but allows Black a strong attack: 17...♗g4!? 18 ♘xg4 hxg4 19 ♘h2 ♘xh4 20 gxh4?! [20 ♘xg4! is stronger, 20...♕d8!? 21 gxh4 {21 ♗h1!?} 21...♕xh4 22 ♗c1? {22 f3 ♘f6 23 ♘xf6+ ♖xf6 24 ♖e1 is more testing} 22...♘f6 23 ♘xf6+ ♖xf6 24 f4 ♖h6! and Black can force a draw—Bücker. 25 ♕f3 ♕h2+ etc.] 20...♕xh4 21 f4 g3 22 ♘f3 ♕h5 23 ♗c1 ♘f6 and the attack eventually won through, Morgado-Gunderam, corr. 1970) 17...♘f4, Diepstraten-Pot, corr. 1978, and now there is nothing wrong with taking the piece: 18 gxf4 ♕xf4 19 ♘f3 ♗g4 20 ♘xg4 hxg4 21 ♗c1 ♕f5 22 ♘g5 Black has almost nothing for the material.

b) 11 ♗d3 0-0 (or 11...♗e6 12 h3!? [12 0-0 transposes] 12...♘d7 13 ♘g4 [or first 13 ♕e2 0-0-0 14 ♘g4 ♗xg4 15 hxg4 h6 16 g5 with advantage, Grivainis-Heap, corr. 1991] 13...♗xg4 [13...♕f7?! 14 ♘g5] 14 hxg4 ♕e6+ 15 ♕e2 ♕xg4 16 ♔f1! ♘f6 17 ♖h4 ♕d7 18 ♘g5 with advantage, Strautins-Destrebecq, corr. 1990/92) 12 0-0 (or 12 h3 ♘g6 13 ♗xg6?! White stops the knight coming to f4 by eliminating this piece, but the white light-squared bishop is an important piece. [13 ♘g4 is better, 13...♕e7+ 14 ♔f1!? {14 ♕e2 ♘h4 15 ♘xh4 ♕xh4 16 ♗e3 is simpler} 14...♗f5 15 ♗g5, Strautins-Filipovs, corr. 1992, and now 15...♕f7 is fine for Black] 13...♕xg6 14 ♘g4!? [14 ♕d3?!, Grivainis-Krantz, corr. 1991, should be met by 14...♕xd3] 14...♗xg4 [but 14...♗f5 and ...♘d7 is more ambitious] 15 hxg4 ♕xg4 16 ♕d3 h6 17 ♔f1, Strautins-Downey, corr. 1990/93, 17...♕f5 =. 12 c4 ♘g6!? [12...♗e6! 13 ♕b3 may transpose into the main line] 13 ♗xg6 ♕xg6 14 cxd5 cxd5 15 ♕b3 ♘c6?! 16 ♕xd5+ ♔h8, Tanner-Leisebein, corr. 1989, and now 17 0-0 questions the correctness of Black's play) 12...♘g6 13 c3 (13 ♗xg6 ♕xg6, Gross-Zemitis, San Francisco 1968, is also fine for Black) 13...♘f4 14 ♘e1?! (14 ♗c2 retains the bishop) 14...♘xd3?! (14...♕h6! threatens mate on h2, 15 g3 ♘h3+ 16 ♔g2 ♘xf2!? [16...♘f4+!? 17 gxf4 ♗h3+ 18 ♔g1 ♕xf4 looks strong, but White can defend by 19 ♗xh7+! ♔xh7 20 ♕h5+ exchanging queens, with a slight plus] 17 ♖xf2 ♖xf2+ 18 ♔xf2 ♕xh2+ 19 ♘1g2 ♗xg3+ 20 ♔f3 ♗h3 with a strong attack) 15 ♕xd3?! b6! 16 g3 ♗a6 17 c4 b5! 18 b3 bxc4 19 bxc4 dxc4 ∓ Krustkalns-Downey, corr. 1993.

11...0-0

Alternatively, 11...♗e6 12 c5 (12 cxd5 ♘xd5 13 ♘c4 is also liked by *NCO*, 12 ♕b3 0-0 transposes) 12...♗c7 13 ♗d3 0-0 (13...♘d7?! 14 ♗d2 0-0 15 ♕c2 is given as advantageous for White by *NCO*, and, indeed, 15...♗h3!? 16 0-0-0 ♗xg2 17 ♗xh7+ ♔h8 18 ♘xg2 ♕xf3 19 ♖he1! does seem good) 14 ♗d2 ♘g6! (again this typical idea, the knight heads for f4) 15 ♕c2 ♗h3! 16 ♗xg6 hxg6 17 0-0 (17 ♖g1 ♗xh2!) 17...♗xg2 18 ♘xg2 ♕xf3 19 ♕xg6 ♘d7 and Black is only slightly worse, Elburg-Rozzoni, corr. 1999.

12 ♕b3 ♗e6

Destrebecq's suggestion of 12...♔h8!? has found no takers, 13 ♗d2!? (13 cxd5?! cxd5 14 ♘xd5 ♘xd5 15 ♕xd5 ♗b4+ is unnecessarily risky, 13 ♗e2 is preferred by *NCO*) 13...dxc4 14 ♗xc4 ♘d7 15 0-0 ♘b6 16 ♗d3 ♗e6 17 ♕c2 is better for White.

13 c5

To prepare the queen's escape, 13 ♕xb7 ♘d7 14 ♕a6!? (14 c5 ♗f4 is probably best, and transposes, but not 14 ♗e2? ♘b6! 15 c5 [15 ♕a6? ♗b4+ 16 ♔d1 ♗c8 is worse] 15...♗c8 trapping the queen) 14...♘f5!? (14...♗b4+ 15 ♗d2 ♗xd2+ 16 ♔xd2 is possible, as the white king's awkward position will provide Black with counterplay) 15 ♗d2?! ♘xd4 16 ♘xd4 ♕xd4 17 ♕xc6 ♕f4 18 cxd5 ♘e5 19 ♕a6 ♕xf2+ 20 ♔d1 ♖f4 and Black has a powerful attack, Zaniratti-Bartsch, corr. 2000.

13...♗f4 14 ♕xb7 ♘d7 15 ♕b3

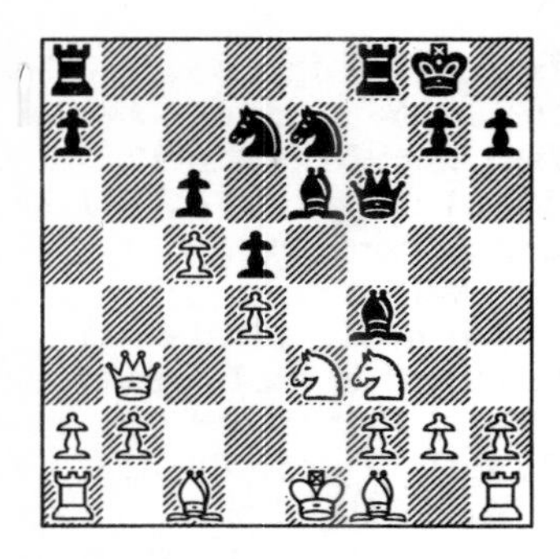

'!' Nunn and *NCO*.

Otherwise, 15 ♗d3 g5 16 h3! (so that when Black plays ...g4, White will obtain the open h-file for his rook; on 16 h4?! g4 17 ♘g5 ♗xg5 18 ♗xh7+ ♔g7 19 hxg5 ♕xf2+ 20 ♔d1 ♖f4 Black has dangerous tactical possibilities against the white king, Priede-Grivainis, corr. 1970) 16...h5 (16...♖fb8!? is an interesting alternative, 17 ♕a6 h5 18 ♕a4 g4 19 hxg4 hxg4 20 ♘g1 ♗xe3 21 ♗xe3 ♖xb2 22 ♖h6 and the active black rook, and open f-file will provide various tactical possibilities for Black, Rozzoni-Koetsier, corr. 1999) 17 ♕b4 g4 (Black cannot afford to hang around, 17...a5?! 18 ♕c3 a4 19 ♗d2 ♗c7 20 0-0-0 and the white king has found safety, Koetsier-Elburg corr. 1999) 18 hxg4 hxg4 19 ♘g1 ♖ae8 20 ♘e2 ♗c7 21 ♖f1 ♗f5 22 ♕c3 ♗a5! 23 ♕xa5 ♗xd3 24 ♘xg4 ♕g6 25 ♘e3 ♗xe2 26 ♔xe2 ♘f5 (the black attack continues unabated) 27 ♕b4 ♕xg2 28 ♔d3 ♖xe3+! 29 ♗xe3 ♕e4+ 30 ♔c3 ♘xe3 31 ♖g1+ ♘g2 and Black is winning, Elburg - Ruggeri Laderchi, corr. training game 1999.

15...g5

15...♖ab8 16 ♕c2 ± *NCO*.

16 h3 h5

Black will try to blast the f-file open.

17 ♕c2

Eyeing h7, as does 17 ♕d3 ♘f5 (perhaps Black should play 17...♖f7, guarding h7, as in the main line) 18 ♗e2 (18 ♗d2! intends long castling, 18...♘xe3 19 ♗xe3 ♗f5 20 ♕d2 and White is fine) 18...♖ae8 19 ♘c2!? ♗xc1 20 ♖xc1 ♘g7!? (20...g4 21 hxg4 hxg4 22 ♘d2 g3 23 fxg3 ♕g7 24 g4 ♘h6 25 ♘f3 ♗xg4 and Black maintains the initiative, Ruggeri Laderchi-Elburg, corr. training game 1999) 21 ♘e3 g4 22 hxg4 hxg4 23 ♕h7+ ♔f7 24 ♖h6 gxf3 25 ♖xf6+ ♘xf6 26 ♕d3 fxe2 is unclear, Tatai - Ruggeri Laderchi, corr. 2000.

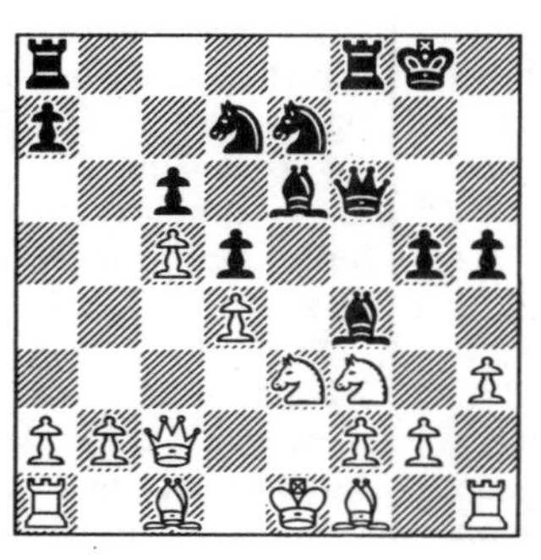

17...♖f7!

Bücker's move, Black guards h7 to revive the threat of ...g4. Other moves have been tried:

a) 17...♖ae8 18 ♗d2 ♘f5 19 ♕c3 g4 20 hxg4 ♘xe3 21 fxe3 ♗g3+ 22 ♔d1 ♗xg4 and Black does not have enough compensation, Tait-Elburg, corr. 1999.

b) 17...♘f5 18 ♗e2 (18 ♗d2! is stronger, 18...g4, otherwise White simply castles, 19 hxg4 ♘xe3 20 ♗xe3 ♗xe3 [20...hxg4?? 21 ♕h7 mate is the point of White's earlier queen move] 21 fxe3 ♗xg4 22 0-0-0 and White has a winning advantage—*NCO*) 18...♖ae8 19 ♗d2 (19 0-0? 'out of the frying pan ...' 19...♗xe3 20 ♗xe3 g4 21 hxg4 hxg4 22 ♘e5 ♘xe5 23 dxe5 ♛h4 and White will soon be mated along the h-line, Faraoni - Ruggeri Laderchi, corr. training game 1999) 19...♘xe3 20 ♗xe3 ♗xe3 21 fxe3 ♗f5 22 ♛d2 g4 23 hxg4 hxg4 24 ♘h4 ♗h7 25 0-0-0 ♛g5 and Black will regain one of his pawns and retain an active set-up, Faraoni-Ruggeri Laderchi, corr. training game 1999.

18 ♗d2 g4 19 hxg4 hxg4 20 ♘g1 ♗e5!!

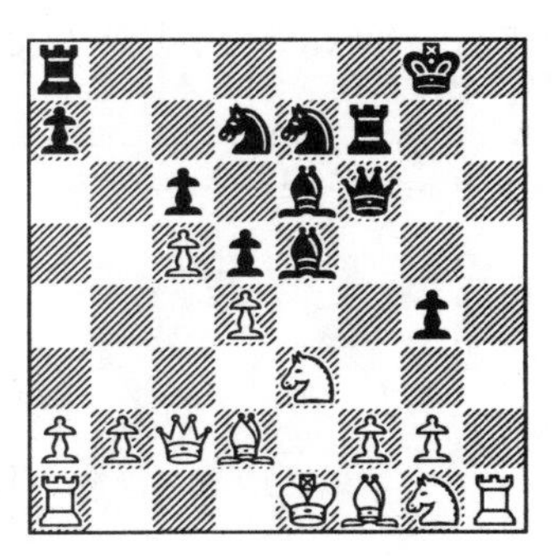

21 dxe5

Black also has good compensation after 21 ♘e2 ♛xf2+ 22 ♔d1 ♗h8 23 ♛d3 ♘f6 24 ♗e1 ♘e4!, and after 21 0-0-0 ♗xd4 22 ♗b4 a5 23 ♖xd4 axb4 24 ♘e2 ♖xa2—my analysis.

21...♛xf2+ 22 ♔d1 ♘f5 23 ♗e2

23 ♘e2 ♛xe3! 24 ♛a4 ♛e4 (or 24...♛xe5 25 ♛xg4+ ♛g7) 25 ♛xc6 ♖af8 26 ♛xe6 ♘g7 obliging White to part with his queen.

23...♛xe3! 24 ♗xg4 ♛d4 25 ♗xf5 ♗xf5 26 ♛c3 ♗g4+ 27 ♘f3 ♛xc3 28 ♗xc3 ♖xf3 29 gxf3 ♗xf3+ 30 ♔c2 ♗e4+ 31 ♔d2 ♗xh1 32 ♖xh1

32 e6?! ♘xc5 33 ♖xh1 ♘e4+ 34 ♔c2 ♘xc3 35 ♔xc3 ♖e8 36 ♖e1 ♔g7, winning the e-pawn, although a draw is probable.

32...♘xc5 33 ♖h6 ♘e4+ 34 ♔d3

This is also likely to be a draw. Many thanks to Stefan Bücker for this original analysis.

C2 7 d3!

This idea of Budovskis, refusing the pawn and playing for the attack, is the modern preference.

7...exd3 8 ♗xd3

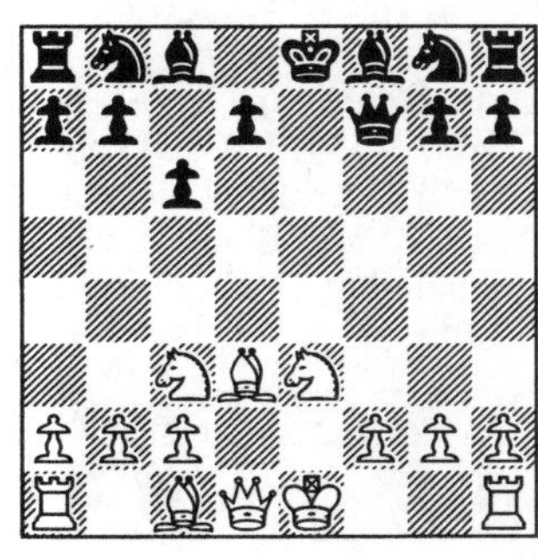

8...d5

Black cannot really do without this move, but might be able to delay it a little:

a) 8...♗b4!? 9 0-0 ♗xc3? (White's dark-squared bishop will make Black regret this; 9...♘f6 is interesting, as if 10 ♗d2 [10 ♘g4—Elburg] 10...d5 might be superior to 8...d5 9 0-0 ♗b4, and 9...d5 transposes to 8...d5) 10 bxc3 ♘e7 11 ♗a3 d5 (11...0-0 12 ♗d6! is quite hopeless) 12 ♖e1 0-0 (12...♔d8 13 ♗xe7+ ♛xe7 14 ♘xd5 +/- Elburg-Diepstraten, corr. 1985) 13 ♗xe7 ♛xe7 14 ♗xh7+! ♔xh7 15 ♛h5+ ♔g8 16 ♘xd5 winning the black queen, 16...♛xe1+ 17 ♖xe1 cxd5 the black pieces are incapable of helping, Sénéchaud-Schirmer, corr. 1992, e.g. 18 ♖e8 ♘d7 19 ♛xd5+ ♔h8 20 ♛h5+ ♔g8 21 ♖e7 ♘f6 22 ♛g6.

b) 8...♘f6 9 0-0 ♗c5?! (the bishop is exposed here; better 9...♗b4 as above) 10 ♘g4! 0-0?

(10...♘xg4 11 ♕xg4 0-0 is better) 11 ♘xf6+ ♕xf6 12 ♕h5! even stronger than (12 ♗xh7+ ♔xh7 13 ♕h5+) 12...♗xf2+ 13 ♔h1 g6 14 ♕e2 ♕h4 15 ♘e4 winning, Tener-Grobe, corr. 1971/72.

9 0-0

If Black is careful, then 9 ♕e2 presents no problems: 9...♗e6 10 ♘f5 ♘d7 11 ♘d4 (11 ♗f4 ♘c5 12 ♘d6+ ♗xd6 13 ♗xd6, Purins-Kozlov, corr. 1977/79, 13...♘xd3+ 14 ♕xd3 0-0-0 =.) 11...0-0-0 12 0-0 (12 ♘xe6 ♖e8 13 0-0 ♖xe6 is fine for Black) 12...♘c5 13 ♘xe6 ♘xe6 14 ♖e1 ♖e8 and Black is very close to equalising, Niemand-Tatlow, corr. 1995.

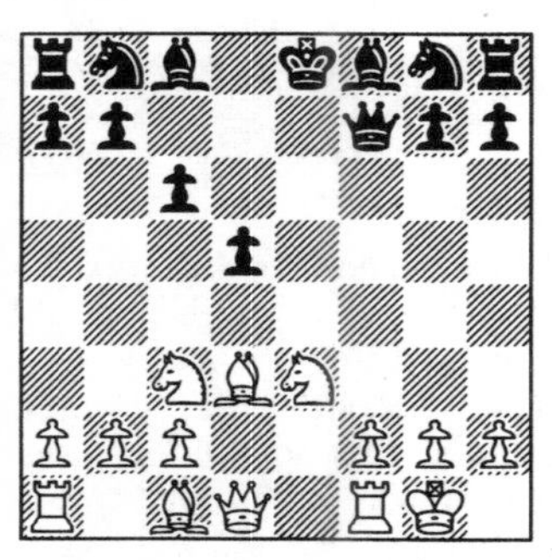

And thus we attain the critical position for Black in this variation. Black has tried most legal moves, but only three of them come close to being satisfactory,

C21 9...♗c5
C22 9...♗d6

A brief round-up of the others, in order of playability:

a) 9...♗b4?! 10 ♘cxd5! (Critical, the other moves are fine for Black: 10 ♘e2 is calmer, but not very effective, 10...♘e7 [10...♘f6!?] 11 c4 0-0 [11...♗e6 12 ♕b3 dxc4 13 ♘xc4 ♘a6 14 ♘f4, Budovskis-Melchor, corr. 1993, 14...♖d8!=, and 14 a3!? b5 15 ♕xb4! 0-0 might favour White, but only slightly] 12 ♕b3 ♗d6 13 cxd5 ♘xd5?! [exchanging the e3-knight helps White's development, 13...cxd5! 14 ♘c3 ♗e6!? {14...♖d8} 15 ♕xb7 ♘bc6 brings Black excellent play for the pawn] 14 ♘xd5 cxd5 15 ♘c3 ♗e6 16 ♘b5 with a slight edge, Kozlov-Gåård, corr. 1994/95. 10 ♗d2!? might be good, lining up threats along the e1-a5 diagonal, but 10 ♖e1 is less effective here, 10...♘e7 [10...♗e6? loses—see 9...♗e6] and now 11 ♘exd5?? cxd5 12 ♘xd5? ♕xd5 13 ♗g6+ loses to 13...♔d8) 10...cxd5 11 ♘xd5 the attack is very dangerous, but I don't know if there is a forced win:

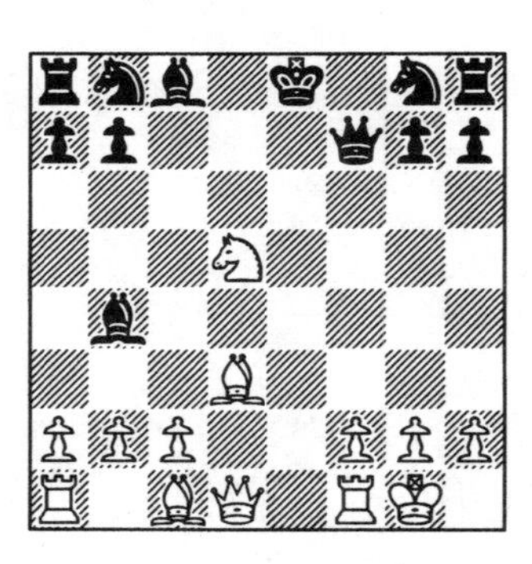

a1) 11...♗c5!? 12 ♗f4 ♔f8 13 ♗c4 ♘c6 14 ♗e3! ♗d6 15 ♘b6 ♗xh2+ 16 ♔h1 ♕f6 17 ♘xc8! (17 ♗c5+ ♔e8 18 ♘xa8 ♕h4 and White will have to face a dangerous discovered check) 17...♕h4 (17...♖xc8!? 18 ♗xg8 ♗e5 19 ♕g4) 18 ♕f3+ ♘f6 19 ♗e6 ♗e5+ 20 ♕h3 ♕xh3+ 21 gxh3 and Black cannot exploit the c8-knight's position, and so is worse, Malmström-Miraglia, corr. 1997.

a2) 11...♗a5? 12 b4 ♗d8 (this loses, but what else? 12...♗e6 13 ♖e1 ♘e7 14 ♗c4 1-0, as 14...♗d8 15 ♖xe6, Krustkalns-Borrmann, corr. 1991, 12...♔f8 13 ♗c4 ♗xb4

14 ♗b3 is also hopeless for Black) 13 ♖e1+ ♔f8 14 ♗c4 ♕d7 15 b5! ♗e7, Littleboy-Borrmann, corr. 1991, when 16 ♗a3! ♗xa3 17 ♕f3+ is decisive.

a3) 11...♕xd5?! 12 ♗g6+ hxg6 13 ♕xd5 ♘c6 14 c3, Svendsen-Sireta, corr. 1997, Black has three pieces for the queen, but his open king is a real problem.

a4) 11...♘c6!? 12 ♘xb4 (alternatively, 12 ♕e2+ ♔f8 13 ♘xb4 ♘xb4 14 ♗c4 ♕f6?! [14...♘d5! 15 ♖e1 ♗d7] 15 ♗e3 ♘c6 16 ♗c5+ ♘ge7 17 ♖fe1 ♗f5 18 ♖ad1 ♖e8 19 ♖d6 ♕g5 20 ♖xc6! bxc6 21 ♕e5 h5 22 ♗xe7+ 1-0, Svendsen-Downey, corr. 1997) 12...♘xb4 13 ♖e1+! (or 13 ♗b5+ ♘c6 14 ♖e1+ ♘ge7 15 ♗xc6+ bxc6 16 ♗g5 0-0 17 ♗xe7 ♕xf2+ 18 ♔h1 when the opposite-colour bishops are unlikely to save Black) 13...♘e7 14 ♗g5 0-0 15 ♗xe7 ♕xf2+ 16 ♔h1 ♘xd3 17 ♕xd3 ♖e8 18 ♗h4 ♕f7 19 ♖xe8+ ♕xe8 20 ♖e1 ♗e6 21 ♕d6 ♔f7 22 ♕c7+ ♔g8 23 ♕xb7 and White's two extra pawns should be enough, Laderchi Ruggeri - Elburg, corr. 2000.

a5) 11...♗d6? transposes to 9...♗c5 10 ♘exd5.

b) 9...♗e6!? is reasonable, avoids all sacrifices on d5, or c4, and may prove to be one of Black's best lines. 10 ♖e1 and:

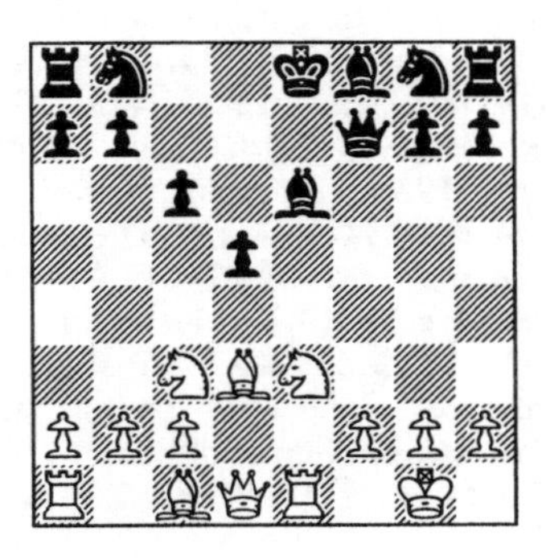

b1) 10...♗e7 11 ♘e2! (seems to be more potent than 11 ♘g4 ♘d7 12 ♕e2 ♗xg4 [12...♘c5!?] 13 ♕xg4 0-0-0 [13...♘gf6 14 ♕e2 ♘c5 15 ♗f5 g6 16 ♗h3 d4?! 17 b4 ♘a6 18 ♗h6! +/- Elburg-Schoppmeyer, corr. 1987] 14 ♗f5 ♘gf6 15 ♕h3 ♗c5 with chances to equalize, Kozlov-Grobe, corr. 1977/78) 11...♗c5!? (11...♘d7?! 12 ♘d4 0-0-0 13 ♘xe6 ♕xe6 14 ♘f5 ♕f6 [14...♕f7?? 15 ♖xe7 1-0, Kozlov-Strelis, corr. 1977, as 15...♘xe7 16 ♘d6+] 15 ♕g4! with advantage Budovskis- Kozlov, corr. 1980) 12 ♘g4 (12 ♘f4!? ♕xf4 13 ♘f5 ♕xf2+ 14 ♔h1 ♔f7 15 ♖f1 picks up the black queen, van den Berg-Hage, corr. 1985, although Black has almost sufficient compensation) 12...♗xg4 (12...♘e7 13 ♘f4 ♗c8 14 ♘e5 ♕f6 15 ♕h5+ g6 16 ♕h6) 13 ♘f4+ ♘e7 14 ♕xg4 0-0 15 ♗e3 with advantage, according to Bücker, although 15...♗xe3 16 ♖xe3 ♘f5 doesn't look so terrible.

b2) 10...♘d7 11 ♗f5 0-0-0?! (11...♗xf5 12 ♘xf5+ ♔d8 avoids the loss of a pawn) 12 ♗xe6 ♕xe6 13 ♘exd5 with advantage, Elburg-Diepstraten, corr. 1990.

b3) 10...♗b4? 11 ♘f5 (not bad, but 11 ♗f5! ♗xf5 12 ♘exd5+ ♔f8 [12...♗e7?! 13 ♖xe7+! ♘xe7? 14 ♘c7+ ♔f8 15 ♕d8+] 13 ♘xb4 just wins, and 11 ♘exd5 cxd5 12 ♕g4 is also pretty effective) 11...♔d7 12 ♘d4 ♗c5 13 ♘xe6 ♗xf2+ 14 ♔h1 ♗xe1 15 ♘c5+ winning, Grivainis-Alloin, corr. 1985.

b4) 10...♘e7!? 11 ♘e2 ♘d7 12 ♘d4 0-0-0 is playable, Diepstraten-Meester, Hilversum 1984.

b5) 10...♗c5? the pressure on f2 does not equal the pressure along the e-file: 11 ♗f5! ♗xe3 (11...♗xf5 12 ♘xf5+ ♘e7 13 ♕g4 is also horrible, but not 13 ♘xe7? ♗xf2+) 12

♗xe6 ♕xf2+?! (12...♗xf2+ 13 ♔h1 ♕f6 14 ♖e2 ♘e7 15 ♗xd5 is superior, but Black can hardly hope to survive) 13 ♔h1 d4 (13...♗xc1 14 ♗xg8+ ♔d8 15 ♗xd5) 14 ♗xe3 dxe3 15 ♗xg8, with a decisive advantage, Tiemann-Alloin, corr. 1986, as 15...♖xg8 16 ♕d4 ♘d7 17 ♖xe3+ is calamitous.

c) 9...♘f6?! fails to keep control of f5, 10 ♖e1 ♗e7 11 ♘f5 ♗xf5 12 ♗xf5 ♘bd7 (obviously 12...0-0?? 13 ♗e6 is out of the question, and 12...g6? 13 ♗e6 ♕g7 14 ♗c8 a6 15 ♗e3 is also crushing, Diepstraten-Purins, corr. 1983/85) 13 ♗f4 (13 ♕d4 ♔f8 [13...♔d8] 14 b4 h6 15 ♗a3 ♗d6 [15...a5!?] 16 ♖e6 is also rather good, Borrmann-Lonsdale, corr. 1991) 13...♔f8 (13...0-0-0? 14 ♕d4 ♘h5 15 ♘b5! 1-0, Sinke-De Boer, corr. 1986; 13...♖f8 14 ♗e6 ♕h5 15 g4 ♕h4? (15...♕g6) 16 ♗g3 ♕g5 17 ♕e2 d4?! 18 ♗xd7+ ♘xd7 19 ♘e4 +/- Kozlov-Lonsdale, corr. 1991, but 13...♔d8 may be the best chance) 14 ♘e2 ♘h5 15 ♗xd7 ♘xf4 16 ♘xf4 ♕xf4 17 ♖e3 with advantage, Kozlov-Gaard, corr. 1989/91.

d) 9...♘h6?! 10 ♘exd5!? (10 ♖e1 is simpler) 10...♗c5? (he might as well take the piece, although 10...cxd5 11 ♗b5+ ♗d7 12 ♖e1+ ♔d8 is not very pleasant) 11 ♕e2+ ♔d7, Grobe-Schwibbe, corr. 1976, 12 ♗xh6 cxd5 13 ♕g4+, winning.

e) 9...d4? 10 ♗c4 ♕d7 (10...♕g6? 11 ♕xd4 ♗d6 12 ♗xg8 ♖xg8 13 ♘c4 1-0, Elburg-Korhonen, corr. 1988. Or 10...♕f6 11 ♘e4 ♕e5 12 ♘g4 with advantage) 11 ♕h5+ ♔d8 12 ♖d1 ♘f6 13 ♕h4 c5 14 b4! b6 15 bxc5 bxc5 16 ♘e4 ♗e7 17 ♘g5 and Black is on his knees, Diepstraten-Alloin, corr. 1983.

f) 9...♗e7?! will transpose elsewhere after both 10 ♖e1 ♗e6! (or 10...♘f6) and 10 ♘exd5 cxd5 11 ♘xd5 ♗d6 12 ♖e1+.

C21 9...♗c5

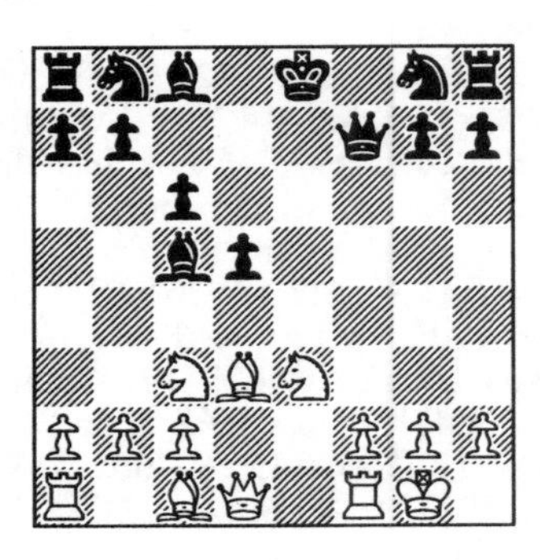

In this main line Black is nearly lost, and there being no obvious improvements for Black, this move must be considered doubtful.

10 ♘a4

Played to put pressure on Black's centre with c4. Others:

a) 10 ♘exd5!? this is less effective here although White still gets two pawns and an attack for his piece, 10...cxd5 11 ♘xd5 (11 ♘b5?! is worse here than in the position with the bishop on d6, as nothing is attacked, 11...♘f6 [11...♗f8? transposes to 9...♗d6 10 ♘exd5] 12 ♖e1+ [12 ♗e3 ♕e7 13 ♗f4 0-0! 14 ♘c7 ♘g4 counterattacking against f2] 12...♔f8 13 ♗e3 ♗xe3 14 ♖xe3 ♘c6 and White's compensation is insufficient) with:

a1) 11...♘c6! (11...♗d6? 12 ♖e1+ ♔f8 [12...♘e7 13 ♗c4 ♕f8? 14 ♖xe7+ 1-0, Littleboy-Riegsecker, corr. 1986, by transposition] 13 ♗c4 ♕g6 14 ♘f4 1-0, Diepstraten-Tiemann, corr. 1990; 11...♘f6?! 12 ♘xf6+ gxf6 13 ♖e1+ ♗e7 14 ♗e4 ♘d7 15 ♗d5 ♕g7 16 ♖e3 with pressure along the central files, Malmström-Niemand, corr. 1995) 12 ♗f4 (12 ♘c7+!? ♕xc7 13 ♕h5+

♕f7 14 ♕xc5 ♗e6!? Tatai-Ruggeri Laderchi, corr. 2000, [14...♕e7!? 15 ♕c3 ♕f6 16 ♖e1+ ♘ge7 17 ♕b3 ♗f5! may be better; if White takes the b-pawn, then Black can castle short] 15 ♖e1 ♘ge7 [15...0-0-0?! 16 b4 ♔b8 17 b5 ♖d5 18 ♕e3 ♘d8 19 ♗c4 wins the exchange, although Black will have some play] 16 ♗g5 ♖d8, unclear) 12...♔f8 (12...♗b6? 13 ♖e1+ ♘ge7 14 ♗c4 ♕f5?! [although if 14...♕g6 then 15 ♘xe7 ♘xe7 16 ♕d5 is crushing anyway] 15 ♘xe7 ♘xe7 16 ♖xe7+! forcing mate, Malmström-Diepstraten, corr. 1994) 13 ♗c4 (13 ♘c7? ♕xf4! 14 ♘xa8 ♘f6, Black already has two pieces for a rook, and will also win the a8-knight eventually, 15 ♗b5 ♗d7 16 ♗xc6 ♗xc6 17 ♕d8+ ♔f7 18 ♕c7+ [White exchanges queens, for if 18 ♕xh8? ♕e4 and there is no defence against mate] 18...♕xc7 19 ♘xc7 ♖c8 and the three pieces soon triumphed, Niemand-Malmström, corr. 1995) 13...♗e6 14 ♗e3 (14 ♗g5 ♘d4!? 15 b4 ♘f6 16 bxc5 ♗xd5 17 ♕xd4 ♗xc4 and the position is messy, but Black is better, De Jong-Sireta, corr. 1994/95) 14...♗d6 15 ♘f4?! ♗xf4 16 ♗xe6 ♗xh2+ 17 ♔xh2 ♕xe6 18 ♖e1 ♕f5 and Black is winning, Diepstraten-Sireta, corr. 1994/95.

a2) 11...♗e6!? is the alternative, 12 ♘f4 (12 ♕e2?! ♔d8 13 ♗c4 [White's attack soon evaporated on 13 ♖d1 ♗xd5 14 ♗e4 ♘f6 15 ♗xd5 ♘xd5 16 c4 ♖e8! 17 ♗e3 ♗xe3 18 fxe3 ♕e7, Laderchi Ruggeri - Elburg, corr. 2000] 13...♘f6 14 ♗g5 ♗xd5 15 ♗xf6+ ♕xf6 16 ♗xd5 ♘c6 17 c3 ♔c7 and Black has overcome the worst of his problems, Kessel-Elburg, corr. training game 1999) 12...♗d7! (12...♘e7?? 13 ♘xe6 ♕xe6 14 ♕h5+ 1-0, Diepstraten-Kozlov, corr. 1991) 13 ♕e2+ ♘e7 14 ♗c4 ♕f5 (14...♕f8!?) 15 ♗e6! (15 ♘d5?! ♔d8! 16 ♘f4 ♘bc6 17 ♘e6+ ♗xe6 18 ♗xe6 ♕e5 19 ♖d1+ ♔c7 -/+ Diepstraten-Krantz, corr. 1991) 15...♗xe6 16 ♘xe6 ♔f7 17 ♘c7 ♘bc6? (Black should prefer 17...♘a6 18 g4 ♕c8 19 ♕f3+ ♔g6 although White is better) 18 g4! Deviation! 18...♕e5 19 ♕f3+ ♔g6 20 ♗f4 ♕f6 21 ♕e4+ ♔f7 22 ♕c4+ 1-0, Nater-Torre, email 1999.

b) 10 ♖e1 For once, this is not in the least bit troublesome for Black: 10...♘e7 11 ♘a4 ♗d6 (11...♗b4!? 12 c3 ♗d6 13 c4 transposes, de Wit-Diepstraten, Hilversum 1990) 12 c4 (12 ♕e2 0-0 = Diepstraten-Tiemann, corr. 1984) 12...0-0 13 ♕c2 ♕h5 14 g3 ♗h3 15 ♗e2 ♕f7 and, with the central pawn and pressure along the f-file, Black is better, Makkinga-Diepstraten, Breda 1987.

c) 10 ♘g4 ♘e7 (10...♘d7!?) 11 ♘e5 ♕f6 12 ♕h5+ g6 13 ♕g5 ♕xg5 = Mercadal-Melchor, corr. 1987/88.

10...♗d6

Although not particularly good, 10...♗e7?! is playable. 11 c4 ♘f6 12 cxd5 cxd5 (12...♘xd5!? 13 ♘xd5 [13 ♗c4 ♗e6 14 ♗xd5 cxd5 15 ♘c3 wins a pawn, for minimum compensation] 13...cxd5 14 ♕c2, Svendsen-Littleboy, corr. 1986, with a plus) 13 ♘c3 ♗e6 14 ♗f5! ♗xf5 15 ♘xf5 ♘c6 16 ♘xe7 ♘xe7 (maybe 16...♔xe7 17 ♖e1+ ♔f8 is best, although White has much the better game, Sireta-Diepstraten, corr. 1997) 17 ♕a4+ ♘c6 (or 17...♘d7 18 ♗g5 ♘c6 19 ♖fe1+ ♔f8 Kozlov-Melchor, corr. 1991, when 20 ♕b5 ♘b6 21 ♗e3 d4 22 ♗xd4 ♘xd4 23 ♕b4+ ♔g8 24 ♕xd4 will win) 18 ♖e1+ ♔d7 19 ♗g5 ♖he8 20 ♕b5 and, again, the d-pawn is lost, Malmström-Diepstraten, corr. 1997.

10...♗xe3? Black cannot afford to concede the defender of his dark squares so easily, 11 ♗xe3 ♘e7 12 ♖e1 0-0?! 13 ♗c5 ♖e8 14 ♕e2 b5 (14...♔f8 15 ♗xh7) 15 ♘c3 a5 16 ♕e3! controlling a7, and winning, Budovskis-Svendsen, corr. 1994/95; 16 ♗xe7? ♖a7 is the point of Black's play.

11 c4

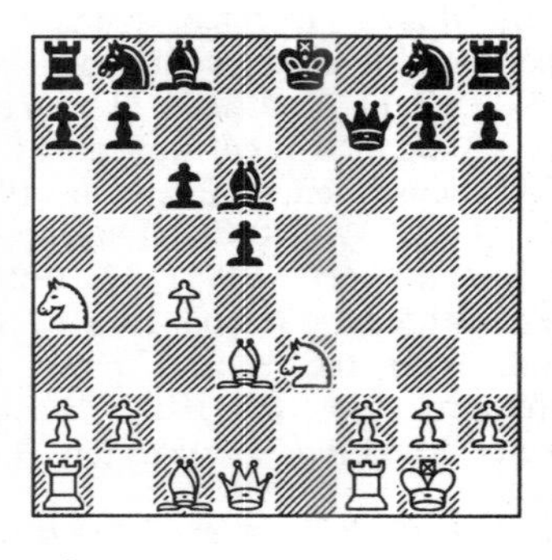

11...♘e7

Black must try to complete his development. Others:

a) 11...d4?! presents Black with overwhelming difficulties:

a1) 12 ♘c2 c5 13 b4! (not 13 ♖e1+?! ♘e7 14 b4 0-0 hitting f2, 15 bxc5 ♕xf2+ 16 ♔h1 ♗xh2 17 ♕h5? [accepting the draw by 17 ♔xh2 ♕h4+ 18 ♔g1 ♕f2+ is more prudent] 17...♘f5 and Black is winning, Svendsen-Tiemann, corr. 1987) 13...b6 (it is all much of a muchness here: 13...cxb4 14 ♘xd4 ♘c6 [14...♘e7 15 ♘b5 ♕f6 16 ♗b2 ±, Kozlov-Tiemann, corr. 1990] 15 ♖e1+ ♘ge7 16 ♘xc6! bxc6 17 c5 ♗c7 18 ♗g5 ♗d8 19 ♕e2 and Black can hardly move, Gåård-Sakellarakis, email 1998, or 13...♗d7 14 ♘xc5 ♗xc5 15 bxc5 ♘c6 16 ♗b2 0-0-0 17 ♘xd4! with advantage) 14 ♗e4 (14 bxc5 first, amounts to the same, 14...bxc5 15 ♗e4 ♗b7 16 ♘xc5 ♗xc5 17 ♗xb7 ♕xb7 18 ♕h5+ 1-0, Vermeulen-Taylor, corr. 1998) 14...♗b7 15 ♗xb7 ♕xb7 16 bxc5 bxc5 17 ♘xc5 ♗xh2+ (17...♕c7 18 ♘e6 ♕f7 19 ♕xd4 1-0, Kozlov-Elburg, corr. 1990) 18 ♔xh2 ♕c7+ 19 ♔g1 ♕xc5 20 ♖e1+ ♘e7 21 ♗a3 unclear, Kozlov-Jackson, corr. 1991.

a2) 12 c5? ♗xh2+ 13 ♔xh2 dxe3 14 fxe3!? (14 ♗xe3 ♘f6 is equal, Krustkalns-Borrmann, corr. 1992, ...♘g4+ is a threat, and Black can use the d5-square) 14...♘f6 15 e4 ♗g4 (the most popular, but others are also adequate: 15...0-0!? 16 e5 ♘g4+ 17 ♔g1 ♕e7? [Black has at least a draw after 17...♕d5! 18 ♖xf8+ ♔xf8 19 ♕f1+?! {19 ♗c2 ♕xd1+ 20 ♗xd1 ♘xe5 21 ♗c2 is very drawish} 19...♔e8 20 ♗xh7 ♕d4+] 18 ♗c4+ ♔h8 19 ♗g5 ♖xf1+ 20 ♕xf1 ♕e8 21 ♖d1 ♘d7 22 e6, with advantage, Elburg-Tiemann, corr. 1990; 15...♗e6!? 16 ♔g1 ♘bd7 17 ♗f4, otherwise Black will establish a knight on e5, 17...0-0-0 18 ♗d6, Borrmann-Gåård, corr. 1991, when Black should exploit the latent d-file pin: 18...♗c4! with good chances) 16 ♕e1 (16 ♕c2 ♕h5+ 17 ♔g1 ♘bd7 18 ♗f4 ♘e5 19 ♖ae1 0-0-0 ∓ Borrmann-Malmström, corr. 1992, 16 ♕b3 ♗e6) 16...♘bd7 17 e5! (17 ♕g3 ♕h5+ 18 ♔g1 0-0 19 ♗e3 ♖ae8 20 ♖f4 ♘e5 ∓, Melchor-Krantz, corr. 1987; whenever the knight successfully reaches the important e5-square, Black will have a plus) 17...♕h5+ 18 ♔g1 ♕xe5 (18...♘xe5?! 19 ♗f5! ♘fd7 20 ♗xd7+ ♔xd7 21 ♗f4 ♘d3?! 22 ♕g3 favours White but 18...♘d5 19 e6 ♘e5 is interesting) 19 ♗f4 ♕xe1 20 ♖axe1+ ♔d8 21 ♗d6 and White has enough play for the pawn, Budovskis-Svendsen, corr. 1990.

b) Meanwhile 11...♗e6 is interesting, 12 ♘c3! (12 cxd5?! cxd5 13 ♘c3 ♘c6! [13...♘e7 transposes to the main line] 14 ♘exd5 [with the knight on c6, 14 ♘b5?! is no problem for Black, 14...♗b8] 14...♗xd5 15 ♘xd5 ♕xd5! 16 ♗g6+ hxg6 17 ♖e1+ [17 ♕xd5 ♗xh2+ draws] 17...♕e5 18 ♗f4 ♘ge7?! [18...♕xe1+ 19 ♕xe1+ ♗e7 is reasonable, after all Black has got two pieces and a rook for his queen, e.g. 20 ♕e4 ♘f6 21 ♕xg6+ ♔f8 with chances for both sides] 19 ♗xe5 ♗xe5 20 h3, Svendsen-Reinke, corr. 1994/95, White is better, the black pieces lack co-ordination, and the king is not safe) 12...♘e7 (12...♘d7? 13 cxd5 cxd5 meets Budovskis' suggestion 14 f4! with advantage, 12...dxc4? 13 ♘xc4! ♗xc4 14 ♗xc4 ♗xh2+ 15 ♔xh2 ♕xc4 16 ♖e1+ ♔f7 17 ♖e4 with a decisive advantage, 12...d4?! 13 ♘e4 ♗e7 14 ♘c2 c5 15 ♖e1 ♘c6 16 ♘g5 ♗xg5 17 ♗xg5 ♔d7 18 b4 is not very pleasant for Black, Vitomskis-Grivainis, corr. 1997) 13 cxd5 cxd5 transposes to the main line.

c) 11...♘f6?! is doubtful, 12 cxd5 (not 12 ♘c3?! d4 13 ♘f5 ♗xf5 14 ♗xf5 ♕xc4 with a reasonable position) 12...cxd5 13 ♘c3 ♘c6 (13...♗e6 14 ♗f5 with advantage to White, who wins the d-pawn again; 13...0-0 14 ♘cxd5 ♘xd5 15 ♘xd5 ♗e6 16 ♘c3 is similarly uninspiring, Owens-Baier, email 1998) 14 ♘exd5 ♘xd5 15 ♗c4! (but not 15 ♘xd5? ♕xd5! [15...♗e6!? is a risky winning try, 16 ♘c3 0-0-0 17 a3 ♘e5 18 ♗e2 ♗b3 19 ♕e1 ♖he8 20 ♘b5 and Black's open king outweighs his active pieces, Niemand-Svendsen, corr. 1991] 16 ♗g6+ hxg6 17 ♕xd5 ♗xh2+ drawing) 15...♗e6 (15...♗xh2+? 16 ♔xh2 ♕c7+ 17 ♔g1 ♘xc3 leaves the black king stranded in the centre, 18 bxc3 ♗d7 19 ♗g5 ♘e7 20 ♕d4 1-0, Svendsen-Crimp, corr. 1997) 16 ♗xd5 0-0-0 17 ♗xe6+ ♕xe6 18 ♕h5 h6 19 ♗e3, Budovskis-Malmström, corr. 1997; Black's compensation for the pawn is non-existent.

12 ♘c3

12 cxd5 cxd5 13 ♘c3 (13 ♖e1? 0-0 14 ♕c2 ♕h5 15 h3 ♘bc6 ½-½ Logunov-Sireta, corr. 1994/96, but Black has a very active, and clearly advantageous, IQP position) will transpose to the main line if Black plays 13...♗e6, and 13...♘bc6 14 ♘exd5 ♘xd5 transposes to (c), above, as 15 ♗c4 wins a pawn, still, Black might have more chances here than in the main line.

12 ♖e1?! 0-0 transposes to the note to 10 ♖e1.

12...♗e6

12...d4? 13 ♘e4 ♗c7, Svendsen-Clarke, corr. 1987, 14 ♘c2 and the d-pawn is lost, as 14...♘f5 15 ♘g5 ♕f6 16 ♖e1+ is awful for Black.

13 cxd5 cxd5 14 ♘b5 ♘c8

Reaching the critical position, Black has been forced into playing an ugly knight retreat; how can White exploit this?

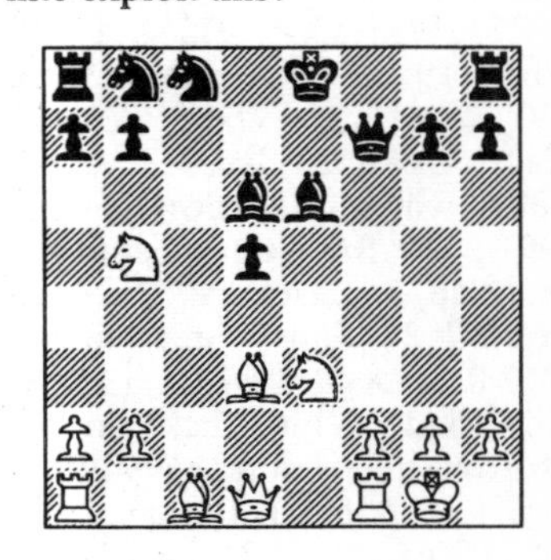

15 f4!

As I suggested, seven years ago, this is very unpleasant for Black, and verges on a forced win. The onward march of the f-pawn will weaken Black's defence of d5, and his king position. Otherwise:

a) Black is not doing too badly after 15 ♘xd6+?! which wins the bishop pair, but helps Black's development, 15...♘xd6 16 b3 (16 ♕c2 is best, and transposes to the next note) 16...♘c6 17 ♗b2 0-0-0!?, Dravnieks-Destrebecq, corr. 1993.

b) 15 ♕c2 is the best alternative, 15...♘c6 16 ♘f5 (16 ♘xd6+!? ♘xd6 17 ♗xh7 0-0-0 18 ♖e1 ♕h5 19 ♘f1 defending h2, when Black's compensation is not enough, Malmström-Clarke, corr. 1997) 16...♗b8 (16...♗e5!? 17 f4 ♗b8 may be more accurate, as the weakness of the g1-a7 diagonal may improve Black's prospects, e.g. 18 ♖e1 0-0 19 ♘fd4 ♗d7 20 ♗xh7+ ♔h8 21 g3?! g5! hitting h7, and f4) 17 ♗d2!? (17 ♘bd4?! 0-0 18 ♘xc6?! ♗xf5 19 ♗xf5 ♕xf5 20 ♕xf5 ♖xf5 = Diepstraten-Grivainis, corr. 1987; 17 ♖e1! is recommended by *NCO*, and in *BCM* Nunn gave 17...♔f8 [17...0-0?! 18 ♘fd4 wins the h7-pawn] 18 ♕c5+ ♔g8 19 ♕c3 although Black is still fighting after 19...♗d7) 17...0-0 (17...♗xf5?! 18 ♗xf5 ♘8e7 19 ♖ae1 ♕h5 [19...a6 20 ♘d4!? ♗xh2+? {20...♕h5} 21 ♔xh2 ♘xd4 22 ♕a4+ ♘dc6 23 ♖xe7+! ♔xe7 24 ♖e1+, winning, Kozlov-Pape, corr. 1991/93, {by transposition} as 24...♔d8 25 ♗g5+ ♔c7 26 ♖e7+ ♘xe7?? 27 ♗f4+ forces mate] 20 h3 0-0 21 ♗g4 ♕h4 22 g3 ♕f6 23 ♗c3 and White has an edge, Kozlov-Sireta, corr. 1994/95) 18 ♘g3 (18 ♘fd4!) 18...g6 19 ♗c3 ♘8e7 20 ♖ae1 a6 21 ♘d4 ♘xd4 22 ♗xd4 and now Black got himself into a tangle with 22...♘c6?! 23 ♗c5 ♖c8 24 ♕e2 ♗e5 25 f4 ♗d4+ 26 ♗xd4 ♘xd4 27 ♕e5 ± Malmström-Destrebecq, corr., but both 22...♘f5 and 22...♗f4 are fine.

c) 15 ♖e1?! 0-0 16 ♕c2 ♕h5 17 ♘xd6?! ♘xd6 18 ♕c7, Riegsecker-Edwards, corr. 1986, 18...♕f7 is fairly level.

d) 15 ♘d4 ♗d7 16 ♘df5 ♗e5 17 ♕b3 ♗xf5 18 ♗xf5 and White has the bishop pair, Logunov-Reinke, corr. 1994/95.

15...0-0

The choice is not a pleasant one:

a) 15...g6? 16 f5 ♗d7 17 fxg6 ♕g7 18 gxh7 with a huge advantage Svendsen-Melchor, corr. 1987/88.

b) 15...♕d7 16 ♕c2 ♘c6 17 ♗xh7 ♘b4 18 ♕g6+ 1-0, Svendsen-Sadeghi, corr. 1991, although Black can play on here.

c) 15...♘c6? 16 f5 ♗d7 17 f6 ♗e6 (this is hopeless, but so is 17...g6 18 ♘xd5) 18 fxg7 ♕xg7 19 ♗f5 ♗xf5 20 ♘xf5 ♗c5+ 21 ♔h1 ♕d7 22 ♕e1+ ♔d8 23 ♕c3 and Black's position is in tatters, Budovskis-Clarke, corr. 1998.

16 f5

16 ♕c2 is also possible, and strong, if less to the point, 16...♕h5 (16...h6? 17 f5 ♗d7 18 ♘xd5 wins a pawn, Sénéchaud-Elburg, corr. 1994/95) 17 ♘xd6 ♘xd6 18 f5 ♖c8 19 ♕a4 ♗f7 20 ♕f4 and White is clearly better, Sénéchaud-De Jong, corr. 1994/97.

16...♗d7 17 ♘xd6!

Introduced by Budovskis, and very effective.

17 f6 g6 (17...gxf6? 18 ♘xd6 ♘xd6 19 ♘xd5 with a crushing advantage Leisebein-Svendsen, corr. 1987) 18 ♘g4 (18 ♗e2 ♗e6? [18...♗xb5! 19 ♗xb5 ♗c5 20 ♔h1 ♗xe3 21 ♗xe3 ♘d6 avoids the worst] 19 ♗g4! ♗xg4 20 ♘xg4

♗c5+ 21 ♔h1 ♕d7 22 f7+! ♔h8 23 b4 the opening of the a1-h8 diagonal spelt the end of the road for Black, Svendsen-Jackson, corr. 1994/95) 18...♗c5+ 19 ♔h1 ♗xg4 20 ♕xg4 ♘c6 21 ♗f4 leaves Black tied up, Svendsen-Griffiths, corr. 1996.

17...♘xd6 18 b3!

White plans to pin the d6-knight by ♗a3. Lein gives 18 ♗c2 (menacing ♗b3xd5) 18...♗c6 19 f6 g6? (a terrible move, 19...♘d7 is clearly superior) 20 ♗b3 ♘c4 21 ♘g4 ♔h8 22 ♗h6 ♖g8 23 ♗xc4 dxc4 24 ♗g7+ forcing mate.

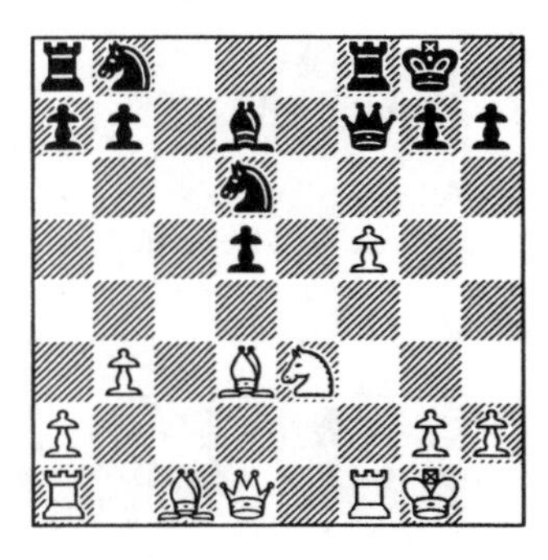

18...♕f6

Black has no decent move:

a) 18...♗c6 19 ♗a3 ♖d8 (19...♖e8 20 ♘g4 ♘e4 21 f6 is not much of an improvement) 20 f6 gxf6 21 ♘g4 1-0, Budovskis-Sireta, corr. 1994/95.

b) 18...♘e4? 19 ♘xd5 ♗xf5? 20 ♖xf5 1-0, Budovskis-Vitols, corr. 1994/95, and the rook is untouchable because of the fork on e7

c) 18...♘c6 19 ♗a3 ♕f6 20 ♘xd5 ♕d4+ 21 ♔h1 ♗xf5 (21...♕xd5?? 22 ♗c4) 22 ♗xf5 ♘xf5 23 ♗xf8 ♖xf8 24 ♕xd4 ♘fxd4 25 ♖xf8+ ♔xf8 26 ♖e1 Black can resign, Budovskis-Melchor, corr. 1994/95.

19 ♗a3 ♖f7

19...♕d4 20 ♕f3 ♕xd3 21 ♗xd6 is no help.

20 ♕f3 ♕e5 21 ♖ad1 ♘c6 22 ♘xd5! ♘d4

22...♘xf5 23 ♗c4 ♔h8 24 ♘c7 wins the exchange.

23 ♕f2 ♕xd5 1-0

Kosten-Elburg, email 2001, as **24 ♗xd6 b5** (24...♕xd6 25 ♗c4 nets an exchange) **25 ♗f4 ♗c6 26 ♗b1** wins the pinned knight.

C22 9...♗d6

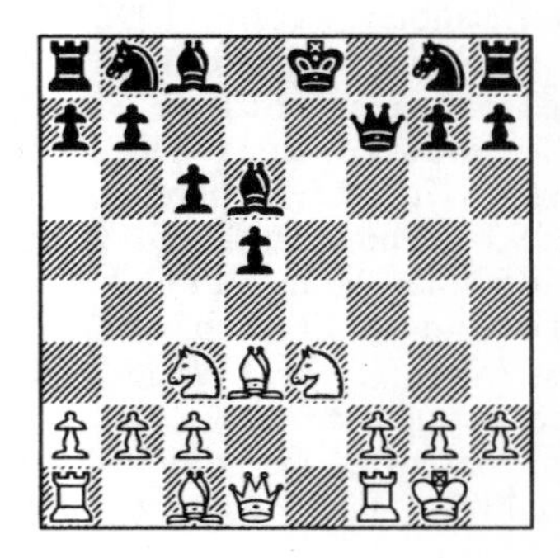

10 ♖e1

Alternatives:

a) The combination 10 ♘exd5!? cxd5 11 ♘b5 is also dangerous, (11 ♘xd5? fails in this position: 11...♗xh2+! [11...♕xd5?! 12 ♗g6+ hxg6 13 ♖e1+ {or 13 ♕xd5 when 13...♗xh2+ draws, 14 ♔h1 ½-½, Borrmann-Crimp, corr. 1995} 13...♕e5 unclear] 12 ♔xh2 ♕xd5 13 ♕e2+ [if 13 ♗g6+?? hxg6+ is check!] 13...♘e7 14 ♗c4 ♕d6+ 15 g3 ♖f8 16 ♗g5 ♘bc6 17 ♖fe1 ♕c5 18 ♗e3 ♕e5 ∓ Diepstraten-Downey, corr. 1992) 11...♗c7 (the anti-developing 11...♗f8?! is the most common, but White appears to win almost by force: 12 ♖e1+ ♔d8 [12...♔d7!? 13 ♗g5 {13 ♗c4?! ♘f6 14 ♗g5 ♔c6 15 ♘d4+ ♔b6 and the king was wandering towards safety, Borrmann-Melchor, corr. training game 1997} 13...♘f6 14 ♗xf6! gxf6 15 ♗c4 ♔c6 16 ♕f3 with a strong attack, Gåård-Magee, corr. 1999] 13 ♗g5+ ♘f6 14 ♗c4 ♕d7 [14...♗e6 15 ♖xe6! ♕xe6 16 ♗xd5 ♕b6 17 ♗xb7+ ♘bd7 18 ♗xf6+ ♕xf6 19 ♗xa8 winning easily, Melchor-Budovskis, corr. 1997] 15 ♗xd5 ♗e7 16 ♖xe7! ♔xe7 17 ♕d4 ♖e8 18 ♖e1+ ♔f8 19 ♕xf6+! The exclamation mark is for beauty! 19...gxf6 20 ♗h6+ ♕g7 21 ♗xg7+ ♔xg7 22 ♖xe8 1-0, Schloegel-Taufratshofer, corr. 1992. Both 11...♗b4?! 12 c3, and 11...♗c5?! 12 ♗e3 only make matters worse) 12 ♖e1+ ♔d8 13 ♗g5+ ♘f6 14 ♗c4 ♗e6, Kristensen-Nicholls, corr. 1998, and now 15 ♖xe6! ♕xe6 16 ♗xd5 ♕e5 (the threat to h2 is a useful resource) 17 ♗xb7+ ♘bd7 18 ♘xc7 ♔xc7 19 ♕f3 ♕xg5 20 ♗xa8 ♖b8! is unclear.

b) 10 ♘e2 is quite feasible, 10...♘f6 (Black doesn't have to worry about the e-file, here, 10...♘e7!? 11 c4 0-0 12 cxd5 cxd5 [the IQP position is the most interesting for Black, but 12...♘xd5!? 13 ♘xd5 ♕xd5 is also possible] 13 ♘c3 ♘bc6!? [an interesting pawn sac, 13...♗e6 14 ♘b5 ♗f4 {14...♖d8} 15 g3 a6 16 ♘d4 ♗d6?! {if 16...♗c7?! then 17 ♘xe6 ♕xe6 18 ♗xh7+ wins a pawn, but 16...♗e5 is fine} 17 ♘xe6 ♕xe6 18 ♗c2 ♘d7 19 ♘xd5! ♘xd5 20 ♗b3 ♘7f6 21 ♗g5 with a small advantage, Kozlov-Morgado, corr. 1977/79] 14 ♘exd5 ♘xd5 15 ♗c4 ♗e6 16 ♗xd5 ♖ad8 17 ♗xe6 ♕xe6 18 ♕e2 ♕xe2 19 ♘xe2 ♗c5 and Black has the initiative, Kozlov-Krantz, corr. 1994/95) 11 c4 (White can also occupy the f5-square, 11 ♘f5 ♗xh2+?? [but not this! 11...♗xf5?! 12 ♗xf5 0-0 13 ♘d4 ♖e8 14 ♖e1 ♗e5 15 ♗e6! ♖xe6 16 ♘xe6 ♕xe6 17 f4 wins the exchange, although Black will have some compensation, but 11...♗e5 is best] 12 ♔xh2 ♕h5+ 13 ♔g1 ♗xf5, Vyskocil-Van Willigen, corr. 1997, and now White could have won a piece on the spot by 14 ♕e1 with the threat of ♘g3+) 11...0-0 12 cxd5 cxd5 13 ♘d4 (13 ♘c3 ♗e6 14 ♘b5 can now be met by 14...♗c5, as c7 is defended by the queen) 13...♘c6 14 ♘ef5 ♗e5 15 ♗e3 and the position is equal, Kozlov-Niemand, corr. 1994/96.

10...♘e7

Now White has a choice between two dangerous sacrifices:

C221 11 ♘exd5!
C222 11 ♘c4!?

If White plays another eleventh move Black will be better.

C221 11 ♘exd5!

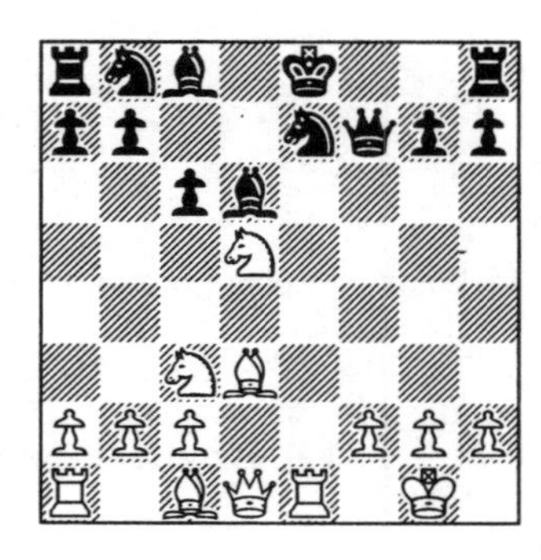

(! *NCO*) White's attention has recently focused on this more direct way of assaulting the solid black centre:

11...cxd5 12 ♘b5

12 ♘xd5?? is a blunder, 12...♕xd5 0-1, Skrastins-Clarke, corr. 1990, as 13 ♗g6+ ♔d8 leaves the queen defended.

12...0-0

With:

a) 12...Bf4?! is the only playable alternative, but it is very difficult for Black. 13 Bxf4 (13 g3? is worse: 13...a6 14 Bxf4 axb5 15 Bxb5+ Nbc6 16 Bd6 Be6 17 Qe2 Kd7 ∓) 13...Qxf4 14 g3 (14 Qh5+?! Kd8 15 Rxe7 Kxe7 16 Re1+ Kd8 17 g3 Qf6 18 Qxd5+ Bd7 19 Nd4 Kc8 20 Ne6 Re8 21 Bf5 Bxe6 22 Bxe6+ Kc7 23 Qa5+ b6 24 Qd5, Salaske-Schreyer, East Germany 1983, when 24...Rd8 is strong, as 25 Qxa8? Nc6 traps the queen) 14...Qf6 15 Nc7+ Kd8 16 Nxa8 b6 (16...Nbc6?! 17 Be4 Bd7 18 Bxd5 Nxd5 19 Qxd5 Kc8 20 Rad1 Rd8 21 Qd6 Qxd6 22 Rxd6 looks pretty miserable for Black, by the time he captures the knight, assuming he manages to, White will have gained a decisive advantage on the kingside, Malmström-Kozlov, corr. 1985) and now:

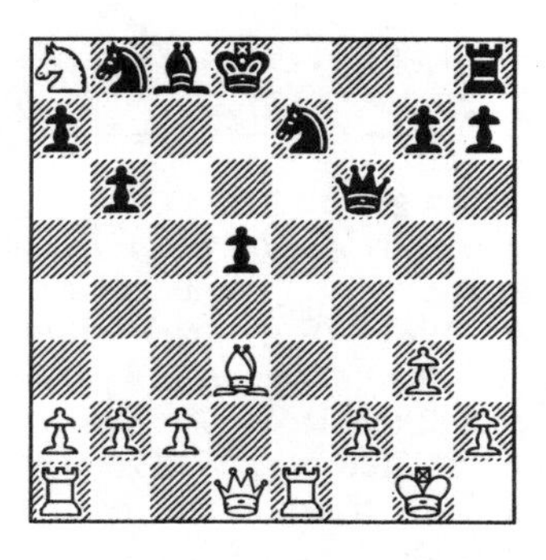

a1) 17 c4! Bb7 18 Nxb6 axb6 19 cxd5 ("White has three pawns to add to his rook, against two black pieces"—Bücker.) 19...Rf8!? (Black cannot afford to go pawn hunting: 19...Qxb2?! 20 Re2 Qa3 21 Bb5 Qc5 22 Bc6 Bc8 23 Rc1 Qd6 24 Qb3, the alternative is 19...Nd7!?, 20 Be4 Rf8 [20...Qxb2?! 21 d6 Nc6 22 Rb1 Qa3 23 Rc1 is strong] 21 Qd2 but with the queens on the board, the black king is a definite liability) 20 Qd2 Qd4!? (Black decides that exchanging queens is his best bet, as then his king may turn out to be strong in the centre) 21 Rad1 Nd7 22 Be4 (Personally, I would prefer 22 Qc2) 22...Qxd2 23 Rxd2 Nf5 24 Bg2 Nd6 (Black wants to find some dark squares for his knights, but White is on the ball) 25 Re6! Rf6 26 Rde2 Nc5 27 Rxf6 gxf6 28 b4 Na4 29 Re6 Ne8 30 a3 b5 31 Re4! and White aims at the h7-pawn, Tiemann-Kosten, email 2001. Black's position is difficult.

a2) 17 Qe2 (+/- *NCO*, although it doesn't say why—a computer assessment, perhaps?) 17...Nbc6 ("with a little advantage to Black" (Budovskis) 17...Bb7?? 18 Nc7) 18 c4!? (Suggested by Melchor, 18 b4 Re8 19 Qe3 Bb7 20 Nxb6 Nd4 21 f4 Qxb6—Malmström) 18...Nd4! (18...Re8?! 19 cxd5? [19 f4! Bb7 20 cxd5 avoids problems on f3] 19...Nd4 20 Qh5 Nf3+ 21 Kg2 g6! 22 Qxf3 [22 Qxh7 Ng5 wins] 22...Bh3+ 23 Kxh3 Qxf3 Black is better; 18...Bb7?! 19 cxd5 Nxd5 [after 19...Nd4 20 Qxe7+ Qxe7 21 Rxe7 Kxe7 22 Nc7, Black will recapture the d-pawn, but remains worse] 20 Be4 Nce7 21 Nxb6 axb6 22 Rad1 and White will probably regain the two pieces for his rook due to the pin) 19 Qxe7+ Qxe7 20 Rxe7 Kxe7 21 Nc7 dxc4 22 Bxc4 Black appears to have quite enough play for the pawn after 22...Rd8 23 Nd5+ Kf8! (23...Kd6 24 Ne3, and on 24...Bb7 25 Rd1) 24 Rd1 Nf3+, the weakness of the white kingside light squares is critical for Black's counterplay, 25 Kg2 Bg4 26 Rc1 Ne5 27 Ne3 (27 Rc3 Bf5) 27...Bf3+ 28 Kg1 Rd2 29 b4 g5 30 a4 Be4 31 h3 Nf3+ 32 Kg2 h5 and White's extra pawn is meaningless.

a3) 17 ♖xe7?! ♕xe7 18 ♗c4 ♗b7 19 ♗xd5 ♔c8 20 ♕g4+ ♘d7 saves the knight from immediate capture, but does not resolve the problem of how to extricate it, 21 ♕f5 (21 ♕f4 ♘c5 22 ♖d1 ♗xd5?! [22...♖d8! 23 ♗xb7+ ♔xb7 24 ♖xd8 ♕xd8 25 ♕f3+ ♔b8 is more straightforward] 23 ♖xd5 ♔b7 24 ♕f3 ♕e4 25 ♕xe4 ♘xe4 26 ♖d7+ ♔xa8 27 ♖xg7 and White has slightly better chances with his three pawns and active rook, for the knight, Van Gameren-Malmström, corr. 1999) 21...♖f8 22 ♗xb7+ ♔xb7 23 ♕d5+ ♔b8 24 a4 ♕c5 about equal, Malmström-Svendsen, corr. 1997.

b) 12...♔d7?? was not one of my better ideas from the first volume!

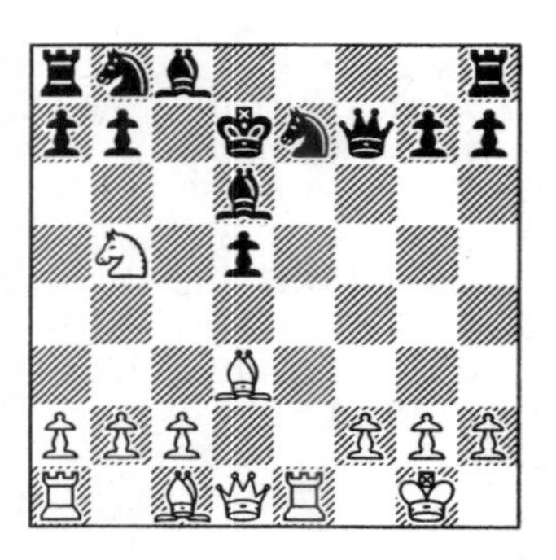

13 ♕g4+ ♔c6 14 ♕a4 ♖f8. Unfortunately, 15 ♗g5! wins: 15...♕xf2+ (15...♗c5 16 ♗xe7 ♕xf2+ [if 16...♗xe7 17 ♘xa7+ ♔c7 18 ♘b5+ ♔d8 19 ♕xa8 is possible, as the back rank is defended] 17 ♔h1 ♗h3 18 ♘c3+ [18 gxh3?? ♕f3 mate] 18...♔c7 19 ♘xd5+ ♔c8 20 ♕e4 wins; 15...♗xh2+ 16 ♔xh2 ♕h5+ 17 ♔g1 ♕xg5 18 ♘xa7+ ♔c7 19 ♘b5+ ♔b6? [Black prefers to get mated rather than lose a rook by 19...♔d8 20 ♕xa8] 20 ♕d4+ ♔c6 21 ♕c3+ ♔b6 22 ♕c7+ ♔a6 23 ♘d6+ ♔a7 24 ♕c5+ b6 25 ♕c7+ ♗b7 26 ♕xb7 mate, Strautins-Svendsen, corr. 1998) 16 ♔h1 ♔d7 (16...♗d7 17 ♗e3 ♕f7 18 ♘xa7+ ♔c7 19 ♕a5+ and mate) 17 ♘xd6+ ♘ec6 18 ♘b5 h5 19 ♕a3 ♖f6 20 ♖f1 1-0, Strautins-Melchor, corr. 1998.

c) 12...♗c5? 13 ♗e3 +/-

d) 12...♕f6? 13 ♕h5+ g6 14 ♗g5 (14 ♕g5 is also convincing) 14...♕xf2+ 15 ♔xf2 0-0+ 16 ♕f3 ♗c5+ 17 ♗e3 ♗xe3+ 18 ♖xe3 ♖xf3+ 19 ♔xf3, White has an extra exchange, Malmström-Niemand, corr. 1994/95.

13 ♘xd6 ♕xf2+ 14 ♔h1

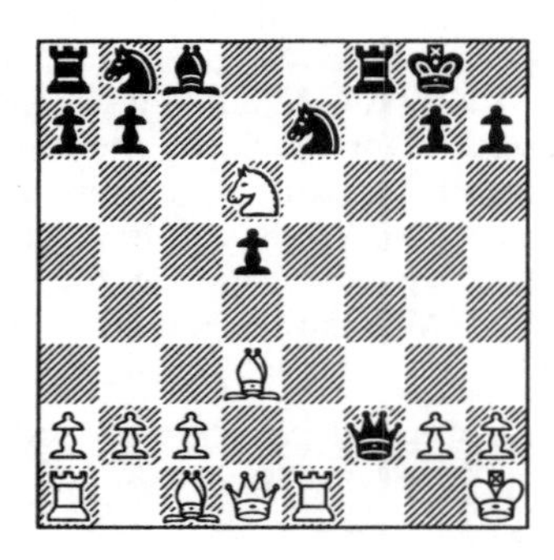

14...♗g4

The only reasonable try, as after 14...♕h4?!, Lambers-Kamitzky, corr. 1987, 15 g3 ♕f6 White wins as per the next game, 14...♕f6?! 15 ♘xc8 ♖xc8 16 ♕g4 ♘bc6 17 ♗g5 ♕d6 18 ♖e6 ♕c7 19 ♖h6 (19 ♖xe7 ♘xe7 20 ♕e6+ is also convincing) 19...♘g6 20 ♗xg6 hxg6 21 ♕e6+ 1-0, Malmström-Melchor, corr. 1997.

15 ♕d2!

15 ♗e3?! ♗xd1 16 ♗xf2 ♗xc2 17 ♗xc2 ♖xf2 18 ♖xe7 (18 ♗b3? ♘bc6 ∓ Elburg-Heap, corr. 1989) 18...♘c6 19 ♗xh7+ ♔xh7 20 ♖xb7, Elburg-Melchor, corr. 1988, when by 20...♖af8 followed by the doubling of rooks on the seventh, Black would draw comfortably.

15...♕h4

The endgame that follows 15...♕xd2 16 ♗xd2 ♘bc6 17 ♘xb7! favours White: 17...♖ab8 18 ♘c5 ♖xb2 19 ♘b3 (the rook is trapped!) 19...♗f5 20 ♗c1 (or 20 ♗c3) 20...♖xc2 21 ♗xc2 ♗xc2 22 ♗a3 ♖e8 23 ♖ac1, Black's compensation for the exchange is insufficient, Strautins-Grivainis/Hayward, corr. 1999.

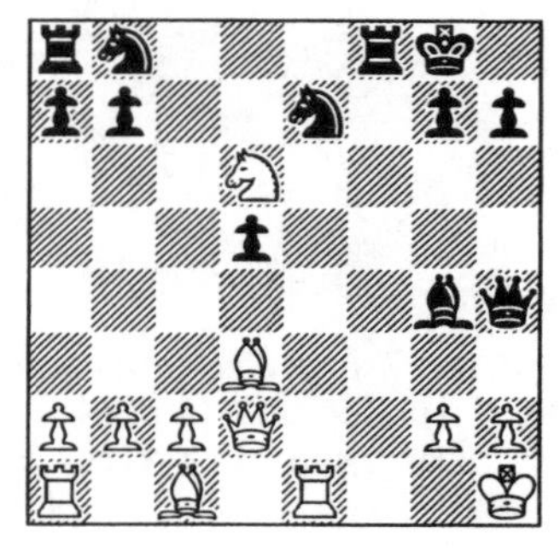

16 b4!

Strautins' idea. White prepares to bring his bishop to the a1-h8 diagonal, whilst at the same time b4-b5 can be a useful resource.

16 ♘xb7?! is too time-consuming, 16...♘bc6 17 b3 (others: 17 ♕c3 d4 18 ♕c4+ ♔h8 19 ♗d2 ♖f2 20 ♘d6 ♖af8 Strautins—the white king is short of defenders; 17 ♘c5 ♖f6! 18 c3 ♖af8 [18...♖h6!] 19 ♕e3 [19 ♔g1?? ♖f2-+ Malmström] 19...♘f5 20 ♗xf5 ♖xf5 21 ♕e6+ ♔h8 22 ♗e3 ♕xe1+! 23 ♖xe1 ♖f1+ 24 ♗g1 ♗xe6 25 ♖xe6 ♖1f6, unclear, Melchor) 17...♖ab8 (rather than 17...♖f6?! 18 ♗a3 ♖h6 19 ♗d6 covering h2) 18 ♘c5, Evans-Stummer, corr. 1994/95, and now Strautins suggests 18...♘d4! 19 ♔g1 ♖b6, swinging the rook over to the kingside, with a powerful attack. 18 ♘a5 is similar: 18...♘d4! 19 ♔g1 ♖b6 20 ♗b2 ♖h6 21 ♕xh6! ♘f3+ 22 gxf3 gxh6 23 fxg4 ♕xg4+ ½-½ Chorfi-Simmelink, corr. 1998.

16...♘bc6

16...♕f6? 17 ♕g5! ♕xa1 18 ♕xg4 ♘bc6 (18...♕f6 19 ♗g5 ♕xd6 20 ♗xe7 ♖e8 [20...♕d7 21 ♕h4] 21 ♗xh7+ wins) 19 ♕e6+ ♔h8 20 ♗g5 ♕xa2 21 ♘f7+ ♔g8 22 ♖f1 ♘d4 23 ♗xh7+ ♔xh7 24 ♕h3+ ♔g6 25 ♘e5+ ♔xg5 26 ♕g4+ ♔h6 27 ♕h4 mate, Strautins-Clarke, corr. 1997.

17 ♗b2 ♖ad8

17...♖f2?! 18 ♕c3 ♕g5 19 ♖f1 ♖af8 20 ♖xf2 ♖xf2 21 ♕e1! ♕f4 22 b5 ♗h3 23 ♗c1 ♕f6 24 bxc6 ♕xa1 25 cxb7 ♘c6 26 gxh3 1-0, Strautins-Destrebecq, corr. 1997.

18 ♕c3 ♕g5 19 ♘xb7 ♖b8

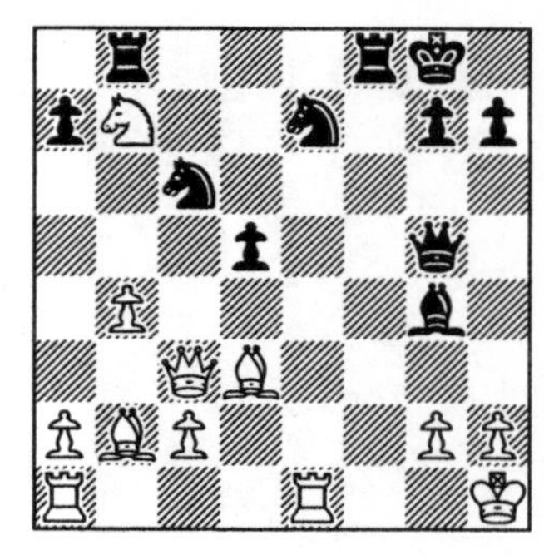

20 b5!

Reaching the critical position for this variation, Ruggeri Laderchi-Radovic, corr. 2000. Black has drawing chances after 20 ♘a5 ♘xb4 21 ♕xg7+ ♕xg7 22 ♗xg7 ♖f7 23 ♗c3 ♘xd3 24 cxd3 ♗f5 due to the opposite-colour bishops.

20...♖xb7 21 bxc6 ♘xc6 22 ♗a3!

22 ♖f1 is also annoying. 22...♖f6! is the best chance, (22...♖xf1+? 23 ♖xf1 is losing, for instance 23...♘b4 24 ♗a3 a5 25 ♕c5) 23 ♖xf6 ♕xf6 24 ♕xf6 gxf6 25 ♗xf6 ♘b4 26 ♗c3 (26 ♖b1 ♗c8 27 ♖e1 ♘xd3 28 cxd3 ♗f5) 26...♘xd3 27 cxd3 ♗f5 28 d4 ♖b1+, drawing.

22...♖c8 23 ♗a6 ♘b8 24 ♕xc8+ ♗xc8 25 ♗xb7 ♗xb7 26 ♖e8+ ♔f7 27 ♖xb8

27 ♖e7+ ♔g6 28 ♖xb7 ♘c6 29 ♗f8 ♕f5 30 ♖xg7+ ♔f6 also favours White.

27...♗c6

27...♗a6? 28 ♖e1 ♕d2 29 ♖f8+ ♔g6 30 ♖e6+ ♔h5 31 h3 threatens mate.

28 ♖c8 ♗b5 29 ♖e1

29 ♖c7+ ♔g6 30 ♗b2 ♕d2.

29...♕d2 30 ♖f8+ ♔g6 31 ♖e6+ ♔h5 32 h3

Again Black is in serious trouble. Black desperately needs an improvement here.

C222 11 ♘c4!?

This guarantees some advantage, although Black may be able to pick his way through the minefield, and draw.

11...dxc4

There is no reason to decline this piece and, anyway, neither 11...♗c7? 12 ♗g5 ♗e6, Tiemann-Criel, corr. 1984, when 13 ♕e2 h6 14 ♕xe6 ♕xe6 15 ♖xe6 hxg5 16 ♖ae1 gives an advantage, nor 11...♗c5? 12 ♗e3 ♗b4 13 ♘e5! with advantage, Kozlov-Nyman, corr. 1990/92, are worth the bother.

12 ♗xc4 ♕g6!?

After this, the best Black can hope for, given correct play, is a drawable ending, a pawn down.

12...♗xh2+! leads to a safer equality. 13 ♔xh2 ♕xc4 14 ♗g5 0-0

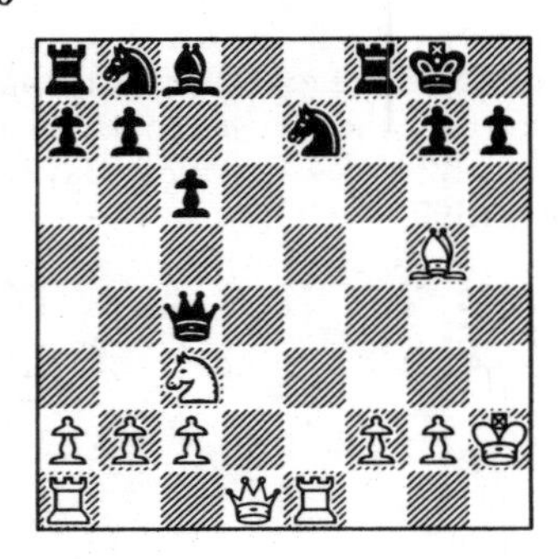

15 ♗xe7 (15 ♖xe7?! is inferior, 15...h6 16 ♖e4 ♕f7 17 ♗h4 ♗f5 18 ♖e3 ♘a6 and I prefer Black, Logunov-Heap, corr. 1994/94) 15...♕f4+! (15...♖e8? 16 ♘e4! ♗e6 17 ♗g5 ♗f7 18 ♘d6 ♖xe1 19 ♕xe1 with advantage, Kozlov-Littleboy, corr. 1991) 16 ♔h1 ♖e8 17 ♗a3 (17 ♕h5! looks stronger, 17...♕f7 [17...♗d7! 18 ♖ad1 ♕f5 is safer] 18 ♕xf7+ ♔xf7 19 ♗a3 and Black suffers from his lack of queenside development, Budovskis-Elburg, corr. 1994/95) 17...♗e6! (must be the best move, 17...♕f7?! 18 ♕f3 [18 ♘e4 is also dangerous, 18...b6 19 ♘d6 ♖xe1+ 20 ♕xe1 ♕h5+ 21 ♔g1, Black has problems with his undeveloped queenside, Budovskis-Kinnes, corr. 1980] 18...♗e6 19 ♘e4! [19 ♕xf7+ ♗xf7 20 ♖xe8+ ♗xe8 21 ♘e4 ♗g6 is equal, Jackson-Malmström, corr. 1990] 19...♕xf3 20 gxf3 ♗f7 [20...♗d5?? 21 ♘f6+] 21 ♘d6 with advantage Budovskis-Krongraf, corr. 1992; 17...♖xe1+ 18 ♕xe1 ♕h6+ 19 ♔g1 ♗e6 20 ♖d1 ± Elburg-Nyffeler, corr. 1989) 18 ♘e4 (not 18 ♖xe6?

♕h4+; 18 ♔g1 [to protect the f-pawn] 18...♘a6 19 ♖e3 ♗g4 20 ♕d2 ♖xe3 21 fxe3 ♕e5, play is level, Adamczyk-Borrmann, corr. 1997; 18 ♖e4 ♕h6+ [18...♕xf2?? 19 ♕d6 wins the bishop, but 18...♕f7 is strongest, keeping the white king on a worse square] 19 ♔g1 ♘a6 20 ♕d4 ♕g6 [20...♖ed8!? 21 ♕e5 ♖e8 22 ♖ae1 ♗f7 23 ♕xe8+ ♗xe8 24 ♖xe8+ ♖xe8 25 ♖xe8+ ♔f7 26 ♖e7+ ♔g8 27 ♖e8+ drawing, Budovskis-Krantz, corr. 1994/95] 21 ♖ae1 ♘c7 22 ♗d6 ♘d5 equalising completely, Budovskis-Kozlov, corr. 1994/95) 18...♘a6 (18...♘d7 19 ♘d6 ♖f8 20 ♖xe6 ♕h4+ 21 ♔g1 ♕xf2+ drawing, Viola-Downey, corr. 1999) 19 ♘d6 ♖ad8?! (19...♖f8! is stronger, as 20 ♖xe6? ♕h4+ 21 ♔g1 ♕xf2+ 22 ♔h1 ♖f4 23 ♖e4 ♖xe4 24 ♘xe4 ♕h4+ 25 ♔g1 ♕xe4 wins a pawn) 20 ♘xe8! (but not 20 ♕c1? ♕xf2 21 ♘xe8 ♖d4!) 20...♖xd1 21 ♖axd1 ♗d5 22 ♘d6, Herbst-Magee, corr. 1999, and now 22...h6 23 c4 ♗xc4 24 ♖e4 ♕g5 menaces ...♕h5+, and keeps play level.

Not 12...♕xc4?! 13 ♕xd6 ♕f7 14 ♗g5 0-0 15 ♗xe7 ♕xf2+ 16 ♔h1 ♖e8 17 ♗h4 with advantage, Budovskis-Morgado, corr. 1977/79.

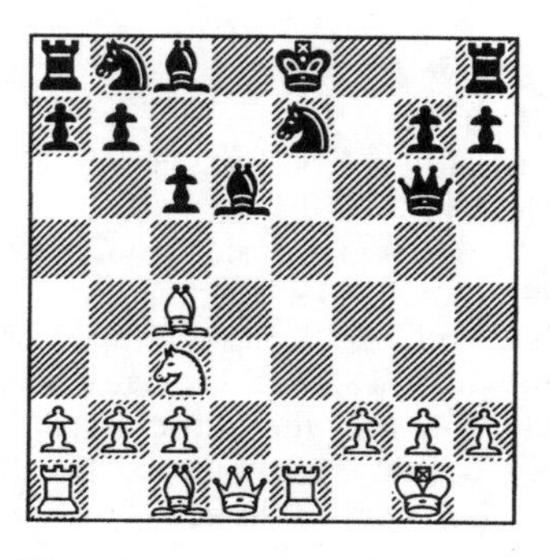

13 ♘e4

This leads to a strong attack.

13 ♗e6 poses less problems, 13...♗xh2+ (13...♗xe6? is clearly worse, 14 ♕xd6 ♔f7 15 ♘e4 h6 16 ♘c5 ♖e8, Svendsen-Clarke, corr. 1989, when 17 ♘xe6 ♘d5 18 ♘d8+ gives him a good pawn more. 13...♗c5!? is an alternative, though, 14 ♗xc8 ♗xf2+ 15 ♔xf2 0-0+ 16 ♔g1 ♘xc8 with a minimal white advantage.) 14 ♔xh2 ♗xe6 15 ♕d6 0-0 (15...♘f5!? 16 ♕xe6+ [16 ♖xe6+?? ♔f7 17 ♕c7+! ♔xe6 18 ♗g5 is unclear, but not 17 ♖xg6?? hxg6+] 16...♕xe6 17 ♖xe6+ ♔f7 is completely equal.) 16 ♕xe6+ (16 ♕xe7 ♗d7 17 ♘e4 ♗f5!? =; 16 ♖xe6 ♕h5+ 17 ♔g1 ♘f5 18 ♕f4 ♕f7 19 ♖e4 ½-½ Grobe-Kozlov, corr. 1994/96) 16...♕xe6 17 ♖xe6 ♘f5 (In this endgame White's bishop should allow him a very slight edge) 18 ♗f4 (there is no lack of alternatives: 18 ♗g5 ♘d4?! [Black should take more care, 18...h6 19 ♗f4 ♘d7 is level.] 19 ♖e4 c5 [19...♘xc2? 20 ♖c1 and the knight is lost] 20 ♗e7 ♖c8 21 ♘d5 and White is getting on top, Herbst-Maltez, corr. 1999; 18 ♖e4 ♘a6 19 b3 ♘c5 20 ♖c4 ♘e6 21 ♘e4 ♖ad8 22 g4?! Too aggressive, 22...♘fd4 23 ♗e3 ♘f3+ 24 ♔h3 ♘e5 and the weakness on f3 allows Black the better prospects, Kozlov-Downey, corr. 1994/97; 18 ♘e2 ♘a6 with a level endgame, Dravieks-Downey, corr. 1992) 18...♘a6 (18...♘d7) 19 ♖d1 ♖ad8 20 ♖xd8 ♖xd8 21 ♖e5 ♘d4 22 ♘e4 and White has a tiny plus, Melchor-Malmström, corr. 1994/95.

13...♗c7 14 ♗g5

14 ♘g5?! is not so worrying, 14...♖f8 15 ♗d3 (15 ♘e6? ♗xe6 16 ♖xe6 ♖f6 17 ♗d3 ♕f7 led to an easy win for Black in Diepstraten-Rittenhouse, corr. 1989; White has

almost no compensation for the piece) 15...♗f5?! (15...♕h6 16 g3 ♕f6 is stronger) and now, instead of 16 ♕e2? ♗d6 17 ♗xf5 ♖xf5, Black is consolidating, Logunov-Downey, corr. 1994/95, 16 ♘e6! ♘a6 17 ♘xf8 ♔xf8 18 ♕f3 is far less clear.

14...♗f5! 15 ♗xe7

15 ♕f3!? ♘d7? (15...♗xe4! 16 ♖xe4 ♕xg5 17 ♕f7+ ♔d8 18 ♖d1+ ♘d7 19 ♗e6 and now Black has the resource 19...♗d6 because of the weak white back rank) 16 ♗xe7 ♔xe7 17 ♘d6+ 1-0, Krustkains-Borner, corr. 1997.

15...♗xe4

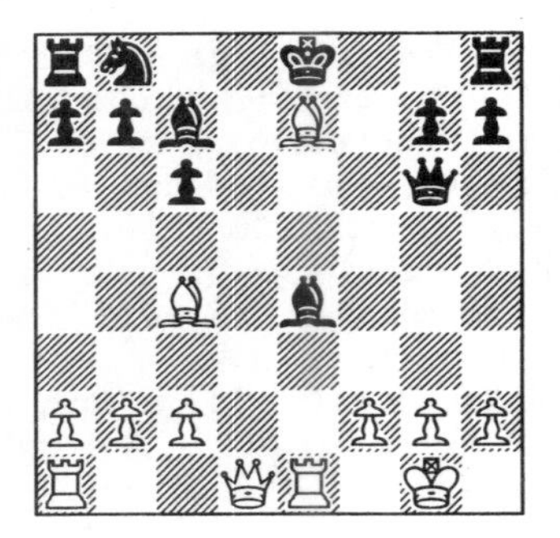

16 ♗g5!

This move is very dangerous for Black.

16 f3 may lead to no more than a draw 16...♔xe7 17 ♖xe4+ ♔f8 18 ♕e2 (18 ♕d2!? ♕d6 19 ♕g5! ♘d7 [19...♕xh2+?? 20 ♔f1 leaves Black without defence to the white mating threats] 20 ♖ae1 with a strong attack, Sénéchaud-Gåård, corr. 1994/95, although Black may be able to defend with 20...b5 21 ♖e7 ♕d4+ 22 ♔h1 bxc4) 18...♘d7 19 ♖e1 ♘f6 20 ♖e7 ♗b6+ 21 ♔h1 ♘d5 22 ♗xd5 cxd5 23 ♖e6 ♕h5 24 g4 ♕f7, De Jong-Downey, corr. 1994/95, and White should take the draw here, by 25 ♖e7 ♕g6 26 ♖e6 ♕f7 etc.

16...♘d7

This is Black's only move.

a) 16...♕xg5? 17 ♖xe4+ ♔f8 18 ♕f3+ ♕f6 19 ♖ae1! (mate on e8 will be a recurring theme) 19...♘d7 (19...♕xf3?? 20 ♖e8 mate) 20 ♕e3 ♗e5 21 f4 ♘b6 22 ♖xe5 ♘xc4 23 ♕c5+ ♘d6 24 ♖e6 and Black is crushed, Budovskis-Niemand, corr. 1994/95.

b) 16...h6? 17 ♕g4 hxg5 (17...♗xh2+ 18 ♔xh2 hxg5+ 19 ♔g1 ♔d8 20 ♖xe4 is also hopeless) 18 ♖xe4+ 1-0, Pape-Logunov, corr. 1994/95, as 18...♔d8 19 ♖d1+ ♗d6 20 ♖xd6+ ♕xd6 21 ♖d4 wins the queen plus some pawns.

c) 16...♔f8? 17 ♕g4 ♗f5 18 ♕e2 ♗d7? (18...♗e6 fends off the mate, but 19 ♕xe6 ♕xe6 20 ♖xe6 is not very encouraging for Black) 19 ♕e7 mate, Budovskis-Clarke, corr. 1994/95.

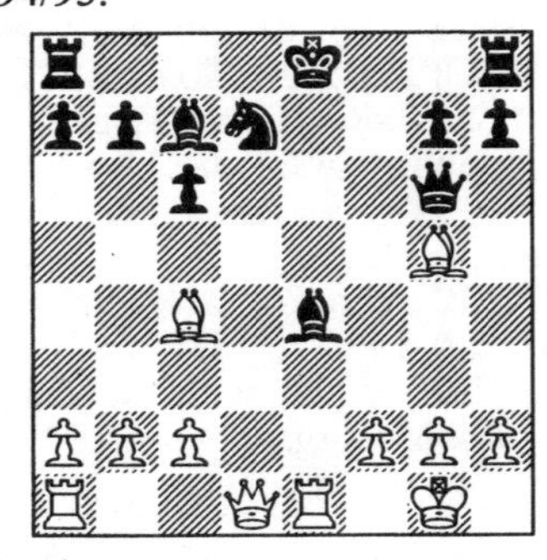

17 ♕g4!

Others:

a) 17 ♗f7+? ♕xf7 18 ♖xe4+ ♘e5! 19 ♗f4 0-0 ∓

b) 17 ♕f3!? ♘c5 18 ♖ad1? (18 b4! ♗e5!? 19 bxc5!? [19 ♕g4] 19...♗xf3 20 ♖xe5+ ♔f8 21 ♗e7+ drawing) 18...♖f8 19 ♕e3 ♖f5 20 h4 ♗f4! and the white attack soon ran out of ammunition, De Jong-Kozlov, corr. 1994/95.

c) 17 ♕d4!? ♘f6 18 ♖xe4+! ♘xe4 (18...♕xe4?! 19 ♗xf6 ♕xd4

20 ♗xd4 0-0-0 21 ♗xg7 is more pleasant for White, although Black has drawing chances) 19 ♖e1 ♕xg5 20 ♖xe4+ ♔f8 21 ♕d7 ♕c1+ 22 ♗f1 ♗b6 23 ♕e7+ (or 23 g3!? when 23...h5? 24 ♔g2! wins, so Black must try 23...h6) 23...♔g8 24 ♕e6+ ♔f8 25 g3 h5 26 ♖e5 (26 ♖f4+ ♕xf4 27 gxf4 ♖h6 28 ♕f5+ as per the previous note) 26...♖h6 27 ♖f5+ ♖f6 28 ♖xf6+ gxf6 29 ♕xf6+ ♔e8 ½-½, Kozlov-Heap, corr. 1994/97.

17...♘c5

17...♘f6? 18 ♕e6+ ♔f8 19 ♖xe4 ♖e8 20 ♕xe8+ ♕xe8 (20...♘xe8?? 21 ♗e7 mate) 21 ♖xe8+ ♔xe8 22 ♖e1+ ♔d8 and with the bishop pair, and an extra pawn, White is winning, Budovskis-Malmström, corr. 1994/95.

18 b4!

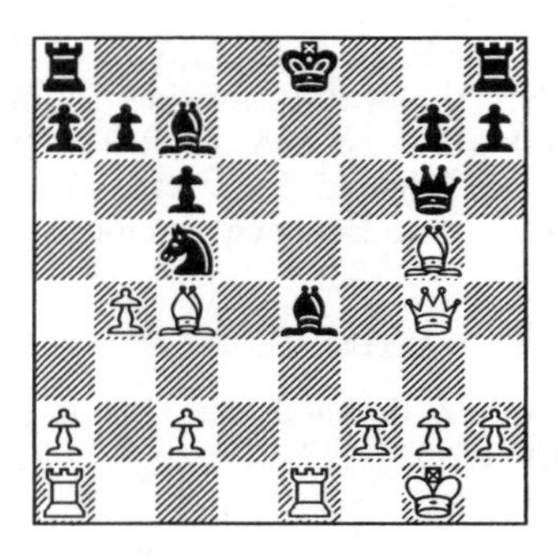

18...h5!

18...♗xh2+? 19 ♔f1! (not 19 ♔xh2 h6 [to capture the bishop with discovered check] 20 ♕h3 b5! [20...♕xg5? 21 bxc5 wins] 21 bxc5 bxc4 22 f3 0-0 and the king escapes!) 19...h6 20 bxc5 hxg5 21 ♕xe4+ (21 ♖xe4+ ♔f8 22 ♖b1 ♖h4 23 ♕f3+ ♕f6 24 ♖xb7 is also strong) 21...♕xe4 22 ♖xe4+ ♔f8 23 ♖d1! (White threatens both g3, trapping the bishop, and ♖d7; the immediate 23 g3? allows 23...♗xg3 24 fxg3?? ♖h1+) 23...♖h4 24 ♖xh4 gxh4 25 g3! Anyway! 25...hxg3 26 ♔g2 gxf2 27 ♔xh2 and White will win, Budovskis-Downey, corr. 1994/97.

19 ♕h4

19 ♕h3!? also promises some advantage, 19...♕xg5 20 bxc5 ♕e5 21 ♗d3 0-0 22 ♗xe4 ♔h8 and Black has some problems with his king, but the opposite-colour bishops, and weakness of f2, make a draw possible, Budovskis-Strautins, corr. 1998.

19...♗d8!

19...♔d7? 20 ♖ad1+ ♔c8 21 bxc5 ♖e8 22 ♗e2 ♖h8 23 ♗g4+ 1-0, Budovskis-Heap, corr. 1994/96.

20 bxc5 ♗xg5 21 ♕xe4+

21 ♖xe4+? ♔f8.

21...♕xe4 22 ♖xe4+ ♔d7

White has an extra pawn, and the more active position, but the opposite-colour bishops, and weak c5-pawn, make a win problematic.

23 h4

23 f4 ♗f6 24 ♖ae1 ½-½ Sireta-Doplmayr, corr. 1995, as 24...♖ae8 25 ♗e6+ ♔c7 26 ♔f2 ♗e7.

23...♗f6 24 ♖b1 ♔c7 25 ♗f7 ♖hd8 26 ♗xh5 ♖h8 27 ♗g4 ♖xh4

White has a slight plus, Strautins-Grivainis, corr. 1997.

Summing up: As about the best Black can hope for after 9...♗c5 is a position with a pawn less, and 9...♗d6 is also difficult, unless Black finds improvements here, I think that 9...♗e6, as well as the line with 8...♗b4!? and 9...♘f6 (or the other way round), are worth investigation.

6 3...♘c6 and other third move alternatives for Black

1 e4 e5 2 ♘f3 f5 3 ♘xe5

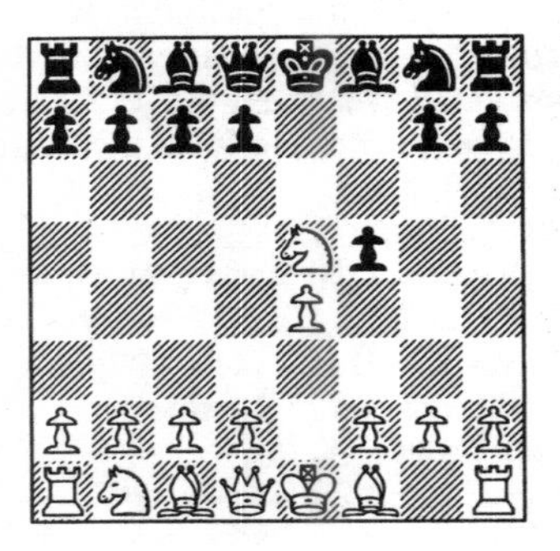

Many Latvian players are not happy to accept the small positional disadvantage, or potential endgame, sometimes entailed by playing 3...♕f6 (considered in the first five chapters of this book) and prefer to continue in a real gambit spirit. Black has several riskier third move options that appeal to these free spirits, of which the strongest, and most popular, is 3...♘c6. Although many of the positions that arise are objectively better for White, they tend to be messy and not without practical prospects for the tactically minded second player, especially considering their undoubted surprise value in over-the-board games, and with the clock ticking away.

A 3...♘c6
B 3...♕e7
C 3...d6
D 3...♘f6

A 3...♘c6!?

Introduced in 1873 by both the Scot G.B.Fraser and the Dane H.Möller. White faces an important choice, and we further sub-divide:

A1 4 ♘xc6
A2 4 ♕h5+
A3 4 d4

White has one other, rare, move in 4 ♘c4? fxe4 5 d4 exd3 6 ♗xd3 ♘f6 7 0-0 d5 8 ♖e1+ ♗e7 9 ♘e3 0-0 10 b3? ♗b4! 11 ♗d2 ♗d6 12 c3 ♘e5, when the white kingside begins to look a bit exposed: 13 ♗f1?! ♘fg4! 14 f3 ♕h4 15 h3 ♘xf3+ 16 gxf3 ♕f2+ 0-1, Bosbach-Hector, Dinard 1985.

A1 4 ♘xc6

White damages the black pawn structure.

4...dxc6

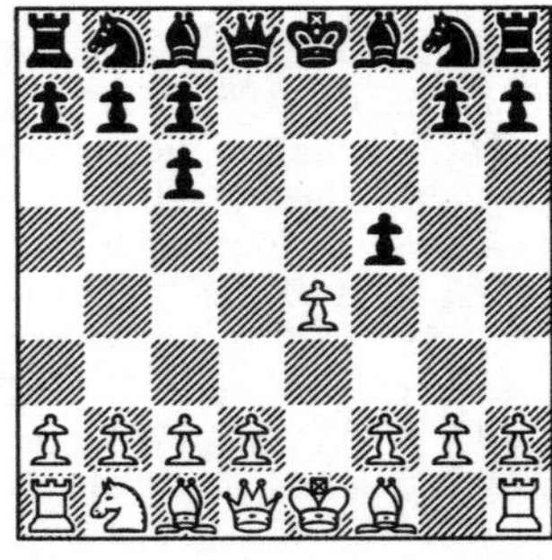

So, Black is a pawn down, what compensation does he have for it?

Well, firstly, he will be able to develop quickly and easily, and secondly, he will have pressure down the open central files, especially after he castles queenside. White has a wide variety of potential fifth moves as Black has no threats as yet—he cannot even take the e4 pawn.

5 ♘c3

There are many alternatives:

a) 5 d4 and,

a1) 5...♕h4, as White no longer possesses his king's knight there is no reason why Black should not avail himself of this aggressive post. Meanwhile, e4 is attacked. 6 e5 (this leaves the white centre rather static, 6 exf5!? transposes to (e), below) 6...♗e6 (6...♕e4+?! ignores the first rule of development, 7 ♗e2!? [7 ♗e3 f4 8 ♘d2 ♕d5 9 ♗xf4 ♕xd4 10 ♗g3 ♕xb2 11 ♗d3 also favours White, Wehr-Schirmer, corr. 1989] 7...♕xg2 8 ♗f3 ♕h3 9 ♗g5 ♗e7 [9...♗d7!?] 10 ♕d3 [menace: 11 ♗xc6+] 10...f4 11 ♗xf4 ♗f5 12 ♗e4 ♕xd3 13 cxd3 and White enjoys a two pawn advantage, Lindstrom-Holm, corr. 1910) 7 c3 (White adds protection to his d-pawn, 7 ♘c3 ♗b4 8 ♗d3? ♕xd4 9 0-0 0-0-0 ∓ Bengtsson-Hector, Swedish ch 1985; not 7 g3?? ♕e4+; 7 ♗e3?!, Massong-Hayward, corr. 1986, allows 7...f4 8 ♗d2 [8 g3?! fxg3 9 fxg3?? ♕e4] 8...0-0-0 9 c3 g5 and Black has good prospects) 7...0-0-0 8 ♘d2! (8 ♗d3 c5 9 ♗e3 c4 10 ♗c2 g5? [10...f4 11 g3!] 11 ♘d2? [missing 11 g3 ♕h6 12 ♕d2 ♗e7 13 h4, winning a further pawn] 11...f4 12 ♘f3 ♕h5 13 ♗d2 g4 with a powerful initiative, Ruben-Sorensen, Copenhagen 1876; 8 ♗e2 c5 [there is also the hyper-aggressive 8...f4?! 9 ♘d2 g5 10 ♘f3 ♕h6 11 h4 ♗e7, Bernard-Hector, Montpellier 1985, when 12 g3 is critical] 9 ♕a4 [9 g3?! ♕e4 10 f3 ♕c6 11 0-0? cxd4 12 cxd4 ♖xd4 ∓ Gilnicki-Monneal, corr. 1953; 9 ♗e3?! f4 10 g3 fxg3 11 fxg3 ♕e4 12 ♔f2 still favours White] 9...♔b8 10 ♗f3 cxd4 11 ♕b5?! [11 ♗e3! keeps the d-pawn] 11...♗c8 12 0-0 d3 13 ♗e3 a6 14 ♕b3 ♘h6 15 g3 ♕e7 16 ♗xh6 gxh6 17 ♘d2? ♕xe5 ∓, Hingst-Stummer, corr. 1991) 8...c5 would then meet 9 ♘f3 (9 ♕c2 h6 10 b3 ♘e7 11 ♗b2 ♘c6 12 ♗c4 ♗xc4 13 ♕xf5+ ♔b8 14 bxc4 cxd4 with counterplay, Müller-Sinke, corr. 1982; 9 g3 is also good, 9...♕e7 10 ♘f3 with the threat of ♗g5, 10...h6 11 ♗g2 g5 12 0-0, Von Otte - Drill, Hessen 1991, and White has almost consolidated) 9...♕e4+ 10 ♕e2 h6 11 ♗e3 g5 12 dxc5! to use the d4-square, 12...♘e7 13 ♘d4 with advantage, Kastner-Drill, corr. 1989.

a2) In the game Punt-Sinke, corr. 1986, 5...c5!? 6 d5 ♘f6 7 ♗b5+ ♗d7 8 ♕e2 fxe4 9 ♘c3 ♗e7 10 ♗g5 0-0 worked out OK.

a3) but 5...♘f6?! is wrong, 6 e5 ♘e4 (on this square Black will have to beware of the move f3, while on 6...♘d5 White will hit Black with a later c4, 7 ♗e2 ♗e6 8 0-0 ♕d7 9 c4 ♘b6 10 b3. White has managed to set-up a large centre, and the black knight is misplaced, De Gleria-Smits, Hengelo 1995) 7 ♗e3 ♗e6 (7...c5?! is not recommended, 8 g3?! [8 d5!] 8...cxd4 9 ♕xd4 ♗d7 10 ♗c4, Duras-Neumann, Hilversum 1903, 10...♗c6 11 ♕xd8+ ♖xd8 12 f3 ♘c5 and Black does not have much for his pawn) 8 g3 (8 f3! is obviously critical, 8...♘g5 9 ♗d3 with a great game) 8...♗d5 9 f3 ♘g5 10 ♗g2 ♘e6 (this is a good blockading square for a knight) 11 ♘c3 (11 ♕d3!?) 11...♗b4 12 0-0 ♗xc3 13 bxc3 f4!? and Black has kingside play, Bering-Henrichsen, Copenhagen 1993.

a4) 5...♕f6!? This is important as it may transpose from what could become Black's best line against 4 d4 (4...♕f6) 6 e5 ♕f7 (6...♕g6 is no better, 7 ♕f3 [7 ♘c3!? ♗e6 {7...♗b4!?} 8 ♘e2-f4 exploits the black queen's position] 7...♗e6 8 ♗d3 ♘e7 9 c4?! [9 ♘c3] 9...0-0-0 10 ♘c3?! [the d-pawn is a problem even after the superior 10 ♗e3 ♕f7 11 ♘d2 h6, intending ...g5 and ...f4] 10...♖xd4 11 ♘e2, Kyroelae-Provoost, Finland-Holland corr. 1980, and now 11...♖d8 is fine) 7 f4 (this move has the merit of controlling g5, 7 ♘d2 [the knight goes to f3 to add defence to the d-pawn] 7...♗e6 8 ♘f3 h6 9 ♗d3 0-0-0 10 0-0 g5 and Black has a good position and can combine the kingside pawn advance with pressure on d4, Downey-Zemitis, corr. 1997) 7...♗e6 8 ♗e3 0-0-0 9 c3 g5!? was interesting, Nyman-Strautins, corr. 1990, although the straightforward 9...♘e7 10 ♗d3 ♘d5 is a good alternative.

b) 5 e5?! ♗e6 (the game Nicolaiczuk-From, Copenhagen 1981, took a different path here: 5...♕d4!? 6 ♕e2 [6 ♗e2?! ♕xe5 7 0-0 ♗e6?, Lauritsen-Henrichsen, Copenhagen 1993, placing too many pieces on the file! 8 ♖e1 and White wins material, 7...♗d6 8 g3 ♗d7 is perfectly good] 6...♗e6 7 ♘c3 [7 c3 may be stronger, 7...♕d7 8 d4 c5 9 ♗e3 with typical play, Van't Land-Van Bree, corr. 1982] 7...♘h6 8 ♕e3 ♗c5 9 ♕xd4 ♗xd4 10 f4 0-0-0 11 d3 g5! 12 ♘e2 ♗b6 13 h3 g4! intending to answer 14 h4 with 14...g3! and play on the kingside) 6 d4 ♕d7 (6...♕h4 transposes to (a) above) 7 ♗e3 0-0-0 8 ♕d2 ♘e7 9 ♕a5 ♔b8 (9...a6!? 10 ♗xa6 ♘d5! is interesting,) 10 ♘c3, Capablanca-Corzo, Havana 1901, (10 d5? b6) 10...c5!? 11 dxc5 ♘c6 with some play for the pawn.

c) 5 ♗c4 ♕h4 6 d3 (the most solid choice, 6 ♕e2 fxe4 7 ♘c3 ♗f5 8 ♗xg8?! ♖xg8 9 ♕c4 0-0-0! 10 d3 [10 ♕xg8? ♗c5 11 g3 ♕g4 12 ♕f7 ♖f8 is strong, but White contrives to lose his queen anyway] 10...♗e7 11 ♘xe4 ♗xe4 12 ♕xe4? ♗b4+ 13 c3 ♖ge8 ∓ Zagt-Sinke, corr. 1982; 6 0-0?! White should avoid committing his king like this, 6...fxe4 7 d3 ♗d6 [7...♗g4!?] 8 g3 ♕h3 9 dxe4 ♗g4!? [9...♘f6] 10 f3 h5? 11 ♗xg8? [Black's attack is not quite sound, and can be beaten off with 11 fxg4 h4 12 ♖f8+! vacating the f1 square for the bishop: 12...♗xf8 13 ♗f1 ♗c5+ 14 ♔h1 hxg3 15 ♗xh3 ♖xh3 16 ♔g2] 11...h4! 12 fxg4 hxg3 13 ♗f7+ ♔d7 14 ♕e2 ♗c5+ 0-1, Tschurgulia-Steinikow, USSR 1988) 6...♘f6 7 ♘c3 fxe4 (7...♗c5!?) 8 ♕e2 ♗g4 9 ♕e3 ♗d6?! (9...♗f5) 10 dxe4 ♗e5 11 ♗d2 ♖f8 12 g3 ♕h5 13 f4 ♗d6 14 e5 0-0-0 15 0-0 (15 ♕xa7 is even stronger) 15...♗e7 16 ♖f2 with advantage, Hazai-Hector, Berlin 1985.

d) 5 ♕h5+!? g6 6 ♕e2 ♗g7! (very dashing, 6...♘e7) 7 exf5+ ♘e7 8 fxg6 ♗f5 9 gxh7 ♕d7 10 ♕h5+? ♗g6 11 ♕h3 ♘f5, Black certainly has a large lead in development for his four pawns, 12 ♕d3 ♕f7 13 ♕c4 ♕f6 14 ♘c3 0-0-0 15 d3 ♖de8+ 16 ♗e3? ♖xe3+! 17 fxe3 ♘xe3 18 ♕a4 ♖f8 19 ♗e2? ♕xc3+! 20 bxc3 ♗xc3 mate, N.N.-Keres, corr. 1940.

e) 5 exf5 ♗xf5 6 d4 (6 d3 ♕d7 7 ♗e3 ♘f6 8 ♘c3 0-0-0 9 ♗e2 ♗d6 10 ♕d2 ♖he8 11 0-0-0 is a sensible approach, Vajda-Pessi, Odorheiu Secuiesc 1993) 6...♕h4 7 ♗e3 (7 ♗d3!? ♗g4 8 ♗e2 ♘f6 9 h3 ♗e6 ±,

Hermann-Thiede, Berlin 1988) 7...0-0-0 8 ♗d3 (8 ♘d2 ♖e8 9 ♘c4 [9 ♘f3?? ♖xe3+] 9...c5 10 ♗e2 cxd4 11 ♕xd4 ♕xd4 12 ♗xd4 ♗xc2 13 ♘e3 ♗e4 = Jacobs-Hector, Seville 1986) 8...♘h6!? 9 0-0 (9 ♗xh6?! ♖e8+) 9...♗g4 10 ♕d2 ♗d6 11 h3 and Black has some activity for the pawn, Prat-Melchor, corr. 1985.

f) 5 d3 will almost certainly transpose into the main line, once White plays ♘c3.

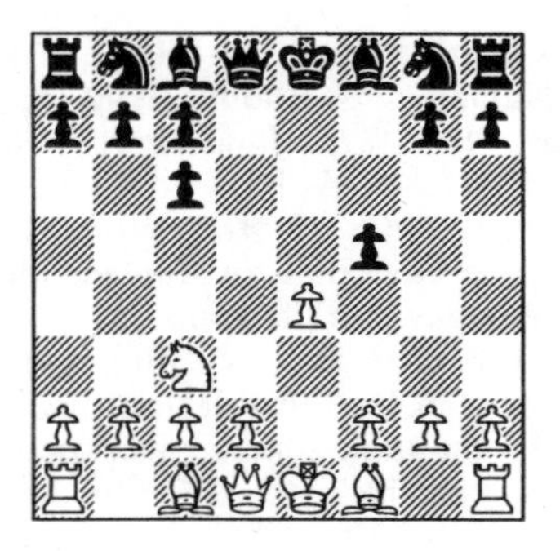

5...♗c5

As White has defended his e-pawn there would be no point playing 5...♕h4 at this juncture, as 6 g3 and ♗g2 is possible. The text is perhaps the most logical, controlling d4 and taking aim at f2, but there is, again, a wide choice:

a) 5...♘f6

a1) 6 exf5 (it seems unnecessary to give back a pawn with 6 d4? fxe4 7 ♗g5 ♗f5 8 ♗c4 ♗e7 9 0-0 ♕d7 = Kinnes-Sprod, corr. 1971/72; but 6 d3 fxe4 [6...♗b4] 7 ♘xe4 ♗e7 8 ♗e2 0-0 9 0-0 is also good, Grivainis-Atars, corr. 1979/80) 6...♗xf5 7 d4 ♗b4 8 ♗d3 ♕e7+! (8...♗g4?! 9 f3 ♗h5 10 ♕e2+ ♔f7 11 ♗c4+ ♘d5 12 0-0 ♖e8 13 ♘e4 [or 13 ♕f2 ♗xc3 14 bxc3 with advantage Elburg-Goldt, corr. 1984] 13...♔g8 14 ♕f2 ♔h8 15 ♗g5 ♗e7 16 ♗xe7 ♖xe7 17 ♖fe1 and White has an extra pawn, and the better position, Malmström-Jansson, corr. 1986) 9 ♗e3, Heap-Stummer, corr. 1994/96, 9...♘e4! 10 ♕f3 0-0 with threats.

a2) 6 e5 ♘g4 7 d4 c5 8 d5!? (8 h3 cxd4 9 hxg4 dxc3 10 ♕xd8+ ♔xd8 11 ♗g5+ [11 ♗d3!?] 11...♗e7 12 0-0-0+ ♔e8 White has a slight edge, Melchor-Bonte, corr. 1998) 8...♘xe5 9 ♕e2 ♕e7 10 ♗f4 ♘g6 (best, 10...♘f7?! 11 ♘b5 g5 12 ♘xc7+ ♔d8 13 ♘xa8 gxf4 14 0-0-0 ♕xe2 15 ♗xe2 ♗d6 16 ♖he1 and Black has no easy method of attacking the a8-knight, Nilsson-Weber, corr. 1990) 11 ♗xc7 ♔d7 12 ♕xe7+ ♗xe7 13 d6 ♗xd6 14 ♗xd6 ♔xd6 15 0-0-0+ ♔c7 16 ♗c4 White has a slight plus, Melchor-Turian, corr. 1995.

b) 5...♕e7?!, popular with some, but it doesn't really fit in with Black's attacking ideals. 6 d3 (6 ♗c4 ♘f6 [6...♗e6 7 ♗xe6 ♕xe6 8 0-0 0-0-0 9 ♕f3!? {9 exf5 ♕xf5 10 d3 ± Kapitaniak-Andersen, corr. 1978} 9...f4? 10 ♕xf4 with advantage, Sinke-van Eijk, corr. 1984] 7 0-0! fxe4 8 d3, Strelis-Harju, corr. 1984, 8...♗g4 9 ♕d2 0-0-0 10 ♖e1, White will win the e-pawn; 6 ♕e2 is always a good idea, White will try to play an endgame, 6...♘f6 7 d3 [7 e5 ♘d5?! Jean-Destrebecq, corr. 1981, when White can play the boring 8 ♘xd5 cxd5 9 d4 and the black position is deprived of its dynamism, but 7...♘g4 is better] 7...fxe4 8 ♘xe4 ♘xe4 9 ♕xe4 ♗e6, Elburg-Oren, corr. 1994/96, 10 ♗e3 and Black has less than nothing for the pawn) 6...♘f6 7 ♕f3 (7 ♗g5 ♗d7 8 f3?! [8 ♕e2] 8...0-0-0 9 ♗e2 h6 10 ♗e3 ♔b8 11 0-0 g5! 12 ♕e1 f4 13 ♗f2 h5 gave Black a nice kingside pawn roller in Janikowski-

Kapitaniak, Poland 1979; 7 ♕e2 fxe4 is also fine, as above) 7...fxe4 8 dxe4 ♗g4 9 ♕f4 0-0-0 10 f3 ♗e6 11 ♗d3 ♕b4 12 a3 with advantage, Harper-Magee, corr. 1991.

c) 5...♗b4 6 ♗c4 (6 e5?! ♕d4 7 ♕e2 ♗e6, Purins-Strelis, corr. 1974/77, but 6 exf5!) 6...♕d4!? (6...♗xc3!? 7 bxc3 ♕h4 is possible) 7 ♗xg8?! (7 ♕h5+ g6 8 ♕e2 is stronger) 7...♗xc3! 8 0-0 ♗xb2 9 c3 ♗xc3 10 ♕b3 ♗xa1 11 ♕f7+ ♔d8 12 ♕f8+, drawing by perpetual a few moves later, Stayart-Bullockus.

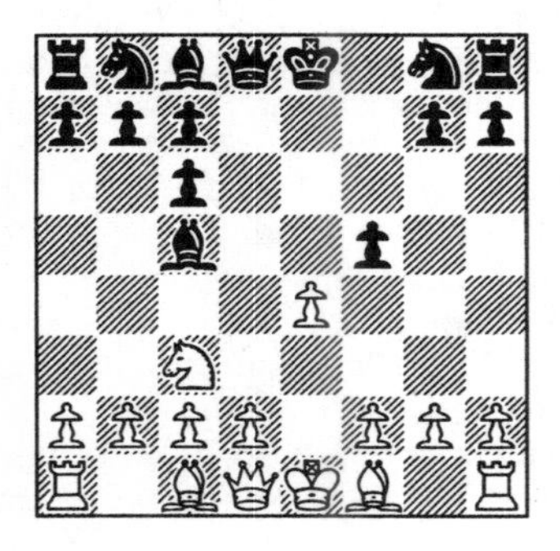

6 d3

Once again, there are several alternatives:

a) 6 ♕f3 ♕e7 (6...♘e7!? worked out well for Black in Dries-Sinke, corr. 1982: 7 ♗c4 ♖f8 8 0-0?! [8 d3 ♘g6] 8...♕d4! 9 ♗b3 [9 ♕e2 f4 10 d3 f3 11 gxf3 ♘g6] 9...fxe4 10 ♕h5+ [10 ♕xe4 loses f2, but was the better choice] 10...g6 11 ♕h4 ♗f5 ∓) 7 ♗e2! (7 d3 ♘f6 8 ♗e3 ♗xe3 9 ♕xe3 0-0 10 0-0-0?! [10 ♗e2] 10...fxe4?! [10...♘g4 11 ♕g3 f4 12 ♕f3 ♘e5 provides genuine positional compensation] 11 ♘xe4 [11 f3! exploits the e-file pin] 11...♘g4 12 ♕e1? [12 ♕g3] 12...♘xf2! 13 ♘xf2 ♕xe1 14 ♖xe1 ♖xf2 15 ♖e2 ♖f8, draw, Bullockus-Stayart, corr. 1977) 7...♘f6 8 exf5 g6! 9 d3! ♗xf5 10 ♗e3 ♗b4 11 0-0!? ♗xc3 12 bxc3 ♗g4 13 ♕g3 ♗xe2 14 ♖fe1 ♘d5 15 c4 ♘xe3 16 ♖xe2 0-0-0 17 ♖xe3 ♕a3 is better for White, though soon drawn in Lamoureux-Kosten, Paris, 1994.

b) 6 ♕h5+ g6 7 ♕e2 ♘e7 8 d3 (8 ♘a4!? ♗d4 9 e5 ♕d5 10 f4 a6 11 c3 ♗a7 12 d4 ♗e6, White is better, but the offside knight is awkward, Downey-Stamer, corr. 1994/97) 8...♗e6 (8...fxe4?! 9 dxe4 ♗d4 10 ♕d3 ♗e6 11 ♘e2 ♗g7 12 ♘f4 with advantage Budovskis-Stummer, corr. 1990) 9 ♗e3 ♗b4 (9...♗xe3?! 10 ♕xe3 ♕d6 11 g3 0-0 12 f4 with advantage Budovskis-Morgado, corr. 1974/77) 10 g3 0-0 11 ♗g2 fxe4 12 dxe4 b5, Grobe-Stamer, corr. 1994/95, 13 ♕d3, White is, not for the first time in this section, a whole pawn to the good.

c) 6 ♕e2 is very similar to the above, except that Black does not have the dark-squared weakness on the kingside. 6...♘e7 (6...♕e7?! Black doesn't really want to play an ending a pawn down, 7 d3 ♘f6 [7...♗d7 8 exf5 0-0-0 9 ♕xe7 ♗xe7 10 ♗e2 ♗xf5 11 0-0 ♘f6 12 ♗e3 with advantage, Budovskis-Grobe, corr. 1977] 8 ♗g5 ♗d4 9 exf5 ♗xf5 10 ♕xe7+ ♔xe7 11 ♗e2 h6 12 ♗d2 and White is a pawn up, Krustkains-Downey, corr. 1991) 7 ♘a4! (7 d3) 7...♗b6 (with the black pawn on g7, 7...♗d4?! is worse, 8 c3 ♗f6 9 e5 and the bishop is gettting kicked around the board) 8 ♘xb6 cxb6 9 d3 0-0 10 ♗d2 ♗e6 11 ♗c3 and White has the bishops to add to his extra pawn, Daurelle-Felber, corr. 1997.

d) 6 ♗c4? Strangely, this is a recommendation of *BCO*, which assesses the position as ± after White's seventh move. I can only think that someone was looking at the wrong position!

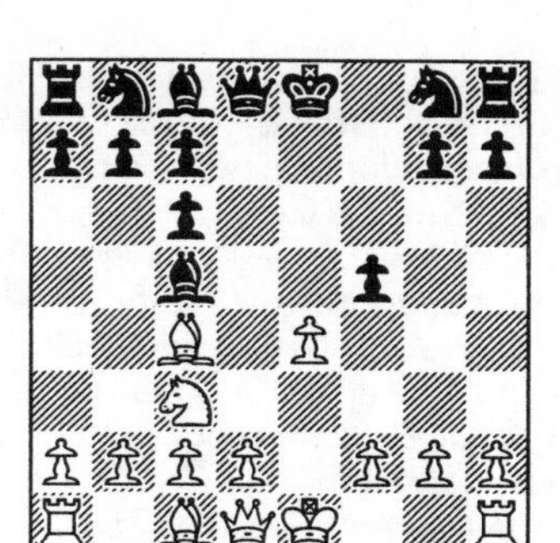

6...♗xf2+ 7 ♔f1 (7 ♔xf2 may represent the best chance, 7...♕d4+ 8 ♔e1 [8 ♔g3? really tempts fate, 8...f4+! 9 ♔xf4 ♘e7 10 ♕e2? {10 ♗f7+ allows White to struggle on a bit} 10...♖f8+ 0-1, Schuttrich-Grobe, corr. 1976] 8...♕xc4 9 d3 ♕e6 10 ♕e2 ♘f6, Burk-Leisebein, corr. 1981, and I really feel that White should take this opportunity to go into the equal endgame by 11 exf5 ♕xe2+ 12 ♔xe2 ♗xf5) 7...♗d4! (the best square for the bishop. 7...♘e7 is good too, 8 d3 ♗b6 [8...♗d4!] 9 ♕e2 f4?! [9...fxe4] 10 ♕h5+ ♘g6 Mathieu-From, corr.; 7...♗b6?! 8 ♕f3 ♕f6 [perhaps best, 8...♘f6 9 d3 ♘g4 10 exf5 ♗xf5, Marquez-Micheloud, corr. 1974/75, 11 ♗f7+ ♔xf7 12 ♕xf5+ =; 8...♕d4 9 d3 ♗d7? {better 9...♘e7} 10 ♗g5 ♘f6 11 ♖e1 0-0-0 12 e5 ♘g4 13 e6 and White is on top, Jedlicka-Walther, corr. 1975] 9 d3 ♗d7 10 ♗f4 0-0-0 11 e5 and White has avoided the worst, Hernandez-Garcia Camejo, corr. 1989) 8 ♗xg8 (8 ♕f3!? ♘e7 [or 8...♕h4] 9 d3 ♖f8 ∓; 8 d3 ♕f6 9 e5 What else? 9...♕xe5 10 ♗d2 ♗d7 and, exceptionally, it is Black who has the extra pawn, Randa-Payot, corr. 1997) 8...♖xg8 (8...♕f6!? is also possible) 9 ♕h5+ g6 10 ♕xh7 ♗e6 11 d3 ♕f6 12 ♔e2 0-0-0 13 ♗f4 ♖d7 14 ♕h3 ♗xc3 15 bxc3 fxe4 ∓ Denaro-Faraoni, corr. 1992.

e) 6 ♗e2 ♘f6 7 e5? (7 d3 transposes to the main line) 7...♕d4 8 0-0 ♕xe5, Pedersen-From, Denmark 1974, is fairly level.

6...♘f6

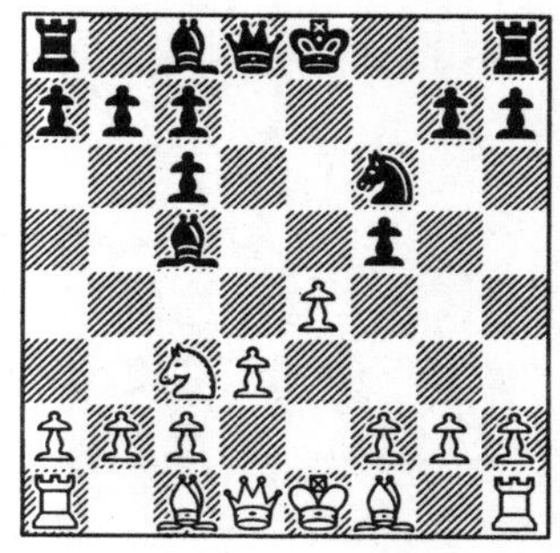

7 ♗e2

In the game Bertram-Stummer, corr. 1991, White played the inferior 7 ♗e3?! ♗xe3 8 fxe3 fxe4 9 ♗e2?! (White can maintain a small plus by 9 ♘xe4 0-0 [9...♘xe4? 10 ♕h5+ g6 11 ♕e5+ ♔f7 12 dxe4 is strong for White] 10 ♘f2) 9...♘d5!? 10 ♕d2 exd3 11 ♕xd3 ♘xc3 (11...♕g5) 12 ♗h5+!? g6 13 ♗xg6+ hxg6 14 ♕xg6+ and had an attack that was probably sufficient to draw, and ultimately won.

7...0-0 8 0-0 fxe4

Alternatively, there is 8...♗d4 9 ♗f3 (a better way of defending e4 than 9 ♗g5 ♗xc3 10 bxc3 fxe4 11 ♗xf6 ♕xf6 12 dxe4 ♕xc3 13 ♕d3 ♕e5 14 ♕e3 g5!?, stopping f4, and limiting White's advantage, Incelli-Elburg, corr. 1992) 9...♕d6 (9...♕e7 10 ♘e2 ♗e5 11 ♘g3 ♗xg3 12 hxg3 fxe4 13 dxe4 ♗e6 14 ♕e2 with a solid pawn more, Harper-Stummer, corr. 1991) 10 exf5 ♗xf5 11 ♗e3 (11 ♘e4—White should not be afraid of exchanges) 11...♗e5 12 g3 ♗xc3 13 bxc3 ♘d5

14 ♕d2 ♗h3, Vargha - Schultz Pedersen, corr. 1979, Black is close to equality.

9 ♘xe4!

To exchange the last two knights. 9 dxe4 is not as good, 9...♕e8 (or 9...♕e7 10 ♗c4+ ♗e6 11 ♕e2 b5! 12 ♗xe6+ ♕xe6 13 ♗g5, Paul-Walther, East Germany 1975, Black should have no problems, i.e. 13...♖ae8 14 ♗xf6 ♖xf6 15 ♖ae1 ♖ef8) 10 ♗c4+ (10 ♗f3 ♕e5!? [10...♕g6] 11 g3 ♗h3 12 ♗f4 ♕e6 13 ♖e1? ♖ad8?! [13...♘g4! is more incisive, 14 ♗xg4 ♗xg4 ∓] 14 ♕e2 [14 ♕c1 ♘g4 15 ♖e2 defends] 14...♘g4 15 ♗xg4?? ♗xg4 16 ♕f1 ♗h3 17 ♕e2 ♖xf4 18 gxf4 ♕g6+ 19 ♔h1 ♕g2 mate, Svendsen-Downey, corr. 1989) 10...♔h8 11 ♗e3, Schuetze-Bondick, corr. 1983, when Black's simplest line was perhaps 11...♗xe3 12 fxe3 b5 13 ♗d3 ♕e5 and the extra white pawn doesn't count for too much.

9...♘xe4 10 dxe4 ♕h4

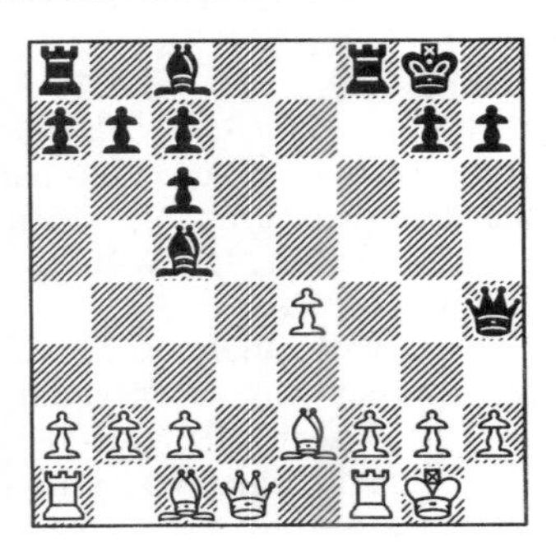

11 ♗c4+

11 ♗e3!? is a simple solution, 11...♗xe3 12 ♗c4+ ♔h8 13 fxe3 ♗g4 14 ♕d4 and White exchanged both sets of rooks to exploit his passed e-pawn(s), Legemaat-Van de Velden, corr. 1996.

11 ♗f3 is more passive, 11...♗e6 12 ♕e2 b5 13 b3 ♗d4 14 ♖b1 and Black's compensation for the pawn is minimal, Brinck Claussen-Schultz Pedersen, Copenhagen 1996.

11...♔h8 12 ♗e3!

Not 12 ♕e2? ♗g4 13 ♕e1 ♖ae8 with strong threats, nor 12 ♕e1? ♗g4 13 ♗e2 (best, if 13 ♗e3? ♗f3! 14 gxf3? ♗d6 15 f4 ♖xf4 mating; if 13 ♗d3 ♖ae8 menaces both ...♗f3, and ...♖e5-h5) 13...♖xf2? (pretty, but not correct, 13...♗xe2! 14 ♕xe2 ♖ae8 wins the e-pawn, with advantage) 14 ♖xf2 ♖f8 15 ♗f3 ♖xf3 16 gxf3 (16 ♗e3! is nasty, 16...♗xe3 17 ♕xe3 and Black's weak back rank scuppers him) 16...♗xf3 17 ♗e3? (if White wants to play for a win, 17 ♕d2! is the move, evacuating e1 for the king) 17...♕g4+ 18 ♔f1 ♕h3+ 19 ♔g1 ♕g4+ draw, Doncevic-Hermann, Bundesliga 1988.

12...♗g4

12...♗xe3 13 fxe3 ♗g4 14 ♕d4 transposes to the note to move eleven.

13 ♕d3 ♖ad8

After 13...♗d6 14 f4 ♖ad8 15 e5 White reminds Black that he has a large kingside pawn majority: 15...♗c5 (15...♗xe5?? 16 fxe5 ♖xd3?? 17 ♖xf8 mate) 16 ♕c3 and Black's case is pretty hopeless, Epstein-Walsh, corr. 1998.

14 ♕c3 ♖f3?

This fails miserably, 14...♕e7 is much better, although Black's dreams of attack are no more.

15 gxf3 ♗xf3 16 ♗e6

The problem, Black has no checks.

16...♗d4

16...♗d6 17 e5.

17 ♕a5

Keeping an eye on g5, and winning, Blaskowski-Stamer, corr. 1988.

A2 4 ♕h5+ g6 5 ♘xg6

White goes for the win of material, which will involve his queen straying away from the defence of her king, although by now it is probably too late to change tracks. 5 ♘xc6?! was played in a game of Keres' considered in A1).

5...♘f6

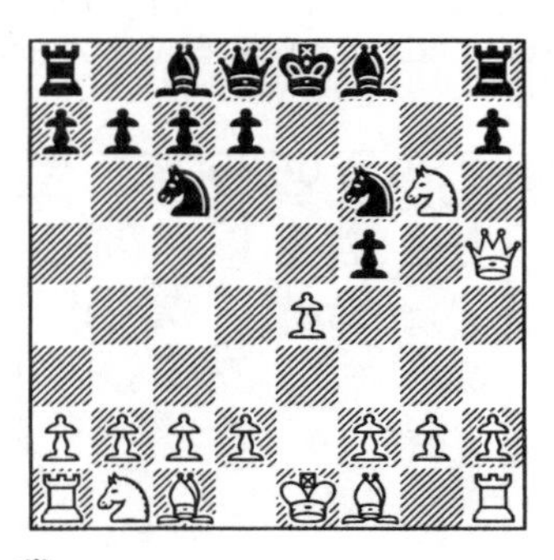

6 ♕h3

It is far from certain that this is stronger than 6 ♕h4, although this last does allow 6...♖g8?! (in addition to the 6...hxg6!? 7 ♕xh8 dealt with later, and 6...d6?! transposing into C) with the following lines:

a) 7 ♘xf8 ♖g4 and

a1) 8 ♕h6 ♖xe4+ with a further sub-division:

a11) 9 ♗e2! ♕e7 10 ♘c3 (10 ♘xh7!? ♖xe2+ [10...♘xh7? 11 ♘c3 ♖e6 12 ♕h5+ ♔d8 13 ♘d5 ♕g7 14 ♕h4+ ♘e7 15 ♘f4 ♖c6 16 c3 ♖h6 17 ♕g3 ♕h8 18 d4, and White had consolidated in Kellerer-Stummer, corr. 1991] 11 ♔d1 ♘g4 [11...♘xh7? allows 12 ♕h5+] 12 ♕g6+ ♔d8 13 ♕g8+ forcing off queens, 13...♕e8 14 ♕xe8+ ♖xe8 15 ♖f1, Vita-Houthuijzen, corr. 1991, when 15...♖h8 16 h3 ♖xh7 17 hxg4 fxg4 offered the best chances) 10...♖xe2+ (10...♘d4 11 ♘xe4 ♕xe4 12 0-0 ♘xe2+ 13 ♔h1 ♘g4, Meshkov-Sukhin, USSR 1977, 14 ♕h4! ♔xf8 15 f3 with extra material) 11 ♘xe2 ♘d4 12 0-0 ♘xe2+ 13 ♔h1 d6 14 ♘xh7 ♘xh7 15 ♕h5+ ♔f8 16 d3 ♘xc1 17 ♖axc1 and White has the better chances, Atars-Morgado, corr. 1976.

a12) 9 ♔d1? ♘g4 10 ♕h5+ ♔xf8 11 ♕xf5+ ♔g7 (11...♔g8 12 d3 d5 13 ♕f3 ♘xf2+ 14 ♕xf2 ♗g4+ 15 ♗e2 [if 15 ♔d2 then 15...♕g5+ 16 ♔c3 ♕g7+ 17 ♔d2 ♖f8 18 ♕c5 ♕g5+ 19 ♔c3 ♕e5+ is strong] 15...♗xe2+ 16 ♕xe2 ♖xe2 17 ♔xe2 ♕e8+ 18 ♔d2 ♕g6 19 ♔c3 d4+ 20 ♔b3 ♘a5+ winning, Capablanca-Corzo, Havana 1901) White is in a bad way: 12 d3 (12 b3 d5 13 ♗b2+ ♔g8 14 ♕f3 ♕h4 15 g3 ♕h5 16 ♗e2 ♘xf2+! 0-1, Gubić-Kurucin, Yugoslavia 1969, as 17 ♕xf2 ♖xe2 18 ♕xe2 ♗g4; 12 c3 d5 13 ♕f3 ♘e3+! 14 ♕xe3 ♖xe3 15 dxe3 ♕h4 gives good chances, Racz-Motyvay, corr. 1967/68; 12 ♗d3 d5 13 ♕f3 ♘xf2+ 14 ♕xf2 ♗g4+ 15 ♗e2 ♖xe2 16 ♕xe2 ♗xe2+ 17 ♔xe2 ♘d4+ 18 ♔d1 ♕g5 0-1, Llorach-Herranz, Barcelona 1981; 12 ♕f3 ♕h4 13 g3? ♘d4! 14 ♕g2 ♘xf2+ 15 ♕xf2 ♕g4+ 16 ♗e2 ♖xe2 17 h3 ♕e4 0-1, Nemo-Kleinerteufel, Sitzbad 1932) 12...d6! 13 ♕f3 ♘xf2+! 14 ♕xf2 ♗g4+ 15 ♗e2 (forced with the pawn on d6 instead of d5, 15 ♔d2? ♕g5+ 16 ♔c3 ♕a5+ mates) 15...♖xe2 16 ♕xe2 ♗xe2+ 17 ♔xe2 ♕h4 0-1, Krenzisty-Borgeson, Denmark 1964.

a2) 8 ♕h3 is less active, 8...♖xe4+ with the same choices:

a21) 9 ♔d1 ♘g4 10 ♕h5+? (tempting, but 10 ♕g3! is stronger, then 10...♕e7 11 ♗d3 d5 12 ♗xe4 dxe4, Bornemann-Mackenzie, New York 1877, when 13 h3 is simplest) 10...♔xf8 11 ♕xf5+ ♔g7 transposing to 8 ♕h6.

a22) and 9 ♗e2 ♘d4 10 ♘c3 (10 ♘xh7?! Mathe-Matwienko, corr. 10...♖xe2+ 11 ♔f1? [11 ♔d1] 11...♘g4 [11...♖e1+! 12 ♔xe1 ♕e7+ 13 ♕e3 ♘xc2+ wins the queen] 12 ♕h5+ ♔e7 13 ♕g5+ ♔f7 when 14 ♕xd8 ♖xf2+ would have been a draw) 10...♕e7 11 ♕d3 (11 ♘xe4!? ♕xe4 12 ♕d3, Grim-Sursock, Malta 1980, 12...♘xc2+ unclear) 11...♘xe2 12 ♘xe2 (12 ♘xe4?! ♘xc1 13 ♖xc1 ♔xf8 14 0-0 fxe4 is very pleasant for Black, Sukhareva-Shtejnikov, Voronezh 2000) 12...♔xf8 13 f3 ♖e5 14 ♔f2?! ♕c5+ 15 ♔f1, messy, Pegoraro-Elstner, Marostica 1995;

b) 7 e5! ♘xe5 (this is not satisfactory, but 7...♖xg6 8 exf6 ♕xf6 [8...♖xf6 9 ♗e2 ♕e7 10 0-0 is clearly advantageous for White, Morgado-Grobe, corr. 1972/75] 9 ♕xf6 [not 9 ♕xh7?? ♕e6+ 10 ♗e2 ♖h6 winning the queen, Weening-Goedhart, corr. 1982] 9...♖xf6 10 c3 d5 11 d4 ♗d7 12 ♗e2 and Black has no discernible compensation for the pawn, Den Hertog-Goedhart, corr. 1982) 8 ♘xe5 ♕e7 9 ♗e2 (9 d4? ♖g4 10 ♕h3 ♖xd4 11 f4 d6 12 ♗b5+ c6 13 0-0 dxe5 14 ♗e2 is very messy, Matwienko-Schuttrich, corr.; 9 f4 ♖g4 10 ♕f2 d6 11 d4 dxe5 12 fxe5 ♘e4 13 ♕g1 ♗e6 is not clear either, Black has a useful advance in development, Steuer-Stummer, corr. 1989) 9...♕xe5 10 d4 ♕e6 (10...♕a5+ 11 ♔d1! ♕b6 12 ♖e1 ♗e7 13 ♗g5 with advantage Müller-Elburg, corr. 1990) 11 ♗g5 ♗b4+ (11...♗e7 12 ♘c3 ♔d8 13 0-0-0 c6 14 ♗d3 with advantage van der Sterren-van der Lijn, Apeldoorn 1978) 12 ♘c3! (getting on with his development, 12 c3 ♗e7 13 ♘d2 d5 14 0-0-0? ♖xg5 15 ♕xg5 ♕xe2 16 ♖he1 ♕a6 17 ♖xe7+ ♔xe7 18 ♕g7+ is unclear, Magee-Stummer, corr. 1991) 12...♘d5 13 0-0-0! ♗xc3 14 bxc3 ♘xc3 15 ♗h5+ ♔f8 16 ♖he1 ♘e4 17 ♖xe4! fxe4 18 ♕f4+ ♔g7 19 d5 ♖f8 20 dxe6 ♖xf4 21 e7 1-0, Chmilewski-Stummer, corr. 1991.

Otherwise, 6 ♕xf5? is a mistake, 6...d6 7 ♕f3 hxg6 8 ♗b5 ♗d7 and the white pawns do not provide sufficient compensation for the piece, Ludvigsen-Sorensen, Aalborg 1872.

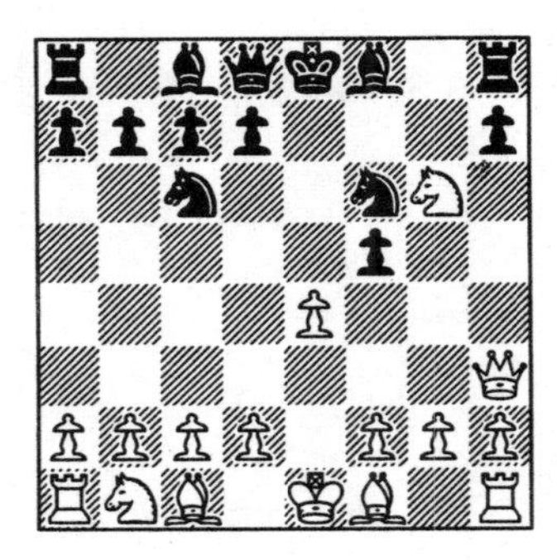

6...hxg6

a) 6...♖g8? does not have quite the same effect in this position, as there will be no ...♖g4 move, forking queen and e-pawn: 7 ♘xf8 (not now 7 e5?! as 7...hxg6 8 exf6 ♕xf6 9 ♘c3 ♗c5 10 ♗c4 ♕e5+ gives excellent compensation for the pawn, Steuer-Stummer, corr. 1990) 7...♕e7 (7...♖xf8 8 exf5 ♘d4 9 ♕e3+ ♕e7 10 ♕xe7+ ♔xe7 11 ♗d3 Steuer-Stummer, corr. 1989; Black will recapture the f5-pawn, but that still leaves him two down) 8 ♘xh7!?, a waste of time, but good anyway, 8...♘xe4?! (8...♘xh7) 9 ♕e3! d5 10 d3 f4 11 ♕xf4 ♘d4? when instead of 12 ♔d1?? ♖xg2! with complications, Petersen-Sorensen, Denmark 1873, 12 dxe4 must win.

b) Objectively 6...fxe4? is insufficient as Black obtains positions similar to the main line but without having captured the knight, but it's fun: 7 ♘xh8 (7 ♘xf8? ♖xf8 8 ♗e2 ♕e7 9 0-0 d5, Black has a strong centre, and two open files for the attack, 10 ♕h4 ♗e6 11 d3 ♘d4 12 ♗d1 0-0-0 13 ♗g5 ♘f5, Masur-Stamer, corr. 1979, 14 ♕f4 h6 with good chances) 7...d5 8 ♕g3 (White impedes Black from playing ...♗g7, and taking the knight. Others: 8 ♕b3 ♗g7 [8...♗d7!? is also interesting, the threat is ...♘d4, and 9 c3 {9 c4?! doesn't look right, 9...♘d4 10 ♕c3 c5 11 ♘a3 (11 d3 ♕e7 12 ♗e3 exd3, Champion-Foutelet, corr. 1982, 13 ♗xd3 and White must surely be better) 11...♕e7 12 ♘c2 ♘xc2+ 13 ♕xc2 d4 14 b4 ♗g7 15 bxc5, Gåård-Maltez, corr. 1999, when I think I would play 15...♗c6, ...0-0-0, and ...♗xh8, with compensation for the exchange} 9...♘e5!? {9...♗g7} 10 d4 exd3 Laganes-van Mulder, Paris 1983, 11 ♕xb7 is random but, assuming Black recaptures the knight fairly soon, he may not have enough compensation for the exchange; 8...♗c5?! 9 ♗b5 ♗d7 10 ♗xc6 ♗xc6 11 ♕g3 ♕e7 12 b4!? with advantage, Strautins-Gaard, corr. 1992] 9 ♗b5 ♗xh8 10 ♘c3 ♕d6 11 0-0 ♘g4 12 g3 ♗e6 with some play for the exchange, Melchor-Stummer, corr. 1990/91; or 8 ♕h4 ♘d4 9 ♘a3 when 9...♗xa3 is probably to be avoided, Black recaptures a rook, but loses his dynamic play, 10 bxa3 ♘xc2+ 11 ♔d1 ♘xa1 12 ♗b2 d4 13 f3, Kozlov-Alberts, corr. 1979, 13...♔e7!? 14 ♗xa1 ♕xh8 15 fxe4 with excellent winning chances; 8 ♕e3 ♘g4 9 ♕f4 ♘ce5 10 h3 ♗d6 11 ♔d1 ♕h4 12 d4 exd3 13 ♗e3 ♘xe3+ 14 ♕xe3 [14 fxe3 ♕h5+] 14...dxc2+ 15 ♔xc2 ♗f5+ 16 ♔c1 0-0-0 and Black will succeed in taking the knight while retaining his attack, Woods-Pierce, corr. 1916) 8...♕e7 (rather than 8...♘d4 9 ♘a3! [9 ♕e5+ ♘e6 10 d3 ♗d6 11 ♕c3 ♕e7 12 ♘d2?, Steuer-Stummer, corr. 1989; objectively, Black should take the draw by 12...♗b4 13 ♕e5 ♗d6] 9...♗xa3 [once again, Black regains material, but loses the initiative, 9...♗d6!? keeps the tension, 10 ♕g7 ♗e6, Schultz. Pedersen-Schuttrich, corr. 1977, 11 c3 ♘f5 12 ♗b5+!? c6 13 ♕xb7 cxb5 14 ♘xb5 with advantage, is one possibility] 10 bxa3 Jensen-Svendsen, corr. 1990, as 10...♘xc2+ 11 ♔d1 ♘xa1 12 ♗b2 with advantage, solving all of White's problems) 9 ♗b5 ♗g7 10 ♘g6 hxg6 11 ♕xg6+ ♔d7 12 a4 a6 13 ♗xc6+ ♔xc6, Jensen-Stummer, corr. 1990; Black has a lead in development, but it is insufficient.

7 ♕xh8 ♕e7

In the game Hindle-J.Littlewood, Hastings 1963, Black played the inaccurate 7...fxe4? and was horribly crushed: 8 d4! ♔f7 9 ♘c3 ♘xd4 (9...d5 10 ♗e3 ♗f5 offers better chances, although Black has little for the exchange) 10 ♗g5 ♘xc2+ 11 ♔d1 ♘xa1 12 ♗c4+ d5 13 ♘xd5 b5 (otherwise, 13...♗g7 14 ♕xd8 ♗g4+ 15 ♔c1 ♖xd8 16 ♘xf6+ ♗e6 17 ♗xe6+ ♔xe6 18 ♘h5 is also hopeless) 14 ♗xf6 ♕d6

15 ♕h7+ ♔e6 16 ♕g8+ ♔d7 17 ♗xb5+ c6 18 ♕f7+ ♗e7 19 ♗xe7 ♕e6 20 ♕xe6+ 1-0.

8 d3!

White must take great care, especially with his queen, who can find herself short of squares:

a) 8 ♕h4 fxe4 (or 8...♘d4 which is also good, 9 ♘a3 fxe4 10 c3 ♘f5 11 ♕h3 d5 with plentiful compensation, Elburg-Svendsen, corr. 1990, but 8...d5?! 9 ♗b5 ♔f7 10 ♗xc6, Kurtovic-Atars, corr. 1974, is less effective) 9 ♗b5?! (9 ♗e2 ♘d4 10 ♗d1 d5 11 0-0 ♘f5 with typical play against the white queen, reminiscent of Svedenborg's line, Vargha-Hammar, corr. 1974, but 9 ♕g3! is a better bet) 9...♘d4 10 ♘a3 c6 11 ♗f1 d5 12 ♕g5 ♗f5 13 ♕e3 ♘e6 14 ♗e2 d4 15 ♕g3 d3 16 ♗d1 ♗h6 17 ♕h4 ♕g7 18 g4 ♘f4 19 ♕g3 dxc2 20 ♘xc2 ♘d3+ 21 ♔f1 ♗f4, when the black pieces were crawling all over White's position, Diepstraten-Sinke, corr. 1984.

b) 8 ♘c3 defends the e-pawn, as per the main line, 8...♘b4 (8...d5?! 9 d4! [♗g5 is coming. Other moves are less promising: 9 d3 ♘b4 10 ♔d1 ♘g4 11 ♗e3 f4 12 h3 fxe3 13 hxg4 exf2 14 a3 dxe4!? 15 axb4 exd3 exposing White's king, Prust-Brondick, corr. 1987; 9 ♗b5 dxe4 10 ♗xc6+ bxc6 11 0-0 ♔f7 12 d3 ♗g7 13 ♕h4 ♗a6 14 ♖e1 ♖h8 and Black has attacking chances on the h-file, Steuer-Stummer, corr. 1989] 9...♘xd4 10 ♗g5! ♘xc2+ 11 ♔d1 ♘xa1 12 ♘xd5 and Black is lost, Rodriguez Capay - Acosta, Amici Sumus 1996) 9 d4!? ♘xe4 10 ♘xe4 ♕xe4+ 11 ♗e3 ♔f7? (Black naturally avoids 11...♘xc2+? 12 ♔d2 ♘xa1 13 ♗d3 [13 ♗h6?? ♕c2+] 13...♕e7 14 ♖e1, but 11...f4!? is feasible, as 12 ♗d3 ♘xd3+ 13 cxd3 ♕e7 14 0-0-0 fxe3 15 ♖he1 [it looks like the black pieces are going to be massacred before they move, but...] 15...e2! 16 ♖d2 ♔f7 17 ♖dxe2 ♕g5+ 18 ♔b1 ♕h5 swapping queens with good chances) 12 ♗d3 ♘xd3+ 13 cxd3 and White is well on top, Perez Cruz-Acosta, corr. 1995.

8...fxe4

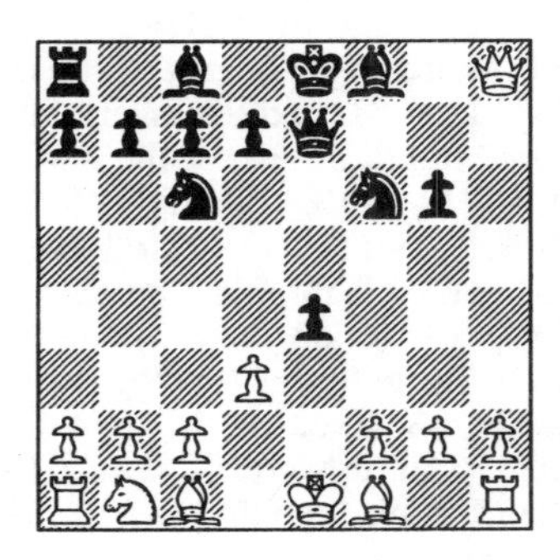

9 ♗e3

This is eminently sensible.

a) 9 ♔d1?! ♘g4 10 ♗e3 d5 11 ♗e2?! (11 h3) 11...d4! (11...♔f7 threatening ...♗g7, 12 ♗xg4 [12 ♕c3? d4! 13 ♕b3+ ♔e8 14 h3 {14 ♗xg4? ♗xg4+ 15 ♔c1 dxe3 16 ♕xb7 looks promising, but 16...♔d7 17 ♕xa8 exf2 and White is busted} 14...♘ge5 15 ♗f4 ♗e6 16 c4 dxc3 17 ♕xc3 ♘xd3 18 ♗xd3 ♖d8 with a venomous attack, Schumacher-Vetter, Porz-Wahn 1980] 12...♗xg4+ 13 ♔c1 exd3, Chmilewski-Svendsen, corr. 1990, when the obvious 14 ♘c3 may keep White on top) 12 h3 (12 ♗xd4? ♘xd4 13 ♕xd4 ♗g7 loses the h1-rook) 12...dxe3 13 hxg4 exf2 14 ♘d2 exd3 15 cxd3 ♗e6 16 ♖h7 ♗f7 17 ♘e4 0-0-0 18 ♘xf2 ♘d4 and the white major pieces are mere spectators to the action, Svendsen-Pape, corr. 1992.

b) 9 d4?! Although a tempo down on the Hindle-J.Littlewood game, this is still viable, 9...♘xd4! (9...♔f7?!, adding defence to the f6 knight, and preparing ...♗g7, evicting the white queen, 10 c3 [10 ♗g5!? ♗g7 11 ♕h4 ♘xd4 12 ♘c3?! {12 ♗c4+} 12...♘xc2+ 13 ♔d1 ♘xa1 14 ♗c4+ d5! {14...♔f8? 15 ♘d5 ♕e5 (15...♕c5?? 16 ♗xf6 ♕xc4 17 ♗xg7+ ♔xg7 18 ♕e7+ mates) 16 ♗xf6 ♗xf6 17 ♕xf6+ ♕xf6 18 ♘xf6 and the a1-knight will be lost} 15 ♘xd5 ♕d6 16 ♗xf6 ♗xf6 draw, Jensen-Magee, corr. 1991, as 17 ♕xf6+ ♕xf6 18 ♘xf6+ ♔xf6 19 ♔d2 =] 10...d5 11 ♗e2 ♗g7 12 ♕h4 ♗e6 13 ♗g5 and Black is an exchange down for nothing, Gåård-Pape, corr. 1994/95) 10 ♗g5 ♘xc2+ 11 ♔d1 ♘xa1 12 ♕xf6 ♕xf6 13 ♗xf6 ♔f7 14 ♗c3 d5 15 b3 ♗g7 16 h3 ♗e6 17 ♔c1, Gaard-Svendsen, corr. 1991, when 17...♘xb3+ 18 axb3 d4 19 ♗a1 ♗xb3 provides Black with an armada of queenside passed pawns

c) 9 dxe4!? is a simple solution to White's problems: 9...♕xe4+ 10 ♗e3 ♔f7 11 ♘d2 (11 ♘c3! ♗b4 12 0-0-0 is promising) 11...♕xc2 12 ♗c4+ d5 13 ♗b3 ♕d3 14 ♗d1, Burk-Leisebein, corr. 1982, 14...♗g4 with some play for the material.

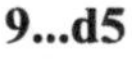

9...d5

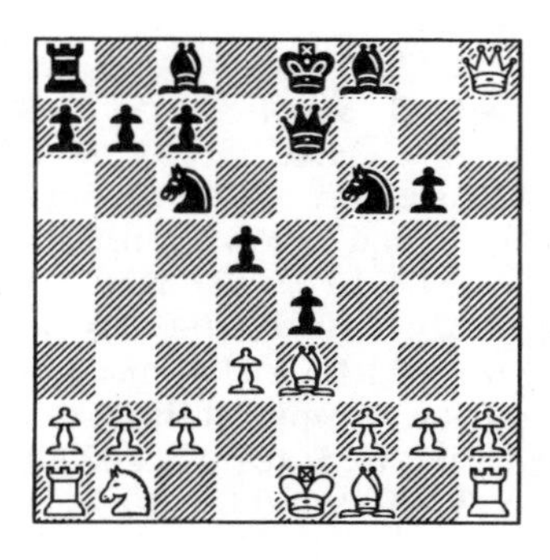

10 ♗c5!

Both finding space for the queen, and exchanging a piece, but there are other reasonable alternatives:

a) 10 ♗e2 exd3 (not 10...♗f5 11 d4 [11 dxe4!?] 11...0-0-0 12 ♘c3 ♘h5!? 13 ♗xh5 ♗g7 14 ♕h7 ♖h8 15 ♗xg6 ♖xh7 16 ♗xf5+ ♔b8 17 ♗xh7 ♗xd4 18 ♗xd4 ♘xd4 19 0-0-0 c5 20 ♘xd5 ♕xh7, Burk-Leisebein, East Germany 1982, when 21 c4 must be good for White) 11 ♗xd3, Geisler-Löffler, corr. 1992, and now Black should try 11...d4!? 12 ♗xg6+ ♔d8 13 ♘c3 dxe3 14 0-0-0+ ♗d7 15 ♖he1 ♕g7 16 ♕xg7 ♗xg7 as White cannot capture on e3 with his rook because of ...♗h6.

b) 10 dxe4 is also promising; 10...♘xe4 11 ♗d3!? (11 ♗e2 is a more staid approach, 11...♗d7?! [11...♗e6 12 ♘c3 {12 f3? 0-0-0! 13 fxe4 ♗g7} 12...0-0-0 is better] 12 ♘c3 and White is soon consolidating, Dupont-Redon, corr. 1991) 11...d4 (as this doesn't work, then Black should consider 11...♗f5) 12 ♗h6! (the discovered check is of no great use to Black) 12...♘g3+ 13 ♔d2 ♘xh1 14 ♗xg6+ ♔d7 15 ♕xf8 ♕xf8 16 ♗xf8 and White's queenside passed pawns will win the endgame, Tait-Elburg, corr. training game 1997.

c) 10 d4?! ♗f5 11 ♕h4?! 0-0-0 12 c3 ♕e6 13 ♘d2 ♗e7 14 0-0-0 ♘g4 15 ♕g3 g5 16 f4 ♗d6 17 ♖e1 ♘xe3 0-1, van Eijk-Sinke, corr. 1984.

10...♕xc5 11 ♕xf6 ♗f5 12 dxe4 ♘d4

If 12...dxe4 then 13 ♘c3 (13 c3?! e3 is less clear) 13...e3 14 0-0-0 must surely be winning as Black is playing without his one and only rook.

13 exf5! ♘xc2+ 14 ♔d1 ♘xa1 15 ♗d3 ♕d6 16 ♖e1+ ♔d7 17 ♕f7+ ♗e7 18 ♖e6 winning, Femmel-Villarreal, corr. 1997.

A3 4 d4

Recommended by Nunn and *NCO*, so this move is likely to become White's most popular.

4...♕h4?

Apart from this, my previous recommendation, which is doubtful, Black has a wide choice:

a) 4...♕f6!? 5 ♘c3 (5 ♘xc6 dxc6 transposes to 4 ♘xc6) 5...♗b4, best, (the game Moreno-Padula, corr. 1980, terminated abruptly: 5...♘xe5? 6 ♘d5 ♕c6 7 dxe5 d6?? [but Black is losing anyway] 8 ♗b5 1-0) 6 ♘xc6?! (6 exf5! ♘xe5 7 ♕e2) 6...♗xc3+ 7 bxc3 ♕xc6 8 exf5 ♕xc3+ 9 ♗d2 ♕xd4 10 ♗d3 ♘e7 11 0-0 0-0 and Black has a reasonable position, Van de Velden-Harper, corr. 1999.

b) 4...♘xe5 5 dxe5 d6 (5...fxe4 6 ♕d5 ♕h4 7 ♗c4 ♘h6 8 ♗xh6 ♕xh6 9 0-0 and Black will experience severe problems completing his development, Van Foreest-Bruin corr. 1881) 6 exf5 ♗xf5 7 ♕f3 ♕c8 8 ♗d3 ♗xd3 9 ♕xd3 ♕d7 (9...dxe5 10 ♕b5+) 10 ♕e4 and White has a pawn more, Ruggeri Laderchi-Stephen, corr. 1999.

c) 4...♕e7?! 5 ♘c3! (5 ♘xc6 ♕xe4+ 6 ♗e2 ♕xc6 7 0-0 d5 8 ♘c3 ♗d7 9 ♗f4, Canfell-Flitney, Canberra 1998, when 9...a6 10 ♗h5+ ♔d8 is uncomfortable for Black, if playable) 5...♘xe5 6 ♘d5 ♕h4!? 7 dxe5! (7 ♘xc7+ ♔d8 8 ♘xa8 ♕xe4+ 9 ♗e3 f4 and Black will recover the a8-knight in due course, when he will have two pieces for a rook) 7...♕xe4+ 8 ♗e2 ♗b4+ 9 c3 ♗a5 10 0-0 and White has a significant lead in development, Vinogradnik-Panchenko, Ukraine ch, Sevastopol, 2000.

d) 4...d6? 5 ♘xc6! now that Black cannot recapture with the d-pawn, (5 ♕h5+!? g6 6 ♘xg6 ♘f6 7 ♕h4 ♖g8 8 ♘xf8 ♖g4 9 ♕h6 ♖xe4+ 10 ♗e3 ♘g4 is messy, Ornstein-Tall, simul, Malmö 1973, but nevertheless, after 11 ♕xh7 White is better) 5...bxc6 6 ♗d3 ♘f6 7 exf5 ♗e7 8 0-0 0-0 9 ♘c3 Black is lost, Klein-Soelter, Bad Meinberg 1986.

e) 4...♘f6?! 5 ♗c4?! (5 ♘xc6 dxc6 6 e5 transposes to 4 ♘xc6, and 5 exf5!? to 3...♘f6) 5...♘xe5 6 dxe5 ♘xe4 7 0-0, Oll-Tasc R30, The Hague 1997, 7...♕e7 with a reasonable position, Black cannot castle kingside, but can try the other side.

5 ♘f3!

White returns the pawn for a lead in development.

5 ♗d3?! fxe4 6 g3 ♕h3?! (6...♕f6 7 ♗xe4 ♘xe5) 7 ♗xe4 ♘f6 8 ♘xc6 dxc6, Melchor-Svendsen, corr. 1992, continuing 9 ♕f3?! and now, instead of 9...♘xe4?! 10 ♕xe4+ ♗e6 11 ♗g5 ±, 9...♗g4! 10 ♕d3 0-0-0 is strong.

5 ♘c3 ♗b4 6 ♘f3 is similar to the main line, except that Black can castle easily: 6...♕xe4+ 7 ♗e2 ♗xc3+ 8 bxc3 ♘f6 9 0-0 0-0 10 ♖e1 ♔h8 11 ♗c4 ♕g4 12 h3 ♕h5 and White

has an edge, Leite-Pinto, Lisbon ch 1997.

5...♕xe4+ 6 ♗e2

NCO evaluates this as +/-, and, indeed, Black does have severe problems with his delayed development, and exposed queen.

6...♗b4+

So that the white knight is denied the c3-square.

6...♘b4?! 7 ♘a3 ♘d5 8 ♘b5 1-0, Ruggeri Laderchi-Owens, corr. 1999, as, for instance, 8...♘gf6 9 0-0 ♗b4 10 c3 ♗e7 11 ♘g5 ♕h4 12 g3 ♕h6 13 ♘e6.

6...d5 7 0-0 ♗d7 8 ♘c3 ♕e6 9 ♘g5 ♕f6 10 ♘xd5 and Black's position has fallen apart, Popović-Kalinski, Zadar 1995.

7 c3 ♗e7 8 0-0 ♘f6 9 c4

9 ♖e1 ♕d5 10 c4 ♕f7 11 d5 is also promising.

9...♘b4

9...0-0 10 ♘c3 ♕g4 11 d5 ♘b4 12 ♘g5 will win material.

10 a3 ♘a6 11 ♘c3 ♕e6 12 ♖e1 d6 13 c5

The black position is creaking, Canfell-Van Mil, Utrecht 1988.

B 3...♕e7?!

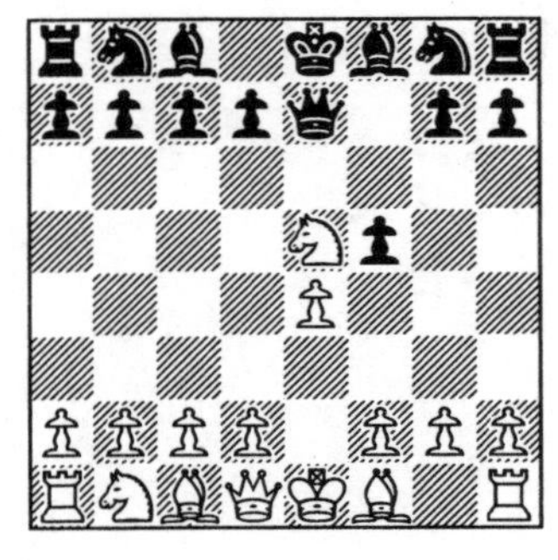

4 ♕h5+

Once again this is the critical reply, although 4 d4 ♘f6 (4...♘c6 transposes to 3...♘c6) 5 ♗c4 is also strong, and less complicated for White. (5 ♘c3?! offers White little, 5...d6 6 ♘c4 ♘xe4! [6...fxe4 7 ♗g5] 7 ♘xe4 ♕xe4+ 8 ♗e2 ♘c6 9 c3, Wijker-Diepstraten, corr. 1982, when Black can try 9...♕xg2!? 10 ♗f3 ♕h3 11 ♕e2+ ♔d8) 5...fxe4 (Black can also play 5...d6 which is analysed in Chapter 9, e.g. 6 ♗f7+! [6 ♘f7 d5 with: 7 ♘xh8 {or 7 ♗xd5?! ♘xd5 8 ♘xh8 ♕xe4+ 9 ♕e2 ♕xe2+ 10 ♔xe2 g6 11 ♖e1 ♗g7 12 ♔f1+ ♔f8 13 ♘xg6+ hxg6 14 c3 b6, Diepstraten-Elburg, corr. 1987} 7...dxc4 8 e5 ♘d5 9 ♕h5+ g6 10 ♘xg6 hxg6 11 ♕xg6+ ♕f7 12 ♕xf7+ ♔xf7 13 c3 ♗e6 and light-squared control, de Boer-Elburg, corr. 1986] 6...♔d8 7 exf5? [for 7 ♗b3! see Chapter 9] 7...♗xf5 8 0-0? dxe5 9 dxe5+ ♘fd7 ∓ Meszaros-Elburg, corr. 1988; 5...♘c6 is considered in Chapter 9) 6 ♗f7+!? (displacing the king, but wasting time, 6 0-0 d5 7 ♗b3 ♗f5 8 c4 ♘bd7 9 ♗f4 slightly favours White, Rubel-Sorensen, Copenhagen 1879; 6 ♗g5! c6? [6...♘c6] 7 ♘c3 transposing to Chapter 12, i.e. 7...d5 8 ♗xd5! winning, De Jong-Stamer, corr. 1994/94; 6 ♘c3! also transposes to Chapter 12) 6...♔d8 7 ♗b3 d5 8 ♗g5 c6 9 0-0 ♘bd7 10 f4 exf3 11 ♘xf3 h6 12 ♖e1 ♕f7 13 ♗h4 ♗d6 14 ♘e5? ♘xe5 15 dxe5 ♗c5+ 16 ♔h1 g5 17 exf6 gxh4 18 c4?! h3 19 cxd5?? (19 g3) 19...hxg2+ 20 ♔xg2 ♕g6+ 21 ♔h1 ♗g4 0-1, Podlesnik-Mohr, Ljubljana 1989.

4...g6 5 ♘xg6 ♕xe4+ 6 ♗e2

White must resign himself to losing his g-pawn, 6 ♔d1? ♘f6 7 ♕h4 (7 ♕h3?, NN-Greco, Italy 1620, [what is a book without at least one reference to the seventeenth century?] 7...♘g4 winning a piece)

7...♕g4+ (7...♘g4!? may be even better, 8 ♗e2? [8 f3 hxg6 9 ♕xg4! is superior] 8...hxg6 9 ♕xh8 ♘xf2+ 10 ♔e1 ♘xh1 11 d3, Slous-Bone, London 1835, and now any sensible queen move like 11...♕e7 should be good for Black) 8 f3?? (of course, 8 ♕xg4 ♘xg4 9 ♘xh8 ♘xf2+ had to be played) 8...♕xg6 ∓ Jonkers-Aartsen, corr. 1982.

6...♘f6 7 ♕h3

The g-pawn needs defence.

7...hxg6 8 ♕xh8 ♕xg2 9 ♖f1 ♔f7

Better to get out of the pin immediately, 9...♘g4 10 d3 (10 ♗xg4 ♕xg4 11 ♕e5+, Liepins-Silavs, Latvia, is possible) 10...d6? 11 ♗xg4 ♕xg4 12 ♗h6 with advantage, Littleboy-Gonsalves, corr. 1990.

10 ♕h4

I'm not sure that this is completely necessary, 10 d4 or 10 d3 are also sensible, aiming to complete White's development, 10...♘c6 11 ♕h4 d5 12 ♕g3?! ♕xg3 13 hxg3 ♘d4 with active play for the lost exchange, Coriell-Hayward, corr. 1988.

10...♘c6 11 c3 b5!

The best way to complete the queenside development and bring the rook to the e-file. 11...♗d6 12 d4 ♘d8?! 13 ♗g5 ♗e7 was far too slow, Hegedus-Kurucsai, corr. 1984.

12 d4 ♗b7 13 ♗g5

13 ♘d2 ♖e8 14 ♔d1 ♘d8 15 ♕g3 ♗d6! with reasonable play for the exchange, Parool-Prins, Holland 1953.

13...♗g7 14 ♗xf6 ♗xf6 15 ♕g3 ♕xg3 16 hxg3 ♖e8 17 ♔d2 b4

Again with some compensation, although objectively not quite enough, Koetsier-Bertoni, corr. 1999.

C 3...d6?

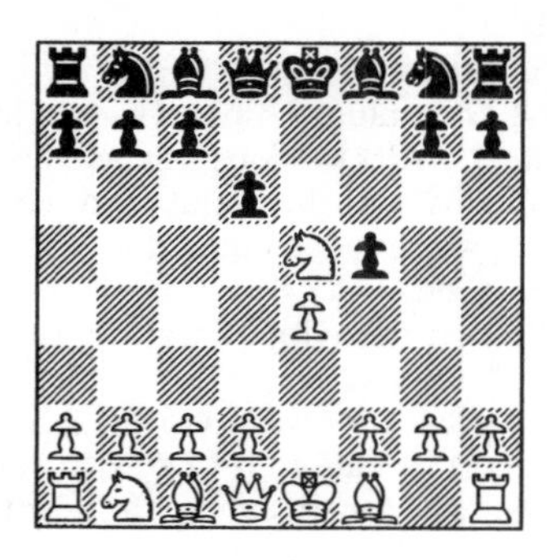

Apparently, this is an idea of Bronstein's, but seems to offer only disadvantages by comparison with 3...♘c6.

4 ♕h5+

This is the only way to refute 3...d6. 4 ♘c4? fxe4 5 ♘c3?! (5 d3 is better) 5...♘f6 6 d3 (6 ♗e2 d5 7 ♘e5 d4! left White facing big problems in Lehman-Diemer, Offenberg 1982, the game continuing 8 ♗c4!? dxc3 9 ♗f7+ ♔e7 10 bxc3 ♕d6 11 d4 exd3 12 ♗f4 d2+! 13 ♔f1 ♗e6! 14 ♘g6+ hxg6 15 ♗xd6+ ♔xf7 16 ♗xc7?! ♘a6 17 ♗f4 ♗c4+ 18 ♔g1 ♖d8 -+.) 6...d5 7 ♘e5 ♗d6 8 d4 ♕e7 9 ♗g5 c6 10 ♗xf6 ♕xf6 with advantage to Black, Landgraf-Kozlov, corr. 1991.

4...g6 5 ♘xg6 ♘f6 6 ♕h4

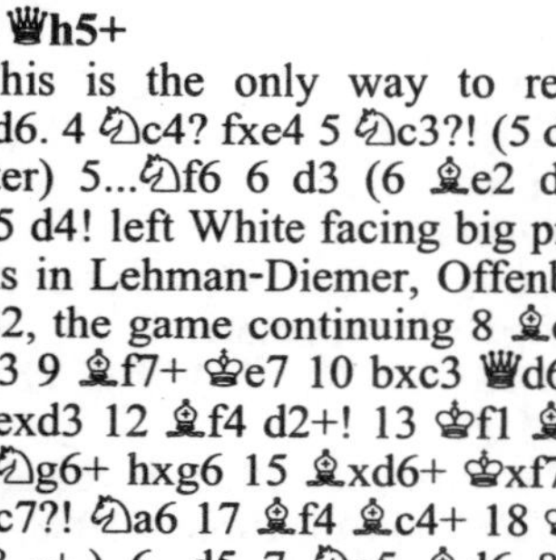

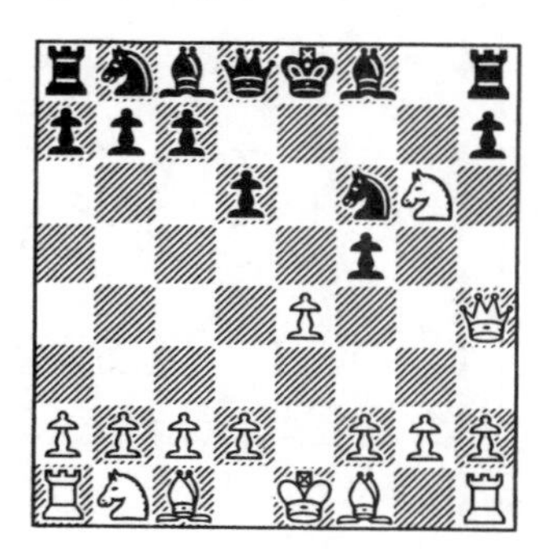

6...♖g8

Sacrificing the exchange is also insufficient:

a) 6...hxg6?! 7 ♕xh8 ♕e7 8 ♗b5+!? c6 9 ♗e2 fxe4 10 0-0 ♗f5 11 f3 and Black has little compensation, Cordoba-Montero, corr. 1975.

b) 6...♘c6!? is interesting as the white queen sometimes has difficulty finding shelter from Black's minor pieces, but a rook is a rook! 7 ♘xh8 ♘d4 8 ♘a3 (8 ♔d1!? fxe4 9 ♗e2 ♘f5 10 ♗h5+ ♔e7 11 ♕h3 ♘h6 12 ♕e3 ♘f5 13 ♕e2 ♗e6 14 d3 ♘d4 15 ♕e3 ♘f5 16 ♕h3 [16 ♕e1! ♘xh5 17 ♗g5+ ♘f6 18 ♕xe4 should win] 16...♘h6 ½-½ (?), Eglitis-Morgado, corr. 1979. White should certainly continue the fight; 8 ♗c4!? ♘xc2+ 9 ♔d1 ♘xa1 10 ♖e1 fxe4??, Viaggio-Morgado, corr. 1978, when White missed the evident 11 ♖xe4+ ♘xe4 12 ♕h5+ ♔d7 13 ♕f5+ and mate next move) 8...fxe4 9 ♗c4? (9 d3 or 9 ♕g3 are far more testing) 9...d5 (9...♗g4?! 10 ♘f7 ♕e7 11 ♘h6 +/- Destrebecq-Viaggo, corr. 1979) 10 ♗xd5 ♕xd5 11 ♕xf6 ♗xa3 12 bxa3 ♘xc2+ 13 ♔d1 ♘xa1 14 ♗b2 (14 ♕xa1 ♗g4+ is unclear) 14...♕xa2 15 ♗xa1 ♕b1+ 16 ♔e2 ♕d3+ ½-½, Downey-Destrebecq, corr. 1996.

7 ♘xf8

7 e5?! is over-elaborate, 7...dxe5! 8 ♘xe5 ♕e7 9 f4, Berg-Aartsen, corr. 1982, 9...♘c6 10 ♗b5 ♗d7 and Black will castle long with a potential attack on the g-file.

7...♖g4

Or 7...♖xf8 8 d3 ♘c6 (8...fxe4 is no better, 9 dxe4 ♕e7 10 ♘c3 with advantage, Houten-de Neef, corr. 1982) 9 ♘c3!? (9 ♗g5) 9...♘d4 10 ♗g5! ♘xc2+ 11 ♔d1 ♗e6?? (11...♘xa1 12 ♘d5 ♕d7 13 ♘xf6+ ♖xf6 14 ♗xf6 ♕a4+ 15 b3 is also hopeless, but at least White has something to think about) 12 ♔xc2 1-0, Morgado-Gabrans, corr. 1976.

8 ♕h6 ♖xe4+

In Bullockus-Grobe, corr. 1973/75, 8...♕e7 was preferred with the follow-up 9 f3 ♖g7 10 ♘xh7 ♖xh7 11 ♕e3?! (but 11 ♕g6+ ♔d8 12 d3 seems more convincing) 11...fxe4 with slight compensation.

9 ♗e2

And certainly not 9 ♔d1?? ♘g4.

9...♖e7

Without the knight on c6, there is nothing for Black here; 9...♕e7 10 ♘c3 and 0-0 with advantage.

10 0-0 1-0

As

10...♖xe2 11 ♘c3 ♖e5 12 d4

...leaves Black material down with a bad position, Sadéghi-Sénéchaud, corr. 1991/92.

D 3...♘f6?!

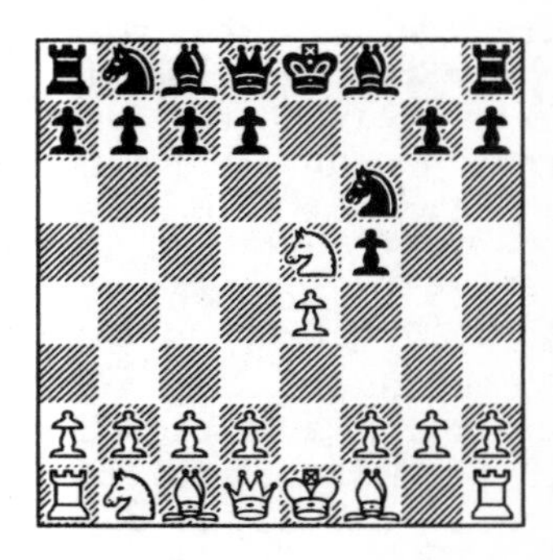

Lowenthal's move. This time there is no need for Black to worry about ♕h5+, but on the other hand, he loses a whole pawn without embroiling White in complex calculations.

4 exf5

Simple and good. 4 ♗c4!? ♕e7 5 d4 transposes into B, whilst 4 ♘c4? fxe4 5 ♘c3 d5 6 ♘e5 d4 (6...♕e7 -+) 7 ♗c4 dxc3 8 bxc3, Sinke-

Elburg, corr. 1987, 8...Qe7 and White can almost resign. 4 Nc3? d6 5 Nc4 fxe4 transposes into C.

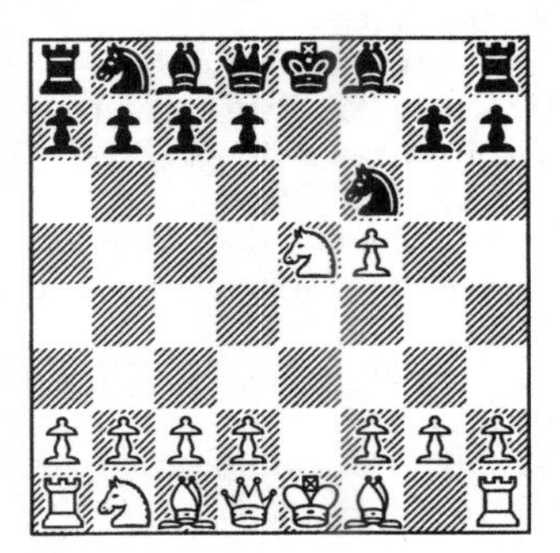

4...Qe7

4...d6 5 Nf3 Bxf5 6 d4 Be7 7 Bd3 Bg4 8 c3 is similar; Black plays a position resembling the French Exchange, without his f-pawn, Budovskis-Gabrans, corr. 1969.

4...Nc6!? goes for quick development; 5 d4!? (5 Nxc6 dxc6 6 Qf3, Gelman-Schuyler, Concord 1995, and now 6...Qd5! and Black will recover one of the pawns, with some play) 5...Qe7 6 Be2 Nxe5 7 dxe5 Qxe5 8 0-0 Bd6 9 g3 0-0 (9...Qxf5 10 Bd3 Qh3 11 Re1+ Be7 12 Nc3 Ng4? 13 Rxe7+! is devastating) 10 Bf4! Qxb2 11 Bc4+ Kh8 12 Bxd6 cxd6 13 Qxd6 Re8 14 Na3! Ne4 (14...b6 is no better, 15 Bf7 Rd8 16 Nc4 Qxc2 17 Ne5 Qc5 18 Qxc5 bxc5 19 Bc4 Rf8 20 Nf7+ Kg8 21 Nd6+ Kh8 22 Rfe1 a5 [22...Rb8?! 23 Rab1 Rb6 24 Rxb6 axb6 25 a4 is almost Zugzwang] 23 Re5) 15 Qd5 Qxa3 16 Rae1 Qf8 17 Rxe4 Rxe4 18 Qxe4 d5 19 Bxd5 Bxf5 20 Qe3 Qc8 21 Re1 Bd7 22 Qd4! 1-0, Kosten-Tiemann, email 2001, as 22...Bc6 23 Re7 Qf8 24 Rf7 Qg8 25 Bb3 Re8 26 f4 is completely crushing.

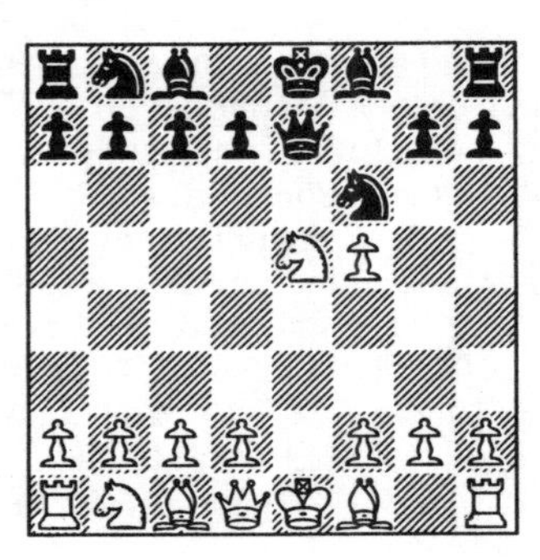

5 Qe2

5 d4?! sacrifices a piece, 5...d6 6 Qe2 (6 f4!? dxe5 7 fxe5 Bxf5 is very speculative, Punt-Elburg, corr. 1986) 6...dxe5 (6...Bxf5?! 7 Nd3 Nc6 8 c3 0-0-0 allows White to escape the loss of the piece, Rogalski-Diepstraten, corr. 1985) 7 dxe5 Nd5 8 Qh5+ Qf7 9 Qxf7+ Kxf7 10 Bc4 c6 11 Nc3?! (11 e6+) 11...Bb4 12 Bd2 Bxc3 13 Bxd5+ cxd5 14 e6+ Kf6 15 Bxc3+ Kxf5. White's proud advanced pawns have disintegrated, Kroonen-Diepstraten, Amsterdam 1989.

5...d6 6 Nc4

6 Nf3 is perfectly reasonable, as well; 6...Bxf5 7 Nd4 Bd7 8 Nc3 Nc6 9 Nxc6 Bxc6 10 Qxe7+ Bxe7 11 Bb5 and Black has no real compensation for his pawn, Müller-Diepstraten, corr. 1985.

6...Bxf5 7 Qxe7+ Bxe7 8 Ne3 Be6 9 d4 Nc6 10 c3

With advantage, Tener-Denny, corr. 1972.

7 3 ♗c4 fxe4 4 ♘xe5 ♕g5 (Poisoned g2 pawn variation)

This is probably one of the sharpest and most extensively analysed opening variations of all. I suppose for this reason alone, the practically minded player may consider that it is not worthwhile making the effort to memorize the complicated variations involved. In addition to that, Black often finds himself subjected to a venomous attack. On the other hand, a variation that might be dubious in correspondence chess (nowadays players often give preference to 4...d5, chapter 8) may well gain untold 'gift' points 'over-the-board'. Black would be most unfortunate to find himself playing against an opponent versed in the theory, and finding a way through the maze of variations with only two hours (or less) on the clock? Forget it!

1 e4 e5 2 ♘f3 f5 3 ♗c4

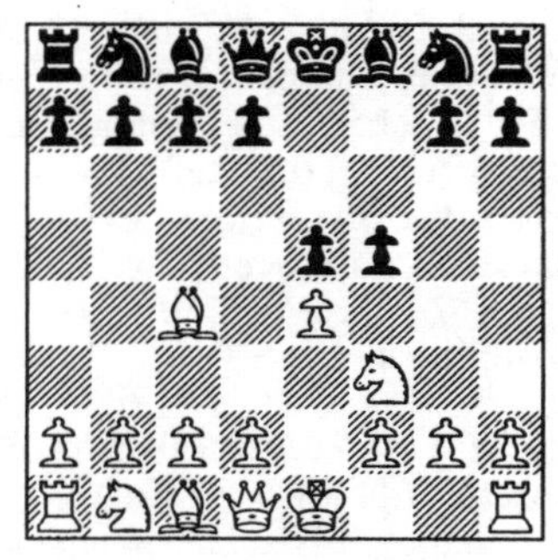

Aiming straight down the a2-g8 diagonal, weakened by Black's second move. This move was the favourite of Paul Keres, and is one that appeals to players of the white pieces who are intent on winning rapidly, and who are not afraid of giving up a few pieces to force mate. The slightest inaccuracy from White, however, and he may find himself material behind with no compensation.

3...fxe4

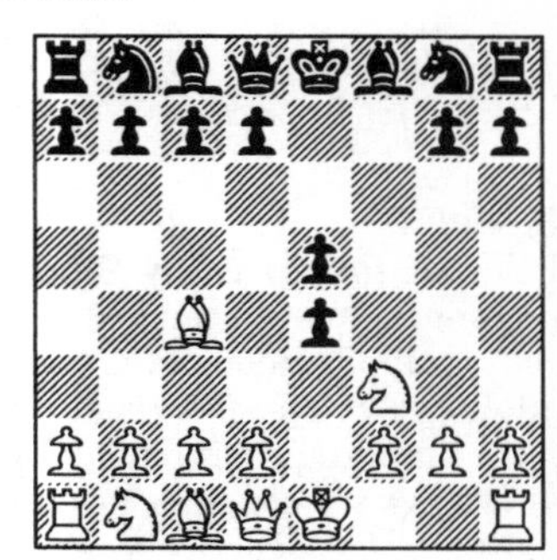

4 ♘xe5

Neither 4 ♗xg8?! ♖xg8 (4...exf3 5 ♗d5 c6 6 ♗xf3 d5 7 0-0 ♗d6, Oren-Diepstraten, corr. 1992, is not bad either) 5 ♘xe5 ♕g5 6 ♘g4 d5 7 h3 ♘c6 8 d4 ♕g6 9 ♗f4 ♗d6 10 ♗xd6 ♕xd6 11 ♘c3 ♗e6 12 ♕d2 0-0-0 ∓ Fischer-Leisebein, East Germany 1987, nor 4 ♘g1? ♘f6 5 ♘c3 ♘c6 6 f3 d5 ∓ Druke-Heap, corr. 1991, are serious alternatives. Further, 4 d4?, a speciality of Breidenbach in the early 80s, is quite unsound, 4...exf3 5 dxe5 (5 ♕xf3 ♕f6 6 ♕h5+ g6 7 ♕xe5+ ♕xe5+ 8 dxe5 ♘c6 is completely hopeless, Dogiel-Löffler, corr. 1991) 5...fxg2 6 ♖g1 d5 (probably the simplest) 7 ♗xd5 ♗b4+! (of course not the immediate 7...♘e7?? 8 ♗f7+) 8 c3 ♘e7 9 ♕a4+, any bishop retreat allows the exchange of queens, 9...♗d7 10 ♗f7+ ♔xf7 11 ♕xb4 ♗c6 12 ♕f4+ ♔e8 13 ♕g4 ♕d3 14 ♗e3 h5! 15 ♕xg7 ♖g8 16 ♕h6 ♗f3 0-1, Breidenbach-Leeners, corr. 1982.

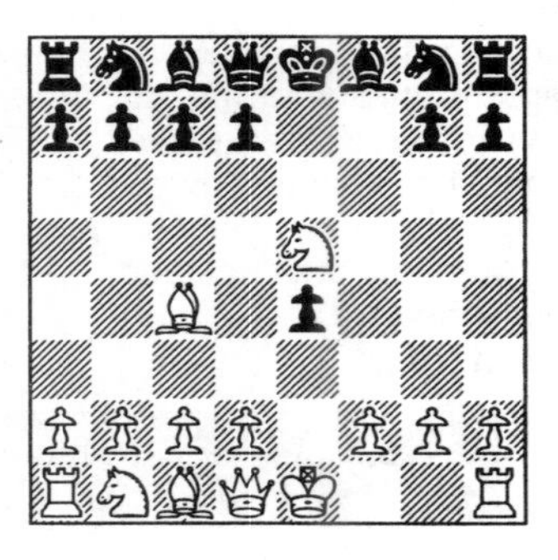

4...♕g5

This was first given by Bilguer as the strongest answer against 3 ♗c4, Black simultaneously counters White's projected ♕h5+ and threatens the important g2 pawn. In the next chapter we consider the key alternative, Svedenborg's 4...d5!, which is likewise not without its problems for both players.

Whilst Blackburne's 4...♘f6?! also sees the light of day occasionally, often with positive results for the second player: 5 ♘f7 (Critical, although White has a choice: 5 ♗f7+ ♔e7 6 ♗b3 d5 is simpler, and causes Black a certain amount of inconvenience, 7 d4 c5!? 8 ♗g5 ♘c6 9 ♕h5?! ♕e8 10 ♕h4?! cxd4 11 ♗xd5 ♘xe5 12 ♕xe4 ♔d6 13 ♗xf6 gxf6 14 f4 ♗f5 15 fxe5+ ♕xe5 16 ♕xe5+ fxe5 and Black has reached a very favourable endgame, not least because of his active king! Gamman-Blackburne, London 1869; but 5 d4?! d5 6 ♗e2 [6 ♗b3! transposes to Chapter 11] 6...♗d6, Hughen-Ortiz, corr. 1968, is too insipid; however 5 ♘c3 is also good, see Chapter 12) 5...♕e7 6 ♘xh8 d5 7 ♗e2 (the alert reader may have noticed that Black is a rook down, but, bearing in mind that the knight on h8 will inevitably be lost, this should only be a temporary state of affairs. Meanwhile, Black has a good development and some potent threats, 7 ♗xd5? for instance, being met by 7...♗g4 8 ♗xb7! [8 ♕xg4? ♘xg4 9 ♗xb7, Strelis-Atars, corr. 1977, is worse, 9...♕h4 10 g3 ♕f6 11 0-0 ♗c5 and White cannot even capture the a8-rook, 12 ♗xa8? ♕f3 winning; 8 f3?! exf3+ 9 ♔f2 ♕c5+ 10 d4 ♕xd5 11 ♘c3 ♕h5 12 gxf3 ♕h4+ and a strong attack, Woll-Amilibia, corr. 1974/77] 8...♕e5!? 9 ♘c3 ♗xd1 10 ♘xd1 ♘d5 11 ♗xa8 c6 12 c3?!, Purins-Amilibia, corr. 1971, when the obvious 12...♘b6 13 ♗b7 ♕e7 is strong, Black wins the b7-bishop, and later the h8-knight. i.e. 14 0-0 g5 15 ♖e1 ♗g7 16 d3 ♕xb7 17 ♖xe4+ ♔f8 18 ♗xg5 ♗xh8 19 ♖e7 ♘8d7 20 ♖xh7 ♗g7, unclear; 7 ♗b3?? ♗g4 8 f3 exf3+ 9 ♔f2 ♘e4+ 10 ♔e3 ♕g5+ 11 ♔d3 ♘f2+ 12 ♔c3 d4+ 13 ♔xd4 ♕c5 mate, Carapelli-Young, Greece 1874; 7 ♗b5+!? is a suggestion of Lein, after 7...c6 8 ♗e2 play is similar to the main line, except that Black can no longer play his knight to c6) 7...♘c6 with the following possibilities:

a) 8 d4 exd3 9 cxd3 ♗g4?! (9...♗f5) 10 ♘c3 0-0-0 11 0-0 ♗e6 12 ♗f4?! d4 13 ♘b5 ♘d5 14 ♗g3 a6, Gamman-Blackburne, London 1869, White certainly stands better here, but went on to lose.

b) 8 ♗h5+? is popular, aiming to get a couple of pawns in return for the knight, but it is very time consuming: 8...g6 9 ♘xg6 (9 ♗xg6+? hxg6 10 ♘xg6 ♕g7 11 ♘h4? [better 11 ♘f4, but 11...♗d6! 12 d3 ♗xf4 13 ♗xf4 ♕xg2 14 ♖f1 ♗g4 is also promising for Black] Gemignani-Pastor, corr. 1971/72, 11...♕h7! 12 g3 ♗g4 13 f3 exf3 14 ♘xf3 ♕e7+ wins) 9...hxg6 10 ♗xg6+ ♔d8 11 ♗h5 ♘e5!? (11...♕g7!?) 12 0-0?! (the king is none too safe here, 12 ♗e2) 12...♕h7 13 ♗e2? (13 d4! is necessary, 13...♘eg4!? [13...exd3 14 ♗g5] 14 ♗xg4 ♗xg4 15 ♕d2! and White has defensive chances, 15 f3?! ♗d6) 13...♗d6 14 g3 (14 h3 ♗xh3) 14...♕h3 15 f3 ♘eg4! 16 fxg4 ♗xg3 17 ♖f2 ♗xf2+ 18 ♔xf2 ♕xh2+ 19 ♔e3 ♕g3+, chasing the king up the board to its demise, Morillo-Ortiz, corr. 1970.

c) 8 0-0 ♗f5 9 d4 0-0-0 10 c3 ♕e6 11 ♗f4 ♗e7 12 b4 ♖xh8 13 a4 g5!?. Objectively White is better, but Black has practical chances, Keast-Borrmann, corr. 1974.

d) 8 d3 ♗f5 9 dxe4! ♘xe4?! 10 ♕xd5!? (greed worthy of a computer! 10 0-0 0-0-0 11 ♗g4 ♕f6 12 ♗xf5+ ♕xf5 13 ♕f3?! is a simpler method, Verolme-Ouwerkerk, corr. 1978, 13...♕xf3 14 gxf3 ♘d6 15 ♘c3 and White should win) 10...♖d8! this is not sound, but is the best prospect, 11 ♕xf5!? (11 ♕f7+ is more circumspect, 11...♕xf7 12 ♘xf7 ♔xf7 13 ♗e3 ♘d4 14 ♗d3 ♗c5 15 0-0 Black is lost, Borrmann-Löffler, corr. 1991) 11...♘d4 12 ♗h5+! (12 ♕h5+?! g6 13 ♘xg6? [13 ♗b5+ is the only possibility, 13...c6 14 ♘xg6 ♘xc2+ 15 ♔e2 ♘c3+ {15...♘g3+ 16 ♔f3} 16 ♔f3 ♘d4+ looks very nasty for White, who is forced to wander along the wrong side of his pawns, but may be playable] 13...♘xc2+ 14 ♔f1 ♖d1+! A superb refutation! 15 ♗xd1 ♘g3+ 0-1, as it is mate next move, Petersson-Ortiz, corr. 1970; 12 ♕f7+? ♕xf7 13 ♘xf7 ♘xc2+ 14 ♔f1 ♔xf7 15 f3 ♘f6 16 ♘c3 ♘xa1 17 ♗f4, Madrid-Ribe, corr. 1983, is quite equal after 17...c6) 12...g6 13 ♗xg6+ hxg6 14 ♕xg6+ ♔d7 15 0-0 ♘e2+ 16 ♔h1 should be winning, nevertheless, in Madrid-Ribe, corr. 1984, there followed: 16...♕h4 17 ♘f7?? (White has a number of good defences, for instance 17 ♕f5+ ♔c6 18 ♕f3 [18 ♘g6? ♘2g3+] or 17 ♘c3) 17...♘xf2+ 18 ♖xf2 ♕xf2 19 ♕d3+ ♗d6 20 ♕d1 (20 ♕h3+ ♔e8 21 ♘xd6+ ♖xd6 forces White to take a perpetual check) 20...♖f8 21 ♘c3 and now 21...♘g3+! 22 hxg3 ♕xg3 23 ♗f4 ♕xf4 24 ♕h5 ♖xf7 is at least equal.

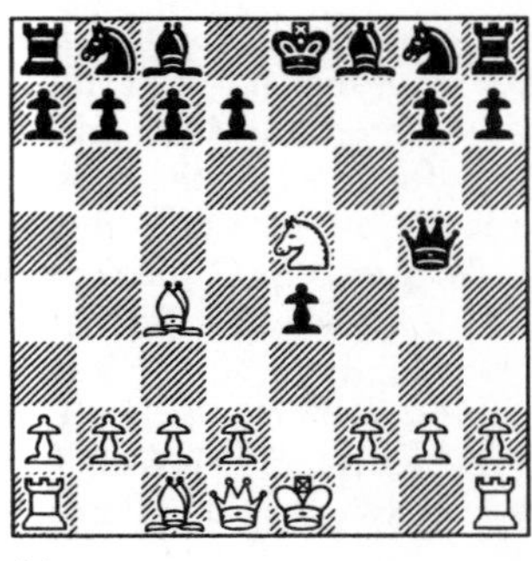

5 d4

Almost forced, as the two 'obvious' alternatives both give White a hard time:

a) 5 ♘f7?! ♕xg2 6 ♖f1 d5! and:

a1) 7 ♘xh8 dxc4 (7...♘f6?! 8 ♗xd5! [8 ♗e2 ♗h3 9 d4 ♕xh2 10 ♗e3, Pemberthy-Pierce, corr. 1915, 10...g6 11 ♕d2 ♗xf1 12 ♗xf1 ♗g7 is good for Black] 8...♗g4 [8...♗h3 is considered below] 9 f3 ♗xf3 10 ♖xf3 exf3 11 ♕xf3 [11 ♗xf3?! ♕g1+ 12 ♔e2 ♕xh2+ 13 ♔f1 ♘c6

14 d4 0-0-0 15 c3 ♘e5 is very dangerous for White, NN-Holwell, corr. 1986] 11...♕g1+ 12 ♔e2 ♕xh2+ 13 ♔d3? [13 ♔f1! c6 14 ♗b3 ♘bd7 15 ♕e2+ has to be good for White] 13...♘bd7 14 ♘f7 ♘xd5 15 ♕xd5 ♕g3+ 16 ♔e2 ♕g4+ 17 ♔e1 ♗e7 with a powerful attack, Vossebeld-Olof, Leusden/Utrecht 1987) 8 ♕h5+ g6 9 ♕xh7 ♗h3! 10 ♕f7+ ♔d8 11 ♕xf8+ ♔d7 12 ♕g7+ (forcing the black king to impede the rook, 12 ♕f7+?! ♘e7 13 ♕xc4 ♘bc6, the knight wishes to come to the f3-square, via e5, 14 ♘f7 ♖f8 15 ♘h6 ♘e5 ∓ Kirchner-Hacker, Switzerland 1965) 12...♘e7 13 ♕d4+ ♔c8 14 ♕xc4 ♘bc6 15 d4 (but now 15 ♘f7? is weaker, as 15...♘d4 is possible, in the other line White could capture this with check) 15...b5! 16 ♕xb5 ♘xd4 17 ♕a6+ ♔d7 18 ♘xg6 ♘xg6 19 ♕a4+ ♔e7 20 ♘d2 ♘f3+ and the white king did not last too long, Rosso-Ruggeri Laderchi, corr. 1998.

a2) 7 ♗xd5 ♘f6 (the most popular move, by far, but maybe not best, 7...♗g4! 8 f3 ♗e7 9 ♕e2, forced, 9...♗h4+ 10 ♔d1 and now 10...♕xe2+ [10...♕xf1+? is flash, but faulty, 11 ♕xf1 ♗xf3+ 12 ♕xf3 exf3 13 ♘xh8 f2 14 ♔e2 ♘c6 15 ♗xc6+ bxc6 16 d3 Perez-Vidal, Spain 1997, and even after best play, 16...♔d7 17 ♗e3 ♘h6 18 ♘d2 ♖xh8 19 ♘f3 Black is worse because of his shabby pawn structure] 11 ♔xe2 exf3+ 12 ♖xf3 ♘f6 13 ♗xb7 ♔xf7 14 ♗xa8 ♖e8+ 15 ♔d3 ♘bd7 and Black has an enormous lead in development and must win; 7...♗h3!? 8 ♕e2 ♘f6 9 ♗xb7 ♔xf7 10 d3?? [White has near equality after 10 ♗xa8 ♗d6] 10...exd3 11 ♗xg2 dxe2 12 ♗xh3 exf1=♕+ 13 ♗xf1 Ironically, it is White who finds himself a rook light! Marshall-Steen, corr. 1995) 8 ♘xh8 ♗h3 (8...♘xd5? 9 ♕h5+; 8...♗g4 transposes to 7...♘f6) 9 ♗f7+ (9 ♗c4? ♘c6 10 c3 ♘e5 11 d4 0-0-0 12 ♗e2? ♘f3+ 13 ♗xf3 ♕xf1+ 14 ♔d2 ♕xf2+ with a decisive attack in Gudju-Betinš, Paris 1924) 9...♔e7 10 ♗c4 (10 ♕e2? ♘c6 11 c3 ♘e5 12 ♗c4 ♘f3+ with the attack, Ziedens-Vitols, Latvia) 10...♘c6 11 d4 ♖d8 12 ♗e3!? (12 b3! looks promising, e.g. 12...♘xd4 13 ♗a3+ ♔e8 14 ♗f7+ ♔d7 15 ♕xd4+ ♔c8 16 ♕c4) 12...♘e5 13 dxe5!? ♖xd1+ 14 ♔xd1 ♘g4 15 ♖e1 ♘xe3+ 16 fxe3 ♕xh2 and White's awkward king position and trapped knight make Black favourite, Crimp-Melchor, corr. training game 1997.

b) 5 ♗f7+?! ♔e7 6 ♕h5!? (6 d4 ♕xg2 7 ♖f1 [7 ♕h5? ♕xh1+ 8 ♔e2 ♘f6 ∓ Thielen-Varga, corr. 1971/72] 7...d6 8 ♗xg8 [8 ♕h5? dxe5 9 ♗g5+ ♘f6 10 dxe5 ♗g4 11 exf6+ gxf6 12 ♗xf6+ ♔xf6 13 ♕d5 ♘c6 and White is material down with a bad position, NN-Sorensen, 1879] 8...♖xg8 9 ♘c4 ♗h3 10 ♘e3, Waller-Quinones, National Open, USA 1996, when 10...♕f3 would be simplest, with a pleasant ending; 6 ♗xg8 ♕xg2!? [6...♖xg8 7 ♘g4 d5 is reasonable] 7 ♖f1 ♖xg8 8 ♕h5, Sanpera-Melchor, La Pobla de Lillet 1997, 8...g6 9 ♕xh7+ ♖g7 10 ♕h4+ ♔e8 unclear) 6...♕xg2!? (6...♕xh5 7 ♗xh5, Alias-Martin Echeandia, Euskadi 2000, 7...♘f6 8 ♗e2 d6 avoids any complications) 7 ♗xg8 (7 ♖f1 ♘f6 is terrible, and 7 ♗e8? ♕xh1+ 8 ♔e2 ♘f6 9 ♕f7+ ♔d8 10 ♘c3, Probst-Lowig, Oeynhausen 1922, 10...♘c6 loses vast amounts of material) 7...♕xh1+ 8 ♔e2 ♖xg8 9 ♘c3! g6 (9...♘c6!) 10 ♘d5+ ♔e8 11 ♕g5 ♗d6 12 ♘f6+ the queen and two knights give the black king a hard time, Rodholm-Herrstrom, corr. 1996.

5...♕xg2

6 ♕h5+

The only correct plan, and one that will involve White in the sacrifice of half of his army.

a) The timid alternative 6 ♖f1? is perhaps the sort of reaction one might expect in an 'OTB' game, 6...♘f6 7 ♘c3 (7 ♗f7+ ♔e7 8 ♗h5?! g6 9 ♗g4 ♘xg4 10 ♕xg4 ♕xg4 11 ♘xg4 of Broquen-Purins, corr. 1968/70, is also to Black's advantage; 7 ♘f7? d5 8 ♘xh8 dxc4 9 ♗f4 ♗g4 10 ♕c1, Pruess-Vinerts, USA 1996, and now Black is in position to win the game, without even bothering to pick up the h8-knight, by 10...♘d5! 11 ♗e3 ♗h3 12 ♘d2 ♗e7 and White has no defence against ...♘xe3, and then ...♗h4+) 7...♗b4 8 ♗f4 d6 9 ♘f7 ♗g4 (9...♖f8! 10 ♘g5 d5 11 ♗e2 h6 wins a piece) 10 ♕d2 ♖f8 11 f3 ♕xd2+ 12 ♗xd2 ♗xc3 13 ♗xc3 ♗xf3 14 ♘g5, Arasola-Susi, Naantali 1993, and with two extra pawns, Black should certainly be able to score the full point.

b) 6 ♗f1? ♕xh1 7 ♕h5+ g6 8 ♘xg6 hxg6 9 ♕xh8 ♔f7 10 ♗e3 d5! (10...♗g7 11 ♕h4 ♘f6?! led to a curious repetition in Douwes-Tissink, Utrecht 1991: 12 ♘d2 d5 13 0-0-0 ♗g4 14 ♗e2 ♕g2 15 ♗f1 ♕h1 ½-½) 11 ♘d2 ♗g4 just in time to stop White castling, 12 ♕e5 ♘f6 13 ♕xc7+ ♘bd7 14 ♗f4 ♖e8 15 ♕xb7 e3 16 fxe3 ♕g1 17 ♕b3 ♗d6! 0-1, Milnes-Mlotkowski, Philadelphia 1911.

6...g6 7 ♗f7+

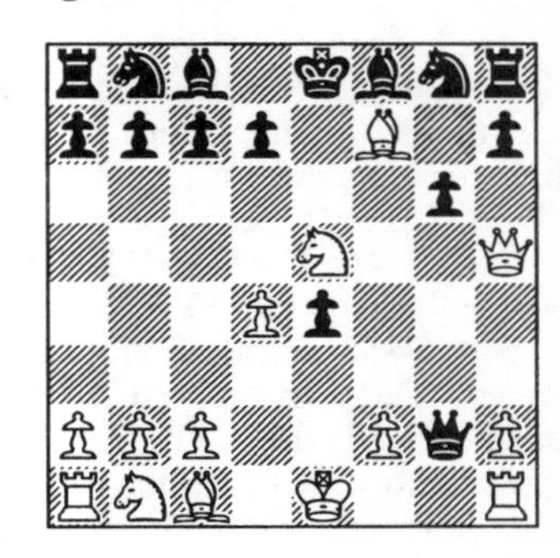

7...♔d8

The black king must try to make himself scarce. 7...♔e7? loses, 8 ♗g5+! (8 ♕g5+ is also strong 8...♕xg5 9 ♗xg5+ ♘f6 10 ♘c3 c6 11 ♘xe4 ♗g7 12 ♗xg6! [12 ♗b3 d5 13 ♘xf6 ♗xf6 14 f4 is nothing special for White, Hayes-Downey, corr. 1991] 12...hxg6 13 ♘xg6+ ♔e6 [13...♔f7!? 14 ♘xh8+ ♗xh8 15 ♘d6+ ♔e6 16 ♘xc8 ♘a6 17 ♘xa7 ♖xa7 certainly favours White, but Black has some chances] 14 ♗xf6 ♗xf6 15 ♘xf6 [15 ♘xh8?! ♗xh8 16 0-0-0 d5 17 ♘g5+ ♔f6 Malmström-Downey, corr. 1992, is less clear] 15...♖h6 [there is little choice, 15...♔xf6 16 ♘xh8 ♔g7 17 ♔d2 ♔xh8 18 ♖ae1 will win a piece] 16 ♘e8 ♘a6 17 ♖g1 and Black soon had to resign, Hage-Svendsen, e-mail 1999) 8...♘f6 9 ♕h4 ♕xh1+ 10 ♔d2 (or 10 ♔e2 ♗g7 when White should avoid 11 ♘c3? when, as Grivainis and Elburg point out, 11...♕f3+! is possible, e.g. 12 ♘xf3 [12 ♔e1? should be answered by 12...♕f5 {rather than 12...♕h1+? which gives White the opportunity to change his mind by 13 ♔d2 transposing into 10 ♔d2!} 13 ♘d5+ ♔f8 14 ♘xf6 ♘c6 with good chances] 12...exf3+ 13 ♔d2 [superior to 13 ♔xf3?! ♔xf7 14 ♕f4 d6 15 ♘d5 ♗f5 16 ♗xf6 ♗xf6 17 ♘xc7 ♘c6 18 ♘xa8 ♘xd4+ Jackson-Downey, corr. 1992, the three pieces being more than a match for the queen] 13...♔xf7 14 ♕f4 d6 15 ♘d5 ♗f5 [rather than 15...♘bd7? 16 ♖e1! and Black is lost] 16 ♗xf6 ♗xf6 17 ♘xc7 ♘c6 18 ♘xa8 ♖xa8 and both sides have chances, Vadot-Sireta, corr. 1994. Instead of all this, 11 ♘d2! increases control of f3, and avoids the black defence, i.e. 11...♕g2 [if 11...♕xa1? 12 ♘xe4 and mate will be swift] 12 ♘xe4 ♔f8 13 ♘xf6 ♘c6 14 ♗d5 etc.) 10...e3+ (trying to confuse matters, 10...♗g7? 11 ♘c3 ♕xa1 12 ♗xf6+ ♗xf6 13 ♘d5+ gives a quick mate) 11 ♔e2 (capturing with the pawn leaves Black an important lateral check: 11 fxe3? ♕g2+ 12 ♔d3 ♕f1+ 13 ♔d2 ♘c6 14 ♘c3 ♕g2+ 15 ♔d3 ♘xe5+ 16 dxe5 ♔xf7 17 ♗xf6 g5 18 ♕h5+ ♔g8 19 ♗xh8 b6! 20 ♗f6 ♗a6+ and, remarkably, Black wins by direct attack, Elburg-Downey, corr. 1991, but 11 ♔xe3 also wins, 11...♗h6 [11...♗g7 12 ♘c3] 12 ♘c3 ♕xa1 13 ♕xh6 ♕e1+ 14 ♔f3 ♕h1+ 15 ♔e2 ♘c6 16 ♕g7 ♘xd4+ 17 ♔d2 and the attack decides, Pape-Melchor, corr. 1994) 11...♗g7 12 ♘c3 ♕g2 13 ♘e4! (White must protect f2, 13 ♘d5+? ♔f8 14 ♗xf6 [14 ♘xe3? ♕e4 15 f4 d6 -/+ Alloin-Downey, corr. 1991] 14...♗xf6 15 ♕xf6 ♕xf2+ 16 ♕xf2 exf2 17 ♘xc7 d6 18 ♗d5 dxe5 19 dxe5 ♔g7 20 ♔xf2 ♖d8 21 c4 ♘c6 22 ♘xa8 ♘xe5 23 ♘c7 and the game is quite level, Stummer-Sireta, corr. 1994/95) 13...♔f8 14 ♗xf6 g5 15 ♕h5! ♕xe4 (if 15...exf2 16 ♘xf2 ♘c6 17 ♗xg7+ ♔xg7 18 ♗d5! wins) 16 ♗xg7+ ♔xg7 17 ♕xg5+ ♔f8 18 ♕d8+ ♔g7 19 ♖g1+ ♕g6 20 ♖xg6+ hxg6 21 ♕g5 1-0, Kozlov-Svendsen, corr. 1991.

8 ♗xg6!

Boldly leaving the h1 rook to its fate, and with check too! The alternatives, though, are either insipid or losing:

a) 8 ♕g5+?! ♕xg5 9 ♗xg5+ ♗e7 10 ♗b3 (neither 10 ♗f4?! d6 11 ♘c4 ♘f6 -/+ Hughen-Dreibergs, corr. 1968, nor 10 h4?! d6 11 ♘c4 ♘c6 ∓ Neukirch-Dukurs, corr. 1968, offer any compensation for the g2 pawn, whilst 10 ♗d5 ♗xg5 11 ♘f7+ ♔e7 12 ♘xg5 ♘f6 13 ♘c3 c6 14 ♗xe4 ♘xe4 15 ♘gxe4 d5, Grob-Tartakower, Meran 1926, favours Black because of the pawn structure) 10...♗xg5 11 ♘f7+ ♔e7 12 ♘xg5 (12 ♘xh8?! ♘h6 [12...♘f6!? is interesting; 13 ♘f7?, Thorn-De Snaijer, corr. 1982, allows 13...♗c1 with advantage, and the superior 13 ♘c3 ♗h4 14 0-0 c6 keeps the knight in the cage, whilst preparing the defence of the e4-pawn] 13 ♖g1 [13 ♘c3?! c6 14 ♘xe4 ♗f6 15 ♘xf6 {there is no escape for the knight: 15 ♘f7?! ♘xf7

16 ♗xf7 ♔xf7 17 ♘d6+ ♔e6 18 ♘xc8 ♘a6 White is lost} 15...♔xf6 16 ♔d2 d5 17 ♖ae1 ♗e6 18 ♖e2 {18 ♖xe6+ ♔xe6 19 ♖e1+ ♔f6 20 ♖e8 still doesn't save the knight, 20...b5 21 a4 a6 22 c3 ♔g7 23 ♗c2 ♘g8} 18...♘a6 19 ♖he1 ♘c7 and the knight is finally captured, when Black's two pieces should make short work of White's rook and feeble pawn, Zirnis-Vitols, Latvia 1972] 13...♗f6 14 ♘xg6+ hxg6 15 ♖xg6 ♘f5 16 c3, Zirnis-Gubats, corr. 1972, 16...c6 and ...d5, with advantage) 12...♘f6 13 ♘c3 c6 (13...♖d8! is a more accurate way to prepare ...d5: 14 ♘gxe4 [14 d5 d6 15 0-0-0 ♗f5 16 ♖he1 ♘bd7 is fine for Black, as White has obstructed his bishop] 14...♘xe4 15 ♘xe4 d5 with good prospects) 14 d5! (White prevents ...d5; 14 ♘gxe4?!, Birkenfelds-Censonis, corr. 1976, 14...♘xe4 15 ♘xe4 d5 with an edge) 14...d6 15 0-0-0 ♗f5 16 ♖he1 c5 17 ♘cxe4 and White has broken through on the e-file before Black can finish his queenside development, Weijers - Van de Casteele, Haarlem 1996.

b) 8 ♗g5+? ♗e7 9 ♗xg6 (9 ♗xe7+? ♘xe7 10 ♕h4 ♕xh1+ 11 ♔d2 [11 ♔e2 d6 12 ♘c3 ♗g4+ 13 ♕xg4 ♕xa1] 11...e3+, Gillis-Pupols, USA 1966, is even worse) 9...♗xg5! (9...♕xh1+? loses, 10 ♔e2 c6 11 ♘f7+ ♔c7 12 ♘d2! [12 ♗xe7 ♕f3+ is less clear-cut, Leiva-Amilibia, corr. 1970] 12...♕xa1 13 ♗xe7 b6 14 ♗d8+ ♔b7 15 ♘d6+ ♔a6 16 ♗xe4 forcing mate, Hazlett-Nakamura, Hawaii ch 1990) 10 ♘f7+ ♔e7 11 ♘xg5 ♘f6 12 ♕h6 ♖g8!? (12...♕xh1+ 13 ♔e2 ♖g8 14 ♗xh7 ♖xg5 15 ♕xg5 ♕f3+ should also be sufficient) 13 ♘c3 c6! (safety first, although 13...♖xg6 14 ♘d5+ ♘xd5 15 ♕xh7+ ♔f6 16 ♕f7+ ♔xg5 17 0-0-0 ♔h6 18 ♕f8+ ♔h5 is probably winning, too) 14 ♘xh7 ♕xg6?! (14...♕xh1+! 15 ♔d2 ♕g2 16 ♘xf6 ♕xf2+ is clear) 15 ♘xf6 ♕xf6 beating off the attack, and remaining a solid piece to the good, for a couple of pawns, Crivosh-Apsenieks, Hungary 1925.

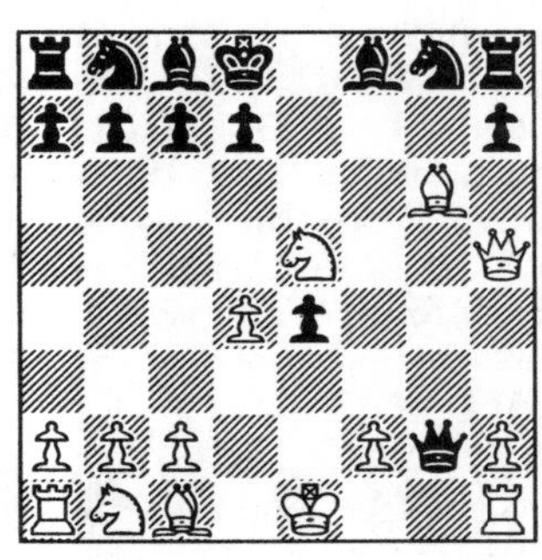

8...♕xh1+

There is little to be gained from not taking the rook, as the alternatives all lose! The analysis of the other moves, some of which emanates from Keres, is as follows:

a) 8...hxg6? 9 ♗g5+ ♗e7 10 ♕xh8 ♕xh1+ 11 ♔e2 ♗xg5 12 ♕xg8+ ♔e7 13 ♕f7+ ♔d6 14 ♕xg6+ 1-0, Heap-Druke, corr. 1991.

b) 8...d6? 9 ♘f7+! (9 ♕g5+ ♕xg5 10 ♗xg5+ ♗e7 11 ♘f7+ ♔e8 12 ♘xh8+ [12 ♗xe7? ♘xe7 13 ♘xh8+ hxg6 14 ♘d2 d5 15 h4 ♗g4 keeps the knight encaged, Scott-Bullockus, corr. 1970] 12...hxg6 13 ♖g1 ♗f5 14 ♗e3 extracts the knight and wins the exchange) 9...♔e7 (9...♔e8? 10 ♘xd6+ 1-0, Robins-Bullockus, corr. 1970) 10 ♗g5+ ♘f6 11 ♘xh8 ♕xh1+ 12 ♔d2 e3+ 13 ♔e2 gives White his standard attack but without being a rook down!

c) 8...♗b4+? Tartakower's idea, but 9 ♔e2! ♕xh1 10 ♗g5+ ♗e7 11

♘f7+ ♔e8 12 ♘xh8+ is devastating.

d) 8...♘f6? 9 ♘f7+ ♔e8 10 ♘xh8+ (10 ♕e5+ ♗e7 11 ♘d6+ ♔d8 12 ♗xe4 ♕g7 13 ♗h6 is also convincing) 10...hxg6 11 ♕xg6+ exchanging queens, with advantage.

e) 8...♗g7? 9 ♘f7+ ♔e7 10 ♕c5+! (10 ♗g5+? changes the entire situation, 10...♔f8 11 ♘xh8 ♕xh1+ 12 ♔d2 ♕f3! 13 ♕xh7? ♕xf2+ 14 ♔c3 ♕xd4+ 0-1, Tallman-Smiley, corr. 1984, exceptionally, it is Black who gives mate!) 10...♔f6 11 ♕f5+ ♔e7 12 ♗g5+ ♘f6 13 ♕e5+ ♔f8 14 ♗xf6 is crushing.

9 ♔e2

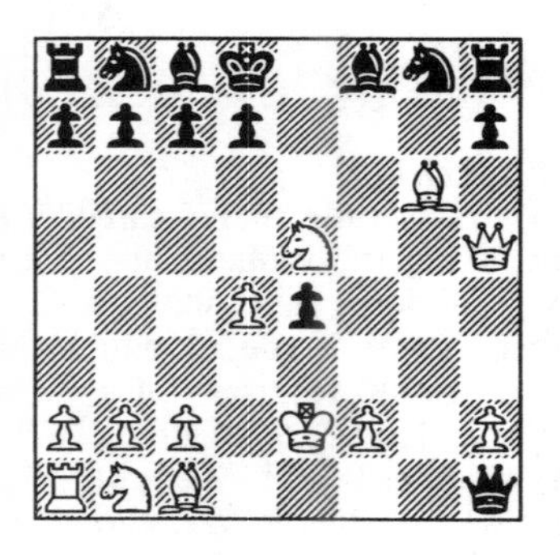

Now we have

A 9...♕xc1
B 9...c6

The alternatives are hopeless:

a) 9...d6? 10 ♘c3! (threatening ♗g5+) 10...♕g2 (10...♗e7 11 ♘f7+ ♔e8 12 ♗xe4) 11 ♗xe4 ♕g7 12 ♘f7+ ♔d7 13 ♗f5+ ♔e8 14 ♘xd6+ 1-0, Morgado-Toro, corr. 1968.

b) 9...hxg6? 10 ♗g5+ ♗e7 11 ♕xh8 ♗xg5 12 ♕xg8+ losing ignominiously.

c) 9...e3? 10 ♘f7+ ♔e8 11 ♘xh8+ hxg6 12 ♕xg6+ ♔d8 13 ♕xg8 c6 14 ♕xf8+ 1-0, Purcell-Summons, corr. 1997.

d) 9...♗g7? may be the best of the bunch, but even so, 10 ♗g5+ (10 ♘f7+?! ♔e7 11 ♕c5+ ♔e8 12 ♗h5?! [12 ♘d6+ draws] 12...♕f3+! 13 ♗xf3 exf3+ 14 ♔xf3 ♔xf7 15 ♕xc7 ♘c6 16 c3 ♘f6 17 ♗g5 ♖f8 18 ♔g2 ♔g8 and Black's pieces should outgun the queen, Stummer-Hunstock, corr. 1989) 10...♘f6 (10...♗f6 loses, but White has to be careful: 11 ♘d2! [11 ♘c3 is also winning; but on 11 ♗xf6+?! ♘xf6 12 ♘f7+ ♔e7 13 ♕e5+ {13 ♕c5+ d6 14 ♕xc7+ ♔f8 15 ♕xc8+ ♔g7 is far from clear} 13...♔f8 14 ♘d2 {14 ♘g5 ♔g7 15 ♗xe4 ♘c6!} 14...♕g2 15 ♘xh8 there is 15...♕g4+ 16 ♔f1 ♕e6 beating off the attack; 11 ♘f7+?! ♔e7 12 ♗xf6+ ♘xf6 transposes to this last line] 11...♕g2 [11...♕xa1 12 ♗xf6+ ♘xf6 13 ♘f7+ ♔e7 14 ♕e5+ ♔f8 15 ♕xf6 leads to mate] 12 ♘f7+ ♔e7 13 ♘xh8 ♕xg5 14 ♕xh7+ winning.) 11 ♕h6! A wonderful tactical shot! 11...♘c6 (11...♕g2? 12 ♕xg7 1-0 Stummer-De Jong, corr. 1994/95, 11...♗xh6?? 12 ♗xf6 mate) 12 ♕xg7 ♘xd4+ 13 ♔d2 e3+ 14 ♗xe3 c5 15 ♕xf6+ ♔c7 16 ♘c3 and mate follows rapidly, Ruggeri Laderchi-Lonsdale, corr. training game 1998.

A 9...♕xc1

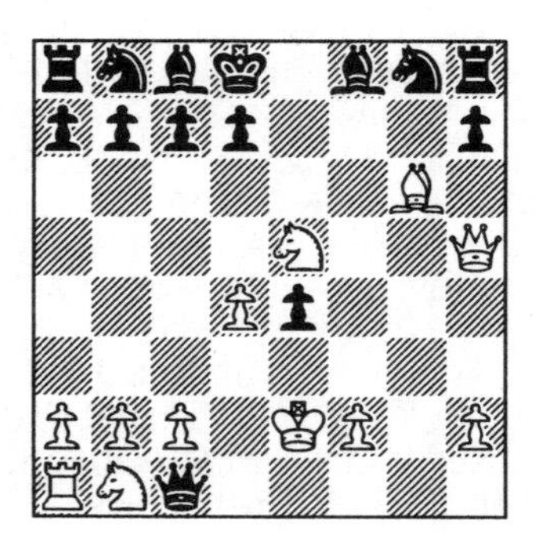

For a long time this was considered Black's best, as White's dark-squared bishop, which seems to form an integral part of White's attacking force, is thereby eliminated. But then Keres showed that White still has a strong attack and it is unlikely that Black can survive as his king is permanently exposed.

10 ♘f7+ ♔e8

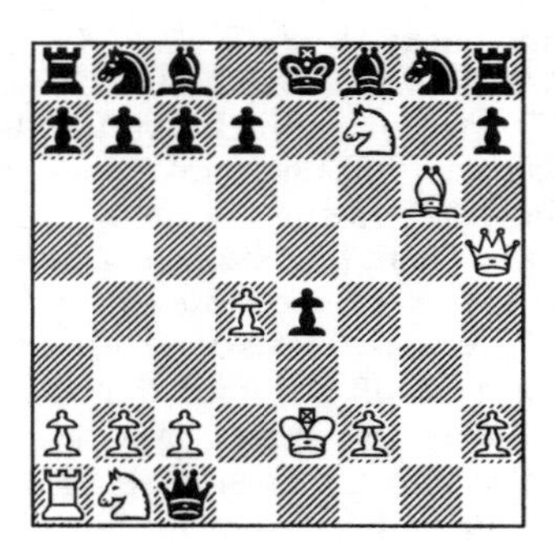

11 ♘xh8+

The strongest continuation, but there are others:

a) 11 ♕e5+!? ♗e7? (this is risky, after 11...♘e7! White should take a draw by 12 ♘d6+ ♔d8 13 ♘f7+ as 12 ♘xh8+? hxg6 13 ♘c3?! ♕xc2+ 14 ♔e1 ♕xb2 is catastrophic, and Black garners a lot of material for his queen after 12 ♘d2?! hxg6 13 ♖xc1 ♖h5 14 ♘g5 d5) 12 ♘d2! (12 ♘c3? ♕xc2+ 13 ♔e1 hxg6 14 ♘xh8 ♕xb2 0-1, Miller-Keres, corr. 1934, 12 ♕xh8 hxg6 13 ♕xg8+ ♗f8 14 ♕xg6 ♔e7 15 ♘e5 ♕h6 defends) 12...♕xb2 (12...♕xa1? 13 ♕xh8 hxg6 14 ♕xg8+ ♗f8 15 ♘e5 wins) 13 ♕xh8 hxg6 14 ♕xg8+ ♗f8 15 ♕xg6 (15 ♘e5!? Keres, 15...♕a3! 16 ♕f7+ ♔d8 17 ♘xg6 ♘c6 seems OK for Black) 15...♔e7 16 ♘h8 ♕xd4 17 ♕f7+ ♔d6 18 ♘b3 (18 ♕g6+ ♔e7 repeats) 18...♕xh8 19 ♖d1+ ♔c6 20 ♕d5+ ♔b6 21 ♕a5+ ♔c6 22 ♘d4+ forces Black to part with his queen.

b) 11 ♘d2!? aims to bring another piece into the fray, 11...♕xb2! the queen must return to defend her king, (11...♕xa1?! 12 ♕e5+!? [12 ♘xh8+ hxg6 13 ♕xg6+ ♔d8 14 ♕xg8 is simpler] 12...♘e7?! [better 12...♗e7 13 ♕xh8 hxg6 14 ♕xg8+ ♗f8 15 ♕xg6 ♔e7 with some chances] 13 ♘xh8+ hxg6 14 ♘xe4 [if queen and knight is a potent attacking force, then how about queen and two knights!] 14...♗h6 [Black is unable to survive by 14...♕xa2 either, 15 ♘f6+ ♔d8 16 d5 ♕a6+ 17 ♔f3 ♕xf6+ 18 ♕xf6] 15 ♘f6+ ♔f8 16 ♘xg6+ ♔f7?! [amazingly, after 16...♘xg6 17 ♕e8+ ♔g7 18 ♘h5+ ♔h7 19 ♕f7+ ♔h8 20 ♕xg6 ♕c1 the attack continues by 21 f4!] 17 ♘h8+ ♔f8 18 ♕h5 and White forces mate, Robins-Reza, corr. 1970; 11...hxg6?! 12 ♕xg6 ♕xd2+? [12...♕xc2 13 ♘xh8+ ♔e7 14 ♕xg8 ♗h6 is a better chance] 13 ♔xd2 ♗b4+ 14 ♔e2 ♘e7 15 ♘d6+ ♔d8 16 ♕e8+ ♖xe8 17 ♘f7 mate, Stummer-Logunov, corr. 1994/95 is very pretty!) 12 ♘xh8+ hxg6 13 ♕xg6+ ♔d8 14 ♕xg8 ♕b5+ 15 ♔e3 ♕f5 16 ♖g1 (16 ♘g6? ♔e8 17 ♘xe4?! d5 18 ♘xf8? allowing Black to wrap up the game quickly, 18...♕xe4+ etc., Polleschi-Walther, corr. 1971) 16...c5! as originally analysed by Betinš, 17 ♘f7+ (17 ♖g5?! cxd4+ 18 ♔e2 ♕f4! [18...d3+!? 19 cxd3 exd3+ 20 ♔f1 ♕f4 21 ♘f7+ ♔c7 22 ♕xf8, Kozlov-Sznek, corr. 1980, is also playable for Black, providing he continues with 22...♘c6] 19 ♖c5? [19 ♘f7+ ♔c7 20 ♕xf8 ♘c6 favours Black, anyway] 19...♘c6 20 ♘f7+ ♔e7 21 ♘g5 e3, Edwards-Gonsalves, corr. 1986, Black is winning; 17 d5?! ♔c7 18 ♘f7 ♕xd5 19

♕xf8 ♕d4+ 20 ♔e2 ♘c6 21 ♖g6 b6 is very easy for Black, Reza-Bullockus, corr. 1971) 17...♔e7 18 ♖g5 ♕h3+! (18...cxd4+ 19 ♔e2 d3+ 20 cxd3 exd3+ 21 ♔e1 ♕xf7 22 ♖e5+ ♕e6 23 ♘f3! ♘c6 is unclear) 19 ♔e2 ♘c6 20 d5 d6 (20...♘d4+ 21 ♔d1 d6 22 ♘xd6 transposes, 22 ♘h8 ♗d7 23 ♘g6+ ♔d8 is playable) 21 ♘xd6!? (21 ♘h8) 21...♘d4+ 22 ♔d1 ♗e6! 23 dxe6 ♔xd6 24 ♕f7 ♗e7 25 ♕f4+ (25 ♘xe4+? ♔c6 26 ♕xe7? ♕f1+ mates) 25...♔c6 26 ♕xe4+ ♔b6 27 ♖g3 ♕h5+ 28 ♔e1 ♖f8 29 ♘c4+ ♔c7 and Black has finally fended off the attack, and is now winning, Magee-Jensen, corr. 1989.

c) It is perhaps important to note that White can force a draw here, if he is so inclined, with 11 ♘d6+ ♔d8 12 ♘f7+.

11...hxg6 12 ♕xg6+ ♔d8 13 ♘f7+

13 ♕xg8? ♕f4 14 ♘g6 ♕f3+ 15 ♔e1 ♔e8 16 ♘e5 ♕f5 17 ♘c3 c6 and White is unable to bring his rook into the game, and is losing, Schmitz-Packroff, East Germany 1968; for 13 ♘d2!? see the analysis for 11 ♘d2.

13...♔e7 14 ♘c3! ♕xc2+

14...♕xa1? 15 ♘d5+.

15 ♔e1

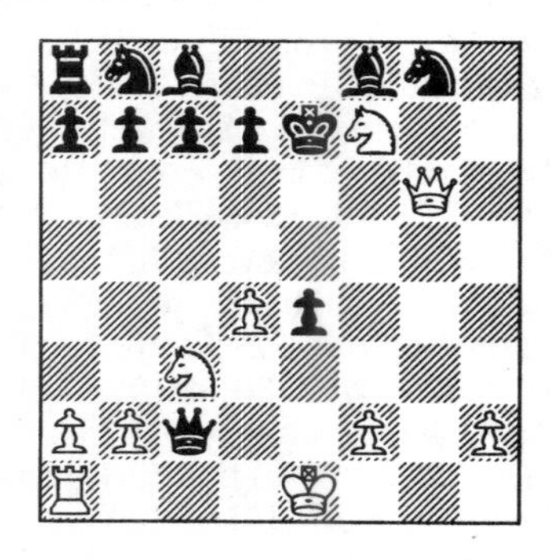

15...d6!

Best, if insufficient. Others:

a) 15...c6? 16 ♘d6! (White must threaten mate, any hesitiation is punished: 16 ♕xg8? ♕xb2 17 ♘xe4 ♕xa1+ 18 ♔e2 ♕xa2+ 19 ♔e1 ♕b1+ 0-1, Scott-Rondon, corr. 1971) 16...♘f6 (16...♕xb2??, Maly-Donny, corr. 1970, allows mate by 17 ♕g5+ ♘f6 18 ♕e5+ ♔d8 19 ♘f7 mate; 16...♔d8? 17 ♕xg8 ♕xb2? permits another sharp mating attack: 18 ♕xf8+ ♔c7 19 ♘e8+ ♔d8 20 ♘f6+ ♔c7 21 ♘fd5+! cxd5 22 ♘xd5+ 1-0, Boisvert-Fellows, Canada 1969) and now White has a choice of wins:

a1) There is some nice analysis in *NCO*: 17 ♘cxe4!! ♘xe4 (17...♕xe4+ 18 ♘xe4 ♘xe4 19 ♕xe4+ ♔d8 is forced, but must be winning for White, as the black pieces are undeveloped) 18 ♕e8+ the queen persecutes the poor black king just with the help of the knight, 18...♔f6 (and on its own: 18...♔xd6?? 19 ♕e5 mate) 19 ♕xf8+ ♔g5 (19...♔g6 20 ♕f7+ ♔g5 21 ♕f5+ transposes) 20 ♕f5+ ♔h6 21 ♘xe4 ♔g7 22 ♕f6+ ♔g8 23 ♘g5 and even giving up his queen will not stop Black from being mated! 23...♕h7 24 ♘xh7 ♔xh7 25 ♔d2 etc.

a2) 17 ♘f5+ ♔d8 18 ♕xf6+ ♔e8 19 ♕g6+ ♔d8 20 ♕g5+ ♔e8 21 ♖c1 ♕xb2 22 ♘d5! 1-0, Malmström-Ruggeri Laderchi, corr. 1998, to avoid mate Black must concede his queen by 22...♕xc1+ 23 ♕xc1 but continuing is hopeless.

a3) 17 ♕g5 ♗g7 (17...♔d8? 18 ♕xf6+ ♗e7 19 ♕h8+; 17...♘a6?? 18 ♕e5+ ♔d8 19 ♘f7 mate, Scott-Richter, corr. 1977/8) 18 ♕xg7+! (this is the only move to win, 18 ♘cxe4?! ♗h8 19 ♘f5+ ♔d8 20 ♘xf6 ♗xf6 21 ♕xf6+ ♔c7 22 ♕d6+ only draws, Heinrich-Kunath, corr. 1981; 18 ♘f5+?! likewise, 18...♔f7! [18...♔e6? 19 d5+ ♘xd5 20 ♘xg7+ ♔f7 21 ♘f5 ♕d3 22 ♖d1 ♕h3 23 ♘xd5, forcing mate, and a very neat one, too: 23...cxd5 24 ♕g7+ ♔e6 25 ♕e7+ ♔xf5 26 ♖xd5+ ♔f4 27 ♕g5+ ♔f3 28 ♖f5+ ♕xf5 29 ♕g3 mate, Hertneck-Hergert, corr. 1988] 19 ♕xg7+ ♔e6 20 ♘h6 ♕xb2 21 d5+ ♘xd5 22 ♕g6+ ♔e7 23 ♘f5+ ♔d8 24 ♕g8+ ♔c7 25 ♕g3+ ♔d8 26 ♕g8+ ½-½, Elburg-Ruggeri Laderchi, corr. 1998) 18...♔xd6 19 ♕xf6+ ♔c7 20 ♕f4+ ♔b6 21 ♖c1 ♕d3 22 ♕d6 ♘a6 23 b4! ♘xb4 24 ♕xb4+ ♔a6 25 ♘d5! cxd5 1-0, Ruggeri-Elburg, corr. training game 1998, because of 26 ♖c3.

b) 15...♘f6? 16 ♘e5 c6 (16...♔e6? 17 ♕f7+ ♔f5 18 ♘d5 ♗b4+ 19 ♔f1 e3 20 ♘xe3+ 1-0, Oyarzu-Macmon, corr. 1981) 17 ♕f7+ ♔d8 18 ♕xf8+ ♔c7 19 ♘f7, menacing mate on d8, 19...♔b6 (19...b5 20 ♕d8+ ♔b7 21 ♘d6+ ♔a6 22 a4! forcing mate, 1-0 Motivay-Barbosa, corr. 1970) 20 ♕c5+ ♔a6 (20...♔c7? 21 ♘b5 mate), Padula-Seri, corr. 1976, when the simplest kill is 21 ♕a3+ ♔b6 22 ♘a4+ ♔a6 23 b4!.

16 ♘d5+

16 ♘g5?! ♘h6! 17 ♘d5+ ♔d8 (17...♔d7!?) 18 ♕f6+ ♔e8 19 ♘h7, Strelis-Donny, corr. 1971, 19...♘f7 20 ♘xf8 ♔xf8 when White must force a repetition by 21 ♕e7+ ♔g7 22 ♕f6+.

16...♔d7 17 ♕xg8

(± *NCO*), 17 ♕f5+ ♔e8 18 ♕g6 ♘a6? (18...♕xb2!? is tempting, and 18...♔d7 offers to repeat), Lescot-Nilsson, corr. 1990, when White can win by 19 ♘e5+! (rather than the 19 ♕xg8? played, 19...♗e6 20 ♘xd6+ ♔d7 winning more bits) 19...♔d8 20 ♕xg8 dxe5 21 ♕xf8+ ♔d7 22 ♕e7+ ♔c6 23 ♘e3, gaining time on the black queen to continue the attack.

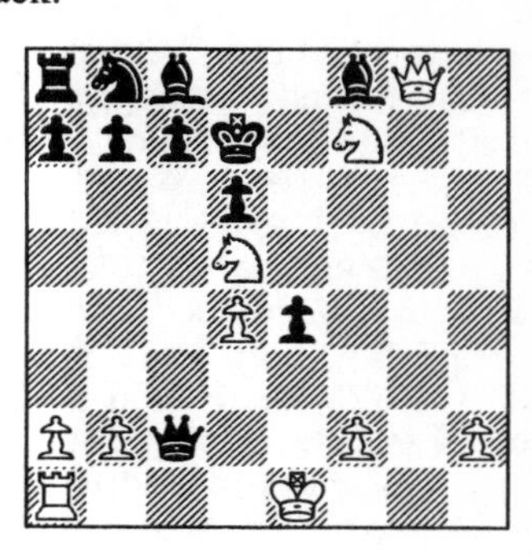

17...♕xb2

As well as this, 17...e3?! aims to bring the queen back to defend, with three possibilities:

a) 18 ♘xe3!? ♕e4!? (18...♕xb2 19 ♖d1 ♕b4+ 20 ♔f1 ♗e7 21 ♘e5+ dxe5 22 dxe5+ ♔c6 23 ♕xc8 is difficult for Black, who can't use his queenside pieces, Clarke-Pape, corr. 1990) 19 ♕xf8 ♘c6 20 ♖d1 ♘xd4 21 ♕d8+?! (21 ♕g7!) 21...♔c6 22 ♘g5 (the point of Black's play is that 22 ♖c1+ ♔b5 23 ♕xc7 is met by 23...♘f3+ 24 ♔e2 ♘d4+ and White cannot avoid the perpetual) 22...♘c2+ 23 ♔d2 ♕b4+ 24 ♔c1 ♘xe3 25 ♕e8+ ♗d7 26 ♕xe3 ♖e8 27 ♕d2 and Black is over the worst, Clarke-Pape, corr. 1994/95.

b) 18 ♘e5+!? dxe5 19 ♕f7+ ♔d6 (sacrificing the queen by 19...♔c6 20 ♕xc7+ ♔xd5 21 ♕xc2 is hopeless, the black king is too exposed) 20 ♘xe3 ♕e4 still looks unclear to me, seven years on, although White can force a draw if he desires, 21 ♕xf8+ ♔d7 22 ♖d1 exd4 23 ♕f7+ ♔d8 (23...♔c6? 24 ♕c4+ ♔b6 25 ♖xd4 wins) 24 ♕f6+ ♕e7 25 ♖xd4+ ♗d7 26 ♕h8+ (26 ♕xe7+? ♔xe7 27 ♘d5+ ♔d8 28 h4 loses, to 28...a5 29 h5 ♖a6 for example)

26...♕e8 27 ♕f6+ ♕e7 (27...♔c8?? 28 ♖h4) 28 ♕h8+ etc.

c) 18 fxe3! is strongest, 18...♕xh2 (the idea is that from here the queen can help defend the king, and also threaten annoying lateral checks.) 19 ♕g4+! (19 ♕xf8 ♕h1+ 20 ♔e2 ♕g2+ 21 ♔d3 ♕xd5 22 ♕d8+ ♔c6 23 ♖c1+ ♔b6 24 ♕xc7+ ♔a6 led to a draw in Nolden-Pape, corr. 1990; 19 ♘g5 ♕g1+ 20 ♔d2 ♕f2+ 21 ♔d3 ♘a6 22 ♕e6+ ♔c6 23 ♖c1+ ♔b5 24 ♘xc7+, Kozlov-Pape, corr. 1993, also seems to lead to a draw on 24...♘xc7 25 ♕c4+ ♔b6 26 ♕xc7+ ♔a6 27 ♕c4+ etc.) 19...♔e8 20 ♕xc8+ ♔xf7 21 ♕f5+ is winning, for example 21...♔e8 22 ♘xc7+ ♔d8 23 ♖c1, winning the exchange.

18 ♖d1

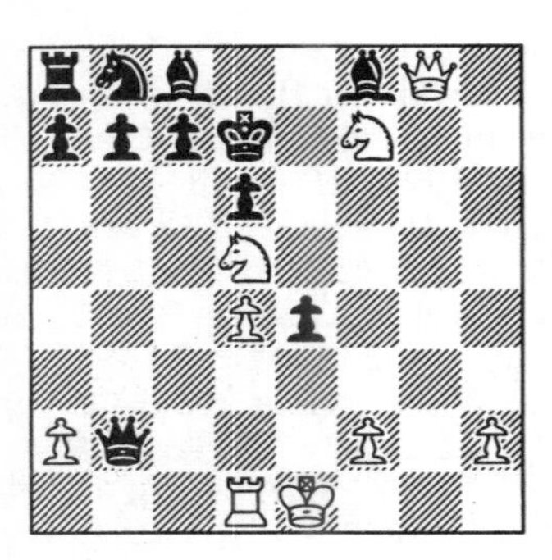

18...♘a6

The key to Black's defences in this line is that he may be able to force a perpetual check when the d5-knight no longer covers the c3-square. So he has to avoid losing material with checks, and the text, an idea of Bartsch, defends the c8-bishop. However, this loses just like the alternatives:

a) 18...c6? loses to a series of forcing checks: 19 ♘e5+! dxe5 20 ♕f7+ ♔d6 21 dxe5+ ♔c5 22 ♕xf8+ ♔b5 23 ♕xc8, Trobatto-Szura, corr. 1974.

b) 18...♗e7?! is also hopeless: 19 ♕g4+ ♔e8 20 ♕xc8+?! (20 ♕g6! ♔d7 21 ♕f5+ ♔e8 22 ♘xc7+ ♔f8 23 ♕xc8+ chases the king to its doom, 23...♔xf7 24 ♕e8+ ♔f6 25 ♘d5+ ♔e6 26 ♘f4+ ♔f5 27 ♕f7+ ♗f6 28 ♘d5) 20...♔xf7 21 ♕f5+ ♔g7 22 ♘xe7 ♘c6? (Black must play first 22...♕c3+! 23 ♔f1, then 23...♘c6 so that he has the resource ...♕c4+) 23 ♕g6+ ♔f8 24 ♕f6+ ♔e8, Maly-Bullockus, corr. 1971, 25 ♘d5! which wins the rook, for instance, 25...♖b8 26 ♕g7 (threatening mate in two).

c) 18...e3?! 19 fxe3 ♕xh2 (19...♕a3!?) 20 ♕g4+ ♔e8 21 ♕xc8+ ♔xf7 22 ♕xc7+ ♘d7 (the best try, for if 22...♔e6, then 23 ♘f4+ ♔f6 24 ♕xb7 wins comfortably) 23 ♕xd7+ ♔g8 24 ♕xb7 with a dominating position, and an extra pawn, White will win, Elburg-Ruggeri Laderchi, corr. training game 1998.

19 ♕g4+!

In the initial game, 19 ♕xf8?! was played instead, and there followed, 19...♔c6 20 ♘e7+ ♔b5 21 ♘xc8 and Black can force a perpetual check: 21...♕c3+ 22 ♖d2 ♕c1+ 23 ♔e2 ♕c4+ 24 ♔e3 ♕c3+ 25 ♔e2 ♕c4+ 26 ♔e1 ♕c1+ ½-½, Benatar-Bartsch, Sweden 1998.

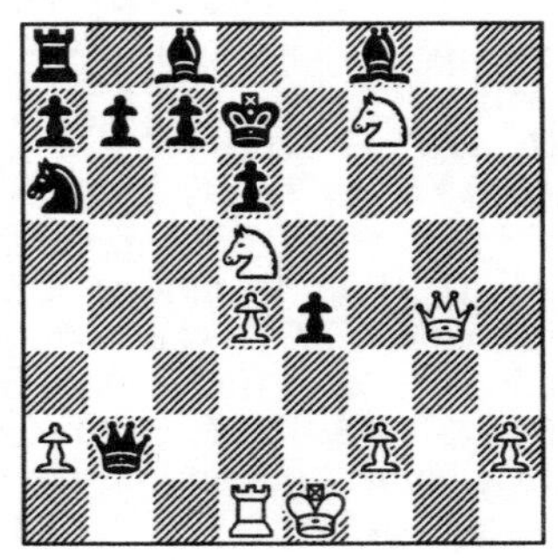

19...♔e8

Unfortunately for Black, Ruggeri Laderchi has analysed this to a forced win for White, and 19...♔c6 likewise, 20 ♘d8+ (20 ♕xe4?! ♗f5! [20...♕a3? 21 ♘d8+ ♔b5 22 ♖b1+ ♔a5 23 ♕c2 menacing ♖b3, and winning] 21 ♕xf5 [Black might be able to bring his king to safety after 21 ♘e7+ ♔b6 22 ♘xf5 ♕c3+ 23 ♔f1 ♘b4 as White has no checks] 21...♖e8+ [Black has few prospects in the ending that arises after 21...♘b4!? 22 ♖b1 ♖e8+ 23 ♘e5+ ♖xe5+ 24 dxe5 ♕xe5+ 25 ♕xe5 ♘d3+ 26 ♔e2 ♘xe5] 22 ♘e3 b6 [the black king is one move from safety on b7] 23 ♕h5!? ♕b4+ 24 ♔f1 ♕b5+ 25 ♕xb5+ ♔xb5, reaching an endgame where Black has chances.) 20...♔b5 21 ♕xe4 ♔a5 22 ♖b1 ♕xa2 23 ♕d3 and Black's only defence against the threats of mate is to give his queen.

20 ♕g6 ♔d7 21 ♘f6+!

Others lead to a draw:

21 ♕f5+ ♔e8 22 ♘f6+ (22 ♕g6 ♔d7 repeats) 22...♔xf7 23 ♘d7+ ♔e8 24 ♕xf8+ ♔xd7 25 ♕g7+ ♔e8 26 ♕g8+ draws.

21 ♕xe4 c5! 22 dxc5 ♘xc5 obliges White to take his perpetual check again, 23 ♕f5+ ♔e8 24 ♘c7+ ♔e7 25 ♘d5+ etc.

21...♔c6 22 ♕xe4+

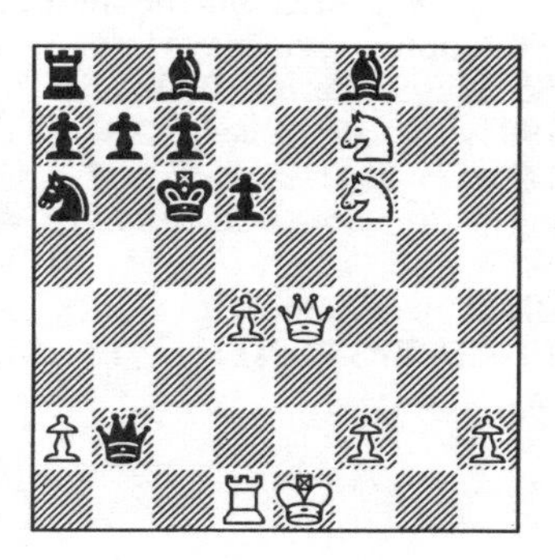

22...d5! 23 ♕xd5+

Black can even win after 23 ♘xd5?! ♔b5 24 ♖b1 (24 ♕d3+ ♔a5 25 ♘c3? ♕xc3+ 26 ♕xc3+ ♗b4) 24...♗b4+ 25 ♘xb4 ♕c3+ 26 ♔d1 ♘xb4 and White quickly runs out of checks after 23 ♘d8+?!, 23...♔b6 24 ♘xd5+ ♔a5.

23...♔b6 24 ♘e5 ♕b4+

24...♕c3+ 25 ♔e2 c5 26 ♖d3 ♕c2+ 27 ♖d2 ♕c3 28 ♘e4 ♕b4 29 ♘c4+ ♔c7 30 ♕e5+ ♔d8 31 dxc5+ ♗d7 32 ♖xd7+! ♔xd7 33 ♕d5+ wins.

25 ♔e2 ♕e7 26 ♕b3+ ♔a5 27 ♖b1 c6 28 ♘e4 ♘b4 29 ♘c5 b5 30 ♕xb4+ ♔b6 31 ♕c3 ♕e8 32 ♖g1

Black has managed to beat off the initial threats, but he remains material down, and undeveloped, Ruggeri Laderchi-Elburg, email 2001.

B 9...c6

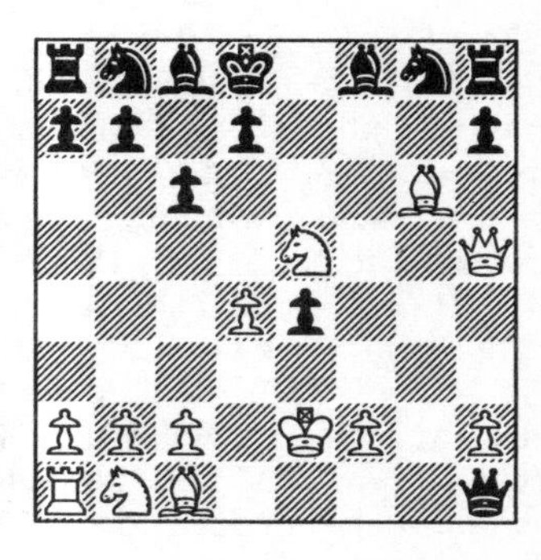

Diemer's move opens a route to the queenside, and possible safety, for the black king.

10 ♘c3!

White brings up the reserves, and menaces the deadly ♗g5+. Alternative moves have been discarded:

a) 10 ♗f4?! d6 11 ♘f7+ ♔c7 12 ♕g5 (12 ♕h4 ♘f6, Kotek-Budovskis, corr. 1970/71, amounts to pretty much the same thing; 12 ♘d2!? ♕xa1!? [this appears to lead to a draw, perhaps 12...hxg6 is a better try, 13 ♕xg6, Rondon-Berthelsen, corr. 1970, and now 13...♗g4+ 14 ♕xg4 ♕xa1 stalls the white attack] 13 ♘xd6! [13 ♕c5? fails to 13...♗g4+ 14 f3 ♗xf3+ 15 ♘xf3 exf3+ 16 ♔f2, Berthelsen-Hochmuth, corr. 1971, when the straightforward 16...hxg6 17 ♘xh8 {17 ♗xd6+ ♔d7 18 ♗xf8 ♖xh2+ forcing mate} 17...♘f6 should bring the game to its conclusion] 13...♗xd6 (13...♗e6!?) 14 ♗xd6+ ♔xd6 15 ♕e5+ ♔d7, Sprod-Bondick, East Germany 1984, and now, rather than losing, White should take a perpetual with 16 ♕e8+ ♔c7 17 ♕e5+) 12...♘f6! (12...♗e7?? 13 ♗xd6+ ♗xd6? 14 ♕d8 mate, Krustkains-Gubats, corr. 1972) 13 ♗h5 (obviously 13 ♕xf6?! ♗g4+ 14 ♔d2 ♕d1+ 15 ♔c3 ♕f3+ 16 ♔d2 ♕xf2+ 17 ♔c3 ♕f3+ 18 ♔d2 e3+ 19 ♔c3 e2+ 20 ♗d3 ♘d7 21 ♗xd6+ ♗xd6 22 ♕xd6+ ♔c8 23 ♘d2 ♕xf7 should win easily) 13...♘bd7 14 ♘xh8 b6 15 c4 ♗a6 winning quickly, Zemzars-Dreibergs, corr. 1960.

b) 10 ♘f7+?! ♔c7 11 ♗f4+ (11 ♘xh8 hxg6 12 ♗f4+ d6 13 ♘xg6 ♘f6 14 ♕a5+ b6 15 ♕d2 ♗a6+ 0-1, Prietz-Atars, corr. 1968 or 11 ♕h4 ♕f3+ 12 ♔e1 ♗e7 13 ♗f4+ ♔b6 ∓ Bauerndistel-Paperle, corr. 1973) 11...d6, the only move, but adequate, as above (but not 11...♔b6??, Scott-Pupols, corr. 1967/68, 12 ♘d2! threatening both mate in two, and the black queen).

c) 10 ♗g5+ ♔c7 11 ♕h4 b6 12 ♗xe4, Carlsson-Gyuricza, corr. 1977/78, 12...♗a6+ 13 c4 ♕g1 and now that his king has found safety on the queenside he will win.

Now there is another divide:

B1 10...♘f6
B2 10...♔c7
B3 10...e3

White appears to have a winning attack after all of these moves, with precise play, but (b) below merits more attention:

a) 10...♕g2?? loses swiftly, 11 ♗g5+ ♔c7 (11...♗e7 12 ♗xe4 ♕xg5 13 ♘f7+ winning, Szilagyi-Alberts, corr. 1979/81) 12 ♗xe4 ♘f6 13 ♗xf6 ♕g8 14 ♘f7 b6 (14...♔b6 15 ♗d8+ ♔a6 16 ♕a5 mate, Moyano-Castro, Barcelona 1980) 15 ♘b5+! 1-0, Melchor-Jackson, corr. 1987/88, as 15...♔b7 16 ♘d8+ ♔a6 17 ♘c7 mate.

b) 10...hxg6!?

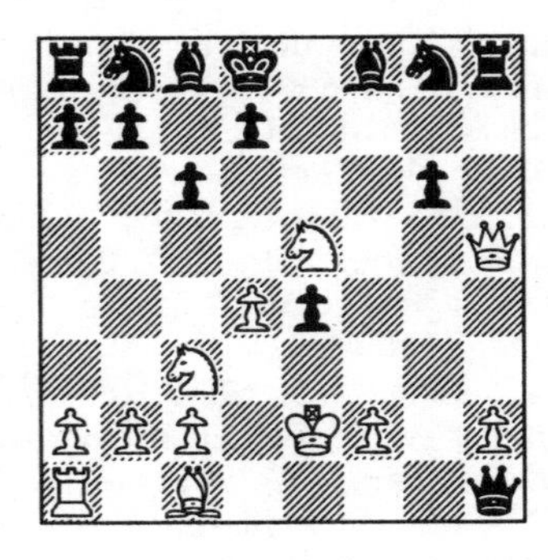

...is very rare, but no immediate refutation is evident: 11 ♕xh8 ♔c7 12 ♕xg8, Perron-Wehmeier, corr. 1993, 12...d6, forced, 13 ♕xf8 dxe5 14 ♕f7+ ♘d7 15 dxe5 ♕f3+, reaching a drawable endgame: 16 ♕xf3 exf3+ 17 ♔xf3 ♘xe5+ 18 ♔g3. Black must simply avoid 18...♗f5? 19 ♗f4 ♖e8 20 ♖e1, by 18...♔b6!?, say.

B1 10...Nf6

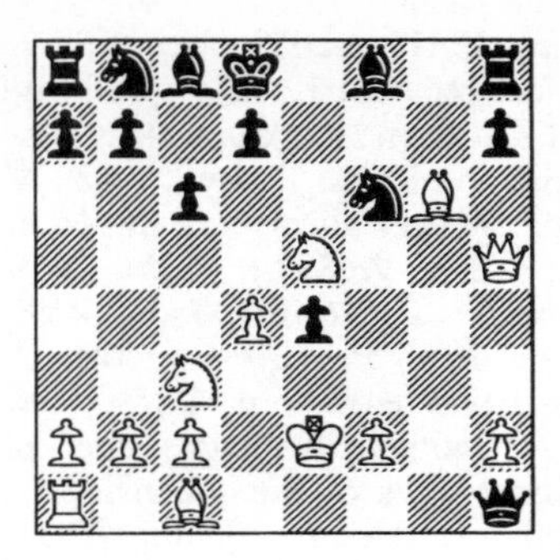

11 Qg5!

Pupol's move seems to be the most efficient.

a) Although 11 Qh4 is not bad, 11...Be7 (11...Rg8? allows a choice of wins: 12 Bg5 [12 Bxe4! is simple, 12...Qg1 13 Bg5 Qxa1 14 Bxf6+ Be7 15 Bxe7+ Kc7, Brieger-Nickel, Washington 1971, when 16 Nc4 decides immediately] 12...Qxa1 13 Bxf6+ Be7 14 Bxe7+ Kc7 15 Nc4 b5 16 Nxe4! [16 Nxb5+! cxb5, Gabrans-Strelis, corr. 1974, is also effective as 17 Qg5! mates] 16...Na6 [16...bxc4 17 Qg3+ Kb7 18 Nd6+ forces mate, 16...hxg6 17 Bd6+ Kb7 18 Nc5 mate and 16...Rxg6 17 Bd8+ Kb7 18 Nc5 mate, likewise, but quicker] 17 Qg3+ Kb7 18 Ned6+ Kb8 19 Ne8+ with mate to follow shortly. 11...Bg7 will probably transpose, 12 Bg5 Qxa1 13 Bxf6+ Kc7!? 14 Nc4! Bxf6? [14...d6 15 Bxg7 Rd8 has to be tried] 15 Qf4+ winning, Zagata-Ikarts, corr. 1993) 12 Bg5 Qxa1 13 Bxf6 Bxf6 (Black might consider 13...b6 14 Bxe7+ Kc7 15 Nf7! [15 Bxe4 Ba6+ 16 Kd2 Rg8 17 Nf7 and now, in Kermeen-Clear, corr. 1987, Black has to move his a6-bishop so that the king can use the a6-square, but the lack of defence on the dark squares doesn't bode well] 15...d5 16 Qg3+ Kb7 17 Nd6+ Ka6 18 Nxd5 Bg4+ 19 Qxg4 cxd5 20 Bxe4! Nc6, Dravnieks-Budovskis, corr. 1970, but 21 Qd7! is crushing; 13...Kc7 14 Nc4?! [14 Bxe7 b6 15 Nf7 wins as per the previous note] 14...b5 15 Qg3+ d6 16 Bxe7 Bg4+ 17 Qxg4 hxg6 18 Qe6 bxc4 19 Bxd6+ Kb7 20 Qf7+ forcing a perpetual check, Gunderam-Pupols, corr. 1970) 14 Qxf6+ Kc7 15 Nc4 (if 15 Nxe4 Rg8? allows mate, 16 Qd6+ Kd8, Reichardt-Geisler, corr. 1990, when White overlooked the obvious 17 Nf7+ Ke8 18 Nf6 mate, but Black can play 15...b6) 15...b6 (15...b5? 16 Nxb5+ cxb5 17 Qe5+ Kd8 18 Qxh8+ Kc7 19 Qe5+ Kd8 20 Nd6 forces a quick mate, Burk-Rebber, corr. 1985) 16 Qe5+ Kd8 (16...d6? lost on the spot in Purins-Eglitis, corr. 1971, 17 Nb5+! as 17...cxb5 18 Qxd6+ Kb7 19 Bxe4+; and 16...Kb7?! is hardly any better, 17 Bxe4 Rg8? [but 17...d5 18 Nd6+ Ka6 19 Nxd5 also wins] 18 Nd6+ Kc7 19 Ndb5+ 1-0, Bronislawa-Blaszczak, corr. 1992) 17 Qxh8+ Kc7 18 Qe5+ Kd8 19 Nd6 Ba6+ 20 Kd2 Qg1?! 21 Nf7+ Kc8 22 Nxe4 1-0, Gunderam-Budovskis, corr. 1970.

b) 11 Nf7+?! Kc7 12 Qa5+ (12 Qe5+?! d6 13 Qxf6 Bg4+ 14 Kd2 Nd7 ∓ Eglitis-Dille, corr. 1968) 12...b6 13 Nb5+! cxb5 14 Qc3+ Nc6 15 Bf4+ d6 16 Rxh1 Rg8! 17 Bxh7! (17 Ne5? dxe5 18 Bxe5+ Kb7 19 Bxf6 Bg4+ 20 Kf1 Rxg6, garnering more than enough compensation for the queen, Herbert-Pupols, USA 1966) 17...Rg7? (17...b4 18 Qe3 still looks unclear) 18 d5 Nxd5? 19 Bxd6+ Kb7 20 Nd8+ Nxd8 21 Bxe4, winning, Kirwald-Bondick, corr. 1985.

c) 11 ♗g5?! probably only leads to a draw, 11...♕xa1 12 ♗xf6+ ♔c7 13 ♘f7 (13 ♘c4!? ♗b4 14 ♗e5+ d6 15 ♘xd6 b6!? 16 ♘xc8+ ♔b7 17 ♗f5?! [17 ♗xe4! ♖xc8 18 ♕f7+ ♔a6 19 ♕c4+ keeps an edge] 17...♕xb2 and eventually it was the white king that found itself mated, Keller-Peperle, corr. 1968) 13...♗b4! (13...b6!? 14 ♕e5+ d6 15 ♘b5+ cxb5 16 ♗d8+ ♔b7 17 ♗xe4+, Djellouli-Ilgart, France 1976, 17...♔a6 unclear) 14 ♕e5+ (14 ♗xh8 hxg6 15 ♕g5 b6 16 ♘xe4?, given by Milić as unclear, despite the fact that 16...♗a6+ 17 ♔f3 ♕h1+ 18 ♔e3 ♕c1+ exchanges queens, and wins! Instead 16 ♕d8+ ♔b7 17 ♘xe4 ♕e1+ 18 ♔f3 and Black may have no better than a draw; but not 14 ♕xh7?! ♗xc3 15 bxc3 ♖f8 16 ♕h4 b5 ∓ Levy-Strobel, Ybbs 1968) 14...d6 15 ♕e7+ ♘d7 16 ♗xh8 ♗xc3?! (16...♕xb2!) 17 ♕d8+?! (17 bxc3!) 17...♔b8 18 bxc3 ♕xc3 and now, instead of Gunderam's 19 ♘e5? ♕xc2+ 20 ♔f1 b5 21 ♘xd7+ ♔b7 and, perhaps surprisingly, White cannot avoid losing material, Destrebecq suggests 19 ♘xd6 when Black must be content with a perpetual: 19...♕xc2+ 20 ♔f1 ♕d1+ 21 ♔g2 ♕g4+ etc. as 21...♕f3+ 22 ♔g1 ♕f8? 23 ♗e8 ♕xd6 allows 24 ♗e5! which is most embarrassing!

11...♖g8

a) If 11...♗e7? then 12 ♘f7+ (stronger than 12 ♗f4 [preferred by *NCO*] when Black can struggle on a few moves, by 12...♕f3+ [12...♕xa1? allowing a forced mate, 13 ♘f7+ ♔e8 14 ♘d6+ ♔d8 15 ♘xb7+ ♗xb7 16 ♕a5+ ♔c8 17 ♕c7 mate, Baer-Reiser, corr. 1975] 13 ♘xf3 exf3+ 14 ♔xf3 hxg6 15 ♖e1 with advantage, the black pieces stuck on the queenside are no help: 15...d6 16 ♗xd6! ♖h3+ 17 ♔g2 ♗xd6 18 ♕xf6+ ♔c7 19 ♖e8 ♖xh2+ 20 ♔g1 b5 21 ♘e4 1-0, Mulleady-Champion) 12...♔e8 13 ♘xh8+ (13 ♘e5+ ♔d8 14 ♗f4 transposes to 12 ♗f4) 13...hxg6 14 ♕xg6+ ♔d8 15 ♘f7+ ♔e8 16 ♘e5+ ♔d8 17 ♗f4! ♕xa1 18 ♘f7+ ♔e8 19 ♘d6+ ♔d8 20 ♕e8+!! forcing mate in a few moves, Borik-Novak, Czechoslovakia 1969, as 20...♘xe8 21 ♘f7 mate.

b) 11...♗g7? is met by 12 ♗xe4 ♕xh2 13 ♕xg7 ♕h5+ 14 ♗f3 ♕e8 15 ♕xf6+ winning, Kozlov-Melchor, corr. 1989/91.

c) And 11...d6? by 12 ♕xf6+ ♔c7 13 ♗xe4! (both 13 ♕xh8? hxg6 14 ♗f4 ♗g4+ 15 ♔d2 e3+, Atars-Tomson, corr. 1974/5 and 13 ♗g5?! ♗g4+, Padula-Tomson, corr., are less emphatic) 13...♕xh2 (13...♕g1 14 ♗g5! ♗g4+ 15 ♔d3 with enormous advantage Kozlov-Melchor, corr. 1989/91) 14 ♘f3 (14 ♕xh8 dxe5 15 ♕xf8 ♗g4+ 16 ♔d3 is also more than sufficient, Heap-Melchor, corr. 1989/91) 14...♗g4 15 ♕xh8 ♘d7 16 ♕xh7 and Black has no compensation for the piece and pawn, Beoto-Bedevia, Cuba 1978.

12 ♕xf6+

12 ♗f4? is not so good: 12...♕f3+! and instead of 13 ♘xf3 exf3+ and 14...♖xg6 ∓, White can play 13 ♔e1!? as pointed out by

Destrebecq, but 13...♖xg6! 14 ♘xg6 ♗g7 15 ♘e5 h6! 16 ♕xg7 ♕xf4 still looks fine for Black.

12 ♘f7+? ♔e8 13 ♘d6+ ½-½, Schendel-Haas, corr. 1988.

12...♗e7 13 ♕f7!

White would be foolish to take a draw here with 13 ♘f7+ ♔e8 14 ♘d6+.

13...♖xg6

After 13...♖f8 14 ♗f4! is very strong, (14 ♕xf8+ also wins, but in a more pedestrian manner: 14...♗xf8 15 ♗g5+ [± *NCO*] 15...♔c7 [15...♗e7 16 ♗xe7+ ♔xe7 17 ♖xh1 hxg6 18 ♘xe4 d5 19 ♘xg6+! leaves White with a two-pawn advantage; 19 ♘g5?! ♗f5 allowed Black to hang on in Scott-Gebuhr, corr. 1972/74] 16 ♖xh1 hxg6, Grava-Budovskis, corr. 1970, was easily winning for White following 17 ♘xg6!) 14...♕xa1 15 ♕e8+ ♔c7, Padula-Oliveira, corr. 1971, and now, instead of 16 ♘c4+? when 16...♖xf4 17 ♕xe7 b6 makes the win problematical, 16 ♘f7+! ♔b6 17 ♕xe7 d6 18 ♘xd6 ♔a6 19 ♘dxe4 wins by a mile.

14 ♗g5

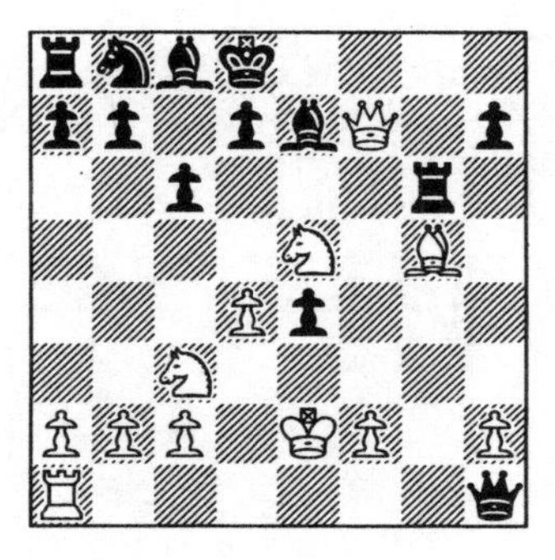

This is winning.

14...♕f3+

Unfortunately for Black, 14...♕xa1? allows a forced mate: 15 ♕xe7+ ♔c7 16 ♕d8+ ♔d6 17 ♘c4+ ♔e6 18 ♕e7+ ♔f5, Atars-Strat, corr. 1970, 19 ♘e3 mate.

15 ♘xf3 exf3+ 16 ♔xf3

16 ♔d3! ♗xg5 17 ♕xh7 is even better.

16...♗xg5

16...♖xg5 17 ♖e1 +/-.

17 ♕xh7

Or 17 ♘e4 ♗e7 18 ♕xh7 ♖e6 19 ♖g1 b5 20 ♖g8+ ♔c7, Pupols-Dreibergs, corr. 1957, 21 ♖e8.

17...♖f6+ 18 ♔g4 ♗d2 19 ♕h8+ 1-0

Purins-Eglitis, corr. 1970/74.

B2 10...♔c7

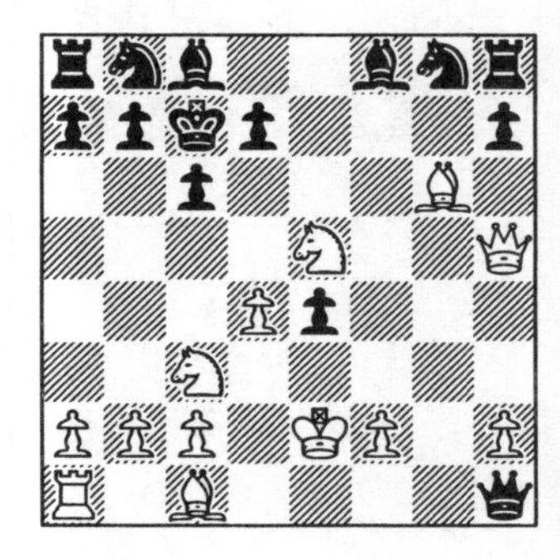

11 ♗f4!

Or:

a) 11 ♗xe4!? ♘f6 12 ♕h4 ♘xe4 13 ♗g5! (White's attack soon petered out after 13 ♘xe4? ♗e7 14 ♕f4 d6 15 ♘f7 ♖f8?!, Siegers-Harju, corr. 1971, but 15...♖g8! 16 ♘fxd6 ♗g4+ 17 ♔d2 ♕d1+ 18 ♔c3 ♕f3+ would have left Black playing an endgame with an extra rook. 13 ♘f7?! ♘xc3+ 14 bxc3, as in the game Ulschmid-Dohner, Mondorf 1962, 14...♗d6?? should have lost on the spot: 15 ♗g5 ♖e8+ 16 ♔d2; instead, Black must flee, 14...♔b6 15 ♘xh8 ♔a6 with advantage) now Black has the choice between 13...♘xg5 (and 13...♘g3+!? when in both cases, it is a question of whether Black can get his pieces coordinated, 14 ♔d3 [otherwise the queen escapes, 14 fxg3? ♕g2+ 15 ♔e3 ♗g7; 14 ♕xg3?! ♕xa1] 14...b6 15 ♖xh1 ♘xh1 which is not too clear) 14 ♖xh1 h6? (14...♖g8!?) 15 f4 ♘e6 16 d5 with a strong initiative, Tomson-Harju, corr. 1971.

b) 11 ♘f7? allows Black his dream: a queen exchange! 11...♕f3+ 12 ♔f1 ♕xh5 13 ♗xh5 ♘f6 14 ♗g5 ♗g7 15 ♗f4+ ♔b6 (15...d6 16 ♗xd6+ ♔d7 is simple enough) 16 ♗e2 a5 17 ♘a4+ ♔a7 18 ♗c7 ♘d5 19 ♗d6 b5 which should bring White's attack to a halt, Padula-Harju, corr. 1971.

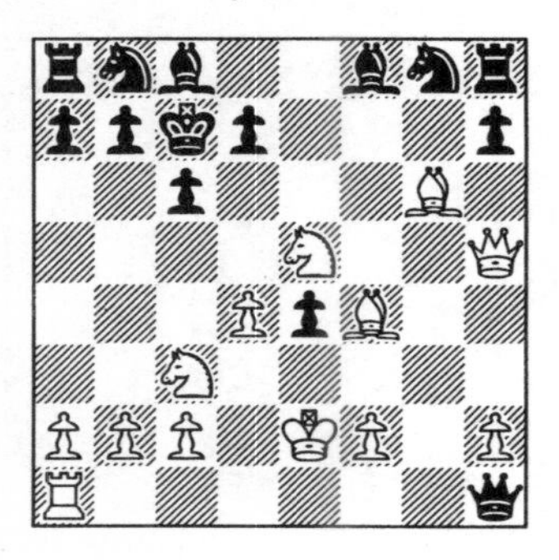

11...hxg6!

11...♕xa1? loses, 12 ♘xd7+! with 12...♔d8 (12...♔xd7 is quickest, 13 ♕f5+ ♔d8 14 ♕xf8+ ♔d7 15 ♕e8 mate, Atars-Tomson, corr. 1973 or 12...♗d6 13 ♕c5! [13 ♘b5+? ♔xd7 {13...cxb5?? 14 ♕c5+ ♔d8 15 ♕xd6 ♘xd7 16 ♗g5+ 1-0, Vitols-Scott, corr. 1970} 14 ♗e8+ ♔d8 15 ♘xd6 ♘f6 16 ♗g5 ♖f8 17 ♕h4 ♔c7 and White's attack is grinding to a stop, Uhlen-Malmström, corr. 1988] 13...hxg6 [there is nothing better, if 13...b6 14 ♘b5+ mates, 14...♔b7 15 ♘xd6+ ♔c7 16 ♘f7+ ♔b7 17 ♘d8+ ♔a6 18 ♕a3+ ♔b5 19 c4+ ♔xc4 20 ♕b3+ ♔xd4 21 ♘e6 mate] 14 ♕xd6+ ♔d8 15 ♗g5+ 1-0 Downey-Svendsen, corr. 1989) 13 ♕e5 hxg6 14 ♕c7+ ♔e8 15 ♕xc8+ ♔e7 16 ♗g5+ ♘f6 17 ♘xf6 ♔f7 18 ♕e8+ ♔g7 19 ♘g4 1-0 as mate follows, Ruggeri Laderchi-Malmström, corr. 1998.

12 ♕g5

The generally favoured move, but Black has recently discovered a useful resource.

12 ♕xh8! is certainly playable, and is probably stronger: 12...♕xa1 13 ♕xg8 d6 (13...g5 is no help, 14 ♕xf8 gxf4 15 ♘f7 f3+ 16 ♔d2) 14 ♕xf8 ♕xb2!? (14...♕g1?, Vitols-Budovskis, corr. 1972, 15 ♘xe4! wins, 15...dxe5? 16 ♗xe5+ ♔b6 17 ♕b4+ ♔a6 18 ♘c5 mate) 15 ♘f7 ♕xc2+ 16 ♗d2 ♗g4+ 17 ♔e1 ♔b6 18 ♕xd6 ♘a6 (Elburg's 18...a5 is better, but 19 ♘e5 e3 20 ♘c4+ ♔a6 21 ♘xe3 is winning) 19 ♘e5, winning, Gubats-Vitomskis, corr. 1970.

However, not 12 ♘c4+? d6 13 ♘b5+ (13 ♕xh8 ♕f3+) 13...cxb5 14 ♕c5+ ♔d8 15 ♗g5+ ♗e7 16 ♕xd6+ ♘d7 17 ♗xe7+ ♘xe7 18 ♖xh1 bxc4 -/+ Oren-Downey, corr. 1992.

12...♗e7

Again 12...♕xa1? is impossible: 13 ♘f7+ ♔b6 14 ♗c7+! 1-0, Ortiz-Amilibia, corr. 1968/69.

13 ♘xc6+ d6 14 ♗xd6+!

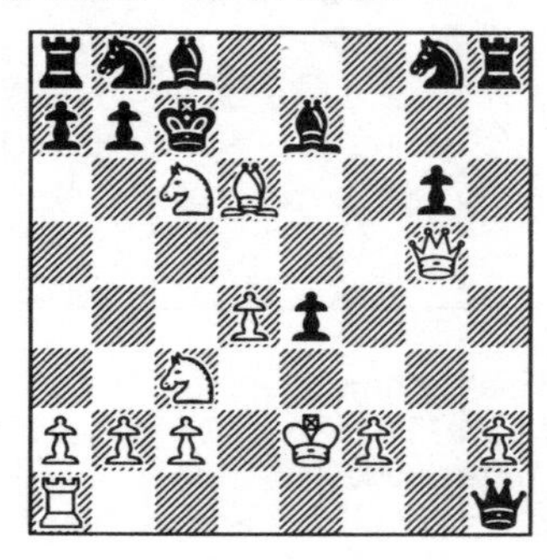

14...Kxd6!

Neither 14...Kd7? 15 Ne5+! Kxd6 16 Nb5+ Ke6 17 Qg4+ 1-0, Grava-Kotek, corr. 1970, nor 14...Bxd6? 15 Qd8+ Kxc6 16 Qxc8+, Downey-Jackson, corr. 1989, are playable.

15 Qc5+! Ke6!

If 15...Kd7 16 Ne5+ Kd8 17 Qa5+! is best, White must find a way to remove his queen from attack whilst giving check, (17 Nf7+ Kd7 18 Qd5+ [18 Ne5+! Kd8 19 Qa5+ transposes into 17 Qa5+] 18...Ke8 19 Rxh1 Nf6 20 Qc4 Bg4+ 21 Ke1 Rh7 which does not look entirely clear to me, Heap-Downey, corr. 1992) and after 17...Ke8 18 Rxh1, *NCO* indicates some advantage to White. 18...Nc6 (18...Na6? 19 Qb5+ 1-0, Behrmann-MacNab, corr. 1995; White maintains a decisive initiative after 18...Nf6 19 Nd5! Bd8 20 Nxf6+ Bxf6 21 Qd5, Malmström-Elburg, corr. 1998) 19 Qa4! (19 Nxc6 bxc6 20 Qc7 Bg4+ 21 Ke1 Rc8 doesn't appear that clear, Black does have two bishops and a rook for the queen and pawns) 19...Nf6 (19...Rb8 20 Nxg6 Bg4+ 21 Ke1 Rh5 22 d5 1-0, Koetsier-Rossell, corr. 1999) 20 d5 b5 21 Qxb5 Ba6 22 Qxa6 Nxe5 23 Qe6 Nf3 24 Rd1 Nh5 25 Qxg6+ Kd8 26 Qxe4 is devastating, Rosso-Rossell, corr. 1999.

16 Qe5+ Kf7 17 Rxh1 Nxc6

17...Bg4+ 18 Kf1 Nxc6 19 Qxh8 Bf5 20 Qh7+ Kf8 21 Nd5 Rd8 22 Nxe7 Ngxe7 23 c3 and the queen and two pawns are stronger than the three pieces, especially as the black king is exposed, Owens-Sakellarakis, corr. 1999.

18 Qxh8 Nf6

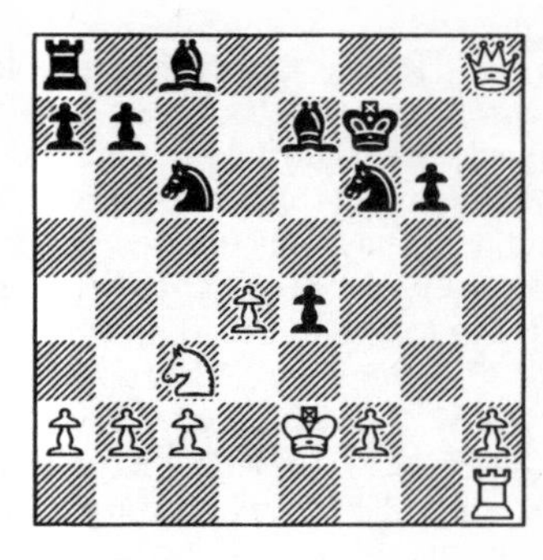

19 Kd2

19 Ke3?! Bf8 20 h3 Bg7 21 Qh4 Elburg-Owens, corr. 2000, and now Black played the tactic 21...Nxd4!? (but 21...Bf5 was also reasonable) 22 Kxd4 g5 23 Qxg5 Nh7+ 24 Qxg7+ Kxg7 25 Nxe4 with a piece for three pawns.

19...Bf8!?

19...Nxd4 20 Kc1 is also playable.

20 d5 Nb4

Unclear, Tiemann-Elburg, email 2001.

B3 10...e3

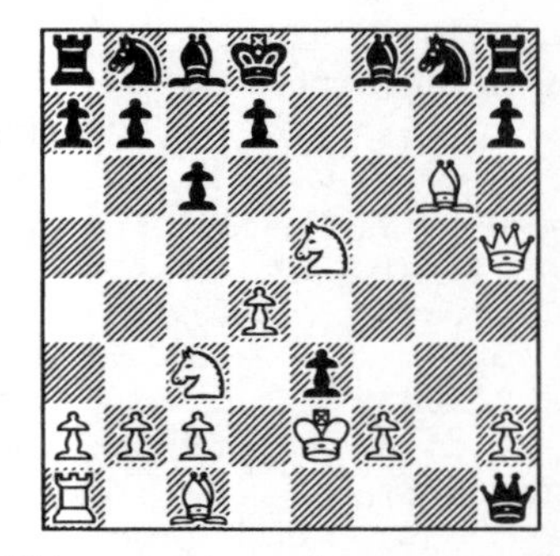

This move, the so called 'blockade attack', was first suggested by Dreibergs.

11 Nf7+

It is now clear that this is White's best move here, either immediately or one move later in (a). The others:

a) 11 ♗xe3 ♕xa1, the position resembles a game between two beginners, one who has developed all his pieces but lost two rooks, the other who has only moved his king and queen! 12 ♕g5+?! (White does better to return to the main line here, with 12 ♘f7+! ♔c7 13 ♕g5, but not 12 ♗g5+? as 12...♔c7 13 ♘f7 b6 14 ♗d8+ ♔b7 15 ♕e5 ♘a6 16 ♘b5 ♖b8 and Black was out of the woods in Murray-Pupols, Sokane Wasch 1966) 12...♗e7 13 ♘f7+ ♔e8! (13...♔c7, transposing into the main variation, is inferior) 14 ♘xh8+ ♔d8 15 ♘f7+ ♔e8 16 ♘e5+ (White took a risk with 16 ♕e5!? in Jimenez Alonso-Miguel, Spain 1995, but the game finished in a draw anyway: 16...hxg6 17 ♕g7 ♘f6 18 ♘e4 ♘xe4 19 ♕g8+ ♗f8 20 ♗h6 d6 21 ♕xf8+ ♔d7 22 f3 ♕h1 23 ♕d8+ ♔e6 24 ♕e8+ ♔f6 ½-½) 16...♔d8 17 ♘f7+ ♔e8 18 ♘d6+ ♔d8 ½-½, Magee-Melchor, corr. 1989/90.

b) 11 ♗e4?! only leads to a draw with best play, 11...♕g1 12 ♗xe3 ♕xa1 (Black gains nothing from keeping his queen in the game, 12...♕g7?! 13 ♘f7+ ♔c7 14 ♕a5+ b6 15 ♘b5+! cxb5 16 ♕c3+ ♘c6 17 ♗f4+ ♔b7 18 ♘d8+ ♔a6 19 a4, trying to bring the rook on a1 into play with decisive effect, 19...♘xd4+ 20 ♔d2 b4? 21 ♕c4+ ♔a5 22 ♕d5+ ♗c5 23 ♕xc5+ bxc5 24 ♗c7+ 1-0, Amilibia-Alberts, corr. 1968) 13 ♘f7+ ♔c7 14 ♕a5+!? (a critical position, 14 ♘xh8? ♕xb2 15 ♗f4+ d6 16 ♕f7+ ♘d7 17 ♕c4 ♘gf6 18 ♗d3 b5 0-1, Ciprian-Sneiders, corr. 1972/4, is no good; and 14 ♕g5?! ♗e7 15 ♗f4+ d6 16 ♗xd6+ ♔d7 17 ♗xe7 ♘xe7 18 ♘e5+ ♔c7 19 ♕xe7+ ♗d7 is OK for Black; but Hergert's suggestion 14 ♗g5!? is dangerous, 14...♘a6 [not 14...b6? which provokes a king-hunt: 15 ♘b5+! ♔b7 16 ♘d8+ ♔a6 17 ♘c7+ ♔a5 following Melchor's analysis, and now 18 ♘xc6+! ♔a4 19 ♕f7 ♕xb2 20 ♕c4+ ♗b4 21 ♗c1 threatening mate by ♕b3+, and winning.] 15 ♗d8+ ♔b8 16 ♕e5+ d6 17 ♘xd6 ♗g4+ 18 f3 ♗xd6 19 ♕xd6+ ♔c8 20 fxg4 ♘h6 and now White can force a draw with 21 ♕e6+) 14...b6 15 ♘b5+ cxb5 16 ♗f4+! (as Melchor points out 16 ♕c3+? ♘c6 17 ♗f4+ ♔b7 18 ♘d8+ ♔a6 19 d5 ♗b4 20 ♕xh8 ♕e1+ is winning for Black) 16...d6 17 ♕c3+ ♔d7 18 ♕h3+ ♔c7 (Black has little choice but to acquiesce to the draw as 18...♔e7? 19 ♗xd6+ ♔xf7 20 ♗d5+ [20 ♕h5+?! ♔e6 is only a perpetual] 20...♔f6 21 ♕h4+ ♔g6 22 ♕g3+ ♔f6 23 ♕f4+ ♗f5 24 h4! forces mate; and 18...♔e8? 19 ♕xc8+ ♔xf7 20 ♗d5+ likewise) 19 ♕c3+ ♔d7 20 ♕h3+ ♔c7 ½-½, Stibal-Croker, corr. 1992.

c) 11 fxe3? is just what Black is hoping for: 11...♕g2+ 12 ♔e1 ♕g1+! 13 ♔e2 d6 (so as to have the annoying possibility of ...♗g4+, later) 14 ♘f7+ ♔c7 15 ♗f5 ♗xf5 16 ♕xf5 ♕xh2+ and ...♘h6 -/+, analysis of Alejandro Melchor (or first 16...♘h6!).

d) ...as is 11 ♔xe3? ♗h6+.

11...♔c7

Now there is a further important choice, between B31 12 ♕g5!, which wins easily, and B32 12 ♗xe3, the traditional main line. otherwise:

a) 12 ♕e5+? loses, 12...d6 13 ♕xh8 exf2 14 ♔xf2 ♕xh2+ 15 ♔f3 ♕h3+ 16 ♔f2 ♕h4+ 17 ♔e3 ♕g3+ 0-1, Plath-Phillips, corr. 1992 .

b) 12 ♕h4! amounts to the same as 12 ♕g5, although *NCO* prefers this particular move order, i.e.

12...♗e7 (12...♘e7?! 13 ♗xe3 ♕xa1 14 ♕f4+ 1-0, Stark-Khulmann, corr. 1980, as mate follows) 13 ♕g3+ d6 14 ♗e4 etc.

c) 12 ♗e4 ♕g1 13 ♗xe3 transposes into B32 above, but not 13 ♕h4?! Borsdorff-Alberts, corr. 1967/69, 13...♗e7 ∓.

B31 12 ♕g5!

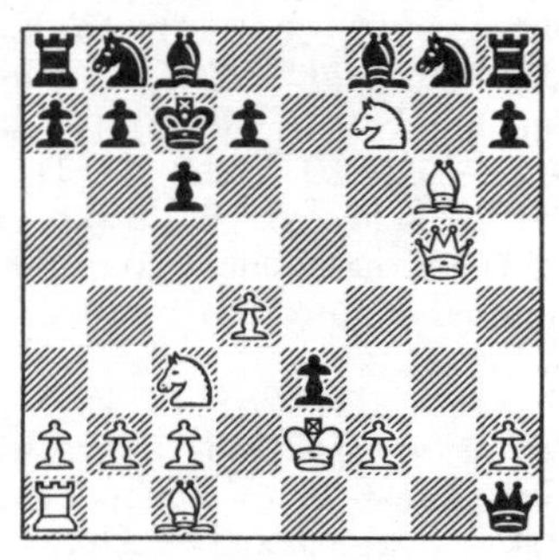

This wins by force.

12...♗e7

12...b6?! 13 ♕d8+ ♔b7 14 ♘e4 ♕xh2 15 ♕xf8 removes Black's dark-squared defence and wins.

13 ♕g3+ d6 14 ♗e4 ♗g4+

Else the queen is trapped.

15 ♕xg4 ♘f6

15...♕xh2 amounts to the same, 16 ♗xe3 ♘f6 17 ♕e6 ♘xe4 18 ♕xe7+ transposes below.

16 ♕e6!

16 ♗xh1 ♘xg4 17 ♘xh8 isn't bad, either, Black has insufficient compensation for the piece, still, that did not stop him from drawing in Lescot-Melchor, corr. 1995: 17...♘a6 18 ♘f7? (18 f3) 18...♖f8 19 f3 ♖xf7 20 fxg4 ♖f2+ 21 ♔xe3 ♖f1 22 ♗e4 ♗g5+.

16...♘xe4

16...♕xh2 changes nothing, 17 ♗xe3! ♘xe4 18 ♕xe7+ ♘d7 19 ♘xe4 and White wins easily, 19...♖he8 20 ♕xd6+ ♕xd6 21 ♘fxd6 ♖e6 22 ♖h1 ♖f8 23 ♖h6 ♖xh6 24 ♗xh6 1-0, Oren-Malmström, corr. 1994/95.

17 ♕xe7+ ♘d7 18 ♘xe4 ♖ae8 19 ♕xd6+ ♔c8 20 ♕f4 winning, Falkowski-Leisebein, corr. 1988.

B32 12 ♗xe3

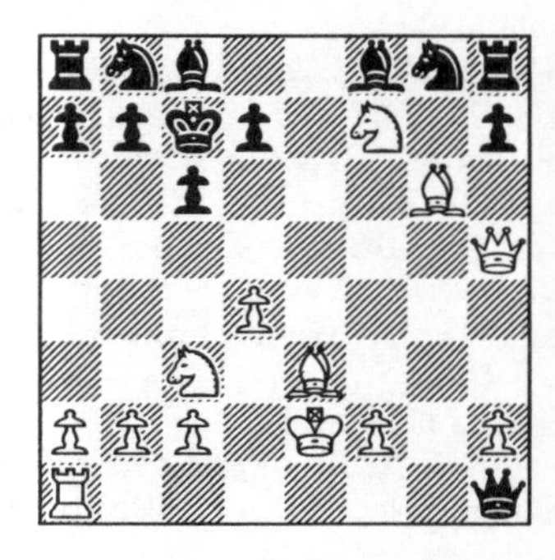

This is very unpleasant for Black, as his king has to go for a walk, but it is not the strongest.

12...♕xa1 13 ♕g5

Threatening mate on d8. In one of the first games in this line, Benner-Dreibergs, corr. 1965, White continued 13 ♗f4+? d6 14 ♕g5? (14 ♘xd6!? is an alternative, 14...♗xd6 leads to a draw, as does 14...♗g4+ 15 ♕xg4 ♗xd6 16 ♗xd6+ ♔xd6 17 ♕f4+ ♔e7 18 ♕f7+ ♔d8 19 ♕e8+ and so on, Boll-Van Dieren, 1978, but 14...hxg6!? may be better, for example 15 ♘de4+ ♔d8 16 ♕xh8 ♗e6 and Black defends) 15 ♗xd6+ ♔xd6 16 ♕e5+ ♔d7 17 ♕e8+ ♔c7 18 ♕e5+ ♔d8 19 ♕e8+ ½-½, Eckenfels-Alberts, corr. 1967) 14...♗g4+! (14...♘e7 was also good in Neukirch-Dravnieks, corr. 1968) 15 ♕xg4 hxg6 16 ♘xh8 (16 ♕e6 ♘d7 17 ♘xd6 Alloin-Keller, corr. 1988, and now Black should win by using the deflection 17...♗xd6 18 ♕xd6+ ♔d8 19 ♗g5+ ♘e7!) 16...♘d7 17 ♕xg6 ♘gf6 18 ♔d2 ♖e8 0-1.

13...♗e7

Black has some choice:

Not 13...b6? 14 ♕d8+ ♔b7 15 ♕xf8 hxg6?! (allowing mate, but 15...♘e7 is also hopeless, 16 ♘d8+ ♔a6 17 ♗d3+ b5 18 ♕xh8) 16 ♘d8+ 1-0, Elburg-Alderden, corr. 1985.

However, 13...b5!? is possible; 14 ♕d8+ ♔b7 15 ♘e4 ♘f6? (15...♘h6!? 16 ♗xh6 d5 is not at all clear) 16 ♕a5! ♘a6 17 ♘d8+ ♔b8 18 ♗f4+ d6 19 ♘xc6+ ♔b7 20 ♘d8+ ♔b8 21 ♕xb5+, stripping the black king bare, Grava-Alberts, corr. 1968.

14 ♗f4+

It is difficult to believe the surprising 14 d5? of Whittemore-Dreibergs, Detroit 1966: 14...d6 (14...♗xg5?? 15 d6 mate) 15 ♕g3 hxg6 16 ♗c5 ♗f5 17 ♘xd6 (17 ♗xd6+ ♔c8) 17...♔d7! 18 ♕e5 ♘a6 19 ♘ce4 ♗g4+, winning.

14...♔b6

Ugly, but essential as 14...d6? 15 ♗xd6+ ♔d7 16 ♕f5+ forces mate, van Loon-de Vries, corr. 1982.

15 ♘a4+ ♔a6

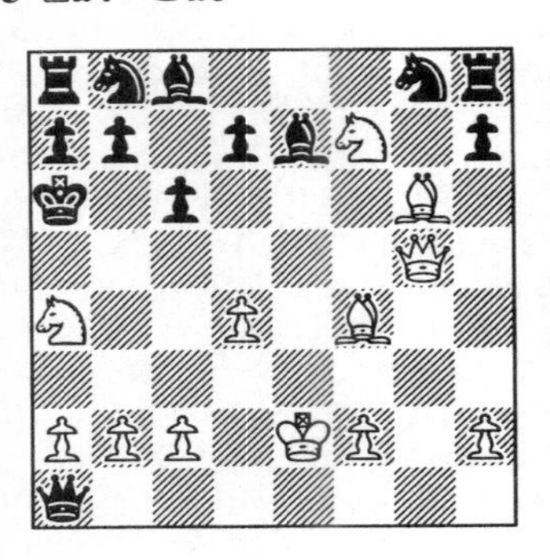

16 ♘c5+

The black king may be out on a limb, but he is only a move from safety, and Black does have two extra rooks, so White cannot afford to hang around:

a) 16 ♗c7? b6! (somewhat superior to 16...b5?? 17 ♕xe7! 1-0, Braczko-Holiman, corr. 1991) 17 ♗d3+ (17 ♕e5 ♘f6?! [17...♕xa2 or 17...hxg6!?] 18 ♗d3+ ♔b7 19 ♗d6 ♕xa2 20 b3 ♗d8?! [20...♖f8 21 ♕xe7 ♖xf7 22 ♕xf7 ♘d5 should win] 21 ♘xh8 ♕a1?? 22 ♘f7 a5 23 ♘xd8+ ♔a7 24 ♕xa5+ bxa5 25 ♗c5 mate, Melchor-Svendsen, corr. 1987/88) 17...♔b7 18 ♕g3 (18 ♗d8? ♘h6! 0-1, Elburg-Rittenhouse, corr. 1990) 18...♕xa2 19 b3 ♘h6 20 ♘xh8 d5 21 ♕e5 ♕a3 22 ♕f4 ♘d7 23 ♕xh6 ♔xc7 and Black has almost consolidated, Stummer-Malmström, corr. 1994/95.

b) 16 ♗d3+? b5 17 ♘c5+ (17 ♕e5 ♕xa2! [17...d6? is worse, 18 ♘xd6 ♗g4+ 19 f3 ♗xf3+ 20 ♔f2! ♗h4+ 21 ♗g3 ♗xg3+ 22 hxg3 ♗d5 and now White forces mate: 23 ♗xb5+ ♔a5 24 ♗xc6 ♘e7, Patron-Ciprian, corr. 1972, 25 ♘c4+ ♔b4 26 ♕xe7+ ♔xc4 27 ♕c5 mate] 18 b3 ♘f6 19 ♘xh8 ♘d5 defending e7, and c7, 20 ♗d2 d6 21 ♕h5 ♘d7 22 ♕xh7 ♘7f6 23 ♕g7 ♗g4+ 24 f3 ♖g8 -/+ Schutz-Leisebein, corr. 1988; 17 ♗c7 ♔b7 18 ♗d8 ♘a6 19 ♗xe7 ♘xe7 20 ♗xb5 ♘c7 0-1, Turian-Melchor, corr. 1995) 17...♔b6! (17...♗xc5 transposes to the main line) 18 ♘d6! ♘f6! (18...♘a6?? is a blunder, allowing mate in five 19 ♘c4+! bxc4 20 ♘a4+ ♔b7 21 ♕b5+ cxb5 22 ♗e4+ 1-0, Repp-Paschitta, corr. 1991) 19 ♘a4+ (19 ♘xb5 ♘d5!? 20 ♗c7+ ♘xc7 21 ♘xc7 ♔xc7! [21...♗xg5? 22 ♘xa8+ ♔a5 23 ♘b3+ ♔a4 24 ♘c5+ draws] 22 ♕xe7 ♕xb2-+ analysis of Miguel) 19...♔c7 20 ♘xb5+ ♔b7 21 ♕xf6 ♖e8! 0-1, Smith-Phillips, corr. 1998.

16...♔b6

Trying to hold on to the dark-squares. 16...♗xc5? loses, 17 ♗d3+ b5 18 ♕xc5 ♕xb2 (this is an attempt to improve on both 18...d6 19 ♗xb5+! cxb5 20 ♕xd6+ ♘c6 21 ♕xc6+ ♔a5 22 ♗d2+ b4 23 ♗xb4+ ♔xb4 24 c3+ 1-0, Tums-Dreibergs, corr. 1966, and 18...♕xa2 19 ♘d6 ♕xb2 [how else to defend against the threat of ♗xb5+ ?] 20 ♗c1 ♕b1 21 ♗d2 ♕b2 22 ♗c3 ♕xc3 23 ♗xb5+ ♔a5 24 ♕xc3+ forcing mate, Harding-Comley, corr. 1986, although 24 ♘c4+ would have saved a few moves) 19 a4 ♘f6 20 axb5+ (20 ♘d6! is quicker) 20...♔b7 21 ♘d6+ ♔c7 22 ♘c4+ ♔d8 23 ♘xb2, winning the queen and the game, Elburg-Rosso, corr. 1998, so still not sufficient.

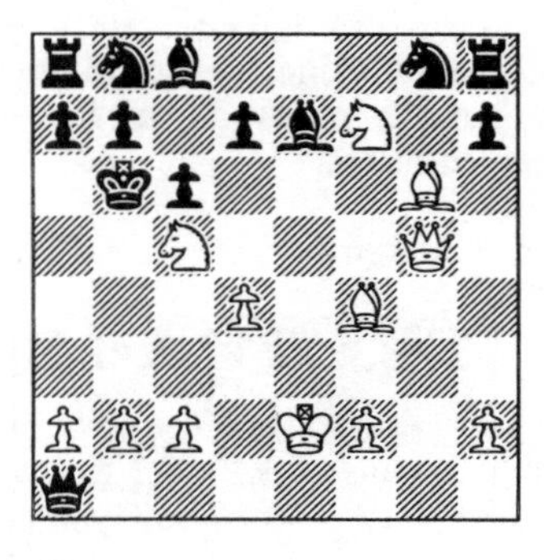

17 ♕g3

As there is no sure win after this, White should prefer Tiemann's 17 ♕e5!, i.e. 17...d6 18 ♘xd6 ♗g4+ 19 f3 ♕xa2 20 ♘c8+! 1-0, Nuutilainen-Rhodes, BPCF v Finland, corr. 1998, as 20...♗xc8 21 ♕c7+ ♔b5 22 ♗d3+ forces 22...♕c4. Parry's 17 ♘d6!? is attractive, but only seems to lead to a draw: 17...hxg6! (17...♗xg5? 18 ♘xc8+ forces mate in 7) 18 a4 (18 ♘xc8+ ♔b5 19 ♘d6+ equal, Turian-Melchor, corr. 1995) 18...♔c7! 19 ♘f7+ ♔b6 20 ♘d6.

17...d6

Miguel has analysed 17...a5!? and it is a good alternative, 18 ♗xb8 ♖xb8 19 ♕xb8 hxg6 (19...♘f6? 20 ♘a4+ ♔b5 21 ♘c3+ ♔b6 22 ♗d3 and 23 ♘a4 mate is difficult to stop) 20 ♕xc8 ♗xc5 21 dxc5+ ♔xc5 22 ♕f8+ ♔b5 23 ♘d6+ ♔c5 24 ♘f7+ repeats.

18 ♗xd6!

After 18 ♘a4+?! the reply 18...♔a6 (forced, as the alternatives allow mate, 18...♔c7? 19 ♗xd6+ ♔d7 20 ♕g4+, 18...♔a5? just takes a few moves more, 19 ♗d2+ ♔a6 20 ♕a3 etc.) 19 ♗d3+ (19 ♘c5+ dxc5 20 ♕a3+ ♔b6 draws) 19...b5 and there is no obvious win.

18...♗xd6?!

This appears to be a fault, as 18...a6! 19 ♗xb8 ♗g4+ 20 f3 ♗xf3+ is unclear.

19 ♘xd6 ♗g4+

There is a threat to c8, but 19...♗e6? is too cooperative, 20 ♘xe6 ♕xa2 21 ♘c8+ ♔b5 22 ♕d3+, mating.

20 ♕xg4 ♘f6 21 ♘c8+!

21 ♕e6! also wins, 21...hxg6 22 ♘c4+ ♔b5 Schmelz-Schirmer, corr. 1997, (22...♔c7 23 ♕e5+ leads to mate) 23 a4+ ♕xa4 24 ♘d6+ ♔a5 25 ♘dxb7+ ♔b5 26 ♘xa4 is overwhelming.

21...♔c7 22 ♕f4+ ♔xc8

De Jong-Malmström, corr. 1994, and now the most efficient win is **23 ♗f5+ ♘bd7 24 ♗xd7+ ♘xd7 25 ♘e6**.

8 Svedenborg's variation 4...d5

1 e4 e5 2 ♘f3 f5 3 ♗c4 fxe4 4 ♘xe5 d5

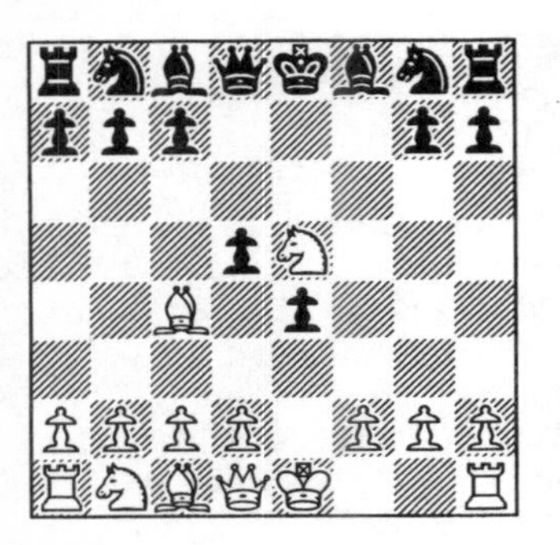

Clearly, this is the move Black would most like to play, expanding in the centre and at the same time shutting out White's king's bishop. White is obliged to play 5 ♕h5+ and enter into the ensuing complications. As is customary, I have named this variation after Svedenborg but, in fact, 4...d5 was already mentioned by Leonardo and Polerio (circa 1575), who gave the continuation 5 ♕h5+ g6 6 ♘xg6 ♘f6 7 ♕e5+ ♗e7 8 ♘xe7 ♕xe7. The line was again quoted by Bilguer (1843), before G.B.Fraser of Dundee analysed the variation 5 ♕h5+ g6 6 ♘xg6 hxg6 7 ♕xh8 ♔f7! 8 ♗e2 ♗g7, unclear, in 1875. It was only in 1970 that the Norwegian Svedenborg re-introduced this line with the improvement 7 ♕xg6+ ♔d7! instead of Fraser's 7...♔e7? 8 d4!.

5 ♕h5+

Obligatory, 5 ♗b3? ♕g5 6 d4 ♕xg2 7 ♖f1 ♗h3 ∓ Barabanov-Kozlov, corr. 1980/82.

5...g6 6 ♘xg6

Which leads us to Black's principal decision...

A 6...hxg6
B 6...♘f6

In A Black offers his king's rook or prepares to defend against an attack, and in B he chooses to play an endgame a pawn down, but with compensation.

A 6...hxg6

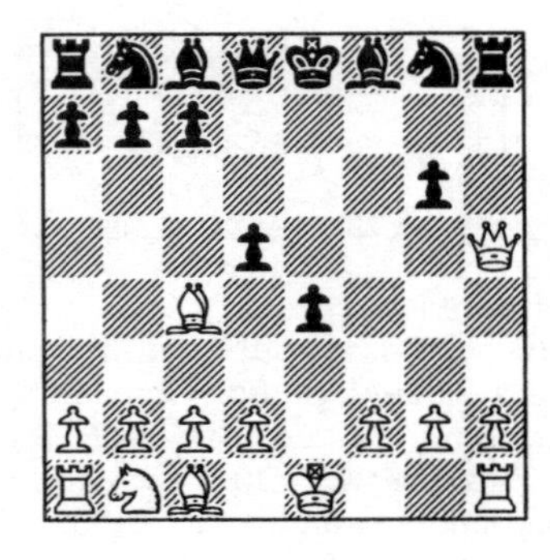

There is now a further sub-division:

A1 7 ♕xg6+
A2 7 ♕xh8

A1 7 ♕xg6+ ♔d7

As mentioned in the introduction, this is the best square for the king: 7...♔e7?! 8 d4 (but not 8 d3?! ♗h6 9 ♗g5+ [9 ♗xh6 ♘xh6 10 ♕g5+ ♔e6 11 ♕g6+ draws] 9...♗xg5 10 ♕xg5+ ♔e8 [10...♘f6!? 11 ♗xd5 exd3 is possible] 11 ♕xd5 [White must refuse the rook, 11 ♕e5+? ♕e7 12 ♕xh8?? exd3+ 13 ♔d2 ♕e2+ winning] 11...♕xd5 12 ♗xd5 exd3 13 cxd3 ♘f6 with chances to both players, Radoszta-Mayo, Buenos Aires 1992) and:

a) 8...♗h6 9 ♗xh6 ♖xh6 (9...♘xh6 10 ♕g5+ ♔e6 11 ♕e5+ ♔f7 12 ♗xd5+ ♔g6, Thorn-De Jong, corr. 1983, and now 13 ♗xe4+ ♗f5 14 ♕g3+ ♔h7 15 ♗xb7 should be sufficient) 10 ♕g5+ ♘f6 (10...♖f6?! 11 ♗xd5 ♘h6 12 ♘c3 ♘f7 13 ♕h4, Grosar-Jacko, Torremolinos 1986, White will find the time to castle long whilst maintaining the attack) 11 ♕xh6 dxc4 12 c3 ♗e6 13 ♘d2 with advantage, Melchor-Oren, corr. 1990.

b) 8...♘f6?! 9 ♗g5 ♘bd7 10 ♗xd5 ♕e8 11 ♕xe4+ ♔d8, Alloin-Steinbach, corr. 1985, 12 ♕xe8+ ♔xe8 13 ♗f3 and the four pawns are likely to outweigh the piece,

c) 8...♕d6?! 9 ♗g5+ ♔d7 (9...♘f6? 10 ♘c3! c6 11 ♘xe4 Black is crushed, Traudt-Vosselman corr. 2000, and others) 10 ♕f5+ ♔c6 11 ♕xc8 dxc4 12 ♕e8+, Bet-Malazs, 12...♔b6 13 ♘d2 ♕d5 14 ♕xf8 is strong.

d) 8...dxc4? 9 ♗g5+ ♔d7 10 ♗xd8 ♔xd8 11 ♘d2 and, although Black has three minor pieces for his queen, his pieces are uncoordinated, his king is exposed, and White has several pawns more. The game Heap-Oren, corr. 1991, is an example of the problems he faces: 11...♘e7 12 ♕xe4 c6?! (12...a5 and ...♖a6 is a possible plan) 13 ♘xc4 ♗f5 14 ♕e5 ♖h6 15 ♕a5+ ♔e8 16 ♘b6 ♖e6+ 17 ♔f1 1-0.

8 ♗xd5

Picking off a third pawn for the piece. Although the black king is awkwardly placed, the white queenside is dormant at present, and the black pieces will develop quickly. White should therefore avoid wasting moves unnecessarily, i.e. 8 ♕f5+? ♔c6 9 ♗xd5+ ♕xd5 10 ♕xf8 ♘d7 (or 10...♗f5 11 ♘c3 ♕e5 ∓, Ballon-Leisebein, corr. 1981) 11 ♕g7 ♕e5 12 ♕f7 b6 ∓, Langheld-Sneider, corr. 1985. Likewise 8 ♕f7+?! ♕e7 9 ♕xd5+ ♔e8 10 ♘c3 ♘f6 11 ♕g5 ♗e6 ∓, Jacquart-Monnard, corr. 1979.

8...♘f6

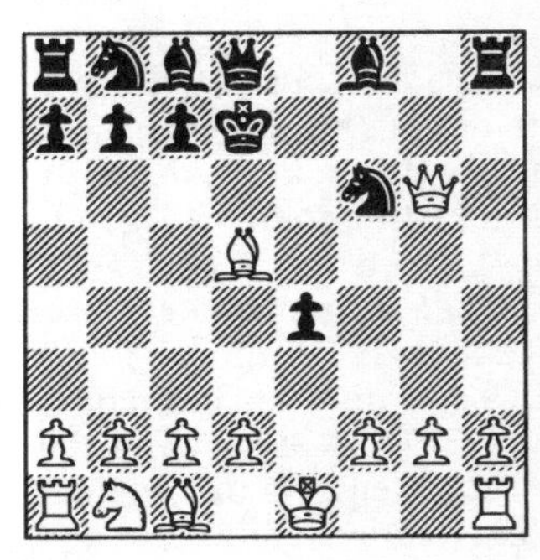

9 ♘c3

For the above reasons 9 ♗xe4?! is bad: 9...♕e7 10 d3 (10 ♘c3?! is best countered by 10...♖g8 11 ♕f5+ ♔d8 12 ♕f3 ♘c6 ∓ see (b), note to move 10 below, rather than 10...♔d8 11 d3 ♖g8 12 ♘d5 ♕xe4+ 13 ♕xe4 ♘xe4 14 dxe4 ♖xg2 15 ♗f4 ♘a6 16 ♗g3, trapping the rook with a slight plus, Trobatto-Kozlov, corr. 1981) 10...♖g8 11 ♕f5+ ♔d8 12 ♕f3 (12 ♕f4 ♘xe4 13 ♕xe4 ♕xe4+ 14 dxe4 ♖xg2 15 ♗e3 ♘c6 ∓, Hickl-Spiegel 1986) 12...♘c6 and:

a) 13 ♘a3! White needs to guard c2; 13...♘e5 (13...♘xe4 14 dxe4 ♘e5 15 ♕c3 ♘d7 is a way of playing for more than a draw, 16 ♕f3 ♘f6 winning the e-pawn, while keeping control) 14 ♕e3 ♘xe4 15 ♕xe4 ♖xg2! 16 ♕xg2 (16 ♗e3? ♕b4+ 17 ♕xb4 ♗xb4+ 18 c3 ♗xa3 ∓ Tiemann-Rasmussen, corr. 1974/75) 16...♘xd3+ 17 ♔d2 (17 ♔d1? allows Black's relatively undeveloped pieces to start a king hunt: 17...♘xf2+! 18 ♕xf2 ♗g4+ 19 ♔d2 ♕d6+ 20 ♔c3 ♗g7+ 21 ♔b3 ♗e6+ 22 ♘c4 [22 c4 ♕d3+ amounts to the same] 22...♗xc4+ 23 ♔xc4 b5+, forcing mate, Garcia-Kozlov, corr. 1979) 17...♗h6+ 18 ♔xd3 ♗f5+ 19 ♔c3 ♕f6+ 20 ♔b3 ♕b6+ 21 ♔c4 ♕a6+ 22 ♔c3 ♕f6+ 23 ♔c4 ♕a6+ 24 ♘b5 ♕a4+ 25 b4 ♕xc2+ 26 ♔d4 ♗g7+ 27 ♕xg7 ♕e4+ ½-½, Müller-Gåård, corr. 1990.

b) 13 c3 ♘e5 14 ♕d1 (so that, if Black captures on e4, the reply dxe4 is check) 14...♔e8! 15 ♖g1 (15 0-0? ♘xe4 16 dxe4 ♗g4 [good, but 16...♕h4! is immediately crushing, as ...♖h8 is coming] 17 f3 [17 ♕d5?, Fiorito-Tiemann, corr. 1978, 17...♘f3+! 18 ♔h1 ♕h4 19 ♗f4 ♖h8 threatens...♕xh2 mating, and there is little White can do about this; 17 ♕a4+ c6 18 ♗f4 ♗e2 19 ♘d2 ♗xf1 20 ♘xf1 ♘f3+ 21 ♔h1 ♖g4 0-1, Jove-Baumann, corr. 1998] 17...♕c5+ [17...♗h3! 18 ♖f2 ♕g7 19 ♗f4 ♗c5 is a simple method of winning an exchange] 18 ♔h1 ♖d8 19 ♕b3? ♘d3!! 20 fxg4 ♘f2+ 21 ♖xf2 ♕xf2 22 ♕e6+ ♗e7 23 ♕xg8+ ♔d7 0-1, Haller-Webe, corr. 1993) 15...♗g4 16 ♕a4+ c6 17 ♗e3 ♘xe4 18 dxe4 ♖d8 19 ♘d2, Topp-Leisebein, Pokalturnier 1987, 19...♘d3+ 20 ♔f1 a6, Black is better.

c) The extent of White's troubles is amply demonstrated by the following games, first Schubert-Leisebein, 1986, 13 0-0? ♘d4 14 ♕d1 ♗h3 15 ♔h1? ♕xe4! -/+.

d) And 13 ♗e3? is no better, 13...♗g4 14 ♕f4 (14 ♗c5 ♕e5, Monsalvo-Grobe, corr. 1975, changes nothing) 14...♘h5 and the queen is trapped in mid-board! 15 ♗c5 ♕xc5 16 ♕d2 ♗g7—two pieces is really too much for four pawns, Edwards-Lonsdale, corr. 1985.

e) 13 ♘c3? ♘d4 14 ♕d1 ♖xg2 15 ♗e3 ♗g4 16 ♕d2 ♘f3+ 17 ♗xf3 ♗xf3, the f3-bishop cuts White in two, 18 ♘e2 ♘d5 and the end is nigh, Siggens-Faldon, corr. 1981.

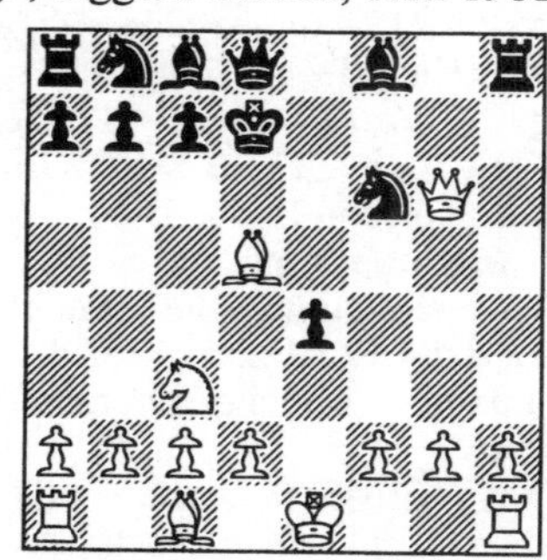

9...♕e7

a) Stronger than 9...♘xd5?! 10 ♘xd5 ♖h6?! (10...c6!, although rare, is the best move, 11 ♕f7+ ♗e7 12 ♘f6+ ♔c7 13 ♘xe4 ♖f8 14 ♕g7 ♗f5 15 d3 ♘d7 16 ♗f4+ ♔c8 17

♗d6, Destrebecq-Carlsson, corr. 1979, and now 17...♗f6 18 ♘xf6 ♖xf6 19 ♗g3 ♘c5 threatens the wicked 20...♘e6, trapping the white queen, with good chances) 11 ♕f7+ ♔c6 12 ♘xc7! ♕xc7 (Black has little choice, as 12...♖f6? 13 ♕c4+ ♗c5 14 ♘xa8 ♗e6 15 ♕c3 ♖xf2 16 b4 +/- Schirmer-Hansson, corr. 1993; and 12...♗c5?? 13 d4 [13 ♘xa8 ♖f6 14 ♕c4 is also effective, as in the previous line] 13...♖f6 14 d5+ ♔b6 15 ♘xa8+ also winning easily, Roszner-Leisebein, corr. 1992) 13 ♕xf8 ♖h7? (13...♖e6 is better) 14 ♕e8+! (14 ♕f6+ ♕d6 15 ♕xd6+ ♔xd6 16 d3 exd3 17 ♗f4+ ♔d5 18 cxd3 ♘c6 and Black has good drawing chances with the opposite-colour bishops, and extra piece, for the four pawns, Nolden-Mage, corr. 1991) 14...♔d5 (14...♔b6 15 d3 is also very unpleasant for Black) 15 d3 ♖e7 16 ♕b5+ 1-0, Kozlov-Zschorn, corr. 1989, as 16...♔e6 17 dxe4 leaves White with four pawns and an attack for the piece.

b) 9...♘c6!? is an alternative, though, 10 d3 ♘e5? (10...exd3 seems fine) 11 ♕f5+ ♔d6 12 ♘xe4+ ♘xe4 13 ♕xe4 ♖h4 14 f4 ♘g4 15 g3 with advantage, Farinas Seijas-Acosta, Lascurain memorial 1995.

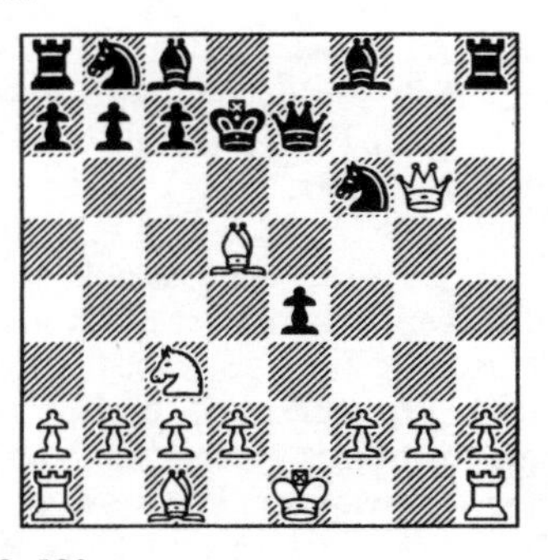

10 d3!

White plays for the attack, opening up the central files and attempting to complete his development as quickly as possible. If he declines to play this pawn sacrifice, he can soon find himself in deep water:

a) 10 b3, White prepares the useful resource ♗a3. There are several possible replies:

a1) 10...♖h6! The strongest. 11 ♕f7 (11 ♕f5+? ♔d8 12 ♕f4 ♖g6 [12...♕g7! is very strong, forking g2 and pinning the c3-knight] 13 ♗b2? [13 ♗c4 still favours Black] 13...♗h6 14 ♕h4 ♘xd5 0-1, Guidi-Minerva, 1991; 11 ♕g3?! ♘c6 12 ♗xc6+ ♔xc6 13 ♘e2 ♗g4 14 ♕c3+ ♔d7 15 d3 ♘d5 16 ♕c4 exd3! 17 ♕xg4+, Thoma-Berg, corr. 1982, and now 17...♕e6! is best, 18 ♕f3 [18 ♕xe6+? ♖xe6 19 cxd3 ♗g7 20 d4 ♖ae8 is overwhelming] 18...♗b4+ 19 ♗d2 [19 ♔f1? dxe2+ 20 ♕xe2 ♕xe2+ 21 ♔xe2 ♖e8+] 19...dxe2 Black has a strong attack.) 11...♕xf7 (11...♘c6? is inferior, 12 ♕xe7+ [12 ♗xc6+?! ♔xc6 13 ♕c4+ ♕c5 favours Black, Svendsen-Hayward, corr. 1990] 12...♗xe7 13 ♗xe4 with four pawns for the piece, and a solid position, White must be favourite; 11...♘xd5 12 ♕xd5+ ♖d6? [12...♔e8 13 ♗b2 c6 is superior] 13 ♗a3! ♖xd5 14 ♗xe7 ♖f5? [14...♗g7 15 ♘xd5 ♗xa1] 15 ♗xf8 ♖xf8 16 ♘xe4, the observation of the previous note applies, Kozlov-Gonsalves, corr. 1986) 12 ♗xf7 ♘c6 (12...♗g7!? 13 ♗b2 ♘g4 14 ♗d5 Niemand-Alloin, corr. 1983, 14...♗d4 15 ♘d1 ♗xb2 16 ♘xb2 ♘f6 is equal) 13 ♗b2 with a new divide:

a11) 13...♗c5! is best as, by attacking f2, Black deters White from queenside castling, 14 h3 (14 0-0? even without queens the king is not safe here, 14...♔e7 15 ♗c4 ♗d6 16 h3 ♗xh3! 17 ♖fe1 [17 gxh3?? ♖g6+ 18 ♔h1 ♖h8] 17...♖g6 winning, De Paz-Miguel, corr. 1995; meanwhile, if either white piece goes to d5, then the c2-pawn is lost, i.e. 14 ♘d5? ♘xd5 15 ♗xd5 ♘b4 16 ♗xe4 ♖e6 17 f3 ♘xc2+ 18 ♔d1 ♘xa1, Hemsley-Crimp, Australia 1994, when White could have retained some hope by playing 19 ♗f5) 14...♗d4 15 0-0-0?! ♗xf2 16 g4 ♗h4 17 ♖df1 ♔e7 18 ♗c4 ♗e6 ∓, Oren-Heap, corr. 1991.

a12) 13...♗d6 is very popular, but it only leads to equality, 14 0-0-0 (14 h3?! ♘e5 15 ♗d5 ♘xd5 16 ♘xd5 b6 17 0-0-0 ♗b7 ∓, Bamber-Jackson, corr. 1987; 14 ♘d5? ♘xd5 15 ♗xd5 ♘b4 16 ♗xe4 ♖e6, Schneider-Vosselman, corr. 1987, 17 d3 ♘xc2+ 18 ♔d1 ♘xa1 19 ♗f5 ♘xb3 20 ♗xe6+ ♔xe6 with every chance of triumphing) 14...♘e5 15 ♗d5 (best, 15 ♘d5? ♘fg4! strands the light-squared bishop, 16 ♗xe5 ♘xe5 17 ♗g8 ♖h8 18 ♘f6+ ♔e7 0-1, Svec-Tiemann, corr. 1979, and 15 ♗c4?! devalues the pawn structure, 15...♘xc4 16 bxc4 b6 17 h3 ♗b7 with a clear edge, Pape-Landgraf, corr. 1990) 15...♘xd5 16 ♘xd5 ♘g4!? (16...b6 is quite playable, 17 ♗xe5 ♗xe5 18 d3 e3!? ½-½, Leisebein-Winckelmann) 17 ♖de1 ♘xf2 (17...♔c6 18 ♘c3 does not change much, Tiemann-Gebuhr, corr. 1978) 18 ♖hf1 ♖xh2? (the main line, but it is inferior, and brings Black problems. 18...♔c6 is best, 19 ♘e3?! [19 ♘c3 ♘g4 20 h3 is level] 19...♘g4 [19...♗xh2!? 20 ♖xf2 ♗g3 and with the exchange for only one pawn, Black is better] 20 ♘xg4 ♗xg4 21 ♖xe4 ♗e6 22 g3 ½-½, Heap-Diepstraten, corr. 1990, but Black can play on if he wants) 19 ♖xf2 ♗g3 20 ♖f7+ ♔d6! (20...♔e6!? 21 ♖f6+! ♔xd5 22 c4+ ♔c5 23 ♖xe4 c6? [23...♗d6 24 ♗a3+ ♔c6 might be better, although the king is still awkwardly placed after 25 ♖e7 ♗d7 26 b4] 24 ♗d4+ ♔b4 25 ♗c3+ ♔a3 [25...♔c5? allows mate by 26 ♗a5! and b4, or d4] 26 c5 b5?? [26...♖h1+ 27 ♔c2 b5 is forced, but even here 28 cxb6 axb6 29 ♖f8 is strong, White will try to bring a rook to the a-file, 29...b5 30 ♖ee8 ♗f5+ 31 d3 1-0, Alloin-Grivainis, corr. 1985] 27 ♖f1! ♖h5 28 ♔b1 1-0 Graber-Leisebein, corr. 1985) 21 ♘xc7 (21 ♖f6+ ♗e6!) 21...♗xe1 22 ♗a3+ ♔e5 23 ♘xa8 ♖xg2 24 ♖e7+ ♔f6 25 ♖xe4 ♗xd2+ 26 ♔b2 ♗f5 27 ♖c4, Svendsen-Gåård, corr. 1989, and others when Black should be able to force a draw easily enough, e.g. 27...a5 28 ♘c7 ♖g1 29 ♗d6 ♗c1+ 30 ♔c3 ♖g2.

a2) 10...c6 11 ♗a3 (or 11 ♗xe4 when, 11...♖g8 12 ♕f5+ ♔d8 13 ♕f3 ♗g4 [stronger than 13...♖g4?! 14 ♗a3! ♕e5? {but 14...♕xa3 15 ♕xf6+ ♗e7 is better} 15 ♗xf8 ♖xe4+? 16 ♘xe4 1-0, Heap-Tiemann, corr. 1991] 14 ♕d3+ [14 ♕e3 ♘bd7 {14...♘xe4 is also fine} 15 d3 ♕g7! 16 ♗b2 ♗b4 17 ♔f1 ♘d5 18 ♗xd5 cxd5 19 ♘a4 ♕g6 20 a3 ♗d6 and Black has an attack, Heap-Krantz, corr. 1993] 14...♘bd7 15 f3 ♗h5 [15...♘xe4 is equally good, 16 ♕xe4 {16 ♘xe4 ♗f5 17 ♕e2 ♕g7 hitting a1, and winning the crucial g2-pawn, Vitols-Borrmann, corr. 1992} 16...♗f5 17 ♕xe7+ ♗xe7 18 g4 ♗xc2 19 d4 ♗h4+ 20 ♔d2 ♗h7 Black has an edge, Delavekouras, Sotiris-Pellen] 16 0-0 ♕g7 17 g3 ♘xe4 18 fxe4 ♗c5+ 19 ♔g2 ♔c7 and White's king position is precarious, Van den Berg-Tatlow, corr. 1996; 11 ♗c4 b5 12 ♗a3 ♕g7 transposes to 11 ♗a3) 11...♕g7 12 ♕xg7+ (12 ♕f5+?

♔d8 13 ♗xf8 ♖xf8 14 ♗e6 ♘d5 15 ♕h3 ♗xe6 16 ♕xe6 ♘xc3 winning, Melchor-Clarke, corr. 1988) 12...♗xg7 13 ♗c4 (13 ♗f7?! ♘g4! [threatening both ...♘e5, and to undermine the c3 knight by ...e3] 14 ♗g6 e3 15 0-0-0?! [15 fxe3 ♘xe3 16 g3 is a better try] 15...♘xf2 [15...♔c7!? 16 fxe3 ♘f2 is another way to take the exchange] 16 dxe3+ ♘xd1 17 ♖xd1+ ♔c7 18 ♗d6+ ♔b6 19 ♘a4+ ♔a5 20 b4+? [White still has chances, by 20 c4 for instance] 20...♔xa4 21 c4 ♔a3! [21...♖h6?? 22 ♗c2+ ♔a3 23 ♖d3+ ♔xa2 24 ♗b1+ ♔a1 25 ♖a3 mate, Alloin-Tiemann, corr. 1985] 22 ♗c2, Elburg-Tiemann, corr. 1989, when 22...♔xa2 23 ♖d3 ♗b2+ 24 ♔d1 ♗f5 is a very strong defence) 13...b5 (also 13...♔c7 14 0-0-0 ♗f5 15 h3 ♘bd7 16 g4 ♗g6 ∓ Alloin-Gaard, corr. 1991; but 13...♘g4 is less effective here, 14 h3 [14 ♗c5? b6 15 ♗e3? b5 16 ♗e2, Alloin-Svendsen, corr. 1990, loses to the elementary 16...♘xe3 17 fxe3 b4 18 0-0! ♔e7 {18...bxc3? 19 ♖f7+ ♔e6 20 ♗c4+ ♔e5 21 ♖xg7} 19 ♘xe4 ♗xa1 when the extra black rook will surely make short work of the four white pawns] 14...e3 15 f4, Löffler-Borrmann, corr. 1991, 15...♔c7 [15...♘f2 16 ♖f1 ♘e4? 17 ♘xe4 ♗xa1 18 c3 favours White] 16 ♗b2 ♗f5 17 ♘d5+ cxd5 18 ♗xg7, Löffler-Borrmann, corr. 1991, 18...♖h7 19 ♗xd5 ♖xg7 20 hxg4 exd2+ 21 ♔xd2 ♖xg4 about equal) 14 ♗e2 ♘d5 (again, 14...♔c7 15 0-0-0 ♗f5, etc., is possible. Although three pawns have the same nominal value as a piece, especially in the endgame, with so many pieces still left on the board and with all the white pawns so far back, Black has the edge in almost all these positions, e.g. 16 h3, Pape-Svendsen, corr. 1990, 16...a5 17 ♗b2 b4 18 ♘a4 ♘bd7 19 g4 ♗e6 and the white knight is sidelined) 15 0-0-0 ♗xc3!? (15...♘xc3 16 dxc3+ ♔e8 is more logical) 16 dxc3 ♔c7 17 ♔b2, Alloin-Malmström, corr. 1990, (17 c4 ♘c3 18 ♗d6+ ♔b6 ∓ Malmström-Borrmann, corr. 1990/91) 17...♗a6 (to deter White from c4) 18 ♗xb5!? ♗xb5 19 c4 ♗xc4 20 bxc4 ♘f6, the game is level.

a3) 10...♘xd5?, as so often, is a mistake: 11 ♘xd5 ♕g7? (11...♕e5 12 ♘f6+ ♔d6 is a better bet) 12 ♘f6+ ♔c6 13 ♕xe4+ ♔b6 14 ♗b2 and Black can resign, Kozlov-Skrastins, corr. 1992.

a4) 10...♕g7!? is a playable alternative, 11 ♗xe4 ♘xe4 12 ♕xe4 ♗d6 (menacing ...♖e8, and stopping White from castling) 13 ♔f1 ♖e8 14 ♕a4+ ♘c6 15 ♗b2, Bravo-Borrmann, corr. 1979, when Black should prepare further development by 15...♔d8.

b) 10 ♗xe4?! As mentioned above this is one pawn too many! 10...♖g8 (10...♔d8?! has already been examined in the note to move 9) 11 ♕f5+ ♔d8 12 ♕f3 ♘c6 (12...♗g4 wasn't too bad either, in Korhonen-Nilsson, corr. 1988: 13 ♕d3+ ♘bd7 14 b3 and now 14...♗f5 15 f3 ♖xg2 is good) 13 0-0 (13 h3 [to stop ...♗g4] 13...♘d4

[13...♘xe4 14 ♘xe4 ♘e5 wins the g2-pawn immediately] 14 ♕d3 c5 15 ♔d1 ♘xe4 16 ♘xe4 ♗f5 17 ♖e1? [because of a tactic the rook fails to defend e4, 17 f3 is forced] 17...♖xg2 18 c3 ♗xe4 19 ♕xe4 ♕xe4 20 ♖xe4 ♖g1+ 21 ♖e1 ♖xe1+ 22 ♔xe1 ♘c2+ 0-1, Garcia-Canal Oliveras, Barbera 1997; 13 d3? ♘d4 14 ♕d1 ♖xg2 is considered in the note to move 9) and now:

b1) 13...♘e5?! is the most popular, but without justification, 14 ♕e3 ♘fg4 15 ♕d4+ (15 ♕e2?! ♘xh2! with advantage, Stegmann-Borrmann, corr. 1992, as 16 ♔xh2?? ♕h4+ 17 ♔g1 ♘g4 wins) 15...♗d7? (15...♘d7 holds the balance) 16 h3 (16 ♕d5 is also strong, 16 d3? less so, 16...♘xh2! 17 ♔xh2?? [17 ♕d5 ♖h8 18 ♕xb7 was the only chance] 17...♕h4+ 18 ♔g1, Naeter-Leisebein, corr. 1982, and for some odd reason, Black refrained from the evident 18...♘f3+ 19 ♗xf3 ♕xd4 !) 16...♕h4? 17 f4? (17 ♗xb7 c6 18 f3 defends, and wins material) 17...♕g3! 18 hxg4 ♘xg4 19 ♖f3 ♕e1+ 20 ♖f1 ♕g3 ½-½, Turczynowicz-Borrmann, corr. 1987, 21 ♖f3 ♕e1+ 22 ♖f1 ♕g3 leads to a repetition.

b2) 13...♘xe4 is a good alternative, 14 ♘xe4 (14 ♕xe4 ♘b4) 14...♘d4 15 ♕f6 (15 ♕d3 ♕g7 16 g3 ♗d7 is also promising) 15...♘xc2 16 ♖b1 ♗h3 and, having holed the white queenside pawn structure, Black has a considerable plus, Krongraf-Stummer, corr. 1980.

b3) ...as is 13...♘d4 14 ♕d3 ♕d6 (14...c5 also looks good) 15 b3 ♘g4 16 f4 ♗d7 17 ♗b2 ♕b6 18 ♔h1 ♘xh2! 19 ♔xh2 ♗c5 and the white king was in a painful predicament, Nyffeler-Elburg, corr. 1988.

c) 10 0-0?! Black has too many open files in front of White's king for this to be playable. 10...♕d6! (the simplest, forking d5, and h2, 10...♘c6 11 ♗xe4 ♘e5 12 ♕g3 ♖g8?!, Drucke-Krantz, corr. 1990, is worse: 13 ♘d5! ♖xg3 14 ♗f5+ ♔e8 15 ♘xe7) 11 g3 (11 f4?! exf3?! [11...♘xd5 12 ♕f5+ ♔c6 13 ♕xc8 ♕h6 is also strong, ...♗c5+ is the main threat, and somewhat simpler] 12 ♗xf3 ♕d4+?! [12...♕xh2+ 13 ♔f2 ♗c5+] 13 ♔h1?? [13 ♖f2 ♔d8 14 d3 is not too clear] 13...♖xh2+ 14 ♔xh2 ♕h4+ 15 ♔g1 ♗c5+ 0-1, Bañon-Melchor, Barcelona 1995; 11 h3 is best, 11...♘xd5 12 ♕f5+ ♔d8 13 ♕xd5 ♕xd5 14 ♘xd5 ♗f5 and White is only slightly worse) 11...♘xd5 12 ♕f5+ ♔d8 (12...♔c6!? 13 ♕xc8 ♕h6 14 h4 ♗d6 is also possible) 13 ♕xd5 ♕xd5 14 ♘xd5 ♗f5, Baranowski-Grobe, corr. 1975, and Black's light-squared bishop is worth more than the white pawns (14...♗e6!?).

d) 10 h3?! does nothing to solve White's problems: 10...c6 (or 10...♘c6 11 ♗xe4 ♖g8 12 ♕f5+ ♔d8 13 ♕f3 transposing to a line above) 11 ♗c4?! b5 12 ♗e2? (White loses control of g8) 12...♖g8 13 ♕f5+ ♔d8 14 ♕f4 ♖xg2 ∓ Druke-Elburg, corr. 1990.

10...exd3+ 11 ♗e3

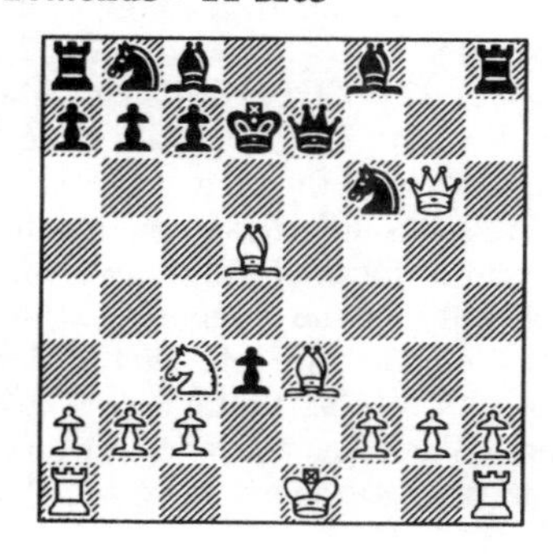

11...c6!

There is a wide choice for Black at this point, and no real consensus as to which move is best. I, however, rather like the text. The idea is to force the bishop away, and then play 12...♗h6xe3. The advantages of this plan are threefold: First, White will be forced to recapture with a pawn on e3, giving him an isolated pawn and closing the e-file. Second, Black exchanges a dangerous attacking piece, and third Black gains control of a lot of dark squares, i.e. his king is safe on c7, and he can install a knight on e5. Here are the alternatives:

a) 11...d2+?!, attempting to cause the maximum inconvenience possible, White will have to castle 'by hand' after 12 ♔xd2:

a1) 12...♕d6 13 ♕f7+ (13 ♗c5?! ♕f4+ 14 ♗e3 ½-½ is a bit limp, Schirmer-Svendsen, corr. 1992; 13 ♗d4 ♕f4+ 14 ♗e3 likewise, although 14 ♔d3!? is feasible; but 13 ♔c1!? is interesting, to vacate the d-file, and then if 13...♘xd5 14 ♕f7+ ♕e7 15 ♕xd5+ ♔e8 16 ♖e1) 13...♗e7 14 ♖ad1 ♖f8 15 ♔c1 ♖xf7 16 ♗xf7 ♕xd1+?! (quite unnecessary: 16...♔c6! 17 ♖xd6+ ♗xd6) 17 ♖xd1+ ♔c6 18 a4! a6? 19 ♘d5 ♗d8? 20 ♘b4 mate, Nyman-Svendsen, corr. 1991.

a2) 12...♕g7 13 ♕d3 ♗d6 14 ♖ae1 ♘c6 15 h4 (15 ♗xc6+?! bxc6, and certainly not 15...♔xc6?? 16 ♕b5 mate) 15...♘b4?! (15...♘e5) 16 ♗e6+? (16 ♕f5+! ♔d8 17 ♕g5 is unpleasant for Black) 16...♔d8 (16...♔e7!? 17 ♕f5 [17 ♗xc8? ♘xd3 18 ♗h6+ ♘xe1 19 ♗xg7 ♘f3+ 20 gxf3 ♖hxc8] 17...♗xe6 18 ♗g5 ♕f7 is unclear) 17 ♕f5 ♗xe6 18 ♕xe6 ♖e8 19 ♕f5 ♖e5 20 ♕f3 ♕g6 21 ♖c1 with balanced play, Melchor-Budovskis, corr. 1993.

a3) 12...♘xd5? 13 ♘xd5 ♕d6 14 ♕g4+! (White also did well with 14 ♕d3 c6? in Melchor-Hayward, corr. 1990, as 15 ♕f5+ wins on the spot, but 14...♘c6 is better) 14...♔c6 15 ♕c4+ ♔d7 16 ♖ad1 b5 17 ♕xb5+ with a big plus, Magee-Hayward, corr. 1991.

a4) 12...c6?! 13 ♗g5! (13 ♗b3 ♔c7 14 ♗f4+ ♔b6 15 ♖ae1 [15 a4!? a5 16 ♗e3+ ♔c7 17 ♖ae1 is also good, Nyman-Borrmann, corr. 1991] 15...♕d8+ 16 ♔c1 a5? 17 ♗g5 ♘bd7 18 ♗e6 ♗e7 19 ♗xd7 ♗xd7 20 ♖xe7 1-0, Pape-Vitols, corr. 1994/95) 13...♗g7 14 ♖ae1 ♕f8 15 ♗f7 ♗h6 16 ♕f5+ 1-0, Nilsson-Stamer, corr. 1993.

b) 11...dxc2!? is somewhat risky but at least it means that White has only two pawns for the piece! 12 ♕xc2 and:

b1) 12...♕h7 13 ♕a4+ (other queen moves: 13 ♕d2!? ♗d6 14 0-0-0 [14 ♗f3 ♘c6 15 0-0-0 ♘e5 16 ♗e2 ♔e7 looks quite reasonable for Black, Elburg-Destrebecq, corr. 1993] 14...♘c6 15 ♗f4 ♘e7 16 ♗xd6 cxd6 17 ♗e4? [17 ♗c6+ bxc6 18 ♕xd6+ ♔e8 19 ♕xf6 ♕h6+ is about equal] 17...♘xe4 18 ♘xe4 ♕xe4! 19 ♕xd6+ ♔e8 20 ♕d8+ ♔f7 21 ♕xh8 ♗f5, the sting in the tail! 22 ♕h5+ ♘g6 0-1, Logunov-Pape, corr. 1994/95; 13

Qb3!? c6 14 Be6+ [14 0-0-0! Nxd5 {14...Bd6 15 Be6+ Kc7 16 Rxd6 Kxd6 17 Rd1+} 15 Nxd5 cxd5 16 Qxd5+ Ke8 17 Rhe1] 14...Kc7 15 Bf4+ Bd6 16 Bxd6+ Kxd6 17 0-0-0+ Kc7 18 Nb5+ cxb5 19 Qg3+ ½-½, Leisebein-Pape, corr. 1995, as White has a perpetual check) 13...Kd8 14 0-0-0 (14 Bg5 Be7 15 Bf3 Nfd7 16 Bf4 Nc5 17 0-0-0+ Bd7 and Black can defend his king by blocking the d7 square. 18 Qc4 Rf8 19 Nd5 Bd6, unclear, Guido-Hector, Geneva 1989) 14...Nbd7 (14...Bd6 15 Bf3 Qd7?, this is not an ideal file for a queen, 16 Nb5 a6 17 Rxd6! cxd6 18 Qf4 Ke7 19 Bd4 1-0, Stummer-Svendsen, corr. 1994/95; 14...Nxd5 15 Nxd5 Bd7 16 Qb3 Kc8 17 Qc4 Bc6 18 Bf4, Stummer-Reinke, corr. 1994/95, when 18...Bh6 exchanges the bishop, with good chances) 15 Bg5 Qf5?! (15...Bh6) 16 Bxf6+! Qxf6 17 Bxb7 Rh4 18 g4 Ba3! 19 Rxd7+ Bxd7 20 Qxa3 Rb8, Dahne-Stame, corr. 1986, and now 21 Qxa7 favours White.

b2) 12...Bh6 exchanging an attacking unit, 13 0-0-0 Bxe3+ 14 fxe3 c6 (opening another central file by 14...Qxe3+? is suicide, 15 Kb1 c6 16 Bxc6+ [flashy, and good, but 16 Rhe1 1-0, Matheis-Kern, corr. 1998, has its points!] 16...Kxc6, Terblanche-Nilsson, corr. 1990, but now 17 Ne4+ Kb6 18 Nxf6 is the most precise) 15 Bxc6+! Kc7 16 Be4 Nc6 17 Rhf1 Be6, Oren-Niemand, corr. 1994/97; Black has avoided the worst, and can now bring his final piece into the action.

b3) 12...Kd8? 13 0-0-0 Nbd7 14 Rhe1 Qg7 15 Nb5 Bd6 16 Bxb7! Bxb7 17 Rxd6, the point, 17...Rc8 (for if now 17...cxd6?? 18 Qc7+ wins) 18 Rd2 and with his king marooned in the centre, and no co-ordination, Black is lost, De Smet-Keller, corr. 1986.

c) 11...Bh6!? can transpose into the main line, but there is one small problem with this particular order of moves

12 0-0! (Black is doing well after 12 0-0-0 Bxe3+ 13 fxe3 c6; and 12 Qxd3 Bxe3 13 fxe3 both transposing, whilst 13 Be4+!? Ke8 14 Bg6+ Kf8 15 fxe3 Nc6 16 0-0 Ne5 17 Qd4 c5 18 Qf4 Kg7 and play is balanced, Stummer-Stamer, corr. 1994/95) 12...Bxe3 (12...c6? 13 Bxh6 Nxd5? 14 Nxd5 cxd5 15 Rae1 is crushing, Jurgenson-Borrmann, corr. 1991, as 15...Qh7? 16 Qe6+ forces mate in six) 13 fxe3 Rf8 (13...Qxe3+!? is risky, 14 Kh1 Nxd5 [14...Nh5?, Logunov-Clarke, corr. 1994/95, with a nasty threat to g3, but there is a large flaw: 15 Bf3 Qe5 16 Bxh5 Rxh5 17 Rf7+ Kd8 18 Qg8+, winning the queen, 18...Qe8 19 Rf8] 15 Nxd5!? Qe5 16 Nf4 dxc2?? [16...d2 17 Rad1 Kd8 18 Rxd2+ Bd7 fights on] 17 Rae1 c1=Q 18 Qd3+ Qd6 19 Qf5+ Kc6 20 Rxc1+ and the black king is cut off from the rest of its forces, and soon dies, Kozlov-Elburg, corr. 1994/96) 14 Qxd3 Ke8 (an unfortunate necessity as 14...c6? loses: 15 Bxc6+! [or 15 Rxf6! Rxf6 16 Bxc6+ Kxc6 17 Qb5+ Kc7 18

♘d5+] 15...♔c7 [15...♔xc6 16 ♖xf6+ ♕xf6 {16...♖xf6 17 ♕b5+ ♔c7 18 ♘d5+} 17 ♕b5+ ♔d6 18 ♘e4+ 1-0, Piazza-Leisebein, corr. 1987] 16 ♖xf6! ♖d8 17 ♗d7! ♖xd7 18 ♘b5+ ♔d8 19 ♕g6 ♕g7 20 ♕xg7 ♖xg7 21 ♖f8+ ♔d7 22 ♖d1+ ♔c6 23 ♖xc8+ ♔xb5 24 ♖dd8 ♖e7 25 h4 1-0, Pfeifer-Dahlhoff, corr. 1990) 15 ♘b5!? (This move asks a lot of questions of Black. White can't afford to hang around, 15 e4?! c6 16 ♗b3 ♘bd7 17 ♕g3 ♘e5 18 ♕h4 ♘fg4 ∓, Jurgenson-Gaard, corr. 1992; and 15 ♖f4?! is also too slow, 15...c6 16 ♗b3 ♗e6! [16...♘bd7 17 ♖af1 ♘e5 18 ♕d4 with strong pressure, Nyman-Dravniek, corr. 1991] 17 ♕g6+ ♔d8 18 ♖d1+ ♘bd7 19 ♘e4?! [19 ♗xe6 ♕xe6 20 ♖e4 ♕f7 is only equal] 19...♗d5! 20 ♗xd5 cxd5 21 ♘g5 ♕xe3+ 22 ♔h1 ♖g8 23 ♕f5 ♖c8 and Black is out of the woods, Krantz-Stamer, corr. 1994/95; 15 ♖ad1 is a very dangerous alternative, 15...♘bd7 16 ♕g6+ ♔d8 17 ♕h6 c6 [17...♔e8!?] 18 ♗e6! ♔e8 19 ♗xd7+ ♗xd7? [19...♘xd7 is the only chance, although the black king is not looking too healthy] 20 ♖d4! ♖f7 21 ♘e4 ♘xe4 22 ♕h8+ ♖f8 23 ♖xf8+ ♕xf8 24 ♖xe4+, winning, Berner-Wegelin, corr. 1988) 15...♘a6? (if the knight comes here to defend c7, then it cannot protect the king on d7, 15...♘xd5? 16 ♕xd5 ♗d7? [a blunder, but if 16...♘a6 then 17 ♖xf8+ ♔xf8 18 ♖f1+ ♔g7 19 ♖f3 also signals the end] 17 ♖xf8+ ♕xf8 18 ♘xc7+ 1-0 Schirmer-Landgraf, corr. 1991; but 15...c6! must be tried, i.e. 16 ♗f7+! [16 ♘d6+ ♔d8 17 ♗f3 ♔c7 and the king is safe] 16...♔xf7 17 ♘c7 [17 ♕h7+? ♔e8 18 ♘c7+ ♔d8 19 ♕xe7+ ♔xe7 20 ♘xa8 b6 and the knight is trapped; Black will eventually have three pieces for a rook and some pawns] 17...♔g7 [17...♕xc7?? 18 ♕h7+ skewers the king and queen] 18 ♘xa8 b6, again the knight is trapped, but this time the black king is under attack, 19 ♖f3 ♗g4 [19...♗b7? 20 ♖g3+ ♔f7 21 ♖f1 ♗xa8 22 ♖xf6+ wins the queen] 20 ♖f4 ♘bd7 21 ♕c3 ♘e5 22 ♖af1 ♗e2 with unclear play. This line needs some tests) 16 ♕g6+ ♔d8 17 ♖ad1 ♘xd5 18 ♖xd5+ ♗d7 19 ♖fd1, 'pin and win'!, Schirmer-Nolden, corr. 1991.

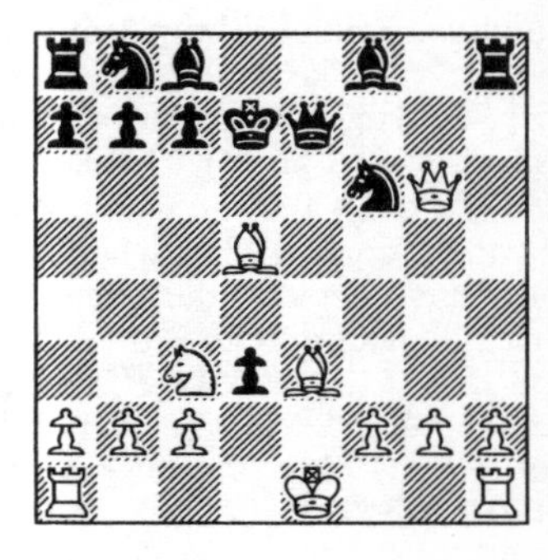

12 ♗b3

It can be important to retain control over the g8 square sometimes, but 12 ♗f3 is also played: 12...♗h6 (12...dxc2!? 13 ♕xc2 ♔d8, is playable but dangerous, 14 0-0-0+ ♘bd7 [14...♗d7 15 ♖he1 ♕h7 16 ♘e4 ♘xe4 17 ♗xe4 ♕xh2?!, too greedy, Melchor-Downey, corr. 1993, 18 ♗f5 and the black king is under fire] 15 ♖he1 ♕h7 an important resource, 16 h3 ♗h6, unclear, Logunov-Grobe. corr. 1994) 13 0-0-0 (or 13 ♕xd3+ ♔c7 14 0-0-0 ♗xe3+ 15 fxe3 ♘bd7! [but not 15...♗e6? 16 ♕d4! ♘bd7 17 ♕f4+ ♔c8 18 ♖d2 ♘b6 19 ♖hd1 with advantage, Nyman-Gaard, corr. 1990, Black has lost the coordination of his rooks, and control of the all-important h2-b8 diagonal] 16 e4

♘e5 ∓ Jackson-Kozlov, corr. 1989/90) 13...♗xe3+ 14 fxe3 ♖g8! (if 14...♔c7?! 15 ♕g3+!) 15 ♕f5+ ♔c7 16 ♕f4+ ♕d6 17 ♕c4, Leisebein-Borrmann, corr. 1985, and now 17...♕e5 18 ♕xd3 ♗e6 and ...♘bd7 ∓ would have been the most straightforward.

12...♗h6!

Continuing the plan, but again, there is no shortage of alternatives:

a) 12...d2+?! 13 ♔f1!? (13 ♔xd2 see above) 13...b6 14 ♗xd2 ♗a6+ 15 ♔g1 ♔c7 16 ♖e1 with a strong initiative, Kozlov-Malmström, corr. 1991/2.

b) 12...dxc2!? is not to everyone's taste (I don't like it!) 13 ♕xc2 ♔d8 (13...♕e5? 14 0-0-0+ ♔c7, Magee-Downey, corr. 1989, when White could have decided the game by 15 ♕d2!, menacing both ♕d8 mate and ♗f4, 15...♗d6 16 ♗d4 ♕f5 17 ♗c2 etc; 13...♔c7?, Herling-van Willingen, corr. 1976, 14 ♘b5+ ♔d8 15 0-0-0+ ♘bd7 16 ♗xa7) 14 0-0-0+ ♘bd7 15 ♖he1 ♕g7, Dissels-Raijmaekers, corr. 1993. White's position looks very aggressive.

c) 12...b6? 13 0-0-0 ♗a6?! (to keep the d-file closed, but lightning strikes elsewhere; better 13...♔c7 14 ♖he1 but White is much better) 14 ♗g5 ♗g7 15 ♘e4 ♖f8 16 ♖he1 and material is lost, Alloin-Strelis, corr. 1983.

13 0-0-0!

The only move to test Black's set-up; after 13 ♕xd3+ ♔c7 14 0-0-0 ♗xe3+ 15 fxe3 ♘bd7 (intending ...♘e5, but 15...♗g4 16 ♖de1 ♘bd7 is a sound alternative) 16 ♕d4 b6 17 ♕f4+ ♔b7 18 ♖df1 ♖f8 the d7-knight is coming to e5, or c5, and Black has an edge, Niewold-Van de Velden, corr. 1997.

13...♗xe3+ 14 fxe3 b6!

Black prepares his king's safety. 14...♔c7?! is inferior, 15 ♕g3+! ♔d8 (15...♔b6 16 ♖xd3 ♘a6?! 17 ♘a4+ ♔a5 18 ♕e1+ 1-0, Magee-Tiemann, corr. 1989; of course, 15...♕d6 is impossible, 16 ♕g7+ picks-off the rook) 16 ♖xd3+ ♘bd7 17 ♖hd1 when Black had to suffer uncomfortable pressure, but managed to defend himself, Magee-Kozlov, corr. 1989.

15 ♖xd3+

Neither 15 ♕xd3+ ♔c7 16 e4 ♘bd7-e5 ∓, nor 15 ♕g3?! ♗a6 ∓ offer anything to White, but 15 ♖hf1 may be best, although Black is fine after 15...♖f8 16 ♖xd3+ ♔c7 17 ♕g3+ ♔b7 18 ♕d6 ♕xd6 19 ♖xd6 ♘bd7 20 ♖f4 ♔c7.

15...♔c7 16 e4

16 ♖f1 ♘bd7 and Black is doing well, he will play ...♗a6 and connect his rooks next go. 16 h3 ♘bd7 17 e4 ♗a6 18 ♖f3 ♖af8 19 ♕g3+ ♔b7 20 ♖e1 ♘e5 ∓, Melchor-Elburg, corr. 1989 (by transposition).

16...♘bd7 17 ♖f3 ♗a6 18 ♖f5 ♖af8 19 ♕g3+ ♔b7

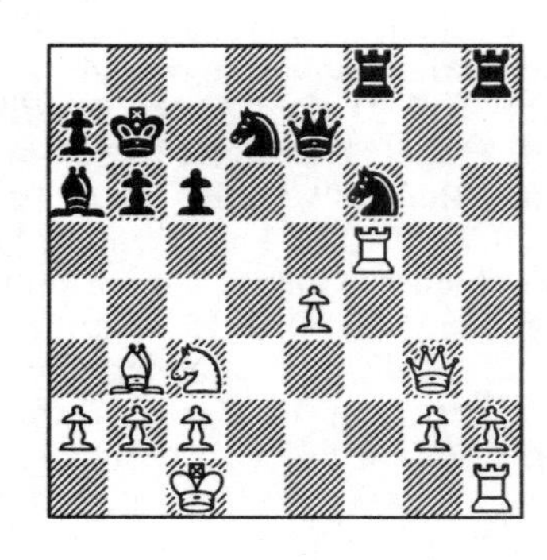

20 ♖e1 ♘c5 21 e5 ♘xb3+ 22 axb3 ♘d7 23 ♖xf8 ♖xf8 24 ♔b1 ♖f1 25 ♖xf1 ♗xf1 26 ♕f3 ♗a6 27 ♕f5 ♘xe5

Black should be winning, Jakobsson-McDonald, corr. 1995.

A2 7 ♕xh8

If White gains no advantage playing for the attack, then perhaps he should just take the rook? However, although it is difficult to demonstrate a forced win for Black, the white position is constantly on the edge of a precipice. White has to take particular care with his queen, and the line has fallen into disuse since I wrote *The Latvian Gambit*.

7...♔f7

Fraser's move, threatening to ensnare the white queen.

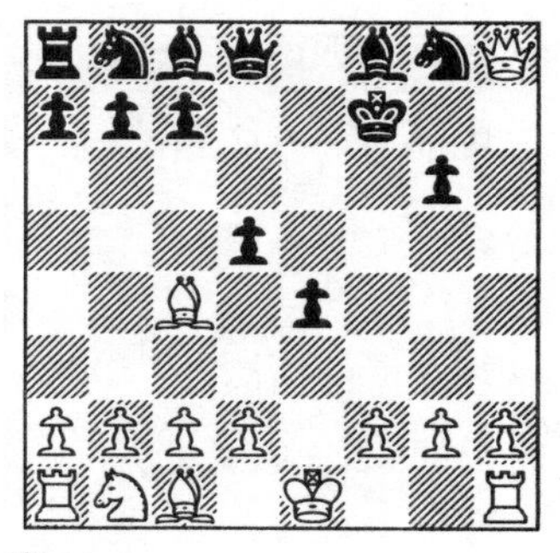

8 ♕d4

The pin on the d-pawn permits White to extract his queen without losing material, although the queen will be mercilessly kicked around the board by the black minor pieces. Oddly, it reminds me very much of a school chemistry experiment to demonstrate Brownian motion. The alternatives are inferior, as the queen finds herself trapped on h7:

a) 8 ♗b3 ♗g7 9 ♕h7 and:

a1) 9...♗e6!, by defending d5, Black prepares ...♘d7-f8 to win the queen. With:

a11) 10 0-0 ♘d7! 11 f3 e3! (the f-file must be kept closed) 12 ♗xd5 (there is nothing else, White needs the h3-square for the queen, and 12 g4? ♘h6 stops her getting there) 12...♗xd5 13 ♕h3, Kaedy-Saunders, corr. 1995, when there is no particular reason Black cannot hold on to his e-pawn thus: 13...e2 14 ♖e1 ♕e7 15 ♔h1 ♖e8 16 ♘c3 ♗xc3 17 dxc3 ♘gf6.

a12) 10 d3?! ♘d7! (the most accurate, 10...exd3 11 cxd3?! ♘d7! 12 g3 [12 g4 is the other possibility to save the queen, 12...♘e5 13 ♕h3 ♗xg4 but the white kingside resembles Swiss cheese!] 12...♘e5 13 0-0? but White is in trouble, anyway, 13...♘f6 0-1, Borrmann-Leisebein, corr. 1985, as 14 ♕h4 ♘f3+, this seems to be the same, but allows White the possibility of 11 ♘d2!) 11 g3 (11 g4!? is again possible, 11...exd3 12 g5!?) 11...♘e5?! (menacing ...♘f6, but now is the time for 11...exd3! and Black is at least equal) 12 ♘d2! exd3 13 0-0 (13 f4! looks right, followed by ♘f3-g5) 13...♕f6!? 14 f4! ♘c4 15 f5 gxf5 Hage-Muysenberg, corr. 1995, unclear.

a13) 10 ♘c3 ♘d7! 11 ♗xd5 (11 ♘xd5!? ♘f8 12 ♘xc7! ♘xh7 13 ♘xe6 ♕c8 is fun, but Black won't be too worried about this) 11...♗xd5 12 ♘xd5 ♘f8 13 ♕h3 ♕xd5 is fairly level, Neukirch-Grobe, corr. 1972.

a14) 10 f4!? ♘d7 (if 10...exf3? 11 0-0, but with the c1-h6 diagonal closed 10...♘h6! must be right, 11 ♘c3?! [11 f5!? ♘xf5 12 d3 ♘d7] 11...♘d7 12 ♘xe4 ♕e7 13 ♘g5+ ♔f6 when the white queen is a goner) 11 f5 (forced) 11...gxf5 12 ♕h5+ ♔f8 13 0-0 ♘c5 14 ♘c3 Clarke-Niemand, corr. 1994/95, and White has managed to sort out his most pressing problems.

a2) 9...c6 is slower, 10 ♘c3 (10 d3? is bad, 10...exd3 11 cxd3 ♗f5 12 0-0 [12 ♗c2? ♕e7+ 13 ♔f1 ♘d7 ∓] 12...♘d7 13 g3 [else ...♘f8 wins] 13...♘e5 14 ♘d2 ♘h6, trapping the queen, Alloin-Diepstraten, corr. 1983/4; 10 f3? exf3 11 0-0 ♕g5! 12 ♖xf3+ ♘f6 13 ♘c3 ♗f5 14 ♖xf5, obviously forced, 14...♕xf5 15 ♕h4 ♘g4 16 h3?? [16 ♘d1 ♗d4+ 17 ♘e3 holds on] 16...♗d4+ 0-1, Züchner-Erler, corr. 1990; 10 0-0 ♘d7 [10...♗f5 11 f3 exf3 12 ♖xf3 also favours White, Clarke-Reinke, corr. 1994/95] 11 ♕h3 ♘h6 12 f3 ♘f6 13 ♕h4 exf3 14 ♖xf3 ♗g4 15 ♖f4 ♘f5 and the black pieces combine beautifully, always gaining time on the white queen or rook, 16 ♕f2 ♗h6, Clarke-Grobe, corr. 1994/95, and now White should prefer the pragmatic 17 d3! ♗xf4 18 ♗xf4 with advantage) 10...♗f5 (10...♕g5!? 11 g3 [and not 11 ♘xe4? ♕xg2 12 ♘g3 ♘f6 13 ♕h4 ♘g4] 11...♘f6 12 ♕h4 ♕xh4 13 gxh4 and Black has a little compensation) 11 d3 (11 g3?! ♘h6 forces 12 g4 ♘xg4 ∓; 11 0-0, White plays for f3, 11...♘a6!? [and not 11...♘d7? 12 ♘xd5!] 12 f3 ♕b6+ 13 ♔h1 ♘f6 14 ♕h4 ♖h8, preparing to give the white king a hard time) 11...exd3 12 cxd3 ♕e7+ 13 ♗e3?! (13 ♔d1! ♘d7 14 ♖e1 is stronger, Koetsier-Rosso, corr. 1999) 13...♘d7 14 0-0-0 ♘f8 15 ♘xd5 cxd5 16 ♗xd5+ ♘e6 17 ♗b3 ♖c8+ and Black has good play, Guillet-Capitaine, Fouesnant 1999.

a3) 9...♕g5? is to be avoided: 10 h4! (10 g3 is worse, 10...♘f6 [10...♘h6?! 11 ♘c3 with advantage Alloin-Fiorit, corr. 1983] 11 ♕h4 ♕xh4 12 gxh4 breaking up the white structure) 10...♕xg2 11 ♗xd5+ ♔f6 12 ♖f1 ♗h3 (12...♘e7 13 ♘c3 ♗h3 14 ♘xe4+ ♔e5 15 ♕xg7+ Elburg-Hayward, corr. 1992) 13 ♗c4 ♘c6 14 d4! (14 b3 is also effective, 14...♖e8? 15 ♗b2+ ♘e5 16 ♗xe5+ 1-0, Hergert-Tiemann, corr. 1989) 14...e3 15 ♗xe3 ♘b4 16 ♘a3 (16 ♗g5+ ♔f5 17 ♕xg7 is even quicker) 16...♕e4 17 0-0-0 ♗xf1 18 ♗g5+ ♔f5 19 ♗xf1 ♘xa2+ 20 ♔b1 1-0, Clarke-Svendsen, corr. 1994/95.

a4) 9...c5?! plans to suffocate the b3-bishop, 10 d3 b5 11 ♘c3 c4 12 ♘xe4! cxb3 13 ♘g5+ ♔f6 14 ♕h4 ♕e8+ 15 ♗e3 bxc2 16 ♔d2 ♘c6 17 ♖he1 and the exposed black king is too great a handicap, Ruggeri Laderchi - Elburg, corr. training game 1998.

b) 8 ♗e2

8...♗g7 9 ♕h7 ♘c6 (...♘d4 is a distinct possibility now that the c2-pawn is undefended, 9...♕g5!? is interesting, 10 g3 ♘f6! 11 ♕h4 ♕xh4 12 gxh4 ♘c6 13 d3 [13 ♘a3] 13...♘b4 14 ♘a3 exd3 15 ♗xd3 ♗g4 16 h3?! ♗f3 17 ♖g1 ♘xd3+ 18 cxd3 ♖e8+ 19 ♗e3 d4 ∓ Melchor-Kozlov, corr. 1985) and it is difficult to know what to suggest for White here:

b1) 10 f3!? ♘d4 11 fxe4! (the best chance, 11 ♘c3? ♘f6 12 ♕h4 ♘xc2+ 13 ♔d1 ♘xa1 14 fxe4 d4 15 ♘d5, Nyman-Owen, corr. 1988, 15...d3 ∓; 11 ♗d1?! ♕g5! 12 0-0 exf3 13 ♗xf3 ♘f6 14 ♗d1 ♗f5 wins) 11...♘xe2? (incorrect, 11...♘f6 12 ♖f1 ♗f5! 13 ♕h4 ♘xc2+ 14 ♔d1 ♗xe4 is unclear) 12 ♖f1+ ♘f6 13 e5 ♗f5 14 ♖xf5! gxf5

15 exf6 ♕xf6 16 ♕h5+ ♔f8 17 ♔xe2 ♕e5+ 18 ♔f1?? (but 18 ♔d1 ♖e8 19 c3 defends easily) 18...♖e8 winning, Szilagyi-Pescod, corr. 1976/78.

b2) 10 d3? ♘d4 11 ♗d1 (11 ♔d1 ♘xe2 12 ♔xe2 ♗g4+ 13 ♔f1 ♗h5 trapping the queen once again, and winning, Dogiel-Borrmann, corr. 1992) 11...exd3 12 cxd3 ♕e7+ 13 ♗e3 ♘f6 14 ♕h4 ♘f5 15 ♕f4 ♗h6 16 ♕f3 d4 ∓, Borrmann-Kozlov, corr. 1979/81.

b3) 10 0-0?! ♘d4 11 ♗d1 ♗f5! (stronger than 11...♗e6? 12 f3 exf3 13 ♗xf3 ♘f6 14 ♗d1 [14 ♕h4? ♘xc2, Strelis-Svendsen, corr. 1990] 14...♕d6 15 ♕h4; 11...♘f3+?! is fun, but unnecessary, 12 ♗xf3 exf3 13 d4 ♗g4 14 ♘d2 fxg2 15 ♔xg2, Kraszewski-Mulleady, corr. 1995, 15...♕e7! 16 f3 ♗h5 when White has to play 17 ♘e4! to save his queen, unclear) 12 d3 (12 f3?! exf3 13 ♗xf3 ♘f6 14 ♕h4 ♘xc2 15 ♘c3 ♘xa1 16 g4 is complicated, but must surely be winning for Black after 16...♘xg4 17 ♕xd8 ♖xd8 18 ♗xg4 ♔e6; 12 c3? ♘e6, menacing ...♘f8, 13 g3 ♘f6 0-1, Haletzki-Stammer, corr. 1979, as 14 ♕h4 g5 15 ♗h5+ ♔g8) 12...exd3 13 c3, Hage-Collins, corr. 1999, 13...♘c2 14 ♗xc2 dxc2 15 ♘a3 when Black has the pleasant choice between 15...♕e7 16 ♗e3 ♘f6 17 ♕h4 ♖h8, and 15...d4!? 16 cxd4?! ♕xd4, trapping the white queen again.

b4) Perhaps 10 ♘a3?! is possible, but 10...♕g5 (threatening ...♘f6) 11 g4!? ♘d4 12 h4 ♘f3+! 13 ♗xf3 ♕e7 14 ♗e2 ♘f6 and again the queen's stay on the board proves to be short-lived.

8...♗e6

Again White must decide whether to put his bishop on e2 or b3.

A21 9 ♗b3
A22 9 ♗e2

Other moves are hopeless, e.g. 9 ♘c3? ♘c6 10 ♕e3 ♗h6 11 ♕c5 dxc4 12 ♘xe4 ♘d4 ∓, Ramazzotti-Destrebecq, France 1984.

A21 9 ♗b3

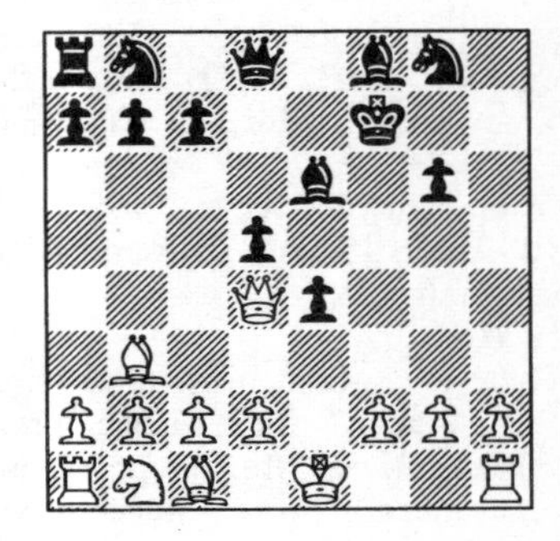

9...♘c6

Black can try to pick up the b3 bishop here, but it might be more trouble than it's worth: 9...c5 10 ♕e3 c4 11 ♗xc4! (the pragmatic decision, 11 ♗a4?! ♕c7!? [11...a6 is also possible 12 c3 ♗h6 13 f4 ♘f6 14 ♗d1 ♘bd7 15 ♕f2 ♕c7 16 0-0 ♘c5 and the hole on d3, with attendant development problems, give Black good play, Fiorito-Niemand, corr. 1983] 12 ♘c3 [12 f4 ♗c5 13 ♕e2 a6 14 c3 ♘f6 15 ♗d1 ♘c6 ∓ Fiorito-Elburg, corr. 1984/85] 12...a6 13 f3 ♘f6 14 fxe4? d4! 15 ♕g5 [15 ♕xd4?? ♗c5] 15...dxc3 16 e5 ♗e7 17 ♖f1 ♗f5 0-1, Korhonen-Elburg, corr. 1988, although this is premature, as after 18 ♖xf5 gxf5 19 exf6 ♗xf6 20 ♕h5+ ♔e6 21 bxc3 b5 22 ♕e8+, say, White has some pawns for the piece) 11...dxc4 12 ♘c3 ♘c6 (12...♗h6 13 ♕xe4 ♘c6 14 d3 ♘f6 15 ♕h4 ♘d4!? 16 0-0 ♘f5 [16...♗g7!?] 17 ♕h3 ♗g7 18 ♕f3 ♕d7 19 ♗e3 cxd3 20 ♖ad1 ♘xe3

21 ♕xe3 ♖h8 22 ♖xd3 ♕c7 23 ♕g3 ♕xg3 and the two black bishops managed to hold their own in the ensuing endgame, Kozlov-Svendsen, corr. 1990) 13 ♘xe4 ♗h6 14 ♕f3+ (14 ♕c5 ♕d5 15 ♘d6+ ♔g7 16 ♕xd5 ♗xd5 17 b3 cxb3 18 c4 ♗xg2 19 ♖g1 should lead to equality, Borrmann-Niemand, corr. 1983) 14...♗f5!? (14...♘f6 is simpler) 15 ♘g3 ♘d4 16 ♕xb7+ ♗d7 17 ♕d5+ ♗e6 Jackson-Kozlov, corr. 1990, 18 ♕xd8 ♖xd8 19 ♔d1 ♘f6 and Black is very active.

10 ♕e3

There is another, bizarre, possibility in 10 ♕h8? ♗g7 11 ♕h7 ♕g5 12 0-0 ♘f6 (as this is good, and simple, there is no real need to consider 12...♘d4!? 13 ♘c3 ♘f3+ 14 ♔h1 ♘f6 15 d4 [better than 15 ♘xe4?! ♘xe4 16 d3 ♘ed2 17 gxf3 ♖h8] 15...♕f5 16 ♕h3 ♕xh3 17 gxh3, Eydan-Eydan, when 17...c6 keeps all the positional pluses) 13 d4 ♘xh7 14 ♗xg5 ♘xg5 -/+ Slater-Karc, corr. 1988.

10...♗h6

11 f4!

Best, otherwise:

a) 11 ♕g3?! ♘f6 12 0-0 (12 ♕h4 ♕h8!? 13 0-0 ♘d4 14 d3?? [14 ♖e1 ♘f5 15 ♕h3 is far superior] 14...♗xc1 15 ♕xh8 ♖xh8 16 ♖xc1 ♘e2+ 0-1, Driscoll-Downey, corr. 1980) 12...♘d4 13 ♖e1, Heap-Elburg, corr. 1991, and now, instead of 13...♘f5 14 ♕c3 ♕d6 15 h3 ♖h8 16 d4 when White had escaped the worst, 13...♘h5! 14 ♕c3 ♗g7 15 ♕e3 ♘f5 16 ♕e2 ♘f4 ∓ is unpleasant.

b) 11 ♕e2? ♘d4 12 ♕d1?! (the bizarre-looking move 12 ♕f1! is better, as g2 is thereby defended, 12...c6 [with the white queen so passive, 12...c5 seems right, e.g. 13 ♘c3 c4 14 ♗a4 a6 15 ♘d1 b5 16 c3 ♘c6 17 ♗c2 ♘e5 with a lot of space] 13 c3 ♘xb3 14 axb3, unclear, Arndahl-Hartsook, National Open 1991) 12...♕g5 13 ♔f1 ♗g4! the most accurate, (13...♘f6 is also strong, 14 ♘c3 ♗g4 15 ♕e1 [possible now that e2 is covered, 15 d3?! ♕h4 16 ♕e1 ♘f3 0-1, Gardner-Fiorito, corr. 1977, although White can continue here] 15...♕h4 16 f3 ♕xe1+ 17 ♔xe1 exf3 18 gxf3 ♖e8+ 19 ♔f2 ♗xf3 20 ♖f1 c6 and Black has good play, Salewski-Borrmann, corr. 1990) 14 ♗xd5+ (14 h4 is no help, 14...♕f5 15 ♕e1 ♗e2+ 16 ♔g1 ♕g4 17 ♖h3 ♕xh3; and not 14 ♕e1? ♗e2+ 15 ♔g1?? ♘f3 mate) 14...♔g7 15 f3?! ♘xf3 ∓ Fernandez-Gayobart, corr. 1990.

c) 11 ♕c5? ♘ge7 12 ♘c3 b6 13 ♕a3 ♘f5 14 d3 ♗xc1 15 ♖xc1 ♕g5 16 0-0 ♘h4 with a swift mate, Harju-Gebuhr, corr. 1975/76.

11...♘ge7

Aiming for f5 to continue torturing the white queen; the more common 11...♘f6 is not so good:

a1) 12 h3!? trying to stop ...♘g4, but it is not necessary, 12...♕d6 (12...♗g7!? 13 c3 ♘e7 14 0-0 ♘f5 15 ♕e1 ♕h8 16 d4?! exd3 17 ♘d2 ♖e8 is very promising, Magee-Clarke, corr. 1990) 13 0-0 ♗g7 14 c3 (14 d4? allows the simple tactic 14...♘g4 15 ♕e1 ♗xd4+ 16 ♔h1

♘e7, Tiemann-Grabner, corr. 1978, and Black has attacking chances) 14...♖h8 15 d3 exd3 16 ♕xd3 ♗f5 17 ♕e3 ♕d7 18 ♖f3 ♗e4 19 ♖g3 ♘e7. Black has a strong, and ultimately decisive, initative, Lawrence-Gillam, corr. 1980.

a2) 12 0-0 ♘g4 13 ♕e1 (13 ♕c5? ♗f8 14 ♕b5?? ♘d4 15 ♕xb7 ♘e2+ 16 ♔h1, Butzelaar-Diepstraten, Hilversum 1989, now the neatest win is 16...♘g3+ 17 hxg3 ♗c5 when a check on h8 forces mate) 13...♕d6 14 d3 ♕c5+ (14...exd3 15 cxd3 ♘b4 is an alternative) 15 ♔h1 e3 16 ♘c3 ♘f2+ 17 ♔g1 ♗xf4 18 ♖xf2!? exf2+ 19 ♕xf2 ♕xf2+ 20 ♔xf2 and White has a sound extra pawn, Wolny-Jablonski, Bydgoszcz 1978.

a3) 12 d4 ♘g4 13 ♕g1 ♗g7 14 c3 ♕h4+ 15 g3 ♕h3 16 f5! (played to free the f4-square; 16 ♘d2 ♘e7-f5, with a light-squared bind on the kingside, Borrmann-Micheloud, corr. 1979/80) 16...gxf5 17 ♗d1 ♖g8?! 18 ♗xg4 ♕xg4 19 ♗f4 ♖c8 20 ♘d2 and at the cost of a pawn White has solved his development problems, Doyle-Evans, corr. 1993.

a4) 12 ♘c3 ♘e7 (12...d4? 13 ♗xe6+ ♔xe6 14 ♕h3+) 13 0-0 ♘f5 14 ♕e1 ♕d6 15 ♘e2 ♘g4 16 h3 ♕c5+ 17 ♔h1 ♖h8 and Black has some play, but the white kingside is solid, Fiorito-Tiemann, corr. 1978.

12 0-0 ♘f5

Black won very quickly in Gemignani-Hamar, corr. 1974, with 12...♗g7 13 c3 ♘f5 14 ♕e2 ♕h4 15 ♕b5?? (but 15 g3! ♕h3 16 ♕g2 is perfectly respectable.) 15...♘cd4! 0-1, as 16 cxd4 ♗xd4+ 17 ♔h1 ♘g3 mate.

13 ♕f2

13 ♕e1 is possibly superior, 13...♕d6 (alternatively, 13...♗f8!? -c5, or first 13...♕h8!?, but not 13...♘cd4? 14 c3 ♘b5 [14...♘xb3 15 axb3 is also good for White] 15 d4 ♗g7 16 ♘a3 ♘bd6 17 ♘c2 ♕h8 and White was doing well, Jackson-Jensen, corr. 1991, although something nasty happened along the h-file, later on.) 14 d3 exd3 15 cxd3 ♘b4 16 ♕d1 ♕c5+ 17 d4 ♕xd4+ 18 ♕xd4 ♘xd4 19 ♘a3, Jackson-Borrmann, corr. 1990, when 19...♗g7 stops the c1-bishop from developing, and promises Black fine play.

13...♗g7

Black can also play 13...♕h8!? 14 ♘c3 ♘cd4 15 d3 e3 16 ♗xe3!? ♘xb3 17 axb3 d4 18 ♗d2 dxc3 19 ♗xc3 ♗g7 but White is better here, Bastian-Destrebecq, Ales 1979.

Destrebecq suggests 13...♗f8, instead, e.g. 14 ♘c3 b6 15 ♕e1 ♗c5+ 16 ♔h1 ♘cd4 17 ♗a4?! c6 18 ♘d1 b5 19 c3?!, Durville-Diepstraten, corr. 1993, when Black missed the shot 19...♘e2!, winning, as 20 ♕xe2 ♘g3+ 21 hxg3 ♕h8+ mates.

14 c3 ♘b4!

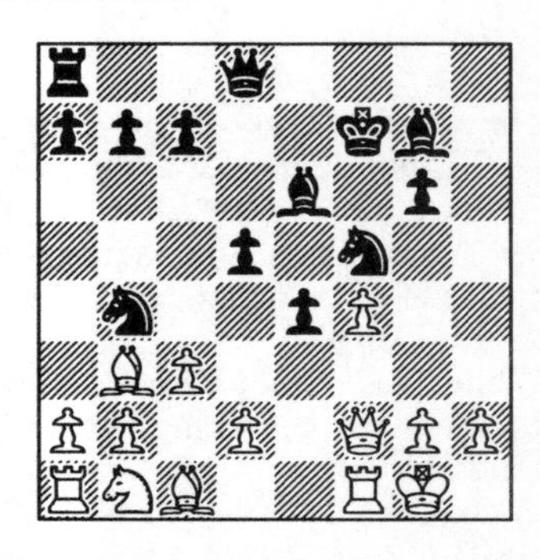

15 d4 ♘d3 16 ♕e2 ♕h4 17 g4

17...♖h8 is a big threat, and the 17 g3 of Reinke-Heap, corr. 1994/96, allows 17...♘xc1 18 ♖xc1 ♘xg3 19 ♕f2 ♘f5 with dangerous play around the white king.

17...♘xc1 18 ♖xc1 ♘h6 19 f5?

19 g5 was the only move, although 19...♘f5 20 ♖f1 ♖h8 is strong, with the menace of ...♘g3.

19...gxf5 20 ♖f1

20 gxf5?? ♕g5+.

20...♘xg4 21 ♗xd5?! ♗xd5 22 ♖xf5+

And now Black faltered on the brink of victory.

22...♔e6? 23 ♖f4

Unclear, Borrmann-Leisebein, corr. 1986, when simply 22...♗f6! 23 ♖xd5 ♖g8 wins.

A22 9 ♗e2

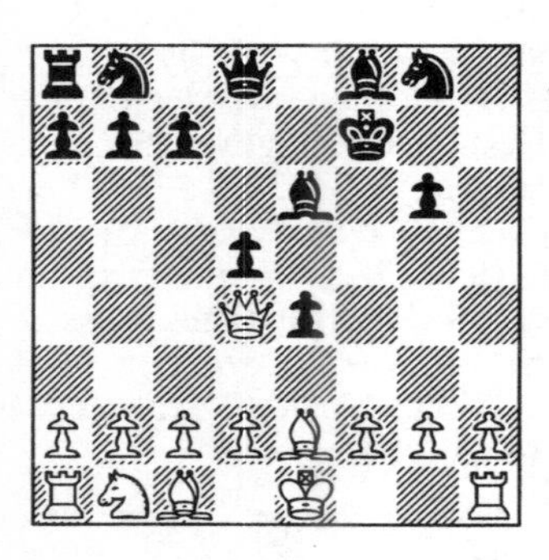

The disadvantage of this move is that c2 is not defended, adding force to moves like ...♘d4, but, on the other hand, from this square the kingside is given assistance.

9...♘c6 10 ♕e3

White has little choice, as 10 ♕a4? leaves the king short of defenders:

a) 10...♗c5 11 ♘c3 (11 d3?! ♕h4 12 0-0? [12 g3 ♗xf2+ 13 ♔d1 only loses a pawn, not the king] 12...♘f6 13 ♘d2 ♘d4 14 ♗d1 ♖h8 15 h3 ♗xh3 16 g3 ♕xg3+ 0-1, Pire-Kolzon, USA 1985; 11 0-0? is always very risky with the h-file open, and no queen to defend, 11...♘d4 12 ♘c3 ♕h4 13 d3 ♘f6 0-1, Moser-Stader, corr. 1979, as there is simply no defence against ...♖h8) 11...♕h4 12 ♘d1 ♘d4 13 g3? ♕f6 14 ♖g1 (what else? 14 ♘c3 loses to 14...♘xe2 15 ♘xe2 ♗xf2+ 16 ♔d1 ♕f3 17 ♖f1 ♗g4 18 ♕b5 ♘f6 and ...a6) and instead of 14...♖e8?, Aker-Magee, USA 1992, 14...♘xe2 15 ♔xe2 ♕f3+ 16 ♔e1 ♗g4 puts an immediate end to White's miseries.

b) 10...♕g5 11 g3 ♗c5 12 ♘c3 (12 ♕b5 ♗b6 13 ♘c3 ♕f5 14 ♖f1, Markus-Melchor, corr. 1982, and now 14...♘d4 almost forces White to play 15 g4 ♕e5 16 ♕a4 ♘f6 when the white kingside is falling apart as 15 ♕a4? ♗d7 16 ♗b5 ♘xb5 17 ♘xb5 a6 wins material) 12...♕f5 13 ♘d1 d4 (to stop the white knight from hopping to e3) 14 ♕b5?, Dartnell-Chadwick, corr. 1981, (14 f3!) 14...d3! (threatening ...♗xf2+, winning the queen) 15 ♕xb7 ♘d4 16 cxd3 exd3 17 ♘e3 ♘c2+ winning.

10...♗h6 11 f4

The pawn is best placed in front of the queen, 11 ♕g3 ♘d4 (11...♘f6?! is slower, and allows 12 0-0 [or 12 c3 perhaps] 12...♘d4 13 ♗d1 ♘f5 14 ♕h3 ♗g7 leaves the white queen exposed, 15 ♘c3? d4 16 ♘b5, Meester-Diepstraten, Hilversum 1981, 16...♘e3) 12 ♘a3 ♗f8!? (an interesting idea, 12...♘f6 is more typical) 13 ♗d1 ♗d6 14 ♕e3 ♕f6 15 0-0?! (Into the lion's den! 15 c3 ♘f5 16 ♕e2 leaves the game open) 15...♘e7 16 c3? (16 h3 ♘ef5 17 ♕c3 ♕e5 is also unpleasant for White) 16...♘ef5 17 ♕e1 ♗xh2+ 18 ♔xh2 ♖h8+ 19 ♔g1 ♘f3+ 0-1, Beaulieu-Saalfeld, corr. 1996, as 20 ♗xf3 exf3 21 g3 g5 and ...♕h6 forces mate.

11...d4

Black can rarely resist this thrust, but 11...♘ge7 is also interesting:

a) 12 g4!? played to control f5, 12...d4 13 ♕g3 d3 14 ♗d1 ♘b4 15 ♘a3 ♕d7 16 c3 ♘bd5 17 0-0, Koskinen-Grabner, corr. 1987, when I would prefer 17...♖f8 to gang up on the f4-pawn.

b) If 12 0-0 then 12...♘f5 13 ♕f2 ♗g7 14 c3 d4 looks sharper than 12...♕d7 13 ♗b5 ♘f5 14 ♕f2 ♗g7 15 c3 ♖h8 of Downey-Nyman, corr. 1993.

c) 12 c3 ♘f5 13 ♕f2, Thomson-Bernard, corr. 1901, 13...d4 (else White will play d4 himself).

d) 12 ♘a3 ♘f5 13 ♕f2 ♗g7 14 c3 d4 15 0-0 (15 ♗b5!?) 15...d3 16 ♗d1, Nilsson-Svendsen, corr. 1998, when 16...a6 keeps White bottled up, he will find it difficult to bring his queenside into the game.

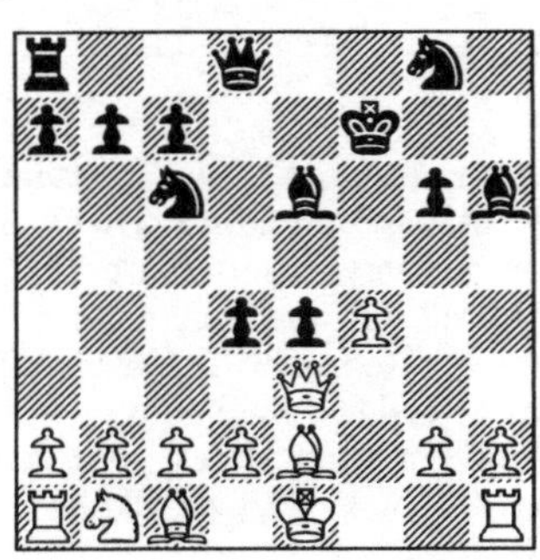

12 ♕f2

On this square the queen is slightly less exposed than after 12 ♕g3 (not 12 ♕xe4? ♗d5 13 ♗c4 [13 ♕d3? ♘b4 14 ♕h3 ♘xc2+] 13...♗xc4 14 d3 ♗d5 15 ♕e2 ♕h4+ 16 ♕f2 ♖e8+ 17 ♔f1 ♕g4, Lonsdale-Borrmann, corr. 1986, and the check on d1 is decisive) when, although Black's position is very promising, he is material down, and the white position is solid. How then to proceed?:

a) 12...♘f6 13 0-0 (instead, 13 d3 ♗f8!? 14 h4!? e3 15 h5 ♘xh5 16 ♗xh5 gxh5 17 ♖xh5 ♕f6 18 f5 ♗xf5 19 ♕xc7+ ♘e7 20 ♕f4 looked unclear in Holecek-Paz, corr. 1972/74, but quickly went Black's way; 13 a4?! looks odd, 13...d3 14 cxd3 ♘d4 [14...♘b4 15 ♘a3 exd3 16 ♗f3 ♕d4! 17 f5 ♗xf5 18 ♕xc7+ ♔f8 19 ♘b5? {19 ♕c3} 19...♘c2+ 20 ♔f1 ♕h4 ∓ Downey-Hayward, corr. 1992] 15 ♗d1 ♘h5?! [15...♘f5 16 ♕f2 exd3] 16 ♗xh5 gxh5 17 ♘a3 h4 ± Downey-Malmström, corr. 1993) 13...♘b4 (13...♘e7!? 14 ♘a3 ♘f5 15 ♕e1 d3 is also reasonable, Mierzynski-Hunstock, corr. 1993) 14 ♘a3 d3 15 cxd3 exd3 16 ♗d1, Simango-Carlsson, corr. 1990, and, instead of grabbing the a2-pawn, I think that Black should play 16...c6 to keep the knight stuck on a3.

b) Apart from the previous line, which is the most popular, but a little slow, Black can essay the ultra-sharp 12...d3!? 13 cxd3 ♘d4 14 ♗d1 (14 ♘a3?! ♘xe2 15 ♔xe2 exd3+ 16 ♔f2 ♘f6 17 ♖e1 ♕d4+ 18 ♔f1 ♗xf4 and White is reeling, Fleckner-Svendsen, Merano 1988) 14...♘f5 (or 14...♘f6!? 15 dxe4 ♘xe4 16 ♕e3 ♕f6! 17 ♕xe4 [not forced, 17 ♘c3 is possible, for instance] 17...♖e8 18 0-0 ♗c4 19 ♕xb7 ♗xf1, Downey-Borrman, corr. 1992, and White is in trouble as 20 ♔xf1 ♕xf4+ 21 ♗f3 ♕xh2 leaves his king looking worried) 15 ♕f2 exd3 16 ♘c3 ♗g7 17 ♕f3 ♘f6 18 ♕xb7 ♘d5! 19 ♗f3 ♖b8 20 ♕xa7 ♗d4 21 ♕a5 ♗b6 22 ♕a4 ♘d4, White has lost time with his queen, and the black pieces are swarming all over his position, Downey-Kozlov, corr. 1989.

c) 12...♘b4 13 ♘a3 d3 is similar to the above, 14 cxd3 exd3 15 ♗f3 ♕d6 (15...♘e7!? 16 ♗xb7!? ♖b8 17 ♕h4? loses instructively, [17 ♗e4!

is necessary] 17...♖xb7! 18 ♕xh6 ♕d4 19 ♔f1 ♘c2! 20 ♘xc2 dxc2, threatening ...♗c4 and White has no defender for his light squares, 21 ♔e1 ♗c4 22 d3 ♖b6 23 ♕h7+ ♔e8 24 ♕h3 ♖e6+ 25 ♔d2 ♕f2+ 26 ♔c3 ♗d5 27 ♕h8+ ♔d7, Lonsdale-Kozlov, corr. 1986) 16 0-0 c6 17 f5 ♕d4+ 18 ♔h1 gxf5 19 ♗h5+ ♔f8 20 ♕g6 ♕f6 was also fine for Black, Bertoni-Malmström, corr. 1999.

12...♘f6

I am surprised that moves like 12...d3!? have not been tried in this position; play may continue: 13 cxd3 exd3 14 ♗d1 ♗g7 when White can no longer castle.

13 0-0

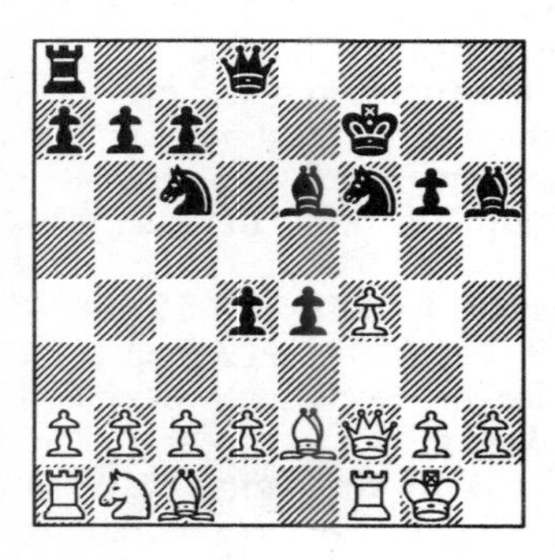

13...d3!?

This is by far the most popular, but is far from obligatory, as, in a way, it does dissipate the space advantage.

14 cxd3 exd3 15 ♗d1

White keeps an eye on c2, but 15 ♗f3 seems fine, 15...♘d4 16 ♘c3 ♗f8 17 ♗xb7?! (walking into the tactics; 17 ♔h1 is safer, when 17...♗c5?! would be met by 18 ♘a4) 17...♖b8 18 ♗a6 (18 ♗e4 is no improvement, 18...♗c5 19 ♔h1 ♘g4 20 ♕e1 [20 ♕g3 ♘e2] 20...♘xh2!) 18...♗c5 19 ♔h1 ♘b3, regaining his rook, Valverde Lopez-Borrmann, corr. 1989.

15...♘d4 16 ♘c3 ♗f8

Bringing the bishop to the important g1-a7 diagonal, rather than the 16...b5?! of Gaard-Leisebein, corr. 1990.

17 ♔h1!

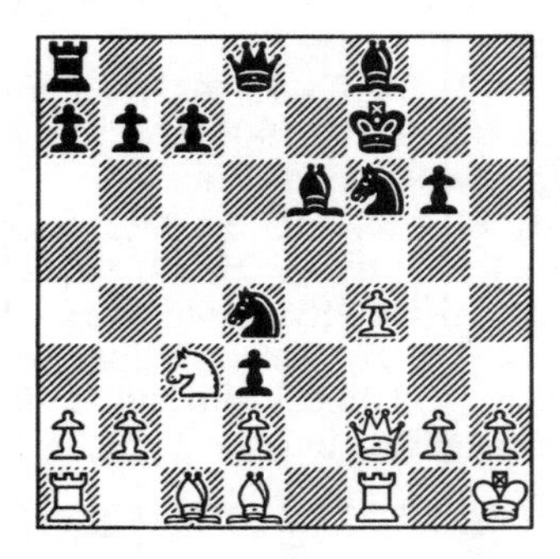

17...♗c5?!

In the light of White's obvious reply, this is premature. Black has to look at ways to prepare this, like 17...b5!? for instance, e.g. 18 ♖e1 ♗c5 19 ♖e5 ♗b6 20 ♕g3 ♘f5 21 ♕e1 ♕d4, menacing another ...♘g3+ mating attack after, say, 22 ♖xe6?? ♘g3+ 23 hxg3 ♖h8+.

18 ♘a4!

Simple, and effective, 18 ♕h4?! ♕h8!? 19 ♕xh8 ♖xh8 with a powerful attack, Scott-Paz, corr. 1974, despite the exchange of queens, 18 ♕e1?! a6 (alternatively, 18...♕h8!? is tempting, 19 ♘e4 [19 ♘a4?? ♕xh2+ 20 ♔xh2 ♖h8+ forces mate] 19...♘xe4 20 ♕xe4 ♘f5 21 ♕xd3 ♕h4 leads to a strong attack) 19 ♘e4! ♘xe4 20 ♕xe4, Nilsson-Evans, corr. 1990, when 20...♘f5! threatens mate, with ...♘g3+, etc. 21 ♕e1 ♕d4 and Black has a strong position.

18...♗e7 19 b3 ♘g4 20 ♗xg4 ♗xg4 21 ♗b2

White has successfully completed his development, and can now exploit his material advantage, Alderden-Goedhart, corr. 1984.

B 6...♘f6

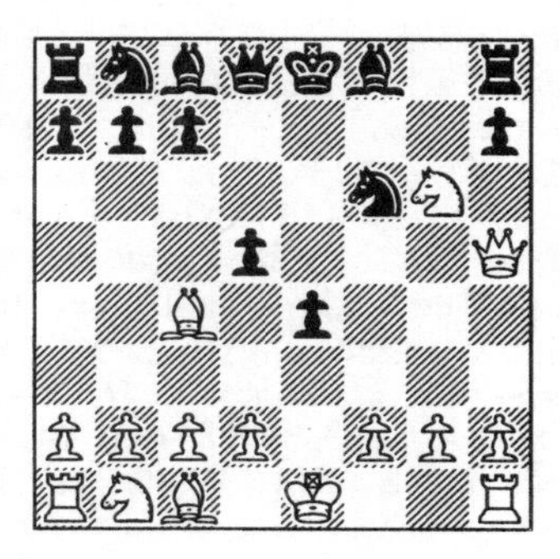

7 ♕e5+ ♗e7 8 ♗b5+!

An important finesse.

a) The immediate 8 ♘xe7 (or first 8 ♕xe7+) is worse because it allows Black to use the c6 square for his queen's knight: 8...♕xe7 9 ♕xe7+?! (this is the last chance for 9 ♗b5+, transposing to the main line) 9...♔xe7 10 ♗e2 (10 ♗b3!? defends the c-pawn, but leaves the bishop on the wrong sector of the board to defend the kingside light squares, 10...♖g8 11 ♘c3 c6 12 g3 ♗h3 13 d3 exd3 14 cxd3 ♘bd7 15 ♗e3, Mayet-Hanstein, Berlin 1837, when 15...♘e5 16 0-0-0 ♘f3 will win the exchange by ...♗g2) 10...♖g8 11 g3 (of course not 11 0-0? ♗h3 12 ♘c3?! ♘c6!? 13 ♘b5 ♖xg2+ 14 ♔h1 ♖ag8 15 d3 ♖2g6 0-1, Lonsdale-Littleboy, corr. 1987) 11...♘c6 (or 11...♗h3 12 ♘c3 ♘c6 13 ♘b5? a6 14 ♘xc7?! ♖ac8 ∓ Moreno-Jurgenson, corr. 1971) after which:

a1) 12 h3 is the best idea, White tries to control the weak h3 and g4 light squares, 12...♘d4 13 ♘a3 c5 14 c3 ♘xe2 15 ♔xe2, Lescot-Turian, corr. 1995, when Black could best exploit his advantage on the light squares by 15...b6 and ...♗a6+, with a likely draw.

a2) 12 d3 ♘d4 13 ♘a3? ♘xe2 14 ♔xe2 ♗g4+ 15 ♔f1 ♔d7 16 ♗d2 ♗f3 17 ♖g1 ♘g4, winning quickly, Vidigal-Clasta, corr. 1974.

a3) 12 0-0?! ♘d4 13 ♗d1 ♗g4 14 ♘a3 ♗xd1 (weakening White's light squares by exchanging their defender) 15 ♖xd1 ♘g4 16 d3 ♖af8 17 ♗e3 ♘f3+ 18 ♔g2 d4 19 ♗d2 ♘h4+! 20 ♔g1 ♖xf2 ∓, Nymann-Koslov, corr. 1991.

a4) 12 c3?! stops ...♘d4, but further exposes the light squares, 12...♘e5 13 ♘a3 ♗h3 (not bad, but 13...♗g4 gains f3 and d3 for the black knights) 14 ♘c2 c5 15 b3 ♗g2 16 ♖g1 ♗f3; Black has a positional edge because of his customary light-squared bind, Zaloznik-Akopian, Bundesliga 1989.

b) Meanwhile, taking the rook is perhaps not as bad as is generally thought: 8 ♘xh8 dxc4, then:

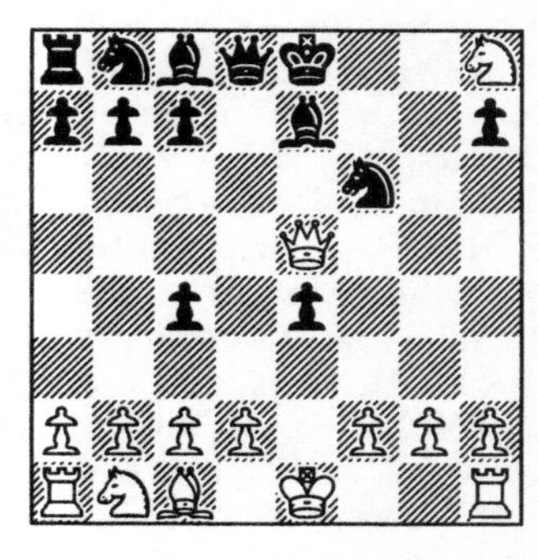

b1) 9 b3! is interesting: 9...♘c6 10 ♕b5 ♗e6 11 ♗b2 ♔f8? (this is not the place for prevarication, 11...a6 is strong, 12 ♕g5 [but not 12 ♕xb7?? ♘a5 -/+] 12...♔d7, best, as Black will capture the knight next go; 12...♘d4!? 13 ♕e5 ♘xc2+ 14 ♔d1 ♕d3 15 ♕xe6 ♘xa1 is messy) 12 ♕g5 ♘d4?! 13 ♕e5!? (13 ♘a3) 13...♘xc2+ 14 ♔d1 ♘xa1 15 ♕xe6 ♕d5 and instead of 16 ♕h3? cxb3 17 ♘c3 ♕c4 18 ♗xa1 bxa2, Cardenas-Rodriguez Izquiero, Cordoba 1992, simply 16 ♕xd5 ♘xd5 17 bxc4 ♗f6, else 18 ♗xa1 18 ♔c1 with advantage.

b2) 9 ♕b5+!?, greedily grabbing another pawn, 9...♘c6 10 ♕xc4, with the further choice:

b21) 10...♕d5 Black decides to play the ending as he will remass the h8-knight and can then play on the light squares, 11 ♕xd5 (11 ♘a3?! ♗e6 12 ♕xd5 ♗xd5, recapturing with the bishop allows Black to defend his e4-pawn, 13 c4?! ♗e6 14 d4 ♘xd4 15 ♗e3 ♗b4+ 16 ♔f1 ♘f5 17 ♗g5 ♔e7 and Black is winning, Crimp-Budovskis, corr. 1999) 11...♘xd5 12 0-0 ♘d4?! (12...♗e6 13 ♖e1 ♔d7 14 ♖xe4 ♖xh8 is more accurate, as Black has a consequent lead in development) 13 ♘a3 ♗f6 14 ♖e1 ♘e6 15 c4 ♘b4 16 ♖xe4 ♗xh8 17 d4 and for once White is clearly on top, Crimp-Niemand, corr. 1999.

b22) 10...♘d4!? is also possible, 11 ♘a3 (11 ♕f7+ ♔d7 doesn't appear to lead anywhere, 12 ♕c4 [12 ♘a3?! ♕xh8 13 0-0 ♔d8, Nilsson-Migala, corr. 1998, and here White has to extract his queen by 14 ♕c4 c5 with a plus for Black] 12...♔e8 13 ♘a3 [White can take a draw with 13 ♕f7+! of course, and he probably should] 13...♗e6 14 ♕c3 as per the main line, Downey-Svendsen, corr. 1990; 11 d3? is a blunder, depriving the queen of several retreat squares, 11...♗e6 12 ♕a4+ [12 ♕c3 ♗b4] 12...b5 13 ♕a6 ♘xc2+ 14 ♔d1 ♕xd3+ 15 ♘d2, Brusey-Simons, England 1992, and Black missed the simplest mate: 15...♘e3+ 16 ♔e1 ♘xg2+ 17 ♔d1 ♗g4+ 18 f3 ♗xf3 mate but found a more convoluted one!) 11...♗e6 12 ♕c3 (12 ♕a4+?! ♔f8!? [12...♕d7 13 ♕xd7+ ♔xd7 is also rather good, and easier to calculate] 13 c3 ♘f5 14 ♘c4 c6 15 ♘e3 ♘xe3 16 dxe3 ♔g7 17 0-0 ♔xh8 18 ♖e1 ♕g8 19 b3? ♗h3 20 g3 ♕g4 0-1, Druke-Svendsen, corr. 1989) 12...b5! (12...♕d5 is also reasonable) 13 b4 (13 ♘xb5? ♘xb5 14 ♕c6+ ♗d7 15 ♕c4 ♘d6 16 ♕b3 ♗f8 and ...♗g7 will gain three pieces for the rook) 13...a5 14 ♗b2 axb4 15 ♕xd4 bxa3 16 ♕xd8+ ♖xd8 17 ♗c3 b4 18 ♗e5 ♔d7 19 0-0 ♖xh8 and White is lost, Downey-Svendsen, corr. 1990, the white a2-pawn is weak, and the a3-pawn is poised for greatness.

b3) 9 0-0 ♘c6 10 ♕g5 ♘d4 11 ♘a3 ♗e6 12 c3? ♘e2+ 13 ♔h1 ♕d3, completely paralysing the white position, Cabral-Gedult, Paris 1971.

b4) 9 ♘c3?! ♘c6 10 ♕b5 ♗e6 11 ♕xb7, Cordir-Barbaut, French ch, Chambery 1994, when 11...♔d7 is good, there is a passing threat of ...a6, and ...♖a7 to cope with, so 12 d4 ♖b8 (12...a6 13 ♘a4) 13 ♕a6 ♕xh8 and the white queen is still not out of the woods.

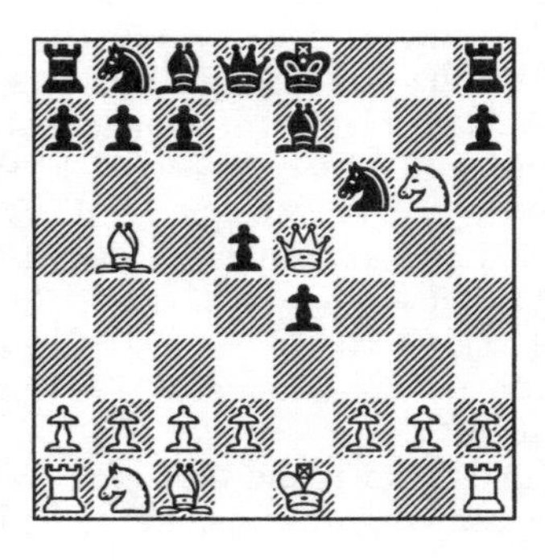

8...c6

In the exciting game, Marshall-Forsberg, New York 1921, Black played 8...♗d7!? 9 ♘xh8?! (somewhat risky, 9 ♘xe7 ♕xe7 10 ♗xd7+ ♔xd7 [10...♘bxd7?! 11 ♕xc7 0-0 12 0-0 {12 b3 is almost certainly very good for White} 12...♖ac8 13 ♕g3+ ♔h8 14 ♘a3 ♘h5 15 ♕e3 ♘f4 16 d3?! {16 ♔h1 is much more circumspect} 16...♕g7 17 ♕g3?? {17 g3 exd3 18 ♔h1 should still favour White, although it is messy} 17...♘e2+ 0-1, Purins-Littleboy, corr. 1983] 11 ♕xe7+ ♔xe7 would have left White a pawn up, but facing some difficulties exploiting it, not the sort of position Marshall would have found at all interesting, of course! 12 d3 ♘bd7 13 dxe4 dxe4 14 ♗g5 ♖hg8 15 ♗xf6+ ♔xf6 16 0-0 and White has a solid extra pawn, Abramauv-Diablo, Minitel 1991) 9...♗xb5 10 ♘c3 (10 ♕e6!? extricates the knight from its tomb, 10...♘c6 11 ♘a3 [11 ♕f7+? is a waste of a check: 11...♔d7 12 ♘c3 ♕xh8 13 ♘xd5 ♖f8 14 ♘xf6+ ♕xf6 and, with his king stranded in the centre, and f2 weak, White is lost, Edwards-Littleboy, corr. 1985] 11...♗a6 12 ♘f7 ♕d7 13 ♘g5 ♘d4 14 ♕xd7+ [14 ♕f7+] 14...♔xd7 15 c3 ♘e2 and White's weak light squares give ample compensation for the exchange, Krustkains-Littleboy, corr. 1986) 10...♗a6 11 d3 ♘c6 12 ♕g3 ♗d6? (improving White's position, Marshall indicates either 12...♘d4, or 12...♕d7 with the idea of 13...0-0-0, as better in his marvellous '*...Best Games of Chess*', for example [12...♕d7] 13 ♗g5 ♕e6 14 0-0-0 0-0-0 15 dxe4 ♘b4 16 exd5 ♕f5 17 ♖d2 ♘h5 18 ♗xe7 ♘xg3 19 hxg3 ♘xa2+ 20 ♘xa2 ♖xh8 21 ♘c3 but White is a bit better here, Doyle-Nilsson, corr. 1994; perhaps Black's best move is 12...♘b4, e.g. 13 0-0 ♘xc2 14 ♖b1 ♗xd3) 13 ♕h4 d4? 14 ♘xe4 ♗e7 15 ♘xf6+ ♗xf6 16 ♕h5+ ♔d7 17 ♕h3+ ♔e8 18 ♕xh7? (after this Black starts gaining the ascendancy) 18...♕e7+ 19 ♕xe7+ ♘xe7 20 0-0 ♗xh8=.

9 ♘xe7

Once again, 9 ♘xh8? is possible, but must be even worse than before, as Black manages to keep his centre intact: 9...cxb5 10 ♘c3 ♘c6 11 ♕g5 ♘d4 12 0-0 b4 13 ♘d1 ♗e6 14 ♘e3 ♔d7 15 c3 ♘e2+ 16 ♔h1 ♕xh8 ∓ Krustkalns-Kozlov, corr. 1986/87.

9...♕xe7 10 ♕xe7+ ♔xe7 11 ♗e2

Sometimes White 'undevelops' his one developed piece with 11 ♗f1!? and this makes some sense, as White can thereby avoid weakening his kingside: 11...c5 (11...♖g8?! does not threaten the g-pawn here: 12 d4 [12 g3?! is wrong, 12...♗g4 13 ♗g2 ♘a6!? 14 b3 ♘b4 15 ♗a3 c5 16 ♗xb4 cxb4 17 a3 ♖ac8 18 axb4 ♖xc2 19 ♘c3 equal, Nolden-Stummer, corr. 1991] 12...exd3 13 cxd3 ♘a6 [13...♗f5 14 h3 ♘bd7? {14...h5} 15 g4 ♗g6 16 f4 and White's pawns are on the move, Malmström-Granik, corr. 1994/95] 14 ♗f4 ♗f5 15 h3 h5 16 g3 ♖ae8 17 ♔d2 ♔f7 18 ♘a3 and Black's compensation is insufficient, Gunderam-Hempel, corr. 1970) 12 d3! (12 g3?! ♘c6 13 ♗g2 ♘d4 14 ♘a3 ♗g4 15 h3 ♗f3 16 0-0 h5! with a powerful initiative, Harju-Destrebecq, corr. 1978) 12...exd3 (12...♗f5?! 13 ♗g5! exd3 14 ♘c3! ♖d8 15 0-0-0! d4?! 16 ♗xd3 ♗xd3 17 ♖xd3 ♘bd7 18 ♘d5+ 1-0, Crimp-Lescot, corr. 1995) 13 ♗xd3 ♖g8 14 0-0 ♗h3 15 ♖e1+ ♔f7 16 g3 ♘c6, Niemand-Budovskis, corr. 1998, and now White could have kept some advantage by 17 ♗e3.

11...♖g8 12 g3

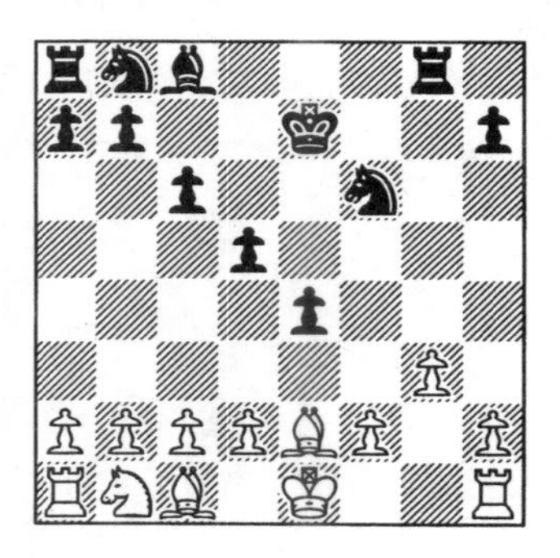

12...c5

If we take stock of the current situation, we see that White has a pawn more and the bishop pair, but that in return Black has a strong centre and good piece play. Further, White's kingside light squares are sensitive. Keres considered that White has a clear advantage, but I think ±/= is somewhere nearer the truth. Black has tried several moves in this position, the text, an idea of Gunderam's, intends ...♘c6-d4. Other moves are:

a) 12...♗f5 trying to dissuade White from playing d3, 13 b3 (better 13 d3! exd3 [13...♘bd7 14 ♘c3 exd3 15 ♗xd3 ♗xd3 16 cxd3 ♘e5 17 ♔e2 ♔f7 18 f4 ♘ed7 19 ♗e3 with advantage, Magee-Stummer, corr. 1990] 14 ♗xd3 ♗xd3 15 cxd3 c5 16 ♘c3 [16 0-0 ♘c6 17 ♘c3 ♘b4 18 ♖d1, Hage-Koetsier, corr. 1999, 18...d4!? 19 ♘e4 ♘xe4 20 dxe4 c4, with potent c and d pawns] 16...♘c6 17 ♗f4 ♔d7 18 0-0-0 d4!? [18...♖ae8 19 ♖he1 ♘d4 20 h3 ♘f3 21 ♖e3 is easier for White, Melchor-Borrmann, corr. 1995] 19 ♘e4 ♘xe4 20 dxe4 b5 21 ♖he1 a5 Gouat-Sireta, corr. 1995, and White is better, but the black queenside pawns certainly provide practical chances) 13...c5 14 ♗a3 ♔d6 15 d4 (15 b4!? b6 16 ♘c3 d4! [16...♘bd7 17 bxc5+ bxc5, Oren-Jackson, corr. 1994/97, 18 d4 exd3 19 cxd3 favours White] 17 ♘a4 ♘bd7 18 bxc5+ bxc5 19 0-0 ♖ab8 and Black's imposing centre is worth a pawn, Oren-Sénéchaud, corr. 1994/95) 15...exd3 16 cxd3 ♘c6 17 ♘c3 ♘d4 18 ♔d2 b5! (18...♖ae8 19 ♖ac1 [19 ♖ae1?! ♗g4 20 f3 ♖xe2+! 21 ♖xe2 ♗xf3 = Melchor-Grivainis, corr. 1992] 19...♖g7?! 20 ♗d1 b6 21 b4 ♖c7 22 bxc5+ bxc5 23 h3 and White is on his way to consolidating, Ruggeri Laderchi-Elburg, corr. training game 1998) 19 b4 c4 20 ♖ae1 a6 21 dxc4 dxc4 22 ♗d1 ♖ae8 23 ♖xe8 ♖xe8 24 f3 ♘d5 25 ♘xd5 ♔xd5 and Black's activity and extra space compensates for the pawn, Melchor-Sénéchaud, corr. 1994/95.

b) 12...♗h3 13 d3 (13 d4?! ♘bd7 14 ♗e3 h5 15 ♘d2 ♘g4 16 ♗f1 ♘xe3 17 fxe3 ♗xf1 18 ♖xf1 ♘f6 19 ♔e2 h4! 20 gxh4 ½-½, Ballard-Cano, corr. 1971/72) 13...♘bd7 14 dxe4 (14 ♘d2?! exd3 15 ♗xd3 ♖ae8 16 ♗e2 ♔d8 17 f3 ♘e5 18 ♔d1 ♖e7 19 b3 ♖ge8 with a strong initiative, Kozlov-Destrebecq, corr. 1981/83; 14 ♗f4 exd3 [if 14...♘c5 then White should play 15 dxe4 rather than 15 ♘c3?!, Faig-Perez Pietronave, Boca ch 1997, when

15...♘e6 16 ♗d2 ♘d4 equalises] 15 cxd3 d4 16 ♘a3 ♘d5 17 ♗d2 ♖ae8 18 0-0-0 White has a plus, Nyman-Destrebecq, corr. 1991; 14 ♘c3?! ♘e5! 15 ♗f4 [15 dxe4 dxe4 16 ♗e3 ♗g2 17 ♖g1 ♘f3+ is fine for Black] 15...♗g2 16 ♖g1 ♘f3+ 17 ♗xf3 ♗xf3 and Black is master of the light squares, Campbell-Stearn, corr. 1994) 14...♗g2 15 ♖g1 ♗xe4 16 ♘a3? (16 ♔d1!? is interesting, White frees the e-file for his rook: 16...♘e5 17 ♖e1 ♔f7 18 ♘d2 ♘fg4!? 19 ♗xg4 ♘xg4 20 f3 ♗f5 21 ♘f1 and White has a clear advantage) 16...♘e5, the knight will reach f3, and Black's opening problems will be solved, 17 f4 ♘f3+ 18 ♗xf3 ♗xf3 19 ♖f1 ♗e4 20 ♗e3 ♘g4 Black has all the play, Melchor-Niemand, corr. 1999.

c) 12...♗g4?!, the idea is to exchange the protector of White's light squares, but I don't like this move for two reasons, one: Black is a pawn down and should therefore not encourage simplification, and two: Black's bishop controls more squares, and has more scope than its counterpart. 13 d3! (White should always try to exchange the e4 pawn, 13 d4 ♗xe2 14 ♔xe2 ♘a6 15 b3 ♔d7 16 ♗a3 ♘c7 ± Schirmer-Stummer, corr. 1991; but not 13 ♗xg4? ♘xg4 14 h3?! ♘e5 15 b3 c5 16 ♘c3 ♔e6 17 ♘b5 ♖c8 18 ♔e2 a6 19 ♘c3 ♘bc6 20 ♗b2 ♘d4+, White virtually forced Black to put his knights on their optimum squares, Kott-Elburg, corr. 1992) 13...♗xe2 (Black can still try to get a knight to f3 via e5: 13...♘bd7 14 dxe4 dxe4 15 ♗e3 ♘e5 but then 16 ♘d2 and f3 is covered a second time, with a plus) 14 ♔xe2 ♘a6 15 h3 (White has other promising options: 15 dxe4 ♘xe4 16 ♘d2 with advantage, or 16 ♗e3 with advantage) 15...♘b4 16 ♘a3 exd3+ 17 cxd3 ♖ae8 18 ♗e3 a5 19 ♗b6 ♖a8 20 ♖he1 ♘d7 21 ♔d2+ with an extra pawn, Krongraf-Stummer, corr. 1990.

13 d3

If White wants to play actively, then 13 b4!? cxb4 14 a3 bxa3 15 ♗xa3+ ♔f7 16 ♘c3 is interesting, 16...♘c6 (16...a6!? 17 f3 ♗h3 18 fxe4 dxe4 19 ♗c4+ ♗e6 20 ♗xe6+ ♔xe6 21 0-0 and White has obtained activity, but at the cost of his pawn, Nyman-Strelis, corr. 1990) 17 ♘b5 ♗h3 (17...♗g4!?) 18 ♘d6+ ♔g6 19 ♘xb7 ♘d4 20 ♗d1 ♗g2 (20...♖gb8!, first, avoids any problems) 21 ♖g1 ♗f3? (21...♘f3+ 22 ♗xf3 ♗xf3 is good, so that if 23 ♗b2 ♖gb8 24 ♖a6? d4 25 ♗xd4 ♖xb7) 22 ♗b2 (22 ♗c5?! ♘e6! [22...♗xd1 23 ♗xd4 transposes to 22 ♗b2] 23 ♗d6 ♘g4 24 ♖a6 ♖ge8 White is playing without his king's rook, Bertoni-Koetsier, corr. 1999) 22...♗xd1 23 ♗xd4 (23 ♔xd1? ♘f3 24 ♖h1 ♖gb8 25 ♗xf6 ♖xb7 is very good for Black, Elburg-Tait, corr. training game 1996) 23...♗xc2 24 ♖a6 ♖gf8 25 ♘c5, Bertoni-Elburg, corr. 1999, the pin on f6 causes Black serious problems.

Alternatively, 13 b3 ♘c6 (13...♗f5 transposes into line (a) of move 12, above) 14 ♗b2 d4 15 d3 ♗f5 16 ♘a3, Fiorito-De Boer, corr. 1984, and now 16...♘b4 17 ♔d2 ♖ae8 is best.

13...exd3

However 13...♘c6?! is worse, 14 dxe4 ♘xe4 15 f3 ♘d4 16 ♘a3 ♘xe2 17 ♔xe2 ♘d6 18 ♗f4 with advantage, Schlenker-Stummer, corr. 1991.

14 cxd3?!

This creates a weakness on d3, White should play 14 ♗xd3! e.g. 14...♗h3 (14...c4 15 ♗e2 ♘c6 16 c3 ♗f5 17 ♗e3 ♖ae8 18 0-0 ♔d7 19 ♖d1 ♗g4 20 ♗xg4+ ♖xg4 21 ♘d2 and Black's compensation is non-existent, Larsen-Nilsson, corr. 1991) 15 ♗f4 ♘c6 16 ♘c3, with a white advantage, Edwards-Riegsecker, corr. 1985; 16...c4 17 ♗e2 ♘d4, followed by capturing on e2, might represent Black's best chance, bringing opposite-colour bishops.

14...♘c6 15 ♘a3 ♗h3

Black has other promising lines, too:

a) 15...a6!? intends to set a queen-side pawn roller in motion, 16 ♗e3 d4 17 ♗d2 ♗f5 18 ♖c1 ♘d7 19 ♘c4 b5 20 ♘a5 ♘ce5 21 b4!, Kuelaots-Erler, corr. 1990, 21...♘xd3+ 22 ♗xd3 ♗xd3 23 bxc5 ♗e4 with equality.

b) 15...b6!? Black will attack d3 from another angle, 16 ♗d2 ♗a6 17 ♘c2 ♔f7 18 0-0-0 ♖ae8 19 ♗f1 d4 and Black's pressure on d3 gives him good chances, Vitols-Budovskis, corr. 1994/95.

16 ♗d2?! ♔d7

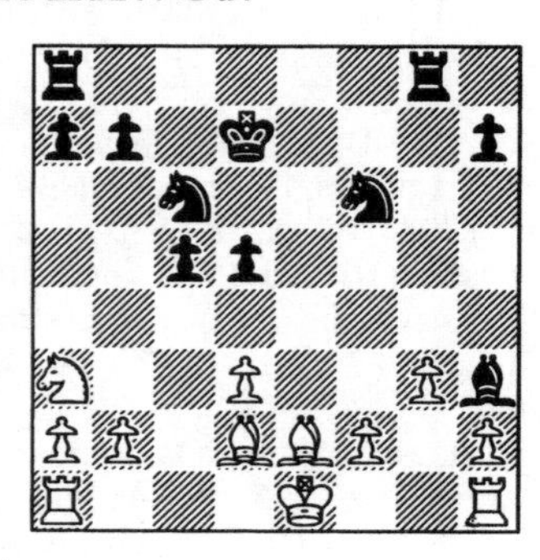

17 ♘c2?

King evacuation was called for: 17 0-0-0 ♘d4 18 ♗f1 ♗xf1 19 ♖hxf1 ♘f3, equal.

17...♖ae8 18 ♔d1 ♘g4 19 ♗e1 ♖gf8 20 f4 ♖e7

White's extra kingside pawns are firmly blockaded and Black has tied White down to passive defence, Elburg-Krantz, corr. 1990.

9 Other replies to 3 ♗c4

1 e4 e5 2 ♘f3 f5 3 ♗c4

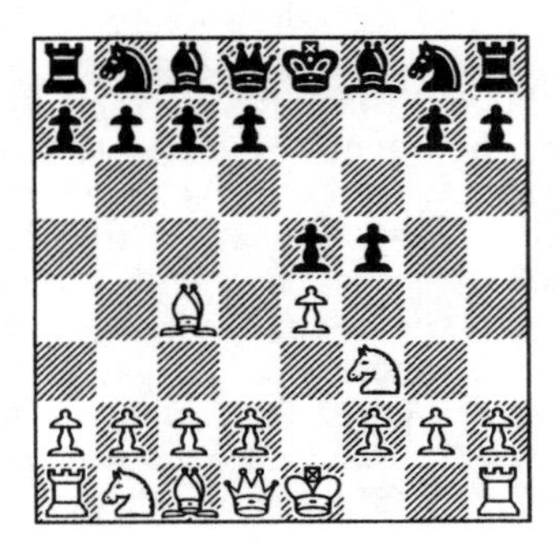

Although the previous chapter showed that Black can obtain a very good position by 3...fxe4 and 4...d5, players of the black pieces still sometimes search for other, less well-known, methods of conducting the defence. These are as follows:

A 3...b5
B 3...♘f6
C 3...♘c6

Otherwise:

a) 3...d6 is perfectly respectable, and transposes to a Philidor counter-attack, e.g. 4 d4 (4 d3?! is insipid, 4...♘f6 5 ♘g5?! d5 6 exd5 ♘xd5 7 ♕f3 c6 8 0-0?! ♗e7 9 h4?! ♕d6! 10 ♖e1 h6 11 ♘h3 0-0 ∓ Belloulou-Kosten, Paris 1993) 4...exd4 5 ♘g5! (5 ♘xd4 fxe4 6 ♕h5+ g6 7 ♕d5 ♕e7 8 ♗g5 ♘f6 = Melchor-Svendsen, corr. 1985) 5...♘h6 6 0-0 (6 ♘xh7!? is risky, 6...♘g4! 7 ♘xf8 ♔xf8 8 ♕xd4 ♘c6 9 ♕d5 ♕e8 with a dangerous lead in development for Black, Sorokin-Maliutin, USSR ch 1991) 6...♘c6 (6...f4!? 7 ♗xf4 ♕f6 avoids the opening of the e-file, Glez-Perez, corr. 1994) 7 exf5 ♗xf5 8 ♖e1+ ♔d7 9 ♗e6+! ♗xe6 10 ♘xe6 ♕h4 11 ♗xh6 gxh6 12 ♕f3 and the threat of ♕f5 causes Black some grief, Zemitis-Svendsen, corr. 1997. But the moves...

b) 3...♕f6? 4 d4 fxe4?! 5 ♘xe5 ♘e7 6 ♗f7+! ♔d8 7 ♘c3 d6 8 ♘xe4 ♕f5 9 ♘g3 ♕f6 10 0-0 with enormous advantage Monsalvo-Barbosa, corr. 1971.

c) and 3...♕e7? 4 d4 (but not 4 ♘c3?! fxe4 5 ♘d5 [5 ♘xe4 c6] 5...♕d6 6 ♘g5 c6 7 ♘c7+? [7 ♘f7 ♔xf7 8 ♘c7+ ♔e7 9 ♘xa8 ♘f6 is also losing, Black controls the centre, and will win the trapped a8-knight; 7 ♘c3 is the best move] 7...♕xc7 ∓ Grotts-Brieger, USA 1971) 4...exd4 5 e5! ♕b4+ 6 ♘bd2 with advantage, Studier-Gunderam, corr. 1959, cannot be recommended.

A 3...b5!?

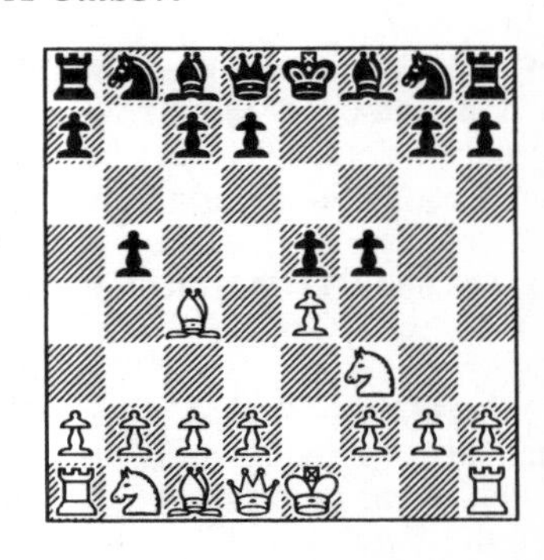

This attempt at distracting the c4 bishop was introduced by Strautins in 1970. The idea is to play similar positions to those of chapter seven but with the presence of a pawn on b5 (and a possible bolt-hole for the black king on b7).

4 ♗b3!?

Not clearly the most persuasive of White's possibilities:

a) 4 ♗xb5? is just what Black is hoping for: 4...fxe4 5 ♘xe5 (5 ♘g1? ♘f6 6 c4 ♗c5 7 ♘c3 0-0 ∓ Tatls-Jozols, corr. 1989; 5 ♗c4!? d5?! [5...♕e7!] 6 ♘xe5 dxc4 7 ♕h5+ g6 8 ♘xg6, Monsalvo-Leeners, corr. 1974, when 8...hxg6 9 ♕xh8 ♘f6 should be fine for Black) 5...♕g5! 6 d4 ♕xg2 7 ♖f1 (not 7 ♕h5+? g6 8 ♘xg6 ♕xh1+ 9 ♗f1 hxg6 10 ♕xh8 ♔f7 ∓ Schwibbe-Atars, corr. 1973) 7...♘f6 (7...c6!? is possibly even stronger, 8 ♗a4 ♗a6 9 c4, Korsmaa-Jackl, corr. 1975, 9...♕xh2 with advantage) 8 ♗f4 c6 9 ♗e2 d6 (9...♗a6 10 ♗xa6 ♘xa6 11 ♕e2 ♘c7 is also pleasant for Black, Atars-Zemitis, corr. 1970) 10 ♘c4 d5 11 ♘e3 (11 ♘d6+ ♗xd6 12 ♗xd6 ♗h3 =; 11 ♘e5 ♗d6 12 c4 0-0 with a good position, Lynch-Nickel, Washington 1972) 11...♕g6 12 c4 ♗b4+ 13 ♘c3 ♗h3 14 ♖h1 ♗xc3+ 15 bxc3 0-0 and the black position is preferable, Strelis-Eglitis, corr. 1977/80.

b) 4 ♗xg8!, swapping this bishop for the unmoved knight on g8 is normally doubtful, but here the tempo gained is important, 4...♖xg8 and:

b1) 5 ♕e2 is the most popular, 5...♕e7 6 ♕xb5 (6 ♘c3 c6!) 6...♘c6 7 ♕d5 (7 ♘c3 fxe4! 8 ♘xe4 g5! 9 g4?! ♖g6 10 c4 ♖b8 was an aesthetic, and effective, method of bringing the black rooks into the fray, Gunderam-Strautins, corr. 1971) 7...fxe4! 8 ♘xe5!? (perhaps too risky, the game Krustkalns-Eglitis, corr. 1977/78, continued 8 ♕xe4 g5!? 9 ♘c3 g4 10 ♘d5 ♕g7 unclear; 8 ♕xg8 is also possible, but just as hair-raising for White, 8...exf3 9 ♕xh7 fxg2 10 ♖g1 [10 ♕g6+? ♕f7 11 ♕xg2 ♗b7 12 ♖g1 0-0-0, White is already helpless against the threat of ...♘d4, 13 ♕g6 ♕xg6 14 ♖xg6 ♘d4 15 ♘a3 ♗xa3 etc., Buckley-Johnsrud, corr. 2000] 10...♘d4 11 ♖xg2 ♗b7 12 ♖g3 0-0-0 and Black has a strong attack on the light squares, Melchor-Strautins, corr. 1997) 8...♕xe5 9 ♕xg8 ♘b4 10 ♔d1 (10 ♘a3?! ♘d3+! 11 ♔e2 ♗a6 with a vicious attack, Grava-Strautins, corr. 1970) 10...d5! menacing ...♗g4, with a strong initiative, rather than 10...♕f5 11 ♖e1 unclear.

b2) 5 exf5! is the best,

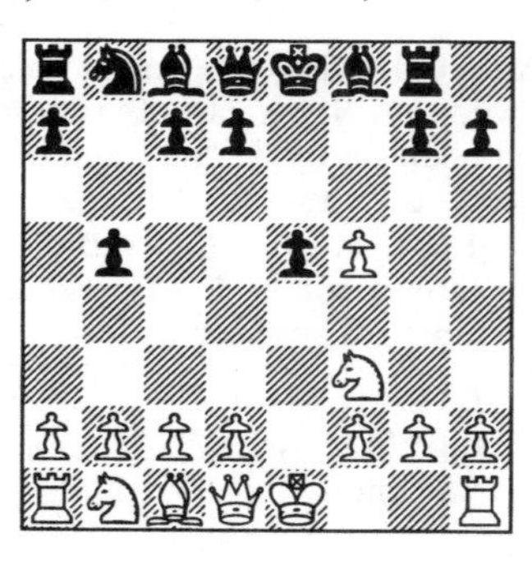

then 5...e4 (5...♘c6 6 ♕e2 ♕e7 7 ♘c3 a6 8 ♘d5 ♕d6 9 c4 bxc4? [9...♗b7] 10 ♕xc4 with discovered threats to the g8-rook that should be decisive, Motivay-Atars, corr. 1970) 6 ♘d4! (6 ♕e2 ♕e7 7 ♘d4 a6 8 ♘c3 ♗b7 Borrmann-Micheloud, corr. 1974/76, doesn't provide much in the way of inconvenience for Black) 6...♕g5 Motivay-Monsalvo, corr. 1970, when the elementary 7 0-0 a6 8 d3 is crushing.

b3) 5 ♘xe5?! ♕e7 6 d4 d6 7 ♘f3 ♕xe4+, Gabrans-Budovskis, corr. 1974/78.

b4) 5 d4 fxe4 6 ♗g5! ♗e7 7 ♘xe5! g6 8 ♗xe7 ♕xe7 9 ♕e2 c6 10 ♘d2, Kozlov-Franco, corr. 1974, gives White an edge.

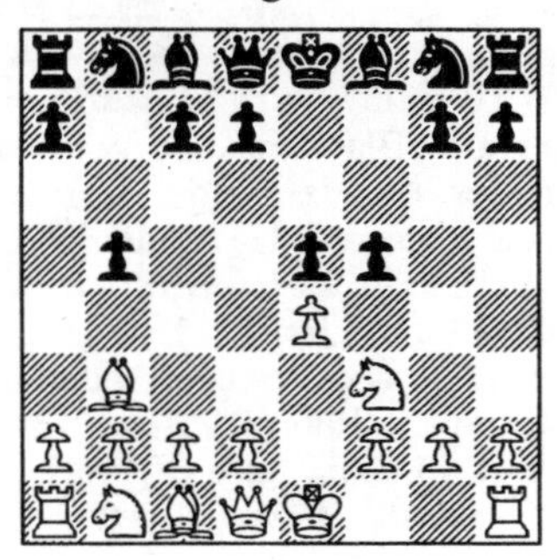

4...fxe4

Crucial to the evaluation of this line, but also 4...d6 5 d4 fxe4 6 ♘xe5!? (6 ♘g5 d5 7 dxe5 c6 8 ♘xe4 Strelis-Alberts, corr. 1978 [8 e6 ♘h6 ± Schild-Bullockus, corr. 1988], when Black should play 8...♕c7 [8...dxe4?? 9 ♗f7+ ♔e7 10 ♗g5+ ♘f6 11 ♕xd8+ ♔xd8 12 exf6] 9 ♘d6+ ♗xd6 10 exd6 ♕xd6 which is not too bad) 6...dxe5 7 ♕h5+ ♔d7 8 ♕xe5 (8 ♕f5+!? appears tempting, but 8...♔c6 9 ♕xe4+ ♔b6 10 ♘c3 [10 ♕xa8?? ♗b7] 10...♗b7 when White might just have enough compensation for the piece, but no more) 8...♗d6 9 ♕e6+? (9 ♗e6+ ♔e8 10 ♕xg7 ♗xe6 11 ♕xh8 ♕h4 is still reasonable for Black) 9...♔c6 10 ♕d5+ ♔b6 11 0-0 ♘f6 and, as the rook is still untouchable, Black is winning, Hebrard-Jester, corr. 1987.

And 4...♘c6?! 5 d4 ♘xd4 6 ♘xd4 exd4 7 ♕xd4 ♕e7 (7...♗b7?! 8 ♘c3 fxe4?! Melchor-Strelis, corr. 1987, 9 ♘xb5 ♖c8 10 ♗f4 is overwhelming) 8 ♘c3 c6 9 0-0 b4 10 ♘b5! cxb5 11 ♗xg8 ♗b7 (11...♖xg8? 12 ♕d5 ♕xe4 13 ♕xg8 ♗b7 14 f3 is winning) 12 ♗d5 ♗xd5 13 exd5 ♔f7 14 ♕d3, White wins a pawn, Bertoni-Rozzoni 1999.

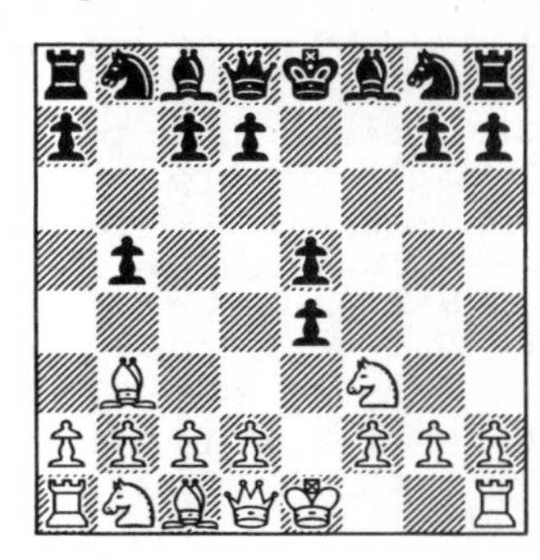

5 ♘xe5

This may not be so wonderful, White has several other contenders for best move here, all based on the weakness of the two white-squared diagonals, a2-g8 and h1-a8:

a) 5 ♘c3!? and:

a1) 5...♘c6 Black's best move, 6 ♘xe5 ♕g5 (6...♘xe5? 7 ♕h5+ ♘g6 8 ♕d5) 7 d4 (this time, 7 ♘f7? is false, 7...♕xg2 8 ♖f1 ♘d4 with a strong attack) 7...♕xg2 8 ♕h5+ g6 9 ♗f7+ ♔d8 10 ♕g5+ ♕xg5 11 ♗xg5+ ♗e7 12 h4 ♘xe5 (12...♘xd4?? 13 0-0-0 c5 14 ♗d5 winning material, Alloin-Strelis, corr. 1987) 13 dxe5 ♗b7 14 ♖h3, Pellegrino-Mathieu, corr. 1975, and others, 14...h6! 15 ♗d2 b4 and Black has no problems.

a2) Of course, not 5...exf3? 6 ♕xf3, forking f7 and a8.

a3) 5...♘h6? is not particularly useful: 6 ♘xe5 ♕g5 7 d4 (7 ♗d5 is also very strong, e.g. 7...♕xe5 [7...c6 8 d4 ♕xg2 9 ♗xe4] 8 ♗xa8 c6 9 0-0 d5 10 d4, White will open play with f3, and Black is a long way from capturing the a8-bishop) 7...♕xg2 8 ♖f1 ♕xh2 9 ♗d5 c6 10 ♗xe4 ♕h3 11 ♘xb5 ♗b4+ 12 c3 ♗a5 13 ♖h1 ♕e6 14 ♕h5+ ♔f8 15

♗xh6 +/- Gaard-Strautins, corr. 1991.

a4) 5...♗b7?! is also doubtful, 6 ♘xe5 ♕g5 and:

a41) With the bishop on b7, 7 ♘f7! ♕xg2 8 ♖f1 is worth serious consideration, and *NCO* even rates this +/-. Let's have a look: 8...♘f6 (8...b4 9 ♘xh8 bxc3 10 ♗xg8) 9 ♘xh8 ♘g4 (9...b4 10 ♘d5) 10 ♘xb5 ♘xh2 11 ♕e2 (11 ♗c4? ♘f3+ 12 ♔e2 ♕g4 deserves to lose!) 11...♘a6 12 d4 ♗e7 13 ♗e3 (13 ♘f7!? ♘f3+ 14 ♔d1 ♘g1 15 ♖xg1 ♕xg1+ 16 ♕e1 ♕g4+ 17 ♔d2 is probably good, too) 13...♘xf1 14 ♕xf1 ♕xf1+ 15 ♔xf1 c6 16 ♘c3 d5 17 ♔e2 ♔f8 and the knight is lost, although White is still better. However, there may be many improvements for White lurking in this analysis, although it is clear that Black still has counterplay.

a42) 7 d4? ♕xg2 8 ♕h5+ g6 9 ♗f7+ ♔d8 10 ♕g5+ ♕xg5 11 ♗xg5+ ♗e7 12 h4 (following 12 ♗xe7+ ♘xe7 13 ♘xb5 d6 14 ♘g4 ♖f8, Jackson-Strelis, corr. 1991, Black has the better chances) 12...d6 13 0-0-0? (13 ♘g4 b4 still favours Black, who has the better structure) 13...♗xg5+ 14 hxg5 dxe5 ∓, Krongraf-Jensen, corr. 1991.

a5) 5...♕e7!? 6 ♘xe4 (6 ♘d5?! ♕d6 7 ♘g5 ♘f6 [if 7...♗b7 then 8 ♘xe4 ♕g6 9 ♘g3 rather than the 8 ♘xc7+?! ♕xc7 9 ♘f7 d5 10 ♘xh8 g6 11 d3 exd3 12 ♕xd3 e4 13 ♕xb5+ ♗c6 14 ♕e2 ♕g7 of Rosso-Viola corr. 1999, which is none too clear] 8 ♘xf6+ ♕xf6 9 ♕h5+ g6 10 ♘xe4 [10 ♕g4 ♘c6] 10...♕xf2+ 11 ♔xf2 gxh5 with a level position, Zerbib-Baudoin, corr. 1997) 6...c6 7 0-0 (7 d4! and if 7...d5? 8 ♘xe5 dxe4 9 ♗f7+ ♔d8 10 ♗xg8 ♖xg8? 11 ♗g5 wins) 7...d5 8 ♘g3 ♗g4 9 h3 ♗xf3 10 ♕xf3 White's lead in development gives him an edge, Dufek-Fritz 3 1996.

a6) 5...d6? 6 ♘xe5! ♕g5 (6...dxe5 7 ♕h5+ g6 [7...♔d7 8 ♕xe5 is also hopeless] 8 ♕xe5+ ♕e7 9 ♕xh8 ♘f6 10 ♘d5 ♘xd5 11 ♗xd5 c6 12 ♗g8 and Black has no compensation for the exchange, Borrmann-Purins, corr. 1983) 7 d4 ♕xg2 8 ♕h5+ g6 9 ♗f7+ ♔d8 10 ♗xg6 ♕xh1+? (10...hxg6 11 ♗g5+ ♗e7 12 ♗xe7+ ♔xe7 puts up much more resistance, although Black is still losing) 11 ♔e2 ♘f6 12 ♘f7+ (12 ♗g5 would have shortened the game somewhat) 12...♔e8 13 ♘xd6+ ♔d8 14 ♘f7+ ♔e8 15 ♘e5+ ♔d8 16 ♗g5 ♕xa1 17 ♗xf6+ leading to mate in a few moves, Alloin-Vlasic, corr. 1988.

b) 5 0-0?! ♕f6! (5...♘f6 6 d4!? [6 ♘xe5 d5 7 d4 transposes to 5 d4] 6...exd4 [6...exf3!? is risky, 7 dxe5 ♗b7 8 exf6 ♕xf6 9 ♖e1+ ♗e7 10 ♗d5 {10 ♘c3!?} 10...♗xd5 11 ♕xd5 c6 12 ♕h5+ ♕f7 with a small plus to Black] 7 ♘xd4 d5 8 ♗g5 c6 unclear, Schmidt-Tiemann, corr. 1978) 6 ♘e1 (6 ♗d5? c6 7 ♗xe4 d5) 6...♕f5!? 7 ♘c3 c6, Jackson-Strautins, corr. 1990, 8 d3!, opening the position with chances of an advantage.

c) 5 d4!? exd4 (5...d5 is also perfectly reasonable, 6 ♘xe5 [6 dxe5!? c6 {6...exf3?! 7 ♗xd5 fxg2 8 ♖g1 leaves Black facing the twin threats of ♗xa8 and ♗f7+} 7 ♘d4 a6 8 a4 c5 9 axb5!? cxd4 10 ♕xd4, Lladors-Esnoala, corr. 1981, when the simplest would have been 10...♘e7 11 ♘c3 ♗b7 with every chance of defending] 6...♘f6 7 0-0 ♗e7 8 ♘c3 c6 9 ♗g5, Lescot-Gåård, corr. 1997, 9...a5 10 a3 ♕b6 and White is only slightly better) 6 ♘xd4 (6 ♘e5!? d5 7 ♕h5+ g6 8 ♘xg6 ♘f6 [8...hxg6!?] 9 ♕e5+ ♗e7 10 ♘xh8

♘c6 11 ♕g5 ♗e6 12 ♕g7 ♕d7 and although temporarily a rook down, Black has a strong position once he castles long, and captures the h8-knight, Clarke-Strautins, corr. 1998) 6...♘f6 7 ♘xb5 d5 8 ♗g5 (8 ♗f4 ♘a6) 8...♗e7 9 ♘1c3 (9 ♗xf6 ♗xf6 10 ♕xd5 ♕xd5 11 ♗xd5 c6 12 ♗xe4 is messy, but might favour White) 9...c6 and the strong black centre promises equal chances, Grivainis-Strautins, corr. 1997.

d) 5 d3! is a good move, and may even be White's best here, 5...♘f6 (5...exd3! 6 ♕xd3 ♕e7 7 ♕xb5 ♘c6 appears stronger) 6 dxe4 and Black will have difficulty developing, Harding-Reed, corr. 1984.

5...♕g5

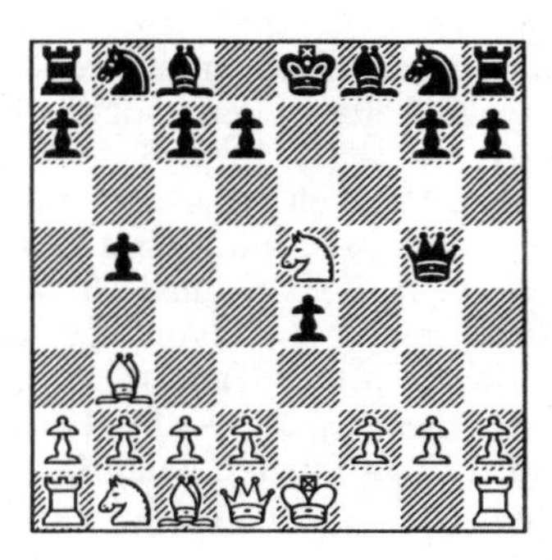

6 d4

Just as in Chapter 7 White is obliged to let his g-pawn go, 6 ♘f7? ♕xg2 7 ♖f1 d5 (necessary, to threaten ...♗g4, and interfere with the f7-knight's defence) and now:

a) 8 ♕e2 ♗g4 9 ♕e3 (Piquero-Cenal corr. 1990, 9 f3!? is the alternative, 9...♕xe2+ 10 ♔xe2 ♗xf3+ 11 ♔e1 ♔xf7 12 ♗xd5+ ♔e8 13 ♗xa8 ♗e7, menacing ...♗h4+, Black has excellent compensation for the exchange) 9...♗h3 10 ♕e2 ♔xf7 (10...♗g4 draws, or forces 11 f3 as per the previous note) 11 ♗xd5+ ♔e8 12 ♗xa8 ♕xf1+ 13 ♕xf1 ♗xf1 14 ♔xf1 c6 which looks fairly level.

b) 8 ♕h5? ♘f6 9 ♕e5+ (9 ♘d6+ ♔d8 10 ♘f7+ ♔e7! 11 ♕g5 ♕xg5 12 ♘xg5 c6 and ...h6 will win the knight) 9...♗e7! (9...♔xf7 10 ♗xd5+ ♘xd5 11 ♕xd5+, Kullesenko-Matwienko, Voronezh 1973, when 11...♔g6! wins because of the threat of ...♗h3, i.e. 12 d4 [12 ♕xa8? ♗h3 forces mate] 12...♗b4+ 13 c3 ♗h3 14 ♘d2 c6 15 ♕e5 ♘d7 16 ♕c7 ♖ac8) 10 d3 ♗h3 ∓, Heiermann-Carlsson, corr. 1981.

c) 8 ♘xh8? ♗g4 9 ♕xg4, forced, (9 f3? exf3 10 ♗xd5 ♗e7 11 ♖xf3 ♗h4+ 12 ♖g3 ♕g1 mate, Taylor-Stewart, corr. 1992) 9...♕xg4 10 ♗xd5 c6 11 ♗f7+ ♔d7 12 ♗xg8 ♘a6 and the white king is too poorly defended, and his king-side pieces misplaced.

d) 8 ♗xd5 ♗g4! (8...♗h3 9 ♕e2 ♘f6 is also playable) 9 f3 (9 ♕xg4?! ♕xg4 10 ♘xh8 c6 transposes to 8 ♘xh8?) 9...♗e7 10 ♕e2 ♗h4+ 11 ♔d1 ♗xf3 12 ♖xf3 ♕xe2+ 13 ♔xe2 exf3+ 14 ♔xf3 ♘f6 15 ♗xa8 ♔xf7 and Black's lead in development makes up for the white bishop pair.

6...♕xg2 7 ♕h5+

White won very quickly in Roiz-Fernandez, Oviedo 1991, following 7 ♖f1? ♘f6 8 ♘c3 (8 ♘f7 ♖g8) 8...♗b4 9 ♕e2 ♗xc3+ 10 bxc3 d5 (10...♗a6!?) 11 ♗a3?! ♗a6? (but 11...c6! 12 f3 ♕xe2+ 13 ♔xe2 a5 wins the b3-bishop) 12 ♗b4?! (12 ♗xd5! b4 13 ♗f7+ ♔d8 14 ♗c4) 12...♗c8?? (12...♘bd7) 13 ♕xb5+ c6 14 ♕c5 1-0.

7...g6 8 ♗f7+

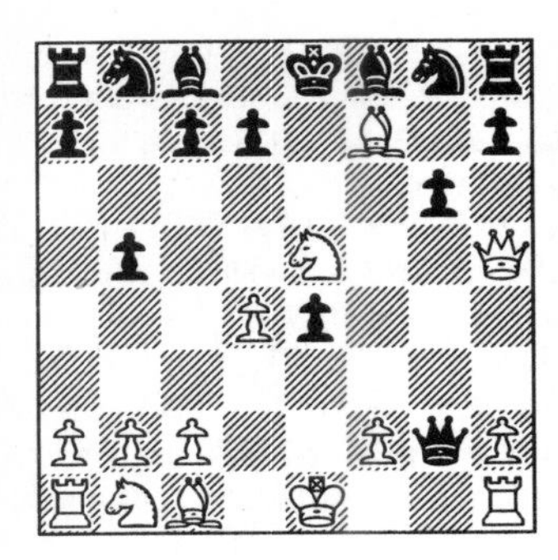

8...♔d8

Strautins' move 8...♔e7? is worse: 9 ♗g5+ (9 ♕h4+ ♘f6 10 ♗g5 transposes) 9...♘f6 10 ♕h4 ♕xh1+ 11 ♔e2 (11 ♔d2?! allows some resources, 11...e3+ 12 ♔xe3?! [12 ♔e2! ♗g7 13 ♘c3 ♕g2 14 ♘e4 should win for White, Melchor-Asensio, Barcelona 1996] 12...♗h6! the only chance, 13 ♘c3! [13 ♗xh6? gives Black a valuable tempo for his counterattack, 13...♕e1+ 14 ♔d3 ♘c6 15 ♘xc6+ dxc6 16 ♘d2 ♗f5+ 17 ♔c3 b4+ 18 ♔b3 ♕xa1 19 ♗g7, O'Keefe-Downey, corr. 1981, 19...♕d1 20 ♕xf6+ ♔d7 21 ♘e4 ♕f3+ 22 ♔a4 ♕xe4 23 ♗xh8 ♕e2 winning] 13...♕xa1 [13...♗xg5+?? 14 ♕xg5 ♕xa1? 15 ♘d5+ mates] 14 ♗xh6 [14 ♘d5+ ♔d8 15 ♕xh6 ♕e1+ 16 ♔f4 ♗a6 is messy] 14...♗b7 [14...♕e1+ 15 ♔d3 ♗b7 16 ♗g5 ♔d8 17 ♗xf6+ ♔c8 18 ♗xh8 ♗g2 19 ♘e2 ♗f1 is less clear] 15 ♗g5 ♕c1+ [unfortunately, it is too late for 15...♕e1+? as 16 ♘e2 wins] 16 ♔d3 ♕xg5 17 ♕xg5 ♖f8 18 ♗xg6 ♖g8, Meldrum-Peet, Scotland-Holland, corr. 1982, and now White could have concluded the game in a number of ways, 19 ♘c6+ ♗xc6 20 ♕e5+ ♔d8 21 ♕xf6+ ♔c8 22 ♗xh7 being possibly the simplest) 11...♗g7 12 ♘c3? (12 ♘d2! is completely decisive, 12...♕xa1 [it is difficult to believe that Black will last long after 12...♕g2 13 ♘xe4 ♔f8 14 ♘xf6; and now 12...♕f3+ is easily dealt with: 13 ♘dxf3 exf3+ 14 ♔d2 d6 15 ♗d5 etc.] 13 ♘xe4 forces mate in a few moves, 13...♘c6 14 ♗xf6+ ♔f8 15 ♗xg7+ ♔xg7 16 ♕f6+ ♔h6, Leiros Vila-Bustos, corr. 1987, 17 ♘g4+ ♔h5 18 ♕g5 mate) 12...♕f3+ (the only try, 12...♕xa1? 13 ♘d5+ [13 ♗xf6+ forces mate in six moves] 13...♔f8 14 ♗xf6 1-0, Garcia-Bravo, corr. 1986) 13 ♘xf3 exf3+ 14 ♔f1! (probably better than 14 ♔d2?! ♔xf7 15 ♕f4 when 15...♗b7 16 ♕xc7 ♗c6 is somewhat stronger than 15...d6? 16 ♕xf3 c6 17 ♘e4 1-0, Thorn Leeson-Wyers, corr. 1985; 14 ♔xf3? ♔xf7 15 ♘e4 ♘d5, Black is defending successfully, Navarro-Baltar Fernandez, corr. 1980) 14...♔xf7 15 ♕f4 ♗b7 (better than 15...♖e8? 16 ♘d5?? [played the wrong way round! First 16 ♗xf6 ♗xf6 then 17 ♘d5 wins] 16...♖e6?? [Black returns the favour, 16...♖e4! 17 ♕xf3 ♗b7 defends, as if 18 ♘xf6 there is 18...♖e1+ 19 ♖xe1 ♗xf3] 17 ♖e1 1-0, Catalan-Herranz, Spain 1985) 16 ♗xf6 ♗xf6 17 ♕xc7 ♗a6? (getting his pieces in a tangle, 17...♗c6 18 d5 ♗xc3, with the king on d2 this would be check, 19 dxc6 ♗f6 20 cxd7 ♖d8 is reasonable for Black, i.e. White must avoid 21 ♕b7? ♘xd7 22 ♖d1 ♔e7 23 ♖xd7+?? ♖xd7 24 ♕xa8?? ♖d1 mate) 18 ♘d5 ♖f8 (18...♖e8 19 ♕f4 ♖e6 20 ♘c7 is also hopeless) 19 ♘xf6 ♔xf6, Torija-Bustos, corr. 1986, when the most precise move order is 20 ♕e5+ ♔f7 21 ♕d5+ ♔g7 22 ♖e1 winning.

9 ♕g5+!

White enters the ending as the rook sacrifice does not work here: 9 ♗xg6? ♕xh1+ 10 ♔e2 ♗a6!

vacating c8 for the king, 11 ♗g5+ ♔c8 (or 11...♗e7 ∓ Padula-Purins, 1971/72) 12 ♗f5 (alternatively 12 ♘c3 ♕xa1 13 ♗xe4 b4+ 14 ♔f3 ♘f6!? 15 ♗xf6 ♗g7 -/+ Benlolo-Sénéchaud, France 1988; or 12 ♘d2 b4+ 13 ♔e3 ♕xa1 14 ♗xe4 ♕e1+ 15 ♔f4 ♘f6 [15...♕xd2+ 16 ♔g3 ♘f6 is more effective] 16 ♗xf6 ♗h6+ winning, Bellin-Sénéchaud, France 1988) 12...♗h6 13 ♗xh6 ♘xh6 14 ♕xh6 b4+ 15 ♔d2 ♕f1 16 ♕e3 ♖f8 and Black has a strong attack and extra material, Bar-Hilbert, corr. 1989.

Also, 9 ♗g5+? ♗e7 10 ♗xg6 ♕xh1+ 11 ♔d2 (11 ♔e2?! ♗a6! 12 ♘d2 [12 ♘f7+ ♔c8 13 ♘xh8 hxg6 14 ♕xg6 b4+ 15 ♔d2 ♕f1 16 ♕xg8+ ♔b7 and White is defenceless against the black mating attack] 12...b4+ 13 ♔e3 ♕xa1 14 ♘xe4 ♕e1+ 15 ♔f4 ♗b7 -/+, Milev-Metodiev, Primorska 1975) 11...♗a6 12 ♘c3 e3+!? 13 ♗xe3 ♕xa1 leaves White a rook down with no attack, Sanchez Rodenas-Pascual, corr. 1981.

9...♕xg5 10 ♗xg5+ ♗e7

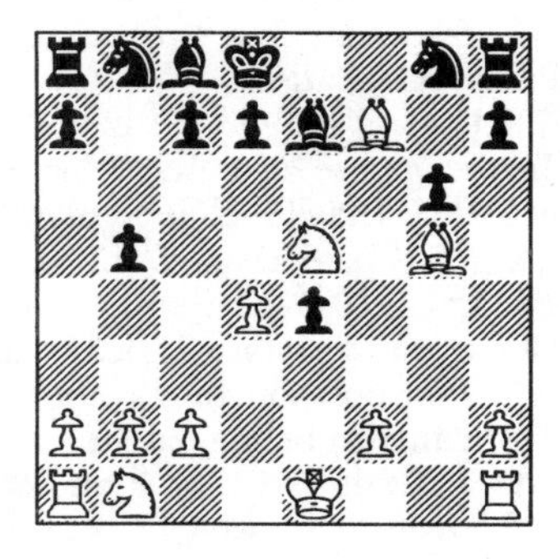

11 ♗d5 c6 12 ♗xe7+

12 ♘f7+?! is bad as ever: 12...♔e8 13 ♘xh8 cxd5 14 h4, Somerset-Ozols, USA 1970, 14...♔f8 and ...♔g7 wins the knight immediately.

12 ♗xe4 ♗xg5 13 ♘f7+ ♔c7 14 ♘xg5 ♘f6 is harmless for Black, who enjoys a superior pawn formation, e.g. 15 ♗d3 ♘a6 16 c3 ♗b7 17 0-0 ♘h5 18 ♖e1 ♘f4 19 ♗f1 ♖af8, Perez Millan-Canal Oliveras, corr. 1992.

12...♔xe7 13 ♗xe4

Anghar-Vincent, France 1977, when 13...♘f6 14 ♗g2 ♗b7 15 0-0 d6 16 ♘d3 ♘bd7 or 16...♘a6 is fairly level.

B 3...♘f6

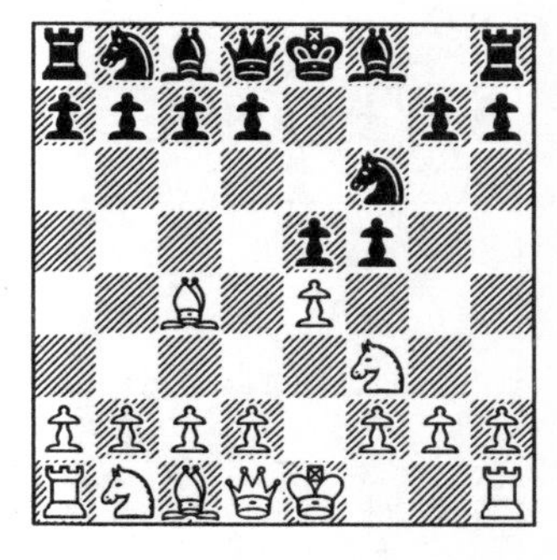

Named after the Argentinian player Morgado who had a number of successes with this variation at the beginning of the 1970s, although the main line had already been cited by Leonardo as long ago as 1575.

4 ♘xe5

Critical, both 4 0-0 fxe4 (4...d5?! 5 exd5 ♗d6 is fun, Feist-Soruco, corr.) 5 ♘xe5 d5, and 4 d4 fxe4 5 ♘xe5 d5 (Chapter 11) are relatively innocuous, but 4 ♘c3 is quite dangerous (see Chapter 12).

4...♕e7

The rook sacrifice 4...fxe4?! was mentioned in Chapter 7

5 d4 ♘c6

With 5...fxe4 we transpose into a line considered in Chapter 6 (from the move order 3 ♘xe5 ♕e7 4 d4

♘f6 5 ♗c4 fxe4) whilst 5...d6 should also be compared to that material, e.g. 6 ♗f7+! (6 ♘f7!? d5 7 ♘xh8 dxc4 8 e5 ♘d5 9 ♕h5+ g6 10 ♘xg6 hxg6 11 ♕xg6+ ♕f7 is fine for Black, Markland-Simm, England 1967) 6...♔d8 7 ♗b3 dxe5 8 dxe5+ ♗d7 9 exf6 ♕xe4+ 10 ♗e3! (better than 10 ♔f1 gxf6 11 ♘c3 ♕g4 12 ♗e3 ♗d6 Pogats-Szilagyi, Hungary 1950) 10...gxf6 (10...f4 11 ♘c3) 11 ♘c3 ♗b4? (11...♕e5) 12 ♗d5 ♕e5 13 ♗xb7 f4 14 ♕d2 with advantage, Downey-Destrebecq, corr. 1992.

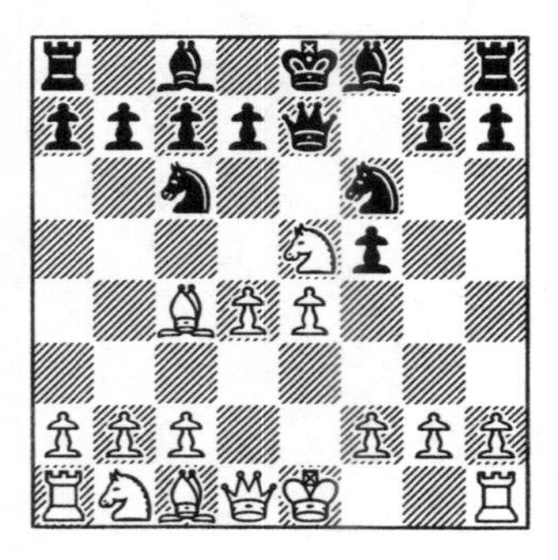

6 0-0

Simple development is the most effective recipe here. The alternatives are:

a) 6 ♘xc6?! ♕xe4+ 7 ♕e2 ♕xe2+ 8 ♔xe2 bxc6 9 ♖e1 d5 = Kotek-Morgado, corr. 1971

b) 6 ♘f7!? d5 7 ♘xh8 dxc4 8 e5 ♘d5 9 ♕h5+ g6 10 ♘xg6 hxg6 11 ♕xg6+ ♕f7 ∓, Pupols-Morgado, corr. 1970/72, and Black has a strong grip on the light-squares.

c) 6 ♗f7+ ♔d8 7 0-0 ♘xe5 8 dxe5 ♘xe4 9 e6 d6 10 ♖e1 ♕f6 isn't so bad for Black, the f7 bishop is not particularly useful, Holthuizen-Diepstraten, Hilversum 1977.

d) 6 ♘c3!? ♘xe5 7 dxe5 ♕xe5 8 0-0 (8 f4?! ♕c5 9 ♕e2 fxe4 10 ♘xe4 ♘xe4 11 ♕xe4+ ♕e7 leads nowhere, Woll-Morgado, corr. 1974) 8...fxe4 (8...♗d6!? 9 g3 fxe4) 9 ♘d5 ♘xd5 10 ♗xd5 c6 11 ♗xe4 ♗e7 (11...d5 12 ♗d3 [12 ♗g6+ ♔d8 13 ♖e1 ♕f6 achieves nothing] 12...♗e7 13 ♖e1 ♕f6 14 ♕h5+ ♔d7 and Black's position is uncomfortable, Grivainis-Diepstraten, corr. 1977, but the king move cannot be avoided, as 14...g6?? loses to 15 ♗g5) 12 ♖e1 ♕f6 13 ♕d3! (John Nunn prefers this in *NCO*; 13 c4 0-0 14 ♗e3 ± Gunderam-Grivainis, corr. 1970) 13...g6 (13...d5 14 ♗xh7 ♔d8 might be better, but is hardly enticing) 14 ♗d2 ♖f8 (14...0-0? 15 ♗c3 ♕xf2+ 16 ♔h1 threatens ♗xg6, and wins quickly) 15 ♖e2, preparing to double rooks along the e-file, Castelli-Grivainis, corr. 1970.

6...fxe4

Rather than 6...♘xe5?! 7 dxe5 ♘xe4 8 ♘c3 ♘xc3 9 bxc3 ♕c5, Schirmer-Sénéchaud, corr. 1992, 10 ♕e2 (10 ♕d3!? with advantage) 10...b6!? 11 ♗e3! ♕xe5?, Kozlov-Sénéchaud, corr. 1994, 12 ♖ae1 and the multiple threats (13 ♕h5+, and 13 ♗g5 to name but two) force immediate resignation.

7 ♗f7+

In the game Eckenfels-Morgado, corr. 1967, Black had good play following 7 ♘xc6 dxc6 8 f3 ♗f5 9 fxe4 ♗xe4 10 ♘c3 0-0-0!, but the best move is certainly 7 ♘c3! with a likely transposition to d), above. 7 ♘f7!? can also be played, of course, 7...d5 8 ♗xd5 ♘xd5 9 ♘xh8 ♕h4 10 f3? ♗d6 11 f4 ♗g4 12 ♕e1 ♕e7 13 c4 ♘xd4! 14 cxd5 ♘c2 15 ♕c3?! (15 ♕g3) 15...♗c5+ 16 ♔h1 ♘xa1 and Black has the edge, Alberts-Grobe, corr. 1971.

7...♔d8 8 ♘xc6+

8 f4?! ♘xe5 9 fxe5 ♕xf7 10 exf6 gxf6 11 ♘c3 d5 12 ♗e3 ♖g8 13

♕d2, continuing by doubling rooks on the f-file with some pressure, Grobe-Padula, corr. 1971/72, but Black is better.

8...bxc6

8...dxc6!?.

9 ♗b3 d5

10 ♗g5 h6 11 ♗f4 ♗g4 12 ♕d2 ♕e6 13 ♘a3

White is a little better, Alvarez-Morgado, corr. 1969.

C 3...♘c6

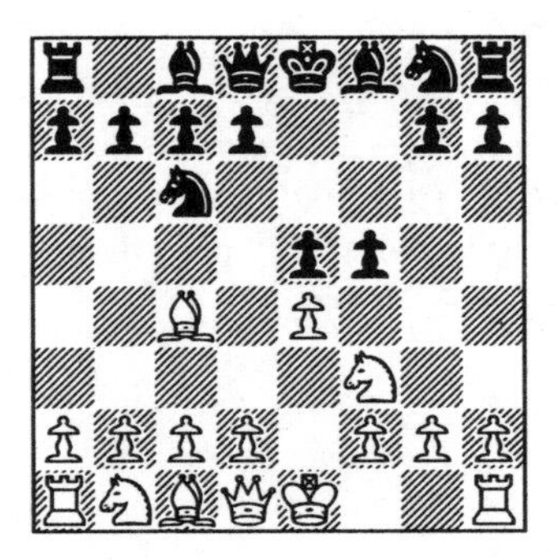

Strictly speaking, this is an Italian Game (1 e4 e5 2 ♘f3 ♘c6 3 ♗c4 f5), and therefore I will only deal with it briefly.

4 d4

I suppose 4 d3 is quite reasonable, 4...d6 (or 4...♘f6 5 0-0 ♗c5 =) 5 ♘g5 ♘h6 6 ♘xh7!? ♘g4!? is unclear Schmidt-Bose, corr. 1964; 6...♖xh7 7 ♕h5+ ♔d7 8 ♕g6 ♘d4 may also be possible; but 4 ♗xg8? giving up the bishop pair, is terrible (actually, I must admit to having played this once, as a lad!) 4...♖xg8 5 exf5 ♕f6 (5...d5! is simpler, as 6 ♕e2 ♗xf5 7 ♘xe5?? ♘d4) 6 0-0 (6 ♘c3 ♕xf5 7 0-0) 6...d5 7 ♖e1 ♗xf5 ∓, Donny-Strelis, corr. 1971/72.

4...exd4

a) The position after 4...fxe4?! 5 ♘xe5 d5 6 ♗b5 ♕d6 (6...♘ge7 is possible) 7 0-0 ♗f5 8 ♗xc6+ bxc6 9 f3 ♘f6 10 fxe4 ♗xe4 11 ♘c3 is very unpleasant for Black, Elburg-Raijmaekers, corr. 1985.

b) And Gunderam's move 4...♕e7?! is too artificial: 5 ♗g5 ♘f6 (5...♕b4+ 6 ♘bd2 exd4 7 exf5 with advantage Padula-Vitols, corr. 1974) 6 ♘c3 ♕b4 (6...fxe4? 7 ♘d5 ♕d6 8 dxe5 ♘xe5 9 ♘xe5 ♕xe5 10 ♗f4 ♕xb2 11 ♖b1 wins material, Rost-Jurack, corr. 1987) 7 ♗xf6 (7 dxe5? ♘xe4 [7...♕xc4 8 exf6 with advantage Zschorn-Schwibbe, corr. 1979] 8 ♗b3 [8 ♕d5 ♘xg5 9 ♘xg5 ♕xb2 may just be good for Black] 8...♘xc3 9 bxc3, Fiorito-Khulmann, corr. 1982, 9...♕e4+ and Black has good chances) 7...gxf6 8 ♗b3 exd4 (8...fxe4 9 ♘d2 ♕xd4 10 ♘d5) 9 a3 ♕c5 10 ♘d5 White has the initiative, Guenzel-Feichtner, corr. 1986.

c) 4...♕f6? 5 ♗g5 ♕g6 6 exf5 ♕xf5 7 dxe5 (7 0-0?! e4 8 ♖e1, Atars-Gunderam, corr. 1970, 8...♘ge7! 9 ♗xe7 ♗xe7 appears to favour Black, who will play ...d5 on his next go if the knight retreats) 7...h6 8 ♗d3 ♕e6 9 ♗e3 ♘ge7 10 0-0 g5!?, Dravnieks-Gunderam, corr. 1971, 11 ♘a3!? a6 (else ♘b5) 12 ♘d4!? ♘xd4 13 ♗xd4 ♘c6 14 ♗c4 ♕g6 15 e6, exposing the black king position.

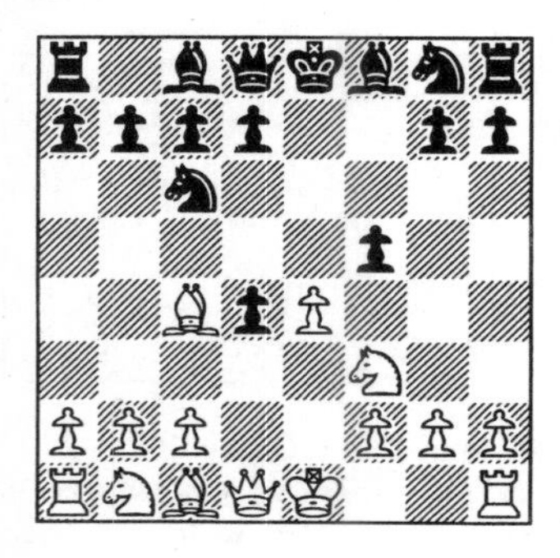

5 ♘xd4

Otherwise,

5 0-0!? fxe4 6 ♘xd4 ♘f6 7 ♗g5 ♘e5!? (if 7...d5 8 ♗xf6 ♕xf6 [8...gxf6!? 9 ♕h5+ ♔e7 is certainly playable, though] 9 ♘b5 might be good for White) 8 ♗b3 c6 9 c4! h6 (9...♗c5? 10 ♘c3 ♘d3? 11 ♘xe4 with advantage) 10 ♗xf6 ♕xf6 11 ♘c3 ♘d3 12 ♘xe4! (White proves himself the equal of the position) 12...♕xd4 13 ♖e1 ♔d8! 14 ♗c2?? (Oops! 14 ♖e3 ♕xb2 15 ♖xd3 left everything to play for) 14...♘xe1! 15 ♕xd4 ♘xc2 16 ♕d1 ♘xa1 17 ♕xa1 d6 18 ♕d1 ♔c7, winning easily, Forte-Kosten, Clermont-Ferrand 1994.

5...♘xd4 6 ♕xd4 fxe4!? 7 ♗xg8?!

7 0-0 is better, 7...♘f6 8 ♗g5 c6 9 ♗xf6 ♕xf6 10 ♕xe4+ ♗e7 11 ♘c3 d6 (11...d5?! 12 ♗xd5 ♗f5 13 ♕e2 wins a pawn, although Black is still alive after 13...0-0-0!) 12 ♖fe1 ♗f5 13 ♕e3 ♔d7 14 ♖e2 ♖he8 15 ♖ae1 and Black is tied up, Gåård-Schott, corr. 1989.

7...♖xg8 8 ♕d5 ♖h8 9 ♕h5+ g6 10 ♕e5+ ♔f7!

10...♕e7?? 11 ♕xh8 +/- Kozlov-Diepstraten, corr. 1977/79.

11 0-0

Not 11 ♕xh8? ♗b4+, 11 ♗g5 ♕e8 12 ♕xc7 ♗g7 =.

11...♗g7?!

11...♕f6 is equal.

12 ♕d5+, Lewis-NN, London 1840, 12...♔f8 13 f3 ♕e7, Black's king is awkwardly placed, but this is not overly serious.

10 3 exf5

1 e4 e5 2 ♘f3 f5 3 exf5

Currently one of the most popular variations, White takes the proffered pawn even though it will entail the displacement of his king's knight. The move was cited by both Polerio in 1575, and by Greco in 1621, and was later analysed by Bilguer in his famous *Handbuch* (1843).

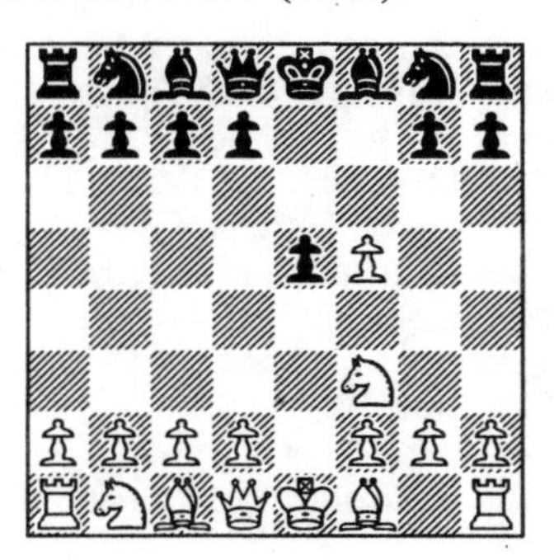

3...e4

The critical reply, although Black has also tried other moves here:

a) 3...d6 is reasonable, transposing into Philidor's Defence. It is not really within the scope of this work, but here is a brief overview: 4 d4 (else Black will simply recapture on f5) 4...e4 5 ♘g5 ♗xf5 (5...♘f6 6 ♘e6 [6 ♘c3 ♗xf5 transposes to 5...♗xf5] 6...♗xe6 7 fxe6 d5 8 g3 c5 9 ♗e3 ♕b6 10 ♘c3, Gonsalves-Kozlov, corr. 1986, when Black can try 10...♕xe6 11 dxc5 ♘bd7) 6 f3 (6 g4!? also promises some advantage, 6...♗g6 7 ♘e6 ♕d7 8 ♘xf8 ♔xf8, Littleboy-Borrmann, corr. 1976) 6...♘f6 (6...♕e7 is safer, 7 fxe4 ♗xe4 8 ♘xe4 ♕xe4+ 9 ♕e2 ♕xe2+ 10 ♗xe2 ♘c6 11 c3 ♘f6 12 0-0 0-0-0 ± because of the bishop pair, Hayward-Downey, corr. 1990) 7 ♘c3 d5 (7...exf3 8 ♕xf3 ♕c8 9 ♗c4 is unpleasant) 8 fxe4 dxe4 (8...♘xe4 9 ♘cxe4 [9 ♘gxe4 dxe4 10 ♗e3 ♗d6 11 ♗c4 ±, Vitols-Maly, corr. 1971/2] 9...dxe4 [9...♕e7? 10 ♗b5+ which is almost winning for White, Hristodorescu-Pessi, Bucharest 1993] 10 ♗c4 ♘c6 Svendsen-Nilsson, corr. 1991, 11 ♗e3 again, clearly better for White) 9 ♗c4 ♘c6!? (9...♗g6 10 0-0 ♘c6?, Jaunozols-Eglitis, corr. 1970, 11 ♘e6 ♕d7 12 ♖xf6! gxf6 13 ♘d5 is devastating) 10 ♗f7+ (10 ♘f7? leads to a draw, but no more, 10...♕xd4 11 ♕xd4 ♘xd4 12 0-0 ♖g8 13 ♘g5 ♖h8 14 ♘f7 ♖g8 etc., Gåård-Oren, corr. 1994/95) 10...♔e7 11 d5 h6 12 ♗e6 ♗g6 13 ♘gxe4 ♘xe4 14 ♘xe4 ♗xe4 15 ♕e2 ♕d6 16 ♕xe4 ♕b4+ 17 ♕xb4+ ♘xb4 18 ♔d1 ♘xd5 19 ♗xd5 ♖d8 20 c4 c6, almost equalising, Magee-Gåård, corr. 1999

b) 3...♘c6!? 4 d4 (or 4 ♗b5 ♗c5 5 ♗xc6? dxc6 6 ♘xe5 ♗xf5 [6...♗xf2+!?] 7 ♕h5+ [7 0-0] 7...g6 8 ♘xg6? hxg6! 9 ♕xh8 ♕e7+ 10 ♔d1 ♗xf2 11 ♕xg8+ ♔d7 12 ♕c4 ♖e8 0-1, Schlechter-Chigorin, 1878) 4...exd4 (4...e4? 5 ♘e5 ♘f6 6 ♗e2 menacing the powerful ♗h5+) 5 ♘xd4 ♘xd4 6 ♕xd4 ♕f6 7 ♕e3+ (7 ♗e3 ±.) 7...♕e7? (7...♘e7 8 ♘c3 ♕xf5) 8 ♘c3 ♘f6 9 ♗d3 with a pawn more, Rossell-Koetsier, corr. 1999.

c) 3...♕f6?! 4 d4 exd4 (4...e4?! 5 ♘e5 ♘e7 [ugly, but if 5...♕xf5 6 ♗c4 with advantage] 6 ♕h5+ g6 7 fxg6 hxg6 8 ♕g5 and White enjoys a sound extra pawn, Tener-Dreibergs, corr. 1965) 5 ♘xd4 ♘e7 6 ♘c3 ♕e5+ 7 ♗e3 ♘xf5 8 ♘xf5 ♕xf5 9 ♗d3 with a lead in development, Miljković-Baier, corr. 1998.

d) 3...♗c5?! is quite popular, 4 ♘xe5 ♗xf2+ 5 ♔xf2 ♕h4+ 6 ♔f3! (objectively stronger than 6 g3 ♕d4+ 7 ♔g2 ♕xe5 8 ♕e2 d6 9 ♕xe5+ dxe5 10 g4 although this is simpler, and also assures an advantage, Vitols-Vashegyi corr.) 6...b5 (the possibility of playing ...b4 provides Black with extra resources, and so this has replaced 6...b6 when 7 d4 ♘f6 8 ♘c3 ♗b7+ 9 d5 0-0 [9...♗xd5+ 10 ♘xd5 ♕e4+ 11 ♔f2 ♕xf5+ 12 ♕f3 is also hopeless] 10 g3 ♘xd5 11 ♘xd5 ♖xf5+ 12 ♗f4 1-0, Gaberc-Rosso, 1970). Nevertheless, the line is still completely unsound, 7 d4 ♘f6 8 ♘c3 ♗b7+ 9 ♔e2 b4, Tiemann-Elburg, corr. 1993, 10 ♘b5 Black has a few checks, but no real compensation for the piece.

e) 3...♘f6 4 ♘xe5 transposes to 3...♘f6 4 exf5 in Chapter 6.

White has four main responses to the attack on his knight:

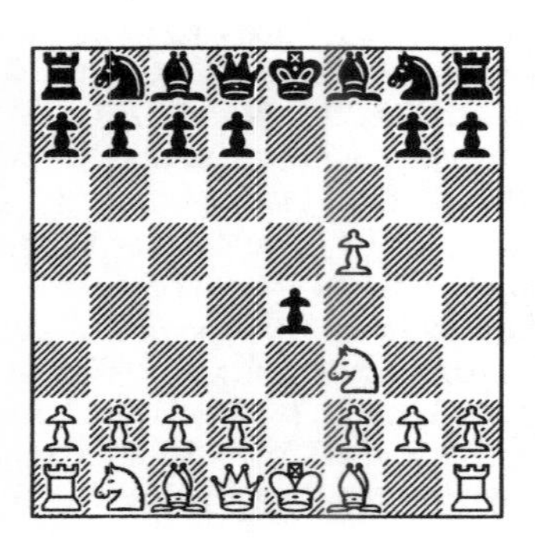

A 4 ♘e5
B 4 ♕e2
C 4 ♘d4
D 4 ♘g1

A 4 ♘e5 ♘f6

Very occasionally, Diepstraten's 4...♕g5!? sees the light of day when, 5 d4! (5 g4!? ♕e7 6 ♘c4 d5 7 ♘e3 d4 8 ♘c4 h5, unclear, Krantz-Diepstraten, corr. 1991) 5...♕xf5 6 ♗c4 ♘c6! with:

a) 7 g4! ♕f6 8 ♘f7 (now this is possible) 8...d5! 9 ♗xd5 ♘xd4 10 ♘xh8?! (10 ♘d2! is more prudent, e.g. 10...♘h6 11 ♘xh6 ♕xh6 12 ♘xe4 ♕b6 13 c3 and White has an extra pawn) 10...♘f3+ 11 ♔f1 ♗xg4 12 ♗f7+ ♔e7 13 ♕d5 ♗h3+ 14 ♔e2 ♘d4+ 15 ♔e3 (15 ♔d2 ♘f3+ 16 ♔e3 ♕b6+ 17 ♔e2 ♘d4+ probably leads to a draw by perpetual) 15...♘xc2+ 16 ♔d2 ♖d8, quite unclear, Geervliet-Diepstraten, Hilversum 1969.

b) 7 ♘f7? is a typical mistake, 7...d5 8 ♘xh8 (8 ♗xd5 is no better, 8...♕xd5 9 ♘xh8 ♗e6 10 ♗f4 0-0-0 11 ♘c3 ♗b4 12 a3 ♗xc3+ 13 bxc3 ♘f6, winning easily, Bakker-Diepstraten, Hilversum 1968) 8...dxc4 9 d5 ♘b4 10 ♘a3 ♘xd5 11 ♘xc4 ♗c5 12 ♗e3 ♘xe3 13 fxe3?! ♕g5 14 ♕d2 ♗e6 15 b3 ♗xc4 and Black can soon recuperate the h8-knight, and win, Oordijk-Diepstraten, Hilversum 1969.

c) 7 ♗f7+ ♔e7 8 g4 ♕f6 9 ♗xg8 (rather than 9 h4?? ♘xe5 10 ♗g5 ♘f3+, winning a piece, Eydan-Svendsen, corr. 1990) 9...♖xg8 10 ♘c3 ♕e6 11 0-0 d5 12 f3 ♘xe5 13 dxe5 c6 14 fxe4 d4 15 ♕xd4 ♕xg4+ 16 ♔h1 ♔e8 messy, Gåård-Malmström, corr. 1994/95.

d) 7 ♘xc6 dxc6 is nothing special.

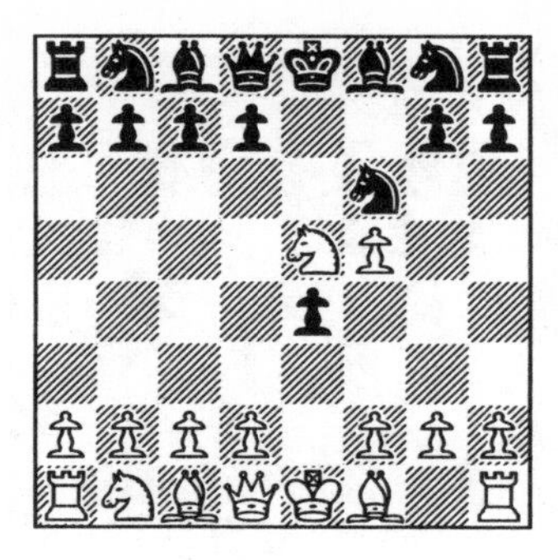

5 ♗e2!

The critical response, threatening the disruptive check on h5.

a) White can also try to hang onto his extra pawn by 5 g4?! although this must be dubious, as Black has more than one strong reply, 5...d6 (also, 5...♛e7!? is strong, 6 ♘c4 d5 7 ♘e3 d4 8 ♘g2 [8 ♘c4?! h5 9 g5 ♘d5 10 h4 ♗xf5 and Black has a massive space advantage, Keiser-Jackson, corr. 1982] 8...h5!? [the logical 8...♘c6 must be good, too, 9 g5 ♘d5 10 ♛h5+ ♚d8, Black is better] 9 g5 [9 ♘f4 may be stronger, 9...♘xg4 10 ♘g6 ♛c5 Criel-Tiemann, corr. 1980, which is unclear, as 11 ♘xh8?? is impossible, 11...d3 and f2 is undefendable] 9...♘g4 10 h4 ♗xf5 11 ♗c4? ♘e5 12 ♗e2 d3 and White is in a bad way, Vashegyi-Grobe, corr. 1970; or 5...♗c5? which is much worse, objectively, but good fun, 6 g5 0-0 7 gxf6 ♛xf6 8 ♘c4?, Danan-Gedult, Paris 1969, and Black already has a forced win! [8 d4 exd3 9 ♘xd3 ♛xf5 10 ♛e2 defends comfortably] 8...♗xf2+! 9 ♔e2 [9 ♔xf2 ♛xf5+ 10 ♔e3 ♘c6 forces mate in two] 9...♛xf5 10 d3 ♛g4+ 11 ♔d2 e3+ winning the queen) 6 ♘c4 d5 (6...h5? is weak, 7 g5 ♘d5 8 ♘c3! ♘xc3 9 dxc3 ♗xf5 10 ♛d5! [10 ♘e3 Neukirch-Alvarez, corr. 1977, 10...♗e6 equal] 10...♛c8, Gubats-Strautins, corr. 1970, when 11 ♘e3! is critical, 11...♗d7 [11...♗h7 12 ♗h3! ♛xh3 13 ♛xb7] 12 ♛xe4+ Black is in a bad way) 7 g5 (7 ♘e5? ♗d6 [this is good, but 7...♛e7! is almost winning, the knight has no retreat] 8 d4 exd3 9 ♘xd3, Morgado-Atars, corr. Betinš Memorial (superfinal) 1976, and now, the typical 9...♛e7+ 10 ♛e2 ♘xg4 wins Black a pawn; 7 ♘e3 d4 8 ♘g2 is uncomfortable for White, but playable) 7...dxc4 8 gxf6 ♛xf6 9 ♗xc4?! (9 ♛h5+ ♚d8 10 d3 leads to rough equality) 9...♗xf5 10 ♛e2? ♘c6 11 ♘c3, Vereb-Eberth, Agria Eger 1999, 11...♘d4 12 ♛d1 ♘f3+ and wins!

b) A more sensible idea is 5 ♘g4 again similar to a King's Gambit (2...♘f6 variation), 5...d5 (but if Black wants some fun he can try 5...♗c5!? 6 ♘c3 d5 7 ♘xf6+ [7 d3 is safer] 7...♛xf6 8 ♛h5+ [8 ♘xd5 ♗xf2+ 9 ♔xf2 ♛xf5+ 10 ♔e1 ♛xd5 favours Black] 8...g6 9 fxg6 [9 ♗b5+ c6 10 ♘xd5!? ♛e5!] 9...hxg6 10 ♛xd5 ♛xf2+ 11 ♔d1 ♗g4+ 12 ♗e2 ♗xe2+ 13 ♘xe2 ♛xg2 14 ♛e5+ ♚d7 15 ♖e1 [15 ♛g7+ ♚c6 16 ♛f6+ forces a perpetual] 15...♜h5, unclear, Melchor-Tiemann, corr. 1991) 6 ♘xf6+ ♛xf6 7 ♛h5+ ♛f7 8 ♛xf7+ ♚xf7 9 ♘c3 c6 10 d3 (10 g4?! h5 11 d3 exd3 12 ♗xd3 hxg4 clearly favours Black, Backhuijs-Den Hertog, corr. 1986) 10...exd3! (10...♗b4 11 dxe4 ♗xc3+ 12 bxc3 ♜e8 13 ♗e3 ♜xe4 ± Melchor-Svendsen, corr. 1990; 10...♗xf5 11 dxe4 dxe4 12 ♗c4+ ♚g6 13 ♗e3 Nilsson-Elburg, corr. 1988, is a little better for White) 11 ♗xd3 ♘d7! 12 ♗f4 ♘c5 13 g4 ♘xd3+ 14 cxd3 ♗c5 (14...g6!? 15 fxg6+ hxg6 16 g5 ♜h3 17 d4 ♗b4 gave Black reasonable play in GromitChess 1.1 - GNU Chess 4.0

computer game 1997) 15 0-0?! h5 16 ♘a4 Chess 4.7-Levy, Toronto 1978, and now Black missed 16...♗e7! 17 h3 hxg4 18 hxg4 ♗xf5! 19 gxf5 ♖h4, skewering the bishop against the knight, and thereby gaining an appreciable advantage.

c) If White does nothing, Black equalizes immediately: 5 d4 d6 6 ♘c4 (6 ♘g4 ♗xf5 7 ♘e3 transposes) 6...♗xf5 7 ♘e3 ♗g6 8 c4 (8 d5 ♗e7 9 ♗e2 0-0 10 ♘c3 ♘bd7 = Colas-Destrebecq, France 1978; 8 h4!? d5 9 c4 ♘c6! 10 ♘c3 dxc4 11 d5 ♘e5 12 ♘xc4 ♘xc4 13 ♗xc4 a6 14 ♗e3 ♗d6 15 h5 ♗f5 16 ♖h4 0-0 ∓ Crouch-Kinderman, London 1978) 8...♗e7 9 ♗e2 0-0 10 ♘c3 ♘c6 11 0-0 ♕d7 with balanced chances, Gibert-Melchor, Spain 1999.

d) 5 d3?! is simply met by 5...d6 6 ♘c4 d5 (6...♗xf5 =) 7 ♘cd2 ♗xf5 8 dxe4, Bychkova-Mikhailova, St Petersburg 1997, 8...♘xe4 (or 8...dxe4) 9 ♘xe4 ♗xe4.

At this point Black has a choice:

A1 5...d6
A2 5...♗e7!?
A3 5...d5?
A4 5...♗c5?!

The themes to bear in mind, in all these lines, are that:

White can win the h8-rook, but that his knight then becomes trapped on h8. If Black can successfully recapture this he may be better. On the other hand, White can often save this piece, by g4-g5-g6, and it is then a question of whether Black has enough compensation for the exchange.

Otherwise, White can play ♘xd6 and then capture the bishop on c8, but it is normally a mistake, as the knight will then also be trapped.

A1 5...d6

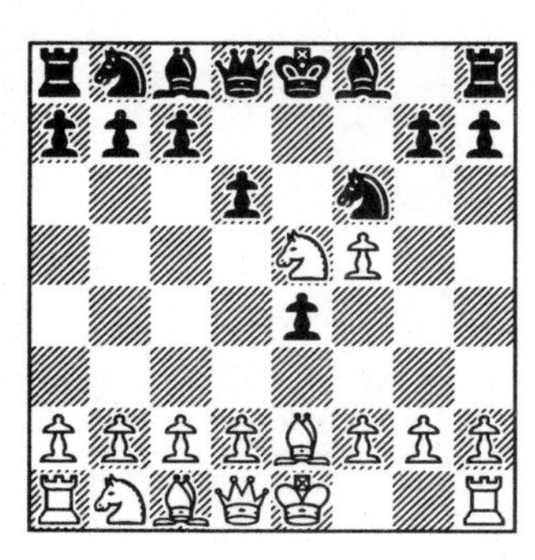

Traditionally the main move, and the most forcing, but bearing in mind that White wants to play ♗h5+ and ♘f7 anyway, it may be that Black has more useful moves.

6 ♗h5+ ♔e7 7 ♘f7

7 ♘c4 ♗xf5 8 d4 ± *NCO*, but 8...♗e6 9 ♘e3 d5 doesn't look particularly worrying for Black.

7...♕e8 8 ♘xh8

a) It is a moot point whether this is stronger than 8 ♘c3, as follows:

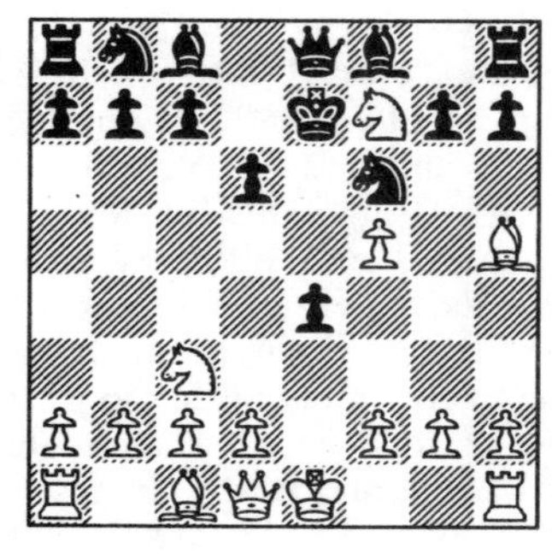

a1) 8...♘xh5 9 ♘d5+ (the most exciting, although 9 ♘xh8 ♘f6 10 g4 c6 [Betinš gives 10...♘c6! 11 g5 ♘d4 12 gxf6+ ♔d8 when, after 13 f7 ♕e5 14 ♕g4? {14 ♔f1 ♗xf5 15 ♔g2!?} 14...♗xf5 15 ♕h4+, Diepstraten-Eglitis, corr. 1977, Black could, indeed, have obtained a powerful position by 15...♔d7 16

♔f1 ♗e7 17 ♕g3 ♖xh8, but White has stronger tries at move fourteen] 11 g5 ♘d5 12 ♕g4 ♔d8, Svendsen-Diepstraten, corr. 1992, is also promising)

a11) 9...♔xf7! 10 ♕xh5+ g6 11 fxg6+ ♔g7 12 ♘xc7

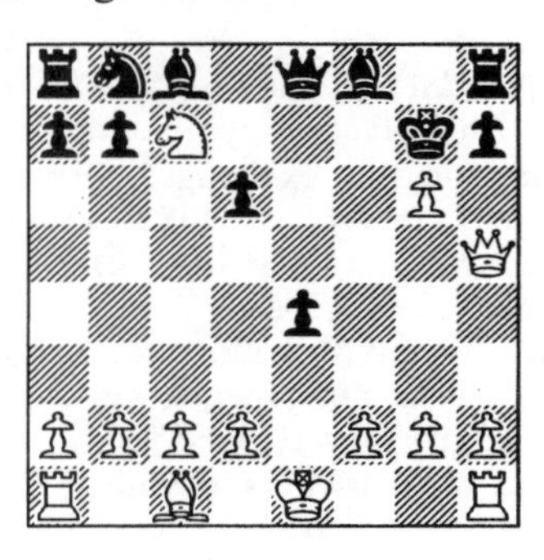

(12 b3?! is less accurate, 12...♕e5 13 ♕xe5+ dxe5 14 ♘xc7 ♗d6 15 ♘xa8 hxg6 16 ♗b2 ♗f5 17 0-0-0 ♖c8!? and, provided he captures the knight soon, Black will have reasonable prospects, Miraglia-Ruggeri Laderchi, corr. 1997) 12...♕e5 (I prefer 12...♕xg6! 13 ♕xg6+ ♔xg6 [13...hxg6?! 14 b4 ♗e7 15 ♗b2+ ♗f6 16 ♗xf6+ ♔xf6 17 ♘xa8 ♘a6, Evans-Reinke, corr. 1994/95, and the white knight escapes, 18 b5 ♘b4 19 0-0 ♘xc2 20 ♖ac1 etc.] 14 ♘xa8 ♘a6 15 d4 ♗e7 16 ♗f4 ♗d7 17 ♘b6 axb6 18 a3; in such a position, where the white rooks have no open files, the black pieces will dominate, Le Deuff-Destrebecq, corr. 1988) 13 ♕xe5+ dxe5 14 ♘xa8 (14 gxh7 ♘c6 15 ♘xa8 ♗d6 [trapping the knight, 15...♘d4!? is more ambitious, 16 0-0 {16 ♖b1!? ♘xc2+!? 17 ♔d1 ♘b4 18 ♘c7 ♗g4+ 19 ♔e1 ♘d3+ 20 ♔f1 ♗c5 is interesting} 16...♘xc2 17 ♖b1 ♗d6 18 b3 ♗f5 19 ♗b2 ♖xa8 and Black is on top, Zeidaks-Budovskis, corr. 1974] 16 c3 [16 c4!? b6 17 d3 exd3 18 ♗e3 ♗e6 19 ♘xb6 axb6 is wild] 16...♗g4 17 h3 ♗f5 18 g4 ♗e6 19 b3 ♖xa8 20 ♗b2 ♔xh7 21 0-0-0 ♖f8 22 ♖h2 ♗c5 Black has good play, Evans-Sireta, corr. 1994/94) 14...♗d6 15 0-0 (15 c4!? [time is of the essence!] 15...♘a6 16 b4, Salenga-Laurinavivius, corr. 1995, 16...♘xb4 17 0-0 ♘d3 is promising for Black, 18 ♖b1 ♔xg6 19 ♘b6 ♗g4!; 15 gxh7 transposes to the previous note) 15...hxg6 16 c4 ♘a6 (if 16...b6 17 a4) 17 b4! White must find a way to free his knight, 17...♗xb4 (17...♗d7 18 c5 ♗e7 is also feasible) 18 ♗b2?! (18 ♖b1!? ♗d6 19 ♖b5) 18...♗d6 19 c5 ♘xc5 20 ♗a3 b6 21 ♖fb1 ♗f5 22 ♘xb6 axb6 23 ♖xb6 ♖a8 and Black has some drawing chances, Charushin-Schreyer, corr. 1986.

a12) 9...♔d7?! is clearly worse, 10 ♕xh5 ♖g8 (10...c6!? is no better, 11 ♘f4 ♖g8 12 ♘e6 ♘a6 13 ♕xh7! ♗e7 [13...♕xf7 14 ♘g5 ♕f6 {14...♕d5 15 ♘e6} 15 ♕xg8 ♕xg5 16 ♕xf8 ♕xg2 17 ♕f7+ ♔d8 18 ♖f1 must be good for White] 14 ♘fg5 with a significant advantage, Zeidaks-Grobe, corr. 1970) 11 f6! (11 ♘f4 ♗e7 12 ♘e6 ♘c6 13 g4!? ♘d8 14 ♘fxd8 ♕xh5 15 gxh5 ♗xd8 16 ♖g1 ♗f6 17 h6 ♔c6 18 ♘xg7 ♗xf5—Betinš, is not so clear) 11...♘a6 (11...c6? is hopeless, 12 ♘e5+! dxe5 [12...♕xe5 13 ♕f7+] 13 f7 ♕e6 14 fxg8=♕ ♕xg8, Vitols-Grobe, corr. 1973, 15 ♕g4+ ♕e6 16 ♕xe6+ ♔xe6 17 ♘c7+; and 11...♕e6? loses immediately, 12 ♘f4 ♕xf6 13 ♕h3+ ♔c6 14 ♕xc8 ♕xf7 15 ♘e6; but 11...♘c6! is Black's best try, 12 ♘f4 [12 ♕g4+ ♕e6 13 ♕xe6+ ♔xe6 14 ♘xc7+ ♔xf7 15 ♘xa8 ♘b4 is not too clear] 12...♘d4 [12...gxf6?? 13 ♕f5+ ♔e7 14 ♘d5+ ♔xf7 15 ♕xf6 mate, Vitols-Gebuhr, corr. 1975] 13 ♕h3+

♔c6 14 ♕c3+ ♔d7 15 ♕xd4 ♕xf7 16 ♕xe4 gxf6 and White is only a pawn up) 12 0-0 (12 fxg7? ♗xg7 13 ♕xh7 ♕xf7 14 ♘f6+ ♕xf6 15 ♕xg8 c6 is good for Black, and 12 ♘e5+? comes one move too soon, 12...♕xe5 13 ♕f7+ ♔c6 14 ♕xg8 ♗e6 15 ♘e7+ ♔b6 which is unclear) 12...♕e6 (12...c6? 13 ♘e5+ dxe5 14 f7 ♕e6 15 fxg8=♕ ♕xg8 16 ♘e3 analysis of Keres 1-0, Popa-Steinhauer, corr. 1985, although, in the game Geisler-Reichardt, corr. 1992, Black reached the same position and decided to play on for a while, 16...♗d6 before resigning) 13 f3 h6 14 fxg7 (14 fxe4!? g6 15 ♕h3 ♕xh3 16 gxh3 c6 17 ♘e7 offers less advantage) 14...♗xg7 15 fxe4 White is better, the black king will have difficulty finding a safe resting place, Pape-Heap, corr. 1994/96.

a2) 8...g6!? 9 fxg6 (9 ♘xh8 gxh5 10 d3, Kell-Nortje, corr. 1997, 10...♗g7 11 dxe4 ♗xh8 12 ♗g5 favours White) 9...hxg6 10 ♘xh8 (10 ♗xg6 ♖g8 11 ♗h5 ♖xg2 12 ♘xd6 ♕xh5 13 ♘xc8+ ♔d7 14 ♕xh5 ♘xh5 15 ♘xe4! ♔xc8 [15...♘c6 16 ♘g3 ♘xg3 17 hxg3 ♗c5 may be stronger] 16 ♘g3 ♘f4 17 d4 ♘h3 18 ♗e3 ♖g1+ 19 ♖xg1 ♘xg1 20 ♘e4 when Black experienced certain difficulties stopping the white pawns, Reinke-Melchor, corr. 1994/96) 10...gxh5 11 ♕e2 ♗g7 (11...d5?! 12 ♕e3!? [12 d3 ♗g7 13 dxe4 is strongest] 12...♗g7 13 ♕c5+ ♔e6 14 ♘b5 ♘a6 15 ♕xc7 ♘xc7 16 ♘xc7+ ♔f5 17 ♘xe8 ♘xe8, unclear, Stummer-Schlenker, corr. 1991) 12 ♘xe4 ♕xh8 may not be to everyone's taste, but is perfectly playable, 13 ♘xf6+ (13 ♘g5+ ♔d7 14 ♕e6+ ♔c6 15 ♕c4+ ♔d7 16 ♕f7+ ♔d8 17 0-0 is a little awkward for Black, but no more, Lindeberg-Nilsson, corr. 1993) 13...♔xf6 14 d4 ♗f5 15 0-0 ♘c6 16 ♕e3 ♔f7 17 ♕b3+ ♔g6 18 c3 with a plus, because of the black king, Pape-Roelofszen, email 1998.

a3) 8...♗xf5?! is worse, though; 9 ♘xd6! (following 9 ♘xh8 ♕xh5 10 ♘d5+ ♔d8 11 ♕xh5 ♘xh5 12 ♘f7+ ♔d7 13 ♘g5 h6 14 ♘e3 ♗g6 15 ♘h3 Black has some compensation for the exchange, Grivainis-Kotek, corr. 1968) 9...♕d7 (9...♕xh5 10 ♕xh5 ♘xh5 11 ♘xf5+ ♔e6 12 ♘g3 ♘xg3 13 hxg3 ♗e7 14 ♘xe4 with a clear advantage, Stummer-Spiegel, corr. 1991) 10 ♘xb7 (or 10 ♘xf5+ ♕xf5 11 ♗e2 with advantage Gubats-Cuba, Latvia) 10...♘xh5 11 ♕xh5 g6 12 ♕e2 is convincing for White, Therkildsen-Zerbib, Tourcoing 1995.

b) 8 d3 is a reasonable alternative, 8...g6 (stronger than 8...♘xh5 9 ♘xh8 ♘f6 [9...♔d8 10 0-0 ♘f6?! {10...exd3} 11 dxe4 ♘c6?! 12 e5! ♘xe5 13 ♖e1 winning a piece, 13...♗e7 14 ♖xe5 ♕xh8 15 c4 with a winning advantage, Haba-Agnos, Bundesliga 1989] 10 0-0 [10 dxe4] 10...♗xf5 11 dxe4 ♗e6 12 ♗g5 ♕b5!? the queen is coming round for the h8-knight, 13 ♗xf6+! [13 ♕d2 is less helpful] 13...gxf6 14 ♘c3 ♕g5 15 ♘d5+ ♔d7 16 f4 ♕g7 17 e5?! [17 f5!] 17...♕xh8 18 ♘xf6+ ♔c8 the position is not so clear, Saavedra-Atars, corr. 1969) 9 ♘xh8 (9 fxg6? hxg6 10 ♗xg6?! [10 ♘xh8 gxh5 11 ♗g5 ♗g7 12 dxe4 ♗xh8 may be slightly better for White] 10...♖g8 11 ♘e5 ♖xg6 12 ♘xg6+ ♕xg6 13 ♔f1 ♗f5 and the white king is more exposed than the black, Basmaison-Sireta, Auvergne IV 1993) 9...gxh5 10 0-0 ♗g7 11 dxe4 ♗xh8 12 ♗g5 with advantage, Malmström-Sireta, corr. 1994/95.

8...Qxh5

As ever, with the king so exposed, it is better to play the endgame.

The move 8...Nxh5?! didn't work out too well in Cano-Ciprian, corr. 1970, 9 g4 (9 d3 transposes to 8 d3 in the last note) 9...Nf6 10 d3 exd3 11 0-0!? dxc2 12 Qxc2 with advantage, the black king is very awkwardly placed.

9 Qxh5 Nxh5 10 g4 Nf6

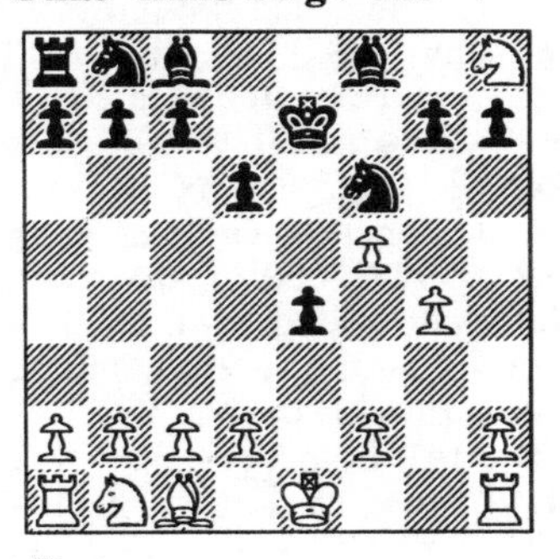

11 Rg1

11 Nc3?! is doubtful, 11...Nxg4 (or 11...c6 12 Rg1 with advantage as the annoying ...Nc6-d4 is no longer possible) 12 Nd5+ Kd7 13 Nf7 Nc6 and ...Nd4 is threatened.

However, 11 h3 is a good, solid alternative, 11...Nc6 12 Nc3 (12 0-0?! Nd4 13 Na3 d5?! [13...g5! 14 fxg6 Bg7 wins the knight] 14 d3 c6 15 dxe4 dxe4 16 Rd1 with advantage, Clarke-Diepstraten, corr. 1998) 12...Nd4 13 Kd1 Nf3 14 d3 exd3 15 cxd3 Bd7 16 g5 Nh5 17 Nd5+ Kd8 18 Nf7+ and White has got over the worst of his problems, Van de Velden-Melchor, corr. 1998.

11...Nc6

The knight threatens to hop into f3 via d4, or e5, and ...Nb4 can also be effective. Black can also win the knight by a well-timed ...g5, and ...Bg7. Meanwhile, White's queenside is undeveloped, and he must try to find some way to either extricate his knight, or gain sufficient compensation for it.

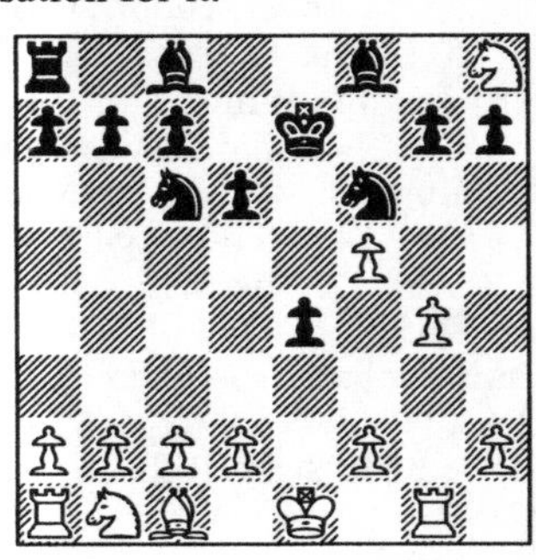

12 Rg3

There are others:

a) 12 Kd1 (to avoid forks on c2, or f3) 12...Ne5 13 h3 Zirnis-Silavs, corr. 1970, when I think I would recapture the knight immediately, 13...g5!? 14 fxg6 Bg7 15 gxh7 Bxh8 16 Nc3 Be6 and, providing Black retains his e4-pawn, the white kingside pawns shouldn't go far.

b) 12 g5? weakens f5 and lets the c8-bishop out. 12...Nh5 (12...Nd5!?) 13 g6 Bxf5 (13...Nd4?? 14 gxh7 Nxc2+ 15 Kd1 Nf4 16 Ng6+ 1-0, Gaard-Knorr, corr. 1990; but Destrebecq's 13...h6! is interesting, as although the h8-knight can go to f7, he cannot return from Black's territory) 14 gxh7 Bxh7 15 Ng6+ Bxg6 16 Rxg6 Ne5 and Black has good play for the exchange, Riegsecker-Lonsdale, corr. 1986.

c) 12 h3 is always a useful move, and I actually think it is the best here, 12...Nd4 (immediately 12...g5 13 fxg6 Bg7 may be better) 13 Kd1 g5!? (13...d5 14 b3 Nf3 15 Rg3 Ke8 16 d3? Bd6 17 Rg2 exd3 18 cxd3 Be5 19 Ke2? [19 Rg3] 19...Nh4 0-1, Borsdorff-Grava, corr. 1968) 14 fxg6 Bg7 15 Nc3 (15 g5?! Nh5 16 gxh7 loosens the white kingside pawns, 16...Bf5 17 g6 Nf3 and White is worse, he will shed all of his advanced pawns,) Ruhbaum-Schreyer, corr. 1979, when 15...♗xh8 16 gxh7 ♗e6 17 d3 slightly favours White.

d) 12 d3?!, Schulien-Glass, corr. 1980, allows the simple 12...♘e5 13 ♔e2 exd3+ 14 cxd3 ♘exg4.

e) 12 ♘c3?!, likewise, 12...♘e5 13 g5 ♘h5 (13...♘f3+ 14 ♔f1 ♘g4 is also reasonable) 14 ♘d5+ ♔d8 15 ♘e3 ♘f3+ 16 ♔f1 ♘xg1 17 ♔xg1 almost equal, Staak-Rubach, Pinneberg 1994.

12...♘d4

12...♘e5!? 13 h3 (the pawn needs defending, 13 ♘c3?, Tiemann-Diepstraten, corr. 1990, is far weaker, 13...♘exg4 14 ♘xe4 ♘xe4! 15 ♖xg4 ♗xf5 16 ♖f4 g6 17 d3 ♘f6 and ...♗g7 with a clear advantage) 13...♘f3+ 14 ♔d1 ♔e8 15 ♘c3 d5 16 ♘b5 ♗d6 17 ♘xd6+ cxd6 18 d3 ♗d7 19 ♗f4 ♔e7 with chances for both sides, Gåård-Diepstraten, corr. 1994/95.

13 ♔d1 g6!

Leading to some long forcing sequences, 13...d5?! 14 d3 ♘f3 15 dxe4 dxe4 is advantageous for White after 16 ♘c3 g6 (16...♘xh2? 17 ♗g5 ♘f3 18 ♘xe4 Garcia-Kapitaniak, corr. 1978) 17 ♘xe4 Black is losing, Szilagyi-Downey, corr. 1976.

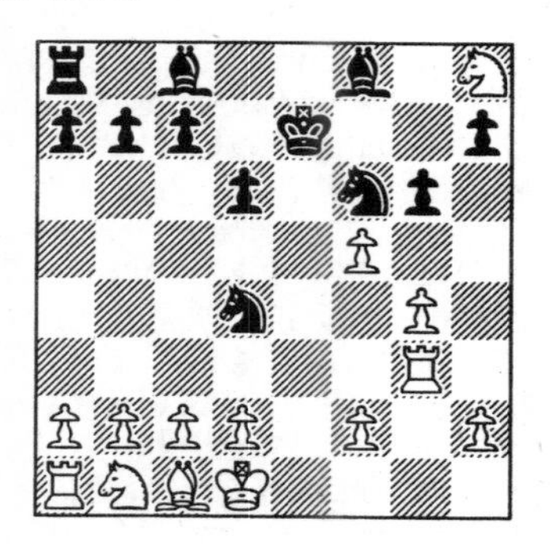

14 c3

This is the only test, others:

a) 14 d3?! is a mistake, 14...gxf5 15 g5 (with advantage—Keres!) 15...♘g4 16 ♗e3 (16 c3? ♘xf2+ 17 ♔e1 ♘xd3+ 18 ♔d1? f4 19 ♖xd3 ♗g4+ 20 ♔e1? ♘c2+ 0-1, Elburg-Heap, corr. 1991) 16...♗g7!? (or 16...f4 17 ♗xd4 fxg3 18 hxg3 ♘e5 19 dxe4 ♗g4+ 20 ♔c1 ♗g7 21 f4 ♘d3+ 22 cxd3 ♗xd4 which is not easy to win, Hansel-Schreyer, East Germany 1985) 17 ♖h3 ♔f8! 18 ♖xh7 this is not too clear, 18...♘f3 19 ♘d2 ♔g8 20 g6 (20 ♖xg7+? ♔xg7 21 ♘xf3 ♘xe3+ 22 fxe3 exf3 is quite hopeless, Grabner-Tiemann, corr. 1978) 20...♗xh8 21 h4, McDonald-Gåård, corr. 1991, when the rook on the seventh, and passed pawns, provide counterplay.

b) 14 fxg6?? is a blunder, 14...♗xg4+ 15 ♖xg4 ♘xg4 ∓ 16 gxh7 ♗g7 17 ♘g6+ ♔f7 18 h8=♕ ♗xh8 19 ♘xh8+ ♖xh8 20 d3 ♘xf2+ 21 ♔d2 e3+ 22 ♔c3 ♘d1+! 0-1, Prietz-Pupols, corr. 1967/68, as 23 ♔xd4 ♖h4+ 24 ♔d5 e2 25 ♗d2 e1=♕ 26 ♗xe1 ♘e3 mate.

c) 14 g5?! is far from critical, 14...♘h5 15 f6+ ♔e8 16 ♖g1? (16 ♖c3 ♗g4+ 17 ♔e1 is superior, although Black is at least equal) 16...♘f3 17 ♖h1, Tortosa-Melchor, Barcelona 1993, 17...♘xg5 winning easily.

14...gxf5! 15 g5

15 cxd4 f4 16 ♖c3 (16 ♖g1?! ♗xg4+ 17 ♔e1 ♗h6 favours Black, Jackson-Pape, corr. 1990) 16...♗xg4+ 17 ♔e1 (17 ♔c2 ♘d5 18 ♖b3 ♗g7 19 ♖b5 ♗e6 20 ♖xb7 ♗xh8 leaves Black with strong positional compensation for the exchange) 17...♖c8!? (17...♘d5! 18 ♖b3 ♗g7 19 ♖b5 ♗e6 20 ♖xb7 ♗xh8 is perhaps simpler, when Black has more than sufficient compensation for the exchange, e.g. 21

♘c3 ♖g8) 18 d3 e3! 19 ♖b3? (19 fxe3 fxe3 20 ♗xe3 ♗g7 21 ♖b3 is much safer, but Black still does have some compensation) 19...♗h6 20 ♖xb7 ♗f3 21 ♖xa7, analysis of Peel (1989), when 21...♖g8 catches White in a mating net, i.e. (Peel's 21...♘d5 is also good) 22 fxe3 fxe3 23 ♗xe3 ♗xe3 24 ♘d2 ♖g1+ 25 ♘f1 ♘d5.

15...♘g4 16 cxd4 ♘xf2+ 17 ♔e2

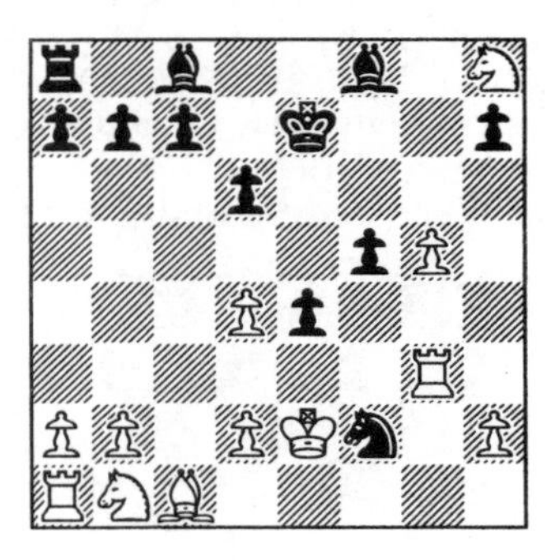

17...f4?!

This doesn't look very logical to me.

17...♘d3! 18 ♘c3 ♗e6 must be fine for Black, his d3-knight is worth a rook. For instance, in the line 19 d5 ♗d7 20 g6 ♗g7 21 ♘f7 hxg6 22 ♘g5 Black is a rook down, but better! 22...♖h8 23 h3 ♗e5 24 ♖g1 ♖h5 and White is playing without his queenside.

18 ♖c3 ♘d3 19 ♖xc7+ ♔e8

With obscure complications analysed at some length by Pupols.

20 ♘c3 f3+ 21 ♔e3 f2 22 ♖f7 ♗e6 23 ♖xf2 ♘xf2 24 ♔xf2, Matz-Leisebein, East Germany 1990, and now 24...♗g7 25 d5 ♗f5 is better for White, but Black has drawing chances.

A2 5...♗e7!?

Probably the better square for the bishop, since, unlike variation A4, White's advance d2-d4 will not gain a tempo.

6 ♗h5+

6 d3 d6 (6...exd3 7 ♗xd3) 7 ♗h5+ ♔f8 8 ♘f7 ♕e8 is similar, 9 ♘xd6!? ♕xh5 10 ♕xh5 ♘xh5 11 ♘xc8 ♗c5 12 dxe4 ♘c6 13 ♘xa7, gaining four pawns for the piece, Wittmann-Gunderam, corr. 1972.

6...♔f8

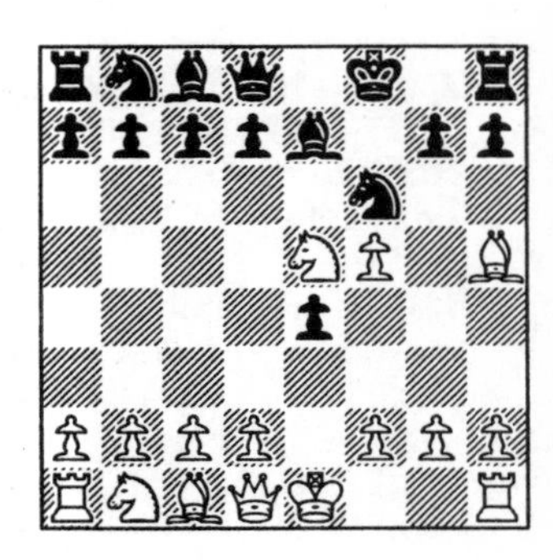

7 ♘c3

This does not seem to offer White much, but neither do the alternatives:

a) 7 d3 exd3 8 ♘xd3 d5 9 ♗g4 ♘c6 10 ♘f4 ♘xg4 11 ♕xg4 ♗f6 12 c3 ♕e7+ 13 ♘e2, Wallwork-Saunders, corr. 1991, 13...♕e5 equal.

b) 7 d4 d6?! risky, (7...exd3 transposes to the above) 8 ♘f7 (8 ♘c4 ♗xf5 9 ♘e3 ♗e6 10 d5 ♗f7 11 ♗xf7 ♔xf7 12 0-0 ♘bd7 13 ♘c3 Jensen-Magee, corr. 1991, doesn't offer White anything. Generally, by comparison with the King's Gambit, the slight inconvenience suffered by Black's king displacement is offset by the tempi White has lost in playing ♗e2-h5-e2) 8...♕e8 9 g4 (the most precise, effectively forcing Black to capture on h5 with his knight, 9 ♘xh8 ♕xh5 10 ♕xh5 ♘xh5 11 g4 ♘f6 12 g5 ♘d5 13 g6 [13 f6 gxf6 14 ♖g1 ♘c6 15 c3 f5 is fine for Black] 13...h6 [13...♗xf5 14 gxh7 ♗xh7 15 ♖g1 ♗f6 is also quite reasonable] 14 h4 ♗xf5 15 h5 ♘d7, whilst the h8-knight is now safe for a moment, it has nowhere to go after f7, Kerstens-Snuverink, Hengelo 1997; 9 ♘xd6 ♕xh5 10 ♕xh5 ♘xh5 11 ♘xc8 ♗h4 12 ♗e3 ♘a6 13 ♘xa7 ♖xa7 White has enough compensation for the piece, Clarke-Stummer, corr. 1994/95) 9...♘xh5 10 ♘xh8, Melchor-Magee, corr. 1989, 10...♘f6 11 g5 forcing Black to concede his knight, as 11...♘d5 12 f6 gxf6 13 ♖g1 ♗f5 14 c3 is awkward.

c) 7 ♘f7?! is premature, 7...♕e8 8 ♘xh8 (this time, 8 g4 is less effective, 8...♘xh5 9 ♘xh8 ♘f4 10 d3 exd3! 11 ♗xf4?! [11 cxd3 is more circumspect] 11...♗b4+ 12 ♔f1 ♕e4 13 ♖g1? dxc2 14 ♕c1 b6 0-1, Pugh-Mamsell, corr. 1978, ...♗a6 is threatened) 8...♕xh5 9 ♕xh5 ♘xh5 10 g4 ♘f6 11 g5 ♘d5 12 g6 h6 (12...♔g8?! 13 ♘f7 d6 14 gxh7+ ♔xh7 Paavilainen-Niemand, corr. 1991, 15 ♖g1 ♗xf5 16 ♘g5+ with chances of an advantage) 13 f3 exf3 14 0-0 ♘c6 15 c3 d6 16 d4 (16 ♖xf3 ♘e5 17 ♖f1 ♘d3 is hardly an improvement) 16...♔g8 17 ♘f7 ♗xf5 18 ♘xh6+ gxh6 19 ♖xf3 ♗xg6 20 ♗xh6, the black pieces are worth more than the rook and pawn, Evans-Clarke, corr. 1994/96.

7...d6 8 ♘f7 ♕e8 9 ♘xh8

There is something to be said for 9 g4! ♘xh5 10 ♘xh8 ♘f6, transposing to 9...♘xh5, but cutting down on Black's options.

Not 9 ♘xd6? ♕xh5 10 ♕xh5 ♘xh5 11 ♘xc8 ♗d8, trapping the knight, Jaunozols-Strautins, Latvia.

9...♕xh5

9...♘xh5!? looks eminently playable: 10 g4 ♘f6 11 g5 ♗xf5!? (11...♘g8? cannot be right, 12 ♘d5 ♘a6, Vitols-Clarke, corr. 1990, 13 ♕g4 c6 14 ♘f4, threatening an appropriate ♘e6+, must be good) 12 gxf6 ♗xf6 13 ♘d5 ♗d8 14 ♘e3 (14 c3?! ♘d7 15 ♘e3 ♘e5 16 ♘xf5 ♘f3+ 17 ♔e2 ♕b5+ 18 d3 ♕xf5 19 dxe4 ♕xe4+ 20 ♗e3 ♘e5 21 ♖g1 ♔g8 and, after recapturing the knight on h8, Black had sufficient compensation for the exchange, Diepstraten-Morgado, corr. 1977) 14...♗d7 15 b3 ♘c6 16 d4 (16 ♗b2 ♔g8 17 ♖g1 ♘e5) 16...♘xd4 17 ♕xd4 ♗f6 unclear, Canal Oliveras-Kozlov, corr. 1998.

10 ♕xh5 ♘xh5 11 g4 ♘f6 12 g5

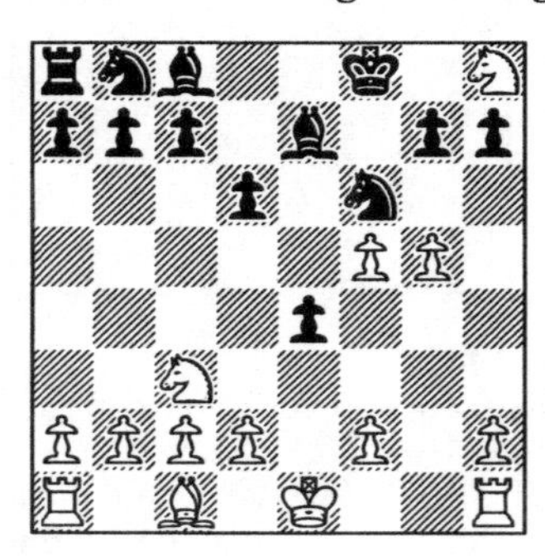

12...♘e8!

12...♘g4 is more active, but after 13 ♘d5 (13 ♘xe4 is also a problem, 13...♗xf5 14 d3 ♔g8 [14...♘e5 15 f4] 15 f4 menacing h3) 13...♗d8 (13...♘a6? 14 f6! gxf6 15 h3 ♘e5 16 gxf6 is worse, Koser-Schirmer, corr. 1993) 14 g6 ♗xf5 15 ♘f7 ♘a6 16 gxh7 ♗xh7 17 ♘xd8 ♖xd8, Black's pawn, and light-squared control, provides some compensation for the exchange, Keskinen-Kilpela, Finland 1997.

13 g6 ♔g8 14 ♘d5 ♗h4 15 ♘f7 ♗xf5 16 d3

Koser-Sénéchaud, corr. 1993, when 16...♗xg6 17 ♘g5 ♗xg5 18 ♗xg5 exd3 would have been reasonable for Black.

A3 5...d5?

This move combines the disadvantage of 5...d6 (the awkward placement of the black king on e7) without the advantage—the immediate attack on the e5-knight. Therefore White has a greater choice of seventh moves, and more than one method of cooking Black's goose.

6 ♗h5+ ♔e7

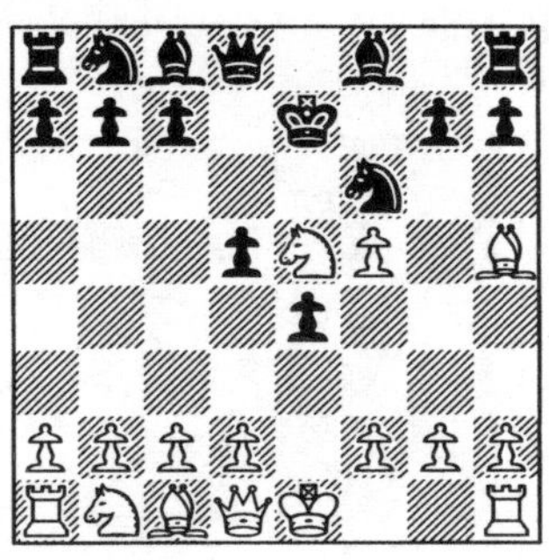

7 d3!

The best, White can capture on e4 when appropriate, to open the central files. There are two other important possibilities:.

a) 7 ♘f7 is less effective, although the knight will be difficult to attack on h8, 7...♕e8 with the further choice:

a1) 8 ♘xh8 ♕xh5 9 ♕xh5 ♘xh5 10 g4 (10 ♘c3 c6 transposes to 8 ♘c3, but 10...♘f6 is perhaps better) 10...♘f6 11 h3 (the tactical 11 ♖g1?! ♘c6 12 ♖g3 ♘d4 13 ♔d1 just helps Black, 13...g6 14 c3 ♘f3 Black has already gained the ascendance, Van Swol-Van Willigen, corr. 1982, as 15 g5 [15 fxg6 ♗g7] 15...♗xf5 16 gxf6+ ♔xf6 17 d3 ♗d6 regains material) 11...♘c6 12 d3 ♔e8 13 ♘d2? (13 ♗g5) 13...♘b4 14 ♔d1 exd3 15 cxd3 ♘xd3 16 ♔e2 ♘f4+ 17 ♔e3 ♗d6 18 ♘f3 h5!? and Black has excellent counterplay, Nobbe-Wynia, corr. 1982.

a2) 8 ♘c3? can transpose, but allows Black a couple of extra possibilities:

a21) 8...g6 9 fxg6 (9 ♘xh8 gxh5) 9...hxg6 10 ♘xh8 (10 ♗xg6? ♖g8) 10...gxh5 11 ♕e2, Downey-Tiemann, corr. 1987, 11...♗g7 12 d3 ♗xh8 13 dxe4 dxe4 14 ♘xe4 ♘xe4 15 ♕xe4+ ♔f7 with every chance in the endgame.

a22) 8...♗xf5!? leaving the d-pawn to its fate, 9 ♘xh8 ♕xh5 10 ♕xh5 (10 ♘xd5+ ♔d6 should transpose) 10...♘xh5 11 ♘xd5+ ♔d6 12 ♘e3 ♗e6, if Black finds time to play ...g6, and ...♗g7, he will be fine, 13 g4!? ♘f4 14 b3 (14 d3 exd3 15 ♘c4+?! does not work, 15...♗xc4 16 ♗xf4+ ♔d7 17 cxd3 ♗d5 18 0-0 ♘c6 and the white knight will be captured by the black rook, after the f8-bishop moves) 14...♘d7 15 d3 (15 ♗b2 ♘e5) 15...♔c6 16 ♘f5 ♗b4+ 17 ♔f1 ♗c3 18 ♖b1 ♘d5 19 dxe4 ♘b4 20 ♗b2 ♗xb2 21 ♖xb2 ♖xh8, unclear, Salvador-Goedhart, corr. 1979.

a23) 8...c6?! is too acquiescent, 9 ♘xh8 (9 d3 ♘xh5 10 ♘xh8 exd3?! 11 0-0 ♔d8 12 ♗g5+ ♘f6 13 ♗xf6+ gxf6 14 ♕xd3 ♗d6 15 ♘xd5 cxd5 16 ♕xd5 ♔c7 17 ♘f7 and White has a raging attack, plus extra material, Modena-Alloin, 1990) 9...♕xh5 10 ♕xh5 ♘xh5 11 g4 ♘f6 12 h3 (12 g5?! just weakens the pawn structure here, 12...♘g4 13 g6 ♗xf5 14 ♘f7 ♗xg6 15 ♘g5 and White has extracted his knight, but at too great a cost, Cimmino-Bonavoglia, Turin 1975) 12...♘bd7 13 d3 ♘e5 and White held the upper hand, Gaard-Jackson, corr. 1992, as it is difficult to see how Black will capture the knight on h8.

b) 7 b3?! c5 (7...♘bd7 8 ♗a3+ c5 9 d4?! [9 ♘f7 ♕e8 10 ♘c3 is tempting] 9...♕c7 10 f4, Polaczek-

Oppitz, Torremolinos 1986, 10...exf3 11 ♗xf3 ♘xe5 12 ♕e2 ♗xf5 is playable.) 8 ♘f7 ♕e8 9 ♘xh8 (9 ♘c3 g6, unclear, Valenti-Redon, corr. 1991) 9...♕xh5 10 ♕xh5 ♘xh5 11 g4 ♘f6 12 g5 ♘h5? (12...♘e8 13 ♘c3 ♘c7) 13 ♘c3 d4 14 ♘xe4 b6 15 ♘g3 and Black is losing, De Boer-Fiorito, corr. 1984.

c) 7 d4?! ♗xf5 8 ♗g5 (8 ♘f7 ♕e8 9 ♗g5 g6 10 ♘xh8 gxh5 11 ♘c3 c6 12 ♕d2 ♗g7 13 ♕f4, Gaillard-Van Mulder, Paris 1996, when 13...♗e6 14 f3 exf3 leaves Black ahead) 8...g6 9 ♘c3!? (interesting; retreating the bishop would also offer some small advantage, i.e. 9 ♗e2 ♗g7 10 0-0 ♘bd7 11 c4 c6 12 ♘c3 h6 13 ♗xf6+ ♘xf6?? [13...♔xf6 is perfectly reasonable] 14 g4 1-0, Burk-Leisebein, corr. 1982; 9 g4!? ♗e6 10 ♗xg6 hxg6 11 ♘xg6+ ♔f7 12 ♘xh8+ ♔g7 13 ♖g1 ♗d6, Black wishes to capture on h8 with his rook, 14 ♘d2 ♘c6 15 c3 ♕d7 16 f3 Kühn-Leisebein, East Germany 1982, and now 16...♗xh2 17 ♖g2 ♖xh8 is unclear) 9...♗g7 (9...gxh5?? 10 ♕xh5 wins immediately) 10 f3!? gxh5 (Black might as well take the piece, although 10...♕d6 is not too bad, 11 fxe4 ♗xe4 12 ♘xe4 dxe4 13 ♗xg6 hxg6 14 ♘xg6+ ♔d7 15 ♘xh8 ♗xh8 16 0-0 with a slim advantage Svendsen-Tiemann, corr. 1990; 10...e3?! 11 g4 ♗e6 12 ♗xg6 hxg6 13 ♘xg6+ ♔f7 14 ♘xh8+ ♕xh8 15 h4 ♘c6 16 ♗xe3, the three mobile white pawns are too strong, Svendsen-Magee, corr. 1991) 11 fxe4 ♗xe4 12 0-0 for the piece White has opened the f-file, 12...♖f8! (this might be the most prudent, 12...♕d6 13 ♕xh5 ♕e6 14 ♘xe4 dxe4 15 ♖xf6! ♗xf6 16 ♗xf6+ ♕xf6 17 ♖f1 ♕e6 18 d5 ♕d6 19 ♘f7 ♕b6+ 20 ♔h1 ♘d7 21 ♕g5+ ♘f6 22 d6+! 1-0, Kozlov-Borrmann, corr. 1992, because of 22...♔d7 23 ♘e5+ ♔xd6 24 ♖xf6+; 12...♕e8 13 ♕e1 ♖f8 14 ♘xe4 dxe4 15 ♕xe4 ♘bd7 16 ♖ae1 ♘b6 17 ♕xh7 1-0, Krantz-Melchor, corr. 1989) 13 ♕e1 ♔e8 14 ♕h4 ♕d6 15 ♖ae1 ♘bd7 16 ♘xe4 dxe4 17 ♖xe4 ♘xe5 18 dxe5?? (18 ♖xe5+ maintained the attack) 18...♘xe4! 19 exd6 ♗d4+ 0-1, Svendsen-Downey, corr. 1993.

7...♗xf5

a) 7...♖g8 is a real computer move, although it may be best, objectively, 8 0-0 (8 dxe4 dxe4 9 ♕xd8+ ♔xd8 10 ♗f7 ♖h8 11 ♗b3 is simple, and effective) 8...♗xf5 9 dxe4 ♗xe4? (9...dxe4! leads to a playable position) 10 ♘c3 ♕d6 11 ♗f4 ♕c5 12 ♗f7 ♖h8 13 ♖e1 and Black has no answer to the attack along the e-file, Risc 2500-Chess Genius 3, Liebert 1993.

b) 7...exd3?!, Black should not open the e-file with his king in such a state, 8 cxd3 (8 0-0!? ♗xf5 9 ♖e1! dxc2 10 ♘f7+ ♔d7 11 ♕f3 cxb1=♕ 12 ♖xb1 and Black is lost, Harper-Pape, corr. 1990) 8...♗xf5 9 ♘f7 ♗g4?! (9...♕e8 10 ♕e2+ ♗e6 11 ♗g5 g6 12 ♘xh8 gxh5 13 f4 ♗g7 14 f5 ♔d7 is slightly better) 10 f3 ♗xh5 11 ♘xd8 ♔xd8 12 0-0 and Black's compensation for the queen is woefully inadequate, Martinez-Thomsen, Copenhagen 1982.

8 ♗g5

By far the most common move here, despite the fact that 8 ♘f7! wins outright: 8...♕e8 9 ♗g5 g6 10 ♘xh8 gxh5 (10...exd3 11 0-0 dxc2 12 ♕xd5 is also hopeless) 11 ♘c3 c6 12 dxe4 dxe4 13 ♕d4 ♗g7 14 ♕b4+ ♔e6 15 ♕xb7 and Black's position is in ruins, Malmström-Vitols, corr. 1994/95.

8...♗e6!

Other, inferior moves:

a) 8...♕d6 9 ♘f7 ♕b4+ (9...♕e6!?) 10 ♗d2 ♕xb2 11 ♗c3 ♕b6 12 ♘xh8 d4 13 dxe4 +/- Stummer-Harper, corr. 1991.

b) 8...g6? 9 dxe4 ♗xe4 10 f3! (even simpler than 10 ♗f3 ♕d6 11 ♘g4 ♘bd7 [11...♗g7 12 ♘c3 ♗xf3 13 ♕xf3 ♕e6+ {13...c6, then 14 0-0-0 ♘bd7 transposes to 11...♘bd7} 14 ♔f1 ♕a6+ 15 ♔g1 ♘bd7 16 ♘xd5+, crushing, Stummer-Krongraf, corr. 1990] 12 ♘c3 ♗xf3 13 ♕xf3 c6 14 0-0-0 ♗g7 15 ♖he1+ ♔f7 16 ♘e4! dxe4 17 ♖xe4 ♕c7 18 ♖xd7+ 1-0, Kühn-Leisebein, East Germany 1982) 10...♕d6 11 ♘g4 ♘bd7 12 fxe4 gxh5 13 ♘xf6 ♘xf6 14 0-0 ♗g7 15 e5 1-0, Radovic-Pape, email 1998.

9 dxe4 dxe4 10 ♘c3 ♕d6 11 ♘g4 h6 12 ♘xf6 ♕xd1+ 13 ♖xd1 gxf6 14 ♗f4 f5 15 ♘d5+ ♗xd5 16 ♖xd5

For once material is balanced, but White has a clear positional advantage, Stummer-Chmilewski, corr. 1991.

A4 5...♗c5?!

Tempting, but it now seems that this is dubious because of the exposed position of the bishop.

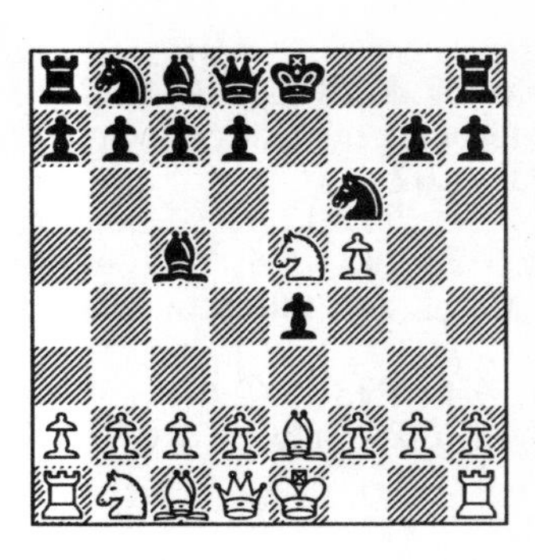

6 ♗h5+

6 d4 should amount to the same, 6...exd3 7 ♘xd3 ♗b6 8 0-0? (the last chance for 8 ♗h5+ transposing) 8...0-0 9 ♘c3 d5 10 ♗f3 c6 11 ♗g5 ♗xf5 12 ♗h4 ♘bd7 Roach-French, corr. 1967/68, Black is already at least equal, and following 13 b3? he could have gained a clear advantage by 13...♗d4.

6...♔f8 7 d4!

Simpler than 7 ♘f7 ♕e8 8 ♘xh8 (8 g4?! ♘xh5 9 ♘xh8 ♘f4) 8...♕xh5 (8...♘xh5!? is also possible, 9 ♕e2 d5 10 d4 ♗b6 11 ♘c3?! [11 g4 ♘f6 12 g5 is more to the point] 11...♔g8! 12 ♘xd5 ♔xh8, unclear, Stummer-Schirmer, corr. 1991) 9 ♕xh5 ♘xh5 10 d3? (the standard 10 g4 ♘f6 11 g5 ♘g4 12 ♘c3 asks more questions of Black) 10...exd3 11 cxd3 ♘f6 with advantage to Black, Vitols-Krauklis, Latvia 1970, as at some point Black will play ...♔g8xh8 with two pieces for a rook.

7...exd3 8 ♘xd3 ♗b6

8...♕e7+ changes little, 9 ♗e2 and: 9...♗b6 10 0-0 d6 11 g4!? h5? (11...♘c6) 12 ♘f4! +/- Koser-Evans, corr. 1993; or 9...d5 10 ♘xc5 ♕xc5 11 ♗d3 (11 ♗e3, Eidan-Oren, corr. 1990, 11...♕b4+ 12 ♘c3 ♗xf5) 11...♔f7 12 0-0 with advantage, Auerbach/Tauber-Antoniadi/Eliascheff, Paris 1917.

9 0-0 ♘c6 10 ♗g5 d6 11 ♖e1

Menacing the black queen.

11...♗d7

11...♘e7 12 ♘e5 ♗e6? (12...♘xh5 13 ♘c6!) 13 ♘g4 ♘xg4 14 ♗xg4 1-0, Stimpson-Hall, corr. 1971.

12 ♘f4 ♘e5 13 ♘d5

With a large plus, Koser-Hansson, corr. 1992.

B 4 ♕e2

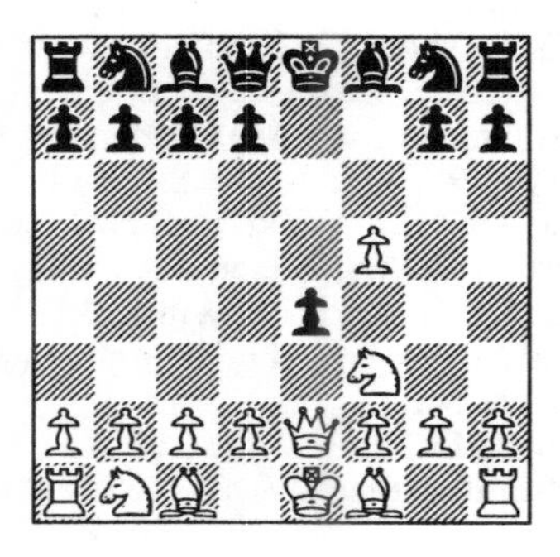

4...♕e7

The move 4...d5 is more in keeping with gambit play, but White can gain an appreciable advantage: 5 d3 (5 ♘d4?! is less logical, and was severely punished in Bertin-Destrebecq, corr. 1978, 5...♘f6 6 f3 c5 7 ♕b5+? [7 ♘e6 ♗xe6 8 fxe6 ♘c6! 9 fxe4? {9 c3} 9...♘d4 10 ♕d1 ♘xe4 and the threat of ...♕h4+ is decisive] 7...♗d7! 8 ♕xb7 cxd4 9 ♕xa8 ♕c7 10 ♘a3? [10 a4 is the only chance, so that 10...♗c6? can be met by 11 ♗b5, but 10...♗d6 is still very good for Black] 10...♗xa3 11 bxa3 ♗c6 ∓ and 11...0-0 may be even stronger, objectively) 5...♘f6 (5...♗xf5!? 6 dxe4 [6 ♘d4 is also tempting, 6...♕d7 and, instead of 7 f3?! ♗g6 8 fxe4 dxe4 9 ♘b3 ♕e7 10 dxe4 ♕h4+ 11 g3 ♕xe4 12 ♗g2 ♕xe2+ 13 ♔xe2 with equality, Müller-Wynia, corr. 1982, 7 ♘xf5 ♕xf5 8 ♘d2 ♘f6 9 f3 wins a pawn, although 9...♘c6 gives Black a lead in development as compensation] 6...dxe4 7 ♘c3 [7 ♕b5+?! ♗d7 8 ♕xb7 {8 ♕h5+ g6 9 ♕e5+ ♕e7 10 ♕xh8 exf3+ 11 ♗e3 ♘f6 is not that clear, the white queen is trapped} 8...♗c6?, Greenwalt-Wall, Dayton 1983, {8...exf3! 9 ♕xa8 ♗c6 is much stronger} 9 ♗b5 ♗xb5 10 ♕xb5+ c6 11 ♕e2 with advantage] 7...♘f6 8 ♗g5 ♗e7 [8...♗b4!? 9 ♕b5+ ♘c6 10 ♕xf5 exf3 11 ♕xf3 ♕e7+ is more interesting] 9 ♘d2 with a small advantage Radikevich-Khavin, Kiev 1937) 6 dxe4 (this is more accurate than the more common 6 ♘c3?! ♗b4 7 dxe4 [7 ♗d2?! 0-0 8 dxe4 ♗xc3 9 ♗xc3 ♘xe4 and Black enjoys a very pleasant position, e.g. 10 0-0-0 {10 ♗e5?! ♘c6 11 0-0-0 ♖e8 leaves Black well on top, Wild-Buchicchio, Saint Vincent Italian Ch (corr.) 1999} 10...♘xc3 11 bxc3 ♗xf5 12 ♕b5, Svendsen-Jackson, corr. 1987, 12...♗e4 White's weakened king position must surely favour Black] 7...♘xe4 8 ♗g5?! [8 ♘g5 is possible, 8...♗xc3+ 9 bxc3 0-0 10 ♘xe4 dxe4 11 ♕xe4! ♘c6 {if 11...♖e8 12 ♗c4+ ♔h8 13 ♗e6} 12 ♗c4+ ♔h8 13 ♗e6 White might just be able to claim an edge] 8...♗xc3+ 9 bxc3 ♕d7! 10 ♘d2 [10 f6 0-0 11 fxg7 ♕xg7 12 ♗d2 ♗g4 hands Black a dangerous initiative] 10...0-0!? 11 ♘xe4 ♕xf5! 12 ♘f6+ gxf6 13 ♗h6 ♖d8 14 ♕e7 ♕e5+ 15 ♕xe5 fxe5, Landgraf-Stummer, corr. 1990, Black's superior pawn structure outweighs White's bishop pair) 6...dxe4 7 ♘c3 ♗b4 8 ♗d2 ♗xc3 (8...0-0!? 9 ♕c4+ ♔h8 10 ♕xb4 ♘c6 11 ♕c5 exf3 12 0-0-0 is also better for White; 8...♗xf5? 9 ♕b5+) 9 ♗xc3 ♗xf5 (9...♕d5!? 10 ♖d1 ♕xf5 11 ♘d4 [11 ♗xf6 gxf6 12

♖d4 is possibly even better] 11...♕c5 12 ♕b5+ ♕xb5 13 ♘xb5 with a clear advantage in the endgame, Destrebecq-Kozlov, corr. 1992) 10 ♘d4 ♗d7 11 0-0-0 with advantage, Destrebecq-Malmström, corr. 1991. Also, 4...♘f6 5 d3 d5 transposes to the above.

5 ♘d4

The odd move 5 ♘g1?! was first played by Borrmann, 5...d5 6 ♘c3 (6 d3 ♗xf5 [6...exd3 7 ♕xe7+ ♘xe7 8 ♗xd3 ♗xf5 is a simple alternative] 7 dxe4 ♕xe4 8 ♘c3 ♗b4 9 ♗d2 ♕xe2+ 10 ♗xe2 ♘f6, quite level, Jackson-Oren, corr. 1994/97) 6...c6 7 ♕h5+ ♕f7 8 ♕xf7+ ♔xf7 9 f3 (9 d3 offers a little plus) 9...exf3 10 ♘xf3 ♗xf5, Black has no problems, Borrmann-Destrebecq, corr. 1990.

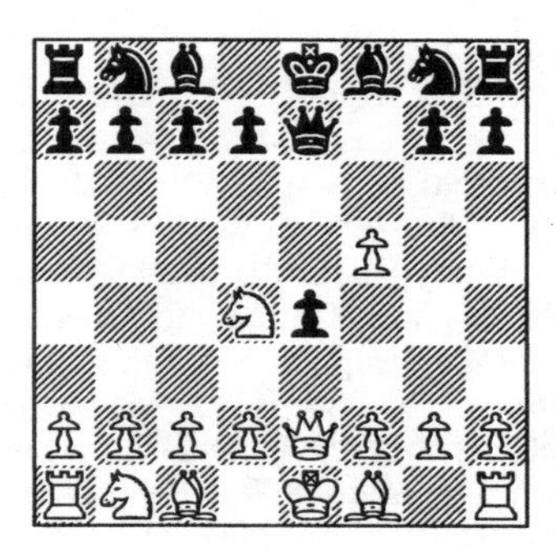

5...♘c6!

Aiming for a speedy development. Other moves are:

a) 5...♘f6!? 6 d3! (the most testing: 6 ♘c3 is inaccurate, 6...d5! [6...c5?! 7 ♘db5 d5 8 d3! transposes to 5...c5; no one has taken up my idea of 6...♘c6!? here, which is similar to 5...♘c6 except that White can no longer play ♕h5+: 7 ♘xc6 [7 ♘db5? d5 and ...a6 ∓, transposes into the Logunov-Kozlov game in the main line, note to move six] 7...dxc6 8 g4 h5! 9 g5 ♘d5 10 ♘xe4 ♗xf5 11 d3 0-0-0 with very good strategical compensation for the pawn, indeed. As any King's Gambit player will know, White's backward f-pawn is quite useless] 7 d3 ♕e5! transposes below) 6...d5 (or 6...exd3?! 7 ♕xe7+ ♗xe7 8 ♗xd3 0-0 9 0-0 with advantage, Bray-Candeias, Portugal 1997; 6...c5? 7 ♘b5 d5 8 ♗f4 [8 ♘1c3 is also good, transposing into 5...c5?!, but this is completely clear] 8...♘a6 9 ♘d6+ ♔d8 10 dxe4 ♘xe4 11 ♘xe4 ♕xe4 12 ♕xe4 dxe4 13 ♘c3 ♗xf5 14 0-0-0+ ♔e8 15 ♗xa6 bxa6 16 ♘xe4 ♗xe4 17 ♖he1 leading to a swift end, Clarke-Evans, corr. 1994/95; 6...♘c6!? 7 ♘xc6 dxc6 8 ♗g5 [8 dxe4 is critical] 8...♗xf5 9 ♘c3 exd3 10 ♕xe7+ ♗xe7 11 ♗xd3 ♗xd3 12 cxd3 0-0-0 is fairly level, Goncalves-Krustkains, corr. 1985) 7 dxe4! (7 ♘c3 ♕e5! 8 ♘e6 ♗xe6 9 fxe6 ♘c6 [9...♗b4! 10 ♗d2 ♘c6 is right, with approximate equality] 10 dxe4 ♘d4? [10...♗b4 is best, again] 11 ♕d1?! [11 f4! ♕xe6 12 ♘b5 ♘xe2 13 ♘xc7+ ♔f7 14 ♘xe6 ♘xc1 15 ♘g5+] 11...dxe4 [it will be no surprise to the astute reader that 11...♗b4 is again best!] 12 ♘e2?! 0-0-0 and Black has the better chances, Garcia Martinez-Busom, Barcelona 1995) 7...♕xe4 (7...♘xe4!?) 8 ♘c3 ♗b4 9 ♗d2 ♕xe2+ 10 ♗xe2 0-0 11 0-0 c5!? 12 ♘e6 ♗xe6 13 fxe6 ♖e8, Bitter-Legouhy, Val Maubuze 1990, and now 14 ♗f3 ♘c6 (14...♗xc3? 15 ♗xc3 ♘e4 16 ♖ad1) 15 ♖fe1 ♘d4 16 ♖ad1 maintains a plus.

b) 5...♕e5?!, Black can ill afford the luxury of another queen move, but it is surprisingly popular, 6 ♘b5 ♘c6? (objectively, this is losing, as is 6...a6?? 7 d4 ♕d5 8 ♘xc7+ Elburg-Kott, corr. 1991; 6...♘a6! is the only try, c7 must be defended 7 f3! [7 d4?! ♕xf5 8 f3 d5 9 ♘d2 ♘f6 10 g4?! ♕g6 11 g5 ♕xg5 12 ♘xe4 ♕h4+ 13 ♕f2 ♕xf2+ Destrebecq-Downey, training game 1993 ∓] 7...d5 8 fxe4 dxe4 9 g4 h5 [9...♗e7?! fails to cause the least irritation: 10 ♗g2 ♗h4+ 11 ♔d1 ♘f6?! 12 d4! ♕e7 13 g5 winning more material] 10 ♘1c3 hxg4 11 d4 ♕xf5 12 ♘xe4 ♗e6? [12...♔d8 has to be played] 13 ♘g3 winning, Malmström-Reinke, corr. 1994/95, as 13...♕d5 14 ♗g2 ♕c4 15 ♗xb7). Now we have:

b1) 7 ♘1c3 ♘f6 8 f4! ♕xf5 (or the invariably played 8...♕xf4 transposing to 7 f4? ♕xf4 8 ♘1c3 ♘f6?, above) 9 ♘xc7+ (9 g4 ♘xg4 10 ♗h3 is also convincing) 9...♔d8 10 ♘xa8 d5 with some vague practical chances for Black, although objectively speaking he is quite lost! 10...♘d4 11 ♕c4.

b2) 7 f4? is worse, 7...♕xf4 8 ♘1c3 ♘f6? (White is also winning after 8...♕xf5? 9 ♘xc7+ ♔d8 10 ♘xa8 ♘d4, Black is relying on this counter-shot, but it amounts to little, 11 ♕c4! ♗c5 [11...♘xc2+?? 12 ♔d1 ♘xa1 13 ♕c7+ 1-0, Svendsen-Schirmer, corr. 1992] 12 b4 ♘xc2+ 13 ♔d1 ♘xb4 14 ♘xe4 and Black is crushed, Destrebecq-Borrmann, corr. 1990; but 8...♔d8! avoids losing a rook, 9 ♘d5 ♕xf5 10 ♘bxc7 ♖b8 and Black is doing alright!) 9 d3 (alternatively, 9 d4!? ♕xf5 10 ♘xc7+ ♔d8 11 ♘xa8 d5? [11...♘xd4 12 ♕d2 ♗c5 13 ♘d1 ♖e8 14 ♘e3! ♘f3+ 15 gxf3 ♗xe3 16 ♕d6 would at least have given White some moves to make, although Black's attack seems to have fizzled-out, anyway] 12 ♗e3, Black is quite lost, Destrebecq-Jackson, corr. 1990) 9...♕e5 (9...♕xf5? 10 ♘xc7+ ♔d8 11 ♘xa8 ♘d4 12 dxe4 ♕e5 [12...♘xe4? 13 ♕xe4! ♘xc2+ 14 ♔d1 ♕xe4 15 ♘xe4 ♘xa1 16 ♗f4 1-0 Landgraf-Spiegel, corr. 1990, the white knight will escape, but not the black one] 13 ♕d3 ♗c5 14 g3 d5 15 ♗f4 Black can resign with a clear conscience, Gåård-Magee, corr. 1989) 10 ♘xe4 ♘xe4 11 ♕xe4 and Black is 'only' a pawn down with a rotten position, not bad for this line! Elburg-Müller, corr. 1991.

b3) However the unplayed 7 d4! just wins on the spot, and renders the rest of this note quite irrelevant! i.e. 7...♘xd4 (7...exd3 8 ♘xc7+ ♔d8 9 ♕xe5 ♘xe5 10 ♘xa8 dxc2 11 ♘c3) 8 f4 ♘xe2 9 fxe5 ♘xc1 10 ♘xc7+ ♔d8 11 ♘xa8 and, as both knights are trapped, White will find himself an exchange to the good, 11...b6 12 ♘c3 ♗b7 13 ♖xc1 ♗xa8 14 ♖d1 etc.

c) 5...c5?! 6 ♘b5 (6 ♕h5+?! ♔d8 7 ♘b5 transposes; 6 ♕c4?! is too artificial, 6...♘a6 7 ♘b3 ♘f6 8 ♘c3 ♘c7 [8...♘b4! 9 ♔d1 d5] 9 ♗e2?! [9 ♕a4] 9...d5 10 ♕a4+ ♗d7 and White has failed to deal with Black's imposing centre, and is worse, Niveau-Rogalski) 6...d5 7 ♘1c3! (best, 7 ♕h5+?! is a waste of time, 7...♔d8 8 ♘1c3 ♘f6 9 ♕g5 a6 10 ♘a3 b5 11 ♘ab1 ♘c6 and Black's space advantage is almost decisive, 12 g4? ♘e5 13 ♗e2, Böhm-Diepstraten, Hilversum 1993, 13...d4, winning a piece; 7 d3 White plays to break-up the black centre, 7...a6 8 ♘5c3 [if 8 ♗g5, Swaffield-Bullockus, corr. 1972, then 8...♕xg5! 9 ♘c7+ ♔f7 10 ♘xa8 ♕c1+ 11 ♕d1 ♕xb2 12 ♘d2 exd3 13 ♗xd3 ♕e5+ with plenty of play] 8...exd3 9 cxd3 ♘f6 10 ♗g5 ♘bd7 11 ♘d2 b5 [11...d4? 12 ♘ce4 with advantage, Bajović-Caroff, Metz Open 1988] 12 0-0-0, Destrebecq-Nyman, corr. 1991, 12...♔f7 13 ♖e1

♕xe2 14 ♗xe2 ♗d6 with fair play for the pawn) 7...♘f6 8 d3 a6 9 dxe4! axb5 (or 9...dxe4? 10 ♗f4! axb5 11 ♘xb5 ♘d5? 12 ♗d6 ♕f7 13 ♕xe4+ ♔d8 14 0-0-0 1-0, Destrebecq-Strautins, corr. 1991) 10 e5 d4?! (Destrebecq analyses 10...b4 11 exf6 ♕xe2+ 12 ♘xe2 ♗xf5 13 ♘f4! ♘c6 14 ♘xd5 0-0-0 15 ♘e3 with advantage; 10...♘bd7 might be the best try, 11 ♗f4 ♖a5 12 exf6 ♘xf6 with a white advantage) 11 exf6?! (11 ♘xb5! is very strong, 11...♘d5 12 ♘d6+ ♔d7 [12...♔d8? 13 ♗g5] 13 ♘f7! ♖g8 14 ♗g5 winning) 11...♕xe2+ 12 ♘xe2 ♗xf5 13 ♘g3 ♗xc2 14 ♗xb5+ ♘c6 15 fxg7 ♗xg7, Destrebecq-Krustkalns, corr. 1991, and Black has almost sufficient compensation.

6 ♘xc6

6 ♘b5?! d5 7 ♘1c3 (on 7 d4 ♗xf5 8 ♗f4 ♖c8 9 ♘1c3 ♘f6 10 0-0-0 a6, the knight is obliged to retreat, and Black already has the upper hand, De Jong-Oren, corr. 1994/95; 7 ♕h5+ ♔d8 achieves little) 7...♘f6 8 d3 a6 9 ♘a3 ♘d4 10 ♕e3 ♘xf5 White is in trouble, Logunov-Kozlov, corr. 1993; 6 ♕h5+ ♔d8 7 ♘xc6+ dxc6 transposes.

6...dxc6

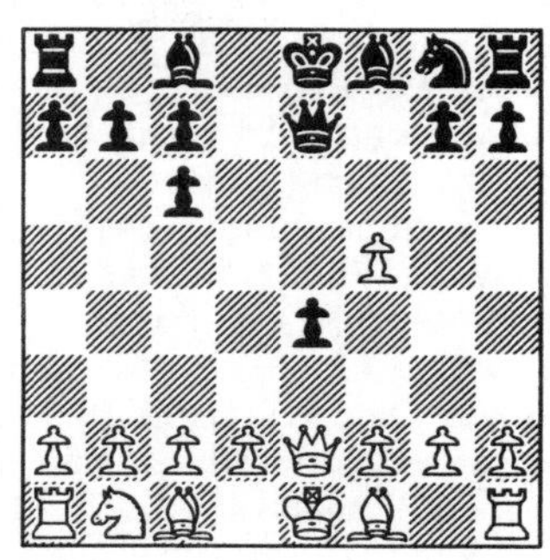

7 ♕h5+

This uses valuable time, but:

a) 7 d3?! seems too acquiescent: 7...♗xf5 8 dxe4 ♗xe4!? (8...♕xe4 9 ♕xe4+ ♗xe4 equalises immediately, 10 c3 ♗c5 11 ♘d2 ♘f6 12 ♗e2 0-0-0 13 ♘xe4 ♘xe4 14 0-0, Oren-Reinke, corr. 1994/97, when 14...♔b8 15 ♗f3 ♖he8 16 ♗f4 a5 favours Black) 9 c3 (9 ♘c3?! ♗xc2 10 ♗e3 ♗g6 11 ♖d1 ♘f6 leaves White without sufficient compensation for the pawn, Jackson-Gåård, corr. 1994/97) 9...0-0-0 10 ♗e3 ♘f6 11 ♘d2 (if 11 ♗xa7 then Black obtains plenty of play by 11...♖e8 12 ♗e3 ♗xb1 13 ♖xb1 ♘d5) 11...♗g6 12 h3 ♔b8 13 ♕f3 ♘e4 14 ♘xe4 ♗xe4 15 ♕e2 ♕f7 with a nice position, Destrebecq-Gaard, corr. 1992.

b) 7 ♘c3 ♗xf5 8 g4! ♗g6!? (8...♗e6 9 ♗g2 ♘f6 10 g5 ♘d5 11 ♕xe4 0-0-0 may be superior) 9 h4?! (9 ♗g2 ♘f6 [or 9...0-0-0 10 ♗xe4 ♕f7 11 d3 ♗b4] 10 g5 ♘d5 11 ♗xe4 ♗xe4 12 ♘xe4 is critical) 9...h6 (9...h5!?) 10 ♗g2 ♘f6 11 g5 ♘d5 and Black is fine, Jensen-Clarke, corr. 1992, as, this time 12 ♗xe4 ♗xe4 13 ♘xe4 is followed by 13...hxg5 14 ♘xg5 ♘b4.

7...♔d8 8 ♘c3

8 ♗e2 ♘f6 9 ♕g5 h6 10 ♕e3 ♗xf5 11 0-0 ♘d5 12 ♕d4 ♕d6 13 d3 ♘b4! (an ending would suit Black fine) 14 ♕c3 exd3 15 cxd3 the black king looks less exposed now 15...♗e7 16 a3 (16 ♕xg7? ♗f6 and ...♘c2 wins material) 16...♘d5 with good play, Psomiddis-Hector, Katerini 1992.

8...♘f6 9 ♕g5 ♕e5! 10 ♗c4

10 ♗e2 h6 11 ♕g3 ♕xf5?! (11...♕xg3 12 hxg3 ♗xf5 is simple, and good) 12 d3 ♗d6 13 dxe4 (13 ♕xg7! ♖h7 14 dxe4) 13...♘xe4 14 ♕h4+ ♘f6 15 ♗d3 ♖e8+ 16 ♘e2 ♕d5 17 0-0 ♗f5, play is balanced, Malmström-Heap, corr. 1994/95.

10...h6 11 ♕g3 ♕xf5?!

Latvian Gambit players like to keep queens on the board, but, as in the previous note, 11...♕xg3 12 hxg3 ♗xf5 is objectively strongest, when Black may even be better.

12 d3 ♗d6 13 ♕xg7! ♖h7 14 dxe4

Malmström-Grobe, corr. 1994/95, 14...♖xg7 15 exf5 ♖xg2, White has an edge.

C 4 ♘d4

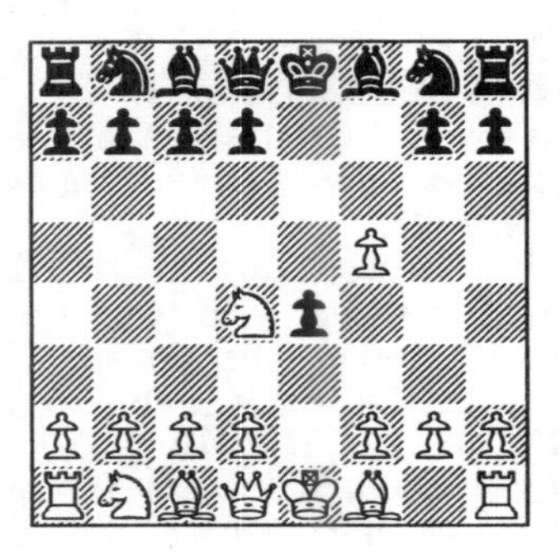

This momentarily defends the f5-pawn, but on d4 the knight is a target for the black pieces.

4...♕f6

This strange queen move is the most popular, and leads to interesting positions, but the mundane 4...♘f6 may be stronger:

a) 5 d3 c5 (5...♕e7 6 ♕e2 transposes into 4 ♕e2) 6 ♘b5 (the 6 ♘b3 of Schiro-Krumins, USA 1973, is best countered by 6...exd3 7 ♗xd3 d5 8 ♗b5+ ♔f7 9 ♗e2 [9 0-0 ♗xf5 is possible, as 9...c4? 10 ♗xc4] 9...♗xf5 10 0-0 ♘c6 11 ♗f4 ♗d6 the game is level, Jackson-Stummer, corr. 1994/95; 6 ♘e2!? may be the best square, 6...d5?! [6...exd3 7 ♕xd3 d5 is simpler] 7 dxe4 ♘xe4, Baas-Diepstraten, Hilversum 1993, 8 ♘f4 ♘f6 9 ♗b5+ ♘c6 10 ♕e2+ is a little awkward) 6...a6 7 ♘5c3 d5? (7...exd3 8 ♗xd3 d5 gives Black a strong, mobile centre, e.g. 9 g4?! c4! and ...d4) 8 dxe4 dxe4 9 ♕xd8+, Downey-Heap, corr. 1992.

b) 5 ♗c4? is the sort of 'obvious' move that White players often choose, after 5...c5 6 ♘b3 d5 7 ♗b5+ (following 7 ♗f1?! ♗xf5 Black already had a clear advantage in Kugler-Farwing, Hamburg 1959) 7...♘c6 (7...♔f7! is possibly even stronger, as ...c4 is threatened, cutting off the bishop's retreat) 8 ♗xc6+ bxc6 9 g4?! a5 10 d4 exd3 11 cxd3 a4 12 ♘3d2 ♕e7+, Daikeler-Sneiders, corr. 1987, and now White had to play 13 ♔f1 to stay in the game.

c) 5 ♗e2, the check on h5 will at least cause Black's king to lose his castling rights, 5...♗c5!? 6 ♗h5+ (or 6 ♘b3 ♗b6 7 0-0?! [7 ♗h5+ ♔f8 causes Black more inconvenience] 7...0-0 8 d4 d5 9 ♗e3 ♗xf5 Black's position is more pleasant, Rabson-Lee, London 1983) 6...♔f8 (6...g6? 7 fxg6 0-0, Simon-Eberth, Felsonyarad 1985, is far too ambitious, 8 ♘f5! and if 8...d5 9 g7 wins the exchange) 7 ♘b3 ♗b6, unclear.

d) 5 f3?! c5?! (5...♗c5 6 ♘b3 ♕e7 appears promising, as 7 ♘xc5 is answered by the Zwichenzug 7...exf3+) 6 ♘b3 d5 7 g4?, Sawyer-Hubbard, corr. 1968, can be countered by, amongst others, 7...c4 (or 7...♘c6 threatening ...c4) 8 ♘d4 ♗c5 when White is in trouble, e.g. 9 ♘e6?? ♗xe6 10 fxe6 ♘xg4.

e) 5 ♘c3 c5 6 ♘b3 d5 7 d3 exd3 8 ♕xd3 (8 cxd3 ♗xf5 9 ♗e2 is already better for Black, Rantanen-Molander, Finland 1993) 8...♕e7+ 9 ♕e2 ♗xf5 10 ♕xe7+ ♗xe7 and Black has no problems, Schroder-Hufschild, Strelasund 1997.

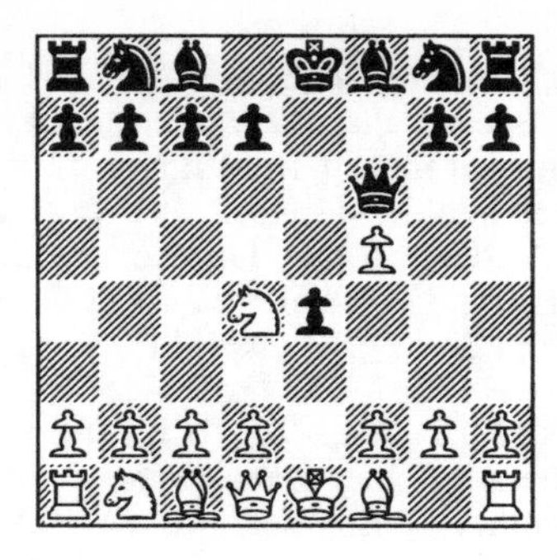

5 c3

The strongest reply, maintaining the knight in the centre.

a) The queen check is certainly too risky here: 5 ♕h5+?! g6 6 fxg6 hxg6 7 ♕d5 ♘e7 8 ♕xe4 (Betinš gives an amusing line: 8 ♕c4 d5 9 ♕c3 ♗g7 10 ♘b5 ♕f7!? 11 ♘xc7+ ♔d8 12 ♕c5 ♘d7! 13 ♕d6 ♗e5 14 ♕e6! ♕g7 15 ♘xd5 [15 ♘xa8? ♘f8 wins the queen!] 15...♘xd5 16 ♕xd5 ♗xb2 17 ♗xb2 ♕xb2 18 ♕a5+? [18 ♕g5+ ♔e8 19 ♕xg6+ draws] 18...b6 19 ♕c3 ♕c1+ 20 ♔e2 ♗a6+ winning) 8...♖h4 9 g4 d5 10 ♕d3 ♖xg4 11 c3 ♘bc6 12 ♗e2 ♘e5 13 ♕e3 ♖e4 (13...c5 14 ♗xg4 ♗xg4 -+) 14 ♕g3 ♗g4 15 f4 ♗xe2? (15...♕a6! wins on the spot) 16 ♘xe2, Evans-Grivainis, Munich 1958, and eventually the American Grandmaster managed to play himself out of the hole he'd gotten into.

b) However, first 5 ♘b5 ♘a6 and then 6 ♕h5+ is possible: 6...g6 7 fxg6 hxg6 8 ♕e2 d5 9 d3 ♗f5 10 dxe4 dxe4 11 g4 ♗e6 12 ♕xe4 0-0-0 13 g5, probably best, (13 ♘xa7+? ♔b8 14 ♗xa6 ♗d5 15 ♕a4 ♗xh1 16 ♗e2 ♗c5 17 ♗e3 ♗xe3 18 fxe3 ♖xh2 0-1, Hansen-Pape, Denmark 1986; 13 ♗g5? ♕xg5 14 ♕xe6+ ♔b8 is also wrong) 13...♗d5! 14 gxf6 (14 ♕g4+ ♕f5 15 ♕xf5+ gxf5 16 ♖g1 ♖e8+ 17 ♗e2 ♖xe2+ 18 ♔xe2 ♗c4+ is also unclear) 14...♗xe4 15 ♖g1 ♘xf6 16 ♘1c3?! ♘b4 and White is in trouble, Romanenko-Dreibergs, USA 1952.

5...c5!?

a) 5...♘e7?! 6 d3 (6 ♕g4!? d5 7 d3 ♘xf5?! [7...♗xf5 8 ♘xf5 ♕xf5 is not too bad for Black] 8 dxe4 ♘d6, Dimmeler-Brunold, Germany 1988, when, 9 ♕h5+ g6 10 ♕xd5 c6 11 ♕g5 leaves White well in charge) 6...♘xf5 7 dxe4 ♘xd4 8 cxd4 ♗b4+ 9 ♘c3, Jackson-Downey, corr. 1987, and White has a strong centre and an extra pawn!

b) 5...♘c6?! is quite common: 6 ♘xc6 (6 ♘b5 ♕e5 7 ♕e2 ♔d8 8 ♘5a3 ♕xf5 led to a mutually difficult position in Downey-Krantz, corr. 1992) 6...dxc6 7 ♕h5+ g6 (this gives more practical chances than 7...♕f7 8 ♕xf7+ ♔xf7 9 g4 h5 10 ♗c4+ ♔f6 11 d3! exd3 12 f3 with advantage Downey-Melchor, corr. 1992) 8 fxg6 hxg6 9 ♕e2 ♗e6 10 ♕xe4 0-0-0 11 d4 ♗d6? (following the better 11...♖e8 12 ♗e3 ♗d6 Black has little compensation for the pawn) 12 ♗g5! ♕xg5 13 ♕xe6+ ♔b8 with advantage Downey-Elburg, corr. 1990.

6 ♘b5 ♕e5

6...♕xf5!? is difficult to believe, nevertheless: 7 ♘c7+ ♔d8 8 ♘xa8 ♘f6 9 ♗b5? (9 d4) 9...a6 10 ♗e2 b5 11 ♘b6 ♗b7 12 a4 ♔c7 13 a5 c4 14 b4 cxb3 15 ♕xb3 ♗c5 16 0-0 ♘c6 17 ♕a2?, White should do something about Black's growing initiative, 17...♘e5 18 ♗a3 ♘f3+!, ripping open the white king's defences, Downey-Diepstraten, corr. 1993.

7 ♗e2

7 ♕e2! ♘a6 8 g4 ♘f6 9 d3 is very good for White, Downey-Borrmann, corr. 1988.

7...a6

7...♘f6 8 d4 exd3 9 ♕xd3 a6?? (9...d5) 10 f4 1-0, Jackson-Borrmann, corr. 1988, Black will lose a rook; 7...♘a6 8 d4 exd3 9 ♕xd3 d5 is a reasonable line.

8 d4 exd3

8...♕xf5?? 9 ♘c7+ 1-0, Downey-Grobe, corr. 1989.

9 f4 ♕xe2+ 10 ♕xe2+ dxe2 11 ♘c7+ ♔d8 12 ♘xa8 b5 13 ♘b6 ♗b7 14 a4 ♔c7 15 a5 ♗xg2 16 ♖g1 ♗f3

...seems very playable for Black.

D 4 ♘g1!?

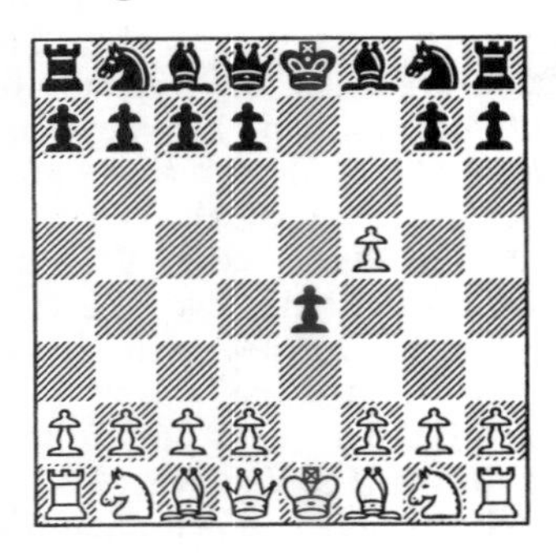

A bizarre idea of the German player Bücker, played with the intention of hanging on to his extra f-pawn. Black is forced to play a King's Gambit accepted with colours reversed, and with the e-pawn slightly further advanced.

4...♘f6

I suppose that any move played in the King's Gambit is also quite playable here, too. Some examples:

a) 4...♕f6?! and:

a1) 5 ♕h5+! g6 6 fxg6 hxg6 7 ♕e2 (7 ♕d5? runs into trouble: 7...♖h5! [7...♖h7!? is also interesting, 8 ♕xg8?! {8 ♘c3!?} 8...♖f7, trapping the queen, 9 ♘h3 d5 10 ♗b5+ c6, Diepstraten, 11 ♗e2 ♗e6! Schiller] 8 ♕xg8 [8 ♕b3 might be the safest, 8...d5 9 d3 ♗c5, Schiller; 8 ♕c4 d5 9 ♕xc7 ♘c6 10 ♗b5 ♗c5 it is clear that the white pieces have strayed too far from home, f2 is undefendable, 11 ♘e2 {11 ♕g3 ♖g5 12 ♕h4 ♖xg2 is also good for Black; 11 f3 ♗b6 12 ♕g3 ♖g5 13 ♕h4 ♖xg2 likewise} 11...♕xf2+ 12 ♔d1 ♘ge7 13 ♕g3 ♕f6 14 ♕e1 ♗d7 15 ♖f1 ♕e5 16 h3 0-0-0 and the white pieces make for a comical picture, Pohl-Wegelin, corr. 1990] 8...d5—forcing White to jettison material in order to extricate his queen—9 g4 ♗xg4 [9...♗e6? 10 ♕xf8+ ♕xf8 11 gxh5] 10 ♗h3 ♗xh3 11 ♘xh3 ♘c6! 12 ♘f4 else ...♘e7 12...♕xf4 13 ♕xg6+ ♕f7 14 ♕xf7+ ♔xf7 15 d3 exd3 16 cxd3, Krongraf-Magee, corr. 1990, 16...♘b4 -/+) 7...♖h5 (7...♖h7?! turned into a fiasco: 8 ♘c3 ♕e5? 9 ♘f3 ♕a5 10 d3 ♗b4 11 ♗d2 d5 12 dxe4 +/- Magee-Nolden, corr. 1991; but 7...d5 8 d3 also favours White) 8 ♘c3 d5 9 d3 ♗b4 10 ♗d2 ♖e5 11 dxe4 dxe4 12 0-0-0 ♕f5? 13 ♕c4 1-0, Magee-Melchor, corr. 1990.

a2) 5 d3 is also strong, 5...♕xf5 (or 5...d5?! 6 ♕h5+ ♕f7 7 ♕xf7+ ♔xf7 8 dxe4 dxe4 9 ♗c4+ ♔e8 10 ♘e2 ♗xf5 11 ♘bc3 c6?! 12 ♘g3 +/- Stummer-Nolden, corr. 1991) 6 dxe4 (6 ♕e2 wins a pawn, see (b) 6...♕xe4+ 7 ♗e2, Melchor-Jensen, corr. 1993 transposing into 4...♕g5.

a3) 5 g4 h5 6 ♘c3 (6 d3 exd3 7 ♗xd3 hxg4 8 ♕xg4 ♘c6 9 ♘c3?! [9 ♕g6+] 9...♘e5 10 ♕e4 ♘e7 11 ♗f4 ♘xd3+ 12 ♕xd3, Hayward-Gaard, corr. 1990, 12...d6 equal) 6...♕e5 (6...hxg4 7 ♕xg4 ♖h4 8 ♕g6+ ♕xg6 9 fxg6 ♗b4 10 ♗c4 ♘h6 11 ♘d5 ♗d6 and the open h-file gives Black some compensation for the pawn, Hayward-Krantz, corr. 1992) 7 ♕e2 hxg4 8 ♘xe4, Hayward-Tiemann, corr. 1990, and after 8...♘c6 9 ♗g2 ♘d4 10 f4 ♕e7

Black will recapture the f5-pawn, when his knight will be well-placed.

b) 4...♕g5 5 d3 (Black is well placed to meet 5 g4: 5...h5! 6 d3 ♕xg4 [6...♕e7?! 7 ♗e3 hxg4 8 ♕xg4 ♘h6 9 ♕xe4?! {9 ♕g6+ ♘f7 10 ♘c3} 9...d5 10 ♕xe7+ ♗xe7 11 ♘c3 c6 and Black has some play for the pawn, Hayward-Grobe, corr. 1989] 7 ♕xg4 hxg4 8 dxe4 d5! 9 ♗f4 [9 exd5 ♗xf5 10 ♘c3 is critical] 9...dxe4 10 ♗xc7 ♗xf5, unclear, Magee-Sénéchaud, corr. 1990) 5...♕xf5 6 dxe4 (going for quick development, but 6 ♕e2!? [Schiller] 6...♘f6 7 ♘d2 d5 8 f3 seems to win a pawn! 8...e3!? might be Black's best try, e.g. 9 ♕xe3+ ♗e7 10 g3!? ♘c6 11 ♗h3 ♕h5 12 ♗xc8 ♖xc8 with free play in return for the pawn) 6...♕xe4+ (6...♕f7? offers little in return for the pawn: 7 ♗e2 ♗c5 8 ♘f3 d6 9 0-0 ♘f6 10 e5 with advantage, Knorr-Schmidt, corr. 1992) 7 ♗e2 ♘f6 (White has a tidy lead in development, so Black should hasten to castle, 7...d5 8 ♘f3 ♘c6? is too slow: 9 0-0 ♘f6 10 ♘c3 ♕f5 11 ♖e1 ♗e7 12 ♗b5 ♗d7 13 ♗g5 ♔f7 14 ♗d3 ♕g4 15 ♖xe7+! ♔xe7 16 ♘xd5+ 1-0, Magee-Pape, corr. 1991; note that 7...♕xg2?? loses to 8 ♗f3 ♕g6 9 ♗h5) 8 ♘f3 ♗c5 (Otherwise, 8...♗b4+!? is a clever idea, attempting to deprive White of the c3 square, 9 c3 [9 ♗d2 0-0 10 0-0 ♗xd2 11 ♕xd2 c6 12 ♘c3 ♕e8 13 ♖fe1 d5 14 ♗d3 ♕d8 ± Melchor-Jensen, corr. 1993, soon drawn] 9...♗c5 10 b4 ♗b6 11 0-0 0-0 12 a4 c6 13 ♘bd2 ♕g6 14 ♘c4 ♗c7 15 ♘d6 ♘e4, Schirmer-Müller, corr. 1986, 16 ♘xe4 ♕xe4 17 ♗d3 with an edge) 9 0-0 0-0 10 ♘c3 ♕f5 11 ♗d3 (the crude 11 ♗c4+ ♔h8 12 ♘g5!?, Bussmeyer-Stamer, corr. 1988, is best countered by 12...b6! [12...♘g4? 13 ♘f7+ ♖xf7 14 ♗xf7 ♘xf2 15 ♕f3] 13 ♘f7+ [13 ♘b5?! d5! 14 ♘xc7 dxc4 15 ♘xa8 ♘a6 traps the a8-knight; 13 ♗d3!?] 13...♖xf7 14 ♗xf7 ♗a6 which regains the exchange) 11...♕h5 12 ♗c4+ ♔h8 (but White's slight development advantage does not count for much) 13 ♗e3 (13 ♖e1?!, Magem Badals-Knox,London 1987, 13...♘g4 forces 14 ♗e3 ♘xe3 15 fxe3 with Black for preference as 14 ♘e4 allows 14...♘xf2 15 ♘xf2 ♗xf2+ 16 ♔xf2 ♕c5+ 17 ♗e3 ♕xc4) 13...d6 (13...c6 was seen in Leeners-Elburg, corr. 1984) 14 ♘b5!? ♘g4 15 ♖e1? (better 15 ♗xc5 ♕xc5 16 ♕d4) 15...♘xe3 16 fxe3 ♗b6 and e3 is a serious weakness, Borrmann-Leisebein, corr. 1986.

c) or 4...♗e7 5 ♕h5+ ♔f8, unclear,

d) but if 4...♗c5?! 5 ♕h5+ ♔f8 6 f6 looks awkward.

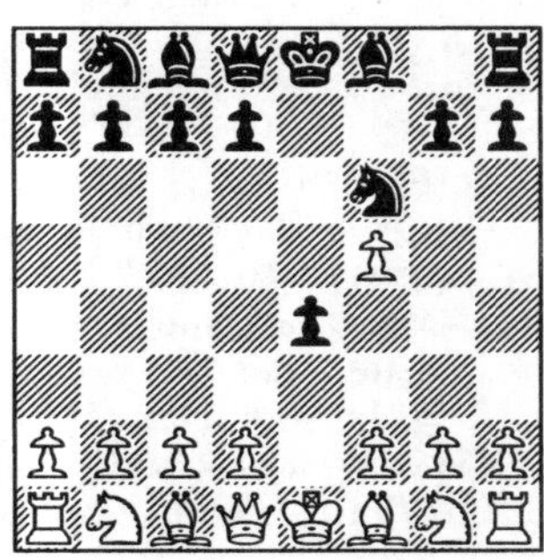

5 g4

Again, by analogy with the King's Gambit, this must be the move to play. Alternatively: 5 d3 ♕e7! (this idea of Kozlov's seems to work better than 5...exd3?! 6 ♗xd3 d5 7 ♕e2+ ♗e7 8 ♘f3 0-0 9 0-0 c5 10 c4! ±, Hergert-Frenzel, corr. 1986; 5...d5 6 dxe4 [Stefan Bücker prefers 6 g4!? exd3 {6...♕e7 7 d4 transposes to 5...♕e7} 7 ♗xd3 ♕e7+

{7...♗c5!? 8 g5!? ♕e7+ 9 ♔f1 ♘e4 10 ♕h5+ ♔d8 is good for Black} 8 ♔f1 ♘c6 {Black hastens to castle queenside, this is simpler than 8...h5!? 9 g5 ♘e4} 9 f3 ♗d7 10 ♘c3 d4 11 ♘e4 ♘e5 12 ♘xf6+ ♕xf6 13 ♗e4 0-0-0, Black has good compensation, as the white kingside is loose, Augustin-Schmidt, corr. 1989] 6...♕e7 [6...dxe4?! 7 ♕xd8+ ♔xd8 8 ♘c3 ♗xf5 9 ♘ge2 ♘bd7 10 ♘g3 {10 ♘d4! gains the bishop pair} 10...♗g6 11 ♗g5 ♗b4 12 0-0-0 ♗xc3 13 bxc3 ♔e7 14 ♗c4, Nikolic-Raty, Bad Niendorf 1989, when 14...h6 15 ♗f4 ♘b6 16 ♗b3 ♖ac8 is fine for Black] 7 ♘c3 ♗xf5 8 ♗g5 dxe4 9 ♗c4 ♘bd7 10 ♕e2 0-0-0 11 0-0-0, Gaard-Clarke, corr. 1991, and now any sensible queen move, avoiding ♘d5, equalises—11...♕e5 for instance) 6 dxe4 (Bücker's preference, 6 d4! is best, 6...d5 7 g4 h5!? [but 7...e3!? is also interesting, e.g. 8 ♗xe3 ♕e4 9 ♕f3 ♕xg4] 8 g5 ♘g8 very aesthetic—the perfect answer to White's fourth move! 9 ♗h3 [9 ♘c3 may be stronger, 9...c6 10 ♗h3 ♕f7 11 f3!? ♗xf5 12 fxe4 dxe4 which is unclear] 9...♕f7 10 c4!?, Jensen-Kozlov, corr. 1989, and now I think Black is better after 10...dxc4 11 g6 ♕f6 12 ♕a4+ ♕c6; 6 ♗e2 d5 7 g4 exd3 8 ♕xd3 ♘xg4 9 ♕xd5 ♘f6 10 ♕d3 ♘bd7 [10...♘c6 is more active still] 11 ♗g5 ♘c5 12 ♕f3 ♗d7 13 ♗xf6 ♕xf6 14 ♕e3+ ♗e7 15 ♘c3 ♗c6 16 ♗h5+ g6 17 fxg6 hxg6 18 ♗f3 0-0-0 19 ♗xc6 ♕xc6 and Black has good play, Malmström-Svendsen, corr. 1990) 6...♕xe4+ 7 ♗e2 ♗c5 8 ♘f3 0-0 9 ♘c3 ♕xf5 10 0-0 d5 11 ♗d3 (11 ♘d4?! ♗xd4 12 ♕xd4 ♘c6 ∓, Svendsen-Kozlov, corr. 1987; 11 ♗g5 c6 12 ♕d2 [12 ♗d3 ♘e4 13 ♕e1 ♖e8] 12...♘e4 13 ♘xe4 dxe4 14 ♗c4+ ♔h8 15 ♘h4 ♕e5 and the offside white knight and active black pieces offer Black excellent play, Pape-Kozlov, corr. 1990) 11...♕h5 12 ♗g5?, Tiemann-Svendsen, corr. 1990, 12...♘g4! and the threat of capturing on f3 leaves White in a terrible mess.

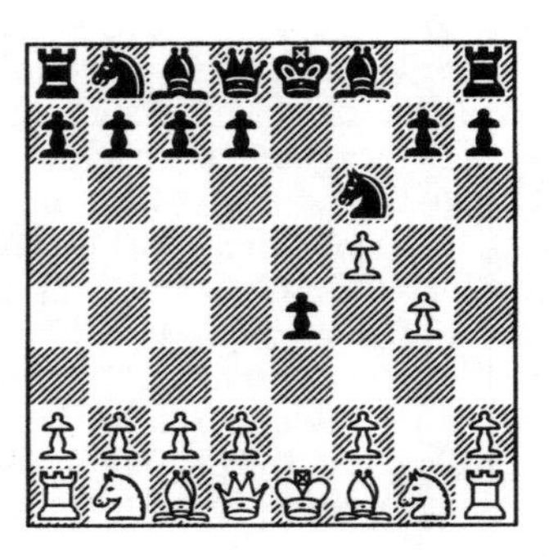

5...♗c5

By far and away the most popular move here, but possibly not the best. The others:

a) 5...h5! 6 g5 ♘g4 7 d4 (7 d3 e3 [7...exd3 transposes] 8 ♗xe3 ♘xe3 9 fxe3 ♕xg5 10 ♕f3 d5 11 ♗h3 is similar, Lomo-Sersch, Gausdal 2000; if 7 h3 Black can play a 'reversed whip': 7...♘xf2!? 8 ♔xf2 ♕xg5 9 d4 ♕xf5+ 10 ♔e1 ♗e7 which looks like it could be fun) 7...e3!? (Not 7...d5? 8 h3 ♘xf2 9 ♔xf2 ♗xf5 10 ♗e3 +/- Hayward-Tiemann, corr. 1990; but 7...exd3 8 ♗xd3 ♗c5 9 ♕e2+ ♔f7 10 g6+ ♔f8 11 ♘h3 [11 ♘f3!? ♘xf2 12 ♗g5 ♕e8] 11...♕h4 12 ♕f3 ♘e5 13 ♕g2 [13 ♕e4!?] 13...♘xd3+ [13...♘bc6! leads to an unclear position] 14 cxd3 d6 15 ♘g5, Pape-Clarke, corr. 1990, and again 15...♘c6 is reasonable) 8 ♗xe3 (8 ♘h3!? is plausible, and avoids losing the g5-pawn) 8...♘xe3 9 ♕e2 (9 fxe3 ♕xg5 10 ♕f3 is also possible, but the text exchanges the queens) 9...♕xg5 10 ♕xe3+ ♕xe3+?! (10...♗e7 has got to be better, why improve the white structure?) 11 fxe3 d5 12 ♗d3 ♗b4+ 13 c3 ♗d6 14 ♘f3 0-0 15 ♘h4 and Black's compensation for the pawn is inadequate, Canal Oliveras-Svendsen, corr. 1997.

b) 5...h6?! seems rather passive, 6 ♗g2 (or 6 d3 ♕e7?! [6...exd3 7 ♗xd3 ♕e7+ 8 ♔f1 b6!? is more combative] 7 dxe4 [7 d4 is not bad, either] 7...♕xe4+ 8 ♕e2 d5 9 ♘c3 ♗b4 10 ♗d2 ♗xc3 11 ♗xc3 ♘c6 [11...0-0 is better] 12 f3 ♕xe2+ 13 ♘xe2 with advantage, Hayward-Zschorn, corr. 1991) 6...♘c6 7 ♘c3 d5 8 f3! exf3 9 ♕xf3 with advantage, Stummer-Landgraf, corr. 1991.

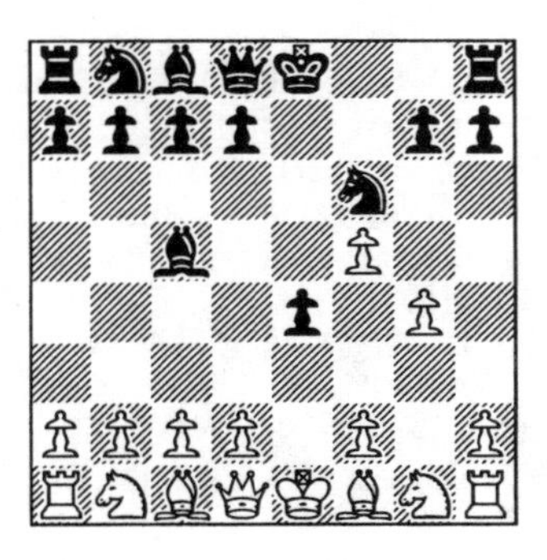

6 g5!

Just like a reversed Muzio Gambit! Other moves:

a) 6 d4? exd3 7 ♗xd3 ♕e7+! 8 ♔f1 (unfortunately for White, if he puts a piece in the way he loses his g-pawn) 8...h5 9 g5 ♘e4 10 ♗xe4 (10 ♘h3?! d5 11 ♕f3 ♕e5 12 ♘c3 ♗xf5 13 ♘f4? ♗g4 0-1, Wittmann-Nyffeler, corr. 1990) 10...♕xe4 11 ♕e2 ♕xe2+ 12 ♘xe2 d5 13 f6 gxf6 14 g6 (after 14 gxf6?!, instead of 14...♗h3+, Borrmann-Svendsen, corr. 1988, there is 14...♘d7 15 ♗g5 ♔f7 16 ♘f4 c6 and, after Black recovers the f6-pawn, he will have a clear edge, as he has fewer pawn islands) 14...♗f5 15 ♘f4 ♘d7 16 c3 0-0-0 with an advantage in development, and chances of winning the g6-pawn, Leeners-Sinke, corr. 1982.

b) 6 ♘c3 0-0 7 g5 ♘e8 (7...d5!? 8 gxf6 ♕xf6 might be worth a shot) 8 ♗c4+?! (8 ♘xe4 ♗b6 9 ♕f3 is more to the point) 8...♔h8 9 d4 exd3 (9...♗b4 is superior) 10 ♗xd3 d5 11 f6, Stummer-Svendsen, corr. 1990, 11...♘xf6! 12 gxf6 ♕xf6 13 ♕e2 ♗xf2+ 14 ♔d1 c6 with two pawns and an attack for the piece.

6...0-0

Black has no choice but to offer his knight as 6...♘d5? 7 ♕h5+ ♔f8 8 ♗c4 c6 9 ♘c3 is pretty miserable. However, 6...♘c6?! might be a better way of doing it, controlling d4, if White had to capture, 7 gxf6 (unfortunately, White also has the pragmatic response 7 ♘c3!) 7...♕xf6 8 d3 d5 9 dxe4 ♕h4 10 ♕d2 dxe4?! (10...♕xe4+!? 11 ♕e2 ♗xf5) 11 ♗b5?? (11 ♕f4! administers a cold shower to Black's thoughts of attack!) 11...e3 12 ♕e2 ♕xf2+ 13 ♔d1 ♗xf5 Melchor-Magee, corr. 1991, White is lost.

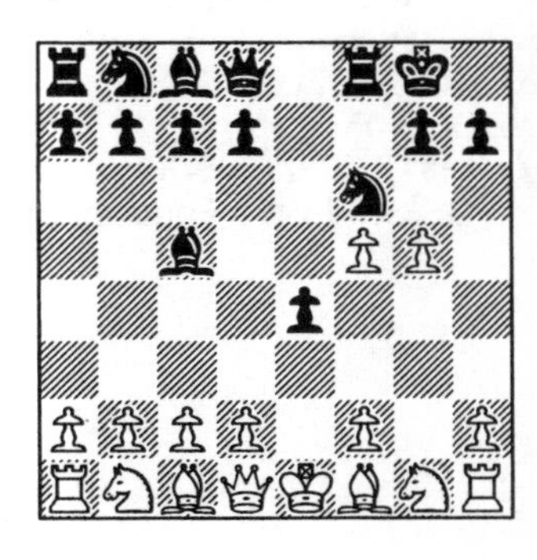

7 d4!

This fine tactical point guarantees White the advantage; the obvious 7 gxf6 gives Black just what he's looking for: 7...♕xf6 8 ♗h3 d5 9 ♘c3? (it is time for 9 d4! ♕xd4 [9...♗xd4 10 c3 ♗xf2+ 11 ♔xf2 ♗xf5 is tempting, but 12 ♔g3! ♕g6+ 13 ♔h4 defends, amazingly enough] 10 ♕xd4 ♗xd4 11 ♘e2 with advantage) 9...♗xf5 10 d4?! exd3 11 ♗xf5 ♕xf5 12 ♕xd3 ♕xf2+ 13 ♔d1 ♕f1+ 14 ♕xf1 ♖xf1+ 15 ♔e2 ♖xg1 -/+ Hayward-Elburg, corr. 1990.

7...exd3

The one drawback of having the e-pawn on e4, instead of e5, is that Black must capture on d3, not d4, 7...♗e7? 8 gxf6 ♗xf6 9 ♘c3 d5 10 ♗h3 ♘c6 11 ♗e3 +/- Magee-Spiegel, corr. 1991.

8 gxf6 ♕xf6

White has no need to fear 8...♕e8+?! 9 ♗e2! dxe2 (9...♕e4 10 ♕xd3! ♕xh1 11 ♕g3 ♖xf6 12 ♗f3 traps the black queen, 12...♗d6 13 ♗xh1 ♗xg3 14 hxg3 when White's two pieces are superior to the black rook) 10 ♕d5+ ♕f7 11 ♕xc5 b6?! 12 ♕e7 ♕xf6 13 ♕xf6 +/- Hayward-Magee, corr. 1991; 8...♖e8+? 9 ♗e2! ♕xf6 (9...dxe2? 10 ♕d5+ ♔h8 11 fxg7+ ♔xg7 12 ♕xc5 is even worse) 10 ♕xd3 d6, Taylor-Hayward, corr. 1987, 11 ♕b3+ ♔h8 12 ♗e3.

9 ♗xd3 d5

9...♖e8+? 10 ♘e2 ♕h4 11 0-0 b6 12 ♘g3 ♗b7 13 ♕h5 puts an end to Black's hopes, Magee-Svendsen, corr. 1991.

10 ♕f3 c6 11 ♘e2

11 ♘c3!? aiming to castle long.

11...♘d7 12 ♘g3?! ♘e5 13 ♕e2 ♗d7 14 0-0 ♖ae8

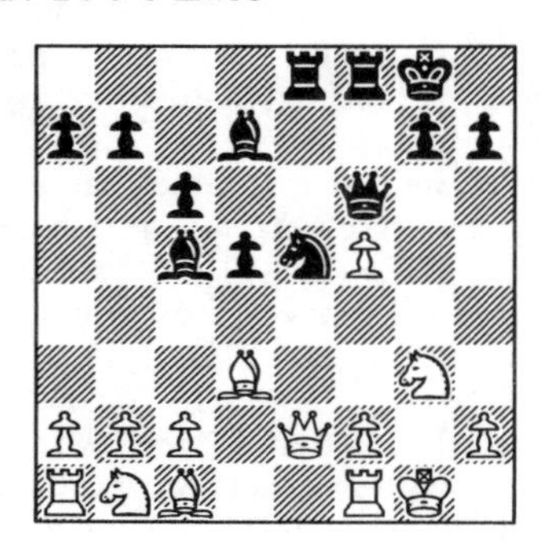

15 ♕d1

15 ♗e3?! ♕h4! 16 ♕h5 ♕xh5 17 ♘xh5 ♗xe3 (Black is not even worse after 17...♘xd3! 18 cxd3 d4 19 ♗d2 ♖xf5 20 ♘g3 ♖f3 as the white pieces are misplaced, and the d3-pawn is lost) 18 fxe3 ♘xd3 19 cxd3 ♖xe3 with some drawing chances, Magee-Harper, corr. 1991.

15...g6?

If 15...♕h4 then 16 ♔g2, but 15...♘xd3!? 16 ♕xd3 ♗xf5 17 ♘xf5 ♕xf5 18 ♕xf5 ♖xf5 is playable, e.g. 19 ♘c3 d4 20 ♘b1 ♖e2.

16 ♗h6 ♖f7 17 ♗e3 ♘xd3 18 ♕xd3 ♗xe3 19 fxe3 ♕xb2 20 ♘c3 with advantage to White, Magee-Kozlov, corr. friendly game 1991.

11 3 d4

A very natural response from White, but it would appear at first sight that Black is well placed to counter this. Indeed he is, but there is more than a drop of poison in this line for the unwary second player, as in the main variations White offers a dangerous piece sacrifice.

1 e4 e5 2 ♘f3 f5 3 d4

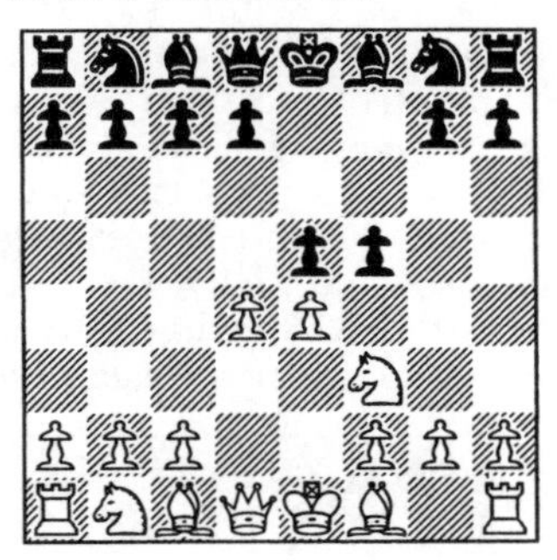

3...fxe4

There seems little reason to search for alternatives at this stage, as the text is obvious and good. For the sake of completeness, though, here they are:

a) 3...d6 again transposes into the Philidor, followed by e.g. 4 ♗c4 (or 4 dxe5 fxe4 etc.) 4...exd4!.

b) 3...exd4?! 4 ♘xd4! (White could also consider playing a sort of 'reversed Falkbeer Gambit' with 4 e5!?, but not 4 ♗c4 which worked out badly in Tiemann-Downey, corr. 1990: 4...fxe4 5 ♘e5 ♗b4+! 6 c3 dxc3 7 bxc3 ♕f6! 8 ♕d5 ♘e7) 4...♕h4 5 ♘xf5 ♕xe4+ 6 ♘e3 ♘f6 7 ♗d3 ♕c6?! (7...♕h4!?) 8 0-0 d5 9 ♘c3 ♘bd7 10 ♘exd5 ♘xd5 11 ♕h5+ g6 12 ♕xd5 ♕xd5 13 ♘xd5 with advantage, Melchor-Diepstraten, corr. 1991.

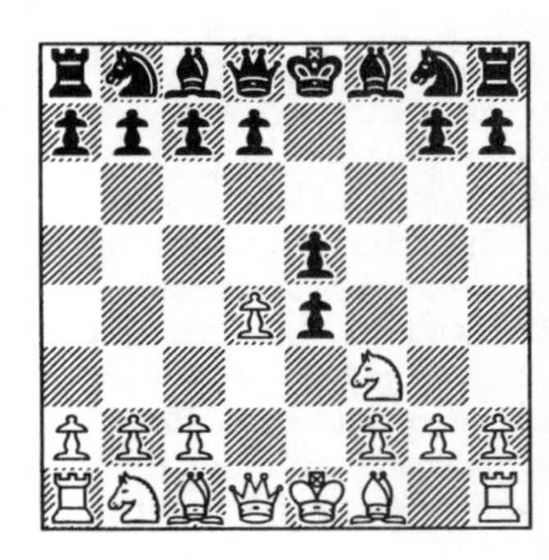

4 ♘xe5

Again, there is no advantage to be gained from spurning this move:

a) 4 ♗g5?! has been played systematically by the correspondence player Diepstraten, but the exchange of a pair of minor pieces only aids Black: 4...♗e7 (4...♘f6 5 ♗xf6?! [5 ♘xe5 transposes to the mainline] 5...gxf6? [5...♕xf6 6 ♘xe5 d6 is good for Black, and is examined in the note to White's main move six] 6 ♘xe5! fxe5 7 ♕h5+ gave White a devastating attack in Diepstraten-Falk) 5 ♗xe7 ♕xe7 (5...♘xe7 is also possible, 6 ♘xe5 d6 7 ♘c4 0-0 8 ♘e3 ♘f5 and if anyone is better, it is Black, Diepstraten-Elburg, corr. 1990) 6 ♘xe5 ♘f6 7 ♘c3 d6 8 ♘c4 (8 ♘d5? is overly aggressive, 8...♘xd5 9 ♕h5+ g6 10 ♘xg6 ♕f7 11 ♗e2, occurred in a 1985 game of Diepstraten, and now 11...♕xg6 12 ♕xd5 ♕f5 won easily) 8...d5 (first 8...0-0 9 ♗e2 d5 might be even more accurate) 9 ♘e3 (9 ♘e5 ♘bd7 10 ♘g4 c6 11 ♗e2 ♘xg4 12 ♗xg4 0-0 13 0-0 ♘f6 ∓, Diepstraten-Budovskis, corr. 1977/9) 9...♗e6 10 ♘a4 ♘bd7 = Diepstraten-Grivainis, corr. 1977/79.

b) 4 ♘fd2!? the 'Zemitis Variation' 4...♕e7! (Black's choices are somewhat limited as 4...exd4?, and 4...d5? are both met by 5 ♕h5+, although 4...d6 5 ♘xe4 ♘f6 6 ♗g5 ♗e7 is also fine) 5 d5 (5 ♕h5+ g6 6 ♕xe5 ♕xe5 7 dxe5 ♗g7 [7...e3!? is interesting, 8 fxe3 ♗g7 9 ♗c4 ♘c6 10 ♘c3 ♘xe5 11 ♗b3 ♘f6 12 0-0 d6 with the superior structure, Zemitis-Grivainis/Hayward, corr. 1997] 8 ♘xe4 ♗xe5 9 ♘bc3 ♘c6 10 ♗e3 ♘ge7 11 0-0-0 a6 and in this type of endgame Black's extra centre pawn should not be underestimated, Zemitis-Strautins, corr. 1999; if 5 ♘xe4 then 5...d5! [5...exd4 6 ♗d3 {but not 6 ♕xd4? d5! -+} 6...d5? 7 ♕h5+] 6 ♘g5 ♘c6! with a great position, Alberts-Bravo, corr. 1979/80, if 7 dxe5 ♕xe5+ 8 ♗e2 ♘f6 9 0-0 ♗c5 ∓) 5...♘f6 6 ♘c3 ♕f7 7 ♘cxe4!? (7 ♘dxe4 ♗b4) 7...♗e7 8 ♗d3?! ♘xd5 with advantage, Zemitis-Grivainis, corr. 1970/72.

c) 4 ♘g5?! exd4 (4...d5 5 dxe5 reached a Philidor position with a tempo more for Black in Lartigue-Alberts, corr. 1971, whilst in the game Spigel-Sawyer, corr. 1988, White tried the enterprising 5 ♘xe4!? dxe4 6 ♕h5+ ♔d7 7 dxe5!? and went on to win, but 7...g6 8 ♕g4+ ♔e8 9 ♕xe4 ♗g7 certainly favours Black. Otherwise, 7 ♕f5+ ♔e8 8 ♕h5+ ♔d7 9 ♕f5+ ♔c6!? [9...♔e8 draws] 10 ♕xe4+ ♔b6 11 ♗e3 exd4 12 ♗xd4+ c5 13 ♗e3 ♘c6 and White has some play for the piece, Alberts-Trobatto, corr. 1979) 5 ♕xd4 (5 ♘xe4 ♘c6 ∓) 5...♘f6 (5...d5 6 ♕e5+ ♘e7 7 ♗e2 is unclear, Redolfi-Atars, corr. 1973) 6 ♘xe4 ♕e7 7 ♘bc3 ♘c6 ∓.

4...♘f6

As in many other lines of the Latvian, Black can also develop his queen to f6: 4...♕f6? but, for once, it is not especially good, 5 ♗c4 ♘e7 (5...c6? 6 ♗f7+! ♔d8 [6...♔e7 7 ♕h5 with the threat of ♗g5] 7 ♗xg8 ♖xg8? 8 ♗g5 1-0, Sénéchaud-Evans, corr. 1992, as 8...♕xg5 9 ♘f7+; and this tactic works well against other moves, as well: 5...♘c6? 6 ♗f7+ [6 ♘f7 ♕xd4 7 ♕xd4 ♘xd4 is also good, although not 8 ♔d2?? b5! unclear, Goedhart-Ten Hove, corr. 1982, but 8 ♘xh8 ♘xc2+ 9 ♔d1 ♘xa1 10 ♗xg8 winning] 6...♔d8 (6...♔e7 7 ♘c3!) 7 ♗xg8 ♘xe5 (again, 7...♖xg8?? 8 ♗g5) 8 dxe5 ♕g6 9 ♕d5) 6 ♘c3 d6 7 ♘f7 ♗e6 8 ♗xe6 ♕xe6 9 ♘xh8 with advantage Saleen-Sticker, Baden-Baden 1987.

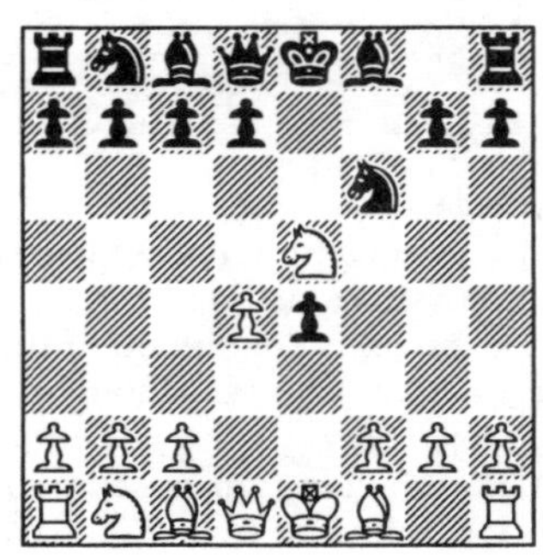

5 ♗g5

Black is ready to expel the white king's knight from e5, how best to react? The text move prepares a sharp piece sacrifice. Other moves:

a) 5 ♗c4 is a sensible move, provoking ...d5, and thus maintaining the knight on e5. White has a clear plan, he will continue with c4 putting pressure on d5, but Black sets up his centre with gain of tempo, 5...d5 6 ♗b3 (6...♗d6 7 ♗g5 [7 0-0 ♘bd7 8 ♘xd7?! ♗xd7 9 f3 c6 10 ♗g5 ♕c7 ∓ Prokopcuk-Ozimok, USSR 1969] 7...c6 8 0-0 0-0 9 ♘c3?! [9 c4!] 9...♕c7 10 ♗f4, Mason-Pollock, London 1887, 10...♘bd7 ∓) 6...♗e6 7 ♗g5 ♗e7 8 0-0 0-0 9 ♘d2 (9 f3—Keres) 9...♘c6!? (perhaps 9...♘bd7!? trying to exchange a couple of pieces, or 9...c5!? 10 dxc5 ♕c7) 10 ♘xc6 = Stockholm-Riga, corr. 1934/36.

b) 5 ♗e2 is very popular, but not very good, Black chases the e5-knight with gain of tempo, and completes his development easily, 5...d6 (Black can avoid the piece sac with 5...♗e7!? as 6 0-0 [6 ♗h5+ g6 7 ♘xg6?! {or 7 ♗e2 d6 8 ♘g4, unclear, Grozshans-Spiegel, corr. 1992} 7...hxg6 8 ♗xg6+ ♔f8 leads nowhere; 6 ♗g5 transposes to the note to Black's fifth move, 5...d6] 6...d6 7 ♘g4 0-0 8 c4 ♘xg4 9 ♗xg4 ♘c6 10 ♗e3 ♗f6 is level, Reefschlaeger-Pirrot, Germany 1996) 6 ♘g4 (6 ♗h5+?! sacrifices a piece, 6...g6 7 ♘xg6 hxg6 8 ♗xg6+ ♔e7 [8...♔d7 might be simpler, 9 ♗g5 d5 10 ♗f5+ ♔e7 11 ♕g4 ♗xf5 12 ♕xf5 ♗g7, consolidating, Marchio-Lutz, Hofheim 1995] 9 ♗g5 ♗h6 10 ♗xf6+ ♔xf6 11 ♗xe4 ♔g7 12 ♕d3 ♘c6 ∓ Alberts-Ortiz, corr. 1967; 6 ♘c4 is an alternative, 6...d5 7 ♘e5 ♗d6 8 ♗f4 ♗e6 9 0-0 0-0 10 ♗g3 c5 11 ♘c3 ♘c6 and Black is already on top, Tornay-Delgado, Catalonia 1994) 6...♗e7 7 ♘c3 d5 and here Hector has faced two moves: 8 0-0 (8 ♘e5 0-0 9 ♗g5 c6 10 0-0 ♗f5 11 g4?, weakening, 11...♗e6 12 ♗e3 ♘fd7 13 f4 exf3 14 ♗xf3 ♘xe5 15 dxe5 ♘d7 ∓ 16 ♗e2 ♖xf1+ 17 ♔xf1 ♘xe5 18 ♗xa7? b6 19 ♕d4 ♘d7 0-1, Moullimard-Hector, Clermont-Ferrand 1989) 8...0-0 9 f4!? ♘xg4 10 ♗xg4 ♘c6 11 ♗e3 ♗f6 12 ♗xc8 ♖xc8 13 g4!? ♘a5! 14 b3 c5 15 g5 ♗xd4 16 ♗xd4 cxd4 17 ♕xd4 ♖f5 18 ♖ad1 ♘c6 19 ♕f2 ♘b4 20 ♘xe4 ♖xc2 21 ♕d4 ♕a5 22 ♖f2 ♖xf2 23 ♘xf2 ♘xa2 24 ♕d3 ♖xf4, Black seems to be getting on top, 25 ♖a1! d4 26 ♕c4+ ♖f7 27 ♘e4 d3 28 g6! hxg6 29 ♕c8+ ♔h7 30 ♕h3+ ♔g8 31 ♕c8+ ♔h7 ½-½, Emms-Hector, Matalascanas 1989.

c) 5 ♘c3 d6 (again, 5...♗e7 is possible, 6 ♗g5 with transposition to a later note) 6 ♘c4 (6 ♗g5 relocates to the main line) 6...d5 (6...♗f5 7 ♗e2 ♗e7 8 0-0 0-0 = Luna-Atars, corr. 1973, or 6...♗e7, ...0-0 =) 7 ♘e5 (7 ♘e3 c6 8 ♗e2 ♗d6 9 0-0 0-0 is pleasant for Black, Evans-Kozlov, corr. 1994/96) 7...♗d6 8 ♗e2 0-0 9 f4 exf3 10 ♗xf3 c6?! (Lein suggests 10...♘c6! instead, 11 ♘xc6 [11 ♗f4 ♖e8] 11...bxc6 12 0-0 ♗f5) 11 0-0 ♕c7?! (11...♗xe5!? 12 dxe5 ♘e8? fails to 13 ♘xd5!, but 12...♘fd7 might be possible, aiming for the blockading square e6 by 13 ♕d4 ♘a6-c7) 12 ♗f4 ♗e6 ±, Clarke-Zschorn, corr. 1990, and not 12... ♘fd7? 13 ♘xd5! cxd5 14 ♗xd5+ ♔h8 15 ♕h5 winning quickly, Kaminskas-Erler, corr. 1995.

d) 5 ♘g4 d5 6 ♘xf6+ ♕xf6 7 ♕h5+ ♕f7 8 ♕xf7+ ♔xf7 =, Marting-Pollock, New York 1889.

5...d6

Should Black wish to avoid the coming complications, then he might try 5...♗e7!?: 6 ♘c3 (6 ♗xf6?! does not work here, 6...♗xf6 7 ♕h5+ g6 8 ♘xg6 hxg6 9 ♕xg6+ ♔f8 10 ♗c4 ♕e7 ∓ as ♘d5 is no longer a problem 11 ♘c3 ♕g7 12 ♕xe4 ♖h4 13 f4 c6 0-1, Magee-Svendsen, corr. 1991; and 6 ♗e2 whilst common, is insipid: 6...d6 7 ♘c4 which transposes to 5...d6 6 ♘c4) 6...d5 (for 6...d6? 7 ♗xf6 see later) 7 f3 exf3 8 ♕xf3 c6 9 ♗d3 0-0 10 0-0-0 ± Stummer-Svendsen, corr. 1991.

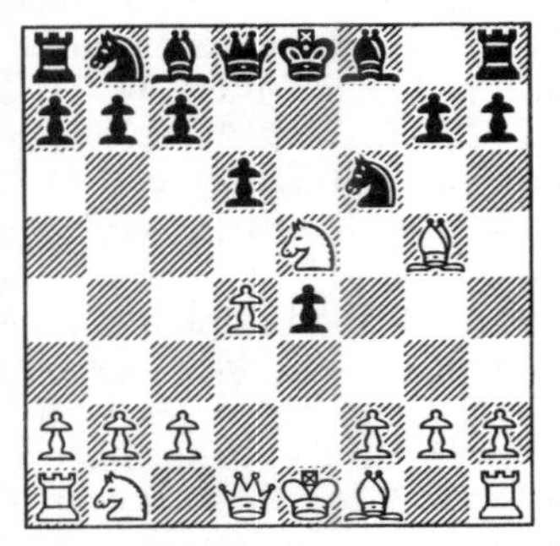

Now, White has to make an important choice. For some time the move of Pupol's, 6 ♘c3 held the sway, but recently 6 ♘d2 has become popular, avoiding the exchange of queens. So, we have:

A 6 ♘c3!
B 6 ♘d2!?

Should White want to avoid the risk involved with either of these, then he can choose 6 ♘c4, but, although it is very common in actual play, it is quite innocuous: 6...♗e7 (6...♗f5 7 ♘e3 ♗g6 8 ♗c4 ♘bd7 9 0-0 c6 10 ♗b3 ♕c7 11 c4 ♗e7 12 ♘c3 0-0 ± Booij-Westerinen, Dieren 1988) 7 ♗e2 (7 ♗xf6?! ♗xf6 8 ♕h5+ g6 9 ♕d5 Navarro-Hammar, corr. 1971, 9...♘c6! 10 c3 ♕e7 ∓; 7 ♘c3 keeps control of d5, and avoids the coming knight manoeuvre, but allows 7...0-0 8 ♗e2 ♕e8!? 9 0-0 b5 10 ♘e3 c6 11 f3 d5! 12 fxe4?! b4! ∓ Christofferson-Petroff, Munich 1936) 7...0-0 8 0-0 ♘d5! (exchanging dark squared bishops gives Black more room, and the king's knight will find a powerful square on f4. Black can also bring his queen to the kingside with 8...♕e8!? 9 ♘e3! [9 ♘c3 b5 as per the Petroff game, above] 9...♕g6 10 ♗h4 c6 11 c4 ♘a6 12 ♘c3 with a slight advantage to White, Drozdov-Nadanian, Krasnodar 1997) 9 ♗xe7 ♕xe7 10 ♘c3 ♘f4 11 ♘e3 c6 12 d5?! c5 ∓ Carlton-Sim, England 1967.

6 ♗xf6?! provides Black with the bishop pair, 'free of charge', so to speak, 6...♕xf6 7 ♘g4 ♕g6 8 ♘e3 ♗e7 9 ♘c3 c6 10 ♗e2 0-0 11 0-0 d5 already favours Black, Schueller-Bukacek, corr. 1989.

A 6 ♘c3

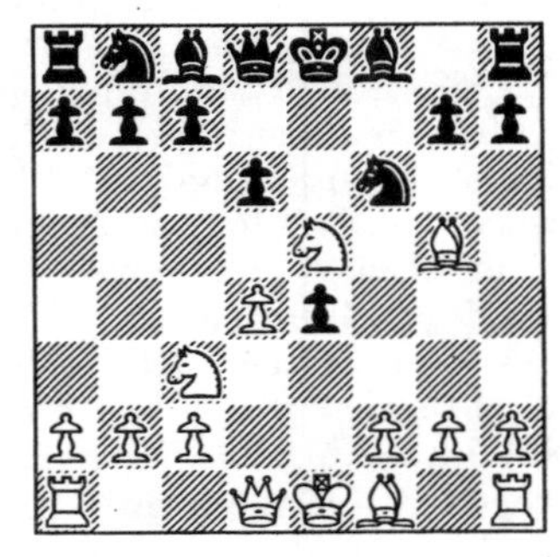

6...dxe5

Black might just as well take this piece:

a) 6...♗e7? 7 ♗xf6 ♗xf6 8 ♕h5+ g6 9 ♘xg6 hxg6 10 ♕xg6+ ♔d7 (10...♔f8 is also hopeless, 11 ♗c4 d5 [11...♕e7? 12 ♘d5] 12 ♘xd5 ♗e6 13 ♘xf6 ♗xc4 14 d5 ♕e7 15 0-0-0 threatening to bring a white rook to the kingside, and winning quickly, Papp-Varga, Hungary 1980) 11 ♘d5 ♖f8 12 ♗e2 (12 ♕f5+ ♔e8 13 ♕xe4+ doesn't hold out any hope for Black, either) 12...♘a6? (12...c5?! 13 dxc5 ♗xb2?? 14 ♕xd6+ is crushing, Blackburne-Pollock; 12...♗xd4 is a better chance, though 13 0-0-0 ♗e5 14 ♕h7+ is still pretty grim) 13

♕f5+ ♔c6 14 ♘e7+ 1-0, it is mate in one, Rechel-Drill, Berlin 1998.

b) 6...♗f5? 7 ♗c4! (7 g4? dxe5 8 gxf5 exd4 9 ♘xe4 ♕e7 ∓ Salnins-Tomson, corr., or even 9...♗b4+ 10 c3 ♕e7) 7...dxe5 8 dxe5 ♕xd1+ 9 ♖xd1 ♘bd7 (9...♘fd7 10 ♘d5 ♘a6 11 ♗xa6 bxa6 12 ♘xc7+ ♔f7 13 ♘xa8 ♗b4+ 14 c3 ♗a5 15 b4 with advantage; 9...h6? 10 exf6! [10 ♗xf6 gxf6 11 ♘d5 might lead to no more than a draw after 11...♖h7 12 ♘xf6+ ♔e7 13 ♘g8+] 10...hxg5 11 ♘d5 ♔d8 12 ♘b6+ ♘d7 13 ♘xd7! with advantage, Carniol-Destrebecq, corr. 1984) 10 exf6 ♘xf6 11 0-0 c6 12 ♖fe1 with a clear advantage, Sénéchaud-Niemand, corr. 1994/95.

c) Destrebecq's 6...c6!? might just be playable, 7 ♘xe4 dxe5 8 ♗xf6 gxf6 9 ♕h5+ ♔d7 (9...♔e7!? may be stronger, 10 dxe5 ♕a5+ 11 c3 ♕xe5 12 ♕h4, Canal Oliveras-Niemand, corr. 1999, and now 12...♗h6 would stop White from castling long) 10 0-0-0 (10 dxe5 ♔c7 11 exf6 b6 with a piece for three pawns, Elburg-Destrebecq, corr. 1991) 10...♔c7 11 dxe5 ♕e8! with the tactical point 12 ♕xe8 ♗h6+ 13 ♔b1 ♖xe8 and if anyone is better, it is Black, Kravitz-Ruggeri Laderchi, email 1998

7 dxe5 ♕xd1+ 8 ♖xd1

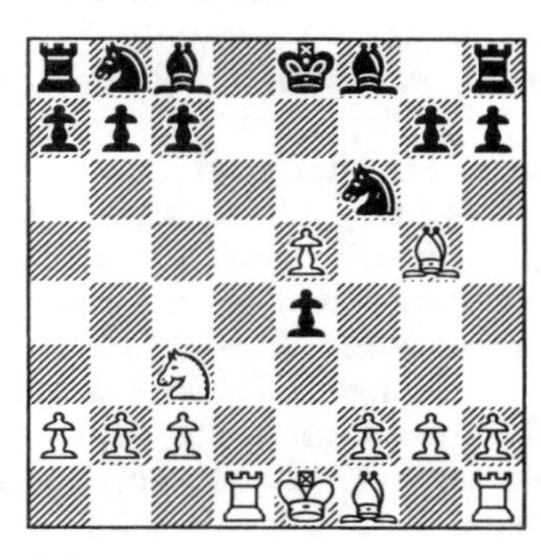

8...h6

a) Black has an alternative in 8...♗g4?!:

a1) 9 ♖d2! h6 (9...♘bd7? 10 ♘b5 0-0-0 11 exf6 gxf6 12 ♗f4 ♗c5 13 ♗xc7 with advantage Schlenker-Stummer, corr. 1991; but 9...♘fd7!? might be Black's best bet, 10 ♘d5 ♘b6 11 ♘xc7+ ♔f7 12 h3 [12 ♗e3 ♘c6! 13 ♘xa8 {13 ♗xb6? ♖c8 equal} 13...♘xa8 with good chances] 12...♗e6 13 ♘xa8 ♘xa8 14 ♖d4 ♘c6 15 ♖xe4 ♗f5 16 e6+? [a blunder, 16 ♖e2 had to be played, but Black is not without chances here] 16...♔g6 17 e7 ♗xe7 0-1, Waldner-Downey, USA 1992) 10 ♗xf6 (10 exf6!? is untried, although play will be similar, e.g. 10...hxg5 11 ♘d5 ♔f7 [11...♔d8 12 fxg7 ♗xg7 13 ♘b6+ ♘d7 14 ♗e2!] 12 ♘xc7 ♘c6 13 ♘xa8 ♗b4 14 c3 ♗a5 15 b4 ♘xb4 16 cxb4 ♗xb4 17 ♗c4+ ♔g6 18 a3 with some advantage) 10...gxf6 11 ♘d5 ♔f7!? (11...♘d7!? has been more successful: 12 ♘xc7+ ♔d8 13 ♘xa8 fxe5 14 h3 ♗e6 15 ♗b5 ♔c8 16 0-0 ♘f6 17 ♖fd1 ± but Black won, Heemsoth-Stamer, corr. 1984 or 12 f3?! 0-0-0 13 fxg4 fxe5 14 ♗c4 ♗c5 = Melchor-Grobe, corr. 1989/91) 12 ♘xc7 ♗b4 13 c3 ♗a5 14 ♗c4+ ♔g6 15 ♘xa8 (in the original game in this line, de Wit-de Zeeuwe, corr. 1989, White continued 15 ♖d6!? ♘d7 16 ♘xa8 ♖xa8 17 ♗d5 ♘xe5 18 ♗xb7 ♖b8 19 ♗xe4+ ♔g7 20 ♖a6?! ♗b6 21 b3?! ♖e8 22 0-0 ♗e2 and Black had gained the ascendancy) 15...♘c6 16 h3! (16 b4?! ♘xb4 17 cxb4 ♗xb4 18 exf6 ♖d8 19 0-0 ♗xd2 20 ♘c7 ♔xf6 with a level position, Tiemann-Elburg, corr. 1991) 16...♘xe5 (what else? 16...♗f5 17 g4 ♘xe5 18 gxf5+ ♔xf5 19 ♗e2 [19 ♖d5! is even stronger] 19...♖xa8 20 ♖g1 leaves Black almost zero compensation for the exchange Melchor-Sénéchaud, corr. 1990, and others) 17 ♗d5 ♗f5 18 ♗xb7 ♘d3+ 19 ♔f1 ♖b8 20 ♗d5, Melchor-Tiemann, corr. training game 1993, and now 20...♗xc3 21 ♖e2 ♘f4 may cause White a few slight problems.

a2) 9 exf6 is another option, White will obtain two pawns and the bishop pair in return for the exchange, 9...♗xd1 10 ♔xd1 ♘d7 (10...gxf6? 11 ♗xf6 ♖g8 12 ♘xe4 ♘d7? [12...♘c6] 13 ♗c4 ♖g6 14 ♖e1 with advantage Sénéchaud-Svendsen, corr. 1991/92; 10...♘c6?! 11 ♘xe4 h6 12 ♗h4 0-0-0+ 13 ♔c1 ♖e8 14 f3 a6 15 ♗c4 g5 16 ♗g3 ♘e5 17 ♗b3 and the black pieces are unable to find good squares, Pape-Malmström, corr. 1994/95) 11 ♘xe4 gxf6 (Black can also flick in 11...h6 12 ♗h4 first) 12 ♘xf6+ ♘xf6 13 ♗xf6 ♖g8 14 ♗b5+ c6 15 ♖e1+ ♔d7 16 ♗f1, Sénéchaud-Gaard, corr., 16...♖e8 and Black shouldn't lose this, although care has to be taken to stop the kingside pawns.

a3) 9 ♗e2? is a blunder, though: 9...♗xe2 10 ♘xe2 h6 11 ♗xf6 gxf6 ∓, Groen-Diepstraten, Hilversum 1983.

b) 8...♘bd7?! 9 exf6 ♘xf6 10 ♗xf6 gxf6 11 ♘d5 ♔f7 12 ♘xc7 is also favourable to White.

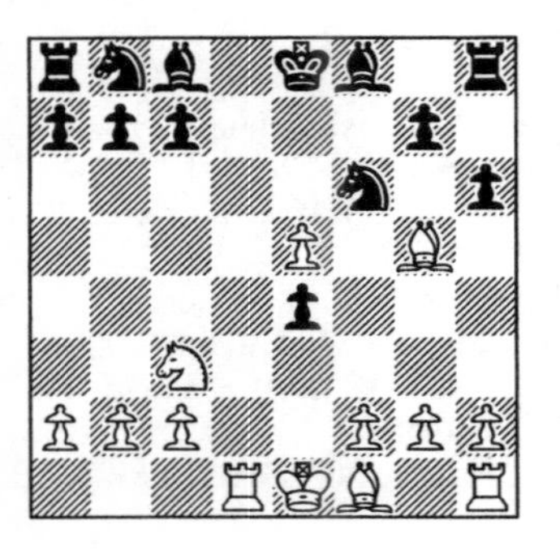

9 ♗xf6 gxf6 10 ♘d5 ♔d7

Taking the unusual step of walking into a double check, but 10...♔f7? 11 ♘xc7 ♗e6 12 ♘xa8 ♗b4+ 13 c3 ♗a5 14 b4 favours White, Schreyer-Sénéchaud, corr. 1992.

11 ♘b6+

Picking up the a8 rook. Whether or not Black can keep the a8-knight trapped is crucial for the assessment of this line.

a) 11 e6+?! is interesting, but can now be considered doubtful: 11...♔d8!! (Black gives White a second chance to use his discovered check! The older move 11...♔c6 is also reasonable: 12 e7 ♗g7 13 ♗b5+ [13 ♘b4+!? ♔b6 {13...♔c5!? takes the king into uncharted, and very murky, waters: 14 ♖d5+! ♔xb4 15 c3+ ♔a4 16 ♗e2 and Black seems to be in some trouble, but after 16...b5! 17 ♗xb5+ ♔a5 18 ♗c6+ ♔b6 19 ♗xa8 ♘d7 Black is OK!} 14 ♘d5+ repeats] 13...♔xb5 14 ♘xc7+ ♔c6 15 e8=♕+ ♖xe8 16 ♘xe8 ♗f8 17 ♘xf6 [though tempting, 17 ♖d8? only succeeds in trapping the rook: 17...♘d7 18 ♘xf6 ♗b4+ 19 c3 ♗a5 winning, Melchor-Oren, corr. 1997] 17...♗f5 18 0-0 ♗g7!? [18...♘d7 19 ♘xd7 ♗xd7 may be even simpler, the two bishops should certainly be more than a match for a rook] 19 ♘d5 ♗h7, with reasonable play for Black, Melchor-Heap, corr. 1993) 12 ♗c4 (12 ♘b6+?! ♗d6 13 ♘xa8 ♗xe6 must be good for Black, the white knight will never escape from its prison) 12...♗xe6 13 ♘f4+ ♗d7 14 ♘g6 ♗g7 15 ♘xh8 ♗xh8 16 0-0?! (even after the superior 16 ♗d5 ♘c6 17 ♗xe4 ♔e7 Black is better) 16...f5 and Black has a solid material advantage, Sénéchaud-Clarke, corr. 1994/95.

b) Perhaps the rare 11 ♘xf6+!? is White's best: 11...♔e6!? (attacking the key e5-pawn, and probably stronger than 11...♔c6?! when the king is misplaced, 12 ♘xe4 ♗e6 13 f4 [13 a4!? is also awkward, 13...♘a6 14 ♗e2 ♔b6 15 f4 ♘b4 16 c3 ♘d5 Goerlinger-Stamer, corr. 1982, when 17 f5! ♗xf5 18 a5+ ♔c6 19 ♗f3 lines up dangerous threats along the h1-a8 diagonal] 13...♗e7 14 ♗e2 ♘d7 Schoppmeyer - Traut, East Germany 1987, and 15 ♘c3! threatens both ♗b5+, and ♗f3+, and looks like it should win) 12 ♘d5 (12 ♘xe4!? ♘c6 [12...♔xe5!? 13 ♗d3 ♗g7 14 0-0 leaves the black king out-on-a-limb, where can it escape to?] 13 f4 ♔f5!?, attacking with the active king! If Black doesn't try this then White has three connected pawns, and good minor pieces, for his sacrifice) 12...♖h7 and now Lein gives 13 ♘f4+ ♔f5 14 g3 (14 ♖d8 ♖h8!) 14...♘c6 15 ♗h3+ ♔g5 which looks fine for Black, but protecting the important e5-pawn by 13 f4! is much more worrying, 13...exf3 14 gxf3 ♘c6 (14...♔xe5? 15 f4+ ♔e6 16 ♗h3+ wins) 15 f4 threatening ♗h3+, so 15...♘b4!? 16 ♘f6, but it looks dangerous for Black.

11...♔c6 12 ♘xa8

Not 12 ♘xc8? ♗c5 and ...♖xc8.

12...fxe5!

Black wants to follow-up with ...♗d6, solidifying his position.

12...b6 is possible, although there is a suspicion that White will garner too many pawns: 13 ♗c4 ♔b7 14 ♘xb6! (14 ♘xc7 ♔xc7 15 exf6 ♘d7 16 f7 ♗g7 17 c3 ♘e5 with some play, Stummer-Magee, corr. 1991) 14...♔xb6 15 exf6 ♘d7 16 f7 ♗g7 17 0-0 with a worse black structure than above, and the three extra white pawns proved too important in Stamer-Kozlov corr. 1994/95; 12...♗e6?? 13 ♗b5+ 1-0, Sénéchaud-Sadéghi, corr. 1991/92.

13 ♗c4 ♗d6

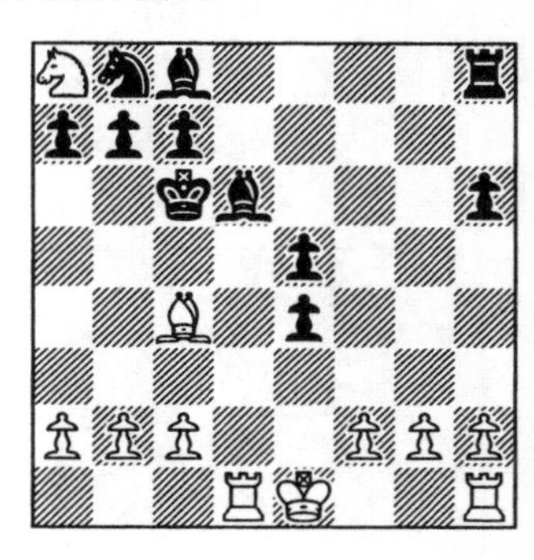

14 ♗d5+

14 a4!? is an idea, menacing ♗b5+, and asking Black how he will complete his development, 14...♗g4!? (this seems to work tactically, the only sensible alternative is 14...♔d7 intending to bring the black king to the safe e7-square, e.g. 15 ♗d5 ♔e7 16 ♗xe4 ♘a6 [followed by ...c6, c8-bishop moves, then ...♖xa8] 17 0-0 c6) 15 ♗d5+ (if 15 ♖d2 then 15...♔d7 looks right) 15...♔d7 16 f3! (16 ♗xb7? ♗xd1 17 ♔xd1 ♘c6) 16...exf3 17 gxf3 ♗f5 18 ♖g1 ♗xc2? letting the knight out, (18...♘c6 19 ♖g7+ ♘e7 20 ♗xb7 ♖b8 is level) 19 ♖g7+ ♔d8 20 ♖c1 ♗xa4 21 ♘xc7 and victory is not far off, Bos-Peters, corr. 1982.

14...♔d7 15 ♗xe4

Destrebecq's 15 c4 is best answered by 15...♘c6! 16 ♗xe4 b6 and ...♗b7xa8.

15...c6

This is successful, but 15...♘a6 and 15...♔e7 are also possible.

16 0-0 ♔e7 17 ♖d3 ♘a6 18 ♖fd1 ♖d8 19 ♖g3 ♘c5 20 ♗h7

The tactic 20 ♖g7+ leads nowhere: 20...♔f8 21 ♖h7 ♘xe4 22

♖h8+ ♔e7 23 ♖xd8 ♔xd8 24 f3 ♔e7! 25 fxe4 b5 and ...♗b7xa8.

20...♘e6 21 c3 ♘g5 22 h4?!

This combination turns out badly for White, but if 22 ♗c2 ♗e6 and ...♖xa8.

22...♘xh7 23 ♖g7+ ♔f6 24 ♖xh7 ♔g6

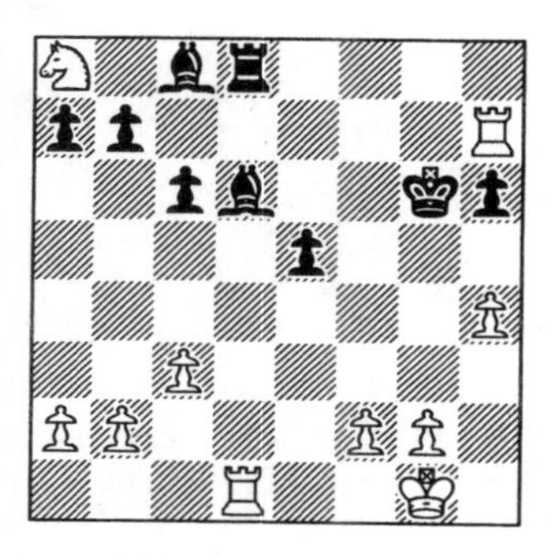

Trapping the rook.

25 ♖xd6+ ♖xd6 26 ♖h8 ♗e6 27 ♖b8 ♖d7

Making sure that the knight never leaves a8; now the active black king decides the game.

28 a4 ♔f6 29 b4 ♖g7 30 a5 ♗d5 31 g3 ♔f5 32 ♖d8 ♔e4 33 ♖e8 h5 34 f4? (34 ♔f1) **34...♖xg3+ 35 ♔h2 ♔xf4 36 ♖f8+ ♔g4 37 ♖f2 0-1**

Piefrusiak-Hector, Swedish ch 1984.

B 6 ♘d2!?

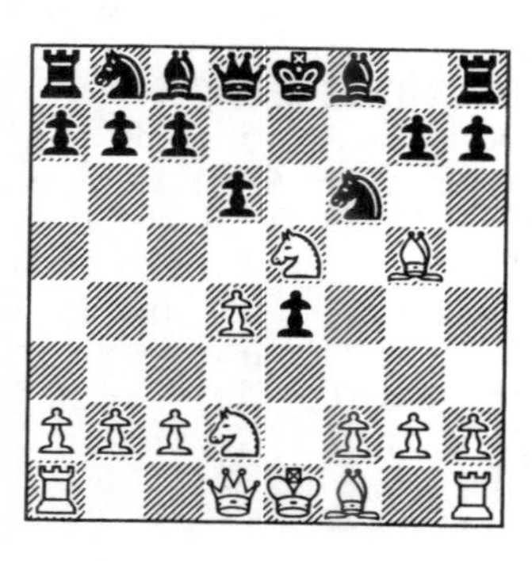

Krantz's speciality, which has recently been much played by Sireta. This is the logical development of the previous variation, White brazenly leaves his knight *en prise* once again, but this time Black is unable to exchange the queens.

6...dxe5

The acid test of the sacrifice is always its acceptance, and in this case avoidance brings its own set of problems:

a) 6...♗f5? 7 ♗c4! dxe5 8 dxe5 ♘bd7 9 exf6 gxf6 10 ♗f4 ♘b6 11 ♕e2 ♕e7 12 0-0-0 0-0-0 13 ♘b3 ♗g7 14 ♗a6!, threatening ♗xb7, with a strong attack, Krantz-Tiemann, corr. 1991.

b) 6...♗e7?! 7 ♗xf6 (this is not as effective as in A but nevertheless White gets a very dangerous initiative) 7...♗xf6 8 ♕h5+ g6 9 ♘xg6 hxg6 10 ♕xg6+ ♔f8! (10...♔d7?! 11 ♘xe4 ♗e7 12 ♘c5+!? dxc5 13 dxc5 ♗xc5 14 0-0-0+ ♗d6 15 ♗b5+ ♘c6 16 ♕g7+ ♕e7 17 ♕xh8! ♕g5+ 18 ♔b1 ♕xb5 19 ♖he1 ♘e7 20 ♕g7 with a continuing attack, Lundkvist-Schreyer, corr. 1984) 11 ♗c4 ♕e7 12 0-0-0 Diepstraten-Jackson, corr. 1994/95, when 12...♕g7 looks safest.

7 dxe5 ♕d5!

Since the first edition, Krantz's suggestion of 7...e3!? has received a number of tries, 8 fxe3 ♕d5 9 ♗xf6 (9 exf6 ♕xg5 10 ♘e4? would then encounter 10...♕xe3+) 9...gxf6 10 exf6 ♗d6!? (there is absolutely no consensus here as to Black's best, 10...♕g5 11 ♕f3 ♗c5 12 f7+ ♔f8 13 0-0-0 ♘c6, unclear, Sireta-Grobe, corr. 1994/96, and after 10...♕e5 11 ♘c4! ♕xf6 12 ♕h5+ ♔d8 13 0-0-0+ ♗d7 14 ♗d3 Black had regained one pawn, but the attack along the d-file is a problem, Sireta-Melchor, corr. 1994/95, however, Sireta's suggestion, 10...♘d7!? is also possible, 11 ♗c4 ♕xg2 12 ♕h5+ [12 f7+ ♔e7 13 ♕f3 ♕xf3 14 ♘xf3 ♘b6 15 ♗b3 ♗e6 is clearly better for Black] 12...♕g6 13 f7+ ♔d8 not allowing White to settle) 11 ♗c4 ♕e5 12 f7+ ♔e7 13 ♕f3 ♘c6 14 0-0-0 ♗e6 15 ♖hf1 ♖af8 and White's attack is insufficient, Sireta-Kozlov, corr. 1994/95.

8 exf6

Better than 8 ♗xf6?! gxf6 9 ♕h5+ ♕f7 10 ♘xe4 ♗e7 (10...♘d7) 11 ♗e2, Diepstraten-Sénéchaud, corr. 1995, when 11...0-0 is simplest.

8...♕xg5 9 ♘xe4

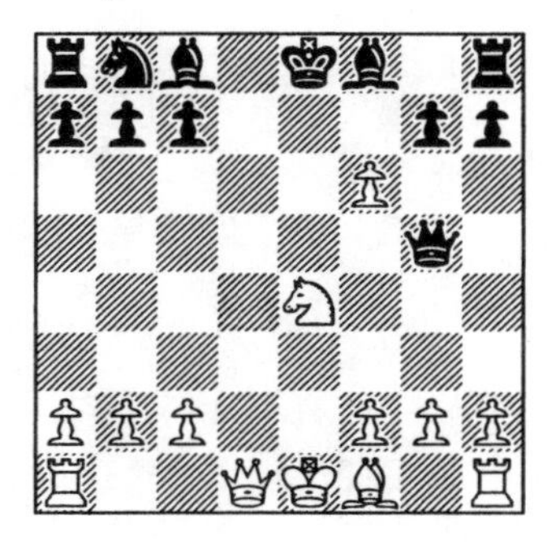

9...♕e5

This allows White to maintain some sort of attack. 9...♕a5+!? is simple and effective: 10 c3 and now 10...♗e6 (not 10...♗f5? 11 fxg7 ♗xg7 12 ♕h5+ ♔e7 13 ♕g5+ ♔f8 14 g4 ♘c6, Krantz-Svendsen, corr. 1989, when 15 ♕xf5+ is certainly very good for White) 11 f4! (preparing g5 for the knight, others are inferior, 11 ♕e2 gxf6!? 12 ♘xf6+ [12 ♘d6+ ♔e7] 12...♔e7 -/+; 11 ♗d3 ♘d7 12 0-0 [12 fxg7 ♗xg7 13 0-0 0-0-0, objectively speaking, White has only two pawns for his piece and nothing else, not even a lead in development, therefore he should lose] 12...0-0-0 13 b4 ♕d5 14 ♕e2 ♘xf6 is hopeless for White, Solinas-Viola, Arzignano Magistrale 1997) 11...gxf6! (the idea is that 11...♕f5?! allows 12 ♗d3 ♕xf4 13 ♕e2 ♗g4 14 fxg7 ♗xg7 15 ♘f6+ ♔d8 16 ♕xg4 ♕xf6 17 0-0-0 with a strong attack) 12 ♘xf6+ ♔e7 (12...♔f7 13 ♘e4 ♗e7 seems simple enough) 13 ♘e4 ♘d7! (13...♗g7 14 ♗d3 ♘c6 15 ♘g5 when, instead of 15...h6? 16 ♘xe6 ♔xe6 17 ♕g4+ ♔f7 18 ♗c4+ ♔f8 19 0-0-0 with a winning light-squared attack, Sireta-Krantz, corr. 1994/95, there is 15...♗g8) 14 ♘g5 ♕b6 15 ♗e2 ♖e8 16 ♕d2 ♔d8 sneaking away to safety on the queenside, Sireta-Budovskis, corr. 1994/96.

10 f7+

A tempo-gaining pawn sac, but 10 ♕f3!? has also been played: 10...♗e6 11 0-0-0 ♘c6 12 ♗a6!? ♘d4 13 ♖xd4! ♕xd4 14 ♗xb7 ♖b8 15 ♗c6+ ♗d7 16 f7+?? (16 ♗xd7+ ♕xd7 17 ♘g5 is far from clear) 16...♔d8 0-1, Terblanche-Stamer, corr. 1993 as 17 ♘c3 ♗xc6 18 ♕xc6 ♗d6 leaves Black a rook up.

10...♔xf7

10...♔e7?! offers no obvious advantage: 11 ♗d3 ♘c6 (the 11...♔xf7 12 ♗c4+ of Sireta-Downey, corr. 1994/96, transposes to 10...♔xf7) 12 0-0 ♗e6 13 ♖e1 ♖d8 14 h4 ♕d5? 15 ♘g5 ♖d6 16 c4 the e-file pressure proving decisive in Sireta-Stamer, corr. 1994/97.

11 ♗c4+ ♗e6

This now seems best, although I still believe that 11...♔g6!? is worth a try: 12 0-0 ♘c6 13 ♕f3 (13 ♘g3?! ♗c5 14 ♖e1?? ♗xf2+! 'the boot is on the other foot'! 15 ♔xf2 ♕c5+ 16 ♖e3 ♖f8+ 17 ♔g1 ♕xe3+ winning, Evans-Doyle, corr. 1993; I think that 13 ♗d3! is best, 13...♔h6

[13...♔f7!? 14 ♗c4+ ♔g6 might be a draw] 14 ♕d2+ g5 15 f4 with some attack) 13...♗e7 14 ♗d3 ♔h6 15 g4 g5 16 ♘g3 ♕f4 17 ♕d5 ♗xg4 18 ♖ae1 ♖ad8 0-1, Melchor-Diepstraten, corr. 1991.

However, bringing the king to the open e-file is dodgy, 11...♔e8?! 12 0-0 ♕xb2? (12...♗e7 13 ♖e1 is less clear) 13 ♕d5 ♘d7 14 ♘g5 ♕f6 15 ♘f7 ♖g8 16 ♖fe1+ ♗e7 17 ♘d6+ cxd6 18 ♕xg8+, regaining material with a strong attack, Sireta Niemand, corr. 1994/95.

12 ♕f3+

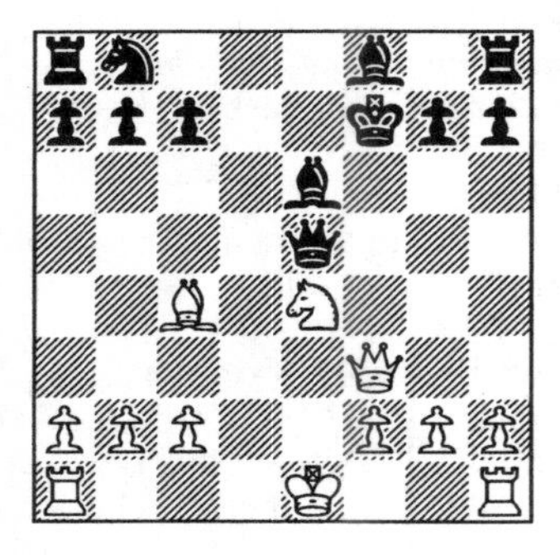

12...♔g8

At the time of my first book on the Latvian, it was not clear which move was strongest, but now important new resources have been found in the main line, the text is clearly best. 12...♔e8?! is too difficult for Black: 13 ♗xe6 ♕xe6 14 0-0-0 ♗e7 15 ♖he1 (training its sights on the poor black king) 15...♘c6 (15...♕h6+ is similar, but leaves the queen offside, 16 ♔b1 ♘c6 17 ♘c5 ♖d8 18 ♘e6 ♖xd1+ 19 ♕xd1 ♕xh2 20 g3! with threats, Krantz-Melchor, corr. 1989) 16 ♘c5 (to come to the key square e6, but 16 ♘c3 has also been effective: 16...♕h6+?! [16...♕f7] 17 ♔b1 ♕xh2? 18 ♘d5 ♖d8 19 ♖d3 ♖d7 20 ♕g4 1-0, Huizer-Owens, corr. 1996; 16 ♘d6+?! is worse, as although the black queen is lost, Black has plenty of pieces as compensation, 16...♕xd6 17 ♖xd6 cxd6 18 ♕g3 ♔f8 unclear) 16...♕xa2 17 ♘e6 ♕a1+ 18 ♔d2 ♗b4+ 19 ♔e2! (an improvement on 19 ♔e3?! from the same two protagonists, ending in a draw) 19...♕a6+ (19...♕xb2?! 20 ♘xc7+ ♔e7 21 ♘d5+ ♔e8 22 ♘xb4 ♕xb4 23 ♔f1+ ♘e7 24 ♕h5+ with advantage, Krantz-Elburg, corr. 1991) 20 ♖d3 ♗d6 21 ♔f1 ♘e5? (21...♘e7) 22 ♖xe5 ♗xe5 23 ♕h5+ ♔e7 24 ♕xe5 ♔f7 25 ♘xc7 ♕a1+ 26 ♔e2 1-0 Sireta-Vitols, corr. 1994/96.

13 ♕d3!

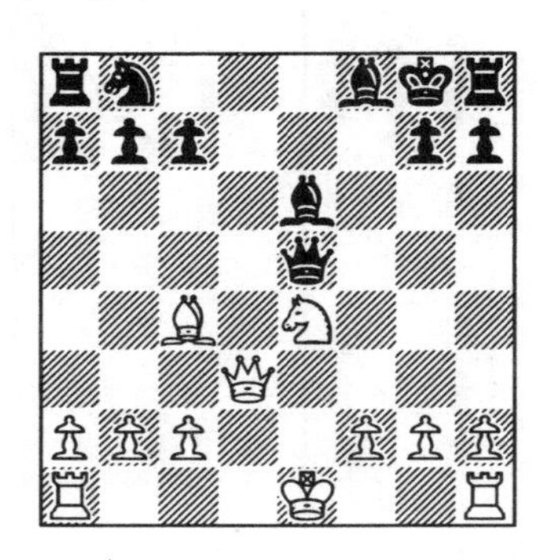

Lining up menaces along the a2-g8 diagonal. 13 ♗xe6+?! allowed Black to fend off the attack in Svendsen-Destrebecq, corr. 1991: 13...♕xe6 14 0-0-0 ♘c6 15 ♘g5? ♕xa2 16 ♖d5 ♕a1+ 17 ♔d2 ♗b4+ 18 ♔d3 ♕a6+ 19 c4 ♖f8 ∓.

13...♘c6!

This now seems to be best, although 13...♗e7 is also a satisfactory reply here, 14 f4 (a key deflection) 14...♕f5! (14...♕a5+ 15 c3 ♕b6 16 0-0-0 ♘a6? [16...♕c6!? 17 ♘c5 ♕xc5 18 ♗xe6+ ♔f8 might just hold on] 17 ♖he1 ♖d8 [17...♔f8 18 ♘g5] 18 ♕xd8+! ♗xd8 19 ♖xd8+ ♔f7 20 ♘g5+ 1-0,

Krantz-Svendsen, corr. 1992) 15 ♘g5 ♗b4+! (to force the c-pawn to 'undefend' the queen, if 15...♕xd3 then 16 ♗xe6+ ♔f8 17 cxd3 gives White a small edge, Krantz-Svendsen, corr. 1992) 16 c3 ♕xd3 17 ♗xd3 ♗d5 18 cxb4 ♘c6 19 0-0 h6 and Black was almost equal, Sireta-Heap, corr. 1994/97.

13...c6!? is another sound idea, 14 0-0-0 (the point is that 14 f4?! is now met by 14...♗xc4 15 ♕xc4+ ♕d5) 14...♘a6 15 f4?! (15 ♖he1 is stronger) 15...♕xf4+ 16 ♔b1 ♗xc4 17 ♕xc4+ ♕f7 18 ♕d4 ♘b4 19 b3 ♘d5 consolidating, Sireta-Downey, corr. 1994/96.

14 f4

14...♗b4+!

To force c3, for the same reason as before. Black was forced to part with his queen after 14...♕f5!? 15 ♘c5! ♖e8 16 ♕xf5 ♗xc4+ 17 ♔d2! (17 ♔f2? g6 18 ♕g5 ♖e2+ [18...♗e7?? 19 ♖he1 ♔g7 20 ♖xe7+ ♖xe7 21 ♖e1 with advantage, in Elburg-Destrebecq, corr. training game 1993] 19 ♔f3 ♘d4+ 20 ♔g3 ♘f5+ 21 ♔h3 ♗e7 22 ♕g4 ♖e3+ 23 g3 ♗e2 wins!) 17...g6 18 ♕g4 ♗xc5 19 ♖ae1 ♖d8+ 20 ♔c1 the undeveloped h8-rook is a problem, Sireta-Elburg, corr. 1994/96.

14...♕a5+? 15 ♔f1!! (to free the e1-square for a rook) 15...♖e8 16 ♘g5 ♘d8 17 ♘xe6 ♘xe6 18 ♖e1 ♔f7 19 ♖e5 ♕b4 20 ♕f5+ ♔g8 21 ♕xe6+ ♖xe6 22 ♗xe6 mate, Krantz-Svendsen, corr. 1991.

15 c3 ♕f5 16 cxb4 ♖d8 17 ♕e2 ♘d4! 18 ♖d1 ♔f8! 19 ♗xe6 ♕xe6 20 ♔f2

The queen versus two rooks position is terrible for White, although there is little choice, as after 20 ♕d3 ♘c6 he drops material.

20...♘xe2 21 ♖xd8+ ♔e7 22 ♖xh8 ♘xf4

With a winning position for Black, Sireta-De Jong, corr. 1994/95.

12 3 ♘c3 Mlotkowski's variation

1 e4 e5 2 ♘f3 f5 3 ♘c3

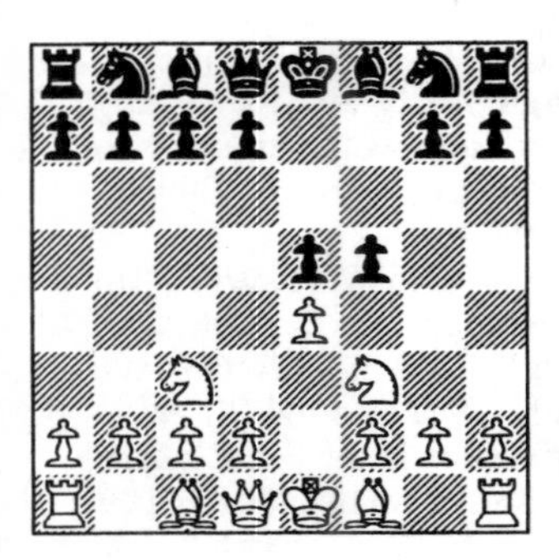

White sensibly continues his development. Although such a move can hardly be critical for the evaluation of the Latvian Gambit, nevertheless Black has to take care. The move was first analysed by the American Mlotkowski in the *BCM* of 1916. Essentially, Black has two main replies:

A 3...♘f6
B 3...fxe4

There are a couple of popular alternatives that really belong to books on other openings:

a) 3...d6, once again, a Philidor's Defence is reached 4 d4 fxe4 5 ♘xe4 ♘f6 (5...d5 6 ♘xe5 dxe4 7 ♕h5+ g6 8 ♘xg6, unclear, is the principal variation) 6 ♘xf6+ (6 ♗g5!? ♗e7 7 ♘xf6+ gxf6?! [but 7...♗xf6 8 ♗xf6 gxf6 =] 8 ♗h6 ♖g8 9 ♗d3 e4 10 ♗xe4 f5 11 ♗d5 ♖g6 12 ♕d2 c6 13 ♗b3 ♖xg2 14 0-0-0 didn't look too good for Black in Melchor-Downey, corr. 1993) 6...gxf6! (always capture towards the centre! 6...♕xf6? 7 ♗g5 ♕e6 8 dxe5 ♘d7 9 ♗d3 ♗e7 10 0-0 with advantage Krantz-Rittenhouse, corr. 1993) 7 dxe5 dxe5! 8 ♘d2! (the endgame after 8 ♕xd8+ ♔xd8 9 ♗e3 ♗g4 10 h3 ♗e6 11 0-0-0+ ♘d7 12 ♔b1 ♗d6 13 ♘d2 ♔e7, is very pleasant for Black, Sebastian-Hector, Aviles 1989) 8...♗e6 9 ♕f3 ♗d5? (9...c6 10 ♘e4 ♗g7 11 ♗e3 0-0 unclear) 10 ♘e4 ♗e7 11 ♗e3 c6 12 0-0-0 ♘d7 13 ♖xd5!! cxd5 14 ♕h5+ ♔f8 15 ♗b5 with a powerful attack, Krantz-Downey, corr. 1991.

b) 3...♘c6 The Three Knights' Game 4 d4 fxe4 (4...exd4?! speeds up White's development: 5 ♘xd4 ♘xd4 6 ♕xd4 d6 7 ♗c4 ♘f6 8 ♗g5 ♗e7 9 0-0-0 with advantage, Svendsen-Melchor, corr. 1988) 5 ♘xe5 ♘f6 6 ♗c4 ♕e7 (a rather clumsy move to have to make, but 6...d5?! meets 7 ♘xd5! ♘xd5 8 ♕h5+ g6 9 ♘xg6 hxg6 [9...♘f6?? 10 ♗f7+! ♔xf7 11 ♘e5+ leads to mate] 10 ♕xg6+ with a strong attack) 7 ♗g5!? (7 ♗f4) 7...♘xe5 8 dxe5 ♕xe5 9 ♗xf6 gxf6 10 0-0 c6? 11 ♘xe4 d5 12 ♘c3 ♗e6 13 ♖e1 ♕d6 14 ♘xd5! ♔f7 15 ♕h5+ ♔g7 16 ♖xe6 ♕xe6 17 ♘e3 1-0, Jensen-Melchor, corr. 1992.

A 3...♘f6

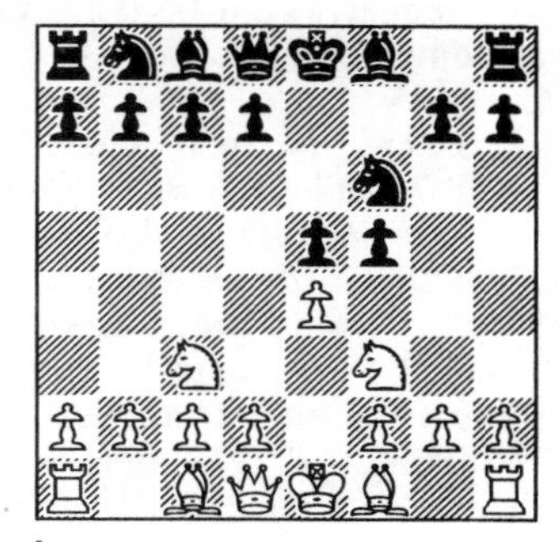

4 ♗c4

The most direct, but there is also:

a) 4 exf5 e4 this will probably resemble variations in Chapter 10, although some options are restricted by the inclusion of ♘c3 and ...♘f6 (Anyway, better to avoid 4...d6?! 5 d4 e4 6 ♘h4 ♗e7 7 g4! [7 ♗g5 0-0 8 g4, Scherbakov-Lomakin, Novokuznetsk 1997, is not so strong, 8...d5! with reasonable play] 7...♘xg4 8 ♕xg4 ♗xh4 9 ♕h5+ ♔d7 10 ♖g1 with a clear advantage Jove-Van Willigen corr. 1998; Destrebecq suggests 4...♕e7!? but it is unnatural, 5 ♗c4 c6 6 0-0 d6 [6...d5? is too weakening, 7 ♖e1 ♘bd7 8 ♗b3 e4 9 d3 and Black has severe problems along the e-file, Oren-Canal Oliveras, corr. 1997] 7 d4 [7 ♖e1 ♗xf5 8 d4 ♘bd7 {8...e4 9 d5!} 9 dxe5 ♘xe5 is also better for White, Wittmann-Gunderam, corr. 1965] 7...e4 8 d5! c5?! 9 ♗d3 blowing the e-file open, Oren-Kozlov, corr. 1994/97) 5 ♘g5! (5 ♘e5 and 5 ♘d4 transpose into Chapter 10, and 5 ♕e2 likewise, e.g. 5...d5 6 d3 ♗b4 7 dxe4 0-0!? 8 ♗d2 ♗xc3 9 ♗xc3 ♘xe4 ∓ Landgraf-Magee, corr. 1991, whilst 5 ♘h4 is a playable alternative: 5...d5 [5...♗b4] 6 d4 ♗e7 7 ♗g5 [7 g4] 7...0-0 8 g4 [8 g3 has also been tried, the f5-pawn can be defended by ♗h3, 8...h6?! {8...♘c6} 9 ♗f4 ♘c6 10 ♘g6 with advantage, Spiegel-Magee, corr. 1990] 8...♘c6 [but a good King's Gambit plan would be 8...c6!, and ...♘e8] 9 ♗b5 ♕d6 10 a3 with some advantage, Gaard-Behrendorf, corr. 1990/92) 5...d5 6 d3 h6?! (6...♗b4!? 7 dxe4 ♕e7 might be playable) 7 ♘e6 ♗xe6 8 fxe6 ♗b4 9 ♗e2 (9 dxe4! 0-0 [or 9...d4 10 a3] 10 e5 ♘e4 11 e7 with advantage) 9...0-0 10 0-0 ♖e8 11 dxe4 ♗xc3 12 bxc3 ♘xe4 13 ♗f3 ♘c6 ±, Melchor-Jensen, corr. 1990.

b) 4 ♘xe5?! d6 5 ♘f3 (5 ♘c4 fxe4 6 d4 ♗e7 is very comfortable for Black, as well) 5...fxe4 6 ♘d4 d5 7 d3 ♗b4 (7...c5 looks like a good move, 8 ♘b3 exd3 ∓) 8 a3 ♗xc3+ 9 bxc3 0-0 10 ♗e2 c5 11 ♘b3 ♘c6 12 0-0 b6 ∓ Nolden-Stummer, corr. 1991.

c) 4 d4 fxe4 5 dxe5!? (5 ♘xe5 d6 [but Black can also try 5...♗b4!?] 6 ♗g5! transposes to the 3 d4 variation; 5 ♘g5 exd4 6 ♕xd4 c6 7 ♘gxe4 d5 8 ♘xf6+ ♕xf6 9 ♕xf6 gxf6= Tudor-Milner Barry, Hastings 1952/53, by transposition) 5...exf3 6 ♕xf3 ♕e7! (6...♗e7? 7 ♗c4! d5 8 exf6 with advantage, Gaard-Tiemann, corr. 1990) 7 ♗f4 (7 ♕e2 ♘g8 8 ♘d5 ♕d8 should be good for Black, despite his lack of development) 7...d6 8 0-0-0 dxe5 9 ♗xe5 ♕xe5 10 ♗c4 Gåård-Kozlov, corr. 1989, and now 10...♕g5+ will win at a canter.

4...fxe4

a) The best reply to 4...♘c6 is probably 5 d4 (5 ♘g5?! d5) with the continuation 5...♗b4!? (5...exd4 6 ♘xd4 ♘xd4 7 ♕xd4 fxe4 8 ♗g5 c6 9 0-0-0 d5 10 ♘xe4 with advantage Svendsen-Gaard, corr. 1992, is a little too easy for White) 6 ♘xe5 (6 dxe5! ♘xe4 7 0-0) 6...♕e7 7 0-0

♗xc3 8 bxc3 fxe4 9 ♗g5?! ♘xe5 10 dxe5 ♕xe5 11 ♗xf6 gxf6 12 ♗d5 ♔d8, and Black managed to hang on to his ill-gotten gains, Svendsen-Krantz, corr. 1990.

b) 4...♘xe4!? has received some attention since I first wrote about the Latvian: 5 ♘xe5 (or 5 ♘xe4 fxe4 6 ♘xe5 d5!? [or even 6...♕f6] 7 ♕h5+ g6 8 ♘xg6 hxg6 9 ♕xg6+ transposing to the main line) 5...♕e7 6 ♗f7+!? (6 d4 ♘xc3 7 bxc3 d6 8 ♗a3 c5 ∓) 6...♔d8 7 ♘d5! ♕xe5 8 d4 ♕d6 9 ♗f4 ♕c6 10 ♗xc7+ ♕xc7 11 ♘xc7 ♔xc7 is very promising for White, Niemand-Destrebecq, corr. 1999.

5 ♘xe5 d5

The alternative 5...♕e7?! is under a cloud at the moment: 6 d4! (discovered by M.Johnson, and much stronger than 6 ♘g4 c6 7 ♘xf6+ gxf6 unclear; or 6 ♘f7? d5) with:

a) 6...♘c6 7 ♗f4 (more incisive than 7 ♗f7+ ♔d8 8 ♘xc6+?! bxc6 9 ♗b3 d5 10 ♗f4 ♕f7 11 0-0 ♗d6 ± Stummer-Sénéchaud, corr. 1991) 7...d6 8 ♗f7+ ♔d8 9 ♗b3 ♗e6 10 d5! ♘xe5 11 dxe6 ♘g6 12 ♗g5 h6 13 ♘d5 ♕e8 14 ♗xf6+ gxf6 15 ♘xf6 ♕e7 16 ♘xe4 with a big plus, Johnson-Clarke, corr. 1989/90.

b) 6...d6 7 ♗f7+!? ♔d8 8 ♗g5 c6 9 ♗b3 ♗e6 10 0-0 ♗xb3 11 axb3 ♔c7 12 ♕d2! ♕e6 13 ♘c4 ♘bd7 14 f3 exf3 15 ♖ae1 ♕f7 16 ♖xf3 with advantage, Krantz-Grivainis, corr. 1991.

c) 6...exd3? 7 0-0 dxc2 8 ♕d2 ♕b4 9 ♖e1 ♗e7 10 ♕g5 d5 11 ♕xg7 ♖f8 12 ♘d3 ♕d6 13 ♗f4 1-0, Strelis-Alloin, corr. 1992.

d) 6...c6 7 ♗g5 d6 (7...d5?! 8 ♗xd5 ♘xd5 9 ♘xd5 with advantage—Johnson) 8 ♗f7+ ♔d8 9 ♗b3! with advantage Krantz-Grivainis, corr. 1991.

6 ♘xd5!

Any retreat would be tantamount to an admission of defeat.

6...♘xd5

Black has no real choice, as 6...♗e6 7 ♘f4 (7 ♘xf6+ ♕xf6 8 ♗xe6 ♕xe5 9 ♗c8 is also winning easily, Krantz-Svendsen, corr. 1994/95) 7...♕d6 8 ♘xe6 ♕xe5 9 0-0 ♗d6 10 g3 should be winning, Borsdorff-Callinan, corr. 1968.

7 ♕h5+ g6 8 ♘xg6 hxg6

Again Black must face the music, 8...♘f6?! seems to lose: 9 ♕e5+ ♗e7 10 ♘xh8 ♘c6 11 ♗f7+ ♔f8 12 ♕g5 ♗d6 13 ♗b3! (the best way of extracting the knight, 13 ♕h6+? ♔e7 14 ♕g7 ♕f8 15 ♕xf8+ ♔xf8 16 d3 ♘b4 with some chances, Franck-Druke, corr. 1989) 13...♕e7 14 ♘f7 ♗c5 (14...♘g4?! 15 h3 ♕xg5 16 ♘xg5 ♘f6 17 0-0 ♗f5 18 f3! winning, Krantz-Druke, corr. 1990) 15 ♘h6 ♘d4 and now as well as 16 0-0, Strelis-Destrebecq, corr. 1991, 16 ♘g8 ♘xc2+ 17 ♔d1 is immediately decisive.

9 ♕xg6+

The coming attack resembles that of chapter eight.

9 ♕xh8?! ♕f6 should be OK for Black, 10 ♕xf6 (10 ♕h7?! ♗e6 11 d3?! ♗b4+ 12 ♔f1? [12 ♔e2] 12...♗c5, soon winning, Arguelles-Barros, corr. 1971) 10...♘xf6 11 d3 exd3 12 ♗xd3 ♔f7 13 0-0 ♗d6 14 ♗d2 ♘c6 and the black knights are quite the equal of the rook and pawns, Leeners-Alderden, corr. 1982.

9...♔d7

If instead 9...♔e7!?, then 10 d3!? (10 ♕g5+ ♔e8 11 ♕e5+ ♕e7 12 ♕xh8 ♘f4 might give some counterplay) 10...e3 11 ♕g5+, Niemand-Canal Oliveras, corr. 1998, and now 11...♔e6!? might be worth trying.

10 ♗xd5

White has an interesting possibility here: 10 ♕f5+ ♔c6 11 ♗xd5+ ♕xd5 (or 11...♔b6!?) 12 ♕f6+ ♗e6 13 ♕xh8 ♘d7 unclear.

10...♕e7

10...c6 is currently more popular, 11 ♗xe4 ♔c7 (the king reaches a relatively 'safe' square) 12 d4 ♗d6 13 ♗g5 ♕f8 14 h4 ♗g4 with a sharp material imbalance, Melchor-Destrebecq. corr. 1997).

11 ♕xe4

With four pawns for the piece, White can consider playing the endgame here.

a) 11 d3?! exd3+ 12 ♗e3 dxc2 (Black can go into another ending: 12...c6! 13 ♗b3 d2+ [13...dxc2] 14 ♔xd2 ♕d6+) 13 ♕xc2 ♕e5 14 0-0-0 ♗d6 ½-½, Melchor-Krongraf, corr. 1991, again somewhat premature one feels, as both sides have reason to continue.

b) 11 ♗xe4 ♖h6 12 ♕f5+ ♔d8 13 ♕f3 ♘c6 14 d3 ♘d4 15 ♕d1 ♖g6 is unclear, Malmström-Collins, corr. 1999.

11...♖h4 12 ♕xe7+ ♗xe7 13 g3 ♖h5 14 ♗e4 ♘c6 15 f4 ♗f6 16 c3 ♔d6 17 d3 ♗d7 18 ♗e3 ♘e7 19 0-0-0 c6 ½-½, Evans-Koser, corr. 1993, although there is plenty of play left at the end.

B 3...fxe4

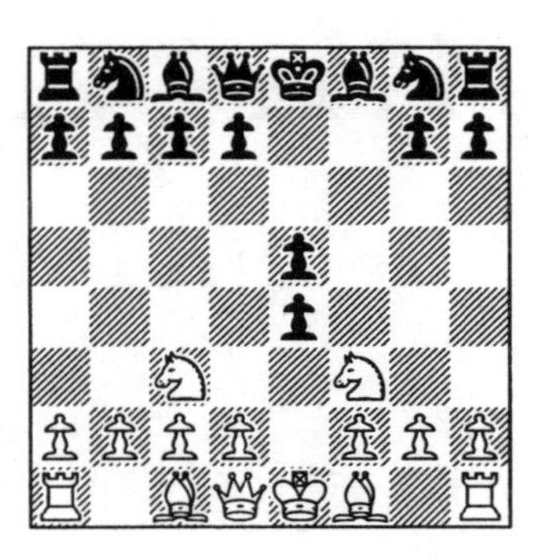

4 ♘xe5

The natural move 4 ♘xe4?! is significantly worse: 4...♘f6 (4...d5 is also good, as 5 ♘xe5? loses a piece to 5...♕e7, and 5 ♘c3 e4 6 ♘d4?! ♘f6 7 ♗e2?! c5! 8 ♗b5+? Delavenne-Destrebecq, France 1977, 8...♔f7 winning a piece) 5 ♘xf6+ ♕xf6 6 d3 ♗c5 7 ♗e2 0-0 8 0-0 ♘c6 9 c3 d5 10 ♗g5 ♕g6 11 ♗h4 h6 12 ♗g3 ♗d6 ∓ Danielsson-Hector, Umea 1990.

4...♕f6

Once again, the obvious move 4...♘f6?! brings problems, as 5 ♘g4! wins a pawn (5 ♗c4 is not bad either and transposes into A; 5 d4 d6 [but 5...♗b4 6 ♗e2 d6 is safer] 6 ♗g5 transposes into Chapter 11) 5...♘c6 (there is nothing better, 5...♕e7 6 ♘xf6+ gxf6 7 ♕g4 with advantage, Spiegel-Landgraf, corr. 1991; 5...♗b4 6 ♘xf6+ ♕xf6 7 ♘xe4 ♕e5 8 ♕e2 with advantage Destrebecq-Kozlov, corr. 1982/86; and 5...♗e7 6 ♘xf6+ ♗xf6 7 ♘xe4 0-0 8 ♗e2 [8 ♘xf6+ ♕xf6 9 ♗c4+] 8...d5 9 ♘xf6+ ♕xf6 10 0-0 ♘c6 11 c3 d4 12 d3 ± Tiemann-Elburg, corr. 1990) 6 ♘xf6+ (6 ♗c4 is also good) 6...♕xf6 7 ♕h5+! (7 ♘xe4? loses in this instance to 7...♕e5 8 ♕e2 ♘d4) 7...g6 8 ♘xe4? (as Franz Destrebecq points out, 8 ♕d5! wins the e-pawn under somewhat more favourable circumstances: 8...♘b4 9 ♕xe4+ ♕e7 10 ♕xe7+ ♗xe7 11 ♔d1 with advantage) 8...♕e7 9 ♕e2 ♘d4 10 ♕d3 ♗g7 11 c3 d5 12 cxd4 dxe4 ∓, Schirmer-Koser, corr. 1993.

One other move worth noting is Doyle's idea 4...g6?! with the possible follow-up 5 ♗c4 (5 ♘xe4! ♕e7 6 d4 looks more worrying, i.e. 6...♘c6 7 ♗g5 ♕e6 [7...♕b4+? 8 c3 ♕xb2?? 9 ♘c4 ±] 8 f4 with advantage) 5...♕g5 6 ♘f7 ♕xg2 7 ♖f1 c6 8 ♘xh8 d5 9 ♗e2 ♗g7 10 d3 ♕xh2

11 dxe4 d4 with a certain amount of compensation.

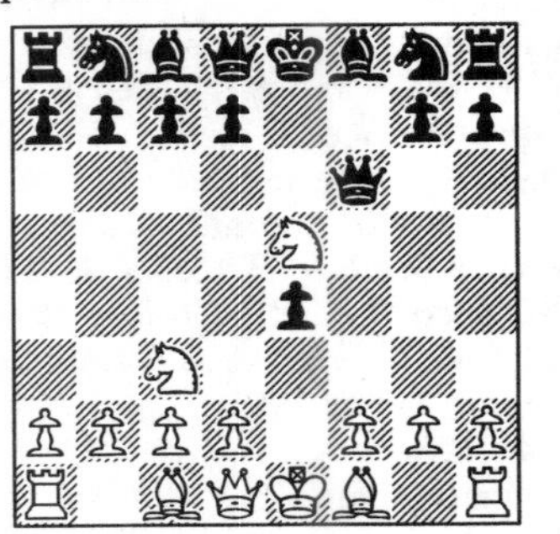

White faces another major choice:

B1 5 f4!?
B2 5 d4

Otherwise, we transpose directly into chapter five if White chooses 5 ♘c4!, and another possibility is 5 ♘g4 although the knight is not particularly well placed here: 5...♕g6 (5...♕e6?! 6 ♘e3 ♘f6 7 ♗c4 ♕b6, Evans-Schirmer, corr. 1992, is too awkward) 6 d3 (6 ♘d5 ♗d6 7 d3 c6 8 ♘c3 ♗b4 9 ♗d2 d5, hitting the exposed knight on g4, Walker-Dravnieks, corr. 1955/56, is fine for Black; 6 ♘e3 ♘f6 7 d3 ♗b4 leaves Black better placed than in Chapter 3) 6...d5 7 h3 ♗xg4?! (7...♗b4) 8 hxg4 exd3 9 ♗xd3 ♕e6+ 10 ♕e2 with an edge, Borsdorff-Strautins, corr. 1969.

B1 5 f4!?

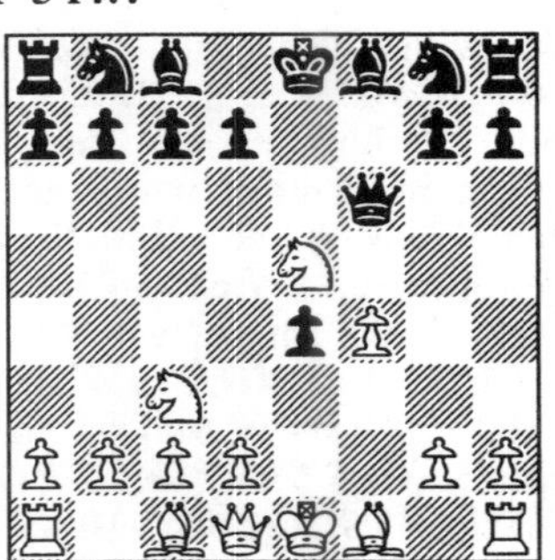

This newish move has become very popular in the last few years, and has scored nearly 100%!

5...exf3

And not 5...♕xf4? 6 ♕h5+ g6 7 ♘xg6 hxg6 8 ♕xh8, Niemand-Clarke, corr. 1999.

6 ♘xf3 ♕e6+

The queen is misplaced on the open f-file, 6...c6?! 7 d4 d5 8 ♗e2 ♗d6 9 0-0 ♕d8 10 ♘g5 ♘f6 11 ♗h5+ g6? 12 ♕e2+ ♔d7 13 ♗g4+ 1-0, De Jong-Van de Velden, 1998.

7 ♗e2 ♘f6 8 0-0 ♗e7 9 d4 d5 10 ♖e1

10 ♗f4!? may be superior, 10...c6 (10...♕b6!?) 11 ♕d2 0-0 12 ♖ae1 gives White a useful lead in development, Oren-Grivainis/Hayward, corr. 1997.

10...0-0

10...♕d6 11 ♗b5+!? c6 12 ♕e2 cxb5 13 ♘xb5 ♕d8 14 ♗f4 ♘a6 15 c4 is dangerous, but Black managed to defend, Krantz-Budovskis, corr. 1994/95.

11 ♗c4!? ♕d6 12 ♘xd5 ♘xd5 13 ♗xd5+ ♕xd5 14 ♖xe7

Krantz-Jackson, corr. 1994/95, when Black could have obtained a useful initiative by 14...♘c6! 15 ♖e3 (15 ♖xc7?! ♕d6) 15...♗g4.

B2 5 d4

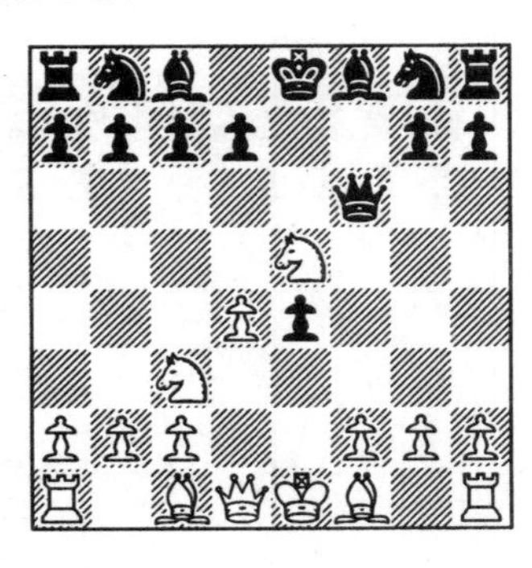

5...exd3

Both 5...d6? 6 ♘d5 ♕d8 7 ♕h5+ g6 8 ♘xg6 hxg6 9 ♕xh8 ♔f7 10 ♗c4 ♗e6 11 ♕h7+ ♗g7 12 ♘f4! ♗xc4 13 ♕xg6+ ♔f8 14 d5 1-0, Krantz-Hayward, corr. 1990, and 5...♗b4? 6 ♕g4 ♗xc3+ 7 bxc3 ♘e7 8 ♗g5 d5 9 ♗xf6 ♗xg4 10 ♗xg7 1-0 Diepstraaten-Izuel, corr., leave Black with difficult problems.

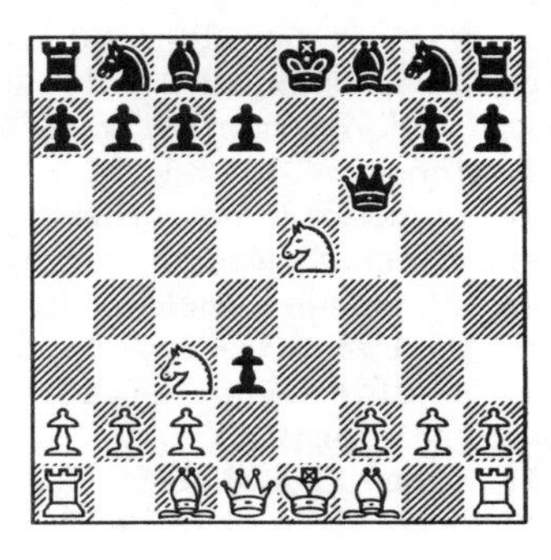

6 f4!?

Somewhat sharper than the alternative 6 ♘xd3, although this, too, has been successful in practice: 6...d6 (6...♕e6+? is worse: 7 ♗e2 ♘f6 8 0-0 ♗e7 9 ♖e1 g6 10 ♗f3 ♕f7 11 ♗h6 d6 12 ♘b5, with advantage, Wundt-Dravnieks, corr. 1992; but 6...c6!? 7 ♗e2 [7 ♕e2+ ♗e7 8 ♘e4 ♕e6 9 ♗f4 d5 10 ♘d6+ Wibe-Svedenborg, Norway 1978, gives an edge] 7...d5 8 0-0 [8 ♗f4!?] 8...♗d6 9 ♗h5+ g6 10 ♖e1+ ♘e7, Lefhaili-Kosten, Reims 1994, is nothing special for White) 7 ♕e2+ ♕e6 8 ♘d5 ♕xe2+ 9 ♗xe2 ♘a6 10 ♘3f4 ♔d8 11 ♗d2! c6 12 ♗xa6 bxa6 13 ♗a5+ ♔d7 14 ♘c7 ♖b8 15 ♘fe6 ♘f6 (15...♗e7?! 16 0-0-0 ♗f6 17 b3 ♔e7 18 ♖he1 with advantage, Downey-Svendsen, corr. 1991) 16 0-0-0 d5 17 c4? (17 ♘xf8+ ♖xf8 18 ♖he1 avoids getting the knights trapped) 17...♗b4 18 ♗xb4 ♖xb4 19 cxd5 cxd5 20 ♔b1 ♔d6 21 ♖he1 ♖c4 22 ♖c1 ♖xc1+ 23 ♔xc1 ♘e8 24 ♘xe8+ ♖xe8 0-1, Svendsen-Clarke, corr. 1994/95.

6...dxc2

There is no reason Black shouldn't take this pawn, but 6...♗b4 is also possible, 7 ♗xd3 (7 ♕xd3 is not so logical, Tiemann-Melchor, corr. 1990, continuing: 7...d6 8 ♕b5+ ♘c6 9 ♘xc6 ♗xc3+ 10 ♔f2 a6 unclear) 7...d6 8 0-0!? ♗xc3 9 bxc3 ♘e7 (I now feel that it is best not to take the piece, Keres gives 9...dxe5?! 10 fxe5 ♕b6+ [perhaps it is better to save this check by 10...♕e6!?, stopping ♗c4, and defending the kingside, in particular f7, 11 ♗a3 ♘d7!? 12 ♕h5+ g6 13 ♕h4 with strong pressure for the piece] 11 ♔h1 ♘e7 12 ♗a3 ♕e6 [12...♗e6?! 13 ♕h5+ g6 14 ♕h4 leaves Black in severe trouble, 14...c5 15 ♕f6 ♖g8 16 ♖ab1 1-0, Niemand-Vitols, corr. 1994/95] 13 ♕h5+ g6 14 ♕h4 with an annoying threat of infiltration on f6, Niemand-Malmström, corr. 1994/98) 10 ♗a3!? (10 ♘g4 ♗xg4 11 ♕xg4 ♘bc6 [11...♘d7 12 ♗e3 ♕xc3 13 ♖ab1 0-0 14 ♗xa7 with advantage, Littleboy-Alberts, corr. 1977/79] 12 ♖b1 ♖b8 [12...♕xc3? 13 ♗b2 ♕c5+ 14 ♔h1 ♕d5 15 ♗xg7 1-0, Svendsen-Magee, corr. 1990] 13 ♗b2 0-0 14 ♖be1 ♘f5 with Black's superior structure offsetting the bishops, Nolden-Kozlov, corr. 1990) 10...0-0 11 ♖b1 ♘bc6 12 ♘xc6 (12 ♕e2!?) 12...♘xc6 13 ♕h5 g6 14 ♕h6 ♖b8 (14...♘d8! is worth serious consideration, menacing to trap the white queen) 15 c4 ♕g7 16 ♕h4 ♗f5 17 ♗b2 with advantage, Krantz-Kozlov, corr. 1992.

7 ♕xc2 ♗b4

7...♘c6 is an alternative, 8 ♘d5!? ♕d6 9 ♕e4 ♘ge7 10 ♗c4 ♘xd5 11 ♘xc6+ ♕e6 12 ♘e5 ♗b4+

(12...♘f6!?) 13 ♗d2 ♗xd2+ 14 ♔xd2 ♘f6 15 ♕d4 d5 (15...c5!?) 16 ♖ae1, Krantz-Strautins, corr. 1990, and now 16...0-0 is unclear.

8 ♗c4

8 ♗e3?! d6 9 0-0-0 ♗xc3 10 ♕xc3 dxe5 11 ♗b5+ ♘c6 12 fxe5 ♕g6 13 ♖hf1 ♘ge7 14 ♖f3 ♗e6 and Black eventually came out on top, Krantz-Heap, corr. 1993.

8...♘e7 9 0-0

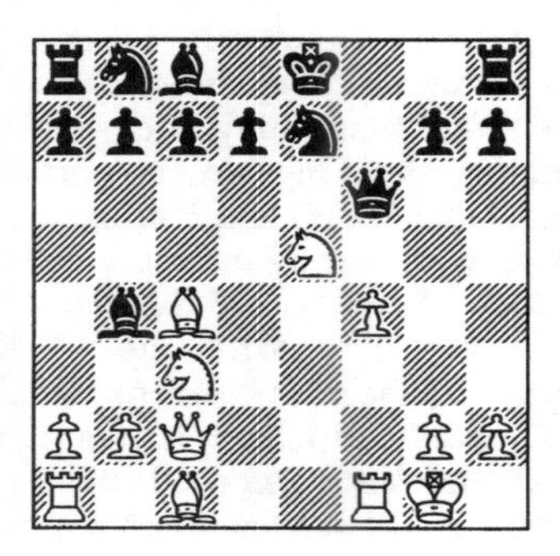

9...♗xc3 10 bxc3

10 ♗f7+ misplaces the black king, but does nothing for White's minor piece arrangement, 10...♔d8 11 bxc3 d6 12 ♖d1 ♘d7 13 ♘xd7 ♕xf7!? 14 ♘e5 ♕f6 and Black's solid structure and pawn extra give him the advantage, Pape-Sireta, corr. 1994/96.

10...d6

10...d5!? 11 ♗d3 ♗f5 12 ♖b1 b6 13 c4 0-0 14 ♗b2 ♕d6 15 ♖bd1 gives White sufficient compensation, Stamer-Gåård, corr. 1994/95.

11 ♘f3

11 ♗a3!? is more fun, and almost certainly stronger, 11...dxe5 (11...♗f5 looks safer) 12 fxe5 ♕g6 (12...♕b6+ 13 ♔h1 ♗d7 14 ♖ad1 is also unpleasant for Black) 13 ♕xg6+! and instead of 13...hxg6? 14 ♗f7+ winning, Melchor-Reinke, corr. 1994/95, 13...♘xg6 14 ♗f7+ ♔d7 15 ♖fd1+ ♔c6 16 ♗d5+ may be playable for Black.

11...♘bc6 12 ♗e3 ♗f5

12...♗e6 13 ♗d3 0-0-0 14 ♘d4 ♘d5!? is also playable, Stamer-Sireta, corr. 1994/96.

13 ♕b3 0-0-0 14 ♘d4 ♘a5 15 ♕b5 ♘xc4 16 ♕xc4 d5

16...c5!?.

17 ♕c5 b6

...with Black for preference, Stamer-Elburg, corr. 1994/95.

13 Unusual third moves for White

We have already examined a large variety of possible third moves for White, but there are some players who disdain theoretical correctness and who always search for a different route. So, we have five less usual possibilities:

A 3 d3
B 3 b4
C 3 c4
D 3 g4
E 3 ♕e2
F 3 b3

The only common factor is that none of the moves offer White any advantage!

A 1 e4 e5 2 ♘f3 f5 3 d3

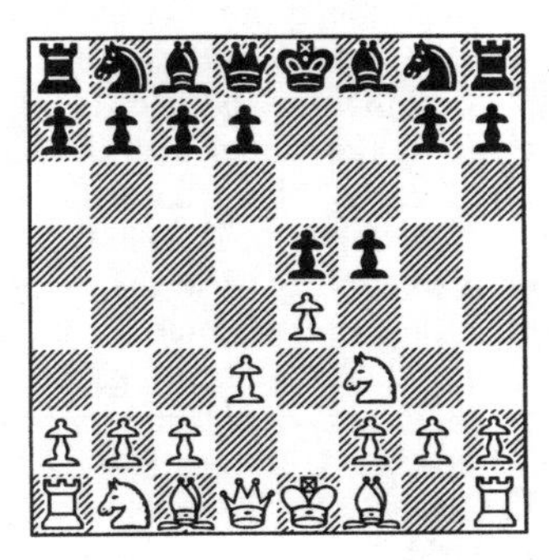

This is a solid, if passive, choice but it is the type of reply weaker players are likely to make over-the-board. So much so, that this move is played more often than all the other moves in this chapter put together!

3...♘c6

Black can just as well play the prudent 3...d6 4 ♘c3 ♘f6 5 g3 (in the game Nicholas-Simons, England 1991, White took his passive start to its logical conclusion: 5 ♗d2?! ♗e7 6 ♗e2 0-0 7 h3 ♘c6 8 ♘h2 f4 9 ♘g4 ♘d4 10 ♘xf6+ ♗xf6 11 ♗g4 ♗h4 12 ♘d5?! c6 13 ♘c3 ♕f6 14 ♘e2? f3 -+) 5...♗e7 6 ♗g2 (6 h4!? c6?! 7 ♗h3 fxe4 8 ♗xc8 ♕xc8 9 dxe4 h6 10 ♗e3 b5 11 a3 a5 12 b3 ♘a6, unclear, Vandervort-Diemer, Holland 1983) 6...♘c6 7 0-0 0-0 8 exf5 ♗xf5 9 ♘h4 ♗g4 10 f3 ♗e6 11 f4 d5!? 12 ♘f3 e4 13 dxe4 d4!? (13...♘xe4 14 ♘xe4 dxe4 15 ♕e2 ♗d5 is a good alternative) 14 ♘g5 ♗c4 15 ♘e2 ♗c5 with a certain amount of compensation for the pawn, Davies-Vasyukov, Grested 1990.

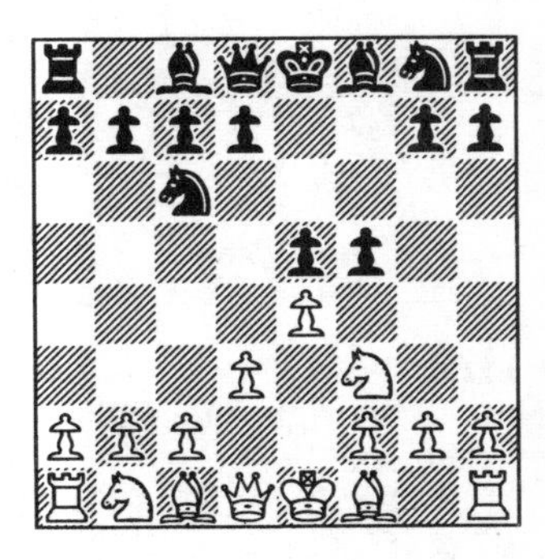

4 ♘c3

a) Giving up the centre by 4 exf5!? is possible, 4...d5 5 ♕e2 (5 ♗g5 ♗e7 6 ♗xe7 ♘gxe7 is favourable to Black; and 5 g4 fails to hold on to the pawn after 5...h5) 5...♕d6!? (if instead 5...♗d6 then 6 ♘xe5 ♗xe5 7 f4 ♗xf5 8 fxe5 ♕e7 leads to a rough equality, but the pawn sac 5...♗xf5!? is interesting, e.g. 6 ♘xe5 ♘d4 7 ♕d1 ♕f6 8 ♘f3 ♗g4) 6 b3 ♗xf5 7 ♗b2 d4 8 ♘bd2 0-0-0 9 0-0-0 with chances to both sides, Geertse-Diepstraten, corr. 1982.

b) Whilst White was horribly mauled in the game Dousse-Hector, Geneva 1986, after 4 c3 ♘f6 5 ♗g5?! d6 6 ♘bd2 h6 7 ♗xf6 ♕xf6 8 g3 g5! 9 exf5 ♗xf5 10 ♕e2 0-0-0 11 0-0-0 d5 12 ♗g2 ♗c5 13 ♘b3 ♗b6 14 ♖hf1 a5! 15 d4? (a gruesome opening of the b1-h7 diagonal!) 15...♗h7 16 ♘e1? (16 ♘xe5 ♘xe5 17 dxe5 ♕f5 18 ♔d2 ♖he8 19 ♘d4 is the best chance) 16...exd4 17 ♘xd4 ♗xd4 18 cxd4 ♘b4 19 b3 ♖he8 20 ♕b2 ♕c6+ 21 ♔d2 ♕a6 22 a3 ♖e2+ 0-1.

4...♘f6

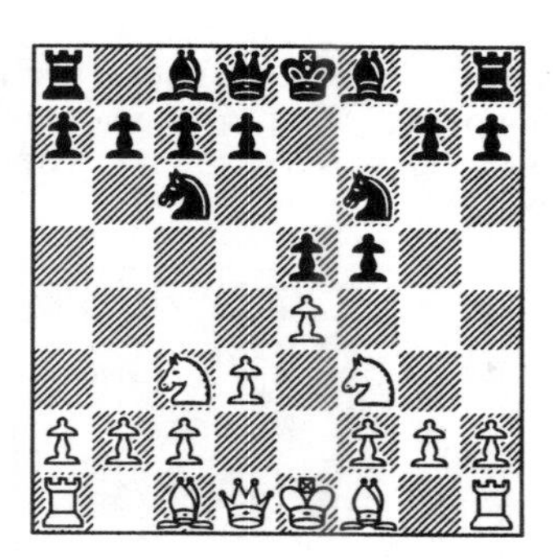

5 exf5!

Now is the right moment for this move. Others:

a) 5 ♗e2 d5!? (5...♗b4 6 exf5 d6 7 ♗d2 ♗xf5 8 a3 ♗xc3 9 ♗xc3 0-0 is pleasant for Black, Hultin-Nyholm, corr. 1994) 6 ♗g5 ♗b4 7 exd5 ♕xd5 8 ♗xf6 ♗xc3+ 9 bxc3 gxf6 10 ♘h4 0-0 11 0-0 ♘e7 12 c4 ♕d6 13 f4 ♘g6 14 ♘xg6 hxg6 15 fxe5 fxe5 ∓, Bezilko-Hector, Cappelle-la-Grande 1988.

b) 5 ♗g5 ♗b4 6 ♗e2 d6 7 0-0 ♗xc3! 8 bxc3 fxe4 9 dxe4 ♗e6 10 ♘d2 0-0 ∓ Svendsen-Destrebecq, corr. 1991.

5...d5!?

This is OK, but 5...d6 is also possible, 6 d4 (6 ♘h4!? ♗e7 7 g4 ♘xg4 8 ♕xg4 ♗xh4 9 ♕xg7 ♗f6 10 ♕g4 ♘d4 11 ♕h5+ ♔d7 is unclear) 6...exd4 7 ♘xd4 ♘xd4 8 ♕xd4 ♗xf5 9 ♗d3 ♗xd3 10 ♕xd3 c6 11 0-0 ♗e7 12 ♘e2 d5 13 ♘d4 ♕d7= Lerner-Bareev, USSR 1986, by transposition.

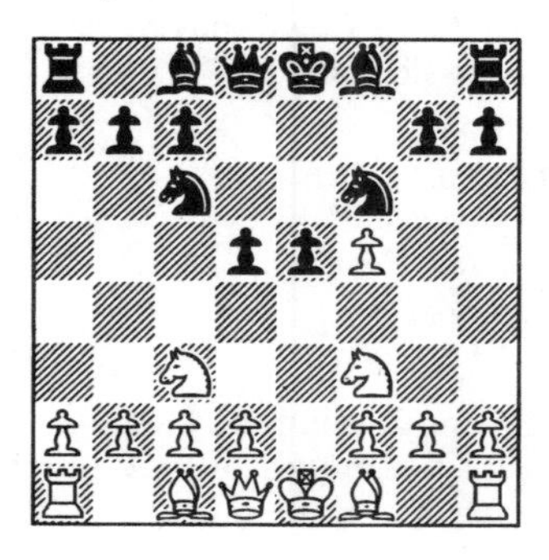

6 d4!

As Destrebecq points out, holding on to the pawn by 6 ♘h4!? allows the combination 6...♘d4!? 7 g4 ♘xg4 8 ♕xg4 ♕xh4 9 ♕xh4 ♘f3+ 10 ♔e2 ♘xh4 11 ♘xd5 ♗d6 equal, i.e. 12 f6 ♗g4+ 13 ♔e3 0-0 with good chances against the exposed white king. Nevertheless, 6...♗e7 looks good, 7 ♗g5 0-0 8 g3 h6 with good play, and 6...d4 has its points, as 7 ♘e4 ♗b4+ forces 8 ♘d2 (as 8 ♗d2? loses to 8...♘xe4).

6...exd4

6...e4?! 7 ♘e5 ♗xf5 8 ♗b5 ♗d7 9 ♗g5 with advantage.

7 ♘xd4 ♘xd4 8 ♕xd4 ♗xf5 9 ♗g5 ♗xc2

White's advantage is minimal after 9...♗e7 10 0-0-0 c6 11 ♕e5 ♗g6 12 ♖e1, but exists.

10 ♖c1 ♗g6 11 ♗xf6 ♕xf6 12 ♕e3+

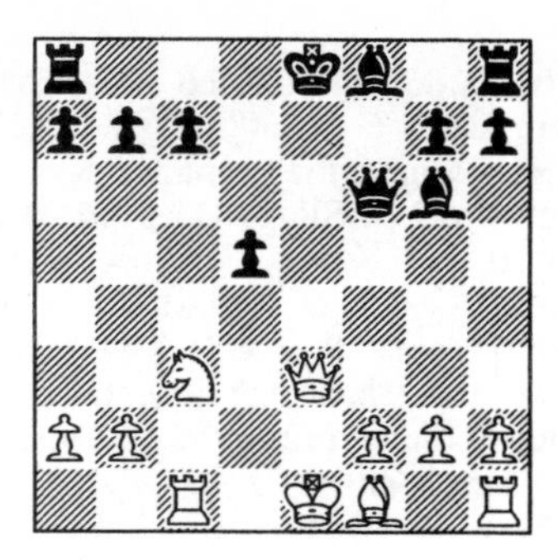

12...♔f7?

A tactical miscalculation, Black is fine following 12...♕e7 13 ♕xe7+ ♔xe7! 14 ♘xd5+ ♔d7 15 ♘xc7 ♗b4+ 16 ♔d1 ♖ad8 17 ♗b5+ ♔e7+ and his bishops may even give him the advantage.

13 ♘xd5 ♗b4+ 14 ♘xb4! ♖he8 15 ♗c4+ ♔f8 16 0-0

The point.

16...♖xe3 17 fxe3 ♗f5 18 g4

Winning a further piece for the queen, Taimanov-Zaichik, Leningrad 1989, Interestingly, this game, like at least one other in this section, actually started as a Dutch Defence: 1 ♘f3 f5 2 d3 ♘f6 3 e4 e5.

B 3 b4?!

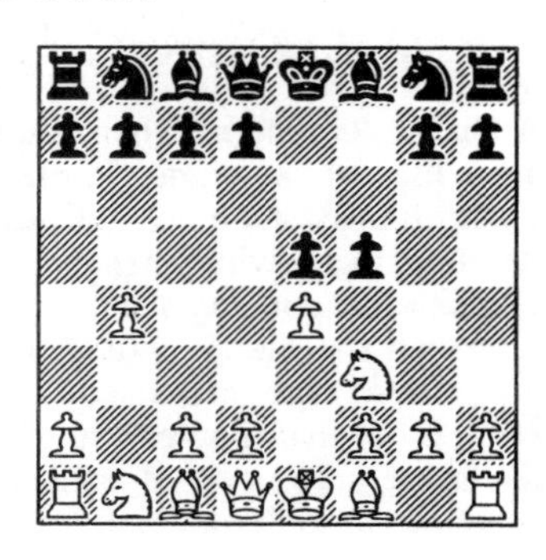

A move much loved by the French player Sénéchaud.

3...fxe4

Alternatively, 3...♗xb4 4 ♘xe5 ♘f6 (4...♕e7 5 ♕h5+ g6 6 ♘xg6 ♕xe4+ 7 ♗e2 ♘f6 8 ♕g5 ♖g8 9 ♕xf6 hxg6 10 ♗a3 ♕xg2 11 ♕e5+ ♔d8 and White forces a perpetual, Sénéchaud-Clarke, corr. 1990) 5 ♗c4 ♕e7 6 ♗b2 d6 7 ♘d3 ♕xe4+ (7...♗a5?! 8 e5 d5?! 9 0-0 ♘g4 10 ♗xd5 ♕h4 11 h3, beating off the attack with a crushing advantage, Sénéchaud-Logunov, corr. 1990) 8 ♕e2 ♗a5 9 ♘c3 ♕xe2+ exchanging queens, when White's compensation for the pawn is not sufficient, Sénéchaud-Schreyer, corr. 1990.

3...d6 4 d3 ♘f6 5 b5 ♗e7 (pawn grabbing by 5...fxe4!? 6 dxe4 ♘xe4 7 ♗c4 c6 is perfectly viable) 6 ♘c3 0-0 7 ♗b2 fairly level, Sénéchaud-Jackson, corr. 1994/95.

4 ♘xe5 ♘f6

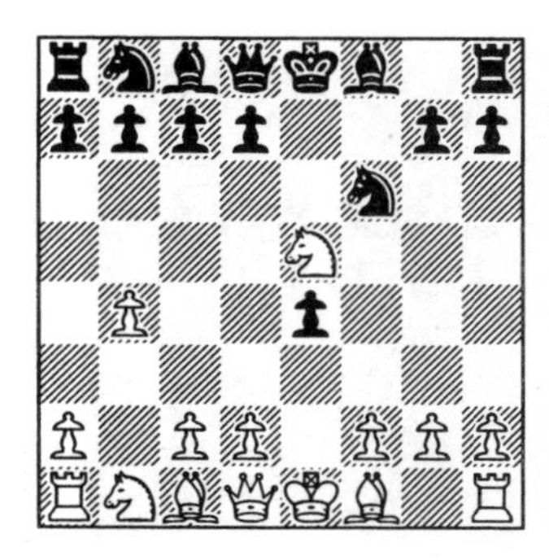

5 c3!?

Quite in keeping with the spirit of the variation, otherwise: 5 ♘g4? ♗xb4 (5...d5 is also good, 6 ♘xf6+ ♕xf6 7 ♘c3 ♕f7 [is this necessary? 7...♗xb4!? is tempting, as after 8 ♘xd5 ♕xa1 9 ♘xc7+ ♔d8 10 ♘xa8 b6 Black will win the a8-knight by ...♗b7] 8 ♖b1 a5 9 a3 ♗d6 10 d3 0-0 11 f3 axb4 12 axb4, Sénéchaud-Magee, corr. 1990, when 12...exd3 13 ♕xd3 ♗xb4 is strong, for 14 ♖xb4 ♕e7+ wins the exchange) 6 ♗b2 ♗e7 7 ♘xf6+ ♗xf6

8 ♗xf6 ♕xf6 9 ♘c3, Sénéchaud-Stummer, corr. 1990, 9...c6! 10 ♕h5+ (10 ♘xe4?? ♕e5 11 d3 d5) 10...g6 11 ♕h6 d5 with a clear Black advantage. 5 d3? d6 -/+ Sénéchaud-Littleboy, corr. 1990.

5...d6

5...d5 6 d4 ♗d6 7 f4?! exf3 8 gxf3?! 0-0 9 ♖g1 ♗f5 10 ♗d3 ♗xd3 11 ♕xd3, Sénéchaud-Svendsen, corr. 1990, 11...♘bd7 and Black enjoys an edge, owing to his superior structure.

6 ♘c4 d5 7 ♘e3 ♘c6 8 b5 ♘e5 9 d4 exd3 10 ♗xd3 ♗c5 11 0-0 0-0 12 ♗a3 ♗xa3 13 ♘xa3 ♕d6 14 ♘ac2

Sénéchaud-Budovskis, corr. 1990, when Black can exploit the weakened white queenside by 14...a6! 15 bxa6 b6.

C 3 c4!?

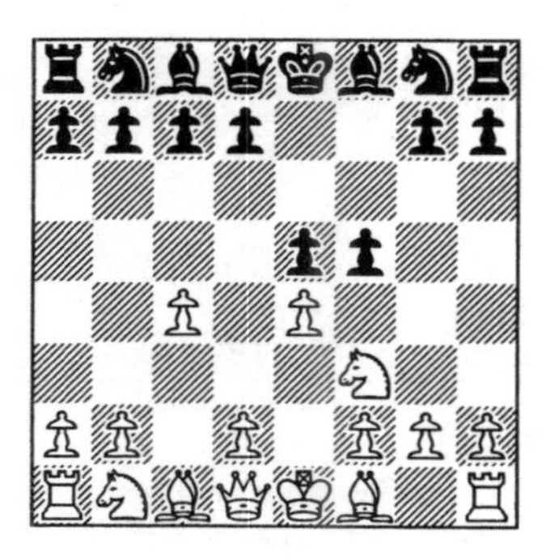

A speciality of Leo Diepstraten, in fact hardly anyone else has ever played this odd move!

3...fxe4

The simplest, although other moves are also satisfactory:

a) 3...♘c6 4 d4 exd4 5 ♘xd4 ♗b4+ 6 ♘c3 ♘xd4 7 ♕xd4 ♕e7 8 ♗d2 ♘f6 9 e5?! d6 and Black will win the e-pawn, Diepstraten-Krantz, corr. 1996.

b) 3...d6 4 ♘c3 ♘c6 (4...♘f6?! 5 exf5 ♗xf5 6 d4 e4?! 7 ♘h4 ♗d7 8 ♕e2 winning the e4-pawn, Kveinis-Antoshin, USSR 1981) 5 d4 ♘f6 6 d5 (6 exf5 ♘xd4 7 ♘xd4 exd4 8 ♕xd4 ♗xf5 is equal) 6...fxe4 7 dxc6?! exf3 8 ♕xf3 ♗g4 9 ♕d3 bxc6 and Black has an extra pawn, Diepstraten-Strautins, corr. 1998.

4 ♘xe5 ♘f6 5 ♘g4

Played to weaken Black's defence of e4.

5...♘a6! 6 ♘c3 ♘c5 7 ♘xf6+ ♕xf6 8 d4 exd3 9 ♗xd3

9 ♗e3 is more accurate.

9...♘xd3+ 10 ♕xd3 ♗b4 11 ♗d2 ♕e5+

Play is quite equal, Diepstraten-Downey, corr. 1997.

D 3 g4?

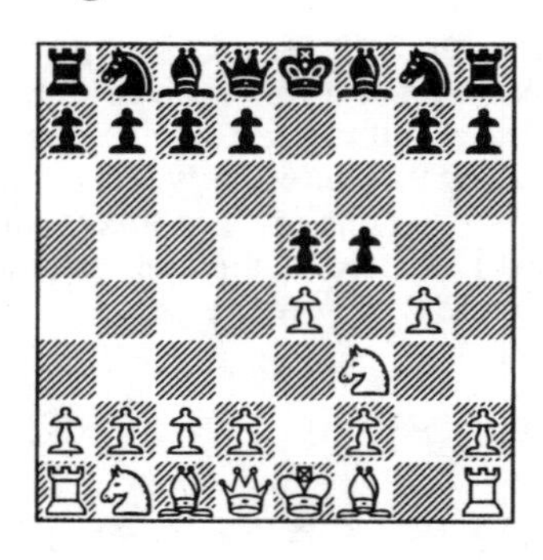

Actually, looking at this move reminds me of a game I played against Mike Basman at Manchester once. I, a mere whippersnapper at the time, after opening 1 e4, replied to Basman's 1...g5?! with 2 f4!?. Tony Miles, who happened to be passing by at that moment, immediately burst into a loud sustained laughter. I can only imagine how he would react to this idea of Sénéchaud's!

3...fxe4 4 ♘xe5 d6 5 ♘c4 d5 6 ♘e3 d4 7 ♘f5

Black is just making pawn moves, while White is just using his knight!

7...♘f6!

7...♗xf5 8 gxf5 ♕h4 ∓ Sénéchaud-Koser, corr. 1993.

8 d3 g6!

I have no idea what is happening after 8...♗b4+ 9 c3 dxc3 10 bxc3 ♗xf5 11 gxf5 exd3!? 12 cxb4 ♕d4 (12...♕d5 13 ♖g1 ♕e5+ is also wild) 13 ♗xd3 ♕xa1 14 ♕e2+ ♔d7 15 0-0, Sénéchaud-Ustinov, corr. 1992.

9 dxe4?! gxf5 10 exf5

Sénéchaud-Evans, corr. 1995, and now 10...♕e7+ 11 ♗e2 ♘xg4 12 ♕xd4 ♖g8 is a rout.

E 3 ♕e2!?

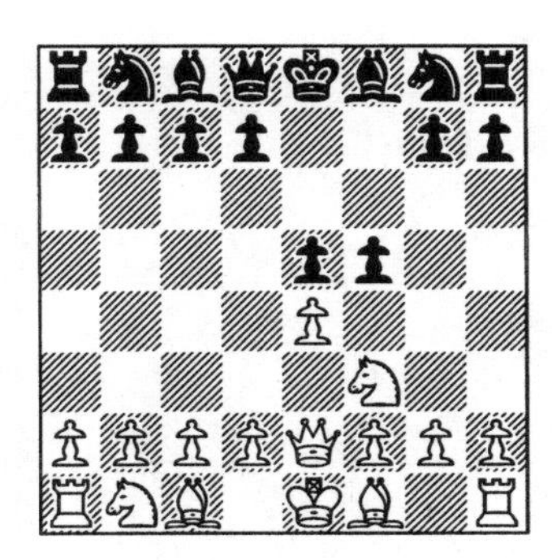

3...fxe4 4 ♕xe4 d6 5 d4

5 ♗c4 ♘f6 6 ♕e2 e4? (6...♗e7) 7 0-0?! (7 ♘c3 ♕e7 8 ♘g5) 7...d5 8 ♗b3 ♗d6 9 d4? ♗g4 ∓ Parker-Destrebecq, corr. 1979.

5...♘f6 6 ♕e2 e4 7 ♗g5 d5 8 ♘fd2 ♗e7 9 c4

With chances to both sides, Viaggio-Carlsson, corr. 1978.

F 3 b3?!

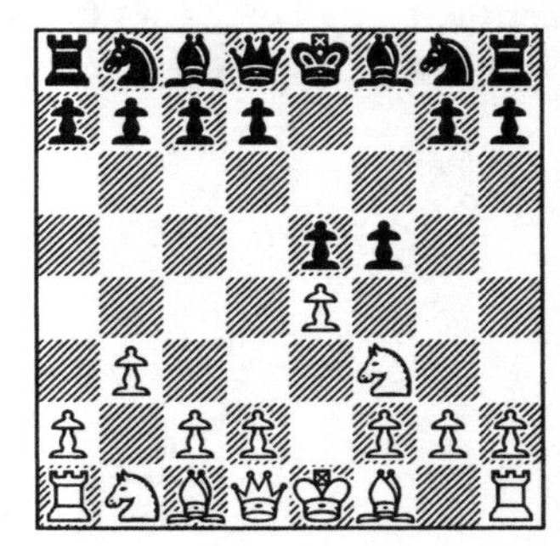

Similar to 3 b4.

3...fxe4

3...♘f6 4 ♘xe5 (4 exf5!?) 4...d6 5 ♘c4 fxe4 6 ♗e2 ♗e7 (6...d5) 7 0-0 0-0 8 ♗b2 ♘c6 9 ♘e3 ♗e6 10 f3 ♕e8 11 fxe4 ♘xe4 12 c4 ♖xf1+ 13 ♕xf1 ♕g6 ∓ Fragola-Laffont, corr. 1992.

4 ♘xe5 ♘f6 5 ♗b2 d5

5...d6 6 ♘c4 d5.

6 c4?! d4 7 d3? ♗b4+ winning, Lebrun-Matwienko, corr. 1973.

Index of Variations